THE
CANONISATION
OF DANIEL DEFOE

P.N. FURBANK & W.R. OWENS

YALE UNIVERSITY PRESS
NEW HAVEN & LONDON
1988

Set in Linotron Bembo by Best-set Typesetter Ltd, Hong Kong
Printed and bound at The Bath Press, Avon, Great Britain

Library of Congress Cataloging-in-Publication Data

Furbank, Philip Nicholas.
   The canonisation of Daniel Defoe.

   Includes index.
   1. Defoe, Daniel, 1661?–1731 — Authorship.   2. Defoe, Daniel, 1661?–1731 — Criticism and interpretation — History.   3. Authorship, Disputed.   4. Canon (Literature)   I. Owens, W.R.   II. Title.
PR3408.A9F87   1988   823'.5   87-23015
ISBN 0-300-04119-5

For
JOHN McVEAGH

OUR THANKS ARE DUE to the following for permission to quote from unpublished material: The Beinecke Rare Book and Manuscript Library, Yale University; Boston Public Library; Columbia University Library; Harry Ransom Humanities Research Center, The University of Texas at Austin; Manchester Leisure Services Committee; William Andrews Clark Memorial Library, University of California, Los Angeles.

Portions of our book have previously appeared in the following journals, and we are grateful to the editors for permission to reprint: chapter 2 was published in *Papers of the Bibliographical Society of America*; part of chapter 6 was published in *The Book Collector*; part of chapter 10 was published in *English Studies*.

Our work has been aided by financial assistance from the Research Committee and the Arts Faculty of the Open University. P.N. Furbank is grateful for financial assistance from the Leverhulme Trust and from the Society of Authors; W.R. Owens is grateful for financial assistance from the British Academy.

Parts of our book have been read in draft form to the Defoe Research Group at the Open University, to an international conference on authorship-attribution at Edinburgh University in 1984, and to the American Society for Eighteenth-century Studies conference at Cincinnati in 1987.

We give our warmest thanks to the following, for encouragement, advice and help of various kinds: Paula Backscheider; Jack Barbera; Frank Bastian; Tony Coulson; Alan Downie; Frank Ellis; Ena Halmos; David Hayton; Mrs George Harris Healey; Erika Langmuir; Dolores Lahrman; Anne Laurence; Bill McBrien; Mrs Alice B. Moore; Shirley Owens; Spiro Peterson; Manuel Schonhorn; Stuart Sim; Wilfrid Smith; Gaby Smol; Ben Spackman; Mrs Emily M. Wood.

Our editors at Yale University Press, Robert Baldock and Gillian Malpass, were most helpful at every stage. We are also grateful to Douglas Matthews, who compiled the index.

Finally, we owe a special debt to Andrew Best, Derwent May and John McVeagh who read and commented on our book in typescript.

CONTENTS

PART I

'What must we do?'
'Stop building.'
The answer came pat...
William Golding, The Spire

DOUBTS ABOUT THE DEFOE 'CANON'

T HE PRESENT BOOK takes its rise from a feeling, which seems to be shared in varying degrees by a number of scholars, that the Defoe 'canon' is a remarkably strange and not very satisfactory construction. It contains, indeed, as odd and as great an assortment of texts as, perhaps, has ever been attributed to one author, and for the larger part these texts have been ascribed on internal evidence alone. Can they really all be by Defoe? It calls for most ingenious mental gymnastics to support this belief. Thus a doubt cannot but occasionally stir in the reader's mind that, from the very beginning, something may have gone wrong — that some error crept in, begetting over the years a long series of further errors, or that the basic principles of attribution adopted have somehow been faulty. It is this doubt that we are wanting to air.

What one always needs to bear in mind with Defoe is that the largest part of his work was published anonymously or pseudonymously and that, though he was a famous man in his day, it was not till sixty years after his death in 1731 that any serious effort was made to draw up a full list of his writings. Sixty years is a long time, indeed it is a lifetime. Thus, when in 1790 his first biographer, George Chalmers, compiled 'A List of De Foe's Works Arranged Chronologically', what he was undertaking was an essay in historical reconstruction. Some of Chalmers's working papers have survived, and in point of devotion and energy he is deserving of admiration, though less kind things will have to be said about his principles of attribution. However, he was, inevitably, working very much by hearsay, at second or third hand, and sometimes relying upon no more than a vague 'tradition among the Booksellers', and as a result his list, which assigned some eighty-one separate books and pamphlets to Defoe, together with an additional twenty that he considered possible or probable attributions, is in some respects fairly speculative. Indeed the verdict of Rodney Baine, the scholar who has examined his papers most closely, is the dispiriting one that 'it should now be clear that Chalmers' assignment of any particular item to Defoe constitutes in itself no evidence that Defoe wrote it'.[1]

What may at least be said of Chalmers's list is that, speculative or not, it was relatively short. Matters, however, were soon to change in this respect. When Walter Wilson, Defoe's next important bio-grapher, compiled a catalogue of Defoe's writings, it ran to about twice the length of Chalmers's, containing 210 items, of which only four were marked as doubtful. Wilson believed his catalogue to be 'much more perfect than any that has been hitherto offered to the public', but he considered that it was still far from being complete.[2] This belief was shared by Wilson's successor, William Lee, who in his 1869 biography of Defoe took earlier bibliographers severely to task, declaring the lists of Defoe's works that they had offered to be '"conspicuous for the absence" of all critical acumen, and even ordinary knowledge of Defoe's stile.'[3] Lee's own list took the number of works in the Defoe canon to 254. Sixty-six of these were marked with an asterisk to indicate that Lee was attributing them for the first time to Defoe.

In the first bibliography of Defoe to be published in the twentieth century, the list compiled by W.P. Trent for *The Cambridge History of English Literature*, the total rose to 382. Trent explained that this was a very conservative total, since his list

> does not take account of nearly 300 books and pamphlets which have been ascribed to [Defoe], but for the authenticity of which I cannot vouch with entire confidence. Many of these are almost as much entitled to be received into the accredited list as most of the items that have been accepted since the times of Chalmers and Wilson; but, for one reason or another, it has seemed best to treat them as plausible ascriptions only and to avoid enumerating them here.[4]

This ever-swifter rate of attribution continued throughout the first half of the present century, culminating in 1960 with the publication of John Robert Moore's *Checklist of the Writings of Daniel Defoe*.[5] The *Checklist*, which appeared in a revised version in 1971, has become the standard reference work. It lists as Defoe's some 570 works, of which fifteen are marked with an asterisk to indicate that the attribution is not certain.

Altogether, then, between 1790 and 1970, the Defoe canon has swollen from 101 items to 570. The fact disturbed Donald Wing, the compiler of the *Short Title Catalogue* for 1641–1700, and, with weary irony, he offered his successor a simple solution to handling anonymous works of the early eighteenth century: '...I suggest to my follower the common sense of putting them all under Daniel Defoe. If we keep on adding twenty or thirty a year to his *corpus*, wouldn't it be time-saving to admit now that he probably wrote them all?'[6]

A crucial feature of the attributions added to the canon since the days of Chalmers is that, as we have said, for the most part they have been based on internal, and especially on stylistic, evidence. We think it can safely be said that there has been nothing quite like it in the history of English studies, though there are some closer parallels in musicology and art history. If, between them, the Defoe scholars have got it right, it has been an amazing achievement; who could deny the epithet 'creative' to such scholarship? Nor, certainly, have we written this book just to mock the efforts of Chalmers and his successors. But when one begins to explore this stupendous edifice, the work of their hands, one cannot help wondering just how well they built — and whether the floors are safe and the roof in no danger of tumbling on one's head.

The edifice has, essentially, been the work of a few notable individuals — men of great confidence in their own abilities and certainly not overawed by, or hampered by piety towards, their predecessors. William Lee rejected many of Wilson's attributions, W.P. Trent many of Lee's, and J.R. Moore many of Trent's. What, on the other hand, was lacking, and not solely for chronological reasons, was much in the way of scholarly commerce between the main Defoe scholars; or at least, as we shall point out, there were one or two damaging failures of communication. What also needs to be remembered is that Chalmers, Wilson and Lee were writing before the professionalisation of literary studies and so did not receive informed criticism on the scale that they would have done later (though one should not over-stress this, for on the whole Defoe was dealt with rather intelligently by Victorian reviewers). Thus, by the time that Trent and Moore came on the scene, much of the work of attribution had been done; and since both Trent and Moore were, by temperament, not 'disintegrators' but accepters, scholars of our own period inherited an even vaster *fait accompli*, and understandably they have felt somewhat inhibited by it. The mere fact that the catalogues of major libraries, quickly or more slowly, come to reflect this weight of new attribution creates a problem for the scholar, all the more so since such catalogues are inclined, and not unreasonably, to follow expert opinion more in adding items than in dislodging them. Again, the sheer multiplication of allusions to Defoe in modern writings about this period by historians, inevitably reflecting the reigning 'canon', is daunting to questioners of this 'canon' and inclined to make them murmur 'too late' to themselves.

As a consequence of this, although scholars like Frank Ellis, Pat Rogers, Spiro Peterson, Henry Snyder and Alan Downie have been doing convincing work in questioning individual items and arguing for their removal from the canon, they have not on the whole called for a general reform or root-and-branch reconsideration.[7] (Indeed, and this is an important point, they have tended to work within the normal scholarly convention of attacking an attribution only if there is a better candidate for authorship to offer.) Likewise, in his list of Defoe's writings in *The New Cambridge Bibliography of English Literature* (1971) that came out between the two editions of Moore's *Checklist*, Maximillian Novak declaredly adopted a conservative approach, though employing an informal code to indicate degrees of probability — 'Almost certainly by Defoe', 'Probably by Defoe', 'Perhaps by Defoe', 'Attributed to Defoe by J.R. Moore', 'Attributed to Defoe by J.R. Moore, but doubtful', etc.

However, one scholar, Rodney Baine, has made an outright attack on the credentials of the existing canon. In a devastating critique of J.R. Moore's arguments for Defoe's authorship of *Robert Drury's Journal*, he wrote, echoing Donald Wing:

> ...it would be strange if from the canon of some 550 works which Mr. Moore has attributed to Defoe, he could not draw adequate parallels in diction, idiom and imagery to prove that Defoe wrote not only Drury's *Journal*, but almost anything published in the century. The wider the Defoe canon becomes, the easier it is to establish other attributions on the basis of style and idiom. We have a widening gyre whose center will not hold.[8]

The only way forward, Baine said, was a re-examination of the entire canon. Professor Baine has moved on to other studies, but we agree with this opinion of his, and it is for such a radical reappraisal that we shall be arguing — if with some diffidence — in the present book.

There is, it is worth pointing out, a reason why this may be the right moment for a reappraisal. It is that only now, for the first time,

are the texts widely available. During the eighteenth and nineteenth
centuries a Defoe expert was almost by definition a Defoe collector,
and indeed a collector on a very extensive scale; and this is something
that relatively few people, in any age, are likely to become — or
indeed, in the logic of things, can become (for it is, after all, a
competitive activity). Nor has the situation been very different for
much of the twentieth century. It is true, at least, that to be a Defoe
expert has been possible only for a scholar with easy and continual
access to a library with a really large Defoe holding, and there are
very few such libraries. This cannot but have implications for the
Defoe canon. A writer in the recent controversy about Shakespeare
and the authorship of the poem 'Shall I die?' had this to say: 'It is not,
finally, the fiat of any particular scholar, nor even the weight of the
internal and external evidence, but a community of readers which
defines a literary canon.'[9] Now whether or not one goes along with
this, it makes one reflect how exceedingly tiny, up to now, has been
the community of readers competent to define, or even give rational
assent to, the Defoe canon. It makes one feel the need to reinterpret
either the term 'canon' or the term 'rational assent'.

Quite recently, however, the situation has changed completely.
The most important single contribution to Defoe scholarship made
by the late J.R. Moore, one might almost suggest, was not his
Checklist of the Writings of Daniel Defoe, but something that followed
upon this: his sponsoring the making and publishing of a microfilm
edition of all the texts listed there.[10] With this microfilm edition in
their possession, scholars anywhere can study the canonical texts of
Defoe almost as easily as they can those of Dickens or Milton. They
can with ease read them and re-read them, and compare them as a
whole or piecemeal and thus get on familiar terms even with this
enormous mass of material, without needing to devote a lifetime to
the task. Accordingly, present-day scholars, through no merit of
their own, are in a better position than their predecessors to question
the canon, should they think there is any need to do so.

We believe there is such a need; indeed, as we have said, we think
it pretty plainly a necessity. So let us begin by noting some of the
reasons why. First there is the fact that, if Moore's *Checklist* is to be
trusted, we must believe that Defoe, who wrote *Robinson Crusoe* and
the other great novels and who, in his *Review* (writing twice or thrice
weekly, sometimes under the most trying circumstances) produced
prose of great verve, intellectual grasp and polemical edge, would
also compose pamphlets of unfathomable dullness or asininity,

incompetent and bungling historical narratives, and quite character-
less hackwork compilations.

Secondly, there is a discomfort or puzzle, quite a severe one, about
consistency. If the *Checklist* is reliable, we must believe, for instance,
the following: that, some time after the publication in 1717 of
Matthew Tindal's *The Defection Consider'd*, which attacked Walpole
and Townshend for resigning from the Whig government and
entering into unholy alliance with the Tories, Defoe, within a single
fortnight in January 1718, produced both a trenchant endorsement of
Tindal (*The Defection Farther Consider'd*) and a furious onslaught on
Tindal for his ill-treatment of Walpole and Townshend (*Some Persons
Vindicated against the Author of the Defection*). Or again, we must
believe that Defoe went to very great and ingenious lengths to help
his erstwhile patron Harley at the time of his fall (*The Secret History of
the White Staff*, 1714–15) and again when his impeachment trial was
coming on (*Minutes of the Negotiations of Monsr. Mesnager*, 1717), yet
that he also produced pamphlets in which Harley, or at least his
ministry, is accused with great virulence of treason and corruption
— and, what is more, that he published eulogistic defences of
Townshend (*An Impartial Enquiry into the Conduct of Viscount
Townshend*, 1717) and of Walpole (*The Conduct of Robert Walpole
Esq.*, 1717), despite the fact that they were Harley's bitter opponents
and accusers. We must also imagine Defoe expressing, in the *Review*
and in later pamphlets, a cogent and idiosyncratic attitude towards
arrest and imprisonment for debt (arguing that, for all the crying
need to humanise its operation, the system was nevertheless essential
to Britain's commercial prosperity), and yet meanwhile publishing
two tracts (*Vox Dei & Naturae*, 1711 and *The Unreasonableness and Ill
Consequences of Imprisoning the Body for Debt*, 1729) that demanded the
abolition of the system.

Then we must picture him contributing, with fine impartiality, to
the Bangorian controversy of 1717–18 from practically every
possible and conflicting angle. It might be worth spelling out this
example in a little more detail. This controversy was provoked by
the Bishop of Bangor, Benjamin Hoadly's *Preservative against the
Principles and Practices of Non-Jurors* (1716), and more particularly by
his strongly Erastian sermon, preached on 31 March 1717 and
published a week or two afterwards, on 'The Nature of the Kingdom
or Church of Christ', in which he denied that Christ had committed
any power or authority to the Church. The high-flying Lower
House of Convocation at once concerted proceedings against Hoadly,

and the headmaster of Eton, Andrew Snape, published a severe remonstrance to him (*A Letter to the Bishop of Bangor*), following it up, after a pacific rejoinder from Hoadly, with the even more abusive *Second Letter*, in which he accused Hoadly of lying and drew the worst inferences from his giving house-room to an ex-Jesuit, Francis de la Pillonniere. By this time or soon after, literally hundreds of pamphlets on the subject had flooded from the press, including attacks on Hoadly by Thomas Sherlock and letters in self-defence from Pillonniere; also, the Bishop of Carlisle and White Kennett (later Bishop of Peterborough) had become locked in bloody combat in the newspapers over things Kennett was supposed to have said, but denied saying, to Hoadly's discredit. Defoe's own contributions to the debate, according to Moore, were as follows:

An Expostulatory Letter, to the Bishop of Bangor (1717): a politely sarcastic rejoinder to Hoadly's *Preservative*.

The Report Reported (1717): a wholehearted defence of Hoadly against Snape's ungentlemanly and unchristian attack.

Observations on the Bishop's Answer to Dr. Snape (1717): a sober tract, accusing Hoadly of ambiguity and saying that he answered some of Snape's criticisms, not all.

A Vindication of Dr. Snape (1717): a needling tract, saying that Snape put his finger on a central weakness of Hoadly's position, which is that, on his own reasoning, he ought to give up being a bishop.

A Reply to the Remarks upon the Lord Bishop of Bangor's Treatment of the Clergy and Convocation (1717): a very punchy tract, violently pro-Hoadly, saying that Snape is to be pitied for having been so soundly trounced by Hoadly and that Thomas Sherlock is a disgrace to the cloth.

A Declaration of Truth to Benjamin Hoadly (1717): an amusing pseudo-Quaker tract, which teases Hoadly with much ingenuity, saying that he will no doubt see the need to give up all his church appointments and emoluments, as a consequence of his own arguments.

The Conduct of Christians made the Sport of Infidels (1717): a fictitious letter from an Armenian merchant to the Grand Mufti, reporting the amazing behaviour of reverend fathers during the Bangorian controversy, of a kind to confirm a good Mohammedan in his own faith.

A Letter to Andrew Snape (1717): a pseudo-Quaker rebuke to Snape for his uncharitable attacks on Hoadly.

Mr. De La Pillonniere's Vindication (1717): an earnest tract, saying that Snape's attempt to blacken Hoadly's reputation by raking up his association with the ex-Jesuit Pillonniere is not only unworthy but irrelevant.

A Letter from the Jesuits to Father de la Pillonniere (1718): a defence of Hoadly and Pillonniere in the form of a bantering pretended letter from Pillonniere's fellow-Jesuits, saying he is letting down the Jesuit cause by acting too honestly.

Dr Sherlock's Vindication of the Test Act Examin'd (1718): only incidentally a contribution to the Bangorian controversy, but speaking of Pillonniere as having been finally discredited and silenced.

A Friendly Rebuke to one Parson Benjamin (1719): a 'Quaker' tract, rebuking Hoadly severely, and without irony, as a trouble-maker and slanderer and as morally inconsistent.

One would be hard put, it must be agreed, to discern any pattern in these twelve tracts, unless it be the pattern of *systematic* self-contradiction. Faced with them, the explanation that would spring to the mind of any uninstructed reader is that they cannot all be by Defoe; and this instinct would deserve respect. To change his or her mind, such a reader would demand some fairly solid evidence that Defoe was responsible for the whole group, and it is not certain how we would satisfy the demand. Is internal evidence, which is what it would mainly be, strong enough for this purpose? And can we specify the evidence, or is it merely that we have faith that Chalmers, Wilson, Lee, Trent or Moore detected such evidence, even though they did not publish it?

Of course, as we need not say, hypotheses can be found — indeed they come thronging — as to how Defoe *might* have come to write all of these tracts. The hypotheses most favoured by scholars when faced by such problems can be summarised thus: Defoe was

1) 'Protean'.
2) a brilliant and highly valued political propagandist, whose support a government or statesman might pay much to procure.
3) a low mercenary hack, who lived by selling himself to political patrons, or alternatively to booksellers, and was thus a professional turncoat.
4) a workaholic, liable from mere excess of restless energy to toss off a lengthy treatise on any subject at a moment's notice or to

orchestrate a many-sided controversy more or less single-handed, impersonating all the contestants.
5) a gratuitous and incorrigible hoaxer.

It will be observed that all these hypotheses, apart from number 2, have an extreme or 'ultimate' quality, making Defoe out to be some kind of monster or unique phenomenon; and they have the disadvantage that, on the basis of them, practically any early-eighteenth-century anonymous work can plausibly be attributed to Defoe. This does not necessarily discredit them, but it must give one a queer and uneasy feeling about them. Michel Foucault has criticised those who, taking the known works of a writer, reconcile any incon-sistencies and heal any ruptures in them by dint of constructing an 'author', whose 'purposes', psychology and 'development' con-veniently supply the unity which the works themselves lack.[11] The warning is a good one. But what shall we say of those who con-struct an 'author' to impose unity on works that may or may not be by the same writer? They would seem to be in greater need of the warning, and indeed to be on a distinctly dangerous path. For in the former case there are at least some rules to the game — the 'author' must give coherence to all the works and to those works only; but in the latter case there appear to be few rules. If one wants to add a new work to the 'canon', it may entail refashioning the 'author', but then, what is to stop one? Only, perhaps, a growing sense that the portrait of the author is growing rather bizarre — and, at least in the case of Defoe, extremely simplified, representing him as a man who might have written practically anything.

Let us scrutinise those five hypotheses. The first would appear to be a fallacy and the result of confusing several different things. The term 'Protean' would be very apt to describe Shakespeare or Dickens or Dostoevsky in respect of their miraculous inventiveness in the creation of character. What would be meant by 'Protean' here is an especial power to 'get into the skin' of such diverse personages; and it is not a belittlement to Defoe to say that, in this respect, he is hardly a rival to these authors. The term can also be applied, less usefully, to a fondness for disguise: for instance, writing a pamphlet, like *The Shortest Way with the Dissenters*, with deliberate intent to deceive, or writing a novel (and this will entail the use of a first-person narrator) in such a manner as to leave it uncertain whether it is fiction or fact. Evidently, Defoe was fond of approaching his readers in disguise. Moreover, he had a respectable talent for impersonation. His high-

flying author in *The Shortest Way* is certainly admirably done. Still,
even here, the achievement lies, quite as much as in the impersonation itself, in the brilliant tactical use to which it is put; and the same
is even more true of his Quaker impersonation in *A Declaration of
Truth to Benjamin Hoadly* (if indeed this tract is his). The Quaker is
established merely by a few deft touches, and the real brilliance of
the tract lies in the mounting comedy of the Quaker's remorseless
encouragement to the unfortunate Bishop to follow his own advice
from the pulpit to its logical conclusion and give up his see and its
emoluments. Further, if it is first-person narration in fiction that we
are thinking of, there is no feat of impersonation in Defoe's novels
quite to compete with Dickens's Esther Summerson or his Mrs
Lirriper; indeed some critics have gone so far as to complain, though
we think unjustly, that Defoe's Moll Flanders and Roxana sound too
much like Defoe himself.

Hypothesis 4 would seem, on consideration, to be a rather
implausible idea, without much to be said for it. As for number 5, it
touches on a tendency genuinely present in Defoe, but if one pursued
it for any distance it would very quickly lead one into fantasy. (Laura
Curtis's 'hoax' theory of *Moll Flanders* is neat but does not carry
much conviction.[12])

This brings us to numbers 2 and 3. What needs to be said at once is
that number 3, in some version or other, is a charge continually
brought against Defoe by his enemies during his lifetime. He was far
from being the only writer to be accused of it, for it was a favourite
piece of mud-slinging in the pamphlets of this period. As W.L.
Payne writes, in an article 'Defoe in the Pamphlets', '"damning
the pamphleteer" was a part of the game'; and he quotes from
Remarks Upon Dr. Hare's Four Letters to a Tory Member (1711):

> Let a man talk, look, tread, or even think a-wry, that is never so
> little disagreeable to those fiery persons...he must expect no
> better quarter than to be stigmatiz'd with the titles of a libeller, a
> prostitute creature, a mercenary wretch, an insolent fellow, a
> villain, and such much more significant language.

Still, Defoe probably had this sort of charge levelled at him more
persistently than any other. What needs to be remembered, of
course, is that he was, anyway, the most widely discussed political
writer of the age. Such, at least, is the opinion of Payne, who, in his
study of pamphlets published between 1700 and 1731, claims that 'no
other writer is mentioned as frequently, or even begins to approach

it: not Roper or Moore or Leslie, not Davenant or Steele or Burney, not Charles King of the *British Merchant*, or John Tutchin of the *Observator*, or Jonathan Swift of the *Examiner*.' Moreover, as Payne notes, Defoe had a peculiar gift for putting people's backs up. 'Whatever Defoe wrote as journalist or pamphleteer counted, hurt, raised hackles.'[13] His sojourn in the pillory made him fair game, and one can sense something symbolic and mythical in the role assigned to him, as the very epitome of the Grub-street arts.

Certainly the charge of mercenariness and 'prostitution' was brought by his adversaries with amazing venom. One may cite the anonymous *A Character of a Turn-coat* (1707), which places him (and Tutchin) among the 'Two-faced Monsters'; or 'The loyal Litany' which abuses this '...vile Presbyterian with a *Jacobite* Face/Who writes on both Sides with an insipid Grace,/Yet demurely on *Sundays* in the Meeting takes Place'; or Abel Boyer's diatribes against this 'mercenary Retainer of Harley, a Scribbler famous for writing upon, for and against all manner of Subjects, Persons and Parties'. In some *Remarks on a Scandalous Libel, Entitl'd A Letter...Relating to the Bill of Commerce* (1713), attributed to Oldmixon, it is said that Defoe might as well 'e'en throw off the Vizard and own himself a *Jacobite* and a Hireling, for there is no Man so dull but to see he will write any thing, do any thing, *Pro* or *Con*, according to the *Cue* that's given him'.[14]

Nor did these allegations cease at Defoe's death. They remained a living anecdotal tradition upon which Chalmers was later to draw, as witness a curious letter of 23 April 1790 from one of Chalmers's informants:

> With regard to Daniel De Foe, I humbly believe he was a *time serving Writer*, especially at the Season he was employed...to conduct the Courant...De Foe's pieces...undoubtedly were numerous & hastily scribled over as the humour of the Day invited or even his necessities required, being t'other day assured by a very knowing old friend of mine, that his Father (a contemporary of our Author) told him, 'that Dan. Defoe had a double Desk where-on one [*sic*] he placed his *own Pamphlet*, & on the other he wrote his *own Answer to it*'.[15]

Defoe, for his part, complained often and bitterly about other people's pamphlets being attributed to him, to the injury of his own reputation. In his best-known apologia, *An Appeal to Honour and Justice*, he writes:

This brings me again to that other Oppression which as I said I suffer under, and which, I think, is of a Kind, that no Man ever suffer'd under so much as my self: And this is to have every Libel, every Pamphlet, be it ever so foolish, so malicious, so unmannerly or so dangerous, be laid at my Door, and be call'd publickly by my Name. It has been in vain for me to struggle with this injury; It has been in vain for me to protest, to declare solemnly, nay, if I would have sworn that I had no hand in such a Book, or Paper, never saw it, never read it, and the like, it was the same thing.

My Name has been hackney'd about the Street by the Hawkers, and about the Coffee-Houses by the Politicians, at such a rate, as no Patience could bear. One Man will swear to the Style; another to this or that Expression; another to the Way of Printing; and all so positive, that it is to no purpose to oppose it.[16]

The matter is given a further and intriguing turn by the fact that some of the most sensational depictions of mercenary pamphleteering come in works that have been attributed to Defoe himself — which would prove, if indeed the works are by him, that he positively encouraged scepticism on his readers' part and found advantage in suggesting the fallibility of all report. We are thinking of *The Secret History of the Secret History of the White Staff* (1715), a curious (and, if by Defoe, immensely ingenious) pamphlet which purports to clear both Harley and Defoe of the authorship of the pamphlets entitled *The Secret History of the White Staff*, written in apparent vindication of Harley after his fall. Harley's enemies, as much as his friends, so says *The Secret History of the Secret History*,

> could not avoid the Snare of taking the Books for genuine, and for a Design of the *Staff* [i.e. Harley] to start something into the World in his own Vindication. The Writers of the Books sitting still all this while, had their leisure to Laugh at Mankind, and to please themselves with thinking how either Side fell into their Snare.... It shall appear that the same People employing other Hands, have been the Editors not only of the Books themselves, but also of several of the Answers to these Books, causing the deceiv'd People to Dance in the Circles of their drawing, while these have enjoyed the Sport of their own Witchcraft.[17]

Or again, there is the amusing passage in the supposititious *Minutes of the Negotiations of Monsr. Mesnager*, in which the French agent Mesnager relates, with relish, how he employed a mercenary English pamphleteer to further French interests:

> Those Writers of Pamphlets in *England*, are the best People of that Kind that are any where to be found; for they have so many Turns to impose upon their People, that nothing I have met with was ever like it; and the People of *England*, of all the People I have met with, are the fondest of such Writings.[18]

What inferences we should draw from these passages will of course depend on whether we believe Defoe was the author of the works in question, a matter we shall come back to later; but on the assumption that he was, what the works seem to be hinting to the reader is, 'Don't be too quick to believe this very pamphlet you are reading, either.'

What we shall also have to examine later is the influence that this theory, so popular with Defoe's adversaries in his own day, that he was a mercenary hack or a writer-on-both-sides, had upon his twentieth-century biographers.

Let us return to our list of hypotheses. Numbers 2 and 3, it would seem, are incompatible and could not easily be true of the same person: a highly valued propagandist will not, as a mercenary hack might do, endanger his reputation and market-value by turning out incompetent work for immediate financial gain. (The fact that such writing would be done anonymously is not a crucial objection: the anonymity of writers could be, and repeatedly was, penetrated.) Again, a highly valued propagandist may very likely possess independent and strongly held convictions of his own; and even if not, it is in his interest as well as his patron's to keep up the fiction that he does and that he cannot just simply be 'bought'. A mercenary hack with a patron, on the other hand, will precisely make it his business to convince his patron that he *can* be bought — lock, stock and barrel. These two thus differ here widely; whilst at the same time neither will be likely to endanger their patron's support by writing indiscriminately on all sides of a question; only a bookseller's 'author to let' (perhaps a somewhat mythical figure?) can be expected to do that. Further, a highly valued propagandist who anonymously publishes opinions that would get him into serious trouble with his patron, were he found out, is hardly likely to be doing it for mercenary motives — though he might be doing it out of honest conviction, or some kind of private revolt against servitude, or out of sheer fun or mischief. In short, we must not imagine that these various conceptions of Defoe can be 'lumped', as possible facets of the same individual.

What is also clear about these 'blanket' conceptions, is that they are resorted to as props or supports by bibliographers or biographers when in a mood of desperation. We need, then, to examine the causes of this desperation. One of them may be that Defoe bibliographers have tended to be 'loners'. (Of course, before the age of photo-copying and microfilming, bibliography was bound to be lonely work anyway.) For a lone individual, though, the bibliographical problem in Defoe must loom as gigantic, and he or she will need much psychological fortification. The famous Defoe scholars solved the problem each in his own way. William Lee, as we shall see, seems to have taken a 'blanket' decision to think the best of Defoe in all possible circumstances and to find in his behaviour the signs of a childlike faith in the Christian revelation and a devotion to 'the Truth as it is in Jesus'. In this project he succeeded completely, at least to his own satisfaction — except in one instance, which was to cause him much chagrin and which will be discussed in a later chapter. What happened with W.P. Trent is different but no less interesting. He began by treating each of the innumerable bibliographical problems in Defoe as an independent case and, to the best of his ability, confronting it without prejudice, in terms of the available evidence and of general human probabilities. Then at some point, in an increasingly chequered and embattled life, he lost his nerve and succumbed to what might be called 'unrealistic cynicism': he allowed himself to believe that Defoe, whom he had once admired, though without idolatry, was a supreme rogue, capable of absolutely any turpitude. (Trent was a 'Southern gentleman', rather hung up about honour, and the suspicion of Defoe's dishonourableness had become too much for him.) The change of attitude simplified his biblio-graphical work, but it also destroyed its poise.

Extreme or 'blanket' conceptions of Defoe, then, it seems to us, do not really cure the uneasinesses prompted by the current canon. These uneasinesses go rather deep and suggest that there may have been something wrong with the whole principle on which the canon has been constructed. Imagining we were back in 1790, with the whole work to do over again, are there not three rules that we should want to observe?

1) In arguing for a new attribution, we should not 'forge chains' of attribution. That is to say, we should be sure not to base any part of

our argument upon an earlier, merely tentative and plausible, attribution or group of attributions, but take care to draw our inferences
solely from works indisputably by Defoe. (There is, of course, quite
a body of such work, though it is relatively small in proportion to
the present huge canon.)

2) If we were adding a new attribution to the canon, by, for example,
including it in a published catalogue, we should invariably give our
reasons for the attribution: are they purely a matter of internal
evidence or probabilities, i.e. similarity of style or ideas, or is there
external evidence?

3) (The most vital and drastic rule.) We should not regard the fact
that a given new attribution seems plausible as in itself a good reason
at all for adding it to the canon (though it might be a sound reason
for adding it to an 'apocrypha'). The reason for this is simple and is
already implicit in rules 1 and 2: the addition of a work to the canon
causes a qualitative change in its status and alters the whole way in
which a later scholar is expected to regard it. The argument for
adding something to the canon has therefore to be enormously more
stringent than the argument for keeping it there, indeed the two
kinds of reasoning are really quite different. If an item is already in
the canon, the duty of later scholars becomes a merely negative one.
They will feel called upon to convince themselves that the attribution is not implausible (and of course if it strikes them as being so,
they will make conscientious efforts to eject it), but the presumption
is all in favour of the item's authenticity. Moreover (see rule 2),
the presumption will gain enormous force from any mystery or
uncertainty surrounding its (the presumption's) origin. It is this that
justifies the use of the term 'canon', with its theological implications,
in the present connection. The inclusion of a new attribution in a
standard bibliography bestows on it an authority as subtle as it is
potent, and much argument about literary attribution is conducted in
terms, not of evidential proof, but of authority. What is more,
authority can exercise a secret influence and often affects participants
in an attribution discussion without their knowing it.

It cannot be said that the above rules have been observed in the
construction of the Defoe canon, and a good deal of our book is
devoted to the history of the canon and of the scholars who created
it, in an effort to demonstrate this. Before this, however, we owe the
reader better reasons for thinking that there is a serious problem at

all, or that, with a little tidying, the existing canon should not content us. This is best done by means of a case-study, and in the following chapter we shall consider *The History of the Wars of Charles XII* (1715), a work first attributed to Defoe by William Lee in 1869.

CHAPTER 2

CASE-STUDY: WILLIAM LEE AND
THE HISTORY OF THE WARS OF
CHARLES XII

At the time of publication of William Lee's *Daniel Defoe: His Life, and Recently Discovered Writings* in 1869, the *British Quarterly*'s reviewer expressed astonishment at the sixty or so new works ascribed to Defoe by Lee. 'We would believe it all if we could', he remarked, but surmised that 'in his [Lee's] eagerness to make discoveries...He has opened both his eyes and his mouth a little too wide, and swallowed a great deal more than he has sufficiently tasted.' What also puzzled this reviewer was Lee's manner of presenting his discoveries: '...if the name of the writer had been upon the title pages, Mr. Lee could not have written in a more positive style concerning them'. Defoe's earlier biographer Walter Wilson had set out the probabilities and difficulties surrounding questionable attributions; 'Mr. Lee...takes a shorter method than this. He says nothing; and an ordinary reader would suppose that the authorship of these works had been acknowledged.'[1]

The reviewer's eye lighted on, among other items, a 400-page *History of the Wars, of His Present Majesty Charles XII*, purporting to be written by a 'Scots Gentleman in the Swedish Service' and published in a year (1715) when Defoe had declared his intention of writing nothing further for some time. 'It is a book, we are told, "hitherto unnoticed by any of his biographers, and almost unknown to the world".' 'But why', asks the reviewer, rather reasonably, 'have none of the biographers noticed it? How is it that nobody, excepting Mr. Lee, ever thought of attributing it to De Foe?'[2]

Defoe scholars have opened their eyes and mouth wider since this reviewer's day, when the Defoe canon was not even half its present size; nevertheless, on his advice, it is worth taking a second look at that *History of the Wars of Charles XII*, which has remained undisturbed in the canon from Lee's day onwards. One thing can be affirmed from the start: this voluminous work, with the 'Continuation' which appeared in the second edition of 1720, has its place in the canon, essentially, for one reason only — that William Lee decided it belonged there. As was usual with him, he offered no reasons, beyond the assertion that the work was 'worthy of standing by the side of the most fascinating productions of his [Defoe's] great genius'. However, knowing Lee, we can safely assume that he was mainly relying on what, in his introduction, he described as 'characteristic modes of expression, abounding in his [Defoe's] works, but scarcely any of them similarly used by any other writer of that age'. It was Lee's view that 'Long and critical study of a great author may result in so full an acquaintance, that his writings will be recognised by the student in a moment, as the voice of a familiar friend.'[3]

This claim of Lee's is a pretty bold one, but it would appear that, in the present instance at least, scholars have been happy to go along with it. The British Museum quickly adopted the ascription, which appeared in their printed catalogue of 1882. W.P. Trent, in his 'Bibliographical Notes on Defoe' published in the *Nation* in 1907 was more cautious, saying that 'a positive verdict' in the matter of this attribution 'should hardly be reached...until a careful study is made of the materials at that time available for a biographer of Charles XII'. It is plain from his own admission, however, in the 'Bibliography' of Defoe which he left unpublished at his death (see p. 83), that Trent himself did not make this 'careful study'.[4] Nor can one recall much published discussion of the credentials of *The History of the Wars of Charles XII*. None the less, the work was included in Trent's Defoe bibliography in *The Cambridge History of English Literature* in 1912, as it was in J.R. Moore's *Checklist of the Writings of Daniel Defoe* of 1960 and by Maximillian Novak in his entry on Defoe in *The New Cambridge Bibliography of English Literature* of 1971.

Lee's confidence in the attribution was whole-hearted, as may be seen when he reverts to the work later in his book. The reader, he writes, will have been surprised at the 'intimate knowledge Defoe possessed as to the history, and especially the military affairs of Northern Europe', a knowledge, he says, further displayed in three other works dealing with mainly Swedish affairs: *Memoirs of a Cavalier* (1720), *A Short Narrative of...Count Patkul* (1717) and *Some*

Account of the Life...of George Henry Baron de Goertz (1719). There is, however, says Lee, a further surprise awaiting the reader. For, according to Lee, all these aforementioned writings 'exhibit a bias in favour of the interests of Sweden', yet in 1723 there was published *An Impartial History of the Life and Actions of Peter Alexowitz, the Present Czar of Muscovy...Written by a British Officer in the Service of the Czar*, a work dealing with the same wars and events but from a pro-Russian point of view, 'and yet bearing the same indisputable proof of Defoe's authorship'.[5] No more than with *The History of the Wars of Charles XII* are we told what the 'indisputable proof' consists in, leaving us to make the same guess as before. However, we may surmise that Lee was helped to this attribution by the fact that, as he noticed, *An Impartial History of Peter Alexowitz* contains extended verbatim quotations from *The History of the Wars of Charles XII*. (They are signalled as quotations by inverted commas and are sometimes referred to as 'the Swedish Account'.)

What we must not fail to observe is that two of those other 'Swedish' tracts which Lee mentions, *A Short Narrative of Count Patkul* and *Some Account of the Life of George Henry Baron de Goertz*, were also first-time attributions by Lee; and though the *Patkul* pamphlet (which is signed 'L.M.') was later restored by Trent to Lord Molesworth,[6] the *Goertz* pamphlet has survived into Moore's *Checklist*.

In the same *Checklist* there are further 'North European' attributions, in particular a forty-page pamphlet, ostensibly pro-Jacobite in tendency, published in 1717 and entitled *A Short View of the Conduct of the King of Sweden*. This escaped Lee's notice but, as Herbert G. Wright pointed out in 1940, is unmistakably a boiling-down, whether by the same author or another, of *The History of the Wars of Charles XII*.[7]

Nor are we done yet; for in 1978 Stieg Hargevik revealed that *The History of the Wars of Charles XII* itself leans heavily on a earlier work, published anonymously in 1704 and entitled *The History of the Expedition of Charles XII, King of Sweeden*. Some of the documents cited in *The History of the Wars of Charles XII* already appear in *The History of the Expedition of Charles XII* (a work three-quarters of which is composed of documents), and several passages of the text of the *Expedition* are reproduced verbatim in the *History*. Because of this, according to Hargevik, there is 'not the slightest doubt' that this work should also be assigned to Defoe.[8] One begins to feel like the man in the Charles Addams cartoon, nervously viewing a factory-line of robots manufacturing yet more robots: 'Sometimes I ask myself "Where will it ever end?"'

*   *   *

Those who wish to accept these 'Swedish' writings as being by Defoe are confronted, clearly, with certain difficulties. *The History of the Wars of Charles XII* is an immensely detailed, blow-by-blow campaign history, replete with facts and figures and what appears to be eye-witness recollections, and it must puzzle us where the author obtained his information, there being no obvious published sources for much of it. Was there leisure in so busy a life as Defoe's for such minute research? On the other hand, even Lee does not suppose that he made it all up. He suggests that Defoe took part of his materials from that 'storehouse of history', the *Review*. However, study of the *Review* hardly bears him out. Anyway, he does not conceive it as possible even for Defoe to have produced both *The History of the Wars of Charles XII* and *An Impartial History of Peter Alexowitz* from the same single body of materials, and he is forced to posit separate undiscovered 'Swedish sources' for the former work and 'Russian sources' for the latter. Further speculation about sources is, he believes, vain. 'Whether any Papers, "By a Scots Gentleman in the Swedish Service", were used by Defoe while preparing the former; or, any Journal or Manuscript, "By a British officer in the Service of the Czar", while writing the latter, must, however probable, always remain uncertain.'[9]

    J.R. Moore's discussion of sources is not much more enlightening, and indeed is somewhat contradictory. In *Daniel Defoe: Citizen of the Modern World* he states that *The History of the Wars of Charles XII* is 'largely based on printed material easily accessible in England', but his note on the second edition in his *Checklist* says that 'internal evidence indicates some special source of information'. On the question of the sources of *An Impartial History of Peter Alexowitz*, his note runs: 'Fictitious attribution to a British Officer in the Service of the Czar; actually based in large part on the notes previously used for *The History of the Wars of his late Majesty Charles XII, King of Sweden* (1720).'[10] The 'notes' are presumably a guess on Moore's part. They reappear in Stieg Hargevik's article, which says that 'Defoe decided to continue his history of these wars from notes, other sources available and his own journalistic reports in the *Review*.'[11]

    It is noticeable that Lee does not discuss the Scots Gentleman or the British Officer as assumed *personae*; which is perhaps another way of saying that he does not much wish to *discuss* these two works at all, nor to suggest what prompted Defoe to write them. This brings us to the much more formidable difficulty that confronts all those who would assign these writings to Defoe. For Defoe wrote a great deal about Charles XII in the *Review* and elaborated there a well-worked-out, balanced but predominantly critical attitude towards him. In Defoe's eyes, Charles was the 'Gothick Hero' who could have done immense things for the Protestant cause, had not vainglory led him astray, and his career prompted serious doubts about the value of heroes in general. We may quote, for instance, the telling words that Defoe wrote of Charles XII in the *Review* of 2 September 1707. Earlier in the year it had seemed likely that Charles might declare war on the Emperor, on behalf of the Emperor's persecuted Protestant subjects — a foolish step, in the eyes of the *Review*, considering the plight of Charles's own Livonian subjects, 'abandon'd to the Tyranny of the *Czar*', and an untimely one that, by diverting the Emperor from the struggle with Catholic France, would have done more harm than good to the Protestant cause. The threat had been averted by the intercession of Marlborough; and on 2 September Mr Review reported in finely ironical style the Emperor's peaceful capitulation to Charles's demands (so disappointing to Charles's more bellicose admirers).

I am told there is sad and lamentable News lately come from Abroad, which may in some Measure lessen the Joy, we are conceiving the Success of *Naples*, or *Thoulon*, and what is this but that the King of S...., *the great* Gothick *Hero*, that was to pull down the *Emperor* and the *Pope*, and do a World of strange things, is like to be satisfied with the Compliances of the *Emperor*, and we are to have no War commenc'd there, to confound the Confederacy in defence of the Protestant Religion; this is sad News indeed...

And now his S.... Majesty, may, perhaps find time, to rescue *Poland* out of the hands of the *Muscovites* if he can — *I ought to say, or rather, which I should think to be as commendable too, and as like a Hero*, he may go and recover *Livonia*, and deliver his own poor Subjects, abandon'd there to the Tyranny of the *Czar*, while their natural King and Protector was so busie, pushing his Glory in *Poland* against King *Augustus*, that he could not, or did not, *which in some Sence is much as one*, think fit to find while, or find Forces to defend them.

If this be to be a Hero — If this be to make a King Great and

Terrible in the World, God Almighty grant, *England* may never be Govern'd by Heroes...[12]

So critical was the tenor of Defoe's comments on Charles in the *Review*, at this period, that they nearly brought him into serious trouble. An official complaint was laid against the *Review* by the Swedish envoy 'Lyencroon', [13] and it was reported gleefully in *Dyer's Newsletter* that Defoe, who was in Edinburgh at this time, was to be arrested by Queen's Messenger. He reacted, however, with much toughness, declaring in two pamphlets (*De Foe's Answer to Dyer's Scandalous News Letter* and *Dyers News Examined*), as well as in the pages of the *Review*, that he could see nothing offensive in what he had written, but if there were, he was happy to answer for it according to the justice of a free country.[14] 'The King of *Sweden* ...has carried it with so high a Hand in some parts of the World, that their Princes deliver up their Subjects bound Hand and Foot for him to use his Pleasure with them. — But *GOD* be Praised, the Queen of England is none of those...'.[15] Some weeks later in the *Review* (6 November) he made handsome personal amends to Charles, praising him as 'a Gallant, a Forward, and an Enterprizing Monarch', but not retracting his criticism of him for negligence in the all-important struggle with France. It was a diplomatic apology rather than a recantation on Defoe's part and it ended with cheerful and none-too-respectful irony:

> When we are free from this War, let him [Charles] take *Vienna* it self, and march from thence, and fetch the *Swedish* Jewels out of the *Santa Casa* at *Loretto*, *Amen*; Let him prosper; I shall pray for his Success, applaud his Glorious advancing the Protestant Cause, as much as any Man living.[16]

Considering, then, the shrewdness and detachment of Defoe's assessment of Charles XII at this earlier period, it is a real puzzle how by 1715 he could have become transformed into Charles's panegyrist and annalist, winning such golden opinions from the King as — so we are told in the 'Continuation' of *The History of the Wars of Charles XII* — 'the Author has too much Modesty to enter upon'; indeed, not only golden opinions, but solid gold ('the Bounty and Goodness of his *Swedish* Majesty to an Author unknown and remote, and testified in the most obliging Manner, upon Account of the Justice done to his Interest and Affairs in that History').[17]

Herbert G. Wright gets round these difficulties by the simple device of ignoring them. According to him, in 1715 Defoe merely thought 'the time ripe' for a history of Charles's achievements. Then in 1717, when the Swedish minister Gyllenborg was arrested for alleged complicity in a Jacobite invasion-plot, Defoe, as a seasoned journalist, saw a further chance of profit. He would abridge his *History of the Wars of Charles XII*, giving it a Jacobite slant — Wright's phrase is, 'adapted his earlier work so that it might appeal to a somewhat different class of reader' — and at the same time would lend it 'an air of actuality' by referring in the preface to recent events. Wright is a little puzzled by the possibility that Defoe may also in the same year have penned *A Short Narrative of the Life and Death of John Rhinholdt Count Patkul*, in which Charles XII is severely censured. However, he is ready to put it all down to Defoe's 'Protean character'.[18]

J.R. Moore at least acknowledges the difficulties. Why, he asks in *Daniel Defoe: Citizen of the Modern World*, should Defoe, a few months before his final reconciliation with the Whigs, choose to publish 'a book with such dangerous political implications' as his *History of the Wars of Charles XII* — a favourable history of 'the archenemy of George I in his Hanoverian domains?' The only answer Moore comes up with, however, is that it was hackwork on Defoe's part, 'Hastily and carelessly thrown together for the booksellers at a time when Defoe was greatly in need of money'. This is a far cry from Lee's estimate of it as a 'volume...worthy of standing by the side of the most fascinating productions of his great genius'.[19]

By contrast, Ernest Rhys, writing in the introduction to the Todhunter translation of Voltaire's *History of Charles XII*, finds *The History of the Wars of Charles XII* a shining example of Defoe's genius for impersonation:

> One interesting point about Voltaire's English associations, in so far as they prepare the way for the writing of his 'Charles XII', has not hitherto been pointed out. It is this: that a history of the 'Wars of Sweden', written by no less a hand than Defoe's, was in existence when Voltaire was studying English literature in London ...Defoe's 'History of the Wars' is written as 'by a Scots gentleman in the Swedish service'. It is a more documentary book than Voltaire's, to all outward appearance; and in it he has written with characteristic fidelity to the make-believe of his literary double the pseudo 'Scots gentleman'. It has much the air of the off-

hand, matter-of-fact military narrator, who does not look for
rhetorical openings, or greatly trouble himself to make the most of
his subject.[20]

(In other words, this seems to say, it was a great feat of the
chameleon-like Defoe to write badly for the length of some four
hundred pages.)

Stieg Hargevik is more brutal. He finds the whole series of 'North
European' writings 'extremely characteristic of Defoe's development as a journalist and a good indication of Defoe's political
engagement as a hack writer'. Defoe, he says, began, in *The History
of the Expedition of Charles XII*, as a eulogist of the Swedish monarch,
but, 'Even if his admiration for Charles XII was basic and great,
Defoe, later on, deliberately turned his coat and exchanged his
eulogy for severe criticism, whenever prompted by profit.' Defoe
turns his coat and becomes a critic of Charles XII in the *Review*, turns
it again in 1715 when he daringly publishes his *History of the Wars of
Charles XII* praising George I's enemy, and then perceives an ideal
opportunity for his talents in the Gyllenborg scandal of 1717, which
allows him to turn a dishonest penny by writing on both sides of the
question — the anti-Jacobite side in *An Account of The Swedish and
Jacobite Plot* and *What if the Swedes Should Come?* and the pro-Jacobite
side in *A Short View of the Conduct of the King of Sweden*. Regrets
overtake him, at the time of the 'Continuation' to *The History of the
Wars of Charles XII*, at having earlier credited Charles with complicity in Jacobite plots; but these regrets soon fade, and, being a
man who 'always used his knowledge of any subject to extract from
it the greatest possible financial gain', Defoe cannot resist exploiting
the growing interest in Peter the Great. Accordingly he revamps his
Charles XII material upon pro-Czarist, that is to say anti-Swedish
lines, to produce *An Impartial History of Peter Alexowitz*.[21]

When literary scholars agree so heartily, as they have done, in
ascribing a string of mutually contradictory 'North European' works
to Defoe, it is hardly for a historian to challenge them; and in consequence the historians of this era in Europe have to make what
sense they can, not merely of these writings, but of the 'Defoe' that
they manifest. For instance, in his *George I, the Baltic and the Whig
Split of 1717* (1969), J.J. Murray attaches a good deal of significance
to Defoe's supposed 'shiftings' and finds him 'a good weather vane
to test the direction of British public opinion toward Sweden'.[22]

*   *   *

Thus there seems a lot to be said for giving a further and close look at that influential attribution of Lee's, *The History of the Wars of Charles XII*. And when one does so, one finds it a puzzle how Lee, or anybody, could have thought it was by Defoe. (If we owe the ascription to a system of attribution based on an author's favourite phrases, then so much the worse for the system.) Two points immediately strike the reader: that the author of this work has no gift at all for narrative; and that this very lengthy history, dealing with events of the highest historical significance, is almost entirely innocent of ideas or reflections.

We shall take the point about narrative first. The style of *The History of the Wars of Charles XII* has a very marked idiosyncrasy: the author continually strews his narration with mnemonic props or promises, 'as above mentioned', 'as we shall see in its place', 'I must take every Thing in its due Order of Time', etc. By dint of repetition, this tic actually grows comic: within the small compass of pages 48-49, for instance, we find 'as I said before', 'as aforesaid', 'and so I shall rid my Hands of the Story as I go on', 'as is mention'd before' and 'as is mentioned already'. What this characteristic indicates, it would seem obvious, is a writer who finds the whole business of historical narration, and of keeping a number of separate stories going, a baffling problem. This could be, in part anyway, through sheer inexperience; and it is noticeable that the 'aforesaids' thin out a little in the later part of the work. At all events, this stylistic oddity seems symptomatic of what any unprejudiced reader must observe: that the author has no grasp of the 'architecture' of historical narrative, no idea of where to place an emphasis, where to condense, where to generalise, where to adopt an 'eagle-eye viewpoint', etc. What he has produced, indeed, is not a history but merely a chronicle.

It is observable, too, that, according to the promise on the title-page, the author often writes as an eye-witness of, or participant in, the events he describes, providing the sort of detail only an eye-witness would be likely to know. This is especially so in his descriptions of battles, which form the main staple of the narrative. Consider, for instance, (to take one example from very many) such a detail-packed passage as this from the description of the Swedish attack on the Russian-held fort at Pitschur, near Narva:

> We immediately caused our Dragoons to alight and attack the Fort Sword in Hand; but having no Cannon, were at a great Loss to know where to begin, the Fort being surrounded with a good

Mote, and regular Works within. But as good Luck would have it, some of our Dragoons attacking a small Redoubt, they carry'd it with small Resistance; and at the same time entring a Half-moon, which covered the Draw-bridge, putting to the Sword about fifty *Muscovites* that defended it; in this Half-moon we very happily found two Pieces of Cannon, which was what we wanted. Our Men immdiately traversing the said Cannon, turn'd 'em against the Draw-bridge, and some of the first Shot having cut the Tackles of the Bridge, which it seems was slung with Ropes, and not with Chains, as it should have been, the Bridge fell down; upon which our Men giving a great Shout, entered the Fort Sword in Hand; but being not above two hundred, and the *Muscovites* within being very numerous, they were driven back, and had like to have all been cut to Pieces before we could come to their Relief. But they maintained the Bridge with the utmost Bravery, sending every Minute to our General for Relief. It happened that an Officer of our Dragoons, who was posted within Call, but with Orders to attack in another Place, perceiving the Distress they were in, sent an hundred of his Men without any Orders, to their Relief, and sent a Dragoon to the General for Orders to go himself, which the Dragoon galloping immediately back, carry'd him Directions to do; and this was the taking of the Place. Our General was unhappily posted on the other Side of the Fort, where he had designed to make his main Attack, not foreseeing the Accident which happened as before. This was the Reason our Men were so long before they were supported, and was the Loss of near two hundred of our brave Dragoons: But as soon as our General came up, the Dragoons he had with him, alighted and joined with them that were engaged before, push'd into the Fort, and making Way for the Horse, they had now no more Business but to cut to Pieces the *Muscovites* that stood in their Way. We kill'd about two thousand Men, the rest fled out of the Fort on the other Side; so the Fort was secured, eight hundred Men left in it, and we returned to our Camp.[23]

It may be objected (no doubt it would have been by Ernest Rhys) that Defoe is an acknowledged master of invented detail. But to this the obvious retort is that Defoe used his invented detail to intensely telling effect, whereas nothing in these laborious battle-accounts could reasonably be called 'telling'. Indeed, though we have no opinion as to whether the author of *The History of the Wars of Charles*

XII was, or was not, a 'Scots Gentleman in the Swedish Service', we can see, *prima facie*, nothing in the book that would rule this out; and the author's many self-references fit perfectly well with the supposition. Nor, in fact, do we wish to pass a harsh judgement on the work, which is in many ways a decent and painstaking effort, which might have had much to offer to a reader living nearer the time. It is just that, everything in it bespeaks the amateur writer; and for the modern reader, it is quite a gruelling task to get through it.

Our second point, that the work is almost entirely devoid of ideas and reflections, is really an extension of the first. For evidently you cannot write meaningful history, you cannot indeed write history proper at all, without possessing ideas; it is they that dictate how your narrative shall be shaped and organised and how you 'make something' of your material. It is unfortunate (for the purpose of comparison) that the only extended history which can unquestionably be ascribed to Defoe is his *History of the Union*, which is a very different kind of enterprise from a military history. Nevertheless it seems paradoxical to suppose that the author of a work so permeated with thought and so full of historical vision as *The History of the Union* (whatever one may think of its truthfulness as a historical record) could also have composed so intellectually vacant a chronicle as *The History of the Wars of Charles XII*. If there were some evidence to suggest this, we should, of course, have to consider it as a possibility; but then, so far as we know, there is not.

*   *   *

It remains for us to draw a moral from the foregoing. Those who would question the attribution of *The History of the Wars of Charles XII* are faced with a difficulty not unusual in Defoe attribution studies — that of having, in a sense, nothing to argue against. For no one, so far as we know, has ever produced any argument for the work's being Defoe's: the fact, if fact it be, has been asserted and accepted as a simple matter of faith. Thus, all that there exists for a doubter to contest is the (somewhat strained and embarrassed) hypotheses and rationalisations resorted to by those whom the fact has puzzled. These have depended, as we have seen, on some of the most cherished 'blanket' notions of Defoe, all of them tending to make of him a kind of monster or, at least, an extreme 'case'. Defoe, so we gather from Lee's account, was a work-maniac who, from sheer abundance of energy, would knock off a minutely detailed history of Charles XII's wars in the time left over from composing *The Family Instructor* and a stream of polemical pamphlets. According to Herbert Wright, Stieg Hargevik and even, in this instance, J.R. Moore, he was a low, mercenary hack and penny-a-liner, willing to produce incompetent and slipshod work so long as it brought in some guineas. Finally, in the view of Ernest Rhys, he was an inspired impersonator. There is much to be said about these 'blanket' conceptions of Defoe, and they are certainly a marvellous help to any argument about attribution. But is it not a precarious case which needs to lean upon them?

Let us suppose for a moment that William Lee had never had the intuition that *The History of the Wars of Charles XII* was by Defoe, or had felt sufficient uncertainty about it not to include it in the main body of his 'Chronological Catalogue', but to relegate it to an annexe of questionable items. Is it not possible that, in that case, the great machine of attribution might never have been set in motion, demanding to be fed with ever more 'Swedish' or 'North European' items? And this, we should remember, would not be a mere matter of a reduction in the size of the canon. For as Michel Foucault has rightly remarked, 'an author's name is not just a proper name like the rest';[24] and it might fairly be said that, without these 'North European' writings and the hypotheses invoked to explain them, we should have a somewhat different 'Defoe'.

CHAPTER 3

PRINCIPLES OF AUTHOR-ATTRIBUTION

WHAT THE PRECEDING CHAPTER illustrates is the 'snowball effect' in attribution. This is only one of the dangers attending the constructing of a canon, though certainly it is an important one, and in due course we shall discuss others. We hope, though, that by now, we have begun to make our case that the Defoe 'canon' is a deeply questionable affair and has been created upon very shaky principles. However, before we say more about the construction of the canon, we need to discuss something logically prior to this, namely the fundamental principles governing author-attribution. We shall do this in a rather general fashion, though coming round to Defoe towards the end of the chapter.

The first rule to observe in regard to author-attribution is the one that Baron Gilbert, in his classic *Law of Evidence*, lays down for a court of law, that it is not necessary to prove a negative:

> And here it is first to be considered, that in all Courts of Justice the Affirmative ought to be proved, for it is sufficient barely to deny what is affirmed until the contrary is proved...
>
> The Civil Law says 'The Proof lies on him who makes the Allegation, for it is against the Nature of Things to prove a negative'.[1]

When an anonymous work is ascribed to an author, the onus of proof lies entirely with the person making the ascription, and, in theory at least, there is no corresponding obligation to disprove it: it may be assumed to be untrue until proved true. It is this that makes the attribution of a work such a momentous business. As we said earlier (p. 15), the argument for adding something to an author's canon has to be vastly more stringent than the argument for keeping it there. For once a work has been included in the canon the whole situation changes radically; there will now be a presumption in favour of its authenticity, and if this is later disputed, the onus of proof will lie entirely with the disputant.

THE FALLACY OF PROVISIONAL ASCRIPTION

It follows that, of the various false steps open to the compiler of an author-bibliography, one seemingly innocuous error is likely, in the long run, to be the most fatal of all. It is to say: 'Let us give this anonymous work to our author until a better claimant comes along.' This was a favourite formula with W.P. Trent, who would write, for instance, of a newly discovered pamphlet: 'since in both manner and matter it strongly suggests Defoe's authorship and apparently is not claimed for anyone else, I adopt it as his until evidence to the contrary is forthcoming'.[2] It was also resorted to by Gary Taylor in the controversy over the supposed Shakespeare poem 'Shall I die?'. ('The cumulative force of the verbal similarities between the poem and Shakespeare's acknowledged works could only be weakened by the identification of another poet whose works provided more and better parallels.'[3]) Why it is fatal is because of that qualitative change which, as we have said, is produced by inclusion in a canon — a change which will take place regardless of any good intentions or mental reservations on the part of the attributor and will infallibly give the new attribution an aura of authority in the eyes of later scholars, tempting them to use it as a basis for further attributions. To contemplate adding a work *temporarily* to the canon is to misunderstand the nature of a 'canon'. Moreover, the motive for doing it would be a wrong one, a quite unjustified eagerness for attribution. The only safe principle, and a precious one, is the negative one: that works do not *need* to be assigned to authors and it does not matter that anonymous works should remain anonymous.

The point is more important than at first sight it might appear, for the error we mention is the consequence of an even more basic mistake, that of thinking that, in the construction of an author-canon, the positive activity of attribution counts for more than the negative one of refusing or rejecting attribution. The mistake is perhaps natural for someone studying, shall we say, the Elizabethan drama, where the assumption is that the identity of most of the working dramatists is known, so that an attribution problem may easily fall into the form of 'Shall we attribute this play to Middleton in preference to Ford or Webster?', that is, into a choice of positive attributions. Its falsity comes out when one considers the very different case of eighteenth-century pamphleteering, where authors, known and unknown, exist in such profusion, and where the fear that only faintly nags at the student of Elizabethan drama, that a work might be by an author nobody has ever heard of, becomes horribly insistent. The decision that such-and-such a work is not by Swift or by Defoe will not, for the most part, involve attributing it to anyone else; and this, we would suggest, is really the most natural state of affairs in author-attribution — lending, as it does, enormous importance to purely negative decisions.

We shall be going on to discuss the various kinds of evidence, and also of reasoning about evidence (the notions of 'accumulation of evidence', 'parallels', etc.), that are commonly met with in attribution. But it is perhaps worth dwelling for a moment on the point that errors encountered here often have their root in a more simple and basic mistake: an over-enthusiasm for attribution — a feeling that it is unnatural for works to go around in an orphaned condition and that even a foster-parent is better than none.

It is worth mentioning here that legal analogies to literary attribution can be misleading. It might be tempting to think that, from a judicial point of view, the correct analogy was with civil procedure, where judgement is supposed to be based on a 'balance of probabilities', but this would be a mistake, and the nearer comparison is with criminal procedure. In a criminal case it is held to be more important that an innocent person should not be convicted than that a guilty one should go free; and in similar fashion, it is far more desirable that a false literary attribution should not be made than that a true one should be made. This is so because the fact of a literary work's not being assigned to any particular author has no important consequences (and *Edmund Ironside* is as good, or as bad, a play, whoever wrote it), whereas any addition to a 'canon', whether correct or mistaken, may have large consequences. A literary attribution does not merely certify a given work as being by a given author; it also, to some degree, redefines the author, so that it becomes plausible to attribute further works to him or her. The legal analogy breaks down here and has to be replaced by a scientific one. Literary attribution is not so much a matter of coming to a verdict as of giving formal adoption to a hypothesis, which will have expanding implications.

EXTERNAL AND INTERNAL EVIDENCE

In the attributing of anonymous works to an author two main kinds of evidence are called upon, 'external' evidence and 'internal'. Arthur Sherbo has defined these as follows:

> Internal evidence concerns itself with style, ideas and areas of interest, verbal parallels and echoes, and peculiarities of spelling and (sometimes) punctuation. External evidence concerns itself with attributions by contemporaries or near contemporaries of the author, place of appearance and publisher (for article and book respectively), and use of a pseudonym or distinguishing mark of some kind.[4]

This definition seems reasonably adequate, but there are at least two complicating factors which need to be borne in mind.

The first is that within external evidence there is one family or sub-division of special significance, which is *witness*. Most ancient legal systems seem to have based themselves mainly on witnesses, so that the task of a judge or jury was to adjudicate according to their assessment of the reliability of witnesses, or maybe according to the willingness of witnesses to commit themselves by oath or combat. In regard to literature, the most natural basis upon which to decide authorship is the witness of a title-page; and thus, in the case of a work whose title-page names no author, it is natural to give a certain amount of credence, in the absence of other and conflicting evidence, to anyone who bears witness to the work's being by such-and-such an author: for instance, a contemporary opponent who accuses such-and-such a person of being the author, or a contemporary bibliographer. Coleridge, indeed, in an article written in 1800, defined 'external evidence' as being no more nor less than the evidence of witnesses.[5] This, however, does not seem to be right, for one can think of many other sorts of external evidence. For example, say that two or three days after the publication of a long anonymous work there appeared an article reviewing it in Defoe's *Review*, showing more intimate knowledge of its contents than a reader would be likely to have gained in so brief a period. This would be external evidence that the work itself might have been written by Defoe. Or again, say that there were a publisher who published very few authors apart from Defoe; then the fact that a given work was published by him might lend a certain support to a suspicion, *based upon other kinds of evidence*, that it was by Defoe. This would be external evidence, and of a legitimate kind, though of course it could never by itself be conclusive.

The second general point to bear in mind is that both external and internal evidence can be decisive *negatively*; whereas neither can be decisive positively and at the most can amount to an extreme probability. Even the most plausible attribution (for instance of *David Copperfield* to Dickens) could in theory be challenged; whereas if it can be proved that a certain work was already in print by 1600 this is conclusive evidence that it was not by Defoe.

It is assumed by some that internal evidence lies nearer the concerns of literary critics, in that it is derived from the literary style and content of a work, whilst by others it is considered too impressionistic and 'unscientific' to be worth much reliance. The status of 'internal' *versus* 'external' evidence was debated hotly at a symposium held at the English Institute at Columbia University in 1958, on the subject of 'Evidence for Authorship'. In an opening paper Arthur Sherbo made extreme claims in defence of internal evidence. He declared: '. . .internal evidence deals with essentials while external evidence deals with accidentals. . .short of an unequivocal acknowledgement by the author himself, the value of internal evidence outweighs any other'. The two kinds of internal evidence he mainly discussed were *style* and *ideas*. He claimed that 'Ideas are more easily recognised and analysed than individual prose styles', and it follows that 'Determination of individual prose styles — this is Johnson's, this is Goldsmith's, and this is Hawkesworth imitating Johnson — is often virtually impossible without the evidence of ideas.'[6]

A succeeding speaker, David Erdman, took a more moderate position and put forward the following two propositions: 1) 'The test of style is always crucial, at least in the negative sense. There are styles which would rule out Marvell as author. . .no matter how impressive the external evidence. It should also be recognized that the test of style *can* be decisive in a positive sense.' 2) Internal evidence works best where two distinct factors concur. 'Parallels can be illusory or coincidental; recognition of the author's signature in characteristic constructional rhythms or in modes of metaphor and metaphysics can be precarious. It is the combination of the two that constitutes the most satisfactory internal evidence.'

Erdman went on to discuss the question of the *calculation* of evidence, how or whether it may be cumulative: 'When parallelisms are rather diffusely scattered than closely associated, it is of course necessary to resort to numbers. But in that case the eligibility of each suffrage requires close scrutiny. Have unrelated commonplaces any cumulative force?...If we must put question marks beside several of the parallelisms, how can a column of 1?+1?+1? be calculated?'[7] In this Erdman was backed up by Ephim G. Fogel, who declared that 'commonplace parallels, unsupported by information about the relative frequencies of the commonplaces in the work of potential candidates, fall into the category of "arguments" which R.W. Chambers calls "so unreliable as not to be arguments at all", zeros which add up to zero no matter how great their number'.[8] In the opposite camp was Arthur Sherbo, who remarked:

> What is overlooked is the fact that each of these minor points gains strength and importance by its very appearance in juxtaposition with the stronger points, and, I would stress, with the other minor points also....I should further suggest...that a series of coincidences results in something more startling and rare than any one coincidence, however weak it may be and however weak the individual coincidences may be.[9]

PARALLELS

We are very much of the Erdman and Fogel school of opinion, and against Sherbo's, as regards 'parallels' and the accumulation of 'parallels', and it will be worth looking a little more closely at this subject, which is one that will dog us throughout our book. A convenient place to start is with the five rules drawn up by Muriel St. Clair Byrne in an article on 'Bibliographical Clues in Collaborate Plays':

1) Parallels may be susceptible of at least three explanations: a) unsuspected identity of authorship; b) plagiarism, either deliberate or unconscious; c) coincidence.
2) Quality is all-important, and parallels demand very careful grading — e.g. mere verbal parallelism is of almost no value in comparison with parallelism of thought coupled with some verbal parallelism.
3) Mere accumulation of ungraded parallels does not prove anything.
4) In accumulating parallels for the sake of cumulative effect we may logically proceed from the known to the collaborate, or

from the known to the anonymous play, but not from the
collaborate to the anonymous;

5) In order to express ourselves as certain of attributions we must
prove exhaustively that we cannot parallel works, images, and
phrases as a body from other acknowledged plays of the period;
in other words, the negative check must always be applied.[10]

To these rules Samuel Schoenbaum, in *Internal Evidence and
Elizabethan Dramatic Authorship* (1966) later added a sixth, namely:
'Parallels from plays of uncertain or contested authorship prove
nothing.'[11]

These six rules are helpful so far as they go, but there seem to be
one or two rather important considerations that suggest further
limitations on what one can hope from attribution by parallels.

The first is suggested by identity-parades and by any kind of
human identification for legal purposes. Accumulation may certainly
play an important part here. Thus, say that in a murder trial several
witnesses believe they saw the culprit, and witness A noticed he had
a limp, witness B noticed he had a scar on the left side of his fore-
head, and witness C noticed that he spoke with a broad Scottish
accent, the cumulative effect of these testimonies could be great and
strongly point to a given suspect; but they would have no force at all
without an item of evidence of another kind, and logically prior, that
is, some fact that could be thought to connect the suspect with the
murder in the first place. (For, after all, the police are not likely to
round up all the men with a limp and a scar and a Scottish accent in
Great Britain.) In similar fashion, literary 'parallels' will have greatly
more force in the presence of a piece of external evidence, however
meagre, which seems to connect a work to an author. Nor will sheer
accumulation be significant here, for the combination of a single
parallel of high 'quality' with a single piece of external evidence
could be most powerful and persuasive. In all this, it needs also to be
remembered that any accumulation of items helping to prove an
identification can always be overturned by a single further item —
such as a further witness who comes forward to attest that the culprit
was over six feet in height (whereas the suspect is diminutive).

A second point concerns rule number 5 and the 'negative check'. It
is conceivable that, with a relatively narrow corpus of writing
like the Elizabethan drama (or Elizabethan poetry), a reasonably
thorough 'negative check', and assurance that there is no other
possible author, is a possibility. But even here one has serious

doubts. For as Robin Robbins pointed out, in the Shakespeare and 'Shall I die?' controversy, if you scale up the parallels in Spenser according to the relative proportion of words in his works as compared with Shakespeare's, they come out as equal in number if not more plentiful, a fact that suggests that there may be other Elizabethan poets with a much smaller output even than Spenser's who would also be candidates, given a suitable proportional adjustment.[12] Thus the application of the 'negative check', even in regard to Elizabethan verse, becomes distinctly problematic; and in regard to eighteenth-century prose we might well be tempted to write it off as altogether impracticable.

A further consideration is that what are normally presented as literary 'parallels' are not likely to occur in sufficiently large quantities for statistical analysis. (This indeed is one of the justifications for the stylometric approach, which concentrates, not on observed 'parallels', but on words or collocations of high frequency; see Appendix on 'Stylometry and Defoe' below, pp. 176–83.) Thus the epithet 'cumulative' here can never have more than an impressionistic or non-verifiable force.

Complementarily, if a disputed work shows a very high incidence of parallels with a single work known to be by a given author (rather than with that author's work in general) this will go along with an increased probability that the work is a plagiarism from the other.

Underlying all discussion of 'parallels', it is important to insist, is the danger of what is known, after Ephim G. Fogel, as the 'salmons in both' fallacy. (Fogel quotes Fluellen's explanation in *Henry V* of how the situations of Macedon and Monmouth 'is both alike. There is a river in Macedon; and there is also moreover a river at Monmouth...and there is salmons in both.' Fluellen's fallacy, says Fogel, 'is rife in current literary scholarship'.) This is the same point as Byrne is getting at in her rule number 2, that 'quality is all-important'. Low-quality parallels, parallels so vague as to possess no real distinctiveness, are really of no significance at all, nor do they acquire any significance by being offered in profusion. One thing common to almost all writers of books to prove that Bacon, etc. wrote Shakespeare's works is their strong faith in sheer quantity when it comes to 'parallels'.[13] However, Byrne's insistence that parallels must be graded according to quality runs into problems also, in that judgements about quality are bound to become somewhat personal. It does not look as if computation will ever do much for us in this business of 'parallels'.

Finally: Schoenbaum's additional rule, that 'Parallels from [works] of uncertain or contested authorship prove nothing', though it is an obvious one, is extremely important and applies even more forcibly in Defoe studies.[14]

THE CALCULATION OF EVIDENCE

The question of how pieces of evidence may be added together is one which has long exercised jurists, and what they have to say seems to have some relevance to these theories about attribution problems. A famous, or infamous, example of the mathematical addition or cumulation of evidence is the rules of procedure introduced in Toulouse in 1670, which specified in advance the value of each piece of evidence, and required the judge simply to add these together, regardless of his own conclusions about the case. For instance, the rules distinguished between *indubitable* or *violent* or *grave* or *light* pieces of evidence. Many *light* pieces of evidence when joined together would make a *grave* one; two *grave* pieces of evidence added up to one *violent* one; one *violent* piece of evidence warranted condemnation to questioning under torture; several *violent* pieces of evidence warranted outright condemnation, especially in the case of serious crimes. In a celebrated and appalling case which attracted the scorn and indignation of Voltaire, Jean Calas, a Protestant, was tried, tortured and executed for the murder of his son — allegedly to prevent his defecting to Rome — according to evidence calculated under this system.[15]

Cogent objections to such attempts to add pieces of evidence together mathematically have been offered by L.J. Cohen in his book *The Probable and the Provable* (1977). Cohen concludes that such formulae work only *if there is a prior probability that the fact suspected is correct.*[16] This of course means that they would not apply to English courts of law, where innocence is presumed and the jury is not supposed to know that the accused already has a police record, etc., and it has a bearing on any attempt to add up pieces of weak evidence, in arithmetical fashion, to support the attribution of a work to an author. If, *prima facie*, the work could just as well *not* be by the author as by him, it is not justifiable to regard one weak piece of evidence as corroborating another. Here perhaps we have a kind of answer to David Erdman's question, 'If we must put question marks beside several of the parallelisms, how can a column of 1?+1?+1? be calculated?'

As for Arthur Sherbo's thesis about the mutual enhancement of bits of evidence, the following from Jeremy Bentham, in his *Treatise on Judicial Evidence*, seems relevant:

> There is nothing in judicial logic more important than the following observation: Circumstantial facts can be cast up into a sum total, only when they are in some measure identical quantities, that is, when they are grouped round the same fact directly, or in an uninterrupted chain; when the mind can follow the connection which unites them without losing sight of it for a single instant; when they all concur to establish, not an opinion or a conjecture, but the existence of a principal fact. Hence [the following] rule: 'Oblige the party, who alleges the facts, to connect them directly with the principal facts, or in an uninterrupted chain with each other'. Wherever the chain is broken, wherever a link is lost, the other links ought to be thrown away.[17]

AUTHORITY

As we have said, the role of authority in the construction and evolution of a literary canon is very large, and larger than one would infer from the theoretical principles expounded by bibliographers. In fact, when Defoe bibliographers discuss their own principles, it is rather rare for them to say much about authority. David Foxon is here an exception. In the introduction to his *English Verse 1701–1750*, he speaks as the author of a general bibliography, and as such, in view of the vastness of the task in hand, as being compelled to a considerable extent to work by 'rule of thumb': '. . .it has clearly been impossible for me to enter at all deeply into the canon of any author either by biographical research or by internal evidence of style'. What his 'rule of thumb' prescribes, he goes on to explain, is respect not merely for evidence, of various kinds, but also for 'cumulative authority':

> When. . .the attribution is merely an unsupported statement in the catalogue of a library or a modern bookseller I have normally recorded but not accepted it. . .I do, however, give weight to cumulative authority — even though, as in the case of Swift, successive editors can be shown to have been united in a misjudgment. Thus, under Defoe I accept *A hymn to the mob* which has been in the canon for a century though external evidence is

lacking, while I reject *A hymn to the funeral sermon* because it rests on the authority of the late J.R. Moore alone.[18]

We find no such expressions of respect for cumulative authority in the introduction to Walter Wilson's *Memoirs of De Foe* or to William Lee's *Daniel Defoe*; nor do we find them in J.R. Moore's article 'Some Remarks on the Assignment of Authorship to Defoe', which is all about the skill of author-recognition at first-hand.[19] Matters are different, however, when these and other scholars come to discuss individual attributions. Here one can find them giving considerable weight to 'cumulative authority', sometimes quite consciously and explicitly, but equally often unwittingly or absent-mindedly.

Schoenbaum is vehement against any respect for authority in attribution: '...responsible scholars', he complains, 'pay to the pronouncements of experts a respect that reasoned demonstration alone can legitimately claim'; and he rebukes J.C. Maxwell for saying that another scholar's 'unargued verdict' on an attribution problem 'carries considerable weight'. 'How', Schoenbaum roundly protests, 'can any unargued verdict carry any weight at all?'[20]

Let us not go quite as far as Schoenbaum — at least, not for the moment — and let us suppose that in attribution, as in religion or in politics, a respect for authority may not necessarily be absurd. Still, what seems most necessary is that, when it exists, its operation should be brought into the light of day. Much alertness is needed to achieve this. One need think only of the incalculable influence of library catalogues. It is not expected even of a major library that it should undertake a fundamental and independent reappraisal of an author's canon; and it may be said to be doing its full duty if it takes care to reflect current scholarly opinion. Nevertheless, and illogically, library catalogues tend to colour our views and are felt to add to the weight of 'cumulative authority'. As we shall see (pp. 117–18), J.R. Moore was keenly aware of this and took elaborate measures, well before the publication of his *Checklist*, to get his attributions adopted by major libraries.

Another means by which attributions can be given authority is by announcing them in an oracular manner. Lee, Crossley, Trent and Moore were all addicted to oracular phraseology and would, on occasion, assert that such-and-such a work was 'unquestionably', 'indisputably', or 'beyond a shadow of doubt' by Defoe. Sometimes, for rhetorical effect, they would even stake their whole reputation on a given attribution, or (as Moore did with *A General History of the Pyrates*), depict the most frightening consequences (no less than the whole canon being put in question) if a particular new attribution were not to be accepted. Nor are these appeals to faith aimed merely at the laity; professional Defoe bibliographers will happily claim support from the oracular pronouncements of their own predecessors. There is involved here a phenomenon of great importance in literary attribution: the wish for an oracle, and the corresponding temptation to set oneself up as such an oracle, whose unsupported judgment can be invoked as authority by fellow-scholars of a later generation.

What may be equally, or even more, important is what we may call silent or unnoticed authority. It is a phenomenon particularly associated with William Lee. In his biography of Defoe, Lee will often introduce a new attribution as if it were a well-attested and unquestioned fact. Then, being an honest man, he may spend considerable effort in attempting to explain the biographical puzzles which arise from the attribution; and this has the effect of diverting the reader, unless particularly alert, from questioning — what is most of all in need of questioning — the attribution itself.

METHODS OF ATTRIBUTION

In attempting to attribute literary works, scholars have employed a wide range of methods: a historical reconstruction of the circumstances of publication of a work, identification of allusions to contemporary events or individuals, literary analysis of language and style, explication of content and purpose, and statistical analysis of linguistic usage. All these methods have been used in the attribution of works to Defoe, but perhaps the preferred method of Defoe bibliographers, at least from William Lee onwards, has been based on the recognition of 'favourite phrases'. In a footnote in his *Life* of Defoe, Lee recorded the following list of favourite expressions, the presence of which, he claimed, indicated Defoe's authorship:

> 'let the World know'; 'I say'; 'of which in its place'; 'When it came to the Push'; 'on that Foot'; 'by the Way'; 'in few Words'; 'it must be confess'd'; 'in short'; 'to that which he answers and says — nothing'; 'upon the whole'; 'says he'; 'Be that as it will'; 'in plain English'; 'the hands of Justice'; 'to that Part'; 'But of this by and by'; 'at Home and Abroad'; ''tis true'; 'and the like'; 'breaking in upon them'; 'all Sorts'; 'to come into their Measures'; 'so nice a

Juncture'; 'the Shortest Way'; 'one of Solomon's Fools'; 'To talk Gospel to a Kettle Drum'; 'Take this with you as you go'.[21]

Similar 'favourite phrases' or 'Defoeisms' were collected by later scholars, including Burch, Secord, Moore, Novak and Bastian, all of them arrived at by simple reading, as opposed to counts made by computer or by using concordances.[22] Various questions of logic are raised by them: for example, it is obvious that such a list ought to be drawn only from works which are unquestionably by Defoe, but it is not always clear that this rule has been observed. One question we can ask ourselves immediately, though: why does instinct tell us that it would not be practicable simply to amalgamate these various lists into one large list? It is because they are the product of different critical responses to Defoe. Lee, Moore, Bastian, etc. each have their own mental image of Defoe as man and writer, and it lurks behind their respective lists.

This system of recognition based upon an author's 'favourite' phrases is not only natural but extremely seductive. All the same, we would suggest that, *taken on its own*, it is quite fatal; indeed, much of the trouble with the work of the Defoe bibliographers seems to lie just here. The objection is not that the method is impressionistic or 'unscientific'; it is rather that it is an attempt at a short-cut, in an area where no short-cut exists. Faced with his giant task, the bibliographer seeks for a quick and handy procedure which will settle many problems out of hand. If enough of Defoe's 'favourite expressions' are present in an anonymous work, this shall be re-garded as a strong — in some cases, a decisive — argument for attri-buting the work to him, without regard to any other consideration. The bibliographer tells himself that this is a highly intuitive skill, only attainable after prolonged immersion in Defoe and not really fully communicable to others or to be summed up in a mere list of 'favourite phrases'. But what we can perceive is that, it is for him also a kind of magic — an 'open sesame', without which, given the limits to human energy, the goal could never be reached.

The dangers of this are rather obvious. In confronting a problem in author-attribution — or at least when considering the making of a positive attribution — it should be strongly urged that there can be no short-cuts. Every such problem needs to be regarded as a unique case and all the approaches that seem relevant need to be tried — the historian's, the biographer's, the literary critic's, and perhaps some others too.

This is not to say that favourite phrases (given that it is established that they are indeed 'favourite') are of no significance. They could in a given case turn out to be highly significant, and so could the many other features of style that scholars have commented upon, for instance, favourite metaphors and similes, particular mis-spellings and grammatical solecisms, favourite anecdotes, Latin tags and French phrases, the treatment of paragraphing, etc.

For that matter, questions of literary value may also be highly significant. How they will enter into attribution arguments needs, however, a little sorting out. One tends to be unrealistic about recognition of authorship in general and to aspire to the impossible. J.R. Moore, in 'Some Remarks on the Assignment of Authorship to Defoe', hypothesises that, 'If we could know the qualities of Defoe's writing as perfectly as we do the few things which we know best, we might be able to recognise it at a glance'; and thereupon he goes further, crediting Defoe with 'a style so distinct that (in its freest expression) it seems to me recognizable by its rhythm alone, and ideas so individualistic that (taken in combination) they set Defoe apart from any other writer who has used the English language'.[23] We believe this to be illusory.

The point, of course, is not confined to Defoe. Let us think, for instance, of William Hazlitt. One could certainly call him a very 'characteristic' writer, for all that, like Defoe, he was a practitioner of the 'plain style'. Yet on reflection one realises that, faced with even his most famous and admirable passages, one could not swear one would have identified them as Hazlitt's (assuming one did not know them) on stylistic grounds alone. (Though of course if some other kind of evidence, from content or context, suggested Hazlitt, the stylistic argument would then weigh very heavily.) On the other hand, there are many kinds of excellent writing which we should not attribute to Hazlitt. This can be an important consideration in questions of attribution, where the relevant argument runs: 'This has the excellence, not of A but of B, not of Hazlitt but of James Mill.' A principle even more important in attribution, however, is the complementary one, which runs that, though Hazlitt no doubt sometimes wrote badly, there are particular kinds of badness of which we can be confident he would never have been capable. A passage of debased Johnsonese, a very long-winded passage, a passage peppered to excess with classical quotations, a pompous, a legalistic, an obtrusively 'quaint' passage may be securely assumed not to be by Hazlitt — except on the supposition that he was writing parody or burlesque. The principle seems a very important one in bibliographic attribution and certainly applies, *mutatis mutandis*, to Defoe. In all these attribution questions, the *negative* principle seems to be the one most necessary to grasp hold of.

It will be seen that we do not go along here with Schoenbaum who, in his *Internal Evidence and Elizabethan Dramatic Authorship*, describes it as a fallacy that, for attribution purposes, anything can be inferred from badness. In Schoenbaum's eyes it was a prime example of Dr Johnson's 'good sense' to have exposed this fallacy, and he quotes approvingly what Johnson wrote apropos of Shakespeare's *Henry VI* plays:

> From mere inferiority nothing can be inferred; in the productions of wit there will be inequality. Sometimes judgment will err, and sometimes the matter itself will defeat the artist. Of every author's works one will be the best, and one will be the worst. The colours are not equally pleasing, nor the attitudes equally graceful, in all the pictures of *Titian* or *Reynolds*.[24]

We hold, on the contrary, that in theory something can be inferred from badness, that is to say from the *kind* of badness involved; and this, of course, has a corollary, which is that nothing can be more important than to be continually sharpening and enriching one's sense of the positive characteristics and virtues of Defoe's thought and style. We shall have something more to say about this in a later chapter.

THE LESSONS FROM ART HISTORY

Author-attribution in literary studies is, you might say, a relatively marginal problem. It crops up in a minor degree with many authors — for instance Swift, Pope, Johnson and Coleridge — but not to very disturbing effect: they would remain the same author with or without the disputed works. The identity of 'Junius' has certainly excited a number of scholars, but here again the issue is not really a disquieting one, since what is in doubt is not so much the integrity of a literary corpus as the name-tag to be attached to it. Undoubtedly there are a few areas of English literature where attribution is a burning issue, notably the Elizabethan and Jacobean drama. Nevertheless it could perhaps be said that the 'Defoe' problem is the most disturbing in English studies; certainly it appears to be the largest in scale. Thus it might be worth seeing if there are lessons to be learned from art history, where such cases are much more common and where, indeed, for experts in certain periods of art, author-attribution could really be said to be a central preoccupation.

The problems are, of course, not exactly the same. In any sphere of art, whether it be literature, music or the plastic arts, it is natural to want to know who is the author of a work. For, as Frank Kermode and others have pointed out, if he or she proves to be a famous name, we shall then look at the work with a different and special sort of attention.[25] However, with painting and sculpture this stress on the author is reinforced and enormously magnified by the fact that paintings (and, generally speaking, sculptures) are unique objects — so that you might possess a Rembrandt, in a way that you could not 'possess' *Middlemarch* or the 'Jupiter' symphony, and this, evidently, must bring money into the question, in a highly significant way. It may also be said that in painting the situation is more favourable to author–attribution than it is in literature. Paintings are perishable objects, which survive only if cherished; and the works of known and highly regarded artists are the most likely to be cherished and preserved — whereas the most despised literary work, being printed in multiple copies, has an excellent chance of survival.

These reservations made, however, art history seems to have some helpful things to say for our purpose. For one thing, the sheer strenuousness of the attributing activity in art, as described by Max Friedländer (1867–1958), the great expert on Netherlandish painting, is very impressive:

> If the determination of the authorship of an individual work of art most certainly is not the ultimate and highest task of artistic erudition; even if it were no path to the goal: nevertheless, without a doubt, it is a school for the eye, since there is no formulation of a question which forces us to penetrate so deeply into the essence of the individual work as that concerning the identity of the author.

Equally striking is the severity of self-criticism demanded:

> If one has made a mistake — which is something that occasionally happens even to a gifted connoisseur — then one must radically and decisively evacuate the falsely judged work of art from one's memory and submit to a purge in the guise of the contemplation of indubitable works by the master. I remember the tragic case of an excellent and conscientious expert who once made a mistake.

He was unable to summon sufficient courage and self-control to confess his mistake to himself; he searched for 'proofs' of his false attribution and as a result ended up in a false position with regard to the master, to whom he once by mistake had assigned something. As a result of this one mistake, which in itself was no disaster, he was bereft of pure and clear notion, and his judgment, at least so far as this master was concerned, lost authority. And that *was* a disaster.[26]

There is perhaps a lesson for literary studies, too, in the way that, in listings, art historians indicate degrees of certainty or specificity in attribution according to an agreed convention.

It is in art history, moreover, that we find the right label for an activity which has been very important to Defoe scholars in the past, that is to say, 'connoisseurship'. When William Lee writes that 'long and critical study of a great author may result in so full an acquaintance, that his writings will be recognised by the student in a moment, as the voice of a familiar friend', he is asserting the claims of connoisseurship.[27] Interestingly, Giovanni Morelli (1816–91), a very influential nineteenth-century champion of connoisseurship, describes his own famous 'method' in attribution in terms that vividly remind us of Lee: 'As most men who speak or write have verbal habits and use their favourite words or phrases involuntarily and sometimes even most inappropriately, so almost every painter has his own peculiarities which escape him without his being aware of them.' According to Morelli, a painter will most clearly reveal himself, and distinguish himself from his imitators, in unstudied features like ears, hands and finger-nails.[28] We are at once put in mind of those lists of 'favourite expressions' compiled by Lee and other Defoe scholars — expressions so habitual as, according to the theory, to escape the author's conscious control.

It is instructive that Morelli's theory of attribution in art was interpreted by his successors in two quite contrary ways: for some, the significance of those finger-nails and ear-lobes was that, through being produced in an unstudied fashion, they were the most complete expression of an artist's sensibility and artistic purposes; for others they were to be prized precisely for their independence of all the qualities in the artist that would cause him to be admired. The interpretation to be placed on William Lee's 'verbal habits' would seem to be somewhere between these two poles, though with an inclination towards the second. (For strict adherence to the second, in literary studies, we need to look to 'stylometry', as described by A.Q. Morton in his *Literary Detection* and other publications. The basic principle or claim of 'stylometry' is that every author has 'habits', distinguishing him or her from all other authors, and that the habits most to be relied on for purposes of recognition are not the authors' more visible and obvious idiosyncrasies, but a purely statistical feature, almost certainly unnoticeable by themselves or others: the rate at which they perform some quite basic verbal operations, common to all users of the language. (For a brief discussion of 'stylometry' in relation to Defoe attribution problems, see Appendix A below, pp. 176–83.)

Curiously, despite the term's eighteenth-century flavour, 'connoisseurship' won a victory over academic 'art history' in the nineteenth century, and Morelli's method continued till quite recently to have important advocates. Indeed, whether by means of his method or not, Morelli seems to have achieved some notable successes in attribution. Nevertheless Friedländer's comment on him is probably just and comes home to us forcefully in regard to Defoe scholarship:

> ... if we look closer, we shall find that he [Morelli] has utilized the much-praised method — the observation of measurably similar forms, notably the ears, the hands, the finger-nails — less for the purpose of arriving at a verdict, than in order to provide evidence subsequently. He points to the individual forms in order to convince the reader of the justness of his attributions: but he, like every successful expert, has formed his opinion from the 'accidental' impression of the whole picture. He had a presentiment of this, and has even hinted at it, when on one occasion he assesses the value of his method — fairly accurately — as being an ancillary device, a means of checking.

Friedländer, moreover, has some excellent words on the human temptations of 'connoisseurship':

> Since nobody can be called upon to account or produce proofs, since everything depends upon confidence and blind faith, it is authority which is demanded, claimed and striven for — at times even created artificially.... The expert appears to the layman to be a magician and a worker of miracles. He thinks this part suits him and he becomes accustomed to indulge in the attitude of the conjuror. He is inclined to assert himself through rhetorical turns

of speech; exclaiming, for instance, 'I put my hand in the fire that this is so', or else, 'Whoever does not see this, must be blind'.

It cannot be denied that this puts us in mind of Lee, Crossley, Trent and J.R. Moore, with their 'unquestionably', 'without hesitation', 'indubitably' and the like.

Finally, it is in Friedländer that we find a golden rule, against what he calls the 'forging of chains':

> One should avoid as far as possible to link up an attribution based on style- criticism with another such attribution — in other words, to forge chains — since, of course, the risk of mistake is always there, and steps must be taken in advance to ensure that error does not produce error. A return to the secure starting-point remains imperative, to a centre from which attributions issue like rays.[29]

It is on the dangers of just such a 'forging of chains', on the part not so much of an individual bibliographer as of succeeding bibliographers, that we insist, with perhaps tedious reiteration, in the present book.

PART II

CHAPTER 4

GEORGE CHALMERS

W E HAVE NOW to trace the history of the Defoe 'canon', or, which is much the same thing, to study the activities of the six men mainly responsible for its construction: George Chalmers, Walter Wilson, William Lee, James Crossley, W.P. Trent and J.R. Moore.

The first true bibliography of Defoe was the work of the Scottish antiquary George Chalmers (1742–1825). Chalmers was a man of aggressively Tory views and, curiously for a biographer of Defoe, nursed a vigorous prejudice against Presbyterians and radicals, as well as anti-slave-trade reformers. He established a legal practice in Baltimore, but, being forced out by the American Revolution, secured in 1786 an appointment as Chief Clerk to the Committee for Trade, in London, a post that left him considerable leisure for literary and antiquarian activities and that he held on to for the rest of his long life, resisting all encouragements to retire.[1] In 1785, 'for amusement during a period of convalescence', he wrote a brief 'Life of De Foe', and five years later, upon its republication in a new edition of *Robinson Crusoe*, he added a 'List of Writings' of Defoe. His list contained 101 items, of which eighty-one were described as 'undoubtedly DE FOE's', and a further twenty were headed 'A List of Books which are supposed to be De Foe's'. However, as the 'undoubted list' included the two volumes of Defoe's own authorised *True Collection* of his works, but listed separately only thirteen of the forty items contained there, the full total of works attributed by Chalmers may be said to have been 128.[2] (Even with this addition, it is a far cry from the 570 or so works attributed in Moore's *Checklist* of two centuries later.)

In the opening paragraph of his 'Life of De Foe' Chalmers made a very reasonable lament:

The lives of literary men are generally passed in the obscurities of the closet, which conceal even from friendly inquiries the artifices

of study, whereby each may have risen to eminence. And during
the same moment that the diligent biographer sets out to ask for
information, with regard to the origin, the modes of life, or the
various fortunes of writers who have amused or instructed their
country, the housekeeper, the daughter, or grandchild, that knew
connections and traditions, drop into the grave.

What applies to biography applies, of course, equally to bibliography, or at least it did so in Defoe's case. By the time Chalmers got
to work the trace had gone cold, though he made a conscientious
exploration of such few bibliographical lists as survived, much the
best of these being the twenty-two ascriptions to Defoe by
Theophilus Cibber (or more probably Robert Shiels) included in
Cibber's *Lives of the Poets* in 1733. He also paid careful, though
cautious, attention to the dubious attributions made by Defoe's
enemies, like Abel Boyer, and the even more dubious ones in
booksellers' catalogues and the catalogues of large libraries. Further,
he made intelligent use of Defoe's allusions to his own writings in the
Review and elsewhere.[3] In all, he came up with some 110 ascriptions
for which there was external evidence, though this evidence varied in
quality, amounting in one or two instances to no more than the fact
that someone had inscribed a copy with Defoe's name, in an early
eighteenth-century hand. To these he then added a further eighteen
ascriptions, ten in his 'certain' list and eight in his 'supposed' one,
arrived at, it would seem, by guesswork, based on Defoe's known
interests and activities or on reasonings from prose style.

   This pioneering list by Chalmers, including its speculative items,
had a good deal of influence on later biographers. The question
therefore naturally arises, what sort of man was Chalmers, and more
particularly what sort of confidence should we be inclined to place in
his powers of judgement in literary attribution? Beyond question he
was energetic, as his enormous list of writings proves. He was also
knowledgeable, and his unfinished history of Scottish antiquities,
Caledonia (1807–1824), is still quarried as a source-book. What counts
rather more for our purposes, however, is the awkward fact that,
during his lifetime, he became a byword for the very vices a bibliographer can least afford: gullibility, obstinacy and shaky (indeed
positively grotesque) reasoning. Poor Chalmers was, throughout his
life, fatally attracted towards identity-disputes, forgeries, and controversies about forgery, and he invariably came to grief. In his
Caledonia he insisted on basing his description of Scotland in Roman

times on the manuscript attributed to a 'Richard of Westminster' ('the Westminster monk, to whom every British antiquary is so greatly indebted for his interesting researches'[4]), though it was in fact a recent forgery by Charles Bertram. He also persuaded himself that the 'Junius' letters were by a young, Irish Grub-street writer named Hugh MacAulay Boyd and in 1800 published a book to this effect,[5] which received very rough treatment all round — the *British Critic* remarking unkindly that there was 'no more cause for suspecting him [Boyd] to have been the writer of the very able letters than is Chalmers's patent imitation of Johnson justification for ascribing to him the great doctor's immortal works'.[6] Undeterred, Chalmers returned to the subject seventeen years later, announcing that his discovery had now reached the condition of 'moral demonstration'.[7] But this is as nothing to his part in the famous Samuel Ireland controversy. When Ireland and his father first exhibited their newly discovered Shakespeare manuscripts in 1795 (among them a letter from Shakespeare to Ann Hathaway, some revised pages of *Hamlet* and the tragedy *Vortigern and Rowena*), Chalmers became one of the documents' most impassioned supporters, bringing various distinguished acquaintances to inspect them. He was thus deeply mortified when, with the devastating critique by Edmund Malone[8] and the first night débâcle of *Vortigern* at Drury Lane, the Shakespeare papers became the laughing-stock of the town. He was, of course, not alone in his mortification, but his response was the most bizarre (though all of a piece with his character). He wrote not just one but two books, six hundred pages apiece, arguing that, though Malone had been technically in the right, it was the supporters of Ireland who had really behaved according to the rules of reason and logic: '. . . the believers were led into their error, by *system*, while the inquirer himself is only right, by *chance*'.[9] By the time the second of these books appeared, even the more friendly reviewers had given him up, and he was pilloried unmercifully in a collection of lampoons and attacks entitled *Chalmeriana*.[10]

That Chalmers should be so notoriously accident-prone in the field of attribution is bound to make one nervous when it comes to his work on Defoe; but indeed 'accident' may be the wrong word, for his errors seem to have been the result of principle. Thus it will be worth our mentioning one or two of the theories or principles asserted by Chalmers in the course of his various controversies. They will be familiar from our earlier chapters. For example, in his dispute with Malone, Chalmers puts forward the odd theory that 'every presumption is evidence till the contrary is made apparent', the implication of this apparently being that there is a presumption in favour of the authenticity of any document — a fact which explains, says Chalmers, why it is so difficult to detect some forgeries by 'fair discussion'.[11] (Malone's methods may have been successful, Chalmers appears to be saying, but they were not 'fair'.) Clearly, what is at work in Chalmers's mind here is a confusion between persons and documents. Under English law a person who is accused of forgery, as he rightly says, 'comes into court with every presumption in his favour',[12] but of course no such rule applies, or possibly could apply, to documents.[13]

Another pet theory of Chalmers's, equally false in our eyes and even more dangerous on the part of a bibliographer, is that positive evidence has an intrinsic superiority over negative evidence. 'I mean', he wrote in his second book on the 'Junius' letters, 'to confine my proofs to the affirmative, without going, in any manner, into negative evidence: If I succeed in my *affirmative proofs*, all *negative* evidence must be in vain; and must, incidentally, preclude any question, as to who did *not* write that notorious publication.'[14] It is noticeable that, so far as one can see, he contradicts himself in the very same paragraph, when he argues that, since the verbal habits of the author of the letters prove him to have been Irish, most of the current candidates for 'Junius' must at once be ruled out. As for his 'affirmative proofs', they consist of a posthumous report at second-hand, that Boyd had once claimed to have been 'Junius', together with a certain number of quite vague 'compatibilities' — with no right, moreover, to the name of 'concatenation', as claimed in the title of the book, being in no way mutually linked.

In regard to Defoe himself, we can identify two of Chalmers's working principles. First, to use Baine's words, he 'followed con-scientiously a policy which has been out of fashion in the twentieth century: he took Defoe at his word'.[15] In particular, he came round to trusting Defoe's assertion in his *Appeal to Honour and Justice* 'That he had written nothing since the Queen's death', and on the strength of it he rejected *The Secret History of the White Staff*, which he had originally recorded in his notebook as 'certainly Defoe's', and allowed Defoe only a very small hand in the *Mercator*. Equally he rejected almost all of Abel Boyer's attributions to Defoe as malicious. Second, he was, as we have said, ready to base attri-butions on stylistic evidence alone, and in his notes he indicated one of his stylistic criteria — not, it must be said, very reassuringly:

'It may be observed that in Defoe's Works he generally throws some part into Dialogue. By attending to this Circumstance and others I think the Knowledge of many of his pieces may be obtained.'[16]

We owe a lot to Chalmers, who did much to rescue Defoe from undeserved neglect, but, from the point of view of method in attribution, it cannot be said that Defoe bibliography got off to an auspicious start, and Rodney Baine's verdict is hard to gainsay:

> ...it should now be clear that Chalmers' assignment of any particular item to Defoe constitutes in itself no evidence that Defoe wrote it. Already Dr Moore in his *Checklist* has rejected ten of the eighty-one items and half of the uncertain twenty. Others are being challenged by the present writer.[17] The failure of Defoe bibliographers to reject or question other items listed by Chalmers constitutes no test for acceptance.[18]

CHAPTER 5

WALTER WILSON

IT WAS NOT till forty years after Chalmers that a new effort was made at a combined biography and bibliography of Defoe, in the shape of Walter Wilson's *Memoirs of the Life and Times of Daniel De Foe* (1830). The book was in fact written with the goodwill of Chalmers, who did Wilson an important favour in lending him his copy of Defoe's *Review*. In sheer scale, however, the contrast between the two enterprises is very striking. Chalmers's 'Life' had been uncharacteristically short, whereas Wilson's was quite vast; and Wilson, in his 'Chronological Catalogue of De Foe's Works', added some eighty items to Chalmers's list (as well as dropping eight).

Walter Wilson (1781–1847) was the illegitimate son of John Walter, the founder of *The Times*. He had a strict Presbyterian upbringing, and in 1797 he became a clerk at East India House, where he got to know Charles Lamb. The two were very different in temperament, Wilson being solemn and sedate ('although not altogether disinclined to pleasantry'[1]) and tending to regard Lamb, his senior by eight years, as dangerously frivolous and lax in regard to religion. Once, during an expedition by boat to Richmond, Lamb got tipsy and indulged in horseplay 'quite unsuited to so unsteady a conveyance in the watery element', nearly having the whole party drowned; and this provoked Wilson to write him a stunning letter of remonstrance on his general conduct. For all this, they became bosom friends — so much so that, at Lamb's suggestion, they adopted the habit of calling each other 'Brother'.

In 1802 Wilson left the East India Company for journalism. Then in 1806 he became a bookseller, specialising in Nonconformist writings, and about the same time he embarked on his ambitious *History of the Dissenting Churches in London*, the first of its four volumes appearing in 1808. His father died in 1812, leaving him a sixteenth share in *The Times*, on the strength of which he qualified at the Inner Temple. He never practised, however, and soon afterwards retired to the West Country, where he became a gentleman farmer and, round about 1822, began work on his *Memoirs of the Life and Times of Daniel De Foe*. His last thirteen years were spent in Bath, where he occupied a handsome house in Pulteney Street and became a magistrate. When his magnificent library, which included some two hundred works attributed to Defoe, was auctioned by Sotheby's after his death, the sale lasted twelve days.

The early-nineteenth-century age of reforms was, one might say, Defoe's moment. The new London University, the new police, could be said to have been fathered by him, in *Augusta Triumphans* and *An Effectual Scheme to Prevent Street Robberies* respectively; and when in 1829 John Cam Hobhouse was proposing parliamentary reform of 'select vestries' he read to the House a long quotation from Defoe's *Parochial Tyranny: or the Housekeeper's Complaint against the Insupportable Exactions of Select Vestries*.[2] Occasional Conformity was once again, and for the last time, in the air, so was the pillory,[3] and so was 'passive obedience'. During the great affair of Queen Caroline's divorce in 1820, the Bishop of London, William Howley, declared that 'the king could do no wrong either morally or physically',[4] and this provoked William Hone to publish a truncated and revised version of Defoe's *Jure Divino* under the title *The Right Divine of Kings to Govern Wrong!*[5]

With intellectual radicals Defoe was much in favour at this period. William Godwin (like Defoe, the product of a Dissenting academy) based a tragedy, *Faulkener*, on the plot of *Roxana*, and when William Hazlitt, near the end of his life, volunteered to review Wilson's *Memoirs* of Defoe for the *Edinburgh Review*, he told the editor that he could treat the subject 'con amore'.[6] For Charles Lamb, whom one might at least call a radical by association, Defoe 'was always my darling', and he was delighted that Wilson should have asked him to contribute a note on Defoe's 'secondary novels' to the *Memoirs*, promising himself 'if not immortality, yet diuternity of being read in consequence'.[7] He ends a later letter to Wilson: 'In the name of dear Defoe, which alone might be a Bond of Union between us, Adieu!'[8] Among the reviewers of Wilson's *Memoirs* one thing was generally agreed, whether in praise or in vilification, which was that Defoe was walking the earth again in the person of William Cobbett.

What we have not yet mentioned, however, is the most important historical consideration for an understanding of Wilson's *Memoirs of De Foe*, the fact that they were written just at the time when the long

campaign against the civil disabilities of Dissenters was achieving
its end. Wilson's heart was with the 'quiet and sober religion' of
old Dissent,[9] and he disapproved of Methodism and evangelical
enthusiasm; nevertheless, the passion of his life was religious liberty.
(One of his few criticisms of his hero Defoe was that he took too
narrow a view of religious toleration, contrasting unfavourably in
this respect with Toland.[10]) He was contemptuous of the 'ridiculous
notion' of orthodox Dissenters 'that they are to be occupied only by
concerns of a religious nature' and held that the only hope of a revival
of Nonconformity (which he thought was in decline) was to identify
religious liberty with civil liberty — 'and then the friends of the latter
will be its firmest supporters'.[11] Thus it was a Dissenter's duty 'never
to lose sight of his situation' and to seize every possible opportunity
of advertising his and his fellow-religionists' wrongs. He himself, as
historian of the Dissenting churches, was, of course, especially well
qualified to take part in the current campaign against the Test and
Corporation Acts, and in 1817 or soon thereafter he became a
member of the influential 'Non-Con Club',[12] the group which gave
the final push leading to parliamentary reform.[13]

As it happened, the motion for repeal of the much hated Acts,
when it was introduced by Lord John Russell in 1828, went through
with quite unexpected ease. Thus Wilson's book, intended as a blow
in an age-old and continuing struggle, was overtaken and, in a sense,
made obsolete by events. He tacitly admits this himself in his
preface, when he asks the reader to bear in mind 'that the whole of
the present work was composed before the late repeal of the
Corporation and Test Acts; and written under the influence of the
state of things as they previously existed',[14] and the fact was held
against him by his reviewer in the *Westminster Review*, who
complained of his 'revival of worn-out circumstances, and the party
spirit in which they are concocted'.[15]

Wilson's book was thus very much the product of a particular
historical moment and it took the form of a prolonged diatribe
against the 'furious churchmen'[16] of Defoe's age and the evil, which
that age illustrated, of all political connection between church and
state. ('In balancing the accounts of nations,' wrote Wilson,
'whatever is gained to the civil government from the influence of the
priesthood, is so much loss to the people.'[17]) Stately and prosy in its
style, the book is simple in its form. For much of the time it simply
introduces one after another of Defoe's political writings, together
with those of his contemporaries or adversaries, giving copious

extracts and explaining their historical bearing. The *Monthly Repository* commented, not too unfairly, that 'The "Life and Times" should rather be entitled the "Times and Life" of *Daniel De Foe*; for it exhibits but a scanty stream of biography meandering through an immense field of political history and disquisition.'[18] Even Hazlitt, who praised the book and admired its robust Whiggish spirit, admitted it was 'spun out at too great a length'; whilst the *British Critic and Quarterly Theological Review*, which disliked Defoe's views as much as it did Wilson's, teased Wilson cruelly over the numerous 'perhapses' and 'probablys' and 'no doubts' in the biographical part of his narrative and complained that 'even the Catalogue of his Works is made out on the same loose principle'.[19]

A point will be seen to be emerging: that Wilson's chosen approach to his task has bibliographical as well as biographical implications. He was, of course, saved from much of the agonising of later bibliographers by the assumption, quite reasonable before the discovery of Defoe's letters to his political employer Charles De la Faye, that his career as political pamphleteer ended in 1715. Moreover, this assumption fed another, which was that Defoe's word could be trusted, and when he denied being the author of some tract, this was evidence that could be relied on. There is, however, an even more significant observation to be made, which is that, granted Wilson's purpose in the *Memoirs*, and his concentration on history and general issues as opposed to personal biography, it might be important to him, but not crucially important, whether a given work was by Defoe or not. This in fact may be seen to be acknowledged in his bibliographical procedure.

In the introduction to his 'Chronological Catalogue of the Writings of De Foe', Wilson makes the claim that his list 'will be found much more perfect than any that has been hitherto offered to the public', and indeed the total of works attributed by him to Defoe (210) is, as we have seen, nearly double the total in Chalmers. This is not surprising, for since Chalmers's day the world had been awash with new Defoe attributions, as a glance at Lowndes's *Bibliographer's Manual* or the *Bibliotheca Britannica* will show and as Wilson, a sometime bookseller, would have been intimately aware. In his text he mentions some attributions suggested by (unnamed) friends, and he records acquiring 'a knowledge of several of De Foe's pieces, with which I was not previously acquainted' (he does not specify which) from the collector Machell Stace, who had been preparing an 'arranged catalogue' of Defoe's works but abandoned it in Wilson's favour.[20] However, it is important to understand the nature of Wilson's claims as an attributor, which is not quite what it would appear. He explains that 'Some of the articles included in the list, appear there, perhaps, with doubtful propriety; and have been inserted rather in deference to common opinion, than from a conviction of their genuineness. These are marked *Doubtful*; and the collectors of De Foe may reject them or not from their collections at their own option'.[21] This, however, is distinctly misleading. For what the reader of the *Memoirs* discovers is that, when Wilson marks an item as 'Doubtful' (which he does only on four occasions), he means that he personally is quite sure that it is not by Defoe, and that, on the other hand, the fact that he includes an item in his 'Catalogue', without marking it 'Doubtful', does not mean that he positively attributes it to Defoe. It may mean, in some cases, no more than that it has been attributed to Defoe and Wilson regards the attribution as just faintly possible.

Of the eighty-odd items he has added to Chalmers's list, thirty-six are, explicitly or implicitly, firm attributions on Wilson's part, and a slightly larger number are tentative, in degrees varying from strong conviction to nearly complete scepticism or the frank admission that Wilson has not in fact seen the work. We shall give a selection of his comments, indicating the catalogue number of the item to which they apply: 'If not penned by De Foe, it was the production of a kindred writer' (41); 'The following work...has been ascribed to De Foe...but upon what ground of probability, the present writer cannot say, having never seen the work' (57); 'The following work ...is very much in the manner of De Foe' (87); 'This seems to have been written by an Englishman, and perhaps by De Foe' (96); 'Although De Foe has commonly the credit of this work, it has been assigned, also, to Lord Somers, and printed with his name; but whether it is correctly given in either case is, perhaps, doubtful' (113); 'The style and spirit of this pamphlet bear strong marks of the pen of De Foe, and the sentiments are congenial with those which he delivered in others of his writings' (130); 'Common fame at the time ascribed this work, but perhaps without any just reason, to De Foe' (146); 'This work, perhaps more from the likeness of the title to that of one of his former pieces than from any weightier consideration, has been sometimes ascribed to De Foe' (160).

It can be seen from this that Walter Wilson has an extraordinarily relaxed attitude towards atrribution. Unlike some later bibliographers he takes no especial pride in swelling the Defoe canon; and we may reflect that, in a sense, this may be no bad thing, and the *British Critic*'s remark about his 'loose principle' in attribution, though true, need not necessarily be considered a condemnation. It also, in Wilson's case, takes the edge off William Lee's complaint that his predecessors showed an 'absence of all critical acumen, and even ordinary knowledge of Defoe's stile',[22] for Wilson's claims to critical skill are really very modest and he is happy to leave many issues in doubt. On the other hand his misleading procedure, by which works are listed by him as if definitely by Defoe, whereas all that he is really asserting is that they are probably, or possibly, or just conceivably by Defoe, plainly proved a confusion and snare to later bibliographers. We shall meet such misunderstandings again as we follow the history of the Defoe canon.

CHAPTER 6

WILLIAM LEE

O NE OF THE MOTIVES for William Lee to write his *Life and Recently Discovered Writings* of Daniel Defoe, published in 1869, was to correct what he thought to be the glaring errors, both bibliographical and ideological, of Walter Wilson — though, as we shall suggest, there were other motives too, perhaps more important ones. Lee came to literary scholarship very late and after a career in an altogether different sphere, as a pioneering Surveyor of Highways in Sheffield and then, from 1849 to 1854, as one of the influential team of inspectors picked by Edwin Chadwick, the sanitary reformer and former Poor Law reformer, to work for his famous and ill-fated General Board of Health. Lee had been born in Sheffield in 1812, his father being a silver-plater, and by the early 1840s, as Surveyor of Highways, he had become a well-known figure, and a byword for energy and public spirit, on the Sheffield scene. His friend, the poet and journalist John Holland, relates how the poet James Montgomery, Sheffield's most notable literary lion, once came into Holland's room choking with laughter at a witticism that had just crossed his mind. Seeing the 'immense piles of square stones' which 'your friend, William Lee, has laid up yonder for paving the streets', he had realised that, when Lee died, the celebrated epitaph made for Sir John Vanbrugh could easily be adapted to suit their 'worthy Sheffielder':

> Lie heavy on him, earth, for *Lee*
> Laid many a heavy load on thee![1]

Among Lee's interests were geology and phrenology, and it appears that, even at this period, he was a keen antiquarian book-collector. He thus naturally became a member of the city's Literary and Philosophical Society, becoming its Honorary Secretary in 1845

— a fact which, to his great indignation, prompted the Board of Highways to dock £100 from his salary, presumably on the grounds that he was dissipating his energies.

He had entered on his career as civil engineer at a time when the 'sanitary idea' was much in the news. In 1842 Edwin Chadwick had published his great *Sanitary Report*, which painted a frightening picture of the condition of Britain's industrial towns and led to the setting up of a Health of Towns Commission. In the Commission's *Second Report*, Lee was invited to write the account of Sheffield, in which he earnestly preached the Chadwickian doctrines of reform and rationalisation. Thus, when in 1848 a General Board of Health, with wide powers, was set up, with Chadwick as its effective head, Lee was a natural choice as one of its Superintending Inspectors.

Four extraordinarily busy years ensued, during which Lee and his four colleagues visited and reported on some 243 places, of which over 182 were 'brought under the Act' and compelled to install a modern system of drainage, piped water and sewage-disposal. Lee's numerous published reports reveal him as an ardent Christian and at the same time, in his approach to social reform, a Benthamite. Of all his tasks the one he most dreaded was visiting common lodging-houses. He would make his inspection at night-time, and the squalor, gambling and sexual promiscuity utterly horrified him. 'I forbear to quote further from these revolting humiliating details of my inspection,' he writes in his report on March in the Isle of Ely. 'Only a sense of duty (and a very painful duty it is) could induce me to witness the physical and moral contamination of the public lodging-houses in this, and the other towns I am called upon to visit.'[2] At Rotherham and Kimberworth he talked with the men and women in a crowded and foetid tramps' lodging-house and learned that they actually enjoyed the tramping life — had lived it for thirty years and could face no other existence — and with a shudder he had to admit: 'There is a kind of fascination about this mode of life.'[3] He was usually ill for a day or two after such visits.

His work involved him in a good deal of conflict and acrimony. His report on Great Yarmouth, for example, provoked an indignant memorial from ratepayers, accusing him of prejudice and corruption; and again, when he challenged the estimate of an engineer engaged to undertake sanitary works in Durham, a furious quarrel and pamphlet war broke out.[4] These quarrels were symptomatic, for the General Board was growing unpopular, and both the virtues and the defects of Chadwick, a bogey figure in some quarters ever since the Poor Law reforms of 1834, were leading to disaster. For his part, Chadwick — it was a point in which Lee perhaps a little resembled him — was always inclined to dismiss criticism as 'senseless clamour'. At length, however, in 1854 the House of Lords voted that it had 'entirely lost confidence in the present members of the Board', and this shattering defeat for Chadwick spelled the end of Lee's public employment also, leaving him with the conviction, expressed in letters to Chadwick, that his chief had been treated with monstrous injustice, and acutely sore at his own dismissal.[5]

He could, of course, return to his private practice as engineer, but he was plainly an ambitious man, and evidently this did not suffice him. We have thus to try to trace the steps by which he came to embark on the totally fresh career of bibliographer and biographer of Defoe. Lee, as we know, had been a bibliophile from his youth, and we have his word for it that the addiction grew on him further in London, with its wealth of bookshops. It had been originally, perhaps, merely a dilettante interest. (He also compiled an extensive collection of matchbox tops, which was sold at auction with his library in 1883.) However, the interest led him in 1857, to obtain a reader's ticket at the British Museum, which suggests a more systematic course of reading; and it is possible that he was then already working on Defoe, in whom he had a long-standing interest going back to the 1830s. At all events, a nice anecdote in his *Life* of Defoe proves that by three years later Defoe was strongly in his mind. It tells how in the year 1860, when the London, Tilbury and Southend Railway was completed, he made a day's excursion to Tilbury in hopes to discover remains of Defoe's tile-works, and how, in a trench cut by the railway company, he found the whole works laid open to view: claypits, drying-floors, foundations of kilns, and heaps of bricks and tiles:

> . . . the narrowness of the bricks, and the peculiar forms of certain tobacco-pipes, found mixed with both, had excited some little wonderment among the labourers. I asked several how they thought these things came there, and was answered by an ignorant shake of the head. But when I said, 'These bricks and tiles were made 160 years since by the same man that made "Robinson Crusoe"!' I touched a chord that connected these railway 'navvies' with the shipwrecked mariner, and that bounded over the intervening period in a single moment. Every eye brightened, every tongue was ready to ask or give information, and every fragment became interesting.[6]

The idea that he should write on Defoe seems, however, to have entered Lee's mind only later — to be precise in the autumn of 1864, and as a direct result of the publication of six remarkable letters by Defoe, recently discovered in the State Paper Office. As is well known, these letters, addressed to Charles De la Faye in the Secretary of State's office between April and June 1718, showed not merely that Defoe's career as a political journalist had not ended with the accession of George I, as had hitherto been believed, but that it had subsequently taken an extraordinary, and apparently rather disreputable, form — no less than taking money from Whig government patrons to masquerade as a Tory and insinuate himself into the management of certain Tory journals, to take the sting out of their attacks on the government.

The letters were printed in two numbers of the *London Review*, with an anonymous commentary savagely hostile to Defoe — accusing him of 'baseness and dishonesty', 'rascality', 'dirty and disreputable work' and the like.[7] Defoe's admirers, who were many and ardent at this period, were much disturbed by the revelations, and not least William Lee. We here put forward a speculation; indeed it is on this hypothesis that the present chapter partly hinges. It is that, quite soon, Lee came to see in the affair an example of the sort of injustice which was all too familiar to him in his own career. Here in Defoe, he told himself, was a man of the utmost goodwill and public spirit, combined with brilliant practical sagacity — a man, it might be said, like Edwin Chadwick, and perhaps to some degree himself also — who had been assailed and misrepresented with the greatest malignancy by his contemporaries and rivals and was now vilified with equal irresponsibility by their modern equivalent. To defend Defoe and wipe his reputation clean was a task very congenial to Lee and an outlet for his own righteous indignation and wounded feelings of ten years before.

So much for hypothesis. It is a fact that Lee set to work some time during the later months of 1864 to examine the journals (*Mercurius Politicus*, *Mist's Weekly Journal*, *Dormer's News-letter*, etc.) on which Defoe had, on his own admission, played a dubious role — his purpose being to ascertain what he had actually, in practice, done, and how far, if at all, it could be called disreputable (or, in his own words, to make possible a verdict of 'Guilty, or Not guilty'). He planned to publish his findings in *Notes and Queries*, the editor of which, W.J. Thoms, was a friend of his and had already published a brief note of his on Defoe. However, as it happened, on 31 December 1864, *Notes and Queries* itself reprinted the six Defoe

Letters, with a brief remark or two by 'L.O.', ending: 'Such are the extraordinary letters, which reveal to us Defoe "bowing in the house of Rimmon"; and in which the future biographer of that remarkable writer will assuredly find material for a new, and I fear not more favourable, view of the moral character of Daniel De Foe.'[8]

Spurred on by this, Lee published five extensive articles in *Notes and Queries*, delivering an emphatic verdict of 'Not guilty'. The first was mainly an attack on the reviewer in the *London Review*, showing, fairly successfully, that he had grossly distorted the evidence against Defoe.[9] In the second he gave a few examples of Defoe's unacknowledged writings done under Tory disguise, promising to publish a substantial selection from them in due course. On the strength of these, he announced 'the somewhat dogmatic judgement' that though Defoe had been 'unwise' to put himself in such a questionable position, these writings showed him in an admirable light. They promoted religion and virtue, contained no trace of pruriency, exhibited impartiality in politics, and presented nothing whatever contrary 'to the liberal principles he had all his life professed'. In short, 'he did nothing to disparage, positively, his moral character as a man, a patriot, and a Christian'.[10]

It will be noticed that Lee, implicitly, is already very sure of his ability to penetrate Defoe's anonymity and recognise his writings in *Mist's Journal* and the like; and before long he asserts this ability with reckless confidence — saying, for instance, that he has 'no more hesitation' in affirming from internal evidence that Defoe wrote the introductory matter to 'Servitude', the poem by Dodsley the footman-poet, than he should have in declaring him the author of *Robinson Crusoe*. (In the same article, another trait of Lee's comes out, when he paints a pathetic imaginary picture of the 'careworn old man', in his 'plain, substantial, and homely' study, turning from the manuscript of *The Compleat English Gentleman* to help, with his failing energies, 'the timid young Footman who humbly beseeches his judgment and advice'.)[11]

From studying the periodicals specifically named in the letters to De la Faye, and working within the date limits indicated in those letters, Lee found himself led on to explore other journals and other periods, as far back as 1712. Meanwhile his pile of transcripts mounted. 'My manuscript of his hitherto unknown writings has... now grown to the capacity of an ordinary octavo volume,' he noted on 25 March 1865; 'My manuscript...now fills many hundred pages of foolscap paper and is increasing daily' (3 June 1865).[12] His aim had widened and it was now to correct the 'distorted and discoloured caricature' of Defoe produced by Walter Wilson, who had portrayed him as 'a bigoted, anti-church, radical Dissenter'.

As we have said in our chapter on Wilson, by the early part of the century Defoe had become very much the hero, if not the property, of political radicals like William Hone, Hazlitt and Godwin. Lee evidently felt the need to rescue Defoe from such hands, and he asserted stoutly that, contrary to Wilson's slanders, Defoe was always 'a liberal Conservative in politics' and, although personally a Dissenter, yet a firm supporter of the Church of England. (His own copy of Wilson's *Memoirs of De Foe* is covered with marginalia furiously attacking Wilson over this issue.) The remainder of his Defoe articles in *Notes and Queries* were devoted to lengthy extracts from *Applebee's Journal*, which he presented as unquestionably by Defoe and were to show his orthodoxy in religion, his wisdom and prudence as a professional journalist and his utter abhorrence of radical republican and king-killing principles.[13]

Lee was working with immense and characteristic energy, and from month to month the scope of his enterprise extended. As a by-product he published, in two numbers of *Notes and Queries*, a chronological list of 'Periodical Publications during the Twenty Years 1712–1732', containing over a hundred titles not included in the table in John Nichols's *Literary Anecdotes*.[14] As his transcripts accumulated, it became an increasing problem what to do about editorial commentary, and eventually he decided that the best solution would be to write a new memoir of the later years of Defoe. This project in turn soon enlarged itself, and he embarked on a complete new 'Life'.

Lee's three volumes (one containing the 'Life' and the other two the 'Recently Discovered Writings') were published by J.C. Hotten in April 1869. The first volume included a 'Chronological Catalogue of Defoe's Works', and in his introduction he declared that, though he did not wish to be 'invidious', the lists of Defoe's works given in the 'Lives by Chalmers, Wilson and Hazlitt were "conspicuous for the absence" of all critical acumen, and even ordinary knowledge of Defoe's stile'.[15] Accordingly he had rejected thirty titles from Wilson's list and twelve from Hazlitt's (and had reinstated seven that Hazlitt had rejected); and he had been enabled to add 'sixty-four distinct Works' to the Defoe canon. To give his reasons for retaining or rejecting each individual book would, he said, have taken up too much space. The truth was: 'Long and critical study of a great author may result in so full an acquaintance, that his writings will be recognised by the student in a moment, as the voice of a familiar friend.' Two things he wished to affirm, 'modestly, but with a strong assurance: — That Daniel Defoe was the Author of all the Works I have ascribed to him; and, that he was not the Author of any of the Works heretofore attributed to him, but which I have omitted.'

The book received, in general, a warm press. In their verdict on Defoe himself the reviewers varied widely, from a lengthy, two-part celebration of Defoe in Dickens's periodical, *All the Year Round*, in which he was lauded as 'a brave, simple, honest, industrious, far-seeing man of genius, one of those noble souls who, with the greatest amount of brain as well as heart, have helped build up the liberties of England', to the lament of the *Athenaeum* that he had performed such a 'vast amount of dirty work'. Reviewers were agreed, however, in two criticisms of Lee: first, that he was an out-and-out idolater of Defoe, so much so that, in the words of the *Saturday Review*, 'His own partiality or admiration makes him indeed scarcely sensible of the havoc which his revelations must inevitably play with the reputation of his idol'; and secondly that he was wildly over-confident in his attributions. 'His boldness in both rejection and adoption is something marvellous,' said the *Athenaeum*, 'though in either case he may be often right.'[16]

Some months later Lee received a lengthy and magisterial, though not unadmiring, review in the *British Quarterly Review*, which spelled out the former reviewers' judgement in more detail. It noted, for instance, the calm way in which, quite without evidence or argument, Lee saddled Defoe with the 400-page *History of the Wars of Charles XII*. The reviewer further objected to the way that Lee went about proving Defoe a zealous supporter of the Established Church — his confidently attributing to Defoe a paragraph and an article in *Mist's Journal* which, said the *British Quarterly* reviewer, 'are evidently the composition of a rabid and unscrupulous Churchman, such as would ordinarily be employed on *Mist's Journal*'. Lee's way of calling in as evidence, to revise our notions of Defoe, 'passages mainly from articles and letters which only he himself has ever suspected to be Defoe's', was, the reviewer said sardonically, 'a novel mode of reasoning'.[17]

Lee could be said to have received just treatment from his reviewers. How he reacted to their strictures on his attributions is not known; but as for the accusation of hero-worship of Defoe, he took it lightly, saying the offence was 'an easily forgiven one'.[18] Nevertheless, he was a man prone to misfortune, and he received two unexpected blows at this time, both of them from his fellow-bibliographer James Crossley.

Crossley was a retired Manchester solicitor who had been a minor *littérateur* in his youth but who in later years had shone mainly as an editor and bibliophile. His library was said to contain 100,000 volumes, and it had been one of his ambitions to assemble a Defoe collection more complete than any predecessor's. Defoe scholars often consulted him and were somewhat in awe of him, and this, we may suspect, was exactly what he desired; for he seems to have been a vain and rather devious man. (When William Hazlitt the Younger was producing his edition of Defoe, he applied for the loan of certain rare works, but, according to W.C. Hazlitt, 'that gentleman declined to lend his copies.'[19]) We shall be examining his career and character in more detail in the next chapter.

Lee had been in contact with Crossley while at work on his book, and Crossley had supplied him with details of Defoe's *Review*, of which he possessed the most nearly complete copy in the country. They had also corresponded, in friendly fashion, about the author-ship of *The Military Memoirs of Captain George Carleton*, both agreeing that Defoe had nothing to do with this work. However, when Lee, in a succession of letters, pressed Crossley for detailed help and advice over attributions, Crossley was evasive, not even answering Lee's anxious plea that he should at least tell him of 'the Titles of any Works by Defoe, that I may yet be unacquainted with'.[20]

The reasons for Crossley's behaviour became plain when he published a notice of Lee's book in *Notes and Queries*. Crossley was polite, saying that 'Every one who has examined them [Lee's three volumes] must be satisfied that the duties Mr. Lee has undertaken have fallen into excellent hands.' The main object of his brief article, however, was to praise his own sagacity in having, as long ago as 1838, identified a book entitled *Due Preparations for the Plague* as being by Defoe, and to express surprise that 'it had escaped the research of Mr Lee'; and secondly, to make the sensational assertion that 'at least fifty more distinct works, hitherto unattributed to Defoe, could be confidently ascribed to him'.[21] This was no vain boast, and we now know which fifty or so works Crossley had in mind; but to announce it in this way, taking Lee entirely by surprise, seems to have been a long-prepared *coup de théâtre* on Crossley's part.

Worse was to follow. In an earlier correspondence about the *Minutes of the Negotiations of Monsr. Mesnager* (the supposed memoirs of the French agent in the Utrecht peace negotiations), which Lee was strongly inclined to attribute to Defoe, Crossley had told Lee of an issue of the periodical *Mercurius Politicus* which quoted a letter from Defoe, in which Defoe apparently denied authorship. Lee naturally asked to be shown it, but Crossley had claimed not to be able to lay his hands on it, his library being in confusion after a move. Lee, in his *Life* had therefore risked asserting that the *Negotiations of Monsr. Mesnager* 'contains, in my judgment, indisputable internal evidence that it came from Defoe's hand'.[22] Now, in an article in *Notes and Queries* for 12 June 1869, Crossley reported that, by a happy chance, he had found his copy of *Mercurius Politicus*, with the relevant issue, and in view of its importance, he would quote from it. It showed Defoe's disclaimer of the Mesnager tract, he said, to be 'distinct and clear', and he professed to believe it ('for I should not like to suppose that Defoe had any secret reservations when making such earnest and even solemn disclaimers'). It thus, he said, left the difficult question, 'who was the contemporary who imitates so well, his style and manner of writing?'[23]

Crossley's blandly innocent article would seem to have been calculated to cause Lee the maximum of embarrassment. Either his boasted mastery in Defoe attribution was in doubt, or his admired hero was a liar. He wrote at once to Crossley, asking for help, and for permission, in his published reply, to quote from Crossley's letters to him (in which presumably he had taken a somewhat different line about the Mesnager tract). Crossley, however, begged to be excused, remarking smoothly: 'In the freedom and carelessness of letter writing many expressions occur which would have been subjected to supervision or put in a more guarded shape if they had been intended to be addressed to the public.' In a reply to a further anxious missive of Lee's, he insisted that his 'respect for the memory of Defoe [was] too great to permit [his] believing him capable of volunteering a deliberate falsehood' and reiterated his theory that Defoe might have had a double — 'a circumstance which if it is ultimately found to have existed', said Crossley, twisting the knife further, 'will be attended with this difficulty that the writer of Mesnager may be also the writer of some of the tracts which you and I have attributed to Defoe'.[24]

Lee's behaviour in this dilemma is of a piece with his character in general. He set to work at once on a 'long and very laborious investigation' lasting many months, eventually publishing the results in two long articles in *Notes and Queries* in February 1870. What he had done was no less than to explore Crossley's theory of a 'double' as a serious possibility:

> With this view, I made out from my extracts of the old journals, from a considerable bibliographical library, and many thousands of pamphlets in my own possession, and from the catalogues of the British Museum, a list of known and anonymous authors of the period, and of such of their works as I had not already examined. Thus prepared I have laboured for several months among such pamphlets and books, with an earnest desire to discover the truth, in whichever direction it might be found; but my only reward is the negative result, that I have utterly failed to discover any contemporaneous imitator of Defoe, or to sift out any book or pamphlet that will bear all the requisite tests of critical comparison, except those written by himself.

Having thus drawn a blank in this inquiry, and having set out the facts surrounding the Mesnager tract as fully and impartially as he could, he left the reader to form his or her own conclusion, but, with great integrity, did not disguise his own — which was that his impeccable hero had told a lie.[25] The whole affair had plainly caused poor Lee a good deal of pain.

One forms a reasonably clear image of Lee through the lens of his *Life* of Defoe. He seems, judging from its pages, to have been a devoted royalist, one who saw a remarkable likeness between Queen Anne's consort Prince George of Denmark and 'the illustrious Prince, whose death our own beloved Queen, and all her sujects, will never cease to mourn'. He was a defender of the Established Church, of which he held Defoe to have been a lifelong 'venerator'; he believed in the need of firmness towards the 'ignorant classes'; and he agreed with Defoe that servants should not be allowed to get above themselves. On the other hand he was a free- trader, finding Defoe 'nearly a century and a half in advance of general public opinion on these topics'; he was a strong advocate of 'progress' — moral, intellectual and material — and believed Defoe's contribution to it could not be over-estimated; and he was a foe to 'the clique of inferior trading busybodies' who still, as in Defoe's day, monopolised local government (a sentiment very natural in a Chadwickian). Like some of his earlier associates on the Sheffield scene, he was a phrenologist and detected in Defoe 'large perceptive faculties, with much Wit, Ideality, Wonder, Eventuality, and Causality; all governed by Conscientiousness and Veneration'. On anything to do with sex he was a most prim, 'respectable' and shockable man, one who considered Defoe's *Conjugal Lewdness* dangerous and 'by no means a book to be placed in the hands of young unmarried persons of the present age', and was driven to explain *Moll Flanders* and *Colonel Jack* by the theory that they were written, not for 'the pure and the delicate', but for convicted thieves and prostitutes to read, for the good of their souls, on the way to the plantations. Above all, he was a fervent evangelical Christian of a somewhat sentimental stamp, who believed that Defoe 'received the truths of Revelation with the simple faith of a child' and that his mission in life was as a 'teacher of the highest morality — the Truth as it is in Jesus'.[26]

None of this account of ours is meant as hostile to Lee, who, as we hope we have suggested, was in some ways a very attractive man — certainly an intensely honourable, high-minded and productive one, who did a good deal for Defoe studies. If he had his limitations as a biographer, they need not worry us too much, for he generally gives us the facts, and we can make our own biographical constructions from them. Where the same limitations matter much more is as they affect him as a bibliographer. That *History of the Wars of Charles XII*, first attributed to Defoe by Lee, is, as we have already remarked, still in the canon, and so are many other of his first-time attributions; and as the *Athenaeum* reviewer said, 'he may be often right', but if so, we cannot help feeling, it is as much by luck as by judgement. A simple-minded and somewhat blinkered man, as Lee assuredly was, is not the best person to penetrate Defoe's secrets; and the thought that so sizeable a portion of the Defoe canon owes its presence there (originally, anyway) to Lee is not reassuring.

It remains for us to consider Lee's long-term influence on Defoe studies. It has certainly been an enormous one, and within it questions of biography and questions of bibliography are almost inextricably intertwined. This is best illustrated by an example. In his *Life* Lee tells us that Defoe, in 1720, having grown increasingly exasperated with his associate Nathaniel Mist, transferred his allegiance to the printer-publisher Ambrose Applebee, 'entering into an arrangement with the owner of "Applebee's Original Weekly Journal", to write Letters Introductory, and take some part in the general management of that paper'. According to Lee's account, Defoe published his first article in *Applebee's Journal*, a playful essay on 'bubbling schemes signed "Oliver Oldway"', on 25 June 1720, and he continued to write weekly articles for the journal until 12 March 1726.[27]

This, however, so Lee informs us, was only one element in Defoe's association with Applebee, for he also worked for him as a crime-reporter and pamphleteer. Applebee, as publisher, specialised in the lives and dying speeches of criminals, and thus it was natural for Defoe, who became increasingly concerned at the spread of crime in Britain, to comment on criminal matters in *Applebee's Journal*. More importantly, it was indirectly through Applebee that he took a new turning as a novelist. Applebee and his deputies had access to Newgate, and thus Defoe got into the habit of visiting and questioning the prisoners there, with the result not only that he was inspired to write some pamphlet lives of rogues but that he conceived the philanthropic plan of writing novels, such as *Moll Flanders* and *Colonel Jack*, for the edification and possible reform of criminals.

In the summer of 1724, Lee continues, Defoe became very closely involved in the great sensation of the hour, the capture, escapes, and recapture of the highwayman John Sheppard. He wrote numerous articles on him in *Applebee's Journal* and paid benevolent visits to him in the condemned cell. This latter he would have done, says Lee, in the person of Mr Applebee: 'I have no doubt that, *as Mr. Applebee*, Defoe visited Sheppard after his condemnation, and seconded the efforts of the reverend Ordinary to impress his mind with a proper sense of religion. I come to this conclusion from the fact that the prisoner seems never to have known Defoe by any other name than "Mr. Applebee".' Defoe, Lee tells us, wrote two pamphlets about Sheppard, and by concerted arrangement the second of them, *A Narrative of All the Robberies, Escapes etc. of John Sheppard*, was actually passed to Sheppard so that it could be ceremoniously handed back by him to Defoe from the hangman's cart, before the eyes of the assembled crowd. (A newspaper report, Lee has to admit, asserted that it was Mr Applebee who appeared on the scene to receive the pamphlet, but he is confident that this must have been Defoe impersonating or representing Applebee.[28])

It is quite difficult for the reader of this stirring and involved narrative to remember that, so far as Defoe is concerned, Lee has produced no hard evidence for it whatever — not even for his ever having been associated with Applebee. The whole construction is built upon stylistic inferences, and Lee's statement in the *Life* should strictly have read: '*Literary-critical considerations prompt me* to the conclusion that, in 1720, Defoe entered into an arrangement with the owner of "Applebee's Journal"', etc. All rests on Lee's conviction that his magic thumb can infallibly detect Defoe's prose style. To this conviction we owe the attribution to Defoe of four or five 'criminal' pamphlets and no less than 355 articles and paragraphs from *Applebee's Journal*, reprinted by Lee among the 'recently discovered writings'.[29] We also owe to it an amazing vision: of an elderly and successful novelist, a one-time victim of the pillory, leaving the comforts of Stoke Newington and intrepidly exhibiting his well-known face to a crowd of thousands, in order to boost the sales of a pamphlet, the authorship of which was to remain secret.

It may be that Lee's conclusions are all correct, though frankly we think it highly unlikely, but his methods certainly leave a lot to be desired. It is, partly, a question of rhetoric. We are safe in assuming that Lee had no intention to deceive; nevertheless his mode of writing tends to be very deceptive. His earnestness and painstakingness in discussing what are declaredly biographical speculations succeed in disguising from the reader that what he asserts, with calm authoritativeness, as biographical fact can be equally speculative and no more than inference, or the end of a whole chain of inferences, from some stylistic intuition. This unconscious rhetoric on Lee's part has had a large influence on the scholars who have drawn on his book, and is we suspect, the main reason for their perpetuating some of his first-time attributions.

CHAPTER 7

JAMES CROSSLEY

THE NEXT IMPORTANT addition to the Defoe canon came, in a complicated and roundabout way, from James Crossley, whom the reader has already encountered in his dealings with Lee. He was born in 1800, the son of a Halifax clothing merchant, and was educated at local grammar schools. Whilst still a boy he developed a passion for literature and especially for collecting antiquarian books. A well-known bookseller and binder in Halifax, Thomas Edwards, did much to encourage the budding bibliophile by lending him copies of rare books which he could not yet afford to buy.

After leaving school in 1816, Crossley moved to Manchester, where he was articled to the legal firm of Thomas Ainsworth. Here began a lifelong friendship with Ainsworth's son, William Harrison, the future novelist (who was later to depict Crossley as Dr Foam, the 'benevolent Physician' and bibliophile, in his novel *Mervyn Clitheroe* (1858)), and the two spent much time together discussing literature and reading in the Chetham Library. Crossley very soon began to write articles on sixteenth- and seventeenth-century literature for *Blackwood's Magazine*. Among his earliest publications were essays on Sir Thomas Browne (a writer on whom Crossley became something of an authority), Sir Thomas Urquhart's 'The Jewell', Thomas Beard's *Theatre of God's Judgments*, *Eastward Hoe* and Mayne's *City Match*, all of these appearing in the 1820s. The works of Browne held a particular fascination for Crossley at this time, and he managed to pass off a forgery entitled 'The Fragment on Mummies' on Browne's editor, Simon Wilkin. (It duly appeared in the fourth volume of the *Works* (1835), with a note by Wilkin explaining that he was publishing the 'Fragment' 'on the authority of Mr. Crossley; but has not been able to find the volume in the British Museum which contained it; nor could he inform me, having transcribed it himself in the Museum, but omitted to note the volume in which he met with it'.[1]) Crossley was also instrumental in the launching of the *Retrospective Review*, which appeared in 1820, a journal representative of a current swing towards nostalgic literary antiquarianism, familiar to us in Charles Lamb and expressive, no doubt, of a reaction against the 'iron realities' of a Reformist and Benthamite age. The principles of the *Retrospective Review* were dear to Crossley's heart, and he supplied a list of nearly 300 works as suitable subjects for articles, and himself contributed several essays. In a review of the scheme of the magazine in *Blackwood's* he declared, with ponderous relish, his impatience with the present idle age:

> ...learning is so widely extended, that, as it is increased in surface, it is lamentably diminished in depth. At present all are readers, and all are superficial readers. It is sufficient with the generality to be acquainted with the glittering novelties of the day, for the blandishments of which the harder and more enduring productions of other periods are neglected.[2]

In 1822 and 1823 Crossley spent some time in London, completing his legal education. There he made the acquaintance of leading literary figures, including Charles Lamb, and he pursued his scholarly investigations in the library of the British Museum. In 1823, on his return to Manchester, he became a partner in the firm of Ainsworth, Crossley and Sudlow, remaining there as a successful lawyer until his retirement in 1860. He rose rapidly in Manchester society, being twice elected president of the Incorporated Law Association of Manchester, president of the Manchester Athenaeum from 1847 to 1850, and a member of the committee which established the Manchester Free Library. Together with Edward Edwards, Crossley was entrusted with the purchase of the new library's initial collection, and he was on the platform, alongside Dickens, Thackeray and Bulwer Lytton, when the library was officially opened in 1852. Crossley greatly enjoyed such public events and the speechifying that went with them. In manner he was a sort of provincial Dr Johnson, much given to the apostrophe 'Sir'. (Dickens, having heard him described by Harrison Ainsworth, identified Crossley at once from his orotund manner of speech.[3])

Crossley was also very prominent in literary and antiquarian circles. He became a member of the Abbotsford Club, the Philobiblon Society, the Society of Antiquaries, the Surtees Society, the Spenser Society and the Lancashire and Cheshire Record Society, holding the office of President in the last two mentioned. But the one which appealed most to him was undoubtedly the Chetham Society, which had been founded at Crossley's own house in 1843. He was elected President in 1848, and played a major role in seeing many of the Society's publications through the press. He also edited a number of volumes himself, notably Thomas Potts's *Wonderful Discovery of Witches* (1845), the *Diary and Correspondence of Dr. John Worthington* (1847, 1855) and *Autobiographical Tracts of Dr. John Dee* (1851). These editions were furnished with an enormous amount of annotation, in which Crossley displayed a formidable knowledge of the by-ways of seventeenth-century literature.

This knowledge was derived, in great measure, from books in his own possession. His acquisitiveness and tenacity as a book collector, not to mention ruthlessness at a bargain, became a by-word. (He made such a nuisance of himself to booksellers by his passion for bargains, that they would sometimes bar him from their shop, until his contrite face at the window induced them to let him in again.) His personal library was reckoned to contain 100,000 volumes, and his Defoe collection, in particular, was said to be the envy even of the British Museum. When the newly formed Library Association held its second annual meeting in Manchester in 1879, John H. Nodal, the Director of the English Dialect Society, gave a paper on 'Special Collections of Books in Lancashire and Cheshire', in which he praised Crossley as the 'possessor of the finest known collection of the works of Daniel Defoe':

> Within two or three, Mr Crossley has the whole of 254 books and tracts enumerated in the list prefixed to Mr Lee's 'Life of Defoe', including the very scarce periodical 'Mercator, or Commerce Retrieved' (1713–14), and the only known copy of 'The Review', in eight volumes quarto, and the first volume of a new series which was never proceeded with (1704–13)....Of the various works above referred to, the collection is believed to have every edition except some of the later impressions of the 'True-born Englishman', 'Robinson Crusoe', and the 'Religious Courtship', which have appeared in chap-books, and in other forms innumerable. In addition to the works contained in Mr Lee's list, Mr Crossley has fifty-two more tracts and books, indubitably by Defoe, and which Mr Lee does not appear to have seen.[4]

The other great prizes of Crossley's Defoe collection were the manuscript of *The Compleat English Gentleman*, and the manuscript correspondence, bound in eight volumes, of Defoe's son-in-law,

Henry Baker. Despite the urgings of Defoe scholars such as William
Lee, Crossley seems to have made no effort to publish *The Compleat
English Gentleman*, even though he recognized it as being the 'most
valuable' item in his collection and described it as Defoe's 'legacy to
the English people'.[5]

Evidently, part of the excitement for Crossley in collecting Defoe
was the possibility of making new attributions, and in 1838 he
published an article in the *Gentleman's Magazine* announcing his
conviction that a book he had recently purchased, entitled *Due
Preparations for the Plague* (1722), was by Defoe: 'The style and
manner of treating the subject are so perfectly Defoe's, that there is
no possible room left for scepticism, and a feeling of surprise is
naturally produced that the work should have been so completely
overlooked.' The attribution is indeed a most plausible one, which
has been accepted by every subsequent scholar, and Crossley was
inordinately proud of his own sagacity in having made this 'not
unimportant discovery', as he termed it.[6] His discovery was given
even wider currency by Harrison Ainsworth, who made extensive
use of *Due Preparations* when writing his novel *Old St. Paul's*,
published in 1841.

When *Notes and Queries* was founded in 1849, Crossley quickly
became a regular contributor on the subject of Defoe. In an article in
1851, for example, he confidently attributed two tracts to Defoe: *An
Effectual Scheme for the Immediate Preventing of Street Robberies* (1731)
and *Street-Robberies, Consider'd* (1728). The first of these is 'beyond
doubt by Defoe', he asserted, and he had 'no hesitation in ascribing'
the second to Defoe. No evidence was offered in support of these
claims, merely an oracular pronouncement that the two pamphlets
were 'written in all Defoe's graphic manner'.[7] A similarly confident
tone is adopted in a later article on Defoe's authorship of the
newspaper entitled *Mercator*. Earlier scholars such as Chalmers and
Wilson had, according to Crossley, misunderstood Defoe's reference
to *Mercator* in his *Appeal to Honour and Justice*. Crossley accepted
Defoe's denial that he was not the proprietor or owner of *Mercator*,
but concluded that 'There cannot...be the slightest doubt to any
one at all acquainted with Defoe's style, or who compares the
Mercator with the commercial articles in the *Review*, that the whole of
the *Mercator*, except such portion as appears in the shape of letters,
and which constitutes only a small part of the work, was written by
Defoe.' We are not told by Crossley, here or elsewhere, what is so
distinctive about Defoe's prose style which makes it so easy to

identify, other than that *Mercator* is 'replete. . .with the vigour, the life and animation, the various and felicitous power of illustration, which this great and truly English author could impart to any subject'.[8]

In subsequent articles Crossley expressed even more forcibly his impatience with, and even contempt for, the work of earlier students of the Defoe canon. 'It is impossible to read Chalmers' and Wilson's *Lives of Defoe*', he writes, 'without being constantly struck not merely by the want of all critical acumen and ordinary knowledge of the characteristics of Defoe's style, which they display, but also by the absence of research on almost every point of importance connected with his career.' In the course of a discussion of Defoe's supposed writings on the Septennial Bill during 1716, he attributes for the first time to Defoe two pamphlets: *Some Thoughts upon the Subject of Commerce with France* (1713), and *Some Considerations on a Law for Triennial Parliaments* (1716). (In the same article, it should be said, he rejects the contemporary attribution to Defoe of *The Triennial Act Impartially Stated*, and offers an explanation of Defoe's, apparently mistaken, assertion that he was the author of another pamphlet, *Arguments about the Alteration of Triennial Elections of Parliament*.[9])

All told, then, Crossley was responsible for six published attributions to Defoe. These represent, however, only a fraction of his total achievement in the field of Defoe attribution, and a great number of further ascriptions of his eventually, by indirect means, found their way into the established canon, and have remained there to this day. As we have seen in the previous chapter, the existence of these unpublished attributions was first revealed by Crossley himself in *Notes and Queries*, in the course of a notice in 1869 of William Lee's *Life* of Defoe, when he claimed to be in possession of 'at least fifty more distinct works, hitherto unattributed to Defoe, but which may confidently be ascribed to him'.[10] The titles of these works were never made public by Crossley, but he compiled a handwritten list of 'Tracts ascribed by me to Defoe which are not in Mr. Lee's List or Wilson's. 61 in Number.'[11] This manuscript list (printed as Appendix B at the end of this book), together with other memoranda of Crossley's, came into the possession of the Defoe scholar George A. Aitken, who in turn put them at the disposal of W.P. Trent. Trent published a series of lengthy articles in the *Nation* in 1907 in which he paid fulsome tribute to Crossley as 'the greatest of all authorities' on the tangled subject of Defoe bibliography. He listed most of the sixty-one titles (actually sixty, since one title was unwittingly repeated by Crossley) with comments of his own, concluding that 'of the sixty-one items in Crossley's list, one is now accepted by all [presumably *Due Preparations for the Plague*], one — "What if the Swedes Should Come?" — is quite generally accepted, two seem to be mistaken ascriptions, and of the fifty-two (or fifty-three) others that I have examined I find only nine about which I have any real doubt'.[12] Trent subsequently included fifty-one of Crossley's attributions in his bibliography in *The Cambridge History of English Literature*, and in the standard *Checklist* by J.R. Moore all but six of the titles on Crossley's list are included.

This is not quite the end of the story, however. The major part of Crossley's personal library was sold at auction in London in two portions, the first in July 1884, the second in June 1885, and among the large collection of 'Defoe and Defoeana' in the second portion were two lots of particular interest. Lot 827 was described as a collection of 172 tracts by, or attributed to, Defoe, in twenty-two bound volumes, with an index and comments in each volume by Crossley. Lot 821 contained twenty-eight works by Defoe, together with about 250 miscellaneous tracts. We have not managed to trace the subsequent fate of the twenty-two bound volumes, but before the sale took place, Edward Riggall, a friend of William Lee's, a London surgeon and keen amateur collector of fine art and books, examined the two lots carefully and recorded the comments written by Crossley in some of the books. Riggall's notes were preserved, and after his death in 1900, when his own library was sold, they were bought by Percy Dobell, who in turn gave them to W.P. Trent in 1912.[13] The notes reveal three more firm attributions, all of them included in Moore's *Checklist*. Crossley, it seems, had been the first to spot that *The Generous Projector* (1731) is a revision of *Augusta Triumphans* (1728). (He wrote in his copy that 'The part at the end relating to Watermen is *not* in *Augusta Triumphans*.') Another tract, *Secret Memoirs of the New Treaty* (1716), is marked as 'by Defoe'; and in his copy of *A Brief Historical Account. . .of the Six Robbers* (1724) he commented: 'Evidently by Defoe. It has every mark of his style. It has not been noticed hitherto by any Biographer.'

So to the sixty attributions in his manuscript list, the five published in *Notes and Queries*, and the one in the *Gentleman's Magazine*, we must add these three, making a total of 69 separate items firmly and specifically attributed by Crossley to Defoe, most of them for the first time. Eight other works owned by Crossley on which he made no comment, but which were included in lots described as 'by Defoe' in the sale catalogue of his library, have subsequently been attributed to Defoe by modern scholars.[14] His comments on a further three works which also are now in the canon show that he thought these likely to be by Defoe, but he had not fully convinced himself.[15] (Perhaps for the sake of completeness we should add that two items now in the canon were specifically rejected by Crossley.[16])

The quality of Crossley's contribution to the Defoe canon, his methods of attribution, and the means by which he made his influence felt are all matters of some importance in our story. As to their quality, our own impression is that it is very varied. He began rather impressively, by spotting *Due Preparations for the Plague*, which is an important, and extremely convincing attribution. Similarly, his attribution to Defoe of three pamphlets on the 'calico' controversy of 1719–20, *The Just Complaint of the Poor Weavers* (1719), *A Brief State of the Question, Between the Printed and Painted Calicoes and the Woollen and Silk Manufacture* (1719) and *The Trade to India Critically and Calmly Consider'd* (1720) seems potentially very plausible. The pamphlets' advocacy of a ban on the use and wearing of calicoes, as the sole remaining defence of the British weaving industry and a cure for the drain on British bullion, would follow on entirely naturally from Defoe's already protectionist analysis of the East India trade that appeared in the *Review* for 29 January and 12 February 1708, and the style is nowhere incompatible with Defoe and in places distinctly suggestive of him. It is highly creditable of Crossley to have discovered these pamphlets, whatever conclusion one were to come to about their right to be added to the Defoe canon.

On the other hand, one or two of his other attributions strike one as distinctly wild. Some of these have since been assigned to other authors; for instance *An Account of the Obligations the States of Holland have to Great Britain* (1711), a virulently anti-Dutch tract, altogether unlike Defoe's habitual attitude towards the Dutch, is now widely attributed to Robert Ferguson (under whose name it is listed in the British Library catalogue). Elsewhere among his list of sixty works is a lengthy narrative entitled *The Tryal and Sufferings of Mr. Isaac Martin, who was put into the Inquisition in Spain, for the sake of the Protestant Religion* (1723). According to the title-page, this sensational piece of anti-Catholic propaganda was written by Martin himself, and was 'Dedicated to his most sacred Majesty, King George, by whose gracious Interposition he was releas'd'. It comes furnished with a testimonial signed by fifteen Anglican bishops, certifying the veracity of Martin's story and recommending him as 'a great object of Charity'. The book, which gives an account of Martin's interrogation and treatment in prison, ends with an apology for his lack of experience as a writer, but claims that he has been advised to publish his story by 'several worthy Bishops and Clergymen' (p.108). Following the main text is an 'Advertisement' inviting orders for copies of the book, to be sent to 'Isaac Martin, at Mr. Scale's, at the Pearl and Dolphin in Green-Street near Leicester Square'.

On the face of it, there would seem to be no reason whatever to connect Defoe with this work. This proves no obstacle to Crossley, as we see from his comment written in his own copy of the book:

> This has been considered a genuine account. It is, however, I have not the slightest doubt, one of Defoe's popular dressings of a meagre subject. The reputed author (Martin) calls himself an illiterate, and how is it possible he would, after the lapse of so many years record long conversations which he had no means of taking down at the time. These conversations have all the impress of Defoe, and were doubtless drawn up by him from a few hints with a charitable view of benefiting the sufferer and making a work which would be saleable. Taylor was the publisher of R. Crusoe.

Perhaps all we need to say here is that no subsequent bibliographer has followed Crossley in crediting Defoe with *The Tryal and Sufferings of Mr. Isaac Martin*.

CHAPTER 8

W.P. TRENT

TO A QUITE baffling degree, a Defoe biographer is compelled also to be a Defoe bibliographer, and how to co-ordinate these two roles is a problem that has never yet been satisfactorily solved. The deepest objection to Lee's work lies here. For, whereas in Wilson narration and attribution are left, to some extent at least, as distinguishable strands, in Lee they present an inextricable knot — so that, for much of the time in reading Lee one cannot tell which of the two one is being offered. (Is Lee asserting that Defoe wrote a particular tract because he was a certain kind of man, or is he asserting that he must be a particular kind of man because he wrote a certain tract?)

It was only gradually that the next major Defoe biographer/bibliographer, W.P. Trent, discovered the problem. When at last he realised it, however, in all its intractability, he faced it with much bravery. In 1905 he set out to write a life of Defoe, with (in the Lee and Wilson manner) a new bibliography as an appendix. By 1912 he had found it necessary to produce not only a massive biography but, as companion to it, a *catalogue raisonné* of Defoe's works at least four times as long, in which a detailed justification was given for every one of the attributions it contained. The whole amounted to over 3,000 pages. He then believed the combined work ready for publication, but thirteen years later he was still revising and adding to it, by now nearly despairing of ever seeing it in print. Nor was it ever printed, and it remains, safe but neglected by scholars, in the vaults of the Beinecke Library. Trent's is a tragic story, which throws much light on the issues we have been discussing in this book.

William Peterfield Trent was a Southerner, born in 1862 amid the siege of Richmond, Virginia. His father, a physician, sacrificed his position and wealth to the Southern cause, leaving the disinherited

Trent with an ambivalent attitude towards the Old South and a deeply ingrained prejudice against war, as a barbaric survival. He attended the University of Virginia and the Johns Hopkins University and in 1888 joined the University of the South (Sewanee) as a professor of history and of literature. Trent — at this time 'an exceedingly cocky young man',[1] given to terse and subersive wit and reputed an agnostic — caused the Sewanee authorities a certain amount of alarm, and he did so considerably more when, in 1892, he published a life of the Southern novelist William Gilmore Simms, in which he was savagely critical of ante-bellum Southern culture. This caused a local furore. The Southern press fell on him with the epithets 'blackguard', 'traitor', 'disloyal son of the south', his mother was cut by her neighbours in the streets of Richmond, and for a time his own position at Sewanee was in jeopardy. (It was none the less in the same year that he became founder-editor of the still-flourishing *Sewanee Review*, contributing to it over the next decade a flood of articles on literature, politics and history.) In 1898 he was in hot water again, for his 'unpatriotic' opposition to the Spanish–American war. He was by now beginning to feel an exile in 'provincial' and *bien-pensant* Sewanee, but, fortunately, his book on Simms had found an influential admirer in Theodore Roosevelt; and in 1900, partly through Roosevelt's influence, he was offered a post at Columbia University and decided to sever his links with the South.

Hitherto his ambitions had been as a teacher and populariser. The theme that runs through his early writings, as it does his character, is 'idealism'. He was a man in whose life the word 'noble' continually crops up, and who in later years would tell his students that 'the only things that mattered in this world were babies and great style'.[2] In his little biography of Robert E. Lee, he describes the Southern general as 'a peerless exemplar of all that is honourable and pure and exquisite and noble in human life and character', and speaks of the surrender to Grant at Appomatox as illustrating, 'as perhaps no similar event has ever done, the essential nobility of human nature'.[3] Trent was a battler, an irascible Quixote, gnawed by inner fears[4] and always inclined to find himself in a party of one. For his friend and pupil Carl van Doren this 'kind, fierce, gray Virginian lion' was 'a philosophical statesman' and 'the noblest man I ever knew'.[5]

Soon after his arrival in Columbia, Trent, somewhat by accident, became interested in Defoe. He had been invited to give an extramural lecture on some popular subject and had chosen *Robinson Crusoe* and its author. It offered him a glimpse of the innumerable scholarly problems presented by Defoe, and it seems to have given him the impulse, which he had not felt before, to make his mark in exact scholarship. By 1905 he was deeply embroiled in Defoe and attribution problems, was acquiring a library of eighteenth-century tracts and was in correspondence with Defoe experts such as T.J. Wise, H.S. Foxwell and George A. Aitken. Aitken showed him a copy of the Crossley list of sixty new Defoe attributions, and Percy Dobell subsequently gave him the Riggall notes taken at the Crossley sale (see pp. 79–80 above), thus putting him in a favourable position to re-assess the standard list of attributions by William Lee. His work was sufficiently advanced by 1907 for him to publish a series of articles in the New York *Nation*[6] setting out the Crossley attributions, most of which he himself supported, and adding a series of tentative or positive attributions of his own. The articles were, he explained, in the nature of an interim report, to provoke corrections and suggestions before his forthcoming bibliography of Defoe.

There was in a way, one feels, an unhappy fatality in a man of Trent's outlook and temperament taking on what he himself called 'perhaps the most tangled subject in English bibliography'.[7] In his *Nation* articles he adopts a mildly facetious tone: he describes how he began 'only with the intention of dipping into the subject, soon found myself getting deeper and deeper in, and at last was completely over my head', though there now seemed 'some chance of my emerging'. His conclusion is in the same cheerfully ironic vein:

...some of Crossley's attributions I have yet to find; twenty of those I have found seem most probably to be Defoe's, although I should like to suspend judgement until I can re-examine them in the light of recent experience; there are at least thirty of the pamphlets included in my lists of strongly suspected and of less probable, but still very possible tracts which have to be reckoned with; and finally there are a dozen or more short performances in prose attributed to Defoe in the catalogues of libraries to which I hope to give some attention later. I should not like therefore to promise that I will stop the bibliography I am preparing short of 350 items, and there seem to be almost, if not quite, as many rejections to be enumerated. I really do not know who is most at fault, Defoe for writing so much or myself for spending so much time over these musty old pamphlets. Yet, if the truth needs to be told, I enjoy the task, and I hope that those readers of the *Nation* who are willing to humour a 'crank', and are able to help him, will examine the following list of *desiderata*, and give any information they have about any item.[8]

What one cannot but notice is that Trent's picture of himself, as a harmless 'crank' and bibliophile, poking about for his amusement among dry-as-dust tracts, does not fit too well with the generous educator or the Quixotic battler for noble causes. Moreover, during these first two years or so of his Defoe studies, Trent had suffered a painful shock. He had begun with a notion of Defoe as an honourable and maligned man, but after some time had reached the conclusion that, on the contrary, he was an absolute rogue, capable of almost any duplicity — and further that a refusal to admit this fact had stultified Lee and Crossley's work in attribution. 'As...my bibliographical investigations were pushed further and deeper,' he writes in his unpublished biography,

> I became more and more impressed by the fact that previous students in attributing three fourths of Defoe's works to him upon the joint basis of traditional ascription and internal evidence had established a canon of procedure which they violated with complete *sang froid* whenever they found that by following it they were compelled to ascribe to their hero works which by no process of legerdermain they could represent as creditable to his character.[9]

The discovery was a disagreeable one but, Trent argued to himself, it had to be faced. The generous faith of Lee and Crossley must be abjured, and a stance of scepticism, of almost bottomless cynicism, must be adopted. It was a matter of courage and honour; and henceforth the words 'courage' and 'cowardice' will figure repeatedly in Trent's bibliographical discussions. Did Defoe write the salacious *History of Prince Mirabel's Infancy* (1712)? The question poses itself to Trent as one of bibliographical valour.

> Gradual realisation...of the chameleon-like qualities of Defoe, and greater familiarity with the cadences of his sentences and the subtler features of his style, combined with a growing conviction that he wrote the 'History of the Proceedings of the Mandarins and Proations' and that that could not be separated from the 'History' of Prince Mirabel, resulted finally in breaking down my hesitation and in stiffening my determination to assign him the present work with full recognition of the fact that to charge him with its authorship was equivalent to asserting that he had lost all sense of shame.[10]

What one perceives on Trent's part here is all the symptoms of disappointed idealism, and this is a very dangerous state of mind for a bibliographer. The conception of Defoe's character that he arrived at was not, in fact, as extreme as we have suggested. He finds various excuses for him (among them indeed, that Defoe himself might have been a disappointed idealist) and retains some affection for him and his so 'human' failings: to the end, with a touch of social condescension, he allows him to be 'The greatest of plebeian geniuses'.[11] Nevertheless, in any particular attribution problem, the fear to be found failing in courage or be seen to flinch from the blackest possible conclusion as regards Defoe presents itself as a moral challenge to Trent, and such fear is an emotion quite as likely to disturb objective judgement as its opposite. There is a great deal to be said in praise of Trent's bibliographical work, and in one respect at least (his realising that reasons must be given for any new or even disputable attribution) it is more deserving of our admiration than that of his successor, J.R. Moore.

Nevertheless, as we shall suggest, it was weakened and half-wrecked by this temperamental flaw — one which had this in common with the rather different foibles of Lee and Crossley, that it served as a stimulus to more and *yet more* attribution. If Defoe is thought capable of writing more or less anything, the conviction is liable to grow that he wrote more or less everything.

Trent's name as a Defoe expert was spreading, and round about 1910 he was invited to write the Defoe chapter, with its bibliography, for the great *Cambridge History of English Literature*. For whatever reason, in the next year he suffered a minor nervous breakdown, and friends were inclined to blame it on his Defoe studies, which seemed to be changing him from a hospitable and clubbable man into a recluse. 'Damn Defoe, or at least his demoralising influence on you!' his friend Henry Holt wrote to him as early as 1908; and in a later letter he asked Trent, who was now complaining rancorously about the carelessness of other scholars, 'I wonder if you're getting to be a little excessive on the topic of superficiality?'[12] Trent battled on, and the *Cambridge History* chapter was written, appearing in 1912. Its most important feature was in fact its bibliography, which added many titles to, and rejected a few titles from, William Lee's list and for nearly thirty years imposed itself as the standard bibliography. In the following year he wrote wryly to his friend Yates Snowden: 'I have in ms. — fairly and in shape for publication — a biography and bibliography that will fill six large and deadly volumes. Think of a Southerner writing that much, after all that has been said of our laziness!'[13]

The Great War gave another adverse turn to Trent's fortunes. As a lifelong Anglophobe, Trent regarded Germany as, if anything, the injured party in the present conjuncture. Thus from the start he argued passionately against American intervention, but more particularly, to the outrage of his Columbia colleagues, against intervention on the British side; and matters became even more fraught when, in the New York *Staats-Zeitung* for 6 March 1915, he published a hymn in praise of Germany, reprinted next day in the *New York Times*. There were heated exchanges in the commonroom, several friends broke with him, he withdrew from all his clubs; and in a mood of intense dejection, he came near to resigning from his chair. The long-term result was that he withdrew even more into what he called his 'beloved dusty pamphlets'. It is significant, and a bad omen, that by now he had ceased to publish scholarly articles on Defoe. In 1916, however, beginning to doubt if his great work would ever find a publisher, he carved two more-saleable products out of it: an edition of *Robinson Crusoe*; and a potted version of his biography, combined with extracts from Defoe's writings, entitled *Defoe: How to Know Him* in the Bobbs-Merrill 'How to know Him' series. In his prefatory note he warned the reader that every month, as he read further in eighteenth-century pamphlet literature, he found reason to revise what he had written earlier: 'Hence I am likely to be the first person to call into question details in the record of Defoe's extraordinarily complicated career as I have given them in the following pages.'[14]

Some years earlier, Trent had initiated the scheme of what became the great Columbia edition of Milton, and for a year or two towards the end of the war, as editor-in-chief, he had some respite from his Defoe studies. He was also involved at much the same time, in collaboration with some Columbia colleagues, on *The Cambridge History of American Literature*. Defoe soon reclaimed him, however, and by the end of 1920 he was describing himself to Mark van Doren as 'an elderly gentleman who seems entirely absorbed in the task of gathering bibliographical samphire on a lonely cliff'.[15] With failing energies he laboured on, re-reading disputed pamphlets for the third, or the tenth, time and comparing his new conclusions on their authorship with those of fifteen years before. In 1921 his wife died; his book-collecting was beginning to impoverish him; and there were more nervous breakdowns, as his *magnum opus* still obstinately refused to finalise itself. Eventually, in Paris in the summer of 1927, having delivered a flaming public speech demanding a reprieve for Sacco and Vanzetti, he had a stroke, which left him for the remaining twelve years of his life confined to a wheel chair, more or less incapable of handling a pen.

Our story is not quite done. When Trent realised he could never work again, he bestowed his Defoe manuscript on an ex-pupil of his, H.C. Hutchins, on the understanding that Hutchins should give it a final tidying and attempt to have it published. At the same time, no doubt partly to pay for medical treatment, he sold his enormous Defoe collection to the Boston Public Library. Hutchins, at some point thereafter, had the manuscript typed, and over the ensuing years he duly made sporadic, but unsuccessful, efforts to find a publisher. He also seems to have drawn on the bibliography himself when, in 1930, he was invited to compile the Defoe entry in *The Cambridge Bibliography of English Literature* — at all events some fourteen of the new attributions included in his list appear also in Trent's manuscript.

Hutchins, however, was a somewhat secretive man [16] and seems not to have encouraged other scholars to examine the Trent papers. There thus came about a curious hiatus between the work of Trent and that of J.R. Moore. According to Moore's account, it was Trent's marginalia in some copies of Defoe's works that gave him his 'first insight into the attribution of anonymous and pseudony-mous writings',[17] and he was also strongly influenced by Trent's attributions in the *Nation* articles and the *Cambridge History* list of 1912. He was aware of the existence of the manuscript, but, without ever having seen it, concluded that Trent's final word on Defoe attribution was contained in his published pieces and had been incorporated into Hutchins's *Cambridge Bibliography* list of 1940; whereas the truth was that Trent, in the years after his *Cambridge History* list of 1912, had made some seventy-nine new attributions, in many cases anticipating Moore, and only a handful of these had found their way into Hutchins's *Cambridge Bibliography* list. Just how false an idea Moore had, and helped to disseminate, of Trent's work can be seen from a letter he wrote in 1952 to Zoltán Haraszti, the Librarian of the Boston Public Library:

To answer your inquiry about Trent's manuscript, I shall have to be *very frank*:
For a number of years Trent hoped to publish a combined bio-

graphy and bibliography. He kept listing this in successive issues of *Who's Who in America*, always referring to it as a forthcoming work in TEN VOLUMES. The gist of his real findings appeared in his brief volume for Bobbs-Merrill, in his chapter for the *Cambridge History of English Literature*, in his bibliography for that chapter, and in the revised bibliography for *CBEL* which was put out by Henry C. Hutchins with his assistance. I don't honestly think Trent went much farther than that — and that is where I started. . . As far as I know, Trent's manuscript contains nothing additional, except a mass of bibliographical data which it would not pay any-one to print. A friend of mine, writing a thesis at the University of California, got permission to use photostatic sheets of Trent's final material on *The Complete English Tradesman*, and he found it of little or no value to him.[18]

Thus, all the time that he was preparing his own *Checklist*, Moore never set eyes upon, and did not make much effort to see, the vast manuscript in which Trent had covered so much of the same ground and arrived at so many of the same attributions. It is not the least odd of the incidents in the strange history of the construction of the Defoe canon.

A RAGE FOR ASCRIPTION

When Trent addressed himself to the bibliography of Defoe, the accepted canon was still, broadly speaking, that represented by the 'Chronological List' of William Lee; and the single most important fact about Trent's own work is that he regarded Lee's list as trust-worthy. The list might, he supposed, include a few incidental mis-ascriptions, but what was mainly wrong with it, in Trent's eyes, was not what it contained but what it left out. The fact is slightly surprising, for Trent was in the habit of accusing Lee of a whole series of bibliographical and biographical vices. Lee, in his opinion, was extremely inaccurate; he could not be relied upon to transcribe a title-page at all faithfully — even, sometimes, adding a date from guesswork — and would give bibliographical descriptions of works he had never actually seen. Further, he would display an 'Olympian calm of certainty', denied to weaker mortals, in singling out the tracts by Defoe from a swarm of similar ones and in detecting Defoe's hand in certain paragraphs (but not others) in periodicals, though sometimes revealing later that he had changed his mind or forgotten what he had once thought.[19] As a biographer he would plunder Wilson without acknowledgement and would mix up fact and inference in such a way that no one could tell which was which.[20] Worst of all, Lee would unashamedly violate his own principles of attribution whenever there was any danger of bringing discredit on his hero Defoe; indeed, on occasion, so naive was his defence of Defoe's shining character that the only adequate answer was 'a bowing of the head in silent prayer'.[21] It was this last trait that, for Trent, represented Lee's one serious weakness as an attributor, a weakness he shared with Crossley; and its effect was merely negative, it inhibited him from making certain needful attributions. In positive attribution Lee's instincts, according to Trent, deserved great respect; indeed, in Trent's experience, 'he was rarely wrong in making a positive ascription'.[22]

Our own feelings about the Defoe canon, as represented by Lee's list, are — we need not say — very different, and it seems to us already a most questionable construction, produced by 'chain-forging' on a reckless scale. Thus we regard Trent's acceptance of it as a fatal step. But at all events, fatal or otherwise, it proved important, for Trent's influence was great. For one thing, it was Trent who, in his *Nation* articles, first put Crossley's list of sixty new attributions into currency — with, on the whole, warm endorsement from himself. (If Trent respected Lee's judgement in attribution, he came to respect Crossley's even more, indeed to regard it with some awe, despite the fact that Crossley rarely offered his reasons — or maybe partly because of this.) Thus Trent's *Cambridge History* list of 1912, which comprised 382 items (incorporating fifty-one new attributions from Crossley as well as several suggested by T.J. Wise and H.S. Foxwell[23]), represented a very considerable enlargement of the canon,[24] and the signs are that J.R. Moore, when beginning work on his *Checklist*, leaned heavily on this list. Nor did Trent's influence end there, for Hutchins's list for *The Cambridge Bibliography of English Literature*, which again was of importance to Moore, contained, as we have seen, quite a few of the many new attributions that Trent had gone on to make in the years after 1912, and it is reasonable to suppose that Hutchins derived them from Trent. Trent was thus one of the main architects of the Defoe canon, and he shared at least one important tendency with Lee, Crossley and Moore: namely, a rage for ascription. For all his mockery of Lee, what Trent particularly admired in him was his positiveness in attribution; and it puzzled him that Wilson, for whom otherwise he had much respect, could bear to be so hesitant and unzealous in this part of his duties.

TRENT'S WORKING METHODS

In the first of his *Nation* articles Trent described himself as depending, for the detection of Defoe's authorship, on 'numerous and very minute tests — which cannot be described here',[25] and later on he mentions 'about twenty different tests derived from my study of Defoe's undisputed writings'.[26] This caused J.R. Moore to ask why Trent did not reveal these tests to the public;[27] but, whatever Moore may have suspected, these tests were no phantasm, and indeed they lay at the heart of Trent's working methods. The tests are of a very down-to-earth nature and are essentially a matter of looking, in each disputed work, for certain habits of style which Trent believed characteristic of Defoe. We have not discovered that he ever reduced them to a rigid list, but they include, first of all, certain favourite solecisms of Defoe's (or what Trent calls 'false concords'), in particular 'neither' followed by 'or' and the use of 'who' for 'whom'. These, according to Trent, could automatically be expected in a work by Defoe, and their absence would be an obstacle, though not an insuperable one, to attributing a work to him. (They represent 'tests' in the simple sense that Trent looks for these features in each disputed work, as a matter of routine.) Then again he had identified a whole string of 'favourite terms of expression' or 'earmarks'. These are evidently in a somewhat different category, from a logical point of view, for we are not to expect all of them to appear in every work by Defoe, though the assumption is that we can confidently expect some of them. Among them are one or two which are held to carry particular weight. Thus, the phrase 'over the belly' or 'over his belly', according to Trent, 'almost warrants one in taking an oath to Defoe's authorship of any book or pamphlet in which it occurs'.[28]

It is not plain what relevance, if any, the figure of 'about twenty' has to this collection of 'favourite' phrases. If we were to put together all of the 'favourite terms of expression' cited here and there by Trent, they would come to vastly more than twenty; but on the other hand he does not seem to be saying that, on average, in any given work, we should expect to find twenty of the various 'favourite terms of expression' or twenty occurrences of 'favourite forms of expression'.

Beyond these 'earmarks' and 'favourite terms of expression' lie some more general criteria, such as that Defoe's style may be expected to be 'homely' and 'garrulous', that he will display 'inquisitiveness' and a 'half-shrewd, half childish attitude towards the workings of Providence',[29] that he is a 'consummate casuist'[30] and that he has a fondness for quoting himself and for passing comments, as if by a stranger, on the author of the *Review*.

It will give the reader a better idea of Trent's method, and especially this aspect of it, if we give an example. Here are some passages from his eight-page note on *A Vindication of the Last Parliament* (1711), an anti-Sacheverell tract which does not appear in Moore's *Checklist* or in Trent's own list in *The Cambridge History of English Literature*:

> The only ascription to Defoe known to me is a tentative one made in B.H. Blackwell's Catalogue No. 155, containing the second portion of Mr C. E. Doble's collection (No. 345). As the book is twice used as if Defoe's in the manuscript notes in Mr Doble's copy of Bohn's edition of Carleton's 'Memoirs'... now owned by me, I infer that that most competent student of Defoe had little or no doubt with regard to the latter's authorship of the present item. I have none. ...
>
> The evidence that the body of the book is by Defoe is very strong in point of substance and perhaps equally strong in point of style. Once more we are told that all the sects wish the Church of England to be supreme (p. 7); again we have repeated attacks upon Leslie and upon the senders up of fatuous addresses to the Queen; once more the Presbyterians are defended from the charge of having murdered Charles I. Probably the most telling points in favour of Defoe's authorship are the passages in which he himself is referred to in the third person — passages which perhaps account for the fact that the book has been so long omitted from his bibliography.... For, as we have often seen, it is Daniel Defoe who is most likely at this period to refer without malice and insult to Daniel Defoe. It is Defoe who complains here (p. 166), as in the *Review*, of being 'daily threaten'd', who refers to his standing 'in the Pillory by a quick Prosecution, as my Lord of *Sarum* calls it[,] for his *Irony*' (p. 205), who tries apparently to transfer to Sir Simon Harcourt his own notorious phrase 'Wet and Dry Martyrdom' (p. 180). But we need not rely entirely upon such references to our hero in order to support the thesis that the book is one of a numerous progeny. We recognize Defoe in the attack upon mercenary

publishers and pamphleteers, which looks forward to *The Secret History of the Secret History of the White Staff, Purse and Mitre* (p. 88) in the description of Sacheverell and the rabble (p. 103), in the remarks on public credit (p. 104), in the quotation from Queen Anne's first speech from the throne, in the discussion of Occasional Conformity (p. 138), in the defence of the Societies for the Reformation of Manners (p. 233), and in a score of other passages.

The style also is Defoe's despite the writer's, or the printer's care in employing 'neither — nor', and 'whom'. We find frequent use of 'I say', and some use of 'in short', and 'in a word', we recognize Defoe's fondness for 'Grimace' and 'Generals', we encounter also 'being to be trump'd up', 'to rally Fundamentals', 'Anglicanes Rigides', 'I wish I could not say it', 'Oh! *La Belle Raillerie*', 'Alteration, I can't say Improvement', 'Remova', 'to give him his Due', 'to fright', 'go about to', 'a *Dernier Resource*', 'be it as it will', '*The Sense of the Nation*' — emphasized as in former writings of Defoe's — 'to palm so visible a Bite on me', 'bubbl'd and bit', ' 'tis a *Chimaera*', 'no, not', 'remember' for 'remind', '*And a Word or Two by the Bye*', 'what you, and I, and ev'ry good *English-Man* can't think of without Horror', and other words and phrases of which Defoe was fond. In addition the general style is his, and many pages are clearly in his manner, e.g. the story of the bawd (p. 89), and of the visit of Sir Peter in Hartfordshire (p. 153).[31]

That, on reading Trent, logical doubts clamour at one has to be admitted: for instance, as to why the absence of false concords does not argue against Defoe's authorship as much as their presence argues for it; or as to how these different categories of evidence from 'tests' are thought to 'add up'; or even more basically, as to whether 'tests' is not just too ambitious a term for such a procedure. However, Trent applies his tests with such diligence and with such faith that it will become us to treat them gently and try at least to think ourselves into his system. Some of our questions of logic are, anyway, answered by Trent himself, in a passage discussing the problems of serial attribution.

The upshot of this whole discussion seems to be that it is not only very difficult to disentangle the special gordian knot constituted by these pamphlets on the Triennial Act [i.e. the pamphlets provoked by the Whig government bill in 1716 to repeal the Act for Triennial Parliaments], but exceedingly necessary to keep a wary eye on one's footsteps as one picks one's way through the entire pamphlet literature of this swarming epoch. The nicest adjustment of one's scales — to change the metaphor suddenly — is continually required, and one has always to be sure that an adequate amount of the necessary constituent elements is present. Sometimes one can afford to dispense with a small amount of such an element as peculiarly idiosyncratic style when one can point to an extraordinarily large amount of convincing substance and to the absence of any alien elements; but, when, as in the case of the two 'Letters' to a friend in Suffolk,[32] questions arise with regard both to substance and to style, and when, if we accepted them, we should be in duty bound to wonder whether we ought not to accept one or two others, including 'An Humble Petition from the October-Club to a Certain Eminent M--r of the H. of C--s concerning the Triennial Bill' which was published on April 25, 1716, the day before the bill passed the Commons, even the most expert weigher, the most cautious reader — to combine one or two metaphors — may well — to employ another — hoist his sails and point for a neighbouring and less jagged promontory.[33]

From this it becomes plain that any 'weighing' or 'adding up' involved in Trent's method will be purely intuitive, and an 'adequate', a 'small' or an 'extraordinarily large' amount are not concepts that anyone will pretend to measure. There is something decently pragmatic and not unacceptable in Trent's tone here. (Though one must remember that the Triennial pamphlets are notoriously a bibliographer's nightmare, and Trent is writing in a chastened mood.)

Another passage from Trent is much more disconcerting.

It should be borne in mind that when I catalogue words and phrases continually used by Defoe, I make no claim that they are peculiar to him. They are merely characteristic of his style, and useful, along with other features of style, with details of substance, and with tone of utterance, in helping to answer the question whether or not he wrote a work under consideration. Students of his writings have constantly employed such tests — cf. Lee's rather unsatisfactory list of expressions. That merely taken by themselves words and phrases would be of very little value as tests emerges from the fact that the following list is taken from the pamphlets of Trenchard that Defoe answered: — 'Neither – or', 'being to be rais'd', 'I say', 'in short', 'I believe I may venture to say', 'to fright', ''tis all one'. Yet no trained investigator would, I think, confuse Trenchard's style with Defoe's.[34]

This, it must be said, is very disturbing; for if we are to take it literally ('when I catalogue words and phrases continually used by Defoe, I make no claim that they are peculiar to him'), it seems to give up the whole logical basis of Trent's system, leaving him with no more than what he calls elsewhere 'that indefinable something called "my feeling for Defoe"'.[35] (It should be added that these are not problems for Trent alone. They seem to be entailed in any such enterprise of proving works to be by one author on the basis of 'favourite phrases', 'parallels' and compatibilities; and, as we shall see, J.R. Moore, though less frank about the problems, got into just as much trouble over them.)

We have referred to Trent's 'tests' as lying at the heart of his system, but they are by no means the only element in it. His commentary on any work in his bibliography will have a roughly three-part pattern. It will begin with a full transcription of the title-page and a detailed account of the work's early publishing history, with reasonings (based on advertisements and the like) about its exact date of appearance and analysis of variations between early issues or editions. (Trent's formula, a tribute to his own magnificent private collection, is very often: 'The original is rare. I refer to my own copy.') Next will come some account of the genealogy of the attribution, with reference not only to the classic bibliographies but to book-trade catalogues and the sale catalogues of private libraries (such as the Huth catalogue, the Pearson catalogue of Crossley's library, the Henri Labouchère and C.E. Doble sale catalogues, etc.). There will then follow a free-ranging discussion of all the external and internal evidence that Trent regards as supporting an attribution to Defoe, including (but of course by no means restricted to) the results of his 'tests'. The whole commentary may run to as many as forty pages, and rarely occupies less than three.

Where there is no attribution problem and the authenticity of the work is beyond dispute, Trent nevertheless runs through the occurrences of strikingly 'Defoean' phrases, and draws attention to the relationship of the work with others by Defoe. Occasionally, however, he must face the awkward fact that very few 'earmarks' may be observed in a work which, nevertheless, he wishes to claim as Defoe's. For instance, we find the following, in an eleven-page defence of a new attribution, *Considerations on the Present State of Great Britain* (1717):

> It would have been surprising had any of the friendly biographers accepted a pamphlet which is so bitter against Lord Oxford and that Treaty of Peace in favor of which Defoe had written so often and so well. And even if no suspicion of another hand had been aroused on this score, it is clear that any student of Defoe, after reading the first fifty pages, might have felt justified in throwing the tract aside on account of the comparative absence of peculiarly Defoelike touches in the style. I was much tempted to save myself by this method from reading a hundred desultory pages; but, as I had encountered a few suspicious features, it seemed wise to persevere to the end, and I had my reward both in finding that the style and substance began more strongly to suggest Defoe and also in the discovery of a passage in which his hand seemed unmistakable. I cannot say that I am glad to have another bit of proof that Defoe at this period was writing both for and against his former patron, but I am glad to be able to point to this pamphlet as a warning against the application of narrow stylistic standards in the study of the bibliography of a writer as diffuse, versatile, and uneven as Defoe.

Trent recorded his discovery of the decisive passage thus:

> ...when later he passed to discuss the economic condition — for this is a most discursive pamphlet, I felt almost certain that I should find the clinching means of identification for which I had been searching. It came on p. 123 in one of Defoe's favourite metaphors. 'Credit', said this author, 'is like a coy Mistress, she must be courted and dealt gently with, for fear she takes such a distaste as may spoil the whole Design'.[36]

(The attribution was adopted by Hutchins in his listing in *The Cambridge Bibliography of English Literature*, though it does not appear in Moore's *Checklist* or in the *New Cambridge Bibliography*.)

There is something, perhaps quite a lot, to be said for Trent's attribution procedures. That he should recognise a duty to give the reasoning behind each and every attribution to Defoe is to his credit and gives him a lead over all his rivals. Moreover, he is amazingly thorough; and maybe only by such expansiveness can that crucially important asset of a Defoe bibliographer, his memory, really find full play. Against this, one has to say that he can be rather rambling and is a little too fond of pawky jokes: in short, that he belongs rather visibly to the 'gentlemanly' school of scholarship. What matters much more, though, is that — like his fellow-scholars or rivals, Lee, Crossley and Moore — he is a poor critic, and one does not have much faith in his responsiveness to Defoe's qualities as a writer. The spectacle of Trent convincing himself by mechanical and narrowly conceived 'tests' that Defoe was the author of works that, on any other grounds, it would seem madness to attribute to him, cannot but be shaking to one's confidence.

Since we are on the subject of Trent's deficiencies, we may even mention one or two more. He is addicted, as we have already pointed out (p. 30), to what we have called 'the fallacy of provisional attribution'; for example, he will write of a work: 'I adopt it as Defoe's until evidence to the contrary is forthcoming'[37] — just what a bibliographer should *not* do, by our lights. Again, in company with Lee, Crossley and Moore, he abounds in such scare-words as 'unquestionably', 'indisputably' and 'imperative'. Moreover, as is revealed by his working papers, he did not escape the occupational hazard of collectors: that their 'possible' or 'probable' attributions tend to ripen over the years into 'certain' ones. He would, to his credit, conduct his many re-readings of pamphlets 'blind' and without reference to his earlier notes, but the verdict most commonly was: 'on rereading...I was left in absolutely no doubt'.[38]

Then, he was inclined to attribute significance to the words 'By Defoe' or 'Dan. Defoe' on a flyleaf or title-page, if written in an old-enough hand, and to refer to it as 'traditional authority', a rather elementary error for such an experienced bibliographer. Sometimes, too, he would perpetrate these two false moves conjointly, as when he wrote: 'the attribution to Defoe made by the original unknown collecter, which may have had traditional support now untraceable, should not be rejected, unless strong positive evidence in favour of some other author should be forthcoming'.[39]

Trent is also very fond of the 'who but Defoe?' formula: 'And if Defoe did not compose the realistic dialogue on pages 9–14, we shall long be at a loss to know who did,'[40] etc. This is harmless enough as a rhetorical question but, we suggest, most treacherous as soon as it is asked as if in expectation of an answer. Finally, let us notice how, having decided it is 'practically certain' that Defoe wrote a preposterous pseudo-medical tract called *Flagellum: or, a Dry Answer to Dr Hancock's Wonderfully-Comical Liquid Book* (1723), and 'highly probable' that he was responsible for several other contributions on both sides of the same idiotic controversy — indeed, that he orchestrated the whole affair more or less single-handedly [41] — Trent lets these speculations suggest to him, as much as if they were solid fact, that Defoe did it all over again two years later and is the 'Catherine Comb-Brush' who writes a rude answer to his own *Every-Body's Business, is No-Body's Business*.[42] What is gaining flesh here, as speculations breed further speculations, is not so much the certitude of some particular attributions as the spectral body of a monster, the Defoe-who-writes-on-every-side.

CHAPTER 9

JOHN ROBERT MOORE

W E COME, FINALLY, to John Robert Moore, who made the largest contribution of all to the Defoe canon and whose influence is still dominant. Moore was born in Colorado in 1890, the son of an Episcopalian minister. He took his first degree at the University of Missouri, and gained a Ph.D. from Harvard seven years later for a thesis on 'The Omission of the Central Action in the English and Scottish Popular Ballads'. Moore was a burly and energetic man, who promised himself to be able to run a mile at the time he retired, and was famous within his family circle and its neighbourhood as a teller of Brer Rabbit stories. In 1921 a senior colleague at the University of Wisconsin described his character as 'sound as a rock'.[1] He first became seriously interested in Defoe soon after his appointment as an Associate Professor at Indiana University in 1922, when he was asked to build up the library's Defoe collection.

A GENERAL HISTORY OF THE PYRATES

A most important stage in Moore's career as a Defoe scholar came when he convinced himself that many passages in *A General History of the Pyrates* (1724), a work attributed on its title-page to 'Captain Charles Johnson', were 'unquestionably' by Defoe. The idea first came to him in September 1930, and, he would say, he used to lie awake every morning at that period, 'wondering what I would do that day if I found out that Defoe did not write the *History* after all'.[2] He announced his discovery at the 1932 meeting of the Modern Language Association, and over the next six or seven years he engaged, to use his own words, in 'a minute study of the relationship of the *History* to Defoe's previously accepted writings and to the other works which have not been generally recognised as his, to possible sources of the *History*, and to [*sic*] its influence on subsequent literature'.[3] His conclusion, as set out at length in *Defoe in the Pillory and Other Studies* (1939), was that the *History* was substantially Defoe's throughout. It was 'an original work of history', extremely reliable in its information, though 'interspersed with a good many passages of historical fiction and with some of unrestrained romance'.[4]

Considering that the *History* has had such vast literary influence (Moore's own words are, 'it is hardly too much to say that the author of the *History* has created the modern conception of pirates'[5]) Moore, if right, had plainly made a remarkably important addition to the Defoe canon. Equally plainly, it was a major occurrence in his own career.

The terms in which he spoke of this new attribution in 1939 are rather striking — threatening, as they did, alarming consequences if it were not accepted. Defoe's authorship of the *History*, wrote Moore,

> is attested by a greater mass of evidence than can be offered for most of his previously accepted writings. It is related to his other works by ties so numerous and so intricate that they cannot be broken; the author who wrote certain passages must necessarily have been the author who wrote certain others. To deny Defoe's authorship of the *History* would throw open to controversy the whole canon of his works (a canon which has been largely deter- mined by internal evidence and by just such analogies existing be- tween the writings which have been assigned to him).[6]

With the last sentence, at least, the writers of the present book can have no dispute.

This episode of the *General History of the Pyrates* may be said to have coloured and dominated all the rest of Moore's activities as a bibliographer. It confirmed him in a faith in his own intuitions; it committed him to a new biographical account of Defoe's last years; and it was during the six or seven years that he worked on the *History* that he developed his general method and philosophy of attribution. (They are summarised in chapter 5 of *Defoe in the Pillory* as 'Some remarks on the assignment of authorship to Defoe'.) The enthusiastic author of *John Robert Moore: a Bibliography* claims that Moore had found 'proof beyond question' that Defoe wrote the *History*, and he rightly emphasises the large significance of the attribution:

John Robert Moore had established the *History* as the largest and most important unassigned work of Defoe's which had been discovered for two centuries, and he was able, since this book dealt with so many of Defoe's favourite subjects, to use it and the analogues it provided as the basis for later assigning an immense number of other works to Defoe which had been classified as anonymous by the great libraries in whose possession they were. Today there is not an enlightened library in the world which would ask John Robert Moore to defend his new attributions of Restoration and Eighteenth Century books on its shelves, which would not accept his judgment as final, nor which, when handed a statement by him to correct its catalogue, would not put it right into the record. . . . [7]

To form an impression of Moore we need to study this episode rather closely. How good, in fact, was his case for the attribution? Our own verdict will have to be that it was thoroughly unsatisfactory, in ways that are characteristic of much of his work in attribution. We say 'characteristic' advisedly, for questions of character are involved.

To confirm his original inspiration that the *History* was, in part or as a whole, the work of Defoe, Moore was faced with a number of difficulties. For one thing, the whole case for Defoe's authorship had to rest on internal evidence. There was not a single piece of external evidence to support it, and quite a few pieces of such evidence to argue (apparently) against it.

There was, for instance, the problem that Defoe was the author — or at least had been so regarded by William Lee — of a pamphlet about the pirate Avery (*The King of Pirates*, 1719) which gave an account of Avery's life quite different, not only in matters of fact but in tone, from the one in the *History*. Moore's way of explaining this was twofold. He noted that *The King of Pirates* was written in a different spirit from the account in the *History*, a 'bantering' one; and thus 'One would not expect to find close resemblances between the fabulous narrative of *The King of Pirates* and the sober work of "Johnson".' Secondly, he offered a biographical hypothesis. He supposed that Defoe did not resolve to make himself an expert on piracy till a year or two later (indeed specifically halfway through the writing of *Captain Singleton*, after which it became one of the main preoccupations of his declining years). Moreover, so Moore argued, *The King of Pirates did*, from another point of view, resemble the

History and Defoe's work in general. This was a matter of 'parallels', particularly parallels of habits of thought and expression, a point we shall come on to in a moment.[8]

A second difficulty facing Moore was the relationship of the account of the pirate John Gow in the *History* to a pamphlet life of Gow, *An Account of the Conduct and Proceedings of the Late John Gow* (1725), which had been published only a few months earlier and was also attributed by Lee to Defoe. The account in the *History* seems, at certain points, plainly to be quoting from the earlier one, though without acknowledgement. On the other hand the two accounts are markedly different. The chapter in the *History*, though much shorter, contains information not found in the *Account*, especially the crucial detail that Gow had a personal motive for persuading his crew to sail to the Orkneys, namely that there was a girl there whom he wished to marry. Further, it actually contradicts the pamphlet life in one or two particulars.[9]

Now, to the ordinary reader, the relationship of the two accounts would seem to present little problem, a very natural explanation being that the compiler of the *History* had made borrowings from the *Account of the Late John Gow*, combining them with information from other sources. In order to discredit any such explanation, Moore has to resort to some very awkward manoeuvres. He argues that, if the two accounts are by different authors, then it is a matter not of borrowing but of theft. (It is not clear how this is relevant.) But if, on the other hand, he says, the accounts are both by Defoe, and Defoe has rewritten and revised his earlier pamphlet for the purposes of the *History*, then 'we have indisputable evidence for Defoe's hand in the *History* and for his authorship of a considerable part of it'.[10] This does not seem logical; for to suppose that Defoe rewrote his pamphlet for the *History* is, *a fortiori*, to suppose that he had a hand in the *History*: the one supposition can hardly be a proof, let alone an 'indisputable' proof, of the other. As for the disagreement between the two accounts, Moore's rather lame explanation is that this was necessary for purposes of 'disguise'. The pamphlet life 'had to be recast, so that at first sight it would appear to be an entirely new life rather than a reprint of one only recently published. That the disguise was successful is attested by the fact that no previous student has ever discovered it.'[11]

Another difficulty facing Moore, a more serious one, could be solved only by means of a further attribution, and here we have a good example of the 'snowball effect'. In the 'Captain John Bowen' chapter of the *History* there is an account of the famous *Worcester* affair (the unjust execution by the Scots in 1705 of the *Worcester*'s captain, Thomas Green, for alleged piracy and murder); and whereas this account shows no similarity to the description of the affair in Defoe's *History of the Union*, it follows very closely, indeed in parts reproduces word for word, a rare pamphlet, *A Letter from Scotland to a Friend in London*, published in 1705. Moore's way of getting round this is to conclude that this pamphlet must be by Defoe also. However, apart from the immediate convenience to Moore, it is an attribution with little to be said for it and much to be said against it. It would, for one thing, suggest an extraordinary *volte-face* on the part of Defoe. On 26 April in the *Review*, Defoe was taking an extremely statesmanlike, indeed excessively cautious, line about the *Worcester* affair, which had come at a very delicate stage of the Union negotiations. He said there that, considering the conflicting reports in the newspapers, it was essential not to make a hasty judgement on the Scots. Even if (at the worst) there had been a tragic miscarriage of justice, he said, it could have been arrived at by proper legal form, and hence the Scots could not really be blamed. By contrast, *A Letter from Scotland*, published only five days later, assumes that there is no possible doubt of the guilt of the Scots. It is, indeed, a rabble-rousing and virulently chauvinistic piece, plainly intended to stir up ill-feeling between the English and the Scots.[12]

There is, again, in Moore's arguments a clear tendency to 'chain-forging'. One of his five 'principal findings' about the *History* is that it is

> Defoe's only connected account of piracy, a subject which had such a fascination for him that he referred to it in writings throughout nearly his entire life, and he introduced it into eight of his longer narratives. Consequently the *History* is of great value in tracing the interrelations of his romances and in establishing more completely his authorship of the narratives of Captain George Roberts and Robert Drury.[13]

Now, as Rodney Baine has pointed out,[14] Moore bases part of his argument for Defoe's authorship of the *History* on parallels with *Robert Drury's Journal* and also with *An Account of the late John Gow* and *The Four Years Voyages of Capt. George Roberts*; so what we seem to perceive is a 'having-it-both-ways', each of several tentative attributions being made to stand on the others' shoulders. The logic of this can hardly be sound.

As for *The Four Years Voyages of Capt. George Roberts*, Moore is forced to acknowledge that there are important discrepancies between the handling of the same events in this and in the *History* — amongst them being the fact that, in the *History*, Captain Low is represented as the very worst of all the pirates and an unspeakable and bloodthirsty maniac, whereas in *The Four Years Voyages* he is depicted as a model of gentlemanliness and goodwill, plying the captive Captain Roberts with wine and holding late-night conversations with him 'concerning *Church* and *State*, as also about *Trade*'.[15] (In addition, what is not quite insignificant, his name is spelled 'Loe' in the *Four Years Voyages* but 'Low' in the *History*.) Moore's clinching argument for the two works being, none the less, by the same hand, is that, in the *History*, it is briefly mentioned that a member of Howel Davis's crew, a certain Charles Franklin from Monmouthshire, stayed behind and settled in the Cape Verde islands and 'lives there to this day';[16] and the same Charles Franklin figures extensively in the *Four Years Voyages*. But then, assuming that such a Charles Franklin actually existed, is there much here to demonstrate common authorship? Could two authors not have been in possession of the same basic fact about him?

The issue about *Robert Drury's Journal* turns out to be even more damaging to Moore's theories, and we shall come to this later in the chapter. Meanwhile let us consider Moore's discussion of possible sources for the *History*. Here again he runs up against formidable difficulties. He builds much on Defoe's acquaintance with Captain Thomas Bowrey, a trader and voyager and principal owner of the ill-fated *Worcester* who, as is well known, wrote to Defoe in 1708 requesting an interview. Moore describes Bowrey as, eleven years before *Robinson Crusoe*, 'singling out' Defoe as an expert on Selkirk's island, Juan Fernandez; and this leads him to imagine a close future relationship between Defoe and Bowrey, perhaps to the extent of Defoe's being given the run of Bowrey's private papers.[17] However, as George Healey has pointed out very reasonably,[18] the fact that a set of notes by Bowrey on Juan Fernandez has survived among a collection of his papers which also include Defoe's letters to him, is no reason to assume that this is the topic he wanted to discuss with Defoe; nor is there any actual evidence that they had any more dealings with each other, let alone that they became fast friends.

Moore goes on to hypothesise that Defoe knew the famous Captain Woodes Rogers, who was appointed to suppress the pirate colonies in the Bahamas and thus could have given Defoe plenty of information on piracy. Moore admits that there is no evidence at all that the two ever met, nevertheless he surmises optimistically that it is 'extremely likely'.[19]

By contrast, he expatiates at length on the absurdity of supposing that the 'Description of Magadoxa' in the *History* (a detailed account of the topography and monuments of this ancient Muslim city on the east coast of Africa) could really, as is claimed there, be derived from 'an original Manuscript of a Mulatto, who was taken by the Natives, and lived among them sixteen years'.[20] Moore's implication is that the 'Description' is purely a novelistic fabrication by Defoe; however, as has since been discovered, a contemporary manuscript closely corresponding to the 'Description', mulatto author and all, has survived and is to be read in the British Library.[21]

A concept that features prominently in Moore's theories is Defoe's supposed 'notes' or 'materials'. Defoe made his acquisitions from books and perhaps from unpublished manuscripts, but he also, suggests Moore, gained much knowledge from personal conversation with retired pirates. The mass of 'materials' so collected formed the basis not just of the *History* but also of *Robert Drury's Journal*, as well as of some parts of *Plan of the English Commerce*. Thus we are not to think of *Robert Drury's Journal* as 'borrowed' from the *History* but rather as being 'based on a mass of identical information'.[22] 'I do not suggest', he says in a later discussion, 'that the *History of the Pyrates* is a source for *Robert Drury's Journal*; the relationships are too intricate and too close for that. They are by the same author and from the same accumulation of notes, and their relationship is like that of two oil wells bored into the ground in the same field.'[23]

Now, it is a perfectly reasonable supposition that Defoe kept notes; yet for all that, Moore's insistence on them is somehow disturbing. The 'notes' seem a shade too concrete for something we know absolutely nothing about; also we remember the questionable role played by such 'notes' in Moore's discussion of Defoe's supposed 'Swedish' writings (see above, p. 20).

MOORE'S PARALLELS

Ultimately, Moore rests his case for Defoe's authorship of the *History* on 'parallels' (of phrase and idea) with other works. He has assembled them in vast quantity (though reminding us that he could have adduced even more, enough to fill a 'folio volume'[24]), and in this sense he has presented his case very fairly. How we can fairly respond to this case is not too easy a problem, since Moore is really arguing, not just for one attribution, but for several simultaneously, and accordingly his 'parallels' are spread over two chapters of *Defoe in the Pillory* as well as his later *Defoe's Sources for Robert Drury's Journal*.

It will perhaps be best if we concentrate on the chapter specifically devoted to the *History*. What is immediately noticeable here is that one set of parallels is, at first sight, very persuasive: we are referring to the various versions of what Moore calls 'the typical Defoe allusion to the origin of Rome which recurs so often in Defoe's known works and in "Johnson's" *History*'.[25] The allusion to ancient Rome's having been founded by a 'company of public robbers' or 'gang of rovers' comparable to contemporary pirates appears, as Moore shows, in very similar form in the *Review*, *A True Account of the...South Sea Trade*, *The King of Pirates* and the *History*. Unfortunately for Moore's case, however, very little research is required to prove that the allusion was not Defoe's own private property. Its source is, in fact, *De Civitate Dei*, in which St Augustine refers to 'the crew that Romulus called together, by proclaiming freedom from fear of punishment to all such as would inhabit Rome; hereby both augmenting his city, and getting a band of fellows about him that were fit for any villainous or desperate act whatsoever'.[26] For other uses of the allusion in the early eighteenth century, we need look no further than the play *The Successful Pyrate* by Charles Johnson — an author whom, despite his name, Moore has specifically told us it would be absurd to associate with the *History*. In the first scene of the play, the pirate-king Arviragus (i.e. Avery) is spoken of by the admiral, Boreal, in these words: '. . . he has erected himself a Throne, ay, and in the Hearts of his People too; reduc'd *Barbarians* — *Romulus* was made a God for this; yes, and what I think more glorious yet, bound and cemented by civil Laws a Race of Vagabonds, the Outcasts of the Earth'.[27]

Moving on to Moore's next page, we find the following:

The distinction between kings *de facto* and *de jure*, which was common in the controversial writings of the Age of Anne when the succession to the throne was still in question, was commoner in Defoe than elsewhere, underlying his longest poem and much of his other political writing. But it appears again in 'Johnson's' *History*, a decade after the Hanoverian dynasty was peacefully established on the English throne:

De facto is *de jure*, and a crown,
To every man that has it, is his own. (*Jure Divino*, Hazlitt ed.,
p. 58).

if dethroned, the person who did it...became
ipso facto as divine...as he (*Ibid.*, p. viii).

And since they actually are kings *de facto*, which is a kind of
right, we ought to speak of them as such. ('Johnson's' *History*,
p. 35).

There are many Defoe-like phrases in 'Johnson's' life of Avery
which could readily be paralleled from Defoe's other writings, if
not from *The King of Pirates*, such as these:

I do not find they took any ships in their way (p. 26)
nor do I find (p. 28)
clapped her on board (p. 27)
In fine (pp. 28,30)
would do the business very faithfully (p. 30)
And since it will be but a short digression, we will give an
account how they came here. (p. 31)
hunting, etc. (p. 32)
as they afterwards confessed (p. 35)[28]

Frankly, it is a puzzle what significance one can reasonably be asked
to see in the coincident use of such utterly commonplace phrases as
'*de facto*', '*de jure*', 'nor do I find' or 'in fine'. Muriel St. Clair Byrne's
rule, that low-quality parallels possess no significance at all (and
acquire none by any amount of accumulation) seems clearly to apply
here; and the words used by Rodney Baine about some other of
Moore's 'parallels' do not seem too harsh:

Such an unsystematic use of parallels does not even approach serious scholarship. These parallels are frequently not at all close; and
the idioms are sometimes standard....Not only did Mr. Moore
fail to distinguish between what is peculiarly Defoean and what is
merely conventional in contemporary narrative style and idiom;
he also drew for his parallels upon works which have been since
shown to be the work of others.[29]

Moore's discussion of the *History* ends with a long list of cor-
respondences with Defoe's known proclivities and interests: his
belief in courage as the key to conduct, his interest in the techniques

of book-keeping, his advocacy of national encouragement for fisheries, his dislike of religious bickering, his curiosity about earth-
quakes and explosions, his knowledge of the exact terminology
of any trade, his wealth of guidebook information, his professed
contempt for romantic stories, his delight in practical ingenuity, his
invention of supposed native words and names, his delight in
impersonation, his enthusiasm for projects and for languages, his
addiction to horse-racing and cock-fighting, his dislike of the
Portuguese and of South Sea directors, his love of irony and
innuendo, etc.[30] One sees in a way what Moore is up to here, but
what one cannot but feel lacking is any explanation as to how such
items of evidence are to be added together. Are they meant to form
a sum at all? Are they indeed even offered as evidence, or merely
as eloquent decoration of what has been already proved by other
methods?

ROBERT DRURY'S JOURNAL

A General History of the Pyrates, as we have seen, was twinned in
Moore's mind with Robert Drury's Journal. It should be remembered
that the latter work was itself a fairly recent attribution to Defoe. The
first person to consider Defoe's having had some hand in it was
William Lee, who, after much reflection, rejected the idea.[31] Captain
Pasfield Oliver, in his edition of the Journal published in 1890,
thought he detected the hand of Defoe, or of 'one who aped Defoe's
methods very closely'.[32] W.P. Trent was also inclined to believe that
Defoe had some share in it, and he included the work in his Defoe
bibliography in The Cambridge History of English Literature (1912). It
was Moore, however, who first proposed that no 'journal' by Drury
had ever existed or could have existed and that the book was purely a
romance by Defoe. This, of course, was an integral part of his more
general hypothesis: that by 1729, when the Journal was published,
Defoe had made himself a great expert on Madagascar and piracy and
was therefore able to give his romance the greatest possible factual
verisimilitude. Moore wrote a good deal about Robert Drury's
Journal, beginning with a chapter in Defoe in the Pillory and following
this with a complete monograph, Defoe's Sources for Robert Drury's
Journal (1943). The book also involved him in the most serious
controversy of his career, one in which he was decisively worsted.
The story of this controversy, to be comprehensible, needs to be

told in a certain amount of detail. *Robert Drury's Journal* is, or purports to be, an authentic journal, edited for the press by a 'Transcriber' and certified as truthful by a certain Captain William Mackett. Robert Drury claims to be the son of a London innkeeper (proprietor of the well-known tavern 'The King's Head' in Cheapside), and, against his parents' wishes, to have embarked at the age of fourteen as a passenger on an East-Indiaman named the *Degrave*. (On board the same ship, as mate, was John Benbow, son of the famous Admiral Benbow.) The ship founders off the coast of Madagascar, and the crew fall into the hands of the natives, most of them being massacred. Drury, however, escapes with a few others, but only to be recaptured and enslaved; and he is forced to spend some thirteen or so years in the interior of the island, before being rescued by Captain Mackett. Later he makes a second voyage to Madagascar as a slave-trader.

The story has a certain acknowledged basis in fact, so far as regards the voyage and shipwreck of the *Degrave* and the ensuing massacre, reports of these having appeared in the London newspapers in March 1705. A month or so later Narcissus Luttrell recorded in his diary the news that a boy had arrived in England aboard a galley, claiming to be the sole survivor of the massacre.[33] Moore's theory was that the latter news item gave Defoe the idea for a novel, one in which the boy, instead of making a speedy escape, should be enslaved and spend many years in captivity (much as happened in real life to Robert Knox on the island of Ceylon, and Defoe would of course have read the famous narrative of Knox's adventures, published in 1681). It followed, according to Moore's view, that the experiences of Robert Drury, as related in the *Journal*, must be regarded as pure fiction. There had indeed been a real-life Drury, but all that was known about him was that he was a porter at East India House. There was no reason to think that he had ever been to Madagascar (though if he had, it was probably as a pirate); and he was certainly too illiterate to compose a journal. Thus we are safe in assuming, argued Moore, that he gave no more to the novel than his name. Further, though John Benbow left some sort of autobiographical narrative, which was accidentally destroyed in a fire in 1741, it was unlikely that Defoe's novel drew on this in any way; and though a friend of the Benbows called Duncombe claimed many years later that this narrative was read to him by John Benbow's brother William, and it tallied closely with *Robert Drury's Journal*, we are to imagine, said Moore, that any memory he had of it had simply been overlaid by Defoe's vivid narrative. (The fact that, when *Robert Drury's Journal* was first published, William Benbow had just died could be significant. Had Defoe perhaps, surmised Moore, delayed publication till the demise of the one witness who could challenge the *Journal's* authenticity?)[34]

It will be noticed that there was one very vulnerable feature in Moore's whole approach to *Robert Drury's Journal*, namely his unquestioned assumption that the germ of the book lay in that news item recorded by Narcissus Luttrell. It led him into some strange reasoning. That there should be a real journal lying behind the book, he argues, is impossible on several accounts — but among them, because the plot of the book 'flatly contradicts the news item from which it was developed'. His *idée fixe* about the book's conception, as we scarcely need say, has here landed him in a glaring fallacy, one which would ultimately prove his undoing.

What is also striking is that Moore pays no attention to the important fact, which would need some explaining if Defoe were the author of *Robert Drury's Journal*, that the 'Transcriber' goes out of his way to express Deistic sentiments.[35]

Moore's views about *Robert Drury's Journal* eventually came under attack, though in the first place of a fairly mild kind. In an article published in January 1945, A.W. Secord reported that certain of the details of the *Journal* proved to be unexpectedly accurate. For instance, the dating of the *Degrave's* departure for the East Indies and of Captain Mackett's return from Jamaica in 1717 could be shown to be exact; likewise the facts asserted in the *Journal* about Drury's later life received a certain amount of confirmation from the marriage licences of other members of the Drury family. Altogether, Secord suggested respectfully, Moore's account, which he himself had accepted until recently, might be a little too sweeping. Much must still be attributed to Defoe's invention, but 'the framework of the *Journal* has a solider basis of fact than has lately been recognised'.[36]

Moore, in a reply in June the same year, came down very heavily on Secord. He had instinctively taken Secord's article as an attack, not just on his view of *Robert Drury's Journal*, but on something even more precious, his all-important theory about the *General History of the Pyrates*. The drift of his critique may be summarised thus: what need had Secord to go chasing after 'fragments which have come to light here and there' — unrevealing marriage licences or 'scattered notes from the Public Record Office' — when such a fully satisfactory source for the *Journal* had already been established, namely the 'notes' which underlay both it and *A General History of the Pyrates*? Secord has been led into 'a maze of erroneous suppositions', and essentially from one cause. This was his

> scepticism regarding two most important facts underlying *Robert Drury's Journal*: (1) That Defoe wrote 'Johnson's' *History of the Pirates*, the notes for which were so obviously used again as the main single source for the *Journal*. (2) That the *History* is what Defoe declared it to be (and what Professor Edward Channing and other modern historians have affirmed it to be), a trustworthy record of the essential facts about piracy, despite its air of romance.

To expect at this date to ignore Defoe's *History* in studying eighteenth-century piracy, said Moore, 'is to expect better bread than can be baked from dough'.[37]

Moore, who was by now regarded as a leading authority on Defoe, had plainly been ruffled, and privately he put Secord's article down to some ancient personal grudge. It seemed to him mere 'stubborn obtuseness' on Secord's part to go on nagging at a question which had been so satisfactorily settled, and later he would speak of Secord as a disappointed and frustrated man.[38] Secord, for his part, was pained, and also puzzled, for, as he remarked in a reply in November 1945, he had nowhere expressed any opinion about the authorship of the *History* or expressed any doubts about its historical accuracy. All he was urging was that, to test the accuracy of the *Journal*, one might need to go beyond the *History* to other sources of information: 'If it be wrong to bake better bread than the dough of the "History" affords, then all research is at an end.'[39]

Secord laboured on at *Robert Drury's Journal* until his death in 1957 and eventually with amazing success. He found documentary evidence confirming many of the details of Drury's family and origins, as related in the *Journal*, and also, in a Court Minute of the East India Company for 18 March 1730, a 'Request of Robert Drury ...representing he had lived on the island of Madagascar 15 years, that he has now an offer of returning thither in the Sweeds service.' Moore had surmised that the detail, related in the *Journal*, of Drury being left the reversion of a property in Stoke Newington was a whimsical stroke on Defoe's part, suggested by his own address; but in Drury's father's will, eventually traced by Secord, there appeared just such a bequest, leaving the property to Drury's heirs on condition that they had been lawfully begotten upon an English woman (thus, by implication, not to any Madagascan half-breeds). Even more remarkably, Secord discovered that the keeper of the Cape of Good Hope archives had, just before the Boer War, published extensive extracts concerning the *Degrave* affair and its aftermath — including an account of the discovery of John Benbow in Madagascar in December 1707, 'dressed in the same way as the natives there, and [living] as intimately with them as if he also were a native of the country'. There followed a circumstantial account of the crew's capture, their escape with royal hostages, the massacre, etc., evidently obtained from Benbow and closely corroborating many of the details in *Robert Drury's Journal*.

Secord's findings were published in a posthumous collection of his writings in 1961, and in his essay he remarked with some justice, that 'While scholars have been posing conjectures, an embarrassing quantity of documentary evidence has been available.' Instead of searching for primary evidence, 'They have exploited internal evidence: improbabilities, contradictions, impossibilities, and resemblances to Defoe's other narratives. But of Drury they have not learned a single fact.'[40]

By the time this posthumous volume appeared, Moore's *Checklist* had been published, containing merely the following reticent comment on *Robert Drury's Journal*: 'Drury seems to have been a real personage; but he was not possibly the author of the major part of the original narrative which the "Transcriber" professedly recast to "put it in a more agreeable Method".'[41] Secord's volume did not create much stir, and the reviews were generally brief, though approving. They did not stress the catastrophic effect on Moore's theories, which had proved quite false in regard to *Robert Drury's Journal* and had lost their main prop in regard to the *General History of the Pyrates*. Moore greeted the appearance of the book with silence.

MOORE'S LATER CAREER

Moore was forty-nine years old and had been working on Defoe for fifteen years when *Defoe in the Pillory* was published in 1939. Its last five chapters represented his first major foray into the principles and practice of authorship-attribution, and much depended, therefore, on the book's reception. This proved, in fact, rather mixed. F.E. Budd, in the *Review of English Studies*, was enthusiastic and thought that, as regards Defoe's authorship of the *General History of the*

Pyrates, Moore's arguments left 'little doubt that his attribution is correct', and by them Moore had 'secured for Defoe a work not inferior in interest and influence to the *Tour*'.[42] James Sutherland was also cautiously encouraging, saying that, of Moore's various arguments for new attributions, the one in favour of giving the *General History of the Pyrates* to Defoe was 'probably the most convincing', and *if* Moore obtained the assent of scholars to this attribution, he would have 'added an important work to the canon'.[43] A review by Hans H. Andersen in *Modern Philology* was, however, distinctly more sceptical, and mildly ironical. Of Moore's 'parallels' he remarks: 'obviously, the validity of this type of evidence depends altogether on whether the instances in the analogies are peculiar to Defoe — a fact hardly to be ascertained without something like an exhaustive survey of thought and idiom in Defoe's milieu'. Moreover, he says: 'Verbal parallels are admittedly treacherous in that they may merely be the result of borrowing.' He goes on to tease Moore about his shaky logic in his handling of parallels and the untroubled way in which this devotee of similarities was ready to explain a *dissimilarity* (between *The Four Years Voyages of Capt. George Roberts* and the *History*) by 'Defoe's alertness to the advantages of novelty'. However, he says, we may be comforted by the thought that even a convincing attribution neither increases the value of the work itself nor improves Defoe's reputation, 'except for his already too well-recognized industry'. Thus, 'such conjectures in authorship may perhaps after all be a dispensable kind of literary activity'.[44] There was also a more definitely acidulous and hostile reveiw by Mark A. Thomson, in the *English Historical Review*, though this did not appear till the end of the war. It accused Moore of being, like others before him, 'inclined to assume that any book written more or less in the style of Defoe and on a subject in which he was interested must have been written by the author of *Robinson Crusoe*'. This assumption, he remarked, 'though common, is hard to justify' — for do not writers often imitate one another? The kind of argument which Moore uses to prove that Defoe wrote *Robert Drury's Journal* or *A General History of the Pyrates*, could, he said, 'be used to prove that most detective stories, published between 1891 and 1930, in which an eccentric detective and his stupid disciple appear, were written by Conan Doyle. It may be that they will thus be used and two hundred years hence embodied in a new series of *Baker Street Studies*.'[45]

Moore, who was a sanguine man, seems to have been contented

with his book's reception and to have taken it as a general approval of his methods. These methods are very revealing of his character, and we need now to say something about his whole attitude to the world and to scholarship. He was an ebullient and outgoing man, of inexhaustible energy, who thought of scholarship in terms of personal prowess. (Defoe's even more prodigious energy was, it would seem, one of the things that most attracted Moore to him, representing a kind of challenge.) He seems to have been in some ways very simpleminded, with a naive glee in his own achievements and in any tribute or compliment he received. It pleased him to feel that, as regards Defoe, he possessed special powers of divination and detection, and in newspaper interviews he would manage to have himself presented as a Sherlock Holmes-like or magician-like figure. The caption to his picture in the *Indianapolis Star* of 16 April 1961 is: 'Prof. John Moore. Authors can't hide from him.'

He was nevertheless someone who could inspire great devotion and confidence in his abilities. His fellow-Defoe-expert George Healey, an admirable scholar, corresponded lengthily with him over some twenty-five years, becoming and remaining a devoted and admiring disciple. (Perhaps significantly, Moore was always 'Professor Moore' to Healey, though he would sign himself 'George'.) An equally warm, and again slightly paternal, relationship grew up between Moore and the English scholar Frank Bastian, and Moore went to great lengths to advise and encourage Bastian — receiving much scholarly help in return, which he acknowledged generously.

No man, we may guess, could have more enjoyed the scholarly life. He was, however, or at least grew, very impatient with criticism or opposition. In his letters he harped for years on the crimes of a scholar whom he had helped over an article on Defoe's *Tour* but who had failed to send him an off-print — and who, moreover, was determined 'to deny every thing to Defoe which he can't prove to his own satisfaction'.[46] Again, in 1954, when asked to report on an article submitted to *PMLA* by the young Rodney Baine (eventually published as 'The Apparition of Mrs. Veal: a Neglected Account'[47]), he argued so violently against it for accusing Defoe of gullibility and other unwelcome suggestions, that both Nicol Smith and Arthur H. Scouten rebuked him for his roughness.[48] He was also strongly inclined to suspect others of stealing from his work.

Moore wanted to be thought *the* authority on Defoe; and though he worked for some months on W.P. Trent's Defoe collection in the Boston Public Library, he seems to have felt it wisest to know as little as possible about Trent's unpublished papers — which, in view of Hutchins's secretiveness, was not difficult. As we have seen (p. 89), when the librarian of the Boston Public Library asked him his opinion about Trent's papers, his tone implied (what he no doubt believed sincerely) that they were rather a mare's nest. The impression that he gained from Trent's marginalia was that he had been too 'impressionistic in method' and also too irresolute.[49] In a letter to the Clark Memorial Library in 1953, disputing a Defoe attribution in *The Cambridge Bibliography of English Literature* and reporting four new attributions of his own, he wrote:

> It was rather painful to see how Professor Trent attempted to work up a case for Defoe as author of the scandalous *Memoirs [of the Amours and Intrigues of a certain Irish Dean* (1728)], and how he rejected his own findings on the four other tracts because he lost his nerve after he had convinced himself that Defoe wrote them.[50]

Significantly, though these four new attributions were described by Moore as 'demonstrably Defoe's — all four very characteristic throughout', he himself had had second thoughts about one of them by the time he published his *Checklist*.

Corresponding to these traits of character is the rhetorical strategy employed by Moore in his writings. It is a matter of some significance; for it has contributed much to his influence. One thinks first of the odd, rather schoolmasterly and paternalistic, approach to the reader adopted in *Defoe in the Pillory*. His preface begins thus:

> If you only have thirty minutes to give to this book, read the Epilogue and the Synopsis to each chapter.
>
> If you wish to read consecutively, omit the Notes and the Appendix.
>
> If you have read the Notes and the Appendix, and are still, as our author says, 'tempted to think the whole story no better than a novel or romance', I shall be glad to support any statement by further documentation. Perhaps, in the words of our author, 'the truth of it can be no more contested, than that there were such men in the world as Roberts and Blackbeard, who were Pirates'.[51]

Moore's scholarly style, and not just here, is a sort of genial bullying or browbeating. Readers are left in no doubt that agreement is expected of them, and they are not really encouraged to pry into the secrets of the scholarly workshop, which, except to an expert, Moore suggests, would be tediously dry.

What plays an important part in his strategy, again, is the force of accumulation. We have noticed his way of piling up 'parallels' in abundance, regardless of their quality, and one can perceive a similarity between this and the way he planned his *Checklist of the Writings of Daniel Defoe*, which was to form the climax of his career. It was, as indeed some reviewers pointed out, a strange gesture to publish a list containing some 120 new attributions (rising to nearly 140 in the second edition) without, for the most part, providing any indication of the reasoning supporting them, *or even indicating which the new ones were*. It is plain, however, that for Moore this scheme of the *Checklist* had great advantages. The sheer mass of the thing, combined with its reticence or inscrutability, was intended to and did have a shock effect and was calculated to silence or discourage criticism.

*   *   *

The success, as he regarded it, of his *Defoe in the Pillory* launched Moore on an accelerating career of Defoe attribution, with a view to a comprehensive new bibliography. This he originally visualised as an appendix to a new biography of Defoe; but on the advice of friends he decided to separate the two.

By 1952 the number of his new attributions had passed the one hundred mark, and to prepare the ground for the publication of his bibliography he approached a number of major libraries in Britain and America, offering to lend them a copy of his bibliography in draft, to help them in the revising of their Defoe catalogue entry. This offer seems to have been gratefully received by the Huntington Library, the William Andrews Clark Memorial Library, the Indiana University Library, the Boston Public Library (which recatalogued Trent's collection according to Moore's ascriptions), the Bodleian, and the British Museum. The Museum, indeed, feeling understandably nervous over the Defoe entry in its forthcoming catalogue, took up his offer with some eagerness, and the resulting entry was heavily indebted to him. According to his own unabashed account, when the British Museum in 1953 issued their new Defoe listing as a separate publication, it 'was based directly on my list and on my long correspondence with the staff in charge of the revision of this part of the catalogue. The staff accepted all my attributions completely, but (according to their usual cautious practice in print) they preferred to leave as mere attributions what they recognized to be certainties.'[52]

On the strength of this, Moore was given his own reserved seat in the Museum's North Library, and the experience, as he related with relish to a friend, 'changed me from a stranger who read at the B.M. when he happened to be in London to a volunteer member of the staff, who goes "home" when he returns to the Museum for work.'[53]

In giving this kind of help to librarians, Moore required a good deal of acquiescence; and they would sometimes complain of his insisting, with much positiveness, that they must re-assign some pamphlet in their collection to Defoe, and then, a year or two later, asking them with surprise why they had done so. During 1952 and 1953 he supplied the Clark Library with some ninety-eight new attributions, of which twenty-two did not survive to be included in his *Checklist*, and the Boston Public Library with nearly ninety attributions, all but three of which he described himself as 'absolutely certain of', but fifteen of which did not reach the *Checklist*.[54]

On 27 October 1955 he wrote to Healey in the kind of mixed mood, of exultation combined with self-doubt and uneasy theory-spinning, that he must have experienced fairly often as his *Checklist* obstinately refused to take final form:

A bright sky, pleasant air, and about the most successful single day of research I ever had. I have come to know a specialist in the Sacheverell Controversy [presumably Madan], and he has provided some new leads which (like a new key) are opening doors I had never been able to open and even leading to doors that I didn't know were there. I must have identified as Defoe's — positively and without doubt — at least four or five new tracts today alone.

That tends to offset the opposite experience I have been having at times — yesterday morning in particular — when I decided to give up all claim to pamphlets which I had previously assigned to Defoe. But I may have still another change of heart on some of these. The problem is like this: in some of the Triennial-Septennial pamphlets [pamphlets concerned with the bill for repealing the Triennial Parliaments Act, the subject of heated controversy in the spring and summer of 1716] there seem to be pretty sure indications of Defoe's work along with details that don't seem to belong with his work at all. Tonight I am wondering a bit whether (just as Walter Scott quoted his own poetry in some of his novels deliberately to mystify his readers and keep them from assigning the books to him) Defoe might not have thrown in some false scent (I know he did *at times*, as when he professed to disagree in part with the *Review*.) Or could it be that the pamphlets were written in haste by several governmental writers, and that any one pamphlet may contain discordant elements? Or could it be — as certainly *at times* — that Defoe went out of his way to concede, like a good debater, the things his opponent was likely to claim, in order to force acceptance of the point he really argued for?[55]

*   *   *

The preparation of his *Checklist* and of his biography, *Daniel Defoe: Citizen of the Modern World*, had gone hand-in-hand. The biography, however, came out first, being published in 1958; and what the casual reader might not notice is that it quietly anticipates the findings of the *Checklist*. Some twenty or so quite new attributions are woven into the biographical account, but generally speaking with no indication that they are new. Moore is here following the example of Lee, but it is, we cannot help thinking, a misleading method.

We may take as an example Moore's account of *A Short Narrative of the Life and Actions of His Grace John, Duke of Marlborough. By an Old Officer in the Army* (1711) — a eulogistic defence of Marlborough that, though he does not say so, he is the first to attribute to Defoe. He tells us that it was 'Defoe's first venture as a biographer', and this leads him into various assertions about Defoe's development as a writer, especially as regards the title-page ascription to (or, as Moore would have it, disguise of) 'an Old Officer in the Army'. Moore claims that this 'enabled him [Defoe] (without detection by Harley or others) to defend Marlborough at the time when several members of the Ministry were planning his impeachment'. Moreover, it 'solved one of Defoe's most persistent problems as a writer on political subjects: how was he, who drew so largely on information not accessible to the public, to justify his frequent practice of writing "Within Doors"?...It was here that "an Old Officer" was most useful; the general reader would expect him to know what happened in the army or in the court.' Then, says Moore, 'There was still another, and a wider, advantage in the introduction of such a fictitious author, it gave Defoe a literary freedom which he needed in his finest writing.' Under the disguise of a ficticious author he could safely indulge in 'tautology' or 'loose grammatical constructions' or 'meanness of style', without fear of reproof.[56]

This seems distinctly shaky reasoning. Why should Defoe so

much wish to indulge in 'meanness of style'? Why should an 'Old Officer' be expected to have inside knowledge of Court affairs? Why, most importantly of all, should Defoe risk writing such an apologia for Marlborough when, so far as we know, he owed him no particular personal loyalty (nor showed any ten months later, at the time of Marlborough's fall)? It is, moreover, the kind of new attribution which seems particularly likely, in the long run, to beget further attributions. One would need pretty firm grounds to accept such an attribution, whereas, in fact, there is no external evidence at all for it and at least one piece of internal evidence that argues somewhat against it, namely that it seems odd that the Whiggish Defoe should ascribe Marlborough's disgrace in 1692 to invidious discrimination by Whig politicians against 'a true Member of the Church'.[57] Paula Backscheider, in a reprint of the *Short Narrative*, has indeed argued strongly for Defoe's authorship, on the stylistic 'fingerprint' basis, but we do not really feel that she has made her case.[58] However, the point we are concerned with here is not the merits of this particular attribution, but rather the silent manner of its introduction and the collusion, or at least questionable alliance, between Moore the biographer and Moore the bibliographer.

The *Checklist of the Writings of Daniel Defoe*, which was to be the lasting monument to Moore's bibliographical labours on Defoe, was finally published in 1960 by the University of Indiana Press. For several years Moore had been in negotiation with Rupert Hart-Davis, in the hope that his bibliography would be published in the distinguished 'Soho' series. However, the scope of this series called for detailed bibliographical descriptions of each work, whereas Moore, with the support of George Healey, felt that the overriding consideration was to 'get the canon first'.[59]

His *Checklist* was quickly adopted as authoritative by librarians and scholars generally. Some reviewers, it is true, remarked on the fact that many works were attributed to Defoe for the first time without any evidence being presented and indeed without any indication, even, as to which these were. J. Béranger complained that the *Checklist* was only a 'skeleton',[60] and James Sutherland had some rather frosty things to say about Moore's bibliographical methods in general:

> In this *Checklist* Professor Moore has added considerably to the canon, and sometimes quite convincingly. But not always. In the nature of the case many of the pieces that have been, or will be,

attributed to Defoe must remain of uncertain authorship; but Professor Moore is hot for certainties, and has too little patience with dusty answers. Those titles about which he feels some doubt he has marked with a star, but it does not appear frequently enough...in the *Checklist* pieces are sometimes attributed to Defoe, apparently for the first time, without any evidence at all being offered. On what grounds, for instance, is he given a tract called *Miserere Cleri* (1718)? To such objections Professor Moore may reply that he cannot possibly give us all the evidence in a checklist. On such matters, however, it is not enough that justice be done, if it is done; it must be seen to be done.[61]

It will be clear from what we have said so far in this book that we are very much in sympathy with these reactions to the *Checklist* — both the respect paid to the richness of Moore's discoveries (for he undoubtedly turned up many extremely plausible new attributions), and the complaints about the deficiencies of his general method. This method, and Moore's whole approach to bibliography, seem to us to depend altogether too much on the mystery and prestige of 'authority'. There is a fault of principle here which, in the long run, is likely to do more harm even than particular faulty ascriptions.

PART III

CHAPTER 10

DEFOE AND PROSE STYLE

U P TO THIS POINT, our book has been largely destructive. We shall now try in these last five chapters to offer something more positive and constructive, that is to say to exhibit our own pretensions, such as they are, to 'knowing' Defoe as a writer and as a man. For anyone engaged upon literary attribution problems is inevitably concerned with the problem, or challenge, of 'knowing one's author'; though what this means, and how 'knowing one's author' should actually help in attribution-study, will need a little examining, and we shall attempt to explore it in a later chapter. Meanwhile, for the space of the next three chapters, we want simply to put forward a few personal reactions to certain aspects of Defoe's art and personality.

Let us suggest a new way of looking at one aspect of Defoe's prose style. Writing in 1810, Sir Walter Scott gave powerful expression to what, for a long time, was the common view of Defoe:

> It is greatly to be doubted whether De Foe could have changed his colloquial, circuitous, and periphrastic style for any other, whether more coarse or more elegant. We have little doubt it was connected with his nature, and the particular turn of his thoughts and ordinary expressions, and that he did not succeed so much by writing in an assumed manner as by giving full scope to his own.[1]

There are two propositions in Scott's assertion: that Defoe is a one-style writer, and that his style is 'colloquial, circuitous, and periphrastic'. The majority of critics today would regard both propositions as false, but they have a way of creeping back. In many ways the most perceptive and stimulating discussion of Defoe's style is G.A. Starr's 'Defoe's Prose Style: 1. The Language of Interpretation', published in 1974, but even here the ghost of Scott can be found lurking. In the opening paragraphs of his article Starr plays a trick on the reader, printing some lines of 'elevated' dialogue from *The Political History of the Devil* as if they were blank verse. His purpose, he tells us, is to show that 'immethodical homespun garrulity is not Defoe's only style'.[2] This leaves the impression that he thinks 'immethodical homespun garrulity' is, at least, Defoe's usual and most characteristic style. Now this is a very strange, and pretty obviously false, view, and indeed it must to some extent be unintentional on Starr's part. Take a page at random from one of Defoe's pamphlets and treatises, or from the *Review*, and you are most likely to find a skilled orator or expositor at work, very resourceful in all the journalistic skills — the sort of pen that, if you were Harley, you would endeavour to retain in your interest. 'Homespun garrulity' is simply not apt at all and it seems plain that the ghost of Moll Flanders or some other fictional character of Defoe's is haunting the argument. When Defoe is homespun and garrulous we may be sure he is dramatising and impersonating.

There seems also to survive in Starr's remarks, not quite extirpated, the fallacy that Defoe had one style only, a style not very distant from that of the characters in his fiction. The reason why this error can linger in his mind is worth exploring. It is perhaps suggested by his comment on certain other, in his view uncharacteristic and atypical, prose effects in *The Farther Adventures of Robinson Crusoe*. Of these he says: 'With their sustained antitheses and parallelisms, such passages smack too much of artifice to represent Defoe's prose at its best.' The truth is, Starr's model of what would *not* constitute 'homespun garrulity' seems to be the prose of Dr Johnson or Gibbon — or at any rate something formal and 'Ciceronian'. The alternatives, we want to suggest in the present chapter, are by no means so limited.

To begin with, it will be a good idea if we go through a polemical pamphlet of Defoe's, noting briefly some of the qualities and characteristic virtues of its style. We have chosen *The Original Right of the People of England*, first published in 1701 and indisputably Defoe's, since he reprinted it in the *True Collection*. It is an important pamphlet for what it reveals about Defoe's political attitudes at this time, and an excellent piece of writing, in our view, but by no means unique, or even exceptional, in its stylistic characteristics. Most of its stylistic features, indeed, could have been illustrated more strikingly from other works of Defoe's. The main part seems to have been written in the autumn of 1701, and its manifesto-like form, with its succession of very brief single-proposition paragraphs, evidently relates it to the famous manifesto and ultimatum, *Legion's Memorial*, presented to the House of Commons in May of the same year.

One's immediate impression is of the life, the verve, the 'attack' of the whole thing. One notes the close forensic relationship to the reader ('I grant', 'I doubt not', 'It remains to argue from hence', 'And here, if I have any foresight'), the little bits of dramatised speech ('if he won't, let him go about his Business'), the fondness for interpolations ('Nor do I think that in this Discourse I can be supposed to favour that Party, if there be such a Party, which indeed I question'), and the purposeful play with the definition of words ('All are but several terms drawn from and reducible to the great Term, the People of England'). (One recalls Defoe's play with the definition of 'a just Peace', 'the felonious Treaty' in the *Review*.) One finds, too, continual verbal inventiveness; for instance, the clever verbal conceit 'a Press in the Clouds', the freshly minted phraseology of 'We have seen Parliaments concur so with the Fate and Fortunes of Princes, as to comply backwards and forward, in Deposing and Reinthroning alternately two Kings as often as Victory put power into their hands', or such free and resourceful mastery of familiar metaphor as the following: 'The House of Commons in the next Settlement over-Ballanc'd the Lords, and Power being added to one side, toss'd the Upper House quite out of the Scale, absolutely Annihilated the very being of the Peers *as a House*, and voted them out of the Constitution.' Then one observes great, and characteristic, variety of syntax, going with variety of rhythmic organisation (it is exemplified, for instance, in the sentence 'We have seen Parliaments' already quoted), and likewise success in giving a run and spring to whole paragraphs. Finally one notices the cadenced, high-arching and deliberately 'classical' peroration with which the main part of the pamphlet impressively ends:

> The *House of Commons* also are Mortal, as a House; a King may Dissolve them, they may die and be extinct; but the Power of the People has a kind of Eternity with respect to Politick Duration: Parliaments may cease, but the People remain; for them they were originally made, by them they are continued and renewed, from them they receive their Power, and to them in reason they ought to be accountable.

It is with some puzzlement that one turns from such varied and resourceful prose to the way that Defoe's style is sometimes spoken of. We are thinking, for instance, of E. A. James, in his book *Daniel*

Defoe's Many Voices (1972). As the title suggests, James emphatically rejects one of Scott's two propositions, that Defoe was a one-style writer, but he seems to go along fairly happily with the other:

> Even when Defoe does not freight his prose quite so heavily with factual minutiae, he often slips into a rushing style characterized by breathless amplifications, qualifications and asides which produce such a glut of information that he loses sight not only of the point of his sentence but also of any grammatical avenue of escape from it.[3]

'Breathless': the word recurs in Bonamy Dobrée's essay 'Some Aspects of Defoe's Prose', where he comments on a paragraph from Defoe's *Review*: 'It is, as often with Defoe, so urgent as to be breathless; the construction tends to get out of hand, and has to be recalled to order by some desperate means.'[4] It recurs, once again, in an article by J.H. Raleigh which, like Dobrée's, is devoted to high praise of Defoe's style. Raleigh describes Defoe as 'the master of what I shall call, for purposes of giving a condensed definition, the cumulative, periodic, sentence-paragraph'; and, after quoting the description of the death of the Prince's wife in *Roxana*, he comments:

> That final period which Defoe places after the word 'Day' — hitherto in the entire paragraph there are no periods but, rather, commas, colons, and semicolons — may be aptly described as surpassingly fitting and just, and the entire passage is classic Defoe: the fast-moving sentence-paragraph unit, made up of loosely-joined members and narrating a complete action; the rushing, breathless pace, with the clauses tumbling over one another and successively modifying content and tone; the long swelling development, beginning in prosaic scientism (the physicians say she is ill) but, finally, catching the very rhythm of the act of dying, as at the last, the Princess alternates, in successive clauses, between the casting up of earthly accounts (Life) and reckoning on Heaven (Death); and finally the concluding, periodic close, with its alliteration of 'died' and 'Day'.[5]

What we want to argue in the present chapter is that all these accounts of Defoe's prose style (or styles), whether deprecatory or favourable, are askew — and for the same reason: they are led astray by an inappropriate model of what 'good' prose must be. It will be noticed that Raleigh uses the term 'periodic' in describing the sentence-paragraph from *Roxana*, and correctly, for the passage exhibits the defining feature of a 'periodic' sentence, which is that it should reserve its main verb to the end (thus giving the end, very strongly, the function of a logical and rhetorical 'resolution' of all that has gone before). This is the 'teleological' or Ciceronian idea of a sentence, and Defoe, when he wanted, was very capable of constructing sentences and paragraphs on this plan.[6] Neverthless, we would argue, it was not habitual with him; and even in the 'periodic' sentence-paragraph quoted by Raleigh one can also feel the tug of a quite different mode of construction, which we shall call the 'improvisatory'.

It always needs insisting, we feel, that Defoe did not have just one style but many. However, what it may also be possible to show is that, at a deeper level, his various styles are governed by a common project.

Let us examine the following passage (shall we call it a 'sentence' or a 'paragraph'?) from *An Essay Upon Projects* (1697):

> There is, 'tis true, a great difference between *New Inventions* and *Projects*, between Improvement of Manufactures or Lands, which tend to the immediate Benefit of the Publick, and Imploying of the Poor; and Projects fram'd by subtle Heads, with a sort of a *Deceptio Visus*, and *legerdemain*, to bring People to run needless and unusual hazards: I grant it, and give a due preference to the first, and yet Success has so sanctifi'd some of those other sorts of Projects, that 'twou'd be a kind of Blasphemy against Fortune to disallow 'em; witness Sir *William Phips's* Voyage to the Wreck; 'twas a mere Project, a Lottery of a Hundred thousand to One odds; a hazard, which if it had fail'd, every body wou'd have been asham'd to have own'd themselves concern'd in; A Voyage that wou'd have been as much ridicul'd as *Don Quixot's Adventure upon the Windmill*: Bless us! that Folks should go Three thousand Miles to Angle in the open Sea for Pieces of Eight! why, they wou'd have made Ballads of it, and the Merchants wou'd have said of every unlikely Adventure, 'Twas like *Phips* his Wreck-Voyage; but it had Success and who reflects upon the Project?[7]

This strikes us as, in a minor way, a wonderfully fine piece of writing, alive in every detail. The writer has, somehow or other, taken the reader captive so that he can play innumerable variations on his tone, can indulge in a little learned word-play here, and sketch a tiny comedy ('Bless us! that Folks...') there. However, what we want to draw attention to for our present purposes is the sentence-construction. The feature which strikes one is how the passage keeps taking on a new lease of life — seems again and again to be reaching its conclusion and then, with perfect but unexpected logic, manages to postpone its end. What one is witnessing is a remarkable syntactical resourcefulness on Defoe's part, and we may cling to the word 'syntax', though it is straining the word to its limit. Those interpolations that keep thrusting in, saving the sentence ('paragraph'?) from expiry, are syntactically perfectly sound; the logic of the sentence's endless extension is impeccable; and in retrospect the sentence is found to be most beautifully organised and articulated.

The question which arises is, of course, to what extent are we justified in referring to each of the passages so far quoted from Defoe as a 'sentence'? In so far as this is a mere matter of naming — of how you define the term 'sentence' — it is, of course, largely academic. The point, it seems to us, is that it is not *purely* a matter of definition. For it can be argued that part of Defoe's rhetorical or dramatic effect lies, often, in the deployment of unusually large verbal units; and if this is true, then the practice of editors, who, in modernising, tend to replace Defoe's colons with full stops, may be doing a definite injury to Defoe's prose.[8]

Let us return for a moment to the phrase 'in retrospect'. Defoe, we feel, when he embarked on this sentence, had only a vague idea how it would end (genuinely so; it was not merely, though it might have been, an artistic pretence that he did not know). We must not jump to conclusions from this. A little reflection will tell us that to write in this way, which we may call 'improvisatory', is quite common and — as in this case — does not at all imply that the product will have less form and 'architecture' than that of a more premeditated style. Nevertheless, it goes against a certain hallowed tradition in prose-writing, which for want of a better word we may call 'Ciceronian'. The Ciceronian tradition attributes special value to the *end* of sentences, thus to forward planning in general;[9] whereas, as we have seen, much of the effort of the improvisatory sentence is devoted to postponing the end — and, what is more, postponing the decision as to how it shall end. (That we are moving into ideological differences already dimly looms. Defoe's 'projecting' spirit, his Whiggism, his contempt for the past and for tradition:[10] all these could be predisposing factors to such an improvisatory notion of literary form, in which ends are not embryonically contained in beginnings.)

Let us quote another Defoean example of a sentence of the 'last-minute reprieve' or 'deathbed recovery' kind, this time from a different kind of writing, A Journal of the Plague Year (1722):

Such is the precipitant Disposition of our People, whether it is so or not all over the World, that's none of my particular Business to enquire; but I saw it apparently here, that as upon the first Fright of the Infection, they shun'd one another, and fled from one another's Houses, and from the City with an unaccountable, and, as I thought, unnecessary Fright; so now upon this Notion spreading, (*viz.*) that the Distemper was not so catching as formerly, and that if it was catch'd, it was not so mortal, and seeing abundance of People who really fell sick, recover again daily; they took to such a precipitant Courage, and grew so entirely regardless of themselves, and of the Infection, that they made no more of the Plague than of an ordinary Fever, nor indeed so much; they not only went boldly into Company, with those who had Tumours and Carbuncles upon them, that were running, and consequently contagious, but eat and drank with them, nay into their Houses to visit them, and even, as I was told, into their very Chambers where they lay sick.[11]

There are various things to say about this sentence, not all to do with its construction. It may help to avoid confusion, however, it we contrast it with a sentence from the opening paragraph of Locke's *Two Treatises of Government*:

I therefore took it [Filmer's *Patriarcha*] into my hands with all the expectation, and read it through with all the attention due to a Treatise, that made such a noise at its coming abroad, and cannot but confess myself mightily surprised, that in a Book, which was to provide Chains for all Mankind, I should find nothing but a Rope of Sand, useful perhaps to such, whose Skill and Business it is to raise a Dust, and would blind the People, the better to mislead them, but in truth not of any force to draw those into Bondage, who have their Eyes open, and so much Sense about them as to consider, that Chains are but an ill wearing, how much Care soever hath been taken to file and polish them.[12]

This admirable and complex sentence, though many qualities relate it to Defoe and to Defoe's period, emphatically does not belong to the *genre* that we are trying to define, the 'improvisatory sentence'. No matter how, in fact, Locke produced this sentence (certainly a very un-Ciceronian one in its ease and relative informality), in principle it was produced by forward planning: in principle Locke knew what he wanted to say; he was not depending, as Defoe in his improvisatory mood depends, on the fortunes of the pen in the act of composing (combined with confidence that his experience and practice in writing will enable him, as it were retrospectively or *post hoc*, to give form to what fortune offers).

Who springs to mind as the master of improvisation, or at least of the art of simulated improvisation? The answer is Laurence Sterne, and we shall now quote a passage that may be thought to take improvisation to its limits or to give it its classic expression — that is, makes most memorable play with the fiction that a sentence may *want* to end but endless 'cross accidents' keep preventing it from doing so:

> On the fifth day of *November*, 1718, which to the aera fixed on, was as near nine kalendar months as any husband could in reason have expected, — was I *Tristram Shandy*, Gentleman, brought forth into this scurvy and disasterous world of ours. — I wish I had been born in the Moon, or in any of the planets, (except *Jupiter* or *Saturn*, because I never could bear cold weather) for it could not well have fared worse with me in any of them ('tho I will not answer for *Venus*) than it has in this vile, dirty planet of ours, — which o' my conscience, with reverence be it spoken, I take to be made up of the shreds and clippings of the rest; —— not but the planet is well enough, provided a man could be born in it to a great title, or to a great estate; or could any how contrive to be called up to publick charges, and employments of dignity or power; — but that is not my case; —— and therefore every man will speak of the fair as his own market has gone in it; — for which cause I affirm it over again to be one of the vilest worlds that ever was made; - - - for I can truly say, that from the first hour I drew my breath in it, to this, that I can now scarce draw it at all, for an asthma I got in scating against the wind in *Flanders*; - - I have been the continual sport of what the world calls Fortune; and though I will not wrong her by saying, She has ever made me feel the weight of any great or signal evil; - - - yet with all the good temper in the world, I affirm it of her, That in every stage of my life, and at every turn and corner where she could get fairly at me, the ungracious Duchess has pelted me with a set of as pitiful misadventures and cross accidents as ever small *HERO* sustained.[13]

Tristram Shandy strikes most readers, rightly, as — from one aspect — a discourse about discourse, a novel all about the adventures of sentences; and we must be careful what analogies we make with Defoe, a very different sort of writer. Notice, though, that the passage from *Tristram Shandy* is all *about* fortune and freaks of fortune. Here, at least, we need have no fears in drawing a parallel with Defoe whose novels — and not only his novels — dwell continuously on the extreme vicissitudes of fortune.

We may say that Sterne pretends to do what Defoe in fact does. Sterne — rather more, as we feel, a disciple of the forward-planning school, for all his celebration of improvisation — makes it his playful claim that with him it is *all* improvisation: he never looks back at all:

> What a rate have I gone on at, curvetting and frisking it away, two up and two down for four volumes together, without looking once behind, or even on one side of me, to see whom I trod upon![14]

By contrast it is Defoe who really does construct, not just his sentences, but his novels by improvisation, and with whom form — fictional form as well as syntactical form — is almost always *retrospective* form. Distant equally from the forward-planning of a Fieldingesque plot (how inconceivable on Defoe's part to write a *Tom Jones!*), and from the relatively meaningless accumulations of incident of *Gil Blas* (and, dare we say, Smollett?), Defoe invents a destiny for Crusoe, Moll Flanders and Roxana which in retrospect, has form and significance: Crusoe, Moll and Roxana are the sum of their experiences, and the sum is significant. The improvisatory method, where Defoe's inspiration can sustain it, produces very satisfying fictional form; though when inspiration fails, as it does half-way through *Colonel Jack*, the result is catastrophic.

It seems to us, then, that one can fairly take Defoe's way with sentence-construction as expressive of his attitude to narration and to writing generally; and, with the provisos suggested at the beginning of this chapter, this may turn out to have some significance in questions of attribution.

CHAPTER 11

DEFOE AS POET

W<small>E AGREE WITH</small> the common opinion that Defoe was on the whole a very bad poet, and this might seem a reason for ignoring his poetic aspect in the present book. Of course the basic rules of attribution will still hold, and the mere fact that Defoe wrote some bad verse is no reason at all for attributing some more to him.) However, Defoe is that intriguing phenomenon, a bad poet who wrote two inspired poems. We are referring to *The True-Born Englishman* and 'A Hymn to the Pillory'; and there seems some point in our discussing these remarkable works, for they say a great deal about Defoe, in a way that indirectly has a bearing upon attribution. They illuminate, better than almost anything in his prose, one important aspect of his original 'project' in life: his wish to figure as the voice of the 'People'.

It is not clear whether Defoe set out with a specific project as a poet, or if so, what it was. One would at least be hard put to say whom he took as a model. We might have expected it to be Rochester, for Defoe certainly idolized Rochester and was continually quoting him, because, according to John McVeagh, 'the older poet did what Defoe wanted to do as a writer'.[1] But in the actual texture of his verse, apart from a few half-quotations, Rochester's influence does not seem to be very noticeable, nor does that of Defoe's other favourites, Butler, Marvell and Oldham. If anything, he is a little closer to his contemporary Tom D'Urfey, whom he addresses in 'A New Discovery of an Old Intreague' (1691).[2] As for Dryden, Defoe announces in both 'A New Discovery' and *The True-Born Englishman* that he will not imitate Dryden's 'parallels from Hebrew Times'.[3]

Defoe's first published poem, 'A New Discovery of an Old Intreague', has a certain piquancy by reason of its ellipticality and sheer obscurity, which would have been considerable even for his original readers and needs by now the help of a whole book[4] to penetrate; but this is the most one can say in its praise. The truth is, Defoe's equipment as a poet, as revealed in 'A New Discovery', 'Reformation of Manners' or 'The Spanish Descent', is rather nondescript. His couplets are broken-backed and monotonous, nor is there anything interesting in the standpoint from which he abuses individuals in verse; the insults he hurls at them come from the commonest stock of vituperation — gibes at venality, physical ugliness, drunkenness, libertinism and impotence. Nor is this brilliant debater in prose good at reasoning in verse, as witness the lumbering and grotesque *Jure Divino*, though there are, indeed, flashes of power even in this, as when, in one of the several sweeps through history in the poem, he falls into a swingeing and magisterial Drydenesque vein:

> A rhapsody of kings, like him [Egbert] divine,
> As void of right as right is void of line,
> Succeed the king-subduing wretch of course,
> By blood, by fraud, or by a way that's worse...[5]

He keeps this up for some lines more, but having, as one feels, adopted the manner at random, he drops it at random also. What is lacking is not so much capacity as any fit artistic purpose.

It may be that, as a young man, Defoe had quite high ambitions as a poet, as he did in so many other spheres, so that it was not quite a surprise to him when, with the runaway success of *The True-Born Englishman*, he became for a spell the best-known poet of his day. But what is plain is that, if so, he went on writing verse after giving up any such ambitions. It is characteristic of Defoe that he was willing to *use* verse, which is to say misuse or abuse it, and was willing to be *used* as a verse-writer, for any purpose he thought good. Fittingly, his career as poet approaches its end with the production of two enormous and bad poems, *Caledonia* and (if we are to trust the attribution by J.R. Moore) *A Scots Poem*, written in the same two or three months, hand-in-hand with much pamphleteering and undercover activities, and all in the cause of Union with Scotland. The lack of conscience we are imputing is artistic, not ethical.

How then is one to explain his writing two poems of high artistic originality, and indeed genius (for so they seem to us)? Defoe said himself that he wrote *The True-Born Englishman* in 'a kind of rage', provoked by the crass chauvinism of John Tutchin's 'The Foreigners'. He would have here been referring to Part 1 of the poem, for it would appear that the satirical portrait of Sir Charles Duncombe, which provides the set-piece of Part 2, was already circulating in manuscript a year or two earlier, and some other portions, like Britannia's song, may have antedated 'The Foreigners' also. But indeed, in praising *The True-Born Englishman* so highly, one is really thinking of Part 1, which has a quality all of its own and was, it is reasonable to imagine, a sudden inspiration. At all events, the first thing that strikes one about it is how much it is all of a piece and how swiftly, purposefully and irresistibly it runs on. Defoe is ignoring all the cunning devices of the heroic couplet considered as a closed unit: the antitheses and false antitheses, the booby-trap and mutually destructive comparison, and so on. He has found instead a way of making his sentences move in harmony with the couplet form in the most natural way possible — a way suggestive, really, not so much of an Augustan poet as of, say, Byron. His rhythmic uninventiveness is here no handicap. the whole point is a free, unhampered, forward motion, a gradual crescendo of genial comic 'rage'. The geniality and triumphant levity is reinforced by the chiming and semi-comic bisyllabic rhymes; and the poem is spun along and given a sort of spiralling energy by the continual return, swelling in irony at each repetition, of the phrase 'True-Born Englishman'. To be so outrageous while remaining genial is a great achievement. How wonderfully and joyously malign are those lines on the Scots who decamp to England in the wake of James I:

> The Royal Branch from *Pict-land* did succeed,
> With troops of *Scots* and Scabs from *North-by-Tweed*.
> The Seven first Years of his Pacifick Reign,
> Made him and half his Nation *Englishmen*.
> *Scots* from the *Northern* Frozen Banks of *Tay*,
> With Packs and Plods came *Whigging* all away:
> Thick as the Locusts which in *Egypt* swarm'd,
> With Pride and hungry Hopes compleatly arm'd:
> With Native Truth, Diseases, and No Money,
> Plunder'd our *Canaan* of the Milk and Honey.
> Here they grew quickly Lords and Gentlemen,
> And all their Race are *True-Born Englishmen*.[6]

The verb 'Whigging' here is, hedgehog-like, designed to sting whoever takes hold of it, and in this it epitomises the unpartisan and even-handed bloody-mindedness of the whole poem. We are not to suppose that being the voice of the People means buttering the

People up or encouraging them in their prejudices. The immense vogue of *The True-Born Englishman* is proof of a more bracing theory, that by the right approach the People may be bounced out of their prejudices.

An essential point to get hold of is that, from one point of view, the poem is a song. Defoe is writing a satire and a ballad (complete with chorus or refrain) at the same time. This is significant as well as original. Defoe wrote a number of actual political ballads, no doubt with traditional tunes in mind, and they are not bad, but not markedly better than anyone else's. Nevertheless it is no accident that his finest poem should aim at the ballad-like and do it in hybridisation with the 'polite' form of the heroic couplet; and it is a fair guess that he could hope it would be sung by street ballad-singers.

The significance we are aiming at lies in Defoe's desire, very keen at this period and never quite given up, to be 'Legion's' spokesman and the People's voice. (According to Walter Wilson the charges against the Commons in his *Legion's Memorial* were turned into a ballad and publicly cried about the streets.[7]) It is an ambition he certainly succeeded in; and since he also succeeded, though perhaps this time by instinct rather than design, in writing one of the two most popular novels in the language, there seems to be much to explore here. The psychology of the thing seems to be that Defoe wants to be in the middle of things publicly, and to put his great talents at the service of the People (as defined by him), yet at the same time to be anonymous. He courts exposure and yet hides his personality, so that we get no such feeling of him as a person as we do with Swift or Pope. Instead, he wants to construct an artificial personality or presence, made up out of self-quotation and self-repetition: he is to figure in people's eyes as 'Legion's Memorialist', 'The author of The True-Born Englishman', the inventor of tags and phrases become, or intended to become, proverbial. No doubt one must think twice before drawing inferences from eighteenth-century printing-house style, but very often it looks as if Defoe is italicising the lines and phrases he hopes will earn proverbial status. (William Cobbett, though a 'personality' in exactly the way Defoe was not, did something not quite dissimilar.) Much of the trouble in understanding Defoe, and consequently in fixing the canon of his writings, stems from the fact that the personality he presents to us is so completely a construction, allowing us to guess only dimly at the 'real' Defoe. It is this that makes it easy to entertain superstitious notions about him as a prodigy of venality or superproductivity or 'Protean' disguise.

In *The True-Born Englishman* Defoe is not 'reasoning in verse';[8] he is, rather, zestfully expanding upon and embroidering a simple (though profound) argument, stated and grasped from the outset. As a poet he is not interested in discriminations, and hence he has not much use for the antithetical style, as practised by Pope, and his own efforts in this vein are clumsy. His Fancy needs to be liberated by a master idea, and liberation is the feeling most conveyed by *The True-Born Englishman*. He finds himself in an invincible and most exhilarating position, with a valid excuse for insulting everyone in sight: Englishmen for being invidious towards the 'foreigners' they were themselves a generation or so ago; foreigners, for being marauding and locust-like invaders; and Englishwomen for welcoming them. It seems that a Whig and rationalist has this freedom, owning as he does no patriotic allegiance to any homeland save Reason. With a secure home in Reason, he need acknowledge no blood-ties or ties of custom and is excused both pieties and flank-rubbing. Gratitude, of course, is another matter; it was Defoe's great 'positive', being (in his view) a rational tie.

For a man eager to be at the centre of things, Defoe's condemnation to the pillory was another occasion to rise to, and rise to it he did, as we know, magnificently. One warms to Walter Wilson, who speaks of this episode as, unreservedly, a 'triumph'.[9] For what more triumphant than, not just to find himself garlanded instead of pelted with rotten eggs, but to have stage-managed the whole occasion, causing his own defiant 'Hymn to the Pillory' to be circulated among the crowd and recited by ballad-singers, at the foot of the pillory?

The virtues of his 'Hymn to the Pillory' complement those of *The True-Born Englishman*. The poem is, of necessity, very different in tone: not unbridled and joyous but measured, defiant and ancient-Roman. What is common, though, is the note of triumphant conviction. The idea of a 'True-Born Englishman' is made, progressively, to appear as quite limitlessly absurd. The rectitude of the victim of the pillory is, similarly, made progressively to seem utterly and beyond question unimpeachable and of the most vital significance to the People of England. In this context, simple and direct utterance, given weight by force and rhyme, but by its irregular strophes asserting a freedom not unconnected with political freedom, constitutes the needed form. The Pindaric ode, and especially the irregular and improvisatory type as used by Defoe, has had on the whole a bad press,[10] but one may see that Defoe found an ideal use for it, one which in a way anticipated *vers libre*. To the weightiness of the ode, appropriate to a man justifying himself before Heaven and mankind, he adds a spontaneity which suggests that the words are rising to his lips here and now.

If the central standpoint and firm ground of *The True-Born Englishman* is an allegiance to Reason, rendering unnecessary all other allegiances, the central ground of the 'Hymn' is the rights and grandeur of *authorship*. The victim of the pillory asserts these in the most appropriate and convincing way by showing what authorship can do even in such apparently helpless circumstances, how it can turn even the pillory itself to advantage. By a marvellous succession of conceits, cumulative in their effect and imposing one metaphorical metamorphosis on it after another, the pillory is made to stand for all the institutions of society: the pulpit, the stage, the bar, the pageant and the 'opening Vacancys' (in other words, jobs) of a corrupt state system. Here, again, is a poem governed by a single mastering idea or project — to reverse the whole sentence passed upon the victim: to steal the clothes of an unjust State, to demonstrate by the conclusive evidence of successful wit that it is still (and just as much as when the satirist was at liberty) the State that is on trial and the writer who is the prosecutor.

The sublime, imaginative opportunism with which Defoe exploited the pillory extends even further, for it was a supreme opportunity for him to differentiate between the 'Mob' and the 'People'. These were for him opposites, and his commitment to the 'People' was in proportion to his scorn for the 'Mob'. (In Lockean style he held that when mutual contract was dissolved by a despot, 'The Nation's all a Mob'.[11]) It may be agreed, of course, that the 'Mob' is not a thing but a way of regarding things, as indeed is true of the 'People', and one remembers Raymond Williams's remark that there are no 'masses', only ways of regarding people as 'masses'. Defoe gives a neat philosophical turn to a kindred point in 'A New Discovery of an Old Intreague', when he writes:

> And thus the Royal Muster did conclude,
> And the Host dissolv'd into a multitude;
> Meer *Mob* the Matter, Army was the Form,
> So Bees go out a Troop, come back a Swarm.
> So well composed Vapours represent

> Ships, Armies, Battails, in the Firmament;
> 'Till steady Eyes the Exhalation solves,
> And all to its first matter Cloud dissolves.[12]

The significance of the pillory in this respect grows enormous. For
here the powers-that-be are, in due legal form, encouraging the
populace to think of themselves as, and to act as, a 'mob': behave
barbarously, pelt a victim with filth and indulge in indiscriminate
malice. It is, in a sense, a crisis of naming — shall Defoe's fellow-
citizens, who have him at their mercy, designate themselves as the
'mob' or as the 'people'? — and Defoe, with temerity, in the first
stanza of his 'Hymn to the Pillory', takes pains to insult the 'mob'.

> Persons or Crimes find here the same respect,
>   And Vice does Vertue oft Correct,
> The undistinguish'd Fury of the Street,
>   With Mob and Malice Mankind Greet:
>   No Byass can the Rabble draw,
> But *Dirt* throws *Dirt* without respect to Merit, or to Law.[13]

It is a stroke as bold as it is brilliant and makes of Defoe as authentic a
hero as the Bastwick, Prynne and Selden with whom, in his 'Hymn',
he claims fraternity.

CHAPTER 12

DEFOE AS A MAN

T HE PRESENT BOOK is not the place to attempt a complete new portrait of Defoe as a man, even supposing we were capable of it. None the less, it might be worth suggesting a few adjustments to the current picture of him, which seem to us to have a certain relevance to, or be bound up with, questions of attribution. Our four topics in the present chapter will thus be Intellectual Independence, Exposure and Solitude, Belief, and Was Defoe a Turncoat, or a Writer-on-both-sides?

INTELLECTUAL INDEPENDENCE

It is a weakness on the part of Defoe's biographers that they tend to lump together vices or crimes that have no necessary connection, for instance venality and mendacity. Those who would accuse Defoe of venality and lack of principle run up against a major difficulty, in that all the evidence seems to show that he had much intellectual vanity and set great store by his own ideas. This is certainly the impression one gains from the *Review*, with its unwearied advocacy of certain propositions, and from Defoe's habit of self-quotation here and in other of his works. It is what is suggested also by his letters to Harley. In one sense, no doubt, he had a dependent relationship to Harley; but in another he had a rather dominating, or would-be dominating, one. From the beginning he showered Harley with ideas and advice, and one of his earliest acts was to draw up a lengthy document, giving Harley general instructions about how to conduct Cabinet government and to set up a secret service network.[1] Now the habit of giving advice puts a premium on consistency, and it is clear that Defoe valued at least the appearance of consistency, as may be seen from the fuss he sometimes made in the *Review* when trying to reconcile his earlier pronouncements with later ones. A man with intelligently worked-out and idiosyncratic positions is indeed rather unlikely to give them up at a moment's notice or without much struggle.

There is, however, no law in Nature that such a man cannot lie or deceive. Could one hope to sustain the view that Defoe never lied? The evidence against it seems overwhelming, though William Lee gallantly resisted it; and our own opinion is that, for certain purposes, like concealing embarrassing activities from his patron, he was quite capable of brazen mendacity. We also have evidence, from Defoe himself, that he enjoyed play-acting and deception; witness the well-known passage in a letter to Harley about the disguises he expected to assume on his mission to Scotland in 1706.[2] It is plain from the blithe tone of this passage that he took positive pleasure in play-acting, and it is not a very rash surmise that he may sometimes have taken a positive pleasure in lying. It was, however, the deepening conviction that Defoe was a liar that led W.P. Trent to believe him a rogue devoid of all principle. This indicates a naivety in Trent, for reflection soon tells us that many men of high integrity in some other directions (for instance Ford Madox Ford) have been the most appalling liars.

What, again, is perhaps not always sufficiently stressed by biographers is a quality in Defoe which we may, for want of a better phrase, call his intellectual 'contrariness'. It is no accident that one of the earliest episodes in his writing life was, according to his own account, a quarrel with his own Whiggish friends and fellow Dissenters:

> The first Time I had the Misfortune to differ with my Friends, was about the Year 1683, when the Turks were besieging Vienna, and the Whigs in England, generally speaking, were for the Turks taking it; which I having read the History of the Cruelty and perfidious Dealings of the Turks in their Wars, and how they had rooted out the Name of the Christian Religion in above Threescore and Ten Kingdoms, could by no means agree with: And tho' then but a young Man, and a younger Author, I opposed it, and wrote against it; which was taken very unkindly indeed.[3]

This was by no means his last difference with his Dissenting friends, for, as we know, he quarrelled with them persistently, and with much injury to himself, over Occasional Conformity. That, for trying to make Occasional Conformity illegal, the high-flying party

were acting as persecuting knaves, and yet that Occasional Conformity itself was vicious and not only unworthy of sincere
Dissenters but injurious to their political cause, is the sort of
independent, cogently reasoned and, from a certain point of view,
thoroughly perverse and mischievously 'cussed' standpoint that
seems profoundly congenial to Defoe. Some of his best early polemical writing was devoted to expounding it, and he never significantly shifted from it. It seems, morever, to have gone with a sheer,
irresponsible zest for teasing. This at least is what one must conclude
if one accepts with J.R. Moore that Defoe was the author of the
entertaining *Dialogue between a Dissenter and the Observator, Concerning The Shortest Way with the Dissenters* of 1703, in which the
Dissenters are caricatured so unmercifully as the stupid party:

> *OBS.* You Dissenters are in something like Case with the *Pharisees*;
> when the Question was put to them by our Saviour about *Johns*
> Baptism; whether it was from Heaven or of Men. If a man should
> ask you of the *Shortest way* was it wrote for you or against you? If
> you should say for us, you would be ask why then are you so mad
> with the Author? And if you should say against you, the People
> would laugh at you; for all men but you see into it, and that a
> Dissenter wrote it; you must say therefore, we cannot tell, and
> consequently, that you rail at the Author for you can't tell what.
> *DIS.* But we don't count him a Dissenter.
> *OBS.* He has all the marks of a Dissenter upon him, but *want of
> Brains.*[4]

This stance of Defoe's puzzled some of his contemporaries, as it
continued to puzzle W.P. Trent, who — quite unjustifiably, so far as
one can see — depicts it as a youthful folly, a rash commitment on
Defoe's part that, in his more worldly-wise years, he would have
been careful to avoid.[5]

What, again, could be more cheerfully and intelligently 'contrary'
and liable to make Defoe ten enemies for one friend, than the thesis
of his *True-Born Englishman*? Or one may think of the uncomfortable
and self-denying logic of his attitude towards imprisonment for debt:
that it produced tragic evils, was in crying need of reform, yet that as
a system England's prosperity depended upon it and one could not
afford to abolish it.[6] His *Review*, too, was originally founded upon a
thoroughly 'cussed' thesis, namely that the French were at once
England's greatest enemy and a prime example of the horrors of

tyranny and papistry, and, in point of efficiency, resourcefulness and fortitude, a model that the English had much to learn from. This thesis rapidly brought him into trouble from his more stupid adversaries, who asked, simply, could a man who extolled the French be anything but a traitor, probably paid with French gold? This reaction provoked his scorn, but plainly it was also one that he invited. Defoe was a man not only with a fatal attraction to trouble, but with a *penchant* for self-destruction. It will be unwise of us to try to explain such a man's behaviour in terms of simple self-interest or an unwinking eye to the 'main chance'.

One thinks, again, of *Conjugal Lewdness* (1727). It is a work very strongly coloured by Defoe's love of paradox, indeed it may be said to be almost entirely generated by two paradoxes: the verbal paradox of 'matrimonial whoredom' (whoredom practised under the aegis of marriage), under which name so many different crimes are here lumped together; and the richly teasing paradox, laboured so tirelessly by Defoe, that to name or describe immoral things may be in itself a kind of immorality, or at least a temptation to immorality. This is presented as the dilemma of the earnest moralist, but for the reader the book figures at moments as faintly salacious — as it were, a respectable equivalent to the pornography of Curll. *Conjugal Lewdness* is one of Defoe's least attractive works, more or less devoid of gaiety; and we might have been tempted to blame it on the sourness of old age, but in fact, according to Defoe, it was begun thirty years earlier and already finished many years before publication:

> Hitherto he [the author] has been reluctant as to the publishing it, and partly on account of his years, for it was long since finished, and partly in hopes of reformation; but now, despairing of amendment, grown old, and out of the reach of scandal, and of all the pretences to it; sincerely aiming at the reformation of the guilty, and despising all unjust reproaches from a vicious age, he closes his days with this satire...[7]

For all this, it strikes one as a most 'Defoean' work, and especially in its attraction towards dilemmas and logical discomforts. Who but Defoe, one feels, would take such perverse delight in tearing the curtains from the marriage-bed and revealing it, not as the haven of virtue, but as a seething morass of sexual temptation and crime. It is the work, not so much of a fanatical mind, as of a perverse and 'contrary' one.

Let us give a further example, a more subtle but rather striking one, of his 'contrariness'. It will be remembered that Charles Lamb, though he was a devotee of Defoe's novels and had much affection for him as a man, launched, in his essay 'The Good Clerk', a bitter attack on Defoe's *Complete English Tradesman*:

> It is difficult to say what his intention was in writing it. It is almost impossible to suppose him in earnest. Yet such is the bent of the book to narrow and to degrade the heart, that if such maxims were as catching and infectious as those of a licentious cast, which happily is not the case, had I been living at that time, I certainly should have recommended to the Grand Jury of Middlesex, who presented the Fable of the Bees, to have presented this book of Defoe's in preference, as of a far more vile and debasing tendency.[8]

Here is the passage which so outraged Lamb:

> The retale tradesman in especial, but even every tradesman in his station, must furnish himself with a competent stock of patience; I mean that patience which is needful to bear with all sorts of impertinence, and the most provoking curiosity that it is possible to imagine the buyers, even the worst of them, are or can be guilty of. A tradesman behind his counter must have no flesh and blood about him, no passions, no resentment; he must never be angry, no not so much as seem to be so: if a customer tumbles him five hundred pounds worth of goods, and scarce bids money for any thing; nay, tho' they really come to his shop with no intent to buy, as many do, only to see what is to be sold, and if they cannot be better pleas'd than they are at some other shop where they intend to buy, 'tis all one, the tradesman must take it, and place it to the account of his calling, that 'tis his business to be ill used and resent nothing; and so must answer as obligingly to those that give him an hour or two's trouble and buy nothing, as he does to those who in half the time lay out ten or twenty pounds. The case is plain, 'tis his business to get money, to sell and please, and if some do give him trouble and do not buy, others make him amends, and do buy; and as for the trouble, 'tis the business of his shop.[9]

In a sense, of course, we find Defoe's text just as disturbing as Lamb did. Nevertheless, he has quite misread, and failed to appreciate, Defoe's tone. The strange quality of this passage, and of similar ones in the book, derives from the way that Defoe leaves the reader absolutely in a corner. None of the awfulness of the shopkeeper's situation is spared. He *must* act the complete hypocrite, so the argument runs (and nothing could be less hypocritical than Defoe's own attitude here); yet he is offered no emotional outlet or reward — neither to gloat over his money-making, nor to laugh at his customers behind their backs. Defoe is not in the least, as Lamb thought, attempting to seduce or make a degrading philosophy attractive. His tone is not irony, either, but something more original, for which rhetoric does not have a name. There is a self-lacerating quality in his vision here, a queer kind of excitement at the spectacle of a trap without an exit.

EXPOSURE AND SOLITUDE

Peter Earle has made the simple but true remark that 'The Defoe who wrote the novels seems to be a very different one from the Defoe one gets to know in the rest of his works.'[10] Much of the task of a Defoe critic, indeed, is to search for the true connection between these two Defoes. What one can say about them is that they share one peculiar strength, a powerful imaginative feeling for dilemmas. The supreme stroke in *Robinson Crusoe*, it might fairly be said, is the dilemma represented by the footprint in the sand: the issue being that what Crusoe wants most in all the world, human company, is what he must also fear more than anything else in the world. Defoe pushes his point home with enormous force:

> How strange a Chequer Work of Providence is the Life of Man! and by what secret differing Springs are the Affections hurry'd about as differing Circumstance present! To Day we love what to Morrow we hate; to Day we seek what to Morrow we shun; to Day we desire what to Morrow we fear; nay even tremble at the Apprehensions of; this was exemplify'd in me at this Time in the most lively Manner imaginable; for I whose only Affliction was, that I seem'd banished from human Society, that I was alone, circumscrib'd by the boundless Ocean, cut off from Mankind, and condemn'd to what I call'd silent Life; that I was as one who Heaven thought not worthy to be number'd among the Living, or to appear among the rest of his Creatures; that to have seen one of my own Species, would have seem'd to me a Raising me from Death to Life, and the greatest Blessing that Heaven it self, next to the supreme Blessing of Salvation, could bestow; *I say*, that I should now tremble at the very Apprehensions of seeing a Man,

and was ready to sink into the Ground at but the Shadow or silent
Appearance of a Man's having set his Foot in the Island.

One could hardly ask for a more perfect expression of the difficulty
of human existence and of life in society, nor one with wider
applicability to human experience, and especially to psycho-
pathology. (As has often been pointed out, the fact that it is one
footprint and not even a pair is part of what gives the experience
its great strangeness and — from Crusoe's point of view —
'wrongness'.) It seems as if there might be a clue here to Defoe's
character and outlook.

His personality certainly shows a strange tension between exposure and privacy. At one moment at least in his career he was, as
no doubt he wished to be, a leading popular hero: his poem was sung
about the streets, his name was 'Legion' and could make parliaments
tremble, and he turned public exposure in the pillory into a triumph
for himself both as man and as writer. As Mr Review, moreover, he
created an admirable public persona, and was seemingly in excellent
rapport with his readers, coaxing and bullying them with much
familiarity and good temper. On the other hand, as we are constantly
being reminded, he was a man incapable of enjoying the warmth of
human solidarity — repudiating it rather harshly, indeed, and, in his
choice of intellectual positions, seeming almost deliberately to be
flouting its claims on him. He needed to be complete within himself,
and through some hitch in his relations with his fellow-men he was
driven upon secrecy, isolation and the chilly satisfactions and
triumphs of 'banter' — even, in *Conjugal Lewdness*, towards mis-
anthropy. That he was aware of his own tendencies seems plain from
his imaginative handling of 'treaty-making' between individuals, as
if between warring nations. One recalls the striking episode in
Journal of the Plague Year in which a group escapes from plague-
striken London and, having severed all its existing social ties, in-
stitutes treaty-relationships with the town on whose outskirts it
wishes to camp. It was some such awareness, indeed, that equipped
Defoe to write the great epic of solitude. That, despite his laments at
'bowing in the House of Rimmon',[11] he may have half enjoyed his
devious role on *Mist's Journal* seems not impossible; but if so, not for
the venal reasons usually imputed to him but rather because it was
the way he lived anyway — certain of his own cleverness and ultimate rectitude, but on guard against every man, and inclined to tell
himself, with a touch of rancour, 'It's all they deserve.'

It is important to understand the enormous influence of the
episode of *The Shortest Way*, both on Defoe's own subsequent
attitude to the world and on the world's attitude to Defoe. His hoax
was so amazingly successful that those whom he had tricked, both
churchmen and Dissenters, could never forgive him, and in their
furious retaliation it is impossible to disentangle the stupidity from
the malice. The reaction of Defoe's old enemy Tutchin, the 'Whig
martyr' of the *Observator*, is typical: first he is quite taken in and
blames this 'villainous' tract, with some jeers at its bad Latin, on
some member of the 'inferior clergy'; then, having had his eyes
opened to 'the pretty sham', he resorts to sanctimonious railing at
such 'Unchristian and Irreligious' deception.[12] A pattern for the rest
of Defoe's career seems to have been set at this time. A man who
could bring off this hoax might well seem to his contemporaries (and
not just his contemporaries) as capable of anything. Saying what you
do not mean on such a scale as in *The Shortest Way* can, to the simple-
minded, appear blood-brother to writing-on-both-sides, tergiversation and double-dealing of every kind. Defoe, from the time of this
episode onwards, became a portent and a bogy, and thinking about
him tended to be superstitious or mythological, as indeed it has not
quite ceased to be.

The effect on his own attitude to the world may be expected to
have been proportionate. We form an impression of Defoe as an
extremely clever (and in a sense rather solitary) man who felt he had
good reason, intellectually speaking, to despise his adversaries — not
without a lingering incredulity that they could be so crass. Indeed it
is plain that he did despise them; for though his tone towards them
is often plaintive and self-righteous, it is just as often airily and tri-
umphantly mocking. Such a man might easily feel no compunction
about lying, not to mention working off secretive jokes on the
public.

BELIEF

There is something odd, it appears to us, in the way in which certain
scholars write about Defoe and belief, for instance beliefs about the
supernatural. They tend to represent him as a decidedly credulous
man — 'he lived in a spirit world' was the phrase used in a recent
study[13] — and they are inclined to find his works on the supernatural
'archaic' and strange. James Sutherland, indeed, is quite depressed by

them, lamenting that 'Unfortunately there seems to be no good reason for denying to Defoe the authorship of [these] works on the supernatural.'[14] By contrast Rodney Baine, in his *Daniel Defoe and the Supernatural* (1968), approaches the attribution of these works with some scepticism and has argued extremely convincingly for the ejection of *The History of the Life and Adventures of Duncan Campbell* (1720), *The Friendly Daemon, or The Generous Apparition* (1726) and *The Dumb Philosopher* (1719) from the canon;[15] but even he, so it seems to us, takes a strangely literal-minded view of what Defoe is doing in works like *The Political History of the Devil* (1726) and *A System of Magick* (1726).

The obvious objection that must arise in one's mind is, if Defoe is of quite such a credulous turn of mind, how does he come to write *The Political History of the Devil*, which takes such a rollickingly sceptical attitude towards Lucifer — expressing affected sympathy for this poor old gentleman from the lower regions, who lives such a harried life, always at the beck and call of fortune-tellers, witches and conjurors, and who, in point of evil, is left far behind by the unaided malice of mankind. The opening chapter especially of *The Political History of the Devil* strikes us, with all respect to Sutherland, as a genial and admirable piece of fooling, with something rather Dickensian about it. (Dickens was, in fact, very fond of the book.) Moreover, we have elsewhere in the book Defoe's explicit declaration of the utter absurdity of belief in the Devil in a corporeal sense or any belief that would associate him with a physical Hell:

> I must own, that to me nothing can be more ridiculous than the Notions that we entertain and fill our heads with about *Hell*, and about the *Devil's* being there tormenting of Souls, broiling them upon Gridirons, hanging them up on Hooks, carrying them upon their Backs, and the like...[16]

About Hell, indeed, Defoe's position is quite clear: it is that it is no more nor less than exclusion from Heaven.

A general truth seems to be indicated here, that with Defoe, as with many other writers, the question of *genre* has to take precedence over the question of belief, and before drawing conclusions about what a work is saying one needs to be clear what kind of work it is and what the author is 'up to' in it. In the case of *The Political History of the Devil* one will not get very far in understanding or enjoying it until one has registered the fact that it is a satire; and something similar is true of *A System of Magick*. It would be an unwise historian of ideas who extracted 'beliefs' from this latter work without considering its satirical standpoint upon the topic of belief itself. It is a cheerful enquiry into 'bubbling' and gullibility, a work kept going by a system of flirtation with the credulity of readers and postponement of final judgement on the reality of the supernatural. (The intelligent reader, however, soon spots the underlying strategy, according to which scepticism towards marvels reported by hearsay is suspended, but any marvel related at first hand turns out to be a cheat or to be explainable by natural causes.)

Defoe's satirical strategies in this area of credulity can be quite cunning and elusive, as in the early pages of *The Compleat English Gentleman*, where it takes the reader a little time to grasp the point: that an absurd theory about 'blood' in the genealogical sense (the concern of 'the numerous party of old women (whether male or female), idolaters who worship escutcheons and tropheys') is being exploded by propounding an equally preposterous theory about milk.

It is important to know what Defoe's beliefs are, but we are not likely to discover this, except in negative fashion, from studying satirical or 'bantering' works. On the other hand, in *A System of Magick* we can discern an aspect in which Defoe is seriously engaged: it is the aspect of 'credit' — from the point of view not of charlatans and their prey, but of the dilemmas about belief which seem built into all existence. Simon Schaffer has pointed out, very helpfully, the great importance to Defoe of the concept of 'credit', whether in the financial sense, as in his analyses of City finance and the 'national credit', or in the artistic one, as in the giving of credibility to fictions.[17] His point applies equally here. The truly clever stroke of the Devil, so Defoe writes, was, when deciding how to communicate with mankind, to choose the same method employed by God: dreams. By what means shall a God-inspired dream be distinguished from one inspired by the Devil? It is something that, Defoe says, 'he cannot undertake to determine'; and certainly, he concedes, it is quite possible to mistake the one for the other in good faith. Admittedly, the book claims at certain points that there is an answer to this troubling question; but this turns out to be the non-answer that we can judge retrospectively whether a dream or inspiration was of divine origin or otherwise — that is to say, by its fruits. The cunning stroke that Defoe here, satirically or at least halfsatirically, attributes to the Devil has, one feels, a serious fascination for him, as a signal example, if not a paradigm, of the unreliability of all report.

WAS DEFOE A TURNCOAT AND A WRITER-ON-BOTH-SIDES?

In the preceding part of our book we have done our best to sketch the history of the Defoe canon and its construction; and if our account has carried any conviction, and has at all persuaded readers that, by a fatal propensity, this 'canon' (from Defoe's own day on) has been swollen by dubious and impossible attributions, one inference becomes clear: here is a very good reason, even in the absence of all others, why Defoe might earn the reputation of a turncoat or a writer-on-both-sides.

It is necessary, therefore, that we look a little more closely at these charges. It will mean discussing two different accusations. For to be a turncoat and, for base motives, to change your side is evidently not the same as to support two opposing sides simultaneously, and would seem to imply a different motive or set of motives. (For instance, one of the suggestions made is that Defoe, having been forced by his employers to write what he did not believe, would relieve his conscience by secretly publishing a counterblast, in which he expressed his genuine convictions. This, if it ever happened, would evidently indicate that his convictions mattered to him.) Taken together, however, these accusations constitute a very large problem in the study of Defoe, and we shall not pretend to solve it in the present book. However, we may as well be frank about our own opinion, which is that he was most probably neither of these two things, or at least not characteristically and habitually so. We say 'most probably' because we have tried to keep an open mind on the subject. We are not, at least so we hope, hero-worshippers of Defoe, and our view is not so much a conviction as a working supposition. On this teasing topic, indeed, a conviction seems a most dangerous thing; and the unexamined conviction that Defoe was a turncoat and a writer-on-both-sides, and that it would show up a person as naive to suggest otherwise, cannot be said to have been much help to Defoe studies. Indeed, one might suggest that it has done more than anything else (more even than William Lee's unshakable conviction that Defoe was in all ways a perfect Christian gentleman) to introduce confusion.

It will be plain why we need to tackle this subject in the present book. For the supposition that Defoe wrote pamphlets on both sides of an issue, or for base motives retracted previously expressed opinions, is inevitably, in any given instance, a supposition about authorship. Hence the first question to ask, when scholars assert these things of Defoe, is the one we have been labouring in our book:

what are the reasons for believing that he wrote the works that are cited in evidence?

Let us examine a few examples. The historian P.W.J. Riley in *The Union of England and Scotland* (1978) takes a distinctly hostile attitude towards Defoe's activities on behalf of the Union. Defoe's views, he says, have acquired 'undeserved authority'; he 'probably had as little idea as anyone else of the probable effects of union' and 'possibly did not greatly care either one way or the other'; he 'directed his arguments to whatever group seemed in need of persuasion, dismissively countering any criticisms as they appeared'. As a result his inconsistencies were frequent, 'which did not seem in the least to trouble him'. All this, Riley implies, was the natural consequence of his character. 'It was not that he completely lacked scruples, but he was able to control them if there was even half a chance of profit.'[18]

Now, among the pamphlets which Riley cites as evidence of Defoe's oscillations, one (*A Letter to a Friend Giving an Account how the Treaty of Union has been Received here* (Edinburgh, 1706)) is now more or less unanimously regarded as being the work, not of Defoe, but of Sir John Clerk; and another (*A Letter from Mr. Reason, to the High and Mighty Prince the Mob* (1706)) does not appear in any Defoe bibliography and has sometimes been attributed to James Donaldson, though admittedly it is attributed to Defoe, alas without reasons, in W.R. and V.B. McLeod's *Anglo-Scottish Tracts, 1701–1714* (1979). What Riley evidently needs to tell us is why he believes Defoe wrote these pamphlets; and till he does so, his case for Defoe's 'inconsistency', not to mention his irresistible greed, seems decidedly thin.

According to the very different view of another historian, Peter Earle, Defoe 'fervently believed in the importance of the Union to both countries and his arguments for both the economic and political benefits are very convincing'. He was, moreover, according to Earle, 'surprisingly consistent for a man who wrote so much'; indeed 'he was nearly always consistent at the level of generalization of ideas'. However, after his patron Harley's rise to power in 1710 (says Earle), Defoe 'was often forced to write in a vein quite counter to his own beliefs', and he 'salved his conscience by writing anonymous articles in support of those things he really believed in, even attacking articles written by himself in the semi-official *Review* and *Mercator*'. Earle takes a breezy attitude towards Defoe and inconsistency: it was simply 'nonsense' on Defoe's part when he wrote to Harley claiming that Harley had never tried to influence him in what he wrote, even if it were nonsense of which he was 'desperate to try and persuade himself'. This does not prevent Earle from feeling 'enormous respect' for Defoe; and the drift of his account, unlike Riley's, is that Defoe had very genuine beliefs — indeed that he would go to great, and sometimes devious, lengths to voice them.[19]

How, then, does Earle go about to show that Defoe sometimes wrote against his own convictions, though compensating by also secretly writing *for* them? He does so, it strikes us, in an odd way. One of the 'anonymous articles' Defoe is supposed by Earle to have written as a counterblast to the *Review* is *The Secret History of the October Club* (1711); yet this teasing and severe banter on the high-flyers is, so far as one can see, exactly on the same lines as all Defoe's references to the October Club in the *Review*. Another of these 'anonymous articles' is *A Short Narrative of the Life and Actions of. . . Marlborough. By an Old Officer in the Army* (1711). It would certainly strike one as unexpected quixotry on Defoe's part to publish such a panegyric of Marlborough just when Harley's supporters were calling for Marlborough's impeachment; but on the other hand it would not noticeably have conflicted with anything in the *Review*, so it can hardly be construed as Defoe's 'attacking articles written by himself'. (Anyway, as we say elsewhere (pp. 119–20), it seems very unlikely that Defoe wrote this pamphlet.) The third of Earle's examples is *Considerations upon the Eighth and Ninth Articles of the Treaty of Commerce* (1713). As is well known, the proposed Treaty of Commerce, designed by the Tories to reduce tariff barriers between Britain and France, came under violent attack from the Whig opposition in the summer of 1713, as representing Britain's certain ruin as a trading nation; and Defoe's help was enlisted to help defend it in *Mercator*. Earle speaks of *Considerations upon the Eighth and Ninth Articles of the Treaty of Commerce* as being 'written for the other side', which must mean the Whigs, but it is hard to see why, for the tract is actually in favour of the Treaty — merely stipulating respectfully that much will depend upon how, in detail, its proposals are implemented.[20]

Earle has to admit that 'Defoe rightly claimed that he had been consistent in his attitude towards the liberalization of trade with France', a claim that Defoe makes much of in *Some Thoughts upon the Subject of Commerce with France* (1713), where he quotes his published views from as far back as 1704. Thus all that is really left for Earle to say in this context is that 'the Tories forced him [Defoe] to be far more liberal than he would have liked to have been' — which is perhaps true but certainly doesn't make him a turncoat.[21]

J.R. Moore, who took a rosy view of Defoe's character, waves away the imputations of duplicity against him somewhat airily, explaining them largely by the fact that Defoe's 'literal-minded readers' were not accustomed to fictional make-believe and thus reproached him with equivocation, and by asserting that, in his controversial writings, Defoe was 'almost never false to the essential truth as he saw it at that time'. When Defoe seems to be writing in opposition to 'his own honest judgement', Moore explains, 'he is writing playfully or indulging his all-too-dangerous love of irony — except when he is using casuistry for an honorable end'.[22] Considering the wildly clashing pamphlets that Moore was sometimes happy to attribute to Defoe, his explanation does not seem very adequate.

James Sutherland's biography, by contrast, is for much of the time a sustained lamentation over Defoe's mercenary 'stoopings' and tergiversations. For example he attributes the trait of 'moderation' to Defoe, in terms which sound rather praiseworthy, only to redesignate it in the very same paragraph as mercenary trimming, on the grounds that there is no smoke without fire and if everyone accuses a man of time-serving, the accusation must be true. No doubt, says Sutherland, there was a good deal of truth in Defoe's claim that he cared about issues rather than men and that, during the political crisis of 1710, he was not one of those Whigs who 'had rather sink the ship than not have their own pilots steer'; still, we must be realists, and 'one can hardly help suspecting that Defoe's mind was not so much on the Ship of State as on the little boat upon which his own private fortunes were embarked'. It is striking that, after all this, the only failing of substance that Sutherland can pin on Defoe is that, though he was a declared peace-maker, he did not rebuke the Allies and the Government in 1710, when they were throwing away a promising chance of peace. 'If Defoe had really been the independent critic, the man of consistent principles, that he claimed to be, he would surely have spoken out .'[23] Now there may be much force in this criticism, but what it impugns, clearly, is Defoe's courage, not his consistency.

That Defoe was venal and had a propensity to write on both sides is, again, a favourite theme with Maximillian Novak in his *Economics and the Fiction of Daniel Defoe* (1962). 'It is not enough to say that Defoe held certain ideas,' he writes in the preface, 'since more often than not it would be possible to show a pamphlet in which Defoe said exactly the opposite.' Or again, in a later preface to a reprint of the same book, he writes:

On numerous occasions Defoe told lies or half-truths, and there is
no means of explaining away his frequent accommodations with
differing political interests, parties, and patrons. Nor is there any
way of straightening out the canon of his writings on the grounds
that he would not defend Jacobitism or present a favourable picture of natural religion of deism. If it seemed fitting or effective to
have natives worshipping nature or the sun, so be it![24]

Presumably Novak's allusion to deism and 'natives worshipping
nature or the sun' refers to *Robert Drury's Journal*; and here we are at
once brought sharply up against the attribution problem. For we
cannot but think that Rodney Baine is right in the article quoted
earlier when he writes that 'Among the spurious items in the Defoe
canon, one of those most unjustifiably placed and retained there is
Madagascar: or, Robert Drury's Journal.' Baine's demolition of the
case for Defoe's authorship of the work seems to us more or less
unanswerable; and of course one of the features he fastens on is
precisely the overt deism of the 'Transcriber' of Drury's *Journal*.
  Defoe's allegiances, according to Novak, were to 'the middle
class', to trade (rather than to land), to the Whig cause, and to the
Dissenters, of whom he 'made himself the champion. . .throughout
his life'. 'Yet at times', says Novak, 'Defoe was willing to betray all
these causes.' As a Nonconformist, 'he must have hated to betray the
dissenters', but in a letter to Harley he suggested 'methods to bring
about the gradual extinction of all religious dissent in England'.[25]
  The important, and it would seem to us misleading, phrase here is
'at times'. In a letter to Harley of 1704, with its advice on 'Methods
of Mannagement of the Dissenters', Defoe writes from a position in
regard to the Dissenters from which, so far as we can see, he never
wavered: that it was intolerable that Dissenters should be persecuted
for their beliefs; that Occasional Conformity would do neither their
souls not their cause any good; that it would be better for all
concerned if the Dissenters kept out of politics; and that it was
probably only through persecution that his chronically factious
fellow-religionists had ever achieved unity — with the implication
that they might well eventually lose their zest for separation from the
Church.[26] It is a harsh attitude, as well as a complex one, and Defoe
was in some respects a harsh man; but it would be wrong to describe
it as a 'betrayal' and equally, or even more, wrong to suggest that he
adopted it only 'at times'.[27]
  Another, and indeed the most extended, of Novak's chosen
examples of Defoe's tergiversation and of his writing-on-both-sides

concerns his attitude towards free trade. He dismisses Defoe's claim
that he had been an advocate of trade with France long before the
Commercial Treaty of 1713 was thought of and depicts him as only
coming round to free trade with France after 1711, when he was
'once more in the pay of a Tory government', and then so half-
heartedly that, as well as defending the Commercial Treaty in
Mercator, he wrote several anonymous tracts *against* the Treaty.[28]
Now there are several objections to this. For one thing (as Defoe
himself reminds the reader truly and with much unction in *Some
Thoughts Upon the Subject of Commerce with France* (1713)), Mr
Review made a vehement plea for the opening of trade with France
as far back as December 1704:[29]

> Six Year and Nine Year ago, and when the Ministry who then
> Govern'd Affairs had Lock'd and Bar'd all the Doors of Trade
> against *France*, — I ventur'd to tell them in so many Words, That *if
> they had been in their Trading Sences, they would have Traded with
> France all the while they Fought with* France.[30]

Then, among the anonymous pamphlets which Defoe is supposed
to have written against the Treaty, Novak cites *Considerations upon
the Eighth and Ninth Articles of the Treaty of Commerce, and Navigation*
(1713). But, whether or not this is in fact by Defoe,[31] it is not in fact
an attack on the Treaty but rather, as we mentioned above (p. 153), a
temperate defence of it, arguing that, though the Treaty would
undoubtedly greatly injure the Portuguese trade and might also be
thought to endanger Britain's own silk manufacture, these disadvantages could be outweighed by the enormous boost it would
give to England's woollen manufacture — and anyway the Treaty
will allow Britain to protect its silk manufacture after all, for there is
nothing in it to forbid Britain making a *general* increase of protective
duties against silken goods, from whatever country.[32] Thus what the
pamphlet is 'humbly recommending' to the Government on behalf
of the poor silk weavers and their families is not any abandonment of
the Treaty but merely its implementation in the way best for the
weavers' interests.

We should make it plain that we are not here defending any
particular view about Defoe and free trade. All we want to point out
is that Novak has not really made his case, neither as to Defoe's
supposed tergiversation over the issue, nor as regards his writing-
upon-both-sides upon it.

There remains what seems to us the most telling accusation of apostasy against Defoe; also in a way the most potentially damaging one: the charge, made in his own time and renewed by later scholars, that he was the author of two pamphlet attacks on John Toland, *An Argument Proving that the Design of Employing and Ennobling Foreigners, is a treasonable Conspiracy against the Constitution* (1717) and *A Farther Argument against ennobling Foreigners* (1717), which trumpeted the very chauvinistic attitudes that he had ridiculed so savagely in *The True-Born Englishman*.

It would take a long chapter or article to explore all the intricacies of this important episode, but the story runs briefly thus. On 21 January 1717 Toland published, anonymously, a treatise entitled *The State-Anatomy of Great Britain*, framed as a letter to an imaginary foreign diplomat and giving 'A Particular account of its [Britain's] several Interests and Parties. . .and what each of them. . .may hope or fear from the reign and family of King George.' It was evidently designed to catch the eye of the King, who had returned to the country two days earlier, after a six months' absence in Hanover; and it contained some startling proposals, among them that non-jurors should be banished the country; that the King's Hanoverian ministers, the Baron Bernstorff and the Baron Bothmar, should, in violation of the Act of Settlement of 1701, be given English peerages; and that the King should be encouraged in a pugnacious war-policy and in keeping a sizeable peacetime army, to include a 'nursery of experienc'd Officers' in the pay of other countries.[33]

Toland's *State-Anatomy* was answered early in February by a hundred-page pamphlet entitled *An Argument Proving that the Design of Employing and Ennobling Foreigners, is a Treasonable Conspiracy against the Constitution*, in which the 'Arguer' expressed amazement at the 'arrogance' of the author of the *State-Anatomy* in 'dictating to the House of Lords' and plotting to 'prostitute the illustrious Blood of our Nobility' (as if unaware of the 'reproaches' already earned by England's ancient nobility, 'by their being so unhappily mix'd with spurious and Foreign Blood'[34]) and spoke with horror of the insidious design of introducing a standing army in peacetime, 'a thing. . .justly esteemed in all Countries, the first step to the enslaving a free People'. The whole affair, he asserted, must be the conspiracy of a 'wicked Party of Men' who, fearing public exposure by 'some honest and loyal Patriots, who yet remain in the Administration', had made use of Toland to test the temperature of the nation.[35] (This was evidently a hit at the faction of Sunderland, Stan-

hope and the King's German ministers, who had been the victors in
the recent dramatic split in the Whig party.)

The *Argument* prompted Defoe's bitter adversary Abel Boyer, in
his monthly journal, the *Political State*, to accuse Defoe of its
authorship, gleefully pointing out the gross inconsistency between
the 'Arguer's' sentiments about 'blood' and race and those in *The
True-Born Englishman* and also between his wholesale condemnation
of standing armies and the temperate defence of them that Defoe had
made nineteen years earlier in *An Argument Shewing that a Standing
Army with Consent of Parliament, is not Inconsistent with Free
Government*.[36] Meanwhile the rival monthly *Mercurius Politicus*, in
which Defoe is known to have had a hand, printed a scare-story
about the *State-Anatomy*, 'by one Toland *a Socinian*', and praised the
Argument as 'a smart Pamphlet'.[37] Upon this, Toland produced a
second part to his *State-Anatomy*, in which he quoted and
embroidered upon Boyer's attack on Defoe; and the 'Arguer' came
back with *A Farther Argument Against Ennobling Foreigners*. This bore
on its title-page the epigraph

> T--l--nd Blasphemes the Holy-Ghost,
> The Bribed of Bribes Accuses;
> Of Foreign Rogues the Traytor Boasts,
> The King, who was your *Lord of Hosts*,
> The Ra--l *How* abuses.

This was an updated version of a stanza from 'A Letter to a Member
of Parliament' (otherwise 'Ye True-Born Englishmen proceed'),
first published in 1713 and generally attributed to Defoe.[38] However,
the pamphlet itself condemned Boyer's attribution of the *Argument*
to Defoe as a malicious fabrication, Defoe being no more the author
of the pamphlet 'than the Man in the Moon' — and indeed, so the
Arguer had heard say, having been 'sick in bed all the while'. Confirmation of this might have been forthcoming from 'Mr Baker the
publisher', the Arguer added mysteriously, were the latter not 'just
at the point of Death while the pamphlet was at the press'.[39]

Did Defoe write the two pamphlets against Toland? We must
honestly say that, on the evidence, it is impossible to rule it out.
Some parts of the case for it seem very strong; though on the other
hand the supposition entails some extraordinary difficulties. What
seems worth saying, at the outset, is that it seems likely that it was
Boyer who put it into Toland's head that the author of the *Argument*
was Defoe. This was not the first time, nor the last, that Boyer

would saddle Defoe with anonymous works, and by no means all of his ascriptions have stuck.

What calls for note about Toland's treatise, further, is its deliberate unrealism, praising as it does the King's 'penetrating genius' and profound grasp of financial affairs, depicting the Prince of Wales as a most 'dutiful' son (it was common knowledge that he and his father were at each other's throat) and extolling the calm stability of the present adminstration. It seems consistent with this unrealism that neither Boyer nor Toland guessed at Defoe's real situation at this time, namely, that he was actually reconciled with the Whigs and indeed in their employment, though by agreement allowing it to appear that he was still estranged from them.[40] Thus when attributing the *Argument* to Defoe, the only explanation they can come up with is the rather nonsensical one that he was writing at the dictation of Harley and in the Jacobite interest.

Admittedly, it seems probable that, unknown to his employers, Defoe was still conducting a covert campaign to help Harley in his present trouble, but we need impute no political motive to this; and, politically speaking, what we would have expected from Defoe, given what we know of his then-current employment, is what in fact we find in *Mercurius Politicus* — a neutral stance and a cautious refusal to take sides over the Whig split.[41]

By contrast, the Arguer has openly thrown in his lot with the defeated Walpole/Townshend faction, referring to them as the few remaining 'loyal Patriots'. Indeed he goes so far as to risk a very rude and seditious gibe at the monarch, asking whether, if today we give peerages to two Germans, 'At length our Posterity may be offered two Turks' — a hit at King George's two Turkish pages, who were reputed to earn a fortune by their backstairs influence.[42] It is not easy to see why Defoe, who according to his own account, passed into the service of Sunderland upon Townshend's dismissal,[43] should have made such a reckless attack on his new masters.

As for the poetic epigraph to *A Farther Argument*, some cite it as an argument for Defoe's authorship, but it might actually be thought to provide a mild argument against it. For, seeing that *A Farther Argument* is concerned mainly with scotching the idea of Defoe's authorship of the *Argument*, it would seem oddly self-defeating to preface it with a poem associated with his name. Then, certain of the Arguer's comments in *A Farther Argument* are so brutally cavalier towards Defoe's reputation that it is hardly comprehensible that he could have written them himself. For instance: '. . .if it were true that the said *D. F.* had been the Author of all those things, and those [*sic*] too, it had amounted to no more than this: either that he had been wrong before, and was now better inform'd; or second, that he had contradicted himself, and wrote one time one thing and one time another'.[44] As an excuse, this is nearly as damaging as the crime.

As for the arguments on the other side and suggesting that Defoe was indeed the Arguer, they are undeniably strong — among them the fact that Defoe was an old enemy of Toland's and attacked him on several other occasions with great malignity and in a rather similar tone. But above all else, what no one can fail to feel is how extraordinarily unconvincing is the story of his having been 'sick in bed all the while' and of the secret that Mr Baker could have told had he not been dying.

Being influenced by the fact that so many of the other well-known charges of tergiversation against Defoe seem to dissolve under scrutiny, our own opinion, a tentative and provisional one, is that, though Defoe may have written or inspired the *Mercurius Politicus* item, he did not write *An Argument* or *A Farther Argument*. Let us suppose, though, that one were to come to the opposite conclusion and accept that Defoe had, in this instance, rather shamefully betrayed a principle. What it is essential to remember is that even this would be no kind of warrant for assuming that he betrayed his principles right and left, or had none to betray. A 'blanket' assumption of this kind is really no more than a self-indulgence on the part of a bibliographer and no kind of help in arriving at reasoned judgements.

'KNOWING YOUR AUTHOR'

WHAT WE HAVE been doing in the last three chapters is to expose our own claims to 'knowing' Defoe. Why this should have a place in a book on the bibliography of Defoe should be clear, for it is the obvious duty of a Defoe bibliographer always to be trying, with whatever success, to sharpen his or her sense of Defoe's personality and talents. The reason why this is a duty, however, may need a little examination. It is not, or not primarily, we would suggest, to encourage the bibliographer to say: 'There is something peculiarly Defoe-like about this work.' For even a very intense feeling of this kind would not in itself be sufficient grounds for attributing the work to Defoe. (Though, on the other hand, it might add very considerable weight to any argument about attribution based on external evidence.) It is rather that, as we have said earlier, it will equip the bibliographer to say: 'Though Defoe, like other writers, may sometimes write badly, we have here a *kind* of badness that it would be foolish to attribute to him.' Or again that, 'Though Defoe may as a man have had numerous faults, we are confronted here with a *kind* of human shortcoming which it would be unnatural to associate with him.' If subjective judgement is going to be admitted into attribution, this seems to be the healthiest form it can take. We shall venture to give three examples, to make the point plain. They concern the pamphlets *A Vindication of the Press* (1718), *A Letter to the Author of the Flying-Post* (1718) and *An Historical Account of the Voyages and Adventures of Sir Walter Raleigh* (1719), and they turn on the unlikelihood of Defoe figuring as, respectively, an utterer of platitudes, an imbecile and a brazen financial crook.

We consider it extremely unlikely that Defoe wrote *A Vindication of the Press*, a tract (accepted as canonical since W.P. Trent) which presents its author as a 'young Author', as a loyal adherent of the

161

Established Church and despiser of Quaker conventicles, and as a devotee of the contemporary theatre — all things which Defoe plainly was not. Now, if there were any solid evidence suggesting that he wrote the pamphlet, one would have to search for some explanation of the authorial disguise, though this would be hard to find (and it really will not do just to fall back upon his supposed 'Protean' character). However, so far as we know, no such evidence exists, and the tract got into the canon merely because W.P. Trent was shown a copy, the eighteenth-century owner of which had written Defoe's name in it, and decided, on stylistic grounds and because of a reference in it to *The True-Born Englishman*, that the attribution must be correct. But why we cite it as an example is because, apart from its factual incongruities, the tract is from beginning to end a tissue of empty commonplaces, though the subject is one on which we know Defoe to have held strong and original opinions. This we believe to be, in its own right, an argument of some weight against the ascription. (We have argued the case at some length elsewhere so will add no more here.[1])

Our second example shall be *A Letter to the Author of the Flying-Post*, first attributed to Defoe by J.R. Moore. The position here is rather different, for there is circumstantial evidence which at first sight makes Moore's ascription seem very reasonable. The pamphlet is a diatribe against George Ridpath for publishing two anti-Jacobite items in his Whiggish *Flying-Post*, one of them reporting how some Edinburgh Jacobites had been struck by lightning while 'drinking confusion to King George', and the other, in the form of a letter to the Bailiff of Brecon addressed from the Grecian coffee-house, relating an attack by a Jacobite mob on the house of a Presbyterian minister in Brecon. The *Letter* follows on from two letters on similar lines recently published in *Mist's Journal* and like them was a blow in the long-standing war between this journal and the *Flying-Post*.[2] Now Defoe is known to have had an association with *Mist's Journal* at this time and also to have been a bitter personal enemy of Ridpath's. This prompted Moore to regard the pamphlet as a hoax by Defoe, or, as he puts it, 'A bantering quasi-Tory tract in which Defoe ridicules George Ridpath and defends Mist's *Weekly-Journal*'.[3] The theory sounds most plausible — until one reads the tract.

A Defoe scholar once remarked that anybody who could attribute this pamphlet to Defoe must be out of his mind, and one can see why. For the most obvious fact about the pamphlet is that, as a piece of writing, it is quite imbecile, a horrible mixture of ludicrously elephantine witticisms and mere crapulous abuse. Let us try in a few lines to convey the flavour of this pamphlet. Here is the author's idea of a witty score:

> I must have a touch at your Stile and Sense passed by before. How can you say Mr *Mist daily affirms, or daily contradicts*, when his Paper comes out but *once a Week*? Is this the consistent Gentleman that reproves almost every one that he meddles with of Inconsistency, and yet talks at this inconsistent Rate himself?

The joke strikes him as so rich that he pursues it for another half-page:

> But perhaps you'll say by *daily* affirming, and *daily* contradicting, you mean that he does so in his *daily* Conversation as well as in his *weekly* Paper. Then this shows that either you are very Conversant, or that you keep Company with those that are Conversant with one whom you call an Enemy to the Government. And if that be a fair Practice, I leave to all the World to Judge. In short, take it in what Sense you please, you're in the Mire...[4]

Later he falls upon a phrase in the letter from the Grecian coffee-house, where the letter-writers say to the Bailiff of Brecon: 'We presume upon your unparallel'd Goodness, Sir, for a Pardon for this Digression.' It provokes him to this sarcastic sally:

> O that's Witty and Fine. I warrant you thought he would be wonderfully pleas'd with it! I dare say, if ever he read it, he laugh'd heartily at it, as I protest I do at the Instant of Writing this; for 'tis really the *sorriest* I ever read in my Life. ... There's a *Blunder* in your Complement which exalts it wonderfully! I say, a *horrid Blunder*, and perhaps something worse. What do you mean by calling *the Bailiff of* Brecon's *Goodness* (with all due Respect to that Gentleman) or indeed that of any *Subject, Unparalled'd*? This is in plain *English* to make it exceed the *King's Goodness*. See whether your silly Complement is like to run! high indeed! I hope you did not design this for a *High-church Complement*! have a care of that.[5]

The right word for this, indeed the only word, is 'abysmal'.

The first and shorter portion of the pamphlet, which deals with the report of God's vengeance on the Jacobites, has at least one recognisable polemical point to make, though it could hardly be called a telling point; indeed, it is desperately feeble. It is that the account in the *Flying-Post* was illogical in reporting the Jacobites as 'endeavouring to distinguish themselves' (by celebrating the Pretender's birthday) and yet as retiring to a 'Hedge-Tavern' to do so.

> To say that a Set of Men went about to distinguish themselves, and yet retired out of the Way; to me seems to be such a Blunder, that had another said so, you'd have told him smartly in your way, that, *such a Man is advised to learn more Consistency*...[6]

The second portion, commenting on the letter from the Grecian coffee-house, by contrast, offers nothing resembling an argument at all and consists of abuse — flailing, repetitive and dull-witted to a degree.

Now, on the hypothesis that this pamphlet is by Defoe, the possible ways in which one might interpret it would seem to be three. Perhaps the extreme Jacobitism represents Defoe's sincere sentiments; but this seems an absurd supposition. Or perhaps it was a 'banter' intended to be recognised as such, a satirical take-off of a Jacobite intended to bring Jacobitism and high-flying into ridicule. But in that case, it would have been on Ridpath's side, and presumably he would have had to welcome it. Or perhaps, lastly, it was an impersonation intended to deceive readers and to damage Ridpath (these being its sole purposes) by the sheer naked force of its arguments and eloquence; and this, to anyone who knows Defoe's skill as a polemicist, seems if anything the wildest suggestion of all.

For our final example we shall take *An Historical Account of the Voyages and Adventures of Sir Walter Raleigh* (1720). This is a Crossley attribution, and one to which he attached considerable importance. It was indeed an influential ascription, for it was the one that most helped convert W.P. Trent to a faith in Crossley's sagacity. In his *Nation* notes he wrote that it was 'the most important item in Crossley's list'.

> When I began to read it, I could not but believe that the great collector had been egregiously deceived, since the author of the pamphlet claimed, with reference to his hero, to 'have the Honour to be related to his Blood'. But as I read on, however, the style seemed more and more to bear out the ascription, and on the last page I found a statement which tallied so completely with one made by Defoe in a letter to Harley that all my doubts vanished. Later, in other writings of Defoe, I discovered accidentally additional and strong confirmation of the ascription, and I am clear that a better case can be made out for its genuineness than can be

made out for at least three-fourths of the pamphlets and books that are unhesitatingly accepted as Defoe's.[7]

As a result of this strong advocacy of Trent's, the pamphlet seems to have had a warm welcome from later Defoe scholars.

The tract is in two parts. The first claims to be a 'history' of Sir Walter Raleigh, written by one who has 'the Honour to be related to his Blood' and can report family traditions about him. It is offered as a corrective to the inadequate Life of him by Lewis Theobald,[8] but also, as its lengthy title-page indicates, as an account of how the country of Guiana in the Orinoco valley 'might now be with Ease, Possess'd, Planted and Secured to the British Nation'. As a history it is exceedingly sketchy, and its main drift soon appears, which is to assert what a noble inspiration it was on Raleigh's part to contemplate the annexation of Guiana, 'the Richest, most Populous, and most Fertile Country in the World...a Country richer in Gold and Silver than *Mexico* and *Peru*; full of Inhabitants like Great-Britain it self; among whom an infinite Consumption of our Woollen Manu-factures might have been expected'. On Raleigh's own admission, he never succeeded in seeing the interior of Guiana, but 'He had very good Intelligence of the Place and of the People', and he thought it very likely that there was a flourishing Inca civilisation there, and that 'the *M. Ingga* [*sic*] hath built and erected as magnificent Pallaces in *Guiana*, as his Ancestors did at *Peru*'.[9]

What Raleigh had been prevented from achieving, by the treachery of the Spaniards and the weakness of James I, should now, says the pamphleteer, be undertaken by the South Sea Company; and the annexation of this country, with its 'Infinite quantity of gold', would prove the perfect solution to Britain's economic needs and problems. Britain would supply the woollens, and Guiana would provide the gold. On the other hand, if the South Sea Company is not interested, 'another Set of Men...will be found ready to form a Subscription of a Million Sterling for such an Undertaking'. Nothing at all is said about how such an ambitious conquest of this, the 'most Populous, and most fertile Country in the World' should be achieved, except that the inhabitants of this unknown country are 'a Sociable People, fitted in any way to be improved and instructed, and willing to receive a People that would use them kindly'.[10] The author, however, offers to lay before the Company 'a Plan or Chart of the Rivers and Shores, the Depths of Water, and all necessary Instructions for the Navigation, with a Scheme of the Undertaking, which he had the Honour about thirty Years ago, to lay before King *William*, and to demonstrate how easy it would be to bring the Attempt to Perfection'.[11]

It does not take much shrewdness to spot what we have here: it is a fraudulent company prospectus, of the kind that circulated in their hundreds during this year of the South Sea Bubble. Lord Erleigh's description in *The South Sea Bubble* (1933) fits it like a glove:

> The exact prescription employed by South Sea projectors had varied from day to day and from place to place, but its general ingredients had included all the stories current in 1711 of the riches of the South Seas with new and circumstantial embroideries, fantastic forecasts of the wealth of the silver mines of Potosi-la-Paz and fabulous prophecies of the golden harvest to be gathered from the mines of Mexico. 'The exploits of Drake were quoted and the dreams of Raleigh renewed'. To carry conviction to the minds of the cautious and sceptical, maps, plans, and pamphlets were specially prepared to illustrate the marvels of the El Dorado of the South.[12]

Against the suggestion that Defoe was the author of such a prospectus, there is an obvious argument. It is that, throughout his career, he was continually advocating a quite different South American project of his own, the colonisation of the more or less uninhabited lands in southern Chile ('Valdivia') at the other end of the continent. In a lengthy letter to Harley (23 July 1711) (which is presumably the one Trent was thinking of), he elaborates it in much plausible and practical detail, considering it from the agricultural, the meteorological and the political point of view. The second volume of his *A New Voyage Round the World*, published in 1724, is once more all about the scheme; *A General History of Discoveries and Improvements* (1725) devotes the best part of a chapter to it; and *A Plan of the English Commerce* (1728) makes mystifying reference to it.[13] This was *his* South American project, and he loved it too dearly, one feels, to have wished to float a rival one; or at least, not such a perfectly ludicrous and phantasmal one, resembling something out of Jonson's *Alchemist* Anyway — a clinching point — in striking contrast to the blithe tone of the *Historical Account*, Defoe, in *A General History of Discoveries and Improvements*, specifically remarks that any project of permanent conquest of Guiana is notoriously doomed to failure.[14]

What perhaps prompted Crossley to ascribe this tract to Defoe was the remark about laying the scheme before King William, which certainly has echoes for readers of Defoe; but if so, it was flimsy evidence indeed, and, if nothing else, reflection on Defoe's known record as a practical-minded 'projector' ought to be a strong inducement to us to reject this attribution.

* * *

Thus, the negative value of 'knowing one's author' can, in our view, be a considerable one for a bibliographer. Can it have any 'positive' value? Is it, or should one allow it to be, a guide to making attributions to Defoe? In the absence of a prior probability that a given work could be by a certain author, are mere 'compatibilities', however compelling, of any positive evidential value whatever? We have, up to now, argued that they are not; and the example of William Lee, with his sublime confidence in his own powers of Defoe-recognition, is not exactly reassuring.

However, it will be wise not to be too dogmatic here, for one's answer may differ according to whether it is a single work one is concerned with or a group of works. It is our impression that the mere fact that a single work strikes one, even strongly, as Defoe-like, is a quite insufficient reason for attributing it to him. Instinct tells us that *Memoirs of a Cavalier* is a work of fiction by Defoe, and an admirable product of his fictional talent; but if external evidence were to turn up, showing that it was by another writer, we should shrug our shoulders and tell ourselves that instinct is not always to be trusted. As we have said earlier, it is not a matter of the first importance that a work should be fatherless.

The situation may, however, be a little different when one comes to a *group* of works, and for a very good reason. To add *Memoirs of a Cavalier* to the Defoe canon, or for that matter to take it away, will not change our picture of Defoe as author in any essential way; but to add a whole group of works to Defoe, or take such a group away, may well do so. We have in mind a particular group of works, or at any rate a number of works which it is attractive to regard as a group, belonging to the early years of the reign of George I and which may be labelled 'Secret Histories': in particular the three parts of the *Secret History of the White Staff* (1714–15), *The Secret History of the Secret History of the White Staff* (1715), *A True Account of the Proceedings at Perth* (1716), *Secret Memoirs of a Treasonable Conference at Somerset House* (1717) and *Minutes of the Negotiations of Monsr. Menager* (1717). They are all attributed to Defoe in J.R. Moore's *Checklist*, and the first, second and last of them were widely ascribed to him at the time, especially by his enemies, despite his own vehement disclaimers.[15] Obviously, it would matter considerably if we decided that Defoe did not write any of these curious and striking works, and we should be left with a somewhat different 'Defoe'. Equally, of course, it will matter greatly if we accept that he wrote all of them. For the author it would posit would be a formidably bizarre man, up to some very devious tricks — ready, for instance, to debunk his own *Secret History of the White Staff* in a *Secret History of the Secret History of the White Staff* and indeed, as it would appear, deliberately to cast doubt on the reliability of all 'report'.

It is at such a point that the paths of the biographer and the bibliographer divide. For the matter is of such significance to a biographer that he or she will have to take a decision on it, on such calculation of probabilities as seems possible; whereas the bibliographer is under no such obligation. These 'Secret Histories' constitute a particularly intricate bibliographical knot, which certainly cannot be satisfactorily untied by intuitive methods alone or without much laborious ratiocination, and perhaps not even then; and if a bibliographer decides to leave them out of a list of Defoe attributions this will not mean a decision to deny Defoe's authorship, but merely a verdict of 'not proven'.

Nevertheless, in a case such as this, where such fundamental issues about Defoe as a writer are at stake, even bibliographers are likely to be influenced by their sense of 'knowing their author'. (It would hardly be human to ignore it.) It is, at least, true in our own case, and we shall risk a modest suggestion on 'plausible attribution' lines. This is that, on the assumption that these particular 'Secret Histories' are by Defoe (but only on that assumption) they contain one or two jokes of an extremely brilliant, though somewhat private, kind that, according to our view of him, would be entirely in character.

The Secret History of the White Staff cannot but strike one as, in itself, an outstandingly clever performance, in the way that, without apparently white-washing Harley, it manages to throw all the serious blame for the crimes of his ministry upon colleagues or associates like Bolingbroke, Harcourt and Atterbury. One thinks, for instance, of the brilliant 'stroke' by which, so we are told in Part II of the *White Staff*, Harley outmanoeuvered the leading Scottish Jacobites — by having them sent up as representative peers to the Union Parliament, where practically the first thing they had to do was to swear solemn allegiance to the Queen and the Hanoverian succession![16] This is as plausible as (probably) it is fictitious, and the brilliance is most likely to lie, not with Harley, but with whoever is writing the pamphlet.

But what shall we say of *The Secret History of the Secret History of the White Staff*, in which the first two parts of the *White Staff* pamphlets are discredited and the whole affair of these pamphlets, together with the counterblasts to them, such as *The History of the Mitre and the Purse*, are represented as a mere commercial stunt, cooked up by a clique of rascally booksellers, with the aid of Grub-street hirelings ready to write on both sides? The first thing to notice, of course, is that this pamphlet too, in its own way, is protective of Harley's reputation. The honest, truth-seeking Quaker who figures in it does not like Harley's ways and is ready to believe that he is an 'evil man'; but he has to bear witness, as the result of his diligent enquiries, that certain specific charges brought against Harley are probably unfounded. Even more important is the whole cunning strategy of the pamphlet, with its relays of witnesses: the author himself, who begins by crediting the gossip which saddles responsibility for the *White Staff* pamphlets on Harley and Defoe; the earnest Quaker, who regards it as his duty to seek out the truth; and the Quaker's friend, who actually interviews Defoe on his sickbed and receives his 'dying' declaration that he did no more than 'revise two or three sheets' of the *White Staff* pamphlets and knew them to be a booksellers' hoax.[18] The effect, as we have said, is to cast doubt on the reliability of all witness and to hint to the reader: 'Be careful how you trust this very pamphlet you are now reading.' If Defoe wrote this pamphlet and the *White Staff* ones as well, one is both amazed at his reckless ingenuity and attracted by the sublety of the private joke.

Very similar feelings arise in one's mind on reading *Minutes of the Negotiations of Monsr. Mesnager* (1717). These supposititious private memoirs of the French representative in the peace-negotiations of 1711–13 demonstrate once again the rich resources of the 'Secret History' *genre*. The work, published a week before Harley's trial, is, like the *White Staff* pamphlets, an oblique and most cunning defence of him. Mesnager is represented in them as a brilliantly successful secret agent, who finds that, with the aid of Grub-street hacks, he has in general very little difficulty in manipulating British opinion in the French interest, but is inexplicably frustrated at certain points by Harley's indolence. The reader is, of course, tacitly stimulated by this to a whole series of reflections, such as: how well the French do things (Britons could afford to learn from them); how fearfully credulous the general run of Britons are and how many of the pamphlets they so dearly love to read may in fact be enemy propaganda; what a good thing it is that the Peace was in our interest as well as France's; and shall we take Harley's 'indolence' at its face value, or could it have a more praiseworthy explanation?

Perhaps the nicest stroke of all in this subtle production, however, is the passage relating how, when the first of Mesnager's Grub-street employees — a most admirable turner-out of sophistical pamphlets, with 'Words enough, as well qualified to prove non-Entries [non-entities?] to contain Substance, and Substance to be entirely Spiritous, as any I have ever met with'[19] — unfortunately dies on him, Mesnager 'attempted once or twice to furnish my self with another, but could never get one like him, except a certain Person, whom the *Swedish* Resident, Monsieur *Lyencroon*, recommended, and who wrote an excellent Tract in our Interest, entituled, *Reasons why this Nation* [meaning England] *ought to put an End to this expensive War.'* Impressed by this tract, Mesnager sends the author one hundred pistoles through Lyencroon,[20] but 'I missed my Aim in the Person, though perhaps the Money was not wholly lost; for I afterwards understood that the Man was in the Service of the State, and that he had let the Queen know of the hundred Pistols he had received.'[21]

Now, *Reasons Why This Nation Ought to Put a Speedy End to this Expensive War* (1711) is a tract very plausibly attributed to Defoe. Thus, if both it and the *Minutes* are indeed by him, Defoe can be seen to be making a wonderfully entertaining (but almost impenetrably private) joke. That he should be recommended to Mesnager by, of all people his arch-enemy 'Lyencroon', who, in 1707, nearly got him into very serious trouble over his outspoken criticisms of Charles XII; and that his pamphlet *Reasons Why This Nation* should be praised by Lyencroon as 'an excellent Tract in our [i.e. *the French*] interest', are, on this hypothesis, as complicated a piece of teasing of the reader as one could wish for. Our own feeling is that Defoe was a man very capable of such strange private joking, and we confess to a hope that we may credit him with such a dazzling example as this would represent.

CHAPTER 14

TOWARDS A NEW
DEFOE BIBLIOGRAPHY

As WILL HAVE become plain, the doubt with which this book opens has, for us, grown fairly insistent. We feel there is a compelling case for saying that the existing Defoe canon, as manifested in J.R. Moore's *Checklist,* is seriously unsatisfactory and misleading and that there would be something to be said, if the proposal is not too utopian, for trying to make an altogether fresh start. Probably we shall not have persuaded all our readers of this, but in case we have persuaded any, we feel it is up to us to suggest, in a very summary and sketchy manner, how we picture the form that a new bibliography might take.

The starting point, from which the construction of any new bibliography must begin, is the recognition that Defoe's is a very special case. The problem is in part simply one of scale. With the vast majority of authors, the question of attribution does not loom large for the bibliographer. A list of known and accepted writings can be assembled relatively easily, and if there is a handful of dubious attributions these can usually be dealt with separately, in an appendix. Such doubtful works may attract a good deal of scholarly discussion as to their authenticity, but whether or not they are accepted into the writer's canon is a *relatively* insignificant matter, in the sense that their inclusion or exclusion will not radically alter our sense of that writer's achievement. In the case of Defoe, however, the proportion between his known writings and more or less speculative attributions is, and always will be, quite different. For each work which we can be confident that Defoe wrote, there exist two or three more which have been ascribed to him purely on the say-so of some bibliographer and his successors. This means that a bibliography of Defoe, rightly conceived, will need to take a rather unusual form. It will be quite impossible to relegate the speculative

171

items to some sort of appendix; and equally obviously, as we hope by now the reader will agree, the policy adopted by most previous Defoe bibliographers, which was simply to amalgamate the two categories in one seemingly authoritative and comprehensive list, will not do.

Logic therefore suggests that a new Defoe bibliography should be clearly divided as between secure and merely plausible attributions, so that users are always aware of the *status* of any given work. But also, and even more importantly, it suggests that in the case of the 'merely plausible' attributions, the reasoning behind each should be set out. We would suggest some such division as the following:

> Part A—Works By Defoe
> Part B—Works Probably By Defoe
> Appendix—A Select List of Other Attributions

The numbering sequence would begin afresh in each of the two main parts, and would include the alphabetical letter, so that references by scholarly users to items in the bibliography would always reveal which part they appear in.

The crucial question is, of course, how a prospective biblio-grapher, or team of bibliographers (as we ourselves think would be preferable), would decide on the criteria by which a work would be admitted into Parts A and B. (The reader will remember our previous discussion (pp. 14–15) of the three 'rules' which earlier Defoe bibliographers ought, in our opinion, to have followed.) We ourselves should be inclined to take a rather hard line on this matter of criteria, and to say that, for a work to be admitted to Part A, there would have to be some piece of *external* evidence, however slender, linking that work to Defoe. In proposing this as an absolute criterion, as the reader of our book will be aware, we are not intending to devalue the importance of internal evidence, merely to argue that internal evidence, which can acquire enormous weight when combined with even some small piece of external evidence, is never sufficient grounds in itself for a secure, as opposed to an 'arguable', attribution. Equally, of course, we are not in the least suggesting that any given piece of external evidence, taken on its own, must constitute decisive proof of Defoe's authorship. External evidence may be challenged, like any other sort of evidence, and sometimes it may conflict with other evidence.

It is perhaps worth reminding ourselves that the kinds of external evidence which may be considered are many. For example, Defoe occasionally openly proclaimed his authorship, either by publishing a work with his own name attached to it, as in the case of *The History of the Union* (1709), or by reprinting a work in an authorized collection of his writings. Sometimes a reference in one of his letters, or in some other of his own (undisputed) works, provides proof of his having written a certain work; and from time to time the manuscript or holograph of a previously unpublished Defoe work has turned up, such as his *Meditations* (1681) or his 'Historical Collections' (1682).[1] Then there are a number of works which were issued bearing Defoe's intials, like his *Essay Upon Projects* (1697), or a transparent pseudonym, such as 'the Author of the *Review*' or 'the Author of *The True-Born Englishman*', and this provides at least a strong presumption in favour of his authorship — though in itself, no doubt, not quite a conclusive one, since there is nothing to stop another author using such a label to boost the sales of his own book. Again, the fact that a book is claimed by its publisher as being by Defoe, either before or shortly after his death, may, we feel, be regarded as constituting external evidence of his authorship. Equally, contemporary or near contemporary attributions of works to Defoe, whether made by opponents or admirers, represent important external evidence that must be considered.

Just to give the reader a rough indication of the number of works that one might find included in Part A of a new Defoe bibliography, our own estimate is that this might at most amount to some 150 of the over 570 works currently in the canon. The evidence for each of these works is so strong, and so few, if any, of them would be challenged by any serious Defoe scholar, that they could simply be listed, in chronological order, with only the briefest of notes on the evidence for attribution.

When we come, by contrast, to Part B, where the bibliographers would present a list of works which may be, or have been, plausibly attributed to Defoe, but which lack the crucial support of a piece of external evidence suggesting Defoe as author, the shape of the bibliography would have to change. For in this part it would be imperative that the reasoning behind each attribution should be set out, and this might mean writing notes of considerable length. Most of the evidence under discussion would be 'internal', and those features of content and style which seemed to indicate Defoe's authorship would have to be set out in some detail, so that users of the bibliography could make a rational assessment of the probabilities involved.

The major problem for the bibliographers in compiling Part B would be how to weigh the various pieces of evidence for a given work. In some cases the discovery of 'high-quality' parallels of thought and language with known Defoe works might make the argument for his authorship seem very strong indeed. Some works in this part might also be supported by external evidence which the bibliographers felt to be too weak to justify inclusion in Part A, but which nevertheless did make an ascription to Defoe seem reasonable. It would be important to include details of the original source of each attribution and of its subsequent history. The bibliographers ought probably, we think, to take a fairly rigorous line in compiling Part B, only including works for which a reasonably persuasive argument could be presented. (In our view, for example, as we need hardly say, the mere fact that the subject-matter of a given work may be shown to be compatible with Defoe's known opinions or interests would not be sufficient of itself to warrant its appearing in Part B.) Our own, very incomplete investigation suggests that the number of works qualifying for Part B might amount to over fifty, but would probably not be as many as a hundred.

It will be seen, then, that even taking Parts A and B together, the number of works attributed to Defoe in the kind of new bibliography we are proposing would fall a long way short of the total in the current canon. We hasten to make clear, however, that exclusion from Parts A and B would not necessarily imply the impossibility of Defoe's authorship, merely that the attribution had not up to now been adequately defended. Thus the new bibliography would have also to include a fairly lengthy appendix in which a select list of works considered by the bibliographers to be spurious, or for which a sufficient case has never been made, would be presented. As a general rule the appendix would give details of the original source of each attribution, and equally of any book or article in which a plausible case is made out for re-attributing the work to some other author.

As we implied at the beginning of this chapter, the production of a new Defoe bibliography would be a formidable undertaking, not to be entered upon lightly. Our only concern here has been to sketch out a possible structure which might enable the attribution issue to be dealt with adequately. It will be obvious that a host of other problems would have to be considered by those with the temerity to embark on such an undertaking. For instance, how complete a bibliographical description should be offered for each item, and should this differ in extent in the two main parts? Or again, how fully should the publishing history of a work, both during Defoe's lifetime and afterwards, be described? How would the problem of sheer physical unwieldiness created by the policy of giving reasons for attribution (in Part B) be overcome? And, not least, assuming that the new bibliography is compiled by a team of Defoe scholars working in collaboration, how easy would it be to reach consensus? Such questions would have to be answered, but they are not ones on which we feel the need to express opinions in this book.

Whatever the feasibility, or the desirability, of such a new Defoe bibliography, it seems almost in the nature of things that it could never be definitive and that, so far ahead as one can see, there will be movement and migration in the Defoe canon. This indeed could be seen as a mild argument in favour of a new attempt; and it should be remembered that, beyond the obvious arguments, there may be wider reasons why such an experiment might be worth while. We are very far from having a satisfactory edition of Defoe, nor — with all the respect due to James Sutherland's valuable brief 'Life' — have we yet had a full and satisfactory biography of Defoe — and the cause is surely as plain as it is deep-seated? It is the anxiety that assails the editor or the biographer, both consciously and unconsciously, about the canon. The signals emitted by Defoe's works, as represented in Moore's *Checklist*, are unnerving enough to an editor, but to a biographer they must be quite baffling and bewildering; and it may be that only by a purge of the bibliography will it be possible to make sense of the author known as 'Daniel Defoe'.

STYLOMETRY AND DEFOE

As was said in Chapter 3 (p. 46), one important approach to the question of author-attribution is the statistical method known as 'stylometry'. The science or art of stylometry dates back to the mid-nineteenth century, when the mathematician Augustus de Morgan suggested that the disputed authorship of the Pauline Epistles might be settled by comparing the average length of word used in each of the Epistles. De Morgan had some followers, among whom we may mention T.C. Mendenhall, a geophysicist by profession, who, in 1887, in some articles in the periodical *Science*, attempted to identify individual 'word-spectra', or frequency distributions of word-length, in the work of Dickens, Thackeray, J.S. Mill, etc., and later used his method to enter the Shakespeare-Bacon controversy.[1] However, it was not till the advent of the computer, together with twentieth-century advances in statistical theory, that 'stylometry' began to seem, potentially at least, a practicable science. Thus its effective achievements belong to the last twenty or thirty years, and it may be too early to form a decisive judgement on its value.

The basic assumption of stylometry is that authors have individual and distinguishable habits in the use of language, and especially in the particular rate at which they perform operations common to all users of the same language, and that these may be recognised by statistical analysis. For this it will on the whole be necessary to focus upon features of frequent occurrence, since, as in all statistical enquiries, a minimum number of occurrences is required before any valid statistical comparison can be made or a 'habit' distinguished from a freak event.[2] Hence stylometry is likely to study different features of texts from those that interest literary critics or students of 'stylistics' and to concentrate upon unobtrusive, and to the normal eye invisible, phenomena: for instance, shall we say, the relative frequency with which sentences are begun with the word 'the', or the word 'in' is followed by the word 'a'. The hope is that by examination of such features, it can be said with scientific confidence that two texts may, or cannot, belong to the same 'population' — with the implication, subject of course to many important qualifications and reservations, that they may be or cannot be by the same author.

It could be forgiven if the Defoe bibliographer, upon first hearing of 'stylometry' and its claims, might think an easy answer had been found to all attribution problems. This indeed is the way in which stylometry has sometimes been reported in the press, as when an article in the *Observer* for 14 March 1976 announced that 'a new technique...provides for the first time a simple and apparently foolproof way of distinguishing the styles of different writers... The new technique...produces unambiguous results.'[3] Such a notion, it ought to be said bluntly, is a delusion and merely a variant of the superstition that the computer can save us the trouble of thinking. No reputable practitioner would think of talking in such a fashion; and stylometricians such as A.Q. Morton, Anthony Kenny, Alvar Ellegård and M.W.A. Smith are in agreement that conducting any kind of stylometric investigation involves tedious and prolonged labour (not least, that of putting the texts to be studied into machine-readable form), as well as continual wrestling with difficult logical and mathematical problems.[4] The point is borne out spectacularly in the one really substantial attempt so far made to apply stylometric methods to Defoe, namely Stieg Hargevik's *The Disputed Assignment of Memoirs of an English Officer* (2 vols, Stockholm, 1974). Hargevik's investigation, which led him to reject *Memoirs of an English Officer* (otherwise known as *The Military Memoirs of Capt. George Carleton*) from the Defoe canon, took him at least six years and, since his method entailed employing text-samples too large to be put into machine-readable form, required him to read, twice over, a million-word Defoe sample and a million-word 'control' sample from other authors. (In the course of this he counted every occurrence of words beginning with 'i', 'dis' and 'ex' and of numerous selected phrases, collocations, orthographical oddities and foreign expressions.)

Further — though here they are not unanimous — stylometricians are unlikely to present their results as 'unambiguous' and self-sufficient, requiring no support from other and non-stylometric types of reasoning. In fact what is striking about two of the most impressive recent book-length studies in stylometry, Mosteller and Wallace's *Applied Bayesian and Classical Inference: The Federalist*

(1984)[5] and Anthony Kenny's *The Aristotelian Ethics* (1978), is how much labour and ratiocination has gone into the solving of very straightforward and cut-and-dried bibliographical problems. The problem tackled by Mosteller and Wallace was — it being known that some essays in *The Federalist* of 1787–8 are either by Hamilton or by Madison — to decide to which of these two authors twelve of the papers should be assigned; and the question tackled by Kenny was to decide whether the three books common to Aristotle's *Nichomachean Ethics* and his *Eudemian Ethics*, in the form in which these have come down to us, originated as part of the former work or as part of the latter. Both problems, it will be seen, are simple two-candidate ones; and there would seem to be a vast difference in degree of difficulty between such problems (or even multi-candidate ones, of the form 'Assuming this play to be by Shakespeare, Marlowe, Chapman, Middleton, Jonson or Ford, to which of these should we assign it?') and ones in the form 'Is this anonymous work to be attributed to Defoe or to an unknown author?' — that is, ones in which the alternative candidates are not specified and are regarded as forming an unlimited group.

Unfortunately, in the case of Defoe, it is precisely this latter category into which the overwhelming majority of attribution problems fall. This is bound to be the case, seeing that the number of possible authors for an anonymous polemical early-eighteenth-century pamphlet, as opposed to an Elizabethan play, is so large and our knowledge of some of them is so sketchy or perhaps non-existent. Thus, for the Defoe scholar, the question to be asked about stylometry has to be twofold: does stylometry work? and if it does, can it cope (and indeed, does it even claim to cope?) with problems of the type of 'Is this by Defoe, or by an unknown?' (or, as one might express it, of 'Defoe against the world').

The authors of the present book lack mathematical skill, but they have thought it reasonable, for all this, to look at a few of the writings of leading stylometricians with this twofold question in mind — just to see if it would be possible for a non-mathematician to form an opinion. One point soon became clear to us: that the approach to stylometry most obviously fitted to the Defoe problem is A.Q. Morton's, which claims fairly unequivocally (if we have understood it) to be able to deal with problems of the 'Defoe against the world' kind. What it offers is best understood as a negative test: its chief value would be as a means of demonstrating, on statistical grounds, that a given anonymous work is highly *un*likely to be by

Defoe. The assumption underlying such testing would seem to be that an author's unconscious verbal habits constitute a unique and distinctive statistical 'profile', which can be discovered, and against which a disputed text can be measured. And this would seem to entail a corollary, that the *same* set of tests (ones that have proved from experience efficacious in revealing authors' habits) should be applied in every attribution problem, rather than, as is more usual in stylometry, a fresh set laboriously tailored to meet each new case. Now, it is our impression that this is precisely what Morton asserts: and if valid, it must clearly give his method a great advantage over others in sheer practicability. Morton favours three types of test, based respectively on words-in-preferred-positions (the rate, for instance, at which an author uses the word 'the' as the first word of a sentence), on verbal collocations (the rate at which an author follows the word 'and' by the word 'the' or the word 'in' by the word 'a' etc.), and on proportional pairs (the proportion between the frequency of an author's use of one or other of a pair of distantly related words, such as 'all' and 'any'). Some thirty or more specific examples of such tests have, according to Morton, proved, by successive trials, to be reliable discriminators between any two texts by different authors in the same language; though it is essential that, in any given enquiry, a substantial number of independent tests should be applied, so that errors in any given test arising from the operation of chance will be neutralised. Not all the tests, he says, can be expected to discriminate effectively in every case, but a sufficient proportion can always be expected to do so; and the reliability of the inferences drawn from such testing can be assigned a precise value in terms of mathematical probability.

Morton's claim, if we have not misrepresented it, is a pretty large one — much larger than would be made by the majority of his fellow-practitioners. (Nothing in the work of Smith or Kenny, for instance, suggests that they believe an author has a statistical 'profile', which can be established once and for all.) The support for such a claim will clearly need to be very powerful, above all as regards the validity of those favourite tests; and here we run up against a difficulty. For we are no doubt meant to assume that these tests have been validated by a very lengthy series of trials, upon works of known authorship, and we really need to have these trials described in more detail than Morton has seen fit to provide.

To this vague uneasiness, we may add one or two more. On what principle are certain tests rather than others to be relied on? Or by what means shall tests be themselves tested? One feels that some rule must be needed for the selection of tests, but if so, what form should this rule take? Perhaps that certain kinds of tests are intrinsically better than others, because they relate to things which we regard as important in language and writing, as opposed to mere 'accidents'? But this plunges us at once into literary and linguistic judgement, which is precisely the subjective territory from which Morton claims that his method rescues us. Alternatively — and this is Morton's position — it could be on the grounds that continual experiment has shown that certain tests (for whatever reason) have been found to 'work'; and here we are back with the all-important problem of validation.

Morton is fond of likening his method to the most famous of all identification methods, fingerprinting — which, as he rightly says, was no less a 'scientific' discovery because it took biological theory a further hundred years to explain the phenomenon on which it depends: that the ridge-patterning of the skin on fingers is unique to the individual and can renew itself even after the flesh has suffered injury from burns, etc.[7] But this fingerprint analogy is misleading, for when the idea of fingerprinting was eventually hit upon, it was a straightforward matter to validate it, which is not the case with stylometry. We do not know what 'unconscious verbal habits' are in the same unambiguous sense that we know what ridge-patterns in skin are, indeed a good deal of Morton's effort has to be spent on attaching a definable meaning to this contentious notion.

A further worry concerns the concept of 'choices'. Morton likes to speak of verbal collocations as being a matter of an author's 'choices'. To be useful in the determination of authorship, he says, a habit must be one 'apparent in a choice which frequently confronts all authors'.[8] However, it strikes one that this is a misuse of the word 'choice'. 'Choosing' means taking one or more from among a defined and limited set of things. Thus, if we meet an acquaintance in the street, and she says 'How's the rheumatism?' or 'I hear they've arrested Paddy', we should not say that she had 'chosen' these remarks, but merely that she had made them. Though on the other hand, if she were a foreigner learning English and had tried out one of the twenty forms of greeting listed in her language-teaching manual, it would be quite proper to speak of her as having chosen it. In the same fashion, it makes perfect sense to say that, if an author tends to favour the locution 'while' in preference to the equally permissible form 'whilst', he or she is choosing to do so — or perhaps made a choice in the matter many years ago, which has become second nature. Again, an author may every now and then hesitate over the selection of a synonym — shall it be 'hate', or merely 'dislike'? — and this, too, is evidently a choice. But choices play a relatively small part in our use of English, and it would be absurd to speak as if each word in an English sentence came there as the consequence of a linguistic choice. To follow the word 'and' by the word 'the' is not an act of linguistic choice, indeed it is not a linguistic decision at all but rather a matter of meaning — of wanting to say something for which 'and the' is the prescribed expression in English. Of course the stylometrician's retort to this may be that he or she is proceeding *as if* each word in a sentence came there as the result of an act of linguistic choice, but the grounds for doing so would then need to be explained to us.

The whole project of stylometry is, as it were, to take writing by surprise, suppressing all that we know about meaning and language-structure, and Morton is frank about its purely empirical character. 'The question which now arises naturally', he writes, 'is, If it is not the grammatical, linguistic or philological role of words which is being investigated, what is it that is being studied? To this reasonable request the only reasonable reply is that we do not know.'[9] In a way it is quite an appealing project, but what one feels about stylometry is that it must be very important for it that it should never weaken, or allow itself to dabble in the banned topics of meaning and language structure; and it is not plain that Morton, or indeed other stylometricians, are consistent in obeying this rule. Every now and then one finds them lapsing into common-sense considerations — making little adjustments to their calculations because of some fact that comes into their mind about the idiosyncracies of the English language, or formulating hasty generalisations about how accidents of 'subject-matter' or 'context' may disturb statistical regularities. It is at these moments that they are at their least persuasive, and one has a suspicion that they are here just tinkering — toying with matters of which, in their non-stylometric capacity, they have profound and sophisticated knowledge.

Further, one is worried by what one might call 'the spectre of the meaningless'. It must remain a problem or anxiety to us, whether we are really justified in drawing conclusions from phenomena that would by ordinary human standards be regarded as without meaning. The feeling arises in particular over Morton's 'proportionate pairs'. He is quite explicit that these pairs of words are to be found empirically: they 'reveal' themselves in an author's text, and though the words may have some visible relationship in meaning, this is not essential. 'It may be possible to give a rational explanation of why some pairs are linked, the pair *and* and *also* for example, but there are others for which no such simple explanation can be put forward and the point to be grasped is that the observation of such pairs is not dependent on the reason for their presence being known.'[10] (Anthony Kenny, indeed, goes even further and remarks, only half-jokingly, that in theory there is nothing to stop one from studying the proportional frequency of such an ill-assorted pair as 'horse' and 'never'.[11]) To the uninstructed reader there is something thoroughly puzzling in this. For if there is nothing in the two words to indicate that they are related, what is the justification for regarding them as a pair or as being linked? Why are these two words a pair, rather than any others? The 'spectre of the meaningless' here advances out of the shadows.

One last doubt or cavil. It is our impression that, if one wanted to test whether a given anonymous work was likely to be by Defoe or not, the orthodox statistical procedure would be to do this in two stages. First one would validate some tests, and then one would proceed to apply them, and the validation would need to be done upon a different text or set of texts from the one to which the tests were to be applied.[12] Thus, if one were trying to decide whether an anonymous work was more likely to be by Defoe than by another suggested author, e.g., Oldmixon, one would validate one's tests on some known works by Defoe and by Oldmixon before 'applying them to the disputed work. But if no other candidate is proposed and the question that we are asking is of the 'Defoe against the world' type, i.e., 'Could this anonymous work be by Defoe?', how can this rule of procedure be observed? (There is, after all, in the nature of things, no second work by the anonymous author upon which we can validate the tests.)

On the whole, then, though the Morton method cannot but look attractive, it provokes too many doubts and uneasinesses for us to regard it quite as the long-wished-for answer to our bibliographical problems. In saying so we are influenced by the fact that at least one stylometrician, M. W. A. Smith (and actually there have been others) has been very critical of certain aspects of Morton's handling of statistical method, and in a way that carries a certain conviction even to the non-mathematician.[13] More importantly, Smith takes the view that the conclusions of stylometry cannot be quantified in terms of statistical probabilities and, at present anyway, they can be expressed only in 'qualitative' form. It is, in his opinion, a quite unproven hypothesis implicit in Morton's work that (to use Smith's words) 'every author exhibits his own multinomial distribution of the features compared and that the figures compiled for each test are random samples from such distributions',[14] and from this it follows that the values of the chi-square statistic, on which many stylometricians depend, cannot be interpreted as mathematical probabilities relating exclusively to authorship. The chi-square statistic is still of use, but the conclusions drawn from its values can be expressed only in the homely qualitative form that Author A is 'more likely', or 'much more likely', or 'rather less likely' to have written a particular work than Author B. This seems a very radical pronouncement, coming from a mathematician; and if it is correct it suggests to us that stylometry, though potentially an aid in author-attribution, is not yet in a position to replace more traditional approaches.

JAMES CROSSLEY'S MANUSCRIPT
LIST OF ATTRIBUTIONS

B ECAUSE JAMES CROSSLEY'S part in the construction of the Defoe canon is much less well known than that of other bibliographers, we have thought it worth reprinting here the influential list of sixty new attributions which he drew up, sometime between 1869 and his death in 1883. The manuscript survives among the W.P. Trent Papers in the Beinecke Library. We have rearranged the list to present works in chronological order of first publication, and have included Crossley's comments on some of them, as recorded by Edward Riggall during his inspection of Crossley's library when it was being sold. The Moore number is included for those items that appear in his *Checklist*.

1. *Reflections on the Prohibition Act* (1708) [Moore 155]
2. *An Account of the Obligations the States of Holland have to Great Britain* (1711)
3. *The Re-representation* (1711)
4. *An Essay upon the Trade to Africa* (1711) [Moore 210] 'By Defoe, beyond doubt.'
5. *The True State of the Case between the Government and the Creditors of the Navy* (1711) [Moore 215]
6. *A Defence of the Allies and the Late Ministry* (1712) [Moore 225]
7. *Peace, or Poverty* (1712) [Moore 229]
8. *The History of the Jacobite Clubs* (1712) [Moore 232]
9. *Wise as Serpents* (1712) [Moore 236]
10. *A Farther Search into the Conduct of the Allies* (1712) [Moore 242]
11. *Not[tingh]am Politicks Examin'd* (1713) [Moore 249]
12. *A Brief Account of the Present State of the African Trade* (1713) [Moore 263]

13. *Proposals for Imploying the Poor* (1713) [Moore 270]
14. *A Letter to the Whigs* (1714) [Moore 271]
15. *A Letter to Mr. Steele* (1714) [Moore 276] 'Tho' the Title-page states this Tract to have been written by a member of the Church of England, I entertain no doubt that its author was Defoe.'
16. *A Brief Survey of the Legal Liberties of the Dissenters* (1714) [Moore 279]
17. *The Case of the Catalans Consider'd* (1714)
18. *Strike While the Iron's Hot* (1715) [Moore 290]
19. *Memoirs of the Conduct of Her Late Majesty and Her Last Ministry* (1715) [Moore 291]
20. *Burnet and Bradbury* (1715) [Moore 302]
21. *The Fears of the Pretender Turn'd into the Fears of Debauchery* (1715) [Moore 304]
22. *The Second-Sighted Highlander* (1715) [Moore 312]
23. *Some Methods to Supply the Defects of the Late Peace* (1715) [Moore 313]
24. *Some Considerations on the Danger of the Church from her Own Clergy* (1715) [Moore 320] [It should be noted that at one time Crossley held a different view of the authorship of this pamphlet. Riggall records him as having written in his copy 'Scarcely by Defoe. See what is said of the Bill of Commerce at the End.']
25. *An Humble Address to our Sovereign Lord the People* (1715) [Moore 321] 'Indisputably by Defoe. Why not noticed before I cannot tell.'
26. *The Conduct of Some People, about Pleading Guilty* (1716) [Moore 340]
27. *A True Account of the Proceedings at Perth* (1716) [Moore 348]
28. *Secret Memoirs of a Treasonable Conference at S[omerset] House* (1717) [Moore 354]
29. *The Danger of Court Differences* (1717) [Moore 355] 'I attribute this to Defoe. There are many marks of his style, but see in particular p. 30.'
30. *Fair Payment No Spunge* (1717) [Moore 363] 'This is also one of Defoe's, never yet noticed.'
31. *What if the Swedes should come?* (1717) [Moore 364]
32. *The Question Fairly Stated* (1717) [Moore 365]
33. *The Danger and Consequence of Disobliging the Clergy Consider'd* (1717) [Moore 366]
34. *Reasons for a Royal Visitation* (1717) [Moore 367]

35. *Memoirs of Some Transactions during the Late Ministry of Robert E. of Oxford* (1717) [Moore 378]
36. *A Letter to Andrew Snape* (1717) [Moore 383] 'Whether these Tracts [Lee 167, 182 and Snape supra] which form part of the series commencing with the "Letter to Bradbury" are written by Defoe is an extremely difficult question to determine, as there is a want of decisive internal marks.'
37. *A Brief Comment upon His Majesty's Speech* (1718) [Moore 398]
38. *A Continuation of Letters written by a Turkish Spy* (1718) [Moore 406]
39. *The History of the Reign of King George* (1718) [Moore 407] 'Evidently by Defoe, though not noticed by any of his biographers.'
40. *The Just Complaint of the Poor Weavers Truly Represented* (1719) [Moore 416]
41. *A Brief State of the Question, Between the Printed and Painted Callicoes and the Woollen and Silk Manufacture* (1719) [Moore 420]
42. *An Historical Account of the Voyages and Adventures of Sir Walter Raleigh* (1720) [Moore 425]
43. *The Trade to India Critically and Calmly Consider'd* (1720) [Moore 428]
44. *The Causes of the Discontents, In Relation to the Plague, and the Provisions against it, Fairly Stated and Consider'd* (1721) 'I attribute this to Defoe. It has been given to Bishop Gibson.'
45. *Due Preparations for the Plague* (1722) [Moore 447]
46. *A Brief debate upon the Dissolving the Late Parliament* (1722) [Moore 450]
47. *The Interest of Great Britain Consider'd: or, the Herring Fishery Propos'd as the most Rational Expedient for paying our National Debts* (1723)
48. *The Tryal and Sufferings of Mr. Isaac Martin* (1723) [For Crossley's note on this, see above, p. 82.]
49. *The Royal Progress* (1724) [Moore 462]
50. *Some Farther Account of the Original Disputes in Ireland* (1724) [Moore 467]
51. *The Life of Jonathan Wild* (1725) [Moore 471]
52. *A Brief Case of the Distillers* (1726) [Moore 477] 'The internal evidence is so strong that I have no hesitation in attributing this to Defoe, notwithstanding his strong attacks on Gin in "Augusta Triumphans".'
53. *Unparallel'd Cruelty* (1726) [Moore 481]

54. *The Evident Advantages to Great Britain and its Allies from the Approaching War* (1727) [Moore 490] 'I consider these two last [this and Lee 239] as Defoe's from the strong internal evidence. They are certainly written by the same author and published in the same year and by the same publisher as the "Brief Deduction of English Woollen Manufacture".'

55. *A Brief Deduction of the Original, Progress, and Immense Greatness of the British Woollen Manufacture* (1727) [Moore 493]

56. *Some Considerations on the Reasonableness and Necessity of Encreasing and Encouraging the Seamen* (1728) [Moore 497]

57. *Some Objections Humbly offered to the Consideration of the Hon. House of Commons, Relating to the Present Intended Relief of Prisoners* (1729) [Moore 509]

58. *The Advantages of Peace and Commerce* (1729) [Moore 510]

59. *A Brief State of the Inland or Home Trade* (1730) [Moore 512] 'It has every attribute of his [Defoe's] style.'

60. *The Perjur'd Free Mason Detected* (1730) [Moore 515]

1. *George Chalmers.* A large collection of Chalmers's working papers, notebooks and correspondence relating to his work on Defoe is in the 'Aitken-Defoe Miscellaneous' collection at The Harry Ransom Humanities Research Center, The University of Texas at Austin.

2. *William Lee.* Letters from and to Lee, and other manuscript material are to be found in Sheffield Local Archives S.L.P.S. MS, Sheffield Central Library; correspondence with Edwin Chadwick in the Chadwick MSS, the library of University College, London; correspondence with Lee's publisher J.C. Hotten in the Chatto Letterbooks, MS 244/3/5/6/7, the University of Reading library; correspondence with James Crossley in the 'Aitken-Defoe Miscellaneous' collection, The Harry Ransom Humanities Research Center. Lee's copiously annotated copy of Walter Wilson's *Memoirs of the Life and Times of Daniel De Foe* is among the W.P. Trent papers at the Beinecke Library.

3. *James Crossley.* Correspondence and other manuscripts relating to his Defoe interests are in the James Crossley Papers (Misc.), Central Library, Manchester; the Crossley Collection, Chetham's Library, Manchester; and the 'Aitken-Defoe Miscellaneous' collection at The Harry Ransom Humanities Research Center.

4. *W.P. Trent.* The most important collection of Trent's working papers, correspondence and other Defoe materials is in an uncatalogued collection, the W.P. Trent Papers, in the Collection of American Literature, The Beinecke Rare Book and Manuscript Library, Yale University. This includes the typescript of his biography of Defoe, running to over 600 pages of text, and of his bibliography of Defoe's works, running to nearly 3,000 pages.

Letters from and to Trent are in Columbia University library. Other materials, including annotations in his own copies of Defoe works, are in the Defoe Collection in the Boston Public Library.

5. *J.R. Moore*. An extensive, though incomplete collection of Moore's working papers is in the Rare Book Room, the University of Illinois library. A large number of letters to Moore, with some other uncatalogued material, is held in the University Archives at Indiana University, Bloomington. A series of letters from Moore to George Healey is in the possession of Mrs Healey; letters to Frank Bastian are in the possession of Mr Bastian; letters to H.C. Hutchins are in the Beinecke Library. There is correspondence between Moore and the librarians at the Boston Public Library, the Bodleian, and the William Andrews Clark Memorial Library.

The place of publication of books cited, where known, is London, unless otherwise stated. References to works by or attributed to Defoe are to the first edition, unless otherwise stated.

CHAPTER 1

1. Rodney M. Baine, 'Chalmers' First Bibliography of Daniel Defoe', *Texas Studies in Literature and Language*, 10 (1969), p. 567. As Baine points out, Chalmers should in fact be credited with 128 items altogether. See further, p. 51.
2. Walter Wilson, *Memoirs of the Life and Times of Daniel De Foe*, 3 vols (1830), I, p. xxiii.
3. William Lee, *Daniel Defoe: His Life, and Recently Discovered Writings*, 3 vols (1869), I, p. xxiv.
4. W.P. Trent, 'Defoe: The Newspaper and the Novel', *The Cambridge History of English Literature*, ed. A.W. Ward and A.R. Waller (1912), IX, p. 433.
5. J.R. Moore, *A Checklist of the Writings of Daniel Defoe* (Bloomington, Ind., 1960; second edition, Hamden, Conn., 1971).
6. Cited in Baine, 'Chalmers' First Bibliography', p. 548.
7. For a list of attribution studies by these and other scholars, see John A. Stoler, *Daniel Defoe: An Annotated Bibliography of Modern Criticism, 1900–1980* (New York and London, 1984). pp. 303–16.
8. Rodney M. Baine, 'Daniel Defoe and Robert Drury's *Journal*', *Texas Studies in Literature and Language*, 14 (1974), p. 484.
9. Donald W. Foster, letter to *TLS*, 7 March 1986, p. 247.
10. The Writings of Daniel Defoe, University Microfilms International, Michigan.
11. Michel Foucault, 'What is an Author?', in *Textual Strategies: Perspectives in Post-*

Structuralist Criticism, ed. Josue V. Harari (1980).
12. See Laura A. Curtis, *The Elusive Daniel Defoe* (Totowa, N.J. and London, 1984), ch. 4.
13. W.L. Payne, 'Defoe in the Pamphlets', *Philological Quarterly*, 52 (1973), pp. 85–96.
14. See *A Character of a Turn-coat: Or, The True Picture of an English Monster* (broadsheet, 1707); 'The loyal Litany', in Read's *Weekly Journal*, 20 September 1718; *The Political State*, XIII (February, 1717), p. 123; *Remarks on a Scandalous Libel* (1713), pp. 1–3.
15. Letter to George Chalmers from George Paton, in the Beinecke Library.
16. *An Appeal to Honour and Justice* (1715), quoted from James T. Boulton (ed.), *Selected Writings of Daniel Defoe* (1965), p. 189.
17. *The Secret History of the Secret History of the White Staff, Purse and Mitre* (1715), pp. 7–8.
18. *Minutes of the Negotiations of Monsr. Mesnager* (1717; second edition, 1736), pp. 107–8.

CHAPTER 2

1. 'The Later Life of De Foe', *British Quarterly Review*, 1 (1869), pp. 483–519.
2. *Ibid.*, p. 499.
3. Lee, *Daniel Defoe*, I, pp. 250, v–vi.
4. W.P. Trent, 'Bibliographical Notes on Defoe: I', *Nation*, 84 (1907), p. 517; unpublished 'Bibliography', pp. 1189 and 1220 (1715).

5. Lee, *Daniel Defoe*, I, p. 368.
6. 'Bibliographical Notes on Defoe: I', p. 516. As Trent pointed out elsewhere, Sir Walter Scott had in fact assigned the Patkul pamphlet to Molesworth; see W.P. Trent, 'A Talk about Defoe', *Papers of the Hobby Club 1911–1912* (Cambridge, Mass., 1912), pp. 30–31.
7. Herbert G. Wright, 'Defoe's Writings on Sweden', *Review of English Studies*, 16 (1940), pp. 25–32.
8. Stieg Hargevik, 'Daniel Defoe and King Charles XII of Sweden', in *Studies in English Philology, Linguistics and Literature Presented to Alarik Rynell 7 March 1978*, ed. Mats Ryden and Lennart A. Bjork, *Stockholm Studies in English*, XLVI (Stockholm, 1978), pp. 50–63.
9. Lee, *Daniel Defoe*, I, p. 370.
10. J.R. Moore, *Daniel Defoe: Citizen of the Modern World* (Chicago and London, 1958), p. 258; idem, *Checklist* (second edition), pp. 175, 183.
11. 'Daniel Defoe and King Charles XII of Sweden', p. 55.
12. *Defoe's Review*, facsimile ed. Arthur W. Secord (New York, 1938), IV, pp. 345–6.
13. The poet-diplomat Christoffer Leijoncrona (1662–1710), Swedish diplomat in England since 1690, envoy extraordinary from 1703.
14. *Review*, IV, pp. 429–32.
15. *Dyers News Examined as to His Sweddish Memorial against the Review* ([Edinburgh, 1707]), p. 1. Defoe is referring here to the famous episode in which, in resentment at an insult to himself given to the Swedish envoy by Count Zobor, the Emperor's chamberlain, Charles XII high-handedly forced the Emperor to turn Zobor over to him as a prisoner.
16. *Review*, IV, pp. 459–60.
17. *The History of the Wars, of his Late Majesty Charles XII* (second edition, London, 1720), pp. 249–50.
18. Wright, 'Defoe's Writings on Sweden', pp. 25–32. See also idem, 'Some English Writers and Charles XII', *Studia Neophilologica*, XV (1942–43), pp. 105–31.
19. *Daniel Defoe: Citizen of the Modern World*, p. 258.
20. *Voltaire's History of Charles XII., King of Sweden*, trans. W. Todhunter ([1908]), pp. xii–xiv.
21. Hargevik, 'Daniel Defoe and King Charles XII of Sweden'.
22. John J. Murray, *George I, the Baltic and the Whig Split of 1717* (1969), pp. 64–65.
23. *The History of the Wars* (second edition), pp. 65–6.
24. Foucault, 'What is an Author?', p. 146.

CHAPTER 3

1. Baron Gilbert, *The Laws of Evidence* (second edition, 1760), pp. 147–8.
2. W.P. Trent, comment on *An Essay on Credit and the Bankrupt Act* (1707), in unpublished 'Bibliography' of Defoe's works, p. 569; typescript in the Beinecke Library.
3. Gary Taylor, 'A new Shakespeare poem? The evidence', *TLS*, 20 December 1985, p. 1447.
4. Arthur Sherbo, 'Can *Mother Midnight's Comical Pocket-Book* be Attributed to Christopher Smart?', in *Essays on Problems of Attribution*, ed. D.V. Erdman and E.G. Fogel (New York, 1966), p. 284.
5. S.T. Coleridge, 'Intercepted Correspondence', *Morning Post*, 3 February 1800.
6. Arthur Sherbo, 'The Uses and Abuses of Internal Evidence', in *Essays on Problems of Attribution*, pp. 7–8.
7. David Erdman, 'The Signature of Style', in *Essays on Problems of Attribution*, pp. 46, 47, 53.
8. Ephim G. Fogel, 'Salmons in Both, or Some Caveats for Canonical Scholars', in *Essays on Problems of Attribution*, p. 97.
9. Sherbo, 'The Uses and Abuses of Internal Evidence', p. 11.
10. Muriel St. Clair Byrne, 'Bibliographical Clues in Collaborate Plays', *The Library*, fourth series, 13 (1932), p. 24.
11. Samuel Schoenbaum, *Internal Evidence and Elizabethan Dramatic Authorship* (1966), p. 184.
12. Robin Robbins, *TLS*, 20 December 1985, p. 1450.
13. In *The Mortal Moon, or, Bacon and his Masks. The Defoe period unmasked* (New York, 1891), J.E. Roe offers to show, on the strength of linguistic parallels, 'not merely that Lord Bacon was the author of Crusoe, but that he was the author of nearly all the so-called Defoe literature'. References to events happening after Bacon's death, he says, can be explained as later interpolations, such 'garbling' being very common.
14. Cf. the remark by Ephim G. Fogel

(p. 73): 'Unless one can show beyond a reasonable doubt that a given work B is by a known author A, parallels between B and an anonymous work X have little if any value in proving A's authorship of X.'

15. See A. Coquerel, *Jean Calas et sa famille* (Paris, 1869), p. 170n.
16. See L.J. Cohen, *The Probable and the Provable* (1977), p. 108. The whole chapter, 'The Difficulty about Corroboration and Convergence', is illuminating.
17. Jeremy Bentham, *A Treatise on Judicial Evidence*, ed. M. Dumont (1825), p. 189.
18. D. Foxon, *English Verse 1701–1750* (1975), introduction, p. xv.
19. J.R. Moore, *Defoe in the Pillory and Other Studies* (1939; reprinted, New York, 1973), pp. 68–71.
20. Schoenbaum, p. 179.
21. Lee, *Daniel Defoe* (1869), I, p. vi.
22. See Charles Eaton Burch, 'Defoe's Connections with the *Edinburgh Courant*', *Review of English Studies*, 5 (1929), pp. 437–40; A.W. Secord, *Studies in the Narrative Method of Defoe* (Urbana, Ill., 1924); Moore, *Defoe in the Pillory*; Maximillian E. Novak, '*Two Arguments Never Brought Yet*: An Addition to the Defoe Canon', *Notes and Queries*, n.s., 22 (1975), pp. 345–7, and idem, 'Defoe's Authorship of *A Collection of Dying Speeches* (1718)', *Philological Quarterly*, 61 (1982), pp. 92–7; F. Bastian, *Defoe's Early Life* (1981), pp. 307–18.
23. Moore, *Defoe in the Pillory*, p. 70.
24. Samuel Johnson, *The Plays of William Shakespeare* (1765), V, p. 225; cited in Schoenbaum, p. 17.
25. See Frank Kermode, *Forms of Attention* (1985), *passim*.
26. Max J. Friedländer, *On Art and Connoissurship*, trans. J. Borenius (1943), pp. 160, 174–5.
27. Lee, *Daniel Defoe*, I, pp. v–vi.
28. See Giovanni Morelli, *Italian Painters*, trans. C.J. Foulkes (1892), *passim*.
29. See Friedländer, pp. 166–7, 180–81, 175.

CHAPTER 4

1. For an account of Chalmers's life and career, see Grace Amelia Cockroft, *The Public Life of George Chalmers* (New York, 1939).
2. Chalmers's list has been reprinted in Baine, 'Chalmers' First Bibliography', pp. 547–68.
3. For a detailed account of Chalmers's bibliographical work see Baine, 'Chalmers' First Bibliography'. Many of Chalmers's working papers survive in the 'Aitken-Defoe Miscellaneous' collection in The Harry Ransom Humanities Research Center, The University of Texas at Austin.
4. Quoted in Cockroft, p. 202.
5. George Chalmers, *An Appendix to the Supplemental Apology for the Believers in the Suppositious Shakespeare-Papers: being the Documents for the Opinion that Hugh MacAulay Boyd wrote Junius's Letters* (1800).
6. *British Critic*, 16 (July 1800), pp. 16ff.; quoted by Cockroft, p. 198.
7. George Chalmers, *The Author of Junius Ascertained: from a Concatenation of Circumstances: amounting to Moral Demonstration* (1817).
8. Edmund Malone, *Exposure of the Ireland Forgeries: an Inquiry into the Authenticity of Certain Papers Attributed to Shakespeare* (1796).
9. George Chalmers, *An Apology for the Believers in the Shakespeare-Papers, which were Exhibited in Norfolk-Street* (1797), p. 33.
10. See Cockroft, p. 197.
11. *Apology*, p. 19n.
12. *Ibid.*, p. 215.
13. See p. 00 above.
14. *The Author of Junius Ascertained*, p. iv.
15. Baine, 'Chalmers' First Bibliography', p. 558.
16. George Chalmers, notebook, p. 55, in the 'Aitken-Defoe Miscelaneous' collection in The Harry Ransom Humanities Research Center, The University of Texas at Austin.
17. In *Daniel Defoe and the Supernatural* (Athens, Georgia, 1968) Baine produced convincing arguments for rejecting *The Life and Adventures of Duncan Campbell* and *The Dumb Philosopher* from the Defoe canon.
18. Baine, 'Chalmers's First Bibliography', p. 567.

CHAPTER 5

1. Wilson's own words: see his 'Recollections of Charles Lamb' published by

E.V. Lucas in the *London Mercury*, December 1934, p. 147. For details of Wilson's life see also *Gentleman's Magazine*, October 1847; *Christian Reformer; or, Unitarian Magazine and Review*, n.s., 3 (1847), p. 506; *DNB, s.v.* Wilson.

2. See Commons debate, 28 April 1829; Hansard, n.s., 21, pp. 898–9.

3. Thomas Noon Talfourd, the historian of the Lamb circle, claimed to have wakened the national conscience on the subject by his article 'Brief Observations on the Punishment of the Pillory', published in *The Pamphleteer*, VIII (1814), pp. 533–49. The pillory was abolished for all offences save perjury in the following year, though it did not finally disappear from the statute-book till 1837.

4. *The Times*, 12 February 1848.

5. *The Right Divine of Kings to Govern Wrong! Dedicated to the Holy Alliance. By the Author of The Political House that Jack Built* (1821).

6. William Hazlitt, letter to Macvey Napier, 21 July 1829. *Letters*, ed., H.M. Sikes (1979), p. 366.

7. *The Letters of Charles Lamb*, ed. E.V. Lucas, 3 vols (1935), III, pp. 232–3.

8. *Ibid.*, p. 342.

9. *Remarks upon the Present State of the Dissenting Interest with Hints for its Improvement by means of a Consolidated Union. By One of the Laity* [i.e. Walter Wilson] (1831), p. 6.

10. In later years he became a Unitarian, and he regretted some of the more orthodox sentiments he had voiced in his *History of Dissenting Churches*.

11. Walter Wilson, 'An Essay on the Causes of the Decline of Nonconformity', *Monthly Repository* (June and July, 1823), p. 394 (originally a paper given to the Non-Con Club).

12. The club was founded in 1817 by Robert Aspland.

13. See R. Brook Aspland, *Memoir of the Life, Works and Correspondence of the Rev. Robert Aspland of Hackney* (1850), pp. 403–6, 467–8.

14. Wilson, *Memoirs*, p. xiv.

15. *Westminster Review*, 13 (1830), p. 70. The *Wellesley Index* suggests that this reviewer is Edgar Taylor, who had, in fact, been very active in the campaign against Dissenters' disabilities.

16. Wilson, *Memoirs*, II, p. 102.

17. *Ibid.*, p. 495.

18. *Monthly Repository*, n.s., IV (1830), p. 58.

19. *British Critic and Quarterly Theological Review*, no. 18 (1830), p. 75.

20. Wilson, *Memoirs*, p. xxi. See further [Machell Stace], *An Alphabetical Catalogue of an Extensive Collection of the Writings of Daniel De Foe; and of the Different Publications for and against that very Extraordinary Writer* (1829).

21. Wilson, *Memoirs*, p. xxiv.

22. Lee, *Daniel Defoe*, I, p. xxiv.

CHAPTER 6

1. J. Holland and J. Everett, *Memoirs of the Life and Writings of James Montgomery*, 7 vols (1854), VI, 204. For a more detailed account of Lee's early career, see our 'William Lee: Sanitary Reformer and Defoe Bibliographer', *The Book Collector*, forthcoming.

2. William Lee, *Report to the General Board of Health on . . . March* (30 July 1850), p. 36.

3. William Lee, *Report to the General Board of Health on . . . Rotherham and Kimberworth* (22 November 1850), p. 34.

4. See Charles May, *A Letter to the Local Board of Health of the City of Durham, in reply to a Letter from Mr. William Lee, one of the Superintending Inspectors of the General Board of Health* (London, 1852).

5. For details of this episode in Lee's career, see the article cited in note 1 above.

6. Lee, *Daniel Defoe*, I. p. 32.

7. *London Review*, 4 and 11 June, 1864, pp. 590–91, 617–18.

8. *Notes and Queries*, third series, VI (1864), pp. 527–30.

9. 'Daniel Defoe and the "London Review"', *ibid.*, third series, VII (1865), pp. 58–61.

10. 'Daniel Defoe, the News Writer', *ibid.*, third series, VII (1865), pp. 244–6.

11. '"Servitude: A Poem"', *ibid.*, third series, IX (1866), pp. 141–3.

12. *Ibid.*, third series, VII (1865), pp. 245, 431.

13. 'Daniel Defoe, On Assassination of Rulers', *ibid.*, third series, VIII (1865), pp. 101–3. Lee's copy of Wilson is preserved among the W.P. Trent papers in the Beinecke Library.

14. *Ibid.*, third series, IX (1866), pp. 72–5, 92–5.

15. Lee is quoting here from an article by James Crossley, 'Defoe's Pamphlet on

the Septennial Bill', *ibid.*, V (1852), pp. 577–9.

16. See 'A Gentleman of the Press', *All the Year Round* (10 and 17 July 1869), pp. 132–7, 156–61; *Athenaeum* (1 May 1869), pp. 597–8; *Saturday Review* (15 May 1869), pp. 651–2.

17. 'The Later Life of Defoe', *British Quarterly Review* (October 1869), pp. 483–519. W.P. Trent came to the conclusion that the author of this review was A.L. Windsor.

18. 'Defoe: "Mercurius Politicus": Mesnager's "Negotiations"', *Notes and Queries*, fourth series, V (1870), pp. 177–9.

19. W.C. Hazlitt, *The Hazlitts* (1912), Part 2, p. 247.

20. Lee, *Daniel Defoe*, I, pp. 204, 439; letter from Lee to Crossley, 21 July 1866, in the 'Aitken-Defoe Miscellaneous' collection, The Harry Ransom Humanities Research Center, the University of Texas at Austin.

21. 'Defoe's "Due Preparations for the Plague"', *Notes and Queries*, fourth series, III (1869), pp. 402–3.

22. Lee, *Daniel Defoe*, I, pp. 269–70.

23. 'Defoe: "Mercurius Politicus": Mesnager's "Negotiations"', pp. 548–9.

24. Draft copies of two letters from Crossley to Lee, one dated 14 June 1869, the other undated, James Crossley Papers (Misc.), Central Library, Manchester.

25. 'Defoe: "Mercurius Politicus": Mesnager's "Negotiations"', pp. 177–9, 202–5

26 Lee, *Daniel Defoe*, I, pp. xxii–xxiii, 109, 153, 165, 214–16, 365–7, 376, 408–10, 423–5, 428, 432–5.

27. *Ibid.*, p. 338.

28. *Ibid.*, p. 387.

29. Oddly, in the case of two of the 'criminal' pamphlets listed by Lee, *The History of the Remarkable Life of John Sheppard* (1724) and *The True, Genuine, and Perfect Account of the Life and Actions of the Late Jonathan Wild* (1725), he gives no pagination, which suggests that he had never actually seen them. Nor are they the only items in his List of which we may form this suspicion: see for instance items 12, 13, 15, 19, 35, 47, 50, 57, 76, 94, 103, 130, 149 and 158. As for the bibliographical status of all those 'Newly-discovered writings', extracted from periodicals, which Lee assigns to Defoe (they amount to 990 pages, or approximately 396,000 words), this is

something of a puzzle, at least to the present authors. The verdict of the *New Cambridge Bibliography of English Literature* is that 'most are unquestionably by Defoe' though possibly not some of the news items, which appeared in much the same form in all the journals of the time. One would like to see this argued out in more detail.

CHAPTER 7

1. Cited in Samuel Crompton, 'The Late Mr. James Crossley', *The Palatine Notebook*, III (1883), p. 228.

2. *Ibid.*, p. 224.

3. Letter to John Forster, 20 November 1838: 'I guessed Crossley at once, by the "shibboleth of authorship", and the repetition of the "no" which is the style of oratory that regaleth the ears of the Borough-reeve', in *The Letters of Charles Dickens*, I, 1820–1839, ed. M. House and G. Storey (1965), p. 458.

4. *Transactions and Proceedings of the Second Annual Meeting of the Library Association of the United Kingdom held at Manchester, September 23, 24 and 25, 1879*, ed. Henry R. Tedder and Ernest C. Thomas (1880), pp. 144–5.

5. Undated MS in the James Crossley Papers (Misc.), Central Library, Manchester.

6. *Gentleman's Magazine* (October 1838), pp. 370–71.

7. *Notes and Queries*, V (1851), p. 195.

8. *Ibid.*, p. 338.

9. *Ibid.*, V (1852), pp. 577–9.

10. *Ibid.*, fourth series, III (1869), pp. 402–3.

11. The MS is now among the Trent papers in the Beinecke Library.

12. W.P. Trent, 'Bibliographical Notes on Defoe: II', *The Nation*, 85 (1907), pp. 29–32.

13. The MSS are preserved in the Trent papers in the Beinecke Library.

14. These are: *A Letter from a Gentleman at the Court of St. Germains* (1719) [Moore 189]; *The Succession of Spain Consider'd* (1711) [Moore 205]; *An Enquiry into the Danger and Consequences of a War with the Dutch* (1712) [Moore 241]; *An Account of the Conduct of Robert Earl of Oxford* (1715) [Moore 323]; *The Layman's Vindication of the Church of England* (1716) [Moore 352]; *The Conduct of Robert Walpole* (1717)

[Moore 370]; *Some Persons Vindicated Against the Author of the Detection* (1718) [Moore 308]; and *Two Arguments Never Brought Yet* (1718) [attributed to Defoe by Maximillian E. Novak, *Notes and Queries*, n.s. 22 (1975), pp. 345–47].

15. These are: *His Majesty's Obligations to the Whigs Plainly Proved* (1715) [Moore 318]; *The Old Whig and Modern Whig Revived* (1717) [Moore 382]; and *The Case Fairly Stated between the Turky Company and the Italian Merchants* (1720) [Moore 429].

16. These are: *R[ogue]'s on Both Sides* (1711) [Moore 198] and *Minutes of the Negotiations of Monsr. Mesnager* (1717) [Moore 377].

CHAPTER 8

1. See F.T. Walker, 'William Peterfield Trent: a Critical Biography', unpublished Ph.D. thesis, George Peabody College for Teachers (1943), p. 99.
2. See William Haller, 'William Peterfield Trent', *Columbia University Quarterly*, 32 (1940), p. 32.
3. W.P. Trent, *Robert E. Lee* (1899), pp. 42, 119.
4. He was club-footed and once confided to a university friend that he thought he might suffer from hereditary syphilis; Walker, 'William Peterfield Trent', p. 66.
5. Carl van Doren, 'Post-War: the Literary Twenties', *Harper's Magazine*, July 1936, p. 148, and idem, *Three Worlds* (1937), p. 116.
6. This was no doubt through the encouragement of his friend the essayist Paul Elmer More, then Assistant Editor of the *Nation*.
7. W.P. Trent, 'Bibliographical Notes on Defoe: II', *Nation*, 85 (1907), p. 32. For Trent's own account of his deepening involvement in his study of 'The man who has literally haunted me', see 'A Talk about Defoe', *Papers of the Hobby Club 1911–1912* (Cambridge, Mass., 1912) pp. 29–50.
8. 'Bibliographical Notes on Defoe: III', p. 183. The list Trent produced for *The Cambridge History of English Literature* in 1912 contained 382 items, among which were eighteen periodicals. The eventual total in his unpublished bibliography rose to 442 items, exclusive of periodicals.
9. W.P. Trent, unpublished biography

of Defoe, typescript in the Beinecke Library, pp. 370–71. Hereafter referred to as 'Life'.

10. W.P. Trent, unpublished bibliography of Defoe's works, typescript in the Beinecke Library, p. 812 (1712). Hereafter referred to as 'Bibliography'. Pagination of the typsescript is not continuous — there are four sequences — and since items are listed in chronological order of first publication, for convenience we specify the year as well as the page-number.
11. The phrase appears in Trent's chapter on Defoe in *The Cambridge History of English Literature* as well as on the final page of his unpublished 'Life'.
12. H. Holt to W.P. Trent, 19 June 1908, cited in Walker, p. 313; and letter of 29 October 1914, Walker, p. 315.
13. W.P. Trent to Yates Snowden, 6 May 1913, cited in Walker, p. 313.
14. W.P. Trent, *Daniel Defoe: How to Know Him* (Indianapolis, 1916).
15. Letter from W.P. Trent to Mark van Doren, 21 Novemeber 1920, in Mark Van Doren Papers, Rare Book and Manuscript Library, Columbia University.
16. This was a regular topic in letters between J.R. Moore and George Healey. When Healey was invited to edit Defoe's letters, it was rumoured that Hutchins was also contemplating an edition, but for all his tactful approaches, Healey could never get at the truth of the matter.
17. Moore, p. vii.
18. Letter from J.R. Moore to Zoltán Haraszti, 29 January 1952, in Boston Public Library.
19. 'Bibliography', p. 1259 (1716).
20. Trent regarded this as rather endearing and as a fault on the right side: 'It is always, of course, more interesting to allow the imagination some play than to reason in an unemotional fashion, and not only do I bear no grudge against Lee for the trouble he has so often given me by mixing his inferences with his ascertained facts, but I am glad that frequently I have no way of proving his suppositions to be false,' 'Bibliography', pp. 100–101 (1724).
21. *Ibid.*, p. 1107 (1715).
22. *Ibid.*, p. 420 (1706).
23. See the *Nation* articles, *passim*.
24. The *CHEL* list contains 382 items, including 18 periodicals. This is 128 more

than in Lee's list (which, moreover, treats the nine volumes of the *Review* as separate items); and to arrive at the total of new attributions we must add the fifteen items from Lee which Trent rejected.

25. 'Bibliographical Notes on Defoe: I', p. 515.
26. 'Bibliographical Notes on Defoe: III', *Nation*, 85 (1907), p. 180.
27. Moore, *Defoe in the Pillory*, p. 68.
28. 'Bibliography', p. 723 (1711).
29. *Ibid.*, p. 268 (1704).
30. *Ibid.*, p. 176 (1702).
31. *Ibid.*, pp. 702–9 (1711).
32. *A Letter to a Friend in Suffolk, Occasion'd by a Report of Repealing the Triennial Act* (1716) and *A Second Letter to a Friend in Suffolk*, etc. (1716).
33. 'Bibliography', pp. 1279–80 (1716).
34. *Ibid.*, p. 29 (1698).
35. *Ibid.*, p. 1285 (1716).
36. *Ibid.*, pp. 1348–9 (1717).
37. *Ibid.*, p. 569 (1707).
38. *Ibid.*, p. 773 (1711). It must be remembered, though, that when, as did sometimes happen, a later re-reading turned him against an attribution, there will, in the nature of things, be no evidence of this in the completed 'Bibliography'.
39. *Ibid.*, p. 368 (1705).
40. *Ibid.*, p. 1250 (1716).
41. See *ibid.*, pp. 173 ff. (1723).
42. See *ibid.*, p. 117 (1725).

CHAPTER 9

1. See Letter from Karl Young, Chairman of the Department of English at the University of Wisconsin, to C.F. Ward, 20 May 1921, in the Moore papers, University Archives, Indiana University, Bloomington.
2. Quoted in *John Robert Moore: a Bibliography* (Bloomington, Ind., 1961), p. 6.
3. Moore, *Defoe in the Pillory* p. 126.
4. *Ibid.*
5. *Ibid.*, p. 127.
6. *Ibid.*
7. *John Robert Moore: a Bibliography*, pp. 6–7.
8. *Defoe in the Pillory*, pp. 146, 154–60.
9. See *A General History of the Pyrates*, ed. Manuel Schonhorn (Columbia, South Carolina, 1972), pp. 363–4. The *Account*

goes out of its way to assert that the parsimoniousness of the French Captain over the crew's rations, which Gow and his associates make a pretext for murdering him, was not for the benefit of his own pocket; whereas the *History* specifically characterizes the Captain as 'covetous'. See *An Account of the Conduct and Proceedings of the Late John Gow* (1725), p. 2; and cf. *A General History of the Pyrates*, ed. Schonhorn, p. 359.

10. *Defoe in the Pillory*, p. 160.
11. *Ibid.*, p. 161.
12. See *Ibid.*, pp. 147–54. The *Letter from Scotland* is reprinted by Moore, *ibid.*, pp. 192–211.
13. *Ibid.*, p. 127.
14. Baine, 'Daniel Defoe and Robert Drury's *Journal*', pp. 485–6.
15. *Defoe in the Pillory*, p. 175. See *The Four Years Voyages of Capt. George Roberts* (1726), p. 61, and *A General History of the Pyrates*, ed. Schonhorn, pp. 318–36.
16. *A General History of the Pyrates*, ed. Schonhorn, p. 170; *Defoe in the Pillory*, p. 176.
17. *Defoe in the Pillory*, pp. 137–9.
18. See George Harris Healey (ed.), *The Letters of Daniel Defoe* (Oxford, 1955), p. 253n.
19. *Defoe in the Pillory*, p. 144.
20. *A General History of the Pyrates*, ed. Schonhorn, p. 540.
21. British Library, Sloane MS 2992.
22. *Defoe in the Pillory*, p. 180.
23. *Defoe's Sources for Robert Drury's Journal* (1943; rev. edition, New York, 1973), p. 62.
24. *Defoe in the Pillory*, p. 128.
25. *Ibid.*, p. 155.
26. *The City of God*, trans. John Healey, ed. R.V.G. Tasker, 2 vols (1945), I, pp. 115–16.
27. Charles Johnson, *The Successful Pyrate* (1713), act I, scene 1.
28. *Defoe in the Pillory*, p. 157.
29. Baine, 'Daniel Defoe and Robert Drury's *Journal*', pp. 484–5.
30. *Defoe in the Pillory*, pp. 181–8.
31. Lee, *Daniel Defoe*, I, pp. 448–9.
32. *Madagascar, or Robert Drury's Journal*, ed. Captain Pasfield Oliver (1886).
33. See Narcissus Luttrell, *A Brief Historical Relation of State Affairs from September 1678 to April 1714*, 6 vols (Oxford, 1857), V, pp. 542–3.
34. See Moore, *Defoe's Sources for Robert*

Drury's Journal, p. 27.

35. Maximillian E. Novak suggests that deistical sentiments in the *Journal* are evidence of the influence of Thomas Burnet on Defoe; see 'Defoe, Thomas Burnet, and the "Deistical" Passages of Robert Drury's *Journal*', *Philological Quarterly*, 42 (1963), pp. 207–16.

36. A.W. Secord, 'Defoe and Robert Drury's *Journal*', *Journal of English and Germanic Philology*, 44 (1945), p. 68.

37. J.R. Moore, 'Further Notes on Defoe's Sources for "Robert Drury's Journal"', *Notes and Queries*, 188 (1945), pp. 268–71.

38. Letter to Frank Bastian, 10 November 1960, in possession of recipient.

39. A.W. Secord, 'Robert Drury and "Robert Drury's Journal"', *Notes and Queries*, 189 (1945) pp. 178–80.

40. A.W. Secord, '*Robert Drury's Journal*' and *Other Studies* (Urbana, Ill., 1961).

41. Moore, *Checklist*, p. 223.

42. F.E. Budd, in *Review of English Studies*, 16 (1940), pp. 226–8.

43. J. Sutherland, in *Modern Language Review*, 35 (1940), pp. 540–42.

44. Hans H. Andersen, in *Modern Philology*, 39 (1941), pp. 215–17.

45. Mark A. Thomson, in *English Historical Review*, 60 (1945), pp. 258–60.

46. Letter to Frank Bastian, 24 October 1960, in possession of recipient.

47. See Rodney M. Baine, 'The Apparition of Mrs. Veal: A Neglected Account', *Publications of the Modern Language Association*, 69 (1954), pp. 523–41.

48. Letter from D. Nicol Smith, 16 November, 1954, and letter from A.H. Scouten, 12 February 1962, in the University Archives, Indiana University, Bloomington.

49. Moore, *Checklist*, p. vii.

50. Letter to Mrs Edna C. Davis, 18 January 1953, in William Andrews Clark Memorial Library.

51. *Defoe in the Pillory*, p. vii.

52. Letter to Zoltán Haraszti, 10 December 1953, in Boston Public Library.

53. Letter to Frank Bastian, 24 April 1965, in possession of recipient.

54. See letter, enclosing list, to Zoltán Haraszti, 25 April 1952, in Boston Public Library.

55. Letter to George Healey, 27 October 1955, in possession of Mrs Healey.

56. Moore, *Daniel Defoe: Citizen of the*

Modern World, pp. 255–56.

57. See *A Short Narrative of the Life and Actions of His Grace John, Duke of Marlborough* (1711), p. 15.

58. Augustan Reprint Society, no. 168 (Los Angeles, 1974).

59. Letter to J.R. Moore from George Healey, 3 February 1958, in the Moore papers, University Archives, Indiana University, Bloomington.

60. J. Béranger, in *Etudes Anglaises*, 15 (1962), pp. 77–8.

61. J. Sutherland, in *The Library*, 17 (1962), pp. 323–5.

CHAPTER 10

1. Reprinted in *Defoe: the Critical Heritage*, ed. Pat Rogers (1972), p. 75.

2. G.A. Starr, 'Defoe's Prose Style: 1. The Language of Interpretation', *Modern Philology*, 71 (1974), pp. 227–94.

3. E. Anthony James, *Daniel Defoe's Many Voices: A Rhetorical Study of Prose Style and Literary Method* (Amsterdam, 1972), p. 74.

4. Bonamy Dobrée, 'Some Aspects of Defoe's Prose', in *Pope and his Contemporaries: Essays Presented to George Sherburn*, ed. James L. Clifford and Louis A. Landa (Oxford, 1949), p. 180.

5. John Henry Raleigh, 'Style and Structure and their Import in Defoe's *Roxana*', *University of Kansas City Review*, 20 (1953), pp. 128–35. The passage from *Roxana* may be found in the Shakespeare Head edition (Oxford, 1927), I, p. 125.

6. Cf. Coleridge's comment on a passage from *The Farther Adventures of Robinson Crusoe*: 'These exquisite paragraphs in addition to others scattered, tho' with a sparing hand, thro' the novels, afford sufficient proof that De Foe was a first-rate master in periodic style'; reprinted in *Defoe: The Critical Heritage*, p. 84.

7. *An Essay Upon Projects* (1697), pp. 15–16.

8. For further discussion of punctuation in Defoe's works, see our 'Defoe and the "Improvisatory" Sentence', *English Studies*, 67 (1986), pp. 157–66.

9. Classical and medieval teaching about prose rhythm (the theory of the 'cursus') is also mainly concerned with ways of beginning and, especially, ending sentences.

10. On Defoe's 'radical denial of custom and tradition', see Manuel Schonhorn, 'Defoe, the Language of Politics, and the Past', *Studies in the Literary Imagination*, 15 (1982), pp. 75–83.
11. *A Journal of the Plague Year* (1722), pp. 259–60.
12. John Locke, *Two Treatises of Government*, ed. Peter Laslett (second edition, Cambridge, 1967), p. 159.
13. *The Life and Opinions of Tristram Shandy, Gentleman*, ed. Ian Campbell Ross (Oxford, 1983), pp. 9–10.
14. *Ibid.*, p. 237.

CHAPTER 11

1. John McVeagh, 'Rochester and Defoe: a Study in Influence', *Studies in English Literature*, 14 (1974), pp. 328–41.
2. See 'A New Discovery', ll.534–8.
3. 'A New Discovery', ll.92–3; *The True-Born Englishman*, ll.921–4.
4. See M.E. Campbell's very informative book, *Defoe's First Poem* (Bloomington, Ind., 1938).
5. *Jure Divino*, Book 9, ll. 455–8.
6. *The True-Born Englishman*, ll.273–84.
7. Wilson, *Memoirs*, I, p. 414.
8. F.H. Ellis, in his excellent edition, seems to get the poem wrong when he writes: 'At its best it achieves the tones and rhythm of a quiet conversation' (*Poems on Affairs of State* (New Haven and London, 1970), VI, p. 260). There is nothing in the least quiet about this poem.
9. Wilson, *Memoirs*, II, 70.
10. Cf. Samuel Johnson's remark in his 'Life of Cowley' about 'This lax and lawless versification which so much concealed the deficiencies of the barren, and flattered the laziness of the idle. . . .'
11. *The True-Born Englishman*, l.808.
12. 'A New Discovery', ll.381–8.
13. 'A Hymn to the Pillory', ll.17–22.

CHAPTER 12

1. See *Letters*, ed. Healey, pp. 29–50.
2. See *ibid.*, pp. 158–9.
3. *An Appeal to Honour and Justice* (1715), quoted from *Selected Writings*, ed. Boulton, p. 191.
4. *A Dialogue Between a Dissenter and the Observator, Concerning The Shortest Way with the Dissenters* (1703), p. 8.

5. 'After the lapse of two centuries it is permissible to suggest that he was an extremely clever man who had just become fully aware of his power as a debater and had rushed into a controversy in which he had logic and high ideals on his side, but custom and practical considerations against him. As a natural result he alienated many of his fellow Dissenters; but, being at the time a sincere Dissenter himself, and not yet adept in tortuous courses, he could not go over fully to the Church party and reap the rewards, coupled with scorn, that fall to the influential turn-coat. For nearly twenty years he was to be plagued by a monster which he did not precisely create, but to which in its youth he certainly furnished nutriment. To put it less figuratively, by his writings on Occasional Conformity Defoe not only stirred up the enemies of Dissent to more aggressive measures, but he deprived himself to a large extent of a non-conformist support which would have been of great service to him in his journalistic career'; W.P. Trent, unpublished 'Life', p. 51.
6. For further discussion of this point, see our article, 'Defoe and Imprisonment for Debt: Some Attributions Reviewed', *Review of English Studies*, n.s., 37 (1986), pp. 495–502.
7. *Conjugal Lewdness: Or, Matrimonial Whoredom* (1727), preface.
8. Charles Lamb, 'The Good Clerk', in *The Works of Charles and Mary Lamb*, ed. E.V. Lucas, 7 vols (1903), I, pp. 129–30.
9. *The Complete English Tradesman* (1726), pp. 103–4.
10. Peter Earle, *The World of Defoe* (1976), p. 230.
11. See his letter to Charles De la Faye, 26 April 1718; *Letters*, ed. Healey, p. 454.
12. See *Observator*, 23–26 December 1702, and 30 December–2 January 1702–3.
13. See Paula R. Backscheider, *Daniel Defoe: Ambition and Innovation* (Lexington, Kentucky, 1986), p. 118.
14. James Sutherland, *Daniel Defoe: A Critical Study* (1971), p. 231.
15. See Baine, *Daniel Defoe and the Supernatural*, chs 7 and 8.
16. *The Political History of the Devil* (1726), p. 232.
17. Simon Schaffer, 'Defoe's Natural Philosophy and the problem of credit', unpublished paper given to the Defoe

Research Group at the Open University, 4 February, 1986.

18. P.W.J. Riley, *The Union of England and Scotland* (1978), pp. 240–42.
19. Earle, pp. 19, 24, 20, viii.
20. *Ibid.*, pp. 139, 317.
21. *Ibid.*, p. 291.
22. Moore, *Daniel Defoe: Citizen of the Modern World*, p. 174.
23. James Sutherland, *Defoe* (1950), pp. 178, 175. For further discussion of this point, see our article, 'Defoe and the Dutch Alliance: Some Attributions Examined', *British Journal for Eighteenth-Century Studies*, 9 (1986), pp. 169–82.
24. Maximillian E. Novak, *Economics and the Fiction of Daniel Defoe* (1962; reissued, New York, 1976), unpaginated 'Preface to the 1976 Printing'.
25. *Ibid.*, pp. 3–4.
26. *Letters*, ed. Healey, pp. 50–56.
27. One remembers Edmund Calamy's hurt comment on Defoe's *Letter to the Dissenters* (the external evidence for Defoe's authorship of this tract is strong; see *Letters*, ed. Healey, p. 424) of 1713: '. . . this year was published a subtle letter to them [the Dissenters] about their behaviour, which insulted them in a cruel manner'; see *A Historical Account of My Life*, 2 vols (1830), II, p. 274. (It probably never occurred to Calamy that the author might actually be a Dissenter himself.)
28. Novak, *Economics and the Fiction of Daniel Defoe*, pp. 23–4.
29. See *Review*, 12 December 1704: 'I presume to say, Our stopping of Trade with *France*, both during the last War and this, has been a great many Millions Damage to us, and much more so, than it has to them. . . .' Britain, during the last war, was very scrupulous in prohibiting the export of corn and lead to France, but the only result was, it reached France indirectly, enriching the countries which re-exported it. 'Thus has *England* been always kept Poor and Honest, and has always taken care to have a Principal Hand in her own Misfortunes.'
30. *Some Thoughts Upon the Subject of Commerce with France* (1713), p. 4.
31. It is not quite plain why Novak refers to *Considerations*, which is a Lee attribution, as being of 'unquestionable authorship'.
32. We may compare Defoe's remark in a letter to Harley of 19 October 1713: 'Q. May Not The Ministry proceed by Another Method, and if The bill can not

be brought down to the Trade, Bring the Trade up to The Bill'; *Letters*, ed. Healey, p. 417.
33. John Toland, *The State-Anatomy of Great Britain* (1717), p. 60.
34. Evidently a reference to 'The True-Born Englishman'; *An Argument Proving that the Design of Employing and Enobling Foreigners, Is a Treasonable Conspiracy against the Constitution, dangerous to the Kingdom, an Affront to the Nobility of Scotland in particular, and Dishonourable to the Peerage of Britain in general* (1717), pp. 12–13.
35. *Ibid.*, pp. 48, 6.
36. See *The Political State*, February 1717, pp. 142–3.
37. *Mercurius Politicus*, January 1717, pp. 79–80.
38. The earlier version reads: '*Toland* insults the Holy Ghost, / Brib'd *Seymour* bribes accuses, / Good Manners and Religion's lost; / The King who was your Lord of Hosts, / The Raskal *How* abuses.' See *Poems on Affairs of State*, VI, pp. 325–6.
39. *A Farther Argument against Ennobling Foreigners* (1717), pp. 5, 26–7.
40. See his letter to Charles De la Faye of 26 April 1718; *Letters*, ed. Healey, pp. 450–54.
41. It would have been a stance rather similar to that of the amusing *Quarrel of the Schoolboys at Athens* (1717), a tract dealing with the same Whig split and generally attributed to Defoe.
42. See *An Argument*, p. 22.
43. See the letter to De la Faye already cited.
44. *A Farther Argument*, pp. 5–6.

CHAPTER 13

1. See our article, '*A Vindication of the Press* (1718): Not by Defoe?', *Papers of the Bibliographical Society of America*, 78 (1984), pp. 355–60.
2. See *The Flying-Post* (26–28 June 1718), and *The Weekly-Journal* (28 June and 12 July 1718).
3.. Moore, *Checklist*, p. 160.
4. *A Letter to the Author of the Flying-Post* (1718), p. 11.
5. *Ibid.*, pp. 34–5.
6. *Ibid.*, p. 5.
7. W.P. Trent, 'Bibliographical Notes on Defoe: II', *Nation*, 85 (1907), p. 31.
8. See Lewis Theobald, *Memoirs of Sir Walter Raleigh* (1719).

9. *An Historical Account of the Voyages and Adventures of Sir Walter Raleigh* (1720). pp. 29–45.
10. *Ibid.*, pp. 44–45.
11. *Ibid.*, p. 55.
12. Lord Erleigh, *The South Sea Bubble* (1933), p. 65.
13. See *A General History of Discoveries and Improvements* (1725), pp. 269–70, 276–83; *A Plan of the English Commerce* (1728), pp. 367–8.
14. '...all the Country farther South, to the River *Oroonoque*, is evidently out of the Possession or Power of the Spainards, who as often as they have attempted to possess it for the sake of the Wealth and Fruitfulness of it, they have found their Settlements overthrown, their People massacred, and all Hopes taken from them of planting again with security; the Natives being not only Bold and Daring, but so infinitely Numerous, that it wou'd be a kind of Desperation to attempt them, unless it were with powerful Armies regularly supplyed and duly supported to carry on a general Conquest', *A General History of Discoveries and Improvements* (1725), pp. 276–7.
15. See especially the retort to Boyer concerning the *Minutes of the Negotiations of Monsr. Mesnager* reprinted in *Mercurius Politicus*, July 1717, pp. 471–3.
16. See *The Secret History of the White Staff*, Part II (1714), pp. 17–18.
17. *The Secret History of the Secret History of the White Staff* (1715), p. 26.
18. *Ibid.*, p. 16.
19. *Minutes of the Negotiations of Monsr. Mesnager* (1717; second edition, 1736), p. 108.
20. In case any lingering doubt remains that the Mesnager *Minutes* are genuine, it should be noted that 'Lyencroon', i.e. the poet-diplomat Christoffer Leijoncrona, died in April 1710, thus a year or more before *Reasons Why This Nation* had been published.
21. *Minutes*, p. 109.

CHAPTER 14

1. See Maximillian E. Novak, *Realism, Myth and History in Defoe's Fiction* (Lincoln, Nebraska and London, 1983), pp. 18–21. For other recent discoveries of Defoe manuscripts, see J.A. Downie,

'"Mistakes On All Sides": A New Defoe Manuscript', *Review of English Studies*, 27 (1976), pp. 431–7; Frank H. Ellis, 'Notes for an Edition of Defoe's Verse', *ibid.*, 32 (1981), pp. 398–407, and idem, 'Defoe's "Resignacon" and the Limitations of "Mathematical Plainness"', *ibid.*, 36 (1985), pp. 338–54.

APPENDIX A

1. For a fuller account of the development of stylometry, see Anthony Kenny, *The Computation of Style* (1982), ch.1.
2. Opinion differs among stylometricians as to the use that can be made of the most high-frequency features of language of all, like common conjunctions and prepositions. A.Q. Morton's method is to a considerable extent based on their use, but in the form of collocations and in 'preferred' positions, whereas Alvar Ellegård, in *A Statistical Method for Determining Authorship* (Goteborg, 1962), pp. 15–16, writes that 'The words most frequently used in the language — articles, prepositions, conjunctions, and pronouns, as well as the commonest verbs, nouns, adjectives and adverbs, are necessarily about *equally* frequent in all texts, whoever the author. And this means in effect that the large majority of the positively or negatively distinctive words will belong to the frequency ranges below 0.0001, or one per ten thousand.'
3. Quoted by M.W.A. Smith in 'An Investigation of Morton's Method to Distinguish Elizabethan Playwrights', *Computers and the Humanities*, 19 (1985), p. 3.
4. See A.Q. Morton, *Literary Detection* (1978); Anthony Kenny, *The Aristotelian Ethics* (1978) and *The Computation of Style* (1982); Alvar Ellegård, *A Statistical Method for Determining Authorship*, and *Who Was Junius?* (Stockholm, 1962); M.W.A. Smith, 'A Stylometric Analysis of *Hero and Leander*', *The Bard*, 3 (1982), pp. 105–32; 'Recent Experience and New Developments of Methods for the Determination of Authorship', *ALLC Bulletin*, 11 (1983), pp. 73–82; 'The Authorship of "A Lover's Complaint": An Application of Statistical Stylometry to Poetry' *Computers and the Humanities*, 18 (1984), pp. 23–37; and articles cited in

notes 3 above and 12 below.

5. Second and revised edition of *Inference and Disputed Authorship: The Federalist* (1964).

6. Morton himself makes the remark that 'all systems of recognition are negative', in *To Couple is the Custom*, by S. Michaelson, A.Q. Morton and N. Hamilton-Smith (University of Edinburgh, Department of Computer Science, Internal Report (1978), p. 12).

7. See *Literary Detection*, pp. 5–7.

8. *Ibid.*, p. 96.

9. *Ibid.*, p. 15.

10. *Ibid.*, pp. 106–7.

11. *The Computation of Style*, p. 69.

12. In a review of *Authorship Puzzles in the History of Economics* by D.P. O'Brien and A.C. Darnell (1982), Stephen M. Stigler makes much of the fatal consequences of disobeying this rule. See *Journal of Economic History*, 43 (1983), pp. 547–50.

13. See particularly his article, 'An Investigation of the Basis of Morton's Method for the Determination of Authorship', *Style*, 19 (1985), pp. 341–68, in which he writes, apropos of Morton's *Literary Detection*, that 'when so many comparisons of samples by two or more authors by means of tests of typical features fail to reveal differences, the effectiveness of the method itself does become suspect. Also, the failure to mention straightforward but important definitions distinguishes Morton's work from scientific studies.' (p. 355).

14. See article cited in note 3 above, p. 7.

Works by Defoe or attributed to Defoe are entered directly under title. Works included in James Crossley's list (Appendix B) are indexed only if they are commented on in the text. Other works appear under authors' names.

CANADIAN POLITICS

Third Edition

Annual Editions
A Library of Information from the Public Press

Editor

Gregory S. Mahler
University of Mississippi

Gregory S. Mahler is chair of the Political Science Department at the University of Mississippi. He received a B.A. from Oberlin College in 1972, and an M.A. in 1974 and a Ph.D. in 1976 from Duke University. His publications in the field of Canadian politics include many articles and two recent books: *New Dimensions of Canadian Federalism: Canada in a Comparative Perspective* (1987), and *Contemporary* ...
(1988).

Roman Ma...
        Pol...
received a
    M.A.
Ph.D. in
two books

8510

...he Dushkin Publishing Group, Inc.
...e Dock, Guilford, Connecticut 06437

The Annual Editions Series

Annual Editions is a series of over 55 volumes designed to provide the reader with convenient, low-cost access to a wide range of current, carefully selected articles from some of the most important magazines, newspapers, and journals published today. Annual Editions are updated on an annual basis through a continuous monitoring of over 300 periodical sources. All Annual Editions have a number of features designed to make them particularly useful, including topic guides, annotated tables of contents, unit overviews, and indexes. For the teacher using Annual Editions in the classroom, an Instructor's Resource Guide with test questions is available for each volume.

VOLUMES AVAILABLE

Africa
Aging
American Government
American History, Pre-Civil War
American History, Post-Civil War
Anthropology
Biology
Business Ethics
Canadian Politics
China
Commonwealth of Independent States
Comparative Politics
Computers in Education
Computers in Business
Computers in Society
Criminal Justice
Drugs, Society, and Behavior
Dying, Death, and Bereavement
Early Childhood Education
Economics
Educating Exceptional Children
Education
Educational Psychology
Environment
Geography
Global Issues
Health
Human Development
Human Resources
Human Sexuality
India and South Asia

International Business
Japan and the Pacific Rim
Latin America
Life Management
Macroeconomics
Management
Marketing
Marriage and Family
Microeconomics
Middle East and the Islamic World
Money and Banking
Nutrition
Personal Growth and Behavior
Physical Anthropology
Psychology
Public Administration
Race and Ethnic Relations
Social Problems
Sociology
State and Local Government
Third World
Urban Society
Violence and Terrorism
Western Civilization, Pre-Reformation
Western Civilization, Post-Reformation
Western Europe
World History, Pre-Modern
World History, Modern
World Politics

Library of Congress Cataloging in Publication Data
Main entry under title: Annual Editions: Canadian Politics. 3/E.
1. Canada—Politics and Government—1945- —Periodicals. I. Mahler, Gregory S., and March, Roman R., comp. II. Title: Canadian Politics.
ISBN 1–56134–191–6   354.71'005

Third Edition

Manufactured by The Banta Company, Harrisonburg, Virginia 22801

Printed on Recycled Paper

To the Reader

In publishing ANNUAL EDITIONS we recognize the enormous role played by the magazines, newspapers, and journals of the *public press* in providing current, first-rate educational information in a broad spectrum of interest areas. Within the articles, the best scientists, practitioners, researchers, and commentators draw issues into new perspective as accepted theories and viewpoints are called into account by new events, recent discoveries change old facts, and fresh debate breaks out over important controversies.

Many of the articles resulting from this enormous editorial effort are appropriate for students, researchers, and professionals seeking accurate, current material to help bridge the gap between principles and theories and the real world. These articles, however, become more useful for study when those of lasting value are carefully *collected, organized, indexed,* and *reproduced* in a *low-cost format*, which provides easy and permanent access when the material is needed. That is the role played by *Annual Editions*. Under the direction of each volume's *Editor*, who is an expert in the subject area, and with the guidance of an *Advisory Board*, we seek each year to provide in each *ANNUAL EDITION* a current, well-balanced, carefully selected collection of the best of the public press for your study and enjoyment. We think you'll find this volume useful, and we hope you'll take a moment to let us know what you think.

This is the third edition of what we hope will continue to be a widely used source of reading material in the study of Canadian politics, especially at a time when Canada is continuing to face fundamental challenges to its constitutional system. Our goal in assembling this collection has been to include discussion and debate about many contemporary issues that are important in the study of Canadian politics but which, because of their timeliness, may not have received adequate coverage in textbooks and other reference material. The *Annual Editions* concept allows us to include very timely material, and it offers the opportunity to revise and update the contents of a volume periodically. Indeed, only a handful of the articles in this volume appeared in the last edition. Although the amount of material published in the study of Canadian politics has vastly increased in recent years, we are not aware of any collections of readable, up-to-date articles similar to those found in this volume.

The selections in this collection come from a wide range of publications, including daily newspapers, weekly and monthly newsmagazines, and less frequently published sources that deal with discussion and analysis related to news of a political nature, as well as cultural and social issues. In making our selections we have sought to include a wide range of issues and perspectives that cover what we perceive to be important themes in contemporary Canadian politics. Some topics have clearly dominated the political landscape in the last year or two—for example, the proposed changes to the Constitution, or the issue of free trade with the United States and Mexico—and they are very well represented here. Other subjects represented here may have been less visible in national headlines, but are no less important to an understanding of the dynamics of contemporary Canadian politics—for example, the economic problems of Atlantic Canada or questions concerning self-government for Canada's aboriginal peoples.

This book is organized into 10 sections, each dealing with a broad dimension of current political interest in Canada, including (a) the national uncertainty of Canada, (b) the role of the Supreme Court and the Constitution, (c) the parliamentary system, (d) participation and elections, (e) the politics of culture, (f) the regionalism of federalism, (g) Quebec, (h) aboriginal issues, (i) free trade, and (j) defence and foreign policy concerns. Within each section we have endeavored to include material touching upon a wide range of subjects, from a variety of perspectives. It is, unfortunately, inevitable that some subjects that some readers will feel very strongly about will have been omitted from this volume. We again invite you to contact us with your reactions to this collection and suggestions for the next volume by completing and returning the article rating form in the back of this book.

Gregory S. Mahler

Roman R. March
Editors

Contents

Unit 1

Canada: A Nation in Limbo

Four articles discuss the challenges that Canada faces after the failure to resolve the question of Quebec's independence.

Unit 2

The Supreme Court of Canada and the Constitution

Six articles examine ideologies and decisions of Canada's Supreme Court.

The concepts in bold italics are developed in the article. For further expansion please refer to the Topic Guide and the Index.

Unit 3

The Parliamentary System

Six selections examine the fundamental changes in the Canadian parliamentary system.

Unit 4

Participation and Elections

Eight articles discuss the dynamics of elections in Canada and consider the regional differences in political participation.

The concepts in bold italics are developed in the article. For further expansion please refer to the Topic Guide and the Index.

Unit 5

The Politics of Culture

Six articles consider how the unique political future of Canada has developed in recent years despite the tremendous influence generated by its proximity to the United States.

The concepts in bold italics are developed in the article. For further expansion please refer to the Topic Guide and the Index.

Unit 6

The Regionalism of Federalism

Eight selections discuss the vast differences among Canada's provinces.

The concepts in bold italics are developed in the article. For further expansion please refer to the Topic Guide and the Index.

Unit

7

Quebec

Four articles discuss the impact of French Canada on the rest of Canadian politics.

Unit

8

Aboriginal Issues

Five articles examine the ever-increasing issue of aboriginal rights and how this important social problem is being addressed.

The concepts in bold italics are developed in the article. For further expansion please refer to the Topic Guide and the Index.

Unit 9

Free Trade

Nine articles examine the problematic issue of the Canadian foreign trade policy and its relationship with the United States, including NAFTA (North American Free Trade Agreement).

The concepts in bold italics are developed in the article. For further expansion please refer to the Topic Guide and the Index.

Unit 10

Defence and Foreign Policy

Seven selections examine the current and future choices Canada must face with regard to its foreign policy.

The concepts in bold italics are developed in the article. For further expansion please refer to the Topic Guide and the Index.

Topic Guide

This topic guide suggests how the selections in this book relate to topics of traditional concern to students and professionals involved with the study of Canadian politics. It is useful for locating articles that relate to each other for reading and research. The guide is arranged alphabetically according to topic. Articles may, of course, treat topics that do not appear in the topic guide. In turn, entries in the topic guide do not necessarily constitute a comprehensive listing of all the contents of each selection.

Canada: A Nation in Limbo

Canada has tried and failed, for the sixth time in 25 years, to find a way to resolve the question of Quebec's independence. The latest attempt did not win support by a referendum vote on the 26th of October 1992. Roman March's article outlines the complex and acrimonious process that led to the decision to put the Charlottetown Agreement to the voters. The article also explains some of the most important reasons why the referendum failed to pass.

The article by Henry Srebrnik explores yet another model that might help to salvage Canada as a recognizable federal state. Or will the Canadian experiment follow the Austro-Hungarian example? If provincial borders are not sacrosanct, would the attempt to partition Canada and Quebec inevitably lead to violence? Srebrnik claims that: "Secessions may sometimes be bloodless, but partitions are messy."

The next article in this section provides a guide for understanding the context, issues, and substance of the debate over the Constitution.

The article on the complete text of the Charlottetown Agreement contains the substance of what could have been agreed to after the failure of the Meech Lake agreement. Of course, many proposals were left out, or they are watered-down versions of what various actors and groups wanted. One can only assume that this text will form the basis for future constitutional negotiations. However, it is likely that formal negotiations will not begin until after the next federal general election. This election can take place at any time, but it must be held no later than November 1993, when the present government's five-year mandate ends.

Polls indicate that the Conservative Party of Canada faces a very difficult election contest, as the Liberal Party of Canada, led by Jean Chretien, is far ahead of the New Democratic, Reform and Bloc Québécois parties. (Conservatives 17%, Liberals 44%, NDP 18%, Reform 13%, Bloc Québécois 29% in Quebec. Angus Reid-Southan News survey, November 6, 1992, *Toronto Star*.)

The Quebec government is much more fortunate than the federal government, which is led by Prime Minister Brian Mulroney, in that its mandate extends to 1994. It expects to survive until after the federal election, but it is uncertain whether other provincial premiers would be willing to begin negotiations on the Constitution immediately after a federal election. This would be particularly true if no party wins a majority of seats in either the federal or the Quebec elections. The Premier of Ontario, Bob Rae, has stated that he will not be at the negotiating table again until after a federal general election. Only Quebec and, perhaps, the Reform Party might want to reopen constitutional negotiations soon.

Looking Ahead: Challenge Questions

Did the federal and Quebec governments make strategic blunders in allowing a referendum on the Constitution? If so, why?

How will plebiscitary democracy modify the principle of representative democracy?

What does the Charlottetown Agreement indicate about the nature of Canadian federalism?

Canada:

Continuing
Constitutional Crisis

Roman March

Written for Annual Editions: Canadian Politics, *Spring 1993.*

When the Meech Lake constitutional proposals failed to be accepted in June 1990, Premier Robert Bourassa of Quebec was immediately faced with a severe challenge to the stability of his Liberal Party's government from a resurgent nationalist backlash led by the separatist Parti Quebecois. Supporters of Canadian federalism in Quebec were charged with having, once again, manufactured another affront to Quebec's honor, dignity, and pride. It was also argued that once again, Quebec's "reasonable and modest" request for constitutional changes had been rejected by a few anti-Quebec provincial premiers, in particular Clyde Wells of Newfoundland, and a majority of public opinion in English Canada.

The Quebec Liberal Party Youth Wing, which comprises one-third of the party's convention delegates, joined forces with the nationalist wing of the Quebec Liberal Party in denouncing Premier Bourassa for failing to prevent another humiliation of Quebec francophones.

In order to channel and control this nationalist resentment, Premier Bourassa established two major commissions to review Quebec's grievances and to renew the historical struggle to protect Quebec's French language heritage by strengthening the powers of the Quebec provincial government at the expense of a too-powerful federal government. Jean Allaire, as Chairman of the Liberal Party's Constitutional Committee, recommended in his *report*, published 28 January 1991, that the federal government be stripped of some 22 powers. As well, the "central government would exercise exclusive authority" only in "defence and territorial security, customs and tariffs, currency and common debt, [and] equalization [payments to have-not provinces and regions]." Other powers were to be shared between Quebec and Canada. The Allaire proposals were ignored by the rest of Canada, but they received such strong support in Quebec, that it became the standard against which all constitutional proposals were compared.

The second major Quebec commission was cochaired by Michel Belanger and Jean Campeau. This Commission on the Political and Constitutional Future of Quebec was composed of representatives from all of Quebec's political, economic, labor union, educational, cooperative, and cultural sectors. Its *report*, submitted on 27 March 1991, analyzed the history of Quebec's constitutional and political status within the Canadian federation since 1867. It reaffirmed the following fundamental principle, that: "From Quebec's standpoint, the Canadian federal regime was based at the outset on the Canadian duality and the autonomy of the provinces. . . . This Canadian duality, based on relations between French Canadians and English Canadians, is perceived as an underlying principle of the federal regime. The federal union is seen as a pact between these two parties." [pp. 11–12]

The Belanger-Campeau Commission declared also that "the *Constitution Act, 1982*, was proclaimed despite the opposition of the National Assembly [of Quebec] . . . [and] the 1987 Agreement on the Constitution, the aim of which was to allow Quebec to become a party to the *Constitution Act, 1982*, had failed." The Commission then recommended "that a referendum on Quebec sovereignty . . . be held" no later than 26 October 1992. Furthermore, "Should the outcome of the referendum be positive, Quebec will acquire the status of a sovereign state one year . . . after the date of the referendum." [p. 79–80]

The recommendation to hold another referendum on sovereignty, so soon after the failed 1980 referendum, caused consternation among federal and provincial elites. However, the commission did provide the federal and provincial governments, and especially Premier Bourassa, with a way to avoid a Quebec referendum on sovereignty, by also recommending that a special parliamentary commission of the Quebec National Assembly be created "to assess any offer of a new partnership of constitutional nature made by the Government of Canada." [p. 81]

The federal government, Ontario, and the eastern Maritime provinces avidly seized this opportunity to avoid a Quebec referendum on sovereignty by first creating the Spicer Commission, which crisscrossed Canada to solicit public opinion. All provincial governments also consulted their own populace and interest groups to prepare their positions for the next round of federal, provincial, territorial, and aboriginal negotiations. Numerous interest groups, pressure groups, and all political parties also made their wishes known—often in no uncertain terms. Many began with nonnegotiable, "bottom-line" demands.

Even as this flurry of public consultation was under way, the federal government established its own Special Joint Committee of the Senate and House of Commons. This committee reported to the Canadian Parliament on 28 February 1992, with a detailed analysis and a set of recommendations to help the government of Canada formulate concrete proposals for a renewed Canada. This *report* served as a guideline for the actual constitutional negotiations. During its deliberations, the committee received 3,000 submissions and listened to testimony from 700 individuals. As well, a series of six televised national conferences were held early in 1992.

It should be understood that besides the formal hearings of commissions and committees, continuous negotiations were taking place at many levels, mostly behind the scenes and out of the public eye, up to the 26 October 1992 Referendum. There was also the rather bizarre situation in which the Quebec government refused to sit at the formal negotiation table from March 1992 until early August, and it conducted its case through emissaries, observers, cabinet ministers, government officials, aboriginal leaders, and spokesmen for political parties and interest groups. Virtually all those involved used rather hardball tactics in order to manipulate, intimidate, and out-negotiate other participants, and to mold public support. Spin doctors, lobbyists, public opinion pollsters, openmouthed [open-line] shows, and consultants were very busy and well-employed.

Only the most economically dependent provinces in the Maritimes tried to be mediators, rather than "heavies." Clyde Wells of Newfoundland, as usual, adopted a hardline stand and defended the Pierre Trudeau theory of a bilingual, multicultural Canada in which no provinces had a distinct status or special constitutionally entrenched powers.

A series of more formal meetings of first ministers or their spokesmen began in March 1992. A consensus on a set of constitutional amendments was eventually incorporated in the *Consensus Report on the Constitution*, at Charlottetown, and made public on 28 August 1992. The *report*'s six sections began with a Canada Clause that attempted, for the first time in Canada's history, to provide a "short and eloquent statement of our fundamental values." A Canada Clause would guide the courts of Canada in interpreting the entire Constitution. Quebec, as in the failed Meech Lake agreement, was recognized as a distinct society within Canada. However the word "distinct" was now far less open-ended by being carefully defined and limited. The linguistic duality of French and English as the official languages of Canada was affirmed, as well as was Canada as a parliamentary and federal democracy.

The most innovative part of the Canada Clause, unprecedented throughout the Americas, recognized aboriginal governments as one of the three orders of government in Canada. To this end, the inherent right of aboriginal self-government would be recognized and entrenched in the Constitution. Racial and ethnic equality and the equality of female and male persons would also guide the courts in their future interpretation of the entire Constitution, as well as the equality of the provinces.

Part II of the Charlottetown Agreement outlined amendments to the federal Parliament. A Triple-E Senate [Equal, Elected, and Effective] long the "bottom line" for the Western provinces, [this was particularly Alberta's nonnegotiable demand] was to replace the current Senate by assigning six senators to each province. Ontario and Quebec would each lose 18 of their current 24 senators, but these losses in the Senate would be compensated for by Quebec receiving a guarantee of one-quarter of the seats in the House of Commons, with 18 additional seats for Ontario. British Columbia would get an extra 4 seats and Alberta 2 seats, in the House of Commons. Many NO supporters were upset by this "power grab" by the two central provinces of an extra 36 seats.

Other proposed modifications of Parliament dealt with the powers of each house, strengthening the powers of the Commons against the formerly virtually equal formal powers of the Senate. Another proposal would entrench the current composition of the Supreme Court of Canada, such that three of the nine judges would have to come from Quebec. Provinces would be asked to nominate lists of candidates for the Supreme Court to the federal government, which would make the final selection.

There would also be a constitutional requirement to hold conferences of First Ministers [Provincial Premiers and the Canadian Prime Minister] on an annual basis, with aboriginal leaders invited to participate in discussion of items that directly affected their interests.

Other sections of the Charlottetown Agreement focused on fiscal/financial and economic arrangements between the federal and provincial governments, the amending formula, and compensation for transfers of jurisdiction from provinces to Parliament.

All these proposals were, after much intense and often acrimonious bargaining between all participants inside and outside the process, accepted by the Quebec government as a fair and reasonable set of constitutional amendments, which could win public acceptance in Quebec, all other provinces, territories, and among the aboriginal peoples.

Despite initial resolute opposition by the federal government, Ontario, and a few other provinces, it was decided to hold a nonbinding national referendum [actually a plebiscite] on the Charlottetown Agreement. The strategic decision to hold a national referendum was taken so that Quebec would not have its own referendum in isolation from the rest of Canada. There was deep concern that, whatever the results of a Quebec referendum, the rest of Canada would not accept any referendum result as legitimate or binding. It was also thought that a national referendum would make it much easier to sell in Quebec if francophones could see strong support for the agreement in the rest of Canada.

But this did not happen for a variety of reasons. The initial high level of support for the agreement in August 1992 began to collapse very rapidly across Canada.

Why did this support evaporate? Many citizens supported the NO side because they believed that an even better deal could be hammered out. For example, in early October 1992, 84 percent of Quebecers agreed that "Quebecers should be able to demand a better deal from the rest of Canada without being called separatists; and 60 percent agreed that "Bourassa gave away too much in the negotiations," while 27 percent disagreed that he had done so. In British Columbia, 79 percent of those who would vote YES and 95 percent of those who would vote NO disagreed on whether or not "Quebec should be guaranteed at least 25 percent of the seats in the House of Commons." [*Globe and Mail*, Toronto, 10 October 1992, A4].

Many YES supporters feared that another constitutional failure would accelerate the drive toward Quebec sovereignty, and that the division of Canada into two hostile nation-states would lead to the collapse of the economy, interminable recrimination between Quebec and Canada, and an attack on Canadian financial markets

by the same international money-market speculators who had already severely weakened the European monetary system in September 1992.

The Reform Party argued, that a NO vote was essential as it would put an end to constitutional turmoil for a period of five or more years; that the Triple-E Senate would be a hollow sham; and, that the aboriginals were incapable of governing themselves, while aboriginal land claims would incur enormous costs, dislocate existing communities, and threaten corporate and government ownership and/or control of its vital petroleum and forest industries. Reformers also claimed that the social charter was merely a New Democratic Party ploy which would increase the costs of government significantly by adding to the already huge national debt. Finally, many Reformers have always been anti-French, an antivisible minority, and distrustful of the economic and political power of central Canada.

Many feminists voted NO because they feared that the federal government would be unable and/or unwilling to maintain the existing social support network. Many aboriginal women voted NO because they feared the continuation of patriarchal leadership in their communities and subordination of their Charter freedoms to aboriginal community interests as defined by male leaders. Aboriginal women also struggled through court challenges against the continued exclusion of representatives of *all* Canadian women from constitutional negotiations.

These conflicts over individual and collective rights, the structure and powers of federal institutions, and special agendas of interest and pressure groups quickly eroded support for the YES side of the referendum. The first published opinion polls showed that there was a significant level of support for the Charlottetown Agreement during the first week of September. For example, the polling firm Environics reported that on 1 September 1992, 43 percent of Quebecers would vote YES while 39 percent would vote NO in the referendum. In the rest of Canada, 53 percent would vote YES and only 20 percent would vote NO. However, by October 10, the Quebec polling firm CROP reported that the YES vote had dropped to 34 percent in Quebec, while the NO vote had jumped to 50 percent, with 16 percent undecided. Other polls discovered considerable opposition to the agreement in British Columbia and Alberta, where Preston Manning's Reform Party posed a strong challenge to the Progressive Conservative and New Democratic Parties.

This widespread opposition to the agreement carried over into the referendum vote. Only 44.6 percent [6,185,902] voted YES across Canada. The NO votes were 54.4 percent [7,550,732]. As predicted by the polls, Quebec voted NO at 55.4 percent; British Columbia, 68.0 percent; Manitoba, 61.6 percent; Alberta, 60.1 percent; Nova Scotia, 51.1 percent; and the Yukon, 56.1 percent. Prince Edward Island topped the YES votes at 73.6 percent; Newfoundland, 62.9 percent; New Brunswick,

61.3 percent; and the Territories, 60.6 percent. Ontario split 49.8 percent YES and 49.6 percent NO.

The results of the referendum vote indicated that the smaller and poorer Atlantic provinces supported the agreement out of a deep concern that they would suffer severe economic dislocation if the failure of the referendum should hasten Quebec's separation. Western Canada forcefully rejected the agreement on the grounds that it gave too much to central Canada, and in particular to Quebec.

In addition to a split between regions, there seemed to be an urban-rural split. Major urban areas voted strongly YES; rural areas were more likely to vote NO. This may stem from the fact that the multicultural communities are concentrated in the major urban areas such as Montreal, Toronto, Winnipeg, Edmonton, Calgary, and Vancouver. These communities are much more afraid of the economic, social, and cultural dislocations of the break up of Canada.

In summary, the referendum marks yet another stage in the Canadian struggle to find an appropriate process and specific constitutional proposals to amend its various constitutions. All the while, the various constituencies such as political parties, provincial premiers, ethnic groups, feminists, aboriginals, and interest groups struggle to be heard, participate in, and be recognized as important and essential participants, in order to obtain constitutional status and recognition of their agendas.

Canada's Constitution: A New Austria-Hungary in the Making?

Henry Srebrnik

Henry Srebrnik teaches in the Department of Political Science at the University of Calgary. This paper was presented at the ACSUS Conference in Boston, November 1991.

Since the breakdown of the Meech Lake constitutional accord, both English and French Canadians have been engaged in a process designed to see if the country can be salvaged as a recognizable federal state, or whether the "two solitudes," to use the term coined by Canadian novelist Hugh MacLennan, will indeed, after a century and a quarter, choose to go their different ways.

In September 1991 the federal government announced its new proposals for constitutional reform. As well, a number of provinces have established commissions after the collapse of Meech. But this essay will not delve into the minutae of the various federal and provincial constitutional proposals, which may be modified beyond recognition. I want rather to see if it is possible for the Canadian-Quebecois dilemma to be resolved if both sides move towards the kind of "dualism" that, in the Habsburg Empire, resulted in the 1867 "ausgleich" or compromise, and the creation of the "Dual Monarchy."

Both of these admittedly very different states - Canada and Austria-Hungary - had a similar starting point: they were the products of empire, rather than the "national principle." They were formed as a result of imperial acquisitions and the conquest of ethnic groups distinct from that of the ruling imperial dynasty.

The lands that became known as Austria-Hungary were cobbled together over many centuries by the German House of Habsburg. Not until 1804, when the Austrian Empire was proclaimed by Francis II, was there even a common state as such, as opposed to purely dynastic unions.

By the mid-19th century, the Habsburgs ruled over populations of Germans, Hungarian (Magyars), Poles, Italians, Ruthenians (Ukrainians), Croats, Serbs, Slovenes, Czechs, Slovaks, and Romanians, among others. These peoples had ethnically-defined territories, often historical kingdoms that retained ancient rights. The Habsburgs were Holy Roman [German] Emperors and kings of Hungary, Bohemia, and Croatia, among numerous other titles. Yet very often, as well, segments of these nationalities lived in belts of mixed population, areas which would later come into dispute as rival nationalisms–Italian vs. Croatian, Hungarian vs. Croatian, Czech vs. German–clashed within the empire.

Within the Habsburg Empire, even the German-speaking inhabitants viewed themselves as Germans, rather than Austrians. As for the other peoples, they owed loyalty, if at all, to the dynasty as such, and, if and when that diminished, were unwilling to assimilate their own ethnic and linguistic identities into those of the German nationality.

Canada was the eventual union of those North American possessions of the British Crown which did not revolt in 1776: Upper and Lower Canada, Nova Scotia, New Brunswick, Prince Edward Island, Newfoundland, British Columbia, and the Hudson's Bay Company's western and northern territories, known as Rupert's Land.

These colonies were inhabited by settlers from the British Isles, French Canadians, and various aboriginal peoples, later augmented by the arrival of immigrants from all over Europe and, after World War II, the entire world. Though most of these territories were incorporated into Canada by the turn of the century, they remained under the political, legal and ideological hegemony of the British Empire until well into the 1940s. French Canadians were largely concentrated in the old New France—although Quebec had a large English minority. The aboriginal peoples lost all meaningful political sovereignty, and became concentrated on reserves.

There was little sense of Canadian nationhood per se. British Canadians saw themselves as part of a larger entity, the British Empire. (Since English Canada was in effect the creation of the United Empire Loyalists, there was also no commonality of interest with the English-speaking but secessionist American Republic.) French Canadians were a people trying to survive as best

From *Canadian Parliamentary Review*, Spring 1992, pp. 2-5. Reprinted by permission.

they could under British rule. Later immigrants (and natives) had little input in the development of Canadian consciousness until post World War II.

The Habsburg Empire was a multi-national state where the two dominant groups, Germans and Hungarians, were each less than 25% of the total population. Loyalty to the state as such was felt most strongly by what we might today call a nomenklatura–the higher bureaucracy and army. Only slowly did nationalism begin to stir among the peoples of the empire–and, like in Canada, it would often take the form of cultural conflict and "language wars."

In 1848, various nationalities rose in revolt against Habsburg rule, while Austrian Germans themselves sought greater political liberties (and possible union within a greater German nation).

The Habsburgs were pressured into adopting the Kremsier constitution, declaring the various nationalities (and their languages) equal and calling for the formation of a bicameral parliament, the lower house to represent the people, the upper house the various lands.

But this liberal constitution never came into effect. In the historic territory known as the Kingdom of Hungary (the lands of the Crown of St. Stephen), the Magyars (who made up less than 50% of the total population but who had long held a privileged position) proclaimed a constitution in their own Diet. However, nationalists like Louis Kossuth refused the other nationalities those freedoms Hungarians themselves sought. This resulted in resistance on the part of Croats, Serbs, Romanians and Slovaks, and the Habsburgs were finally able to defeat this attempt at creating an independent Hungarian republic.

The Magyars did not give up. For the next two decades, while the Austrian Germans tried to unify the monarchy, the Magyars insisted, not on federalism, but on a Hungary distinct from the other Habsburg lands, and itself centralized and unitary.

After 1866 they got their chance. The Habsburgs were defeated by Prussia and were eliminated from German politics. The weakened Austrian Germans, aware that the Hungarians would if necessary side with the Prussians, in 1867 (the same year as Confederation) agreed to the creation of a dualist political system in which the Hungarians received almost complete independence within their historical frontiers; they would also exercise a role in the larger polity far beyond their numerical or economic strength. None of the other nationalities in either "Austria" (i.e. the non-Hungarian lands of the Habsburgs, whose official name was simply "the kingdoms and lands represented in the Reichsrat [Imperial Council]") or Hungary were consulted. The "ausgleich" was a deal between the Habsburg court and the Hungarian leaders.

The details of the ausgleich are complex, so I will provide only a few of the main points. Three administrative authorities were set up: There was to be a common head of state–Francis Joseph I was now Emperor of Austria and King of Hungary–and a few areas of jurisdiction that would remain under imperial control: the military, foreign affairs (though both parliaments would have to approve international treaties), and a few common financial matters. Three imperial ministries were formed for these. As well, there were certain matters which, while not administered in common, would be regulated jointly upon principles which had to be renegotiated every 10 years: customs legislation, the proportion to be paid by each entity of certain taxes and expenses, a common monetary and postal system, and railway lines affecting both parts of the empire.

In order to deal with such legislation, numerically equal delegations from the two respective parliaments would meet in common once a year, alternately in Vienna and Budapest.

Everything else was now to come under the jurisdiction of Hungary or the lands of the Austrian Reichsrat. Each part of the empire would now have its own constitution, parliament and cabinet (located in Budapest and Vienna, respectively), and official language. There was no common citizenship, nor could either country intervene in the other's domestic affairs.

Austria's constitution, much more liberal than Hungary's, recognized some national and linguistic rights. Within Hungary, despite the enactment of a Nationalities Law in 1868, which on paper allowed minorities to receive education and conduct local governmental affairs in their own language, by 1875 only the Croats retained certain very limited autonomy. The policy would henceforth be one of cultural assimilation: minorities wishing to adopt Magyar culture and language would be accepted, but those wishing to develop their own would be repressed. Magyar was made compulsory in all schools in 1883. By the turn of the century, over 90% of all judges, county and government officials in Hungary were Magyars.

But even within the Austrian lands there was conflict: Germans and Czechs clashed over who "owned" Bohemia: after all, said the German inhabitants, it had been an historic part of the Holy Roman Empire. But, countered the Czechs, these were the lands of the Crown of St. Wenceslaus, as such a Czech entity. These quarrels would extend to matters of language as well, including questions about the use of Czech or German on street signs or on restaurant menus in bi-cultural cities such as Prague.

An attempt in 1871 to grant the Czechs equal status to Germans in a federal Bohemia failed (partly because the Hungarians, not wishing to alter the 1867 arrangements *anywhere* in the empire, blocked it). There were also outbreaks of violence by Germans in Bohemia and Moravia in 1897, when the government tried to introduce bilingualism in the civil service–a move favorable to the

1. CANADA: A NATION IN LIMBO

Czechs, who were more likely to know German than the reverse case.

Indeed, many Austrian Germans, now no longer prominent in wider German affairs, and indeed fearing their own decline within the Dual Monarchy itself (imperial ministries were no longer necessarily under German control), began to declare pan-German sentiments, and looked longingly towards the powerful German Empire next door. Some intellectuals wanted a small, German Austria, attached to Germany by a customs union. A nationalistic pan-German party was formed by Georg von Schonerer in 1885. Germany discouraged such behavior, believing that a united Habsburg monarchy better served Germany's interests than a fragmented group of successor states.

As for the Hungarians, despite the ausgleich, demands for complete independence increased by the turn of the century. Many wanted a separate Hungarian army with Magyar as the language of command, and an end to the customs and monetary union with Austria. Even those who continued to support the ausgleich constantly sought increased influence and privileges in the empire as a whole.

The Hungarians also redoubled their campaigns against minorities within their borders, especially against the Croats. Even private schools for minorities were banned in 1907. The minorities, said Hungarian Prime Minister Stephen Tisza in 1913, had to become accustomed to the fact that they lived in a nation-state, "a state which is not a conglomerate of various races." As already noted, the Magyars also blocked whenever possible ethnic advances in the Austrian lands, lest similar demands be made on them. They considered only themselves and the Germans the two "peoples of state." They needed the Habsburg connection in order to maintain their greater Hungary, while wishing to remain free from Viennese interference.

The national discontent within the empire led to its disintegration after World War I. Two tiny rump states, Austria and Hungary, reduced to their ethnic boundaries, were all that was left to the two ruling peoples of the empire. (The Hungarians did indeed find out they could not leave the Dual Monarchy with all their territory.) Elsewhere, successor states, based on the "national principle," emerged, though often these, too, found themselves with recalcitrant or unwanted minorities.

> All of these conflicts resulted in sterile
> constitutional questions taking
> precedence over the promotion of
> economic unity and industrial
> development. Towards the end, the state
> was held together only by a vast body of
> bureaucrats.

The various constitutional amendments now on the table in Canada are leading us towards a "Austro-Hungarian" solution. But that begs the question: Would a "Dual Canada" which made constitutionally explicit the notion of "two founding nations" follow the same downward spiral as did the Hapsburg Monarchy?

Quebecois, certainly, show ethnocentric tendencies not encouraging to anglophone and allophone minorities, and seem more interested in cultural assimilation than pluralism.

Despite massive emigration since the 1970s, there are still some 800,000 anglophones in Quebec, concentrated mainly in Montreal, and they remain hostile to Quebec nationhood.

The allophones–some 630,000 people-fare little better. While in many ways more integrated into the larger French Canadian society than are the anglophones (many allophones are recent immigrants), they fear Quebec separatism almost as much and also wish to remain within Canada.

In December 1990, a report written by nine prominent members of Quebec ethnic groups said that In Quebec, racism is alive and well and living under the guise of Quebec nationalism. As Quebec moves toward becoming more French, it pushes aside and ignores other cultures, which are not seen as valid. The Quebec concept of integration is really assimilation. It also noted that Quebec identity has begun to be based entirely on race, leading to expressions such as Quebecois "pure laine," literally, of pure wool, i.e. old-stock or "real" French Canadians.

While the Canadian federal civil service employs approximately the same percentage of francophones as comprise the overall population, Quebec's civil service is still overwhelmingly francophone. Though francophones comprise about 83% of Quebec's population, the provincial civil service was, as of March 1990, 99.3% francophone. Montreal's own civil service is less than 1% anglophone–this, in a city where anglophones still make up some 19% of the population.

In March 1991, Cree Chief Billy Diamond warned a House of Commons committee that his people might engage in armed confrontation if the $12.7 billion Great Whale River (James Bay II) project were to be launched. "We are distinct. We are sovereign. We are autonomous," contended Diamond.

This has in turn generated much anger among Quebecois, for whom Hydro-Quebec and the various projects in northern Quebec have become secular icons of the Quiet Revolution, as well as a means to economic development. Quebec Energy minister Lise Bacon warned the Cree in October 1991 that the project would not be permanently blocked.

There are other peoples in Quebec who might also opt for self-determination. Witness the extreme bitterness between the Mohawks of Oka, Kahnawake, and Kanasatake and the Quebec government in 1990. Before it was over, one Quebec provincial police officer had been killed, and 3,700 Canadian troops deployed to keep the peace.

In English-speaking Canada, too, there are voices calling for an end to policies designed to preserve ethnic and linguistic diversity. There is massive discontent with federal policies regarding official bilingualism and multiculturalism, which in many parts of English Canada bears little resemblance to social reality. In the West, especially, people think of French Canadian as simply another ethnic minority, rather than as a "dual partner" in Canada.

> *If dualism does prove unworkable, what are some other potential outcomes? A complete breakup of the country might be economically extremely costly. Nor are there any guarantees that the passions such a situation might unleash could be controlled.*

Historians as well-respected as Jack Granatstein of York University and Desmond Morton of the University of Toronto have both spoken publicly of the potential for civil war, especially if Quebec's secession were to involve more than simple separation of the province from Canada, but might also result in an partition or shifting of borders between provinces to reflect ethnic and linguistic boundaries as happened in Austria-Hungary.

Who, after all, has the right to self-determination? If French Quebecois, then why not also the internal minority of anglophones? Why not natives?

In March 1991, the Equality Party (a newly formed Quebec anglophone-rights party) passed a resolution demanding negotiations on the partition of Quebec should the province declare independence. They called for "the establishment of new provincial boundaries that will maintain the physical integrity of Canada." Presumably a corridor south of the St. Lawrence River, running through the historically English Eastern Townships, and perhaps also including anglophone parts of Montreal, could become a new Canadian province. Some of the towns north of the Ottawa River

also have anglophone populations, and might consider joining this new province, or Ontario.

Others have noted that the entire Quebec north (the Abitibi and Ungava regions) was granted to the province in 1898 and 1912 by the federal government, presumably on the assumption Quebec would remain in Confederation, and therefore should revert to Canada if Quebec goes its own way. Most of the population there is aboriginal, and Ovide Mercredi, chief of the Assembly of First Nations, has said aboriginals would resist severing this territory from Canada.

One of last year's best selling books, *Deconfederation: Canada Without Quebec*, written by University of Calgary academics David Bercuson and Barry Cooper, not only rejects an Austro-Hungarian solution for Canada, calling instead for the departure of Quebec, but also suggests Canada has a right to retain the far north, the South Shore of the St. Lawrence, and perhaps even parts of the Ottawa valley and Montreal.

On the other hand Quebec nationalists maintain claims to Labrador, which is an integral part of Newfoundland province. Nationalists have never reconciled themselves to the 1927 ruling by the Judicial Committee of the Privy Council in London awarding the disputed territory to Newfoundland (then still a British colony), and official Quebec maps and logos typically show the area as part of the province. Also, might not the Acadians of New Brunswick wish to throw in their lot with a sovereign French-speaking state, resulting also in a division of that province?

We know that once people begin to fiddle with borders, violence often follows. Secessions may sometimes be bloodless, but partitions are messy. A sovereign French Quebec may end up, like Hungary, a much smaller state.

The dangers are clear. Another referendum looms in Quebec–but this time, unlike in 1980, both major provincial parties are prepared to see Quebec leave Confederation. So perhaps there are lessons to be drawn for Canada from the Austro-Hungarian experiment, because, as Keith Spicer stated in November 1991, "there are not a lot of chances left for Canada."

The Constitutional Debate

A Straight Talking Guide for Canadians

The mood of Canadians in late 1991 was described by pollsters in a variety of ways, almost all of them negative. Canadians were said to be sour over the economic outlook, intolerant of the regional concerns of other citizens and distrustful of political leaders at all levels of government.

A dangerous cycle, it seems, is now under way in Canada. It begins with the grave doubts people have about Canada's prospects. These doubts often encourage suspicion, prompting Canadians in one region of the country to grow skeptical of the views held by other regions. Suspicion, in turn, leads to an unwillingness to compromise on important issues—an attitude that is fast becoming the most serious stumbling block to resolving our national unity problem. Finally, doubt and anxiety over our ability to achieve lasting national unity contributes to additional economic uncertainty, causing the cycle to repeat itself.

We have the opportunity to break this cycle. The federal government's proposals, released in late September, received close scrutiny before the Special Joint Committee on a Renewed Canada. To assess all these proposals, a series of regional meetings were held across the country in early 1992. Their purpose was to provide Canadians with a forum to express their views on such key constitutional issues as strengthening the economic union, Senate reform, the division of powers and the distinct society clause. Following these meetings, the Special Joint Committee filed its report on February 28.

Recent public polls have suggested that a small majority of Canadians wants an acceptable compromise that will break the current unity deadlock. Indeed, there is the opportunity for a "win/win" outcome to this painful debate. Long-standing constitutional issues are up for discussion, as well as a broad package of economic reforms—reforms that would strengthen the way in which the Canadian economy operates and performs.

The fact that many of these reforms received little initial support among participants at the regional constitutional conferences in no way lessens their importance. Nor does it eliminate the pressing need to continue to work toward their implementation. If even some of them are agreed upon, all Canadians will be better positioned for stronger economic growth in the coming years.

Why should we worry about national unity when the economy is facing such problems?

A growing number of Canadians are asking themselves this very question. In a recent poll conducted by Maclean's magazine and Decima Research, respondents agreed by a three-to-one margin that the recession was a more pressing issue than national unity.

The Canadian economy is indeed going through hard times. Our recovery from the 1990-91 recession has been slower and more painful than expected. Personal and business bankruptcies have both been hitting record highs. Provincial welfare rolls are growing daily. And in 1991, unemployment averaged over 10 per cent. As a result of all this, 1.4 to 1.5 million Canadians are currently out of work.

Canada's long-term economic challenges are also a cause for concern. Our productivity growth lags behind that of the world's most industrialized countries. Spending on research and development is less than half of what most other advanced nations spend, thereby hampering our ability to develop new products and services. And workplace training and technological education are below that of many of our competitors, which robs workers—and country—of the skills needed to prosper and compete in an increasingly technological world.

It is a mistake, however, to argue that because Canada faces serious economic problems, national unity is less important. Such an argument fails to recognize the close connection between political unity and economic health.

For example, in its most recent set of national unity proposals, the federal government has made several constitutional recommendations — such as the removal of interprovincial trade barriers — which are specifically designed to improve economic performance.

The elimination of these barriers would help make Canadian businesses more competitive both internally and in world markets, make it easier for goods, services, skilled workers and professionals to move between provinces and enhance the overall efficiency of Canada's internal market. This is a clear case of how constitutional reform can affect an economy — and do so in a positive manner.

The reverse is also true — that is, political disintegration, or even the appearance of disintegration, can trigger serious economic penalties.

A bitter struggle over the Constitution — regardless of whether or not the country remains intact—could prompt foreign investors to question Canada's future political stability and therefore its attractiveness as a place to invest. This would be unfortunate. Foreign investment contributes to Canadian competitiveness by helping us finance new manufacturing facilities, develop new processes and purchase new equipment. It also contributes to financing our capital needs, including those generated by our fiscal deficits. Loss of faith in our ability to remain united could drive many investors—domestic as well as foreign—to take their money out of Canada, demand higher interest rates on the money they do invest here, or not invest here at all. The consequences of such actions are not pleasant to contemplate. Interest rates would go up. Efforts to reduce deficits would be thwarted. Capital costs would rise. Investment in new plants and equipment would decline. And job growth—now at a standstill—could continue to be adversely affected.

But the relationship between economic and constitutional concerns involves more than simply the loss or preservation of investor confidence. A whole host of urgent economic issues and our ability to deal with them effectively — from unemployment to productivity, from training to the deficit — are affected and jeopardized by Canada's current constitutional crisis. That's because the longer we are mired in constitutional debate and controversy, the more we risk ne-

Recovery from the recession has been slower than expected.

15

glecting the economic problems this country so desperately needs to solve.

At the same time, however, those problems will not be satisfactorily dealt with unless we first take care of the national unity question. Time and again, Canada's history has shown that while national unity issues may lie dormant for a while, they never wholly disappear.

The way out of this dilemma is not to dismiss the need to resolve our constitutional problems or to pretend they are unrelated to economic issues. Rather, the approach we should take is one which recognizes the intimate connection between national unity and the economy and which seeks to achieve a quick, effective and fair resolution — one which all Canadians can live with. Only then will we be able to devote our full energies to the economic challenges we need to meet.

What's so great about Canada, anyway?

People from other countries frequently marvel at Canada's achievements. Yet they are puzzled by the fact that so many Canadians take Canada for granted. Indeed, Canadians seem to have an ingrained habit of belittling themselves and their country. Even in these difficult economic times, we should remember that ours is a most favored nation.

We have the seventh largest economy in the world. Canadians enjoy the second highest standard of living of any country, trailing only the United States and ahead of such nations as Germany and Japan. According to international ratings, Canada is regularly ranked among the top five countries in terms of competitiveness — admittedly, largely on the basis of our wealth of natural resources.

The United Nations Human Development Index, which summarizes a country's relative strengths in national income, literacy and longevity, ranks Canada second among the world's countries, just after Japan. Moreover, across a great range of undertakings — from

international aid to peacekeeping efforts — Canada is a highly respected nation.

Yes, social problems such as poverty exist in Canada and we are only too familiar with our economic difficulties. These must be addressed.

But we must also put them in perspective. Canadian cities and streets are still safe relative to those in the U.S. and elsewhere. The quality and scope of our social services is the envy of the world. Many of our institutions and professions are universally admired.

It was Canadians who discovered insulin; Canadians who built one of the world's best energy, transportation and communications infrastructures, and Canadians who created a nation where the French language and culture can thrive despite being surrounded by more than 200 million people who speak English. It was Canadians who fashioned one of the most tolerant and equitable societies on earth.

It's vital that we work to correct our economic problems and resolve our constitutional difficulties. But as we do so, it's equally important that we do not lose sight of our strengths, achievements and potential as a nation.

There's a lot of talk about Canada as an "economic union." What does it mean?

An economic union occurs when all parts of a country agree to let goods, services, labor and capital move relatively freely and easily within their borders. This freedom of movement generally improves efficiency and living standards.

Despite some restrictions that exist among the provinces, Canada is an economic union because goods and services, labor and capital can move anywhere inside its national boundaries.

There are, however, greater and lesser degrees of economic union. The European Community (EC), for instance, is moving toward an economic union. This effort has generated much comment, excitement and even admiration around the world. But it is important to remember that the EC still has a long way to go before it reaches the level of economic union Canada has already achieved.

At present, for example, EC countries still use their own individual currencies, while Canada has long had a common currency. In many respects, therefore, Canada already has a strong economic union. Of course, that economic union might be considerably weakened in the event of Quebec's separation from the rest of Canada. In that case, instead of being a potential model for what the EC is trying to achieve, Canada would be seen as adopting a less efficient economic arrangement.

Even without the threat of separation, however, Canada's economic union must often endure factors which impair its economic efficiency. For instance, situations exist where the products made in one part of Canada — beer, for example — cannot be sold in another part.

In addition, several governments give preferential treatment to local suppliers, buying their services rather than those of a more qualified, but out-of-province competitor. Certain seemingly harmless provincial standards or qualifications, moreover, can sometimes seriously restrict the sale of out-of-province goods or the employment of out-of-province workers. In each case, these restrictions reduce the efficiency of the Canadian economy and add to the underlying costs to consumers or taxpayers. Estimates of the benefits to be gained by removing these restrictions range as high as 1.5 per cent of GDP, or about $1,500 for a family of four.

The government of Canada's constitutional proposals include recommendations for improving the economic union. Some people have questioned the methods proposed to achieve this goal. Others think the economic benefits to be gained are exaggerated. Despite these doubts, the need to enhance Canada's economic union, particularly in the face of growing international competition, is beyond dispute.

I f economic union is working, why do Quebecers want to restructure their political relationship with Ottawa?

The British North America Act of 1867 (the BNA Act), later renamed the 1867 Constitution Act, created a new nation composed of four provinces. Ontario and Quebec, which had since 1840 been united as one colony, were split into two provinces. French Canadians, who had settled in New France more than 250 years before, had mixed feelings about this new reality. They were uneasy that the BNA Act made French Canada part of a larger nation but confident that the guarantees built into the new constitution, together with the return of the provincial capital to Quebec City, would help them preserve their language, religion and social/cultural values.

Over the years, these mixed feelings continued. French Canadians remained concerned about their future as a French-speaking society within an increasingly English-speaking North America. Responding to this concern, the provincial government throughout the 1960s took an increasingly active role in the social and economic life of the province. As a result, Quebec society changed radically. The creation of Hydro-Québec and the Caisse de dépôt et placement, the establishment of the Quebec pension plan operating in parallel with the Canada Pension Plan, and the continued consolidation of a separate personal and corporate income tax system are some of the significant economic changes which occurred during this period.

These economic transformations were reinforced by parallel changes and developments in education, the arts and business. This cultural flourishing contributed greatly to the confirmation and definition of Quebec as a distinct society.

At the same time, French Canadians realized that they should have greater control over their political future as well as those government policies which help determine that future.

The people of Quebec are keenly aware of the difficulties of preserving a distinct French-speaking culture of six million on a continent where more than 200 million people speak English. Given that Quebec's language and culture have helped contribute to the richness and uniqueness of Canada, many Quebecers feel that it is appropriate that these contributions be valued and preserved.

As a consequence, Quebecers generally look

to the provincial government to ensure that the province remains distinct. In all of their requests to the federal government, successive Quebec governments have sought to advance similar goals and aspirations. These are:

1. Quebecers want to be acknowledged as different and respected as such. They want the "distinct society" clause to be officially recognized, once and for all, as a part of Canada's reality.

2. Quebecers want to remain part of Canada, provided they feel welcome, and so long as they can control the conditions necessary to their future.

In 1986, Quebec maintained that these goals would be satisfied if Canada's Constitution were to grant the following:

1. Recognition of Quebec as a dinstinct society;

2. Increased powers to control immigration into the province;

3. Limitations on federal spending in areas of exclusive provincial jurisdiction;

4. A recognition of the right to veto any constitutional change, and,

5. Quebec participation in the appointment of Supreme Court justices.

Quebecers feel that being just one among 10 provinces is not working, since such an arrangement provides no guarantee for the future preservation of a French-speaking Quebec in Canada. The demands of the Quebec government, therefore, have changed since the demise of the Meech Lake Accord. With the publication of the Allaire Report in 1990, Quebec has focused on a significant shift in responsibilities from Ottawa to Quebec City as a means to guarantee the preservation of Quebec culture and language.

Where the current constitutional debate will end up depends, in part, on all Canadians recognizing that Quebec is serious and wishes to preserve its future as a distinct (French language, civil law and different cultural values) society within a renewed Canadian federation.

Quebecers are asking the rest of Canada to recognize the province's right to decide its own future. They understand that the 1992 provincial referendum will mark a significant point in that decision making process.

Quebec considers its constitutional demands necessary to ensure the preservation of its unique cultural identity. This sentiment is reinforced by the fact that many Quebecers feel they were left out of the 1982 constitutional agreement.

But what about the rest of Canada? What does it want in this current constitutional round?

 f Quebec has its demands, what does the rest of Canada want?

At the outset, it is important to note that there is no "rest of Canada," "English Canada," or any other monolithic group that exists outside Quebec. Canada is a nation of different regions, multiple heritages and diverse values. To some people, the constitutional debate seems only a matter of Quebec demanding rights and the rest of the country deciding whether or not to accept those demands. In fact, there is no generally accepted or universal bloc of opinion outside Quebec. More so than even Quebec, the "rest of Canada" is characterized by a diversity of views and positions.

In terms of constitutional issues, this diversity is quite apparent.

For example, in Ontario the idea of having a "social charter" as part of the Constitution has become a high priority for the provincial government. For many westerners and some residents of Atlantic Canada, on the other hand, forming a "Triple-E" Senate is a key demand. For others, a critical issue is allowing "average Canadians" a voice in the process of constitutional renewal. And in British Columbia, there is a desire for greater "disentanglement" — that is, more responsibilities for the provinces and a diminished role for the federal government.

There's also a diversity of viewpoints concerning the more specific constitutional issue of decentralization. Calls by some people for a greater transfer of federal powers to the provinces are met with concerns from others who question the ability of smaller provinces to assume these powers. Can smaller provinces assure universal access to social programs, for instance? There is also the question of "national standards" — that is, will less affluent provinces be able to ensure the same quality of service that characterized federally-run social programs?

Also, there is the matter of Meech Lake and its aftermath. It is important to remember that the Meech Lake Accord, while not overwhelmingly supported by Canadians outside Quebec, nevertheless represented to many an acceptable resolution of the national unity question. It is not totally accurate to maintain, as many have in Quebec, that the failure of the Meech Lake Accord represented English Canada's rejection of Quebec. Indeed, the accord required unanimous support from all 10 provinces. Between 1987 and 1990, all but Manitoba voted for the accord. Even Newfoundland initially passed the accord prior to reversing its decision after the election of a new provincial government. The response which the majority of provinces gave to Meech Lake, therefore, can hardly be called a "rejection" of Quebec's concerns by the "rest of Canada."

Other Quebecers admit there is diversity of opinion in the rest of Canada, but see it as evidence of confusion, indecision and apathy. This frustrates Quebecers who seek to initiate a dialogue on constitutional renewal.

This perception — erroneous but still common — has implications for the progress of our constitutional negotiations. It could, for instance, increasingly disillusion and disappoint those Quebecers who genuinely want to negotiate a deal but who feel that the "rest of Canada" is too fragmented to put forth a coherent bargaining position.

What seems critical here is that Canadians in all provinces at least try to forge a consensus on the major issues, to acknowledge that not all those issues can be presented in simple "black-and-white" terms and to recognize that a meaningful resolution of the constitutional question will only be possible if views from all parts of the country are heard.

ow do the concerns of Canada's aboriginal peoples relate to the constitutional negotiations?

Canada's aboriginal citizens have been governed under the provisions of the Indian Act, first passed by Parliament in 1876. Since that time,

relations between Canada's first nations and both federal and provincial governments have become increasingly strained. This is because such issues as treaty rights, land claims, and the "inherent" right to self-government have dominated the agenda of many native groups.

In pressing these claims, Canada's first nations refer back to their relationship with the British Crown, which seemed to recognize Canada's native populations as "nations" in their own right. The British North America Act of 1867 granted the federal government authority over Indians and their lands. For more than a century, virtually every aspect of Indian life was controlled by the federal government. Canada's native population did not even get the right to vote in federal elections until 1960.

By the time the Constitution Act of 1982 came into force, several provisions were included for changing the relationship between aboriginals and the federal government. Section 35 of the act recognizes existing aboriginal and treaty rights, including land claims, and extends this recognition to the Indian, Inuit and Métis peoples.

Several attempts between 1982 and 1987 were made to clarify these provisions. By 1987, provincial, federal and aboriginal representatives were unable to progress further in resolving the issues surrounding land claims and other existing aboriginal rights. Indeed, the broader issue of aboriginal land claims will probably continue to evolve regardless of future constitutional developments.

The lack of aboriginal input into the 1982 Constitution Act and a similar exclusion from the 1987 Meech Lake Accord led to a significant increase in aboriginal concern over the process of constitutional reform. This concern came to a head in Manitoba, where the provincial legislature was prevented from reviewing the provisions of the accord by the actions of a single aboriginal representative.

That action simply highlighted the fact that Canada's first nations were determined not to be excluded from the decision-making process.

All parties generally agree that when it comes to the rights of native people the provisions of the Constitution Act of 1982 are inadequate. At present, however, the major stumbling block to moving beyond the 1982 Constitution Act lies in the natives' claim for recognition of the "inherent" right to self-government and the federal and provincial governments' uncertainty about how this would affect the application of existing Canadian laws to Canada's first peoples. Clearing this hurdle will not be easy, as was demonstrated by the claim made in February 1992 by Ovide Mercredi, Grand Chief of the Assembly of First Nations, that native peoples constitute a "distinct society" just as much as Quebec society does.

As it stands now, the federal government has proposed recognizing the aboriginal right to self-government within the Canadian federation. This right would be subject to the Charter of Rights and Freedoms and would be further defined by aboriginal groups, by Ottawa and by the provinces and territories. It could be delayed for up to 10 years. Finally, a committee may be established to review the definition of the right itself.

What kinds of institutional reforms could emerge from the constitutional debate?

Many constitutional issues represent causes and beliefs which are critically important to a number of Canadians. Balance is the key. Constitutional debate is very important. But it should not overshadow the need for action on the Canadian economy.

On issues of social policy, language, economic and regional development, groups in society look to their federal and provincial governments for support and reinforcement. But when many Canadians observe Canada's political structures, they fail to see an adequate reflection of either their personal values or regional realities. Part of the reason for this can be found in the demographic inequities that characterize some of our political institutions.

The House of Commons, as an elected body, provides for representation by population. The most populous parts of the country get the most seats. With the exception of the more heavily populated provinces of Ontario and Quebec, most of Canada's regions maintain that this

structure ensures their needs are not going to be met at the federal level.

Various individuals and groups have suggested that the Canadian Senate has the potential to redress these grievances. Originally, the Senate was intended to act as a counter-weight to the more populist mandate of the House of Commons.

In 1867, with the creation of an appointed Senate for Canada, two provisions were established. The first is that appointments to the Senate were to be made on a regional basis. Today, as a result of this provision, Ontario, Quebec and the West each have 24 senators. The Atlantic provinces have 30 and the territories have one representative each.

The second provision was that an appointed Senate was to be a body that could restrain the excesses of the democratically elected representatives in the Commons. By the early 20th century, however, this latter concept had long outlived its relevance and credibility.

To complicate matters, an appointed Senate, while providing for regional representation, has rarely employed the powers granted to it under the existing Constitution to challenge the elected House of Commons. Thus, whatever potential the Senate may once have had to act as a voice for regional concerns has long since faded away.

For this reason, many Canadians in both the west and the Atlantic provinces are now calling for a Triple-E Senate — elected, equal and effective. Roughly based on the Senate of the United States, this body would be popularly

Many are calling for a "Triple-E" Senate that's elected, equal and effective

elected. It would be composed of an equal number of representatives from all provinces and the territories, and it would have the power to initiate and approve legislation originating in the Commons.

Critics of the plan maintain that such an institution would create problems. The existence of an upper House equal to the House of Commons might, it is said, sometimes lead to a legislative stalemate between the two bodies.

In addition, there are concerns that a Triple-E Senate would allow a province like Prince Edward Island, with its relatively small population, to have the same Senate representation as British Columbia, Ontario or Quebec — an arrangement many consider unfair.

While debate around the need to reform our federal structures continues, the key question is how can Canadians ensure that voices from all regions of this country receive fair treatment in the discussion and formulation of public policy. An elected Senate, for many Canadians, is the vehicle to accomplish this task.

In its most recent proposals, Ottawa has suggested that some accommodation be made toward an elected Senate. Ottawa has proposed the creation of an elected body that would allow for a stronger regional voice than now exists at the federal level. Most legislation would still require the support of both the House and the Senate. A reformed Senate, however, would have the power only to delay, not override, legislation considered to be of "national importance."

The Senate, moreover, could not veto legislation dealing with taxation and spending. To this extent, the new Senate's powers would be more restricted than those of the current Senate.

In addition to Senate reform, it has also been suggested that the House of Commons itself needs some radical surgery. Proposals have been put forth that would require elected members of Parliament to represent the views of their constituents far more accurately and vigorously than they do now — which is often simply to vote exclusively along rigid party lines. Other suggestions for House reform include politically reconfiguring Canada into five regions and then electing representatives to both the House and the Senate from these regions. There is also strong feeling in some quarters that more women and aboriginals should be elected to both the House of Commons and the Senate.

Ottawa has also suggested yet another reform — the inclusion of an additional level of authority in the form of a so-called Council of Federation. This council would be composed of representatives from the federal, provincial and territorial governments and would have responsibility to decide issues of intergovernmental co-ordination and collaboration.

A focal point for the concerns of Canadians, the reform of our representative institutions has been one of the major issues in the constitutional debate.

What does "distinct society" status mean for Quebec?

Perhaps no one issue has been so hotly debated among Canadians as the issue of "distinct society" status for Quebec. Supporters of the concept note that it is simply an affirmation of the obvious. Since the passage of the Quebec Act in 1774, the Roman Catholic religion, the French system of civil law and the French language have characterized Quebec society. This reality has been consistently recognized in law.

Legislation governing Canada, both before and since Confederation, has granted distinctive rights to Quebec. By the mid-19th century, language had grown into the one issue considered essential to protect those rights. And by 1867, language and culture had become so important that they were prominent factors in the creation of the British North America Act, which united the colonies of Ontario, Quebec, Nova Scotia and New Brunswick.

Opponents of a distinct society constitutional clause fear it will give special powers to the Quebec government. They believe that, as a result, Quebec law would not be subject to the guarantees of the Charter of Rights and Freedoms. Similarly, they fear that distinct society status will give Quebec greater powers than other provinces.

In considering the issue of provincial equality it is important to remember, that in many respects Canadian provinces are far from equal in relation to one another. They are not uniform, for instance, in terms of customs, rights or services. Parents in Ontario are able to send their children to either public or separate school systems. This is not true for all provinces. Similarly, while access to our national health care system is universal, the services that each province offers its citizens are not identical. Thus, while equality is a goal of many Canadians, significant differences exist among provinces — differences shaped by the historical, regional and cultural realities that defined each province at the time it joined the Canadian federation.

In recognition of this fact, the federal government's proposals recommend that the distinct reality of Quebec society be acknowledged. This distinct society includes Quebec's civil law tradition, its language and its unique culture. In addition, the proposals recommend that it is the responsibility of all governments to preserve Canada's linguistic majorities and minorities and that Quebec has a special responsibility to preserve and promote its own distinct culture.

Some in Quebec see these recommendations as giving to Quebec less than the Meech Lake Accord offered. On the other hand, some opponents of the distinct society provision, as it was described in the Meech Lake document, think that this new proposal addresses many of their concerns.

 re referendums likely to replace old constitutional amending formulas?

The way Canada changes its Constitution lies at the root of many divisive debates between the federal government and the provinces. Prior to the Constitution Act of 1982, there was no way to amend the Canadian Constitution other than by an act of the British parliament. This inability to change the fundamental law of Canada was one of the driving forces behind then-prime minister Pierre Trudeau's many attempts to "patriate" the BNA Act throughout the 1970s.

With the passage of the Constitution Act in 1982, six different amending formulas were in-

Ottawa's proposals recognize the distinct reality of Quebec

troduced into the Canadian Constitution. Of these, the most significant are:

1. Unanimous consent of the federal government and all provincial governments is required for any change to the monarchy, the Supreme Court and the status of official languages in Canada.

2. Representation to the House of Commons, the selection and powers of the Senate, the establishment of new provinces and minor changes to the Supreme Court require the support of seven of the provinces representing 50 per cent of the population of Canada. This is usually referred to as the 7/50 rule.

Most of the federal government's recent constitutional proposals require the support of seven provinces with 50 per cent of the population. In the case of Meech Lake, the unanimous consent of all the provinces was required within three years. When the provinces of Manitoba and Newfoundland did not ratify the accord, those proposed amendments died.

Neither the Constitution Act of 1982 nor the Meech Lake Accord of 1987 provided for any form of popular participation in new constitutional proposals. Since the downfall of the Meech Lake initiative, much debate has occurred in Canada over the difference between elite and popular input into the constitutional process. This has prompted many Canadians to urge the government to pass a referendum law that would give all Canadians the right to vote on new constitutional structures.

The role of a referendum to ratify or bind the future actions of the federal government has not yet been determined. It is also uncertain how a referendum would function, considering that most of the current constitutional proposals require the approval of provincial legislatures and not the provincial population.

The federal government has at times suggested and at other times backed away from the issue of a national referendum. But legislation providing for a referendum may be introduced into the House of Commons later this year.

In the meantime, the decision to hold a series of regional conferences on the major issues for debate has provided some degree of popular input into the constitutional process that is now under way.

How is the division of powers being affected by the constitutional debate?

All federations divide powers among the various levels of government. In Canada, the federal government and the provinces are each responsible for a different range of government, social and economic services.

Under the 1867 BNA Act, the federal government was responsible for such areas as aboriginal peoples, criminal law, national defence, weights and measures, banking, the national debt, the post office, the regulation of trade and commerce, taxation, the provision of equalization payments to the provinces and the making of laws for the "peace, order and good government" of the country.

The provinces were responsible for health, education, justice, property and civil rights. They also have control over natural resources, the incorporation of provincial companies and contract law.

The BNA Act also provided for several areas of joint responsibility. Today, these responsibilities are shared in such areas as agriculture, immigration, the environment and pensions.

Wherever the Constitution is silent, the federal government is granted the "residual" power to legislate on matters affecting the country as a whole. The provinces have residual powers over purely local or provincial matters. The powers each level of government exercises are determined by the Constitution. Those powers, however, were established some 125 years ago and may not ac-

curately reflect the realities of governing Canada in the late 20th century.

Among the most prominent issues that have been raised over the past several years are the search for greater authority by several provinces, including Quebec, the management of new areas of responsibility (e.g., telecommunications) and the use of the so-called federal spending power.

To some extent, the Meech Lake Accord addressed the division of powers issue. It provided for provincial input regarding both the appointment of new senators and the issue of Quebec's approval of Supreme Court appointments. In addition, the accord put certain limitations on federal spending in areas of provincial jurisdiction.

A more extensive transfer of powers was suggested in early 1991 with the release of the Quebec Liberal party's own report on constitutional issues. Known as the Allaire Report, it recommended that Quebec take over some 22 areas of jurisdiction from the federal government, leaving only defence, customs, currency and equalization payments as Ottawa's responsibility.

In contrast, the federal government's latest proposals recommend that control of certain traditional areas of federal responsibility — such as tourism, forestry, mining, recreation, housing and municipal affairs — could be turned over to provincial governments.

In addition, Ottawa would transfer elements of manpower training, immigration and broadcasting to the provinces. Finally, Ottawa has suggested it would exercise its spending power in areas of provincial jurisdiction only with support of seven of the provinces with 50 per cent of the Canadian population.

Ultimately, however, the question of which level of government provides which specific service is less an issue than that of the need for federal and provincial governments to co-operate— not compete — with each other in giving Canadians the means to create and participate in an increasingly efficient and productive economy.

There's been talk of including a "social charter" in the Constitution. What is it and what would it mean?

Although a social charter was not among the original proposals offered by the federal government, its presence in the Constitution is an idea that has received considerable support from a number of groups.

Advocates of a social charter argue that Canada's historical commitment to values such as universal access to health care, public education and social security is an essential part of our national identity. They have urged that this commitment be protected by formal inclusion in the Constitution.

Critics of this proposal say that a constitution is not an appropriate vehicle for defining social policy. They maintain that the courts would have difficulty in interpreting the charter and in relating it to future legislation, and that the charter itself might limit the power of future governments.

Some supporters of the social charter have acknowledged these problems. To overcome them, they suggest that the charter take the form of a declaration of commitment — a statement that is without legal force but which nevertheless carries considerable moral authority as an affirmation of Canada's most cherished social principles.

Many women's groups want their concerns addressed. What's in the debate for women?

Long after the failure of the Meech Lake Accord, the image of 11 males sitting in a closed room and deciding the fate of an entire nation persists.

Women, as well as men, saw this as a symbol of how women have been excluded from Canada's political decision-making process. As a result, renewed demands were made to change the situation.

In the course of the current constitutional debate, it has been repeatedly suggested that women be allowed to make a greater contribution to the issues under discussion and to the areas those issues affect.

This message was perhaps most effectively put forth in the discussion on parliamentary representation. It was pointed out that women form a majority in Canada — about 52 per cent of the population — but that only a small proportion of elected officials are female.

It was further argued that since women face considerable obstacles to getting elected — ranging from subtle biases against women who run for public office to the constraints imposed by family responsibilities — they should be accorded special treatment as a means of overcoming these obstacles.

Other women argued that they would prefer to be judged and to succeed on their own merits rather than be given special treatment.

While there appears to be no easy resolution to this debate, it is clear that the time has come to give the issue of employment equity in the political arena the same attention and importance it has in the business sector.

Is there anything positive to come from this debate on national unity?

Canada's constitutional debate has produced a number of positive results.

The failure of the Meech Lake Accord in June 1990, for example, demonstrated to many the defects of a procedure that excluded the opinions of "ordinary" Canadians from the constitutional decision-making process. Had such opinions been actively sought, the accord itself may have had a better chance of success.

As a consequence, the discussions which have taken place since Meech Lake — such as the Spicer Commission and the series of public conferences on the federal government's constitutional proposals — have encouraged a greater degree of public participation. This emphasis on popular input and open proceedings is certainly a worthwhile development, especially if it influences areas of the political process that have been out of tune with the public mood.

The debate over constitutional renewal has also helped focus attention on several other key issues, many of which have been either neglected or only partially understood in the popular mind.

Benefiting from comprehensive media coverage, many Canadians now have at least the opportunity to better grasp a number of diverse yet constitutionally relevant topics. These topics include: the West's desire for a Triple-E Senate; the damaging economic effects of interprovincial trade barriers and the need to reduce and even eliminate them; the needless duplication of some government programs and services; the political aspirations of native peoples; the delicate and complex social and economic relationships between Canada's regions, and even the nature of monetary policy . . . to name only a few.

Moreover, by familiarizing themselves with these and other issues, many Canadians have acquired a deeper appreciation not only of the complexity and importance of constitutional change but also of the rich regional and cultural diversity of Canada itself.

The current constitutional debate has sometimes been accused of fostering disunity in the nation. Perhaps this is true if it is used as an occasion for promoting inflexible positions, self-serving ideas and intolerant opinions.

But if approached with a desire to learn and to compromise, then that debate offers a major opportunity to rebuild this country along lines that truly reflect its unique character and that assist Canadians in understanding one another.

Where do we go from here?

Although the timing has come into question lately, the Quebec government says that it still intends to hold a popular referendum on the sovereignty issue this October. The issue is sufficiently sensitive that it is impossible to predict the results at this time. Some polls, however, have indicated that at least two-thirds of Quebec residents believe that separation is likely to happen if a new constitutional arrangement is not agreed upon.

Our present Constitution has never been ratified by Quebec

There are several forms that this new arrangement could take. The ones most frequently mentioned are:

1. Asymmetrical federalism: this arrangement would allow certain powers and responsibilities to be transferred from the federal government to those provinces that consider such powers essential to their economic, political and cultural well-being. Provinces that do not want such powers can allow them to remain in the hands of the federal government.

Such an arrangement would allow Quebec to have more control over its own internal affairs while at the same time allowing those provinces that want to retain a strong central government system to do so.

2. Decentralization: the transfer of certain powers from the federal government to all the provinces. Elements of decentralization can be found in the federal government's recent package of constitutional proposals. It includes recommendations to make labor market training a wholly provincial responsibility. It also includes recommendations to withdraw or curtail federal involvement in such areas as tourism, forestry, mining and recreation.

Decentralization in one form or another has long been part of Canada's political history. Quebec has traditionally been a strong proponent of the concept. And so has Alberta on occasion and British Columbia as well. Other provinces, however, such as those in Atlantic Canada, are generally uncomfortable with the idea on the grounds that decentralization would force them to perform services and assume responsibilities they cannot financially afford.

3. The status quo: in other words, Canada's present constitutional arrangement — the patriated Constitution of April 1982, including a

Charter of Rights and Freedoms, an elected Parliament with representation based on population, an unelected Senate with little real power, and so on.

Even though Canada's present Constitution has been in effect for nearly 10 years, it has never been ratified by Quebec, a province where roughly one-quarter of all Canadians live.

Most parties involved in the current constitutional debate admit that the status quo is not an acceptable solution to our constitutional problem. Indeed, many would argue that it is one of the major causes of that problem.

4. Separation: the term is self-explanatory. Quebec would secede from the rest of Canada and form an independent nation.

 An opportunity to advance our national legacy

Canadians can prevent separation.

If, however, Canadians allow constitutional issues to lead them down the path of anger, suspicion, stubbornness, frustration and apathy, then separation is a real possibility. The danger — and the tragedy — here is that separation might come about not because most Canadians choose or want it, but because we simply allowed it to happen.

There is an additional danger to contemplate. Some Canadians believe that Quebec and the "rest of Canada" would be able to survive quite nicely without each other.

"Let Quebec go," certain people say. "We are going," say some Quebecers. Both groups base their sentiments on the assumption that a fractured Canada would be as economically prosperous as a united Canada.

That is a patently false assumption. Those who advocate or accept the division of Canada are deluding both themselves and others if they think that such divisions can be accomplished without great social and economic cost.

In the event of separation, a strong case can be made that the "new" governments of Canada and Quebec would face considerable difficulties in financing their debts and deficits. And they would likely encounter increasing problems in their ability to stay globally competitive.

Canada's excessive debt and its inability to fully finance that debt domestically have made Canadians more dependent than ever on foreign investment and foreign confidence — especially confidence in our political stability. By the same token, demand for our natural resources has declined and our position as an industrial power has deteriorated in the face of intense global competition. All these things have made national co-operation and collective endeavor essential factors in any drive for competitive success.

Today, more than ever, all parts of Canada need each other and need to support each other.

A country's constitution is never perfect. From time to time it has to be modified and adjusted to meet the evolving requirements of the society it is designed to benefit. What is exceptional in Canada's case is that throughout our history we have consistently and successfully addressed the challenges of constitutional change in ways that enhanced — not undermined — economic security, human rights, political stability and social fairness. And we have done so without revolution, secession or civil war.

Today, Canadians have yet another opportunity to preserve and even advance that legacy. We must seize that opportunity and demand that our politicians and leaders work toward a constitutional solution that is acceptable and fair to everyone — not just one or two regions or groups — and that the result of that solution is not a nation that is dismembered, dismal and feeble, but one that is united, strong, and confident of itself and of its future.

Text of the Charlottetown Agreement

Revised draft: 2:30 p.m. August 28, 1992

. . . Canadians will probably be asked in a national vote to accept or reject a sweeping new set of changes to the country's system of government.

Those changes are all contained in an agreement reached . . . by Ottawa, all provinces, and native and territorial leaders. These national-unity negotiators spent long hours in Charlottetown . . . , poring over the details of their deal, which still has to be translated into legal text.

The Globe and Mail *has obtained the draft wording of that agreement, which is due to be released later. . . .*

I. UNITY & DIVERSITY

A. PEOPLE AND COMMUNITIES

1. Canada Clause

A new clause should be included as Section 2 of the Constitution Act, 1867, that would express fundamental Canadian values. The Canada Clause would guide the courts in their future interpretation of the entire Constitution, including the Canadian Charter of Rights and Freedoms.

The Constitution Act, 1867, is amended by adding thereto, immediately after Section 1 thereof, the following section:

"2. (1) The Constitution of Canada, including the Canadian Charter of Rights and Freedoms, shall be interpreted in a manner consistent with the following fundamental characteristics:

(a) Canada is a democracy committed to a parliamentary and federal system of government and to the rule of law;

(b) the Aboriginal peoples of Canada, being the first peoples to govern this land, have the right to promote their languages, cultures and traditions and to ensure the integrity of their societies, and their governments constitute one of three orders of government in Canada;

(c) Quebec constitutes within Canada a distinct society, which includes a French-speaking majority, a unique culture and a civil law tradition;

(d) Canadians and their governments are committed to the vitality and development of official-language minority communities throughout Canada;

(e) Canadians are committed to racial and ethnic equality in a society that includes citizens from many lands who have contributed, and continue to contribute, to the building of a strong Canada that reflects its cultural and racial diversity;

(f) Canadians are committed to a respect for individual and collective human rights and freedoms of all people;

(g) Canadians are committed to the equality of female and male persons; and

(h) Canadians confirm the principle of the equality of the provinces at the same time as recognizing their diverse characteristics.

(2) The role of the legislature and Government of Quebec to preserve and promote the distinct society of Quebec is affirmed.

(3) Nothing in this section derogates from the powers, rights or privileges of the Parliament or the Government of Canada, or of the legislatures or governments of the provinces, or of the legislative bodies or governments of the Aboriginal peoples of Canada, including any powers, rights or privileges relating to language and, for greater certainty, nothing in this section derogates from the aboriginal and treaty rights of the Aboriginal peoples of Canada."

2. Aboriginal Peoples and the Canadian Charter of Rights and Freedoms

The Charter provision dealing with Aboriginal peoples (Section 25, the non-derogation clause) should be strengthened to ensure that nothing in the Charter abrogates or derogates from Aboriginal, treaty or other rights of Aboriginal peoples, and in particular any rights or freedoms relating to the exercise or protection of their languages, cultures or traditions.

3. Linguistic Communities in New Brunswick

A separate constitutional amendment requiring only the consent of Parliament and the legislature of New Brunswick should be added to the Canadian Charter of Rights and Freedoms. The amendment would entrench the equality of status of the English and French linguistic communities in New Brunswick, including the right to distinct educational institutions and such distinct cultural institutions as are necessary for the preservation and promotion of these communities. The amendment would also affirm the role of the legislature and government of New Brunswick to preserve and promote this equality of status.

B. CANADA'S SOCIAL AND ECONOMIC UNION

4. The Social and Economic Union

A new provision should be added to the Constitution describing the commitment of the governments, Parliament and the legislatures within the federation to the principle of the preservation and development of Canada's social and economic union. The new provision, entitled The Social and Economic Union, should be drafted to set out a series of policy objectives underlying the social and the economic union, respectively. The provision should not be justiciable.

The policy objectives set out in the provision on the social union should include, but not be limited to:
• Providing throughout Canada a health-care system that is comprehensive, universal, portable, publicly administered and accessible;
• Providing adequate social services and benefits to ensure that all individuals resident in Canada have reasonable access to housing, food and other basic necessities;
• Providing high-quality primary and secondary education to all individuals resident in Canada and ensuring reasonable access to postsecondary education;
• Protecting the rights of workers to organize and bargain collectively; and,
• Protecting, preserving and sustaining the integrity of the environment for present and future generations.

The policy objectives set out in the provision on the economic union should include, but not be limited to:
• Working together to strengthen the Canadian economic union;
• The free movement of persons, goods, services and capital;
• The goal of full employment;
• Ensuring that all Canadians have a reasonable standard of living; and,
• Ensuring sustainable and equitable development.

A mechanism of monitoring the Social and Economic Union should be determined by a First Ministers' Conference.

A new provision should be drafted to clarify the possible relationship between the new section and the existing Canadian Charter of Rights and Freedoms.

A clause should be added to the Constitution stating that the Social and Economic Union does not abrogate or derogate from the Canadian Charter of Rights and Freedoms.

5. Economic Disparities, Equalization and Regional Development

Section 36 of the Constitution Act, 1982, currently commits Parliament and the Government of Canada and the governments and legislatures of the provinces to promote equal opportunities and economic development throughout the country and to provide essential public services of reasonable quality to all Canadians. Subsection 36(2) currently commits the federal government to the principle of equalization payments. This section should be amended to read as follows:

Parliament and the Government of Canada are committed to making equalization payments so that provincial governments have sufficient revenues to provide reasonably comparable levels of public services at reasonably comparable levels of taxation.

Subsection 36(1) should be expanded to include the territories.

Subsection 36(1) should be amended to add a commitment to ensure the provision of reasonably comparable economic infrastructures of a national nature in each province and territory.

The Constitution should commit the federal government to meaningful consultation with the provinces before introducing legislation relating to equalization payments.

A new Subsection 36(3) should be added to entrench the commitment of governments to the promotion of regional economic development to reduce economic disparities.

Regional development is also discussed in item 36 of this document.

6. The Common Market

Section 121 of the Constitution Act, 1867, would remain unchanged.

Detailed principles and commitments related to the Canadian Common Market are included in the political accord of August 27, 1992. First Ministers will decide on the best approach to implement these principles and commitments at a future First Ministers' Conference on the economy. First Ministers would have the authority to create an independent dispute resolution agency and decide on its role, mandate and composition.

II. INSTITUTIONS

A. THE SENATE

7. An Elected Senate

The Constitution should be amended to provide that Senators are elected, either at large by the population of the provinces and territories of Canada or directly by the members of their provincial or territorial legislative assemblies.

Federal legislation should govern Senate elections, subject to the constitutional provision above and constitutional provisions requiring that elections take place at the same time as elections to the House of Commons and provisions respecting eligibility and mandate of Senators. Federal legislation would be sufficiently flexible to allow provinces and territories to provide for gender equality in the composition of the Senate.

Matters should be expedited in order that Senate elections be held as soon as possible, and, if feasible, at the same time as the next federal general election for the House of Commons.

8. An Equal Senate

The Senate should initially total 62 Senators and should be composed of six Senators from each province and one Senator from each territory.

9. Aboriginal Peoples' Representation in the Senate

Aboriginal representation in the Senate should be guaranteed in the Constitution. Aboriginal Senate seats should be additional to provincial and territorial seats, rather than drawn from any province or territory's allocation of Senate seats.

Aboriginal Senators should have the same role and powers as other Senators, plus a possible double majority power in relation to certain matters materially affecting Aboriginal people. These issues and other details relating to Aboriginal representation in the Senate (numbers, distribution, method of selection) will be discussed further by governments and the representatives of the Aboriginal peoples in the early autumn of 1992(*).

10. Relationship to the House of Commons

The Senate should not be a confidence chamber. In other words, the defeat of government-sponsored legislation by the Senate would not require the government's resignation.

11. Categories of Legislation

There should be four categories of legislation:

1) Revenue and expenditure bills ("Supply bills");

2) Legislation materially affecting French language or French culture;

3) Bills involving fundamental tax policy changes directly related to natural resources;

4) Ordinary legislation (any bill not falling into one of the first three categories).

Initial classification of bills should be by the originator of the bill. With the exception of legislation affecting French language or French culture (see item 14), appeals should be determined by the Speaker of the House of Commons, following consultation with the Speaker of the Senate.

12. Approval of Legislation

The Constitution should oblige the Senate to dispose of any bills approved by the House of Commons, within 30 sitting days of the House of Commons, with the exception of revenue and expenditure bills.

Revenue and expenditure bills would be subject to a 30-calendar-day suspensive veto. If a bill is defeated or amended by the Senate within this period, it could be repassed by a majority vote in the House of Commons on a resolution.

Bills that materially affect French language or French culture would require approval by a majority of Senators voting and by a majority of the Francophone Senators voting. The House of Commons would not be able to override the defeat of a Bill in this category by the Senate.

Bills that involve fundamental tax policy changes directly related to natural resources would be defeated if a majority of Senators voting cast their votes against the bill. The House of Commons would not be able to override the Senate's veto. The precise definition of this category of legislation remains to be determined.

Defeat or amendment of ordinary legislation by the Senate would trigger a joint sitting process with the House of Commons. A simple majority vote at the joint sitting would determine the outcome of the bill.

The Senate should have the powers set out in this Consensus Report. There would be no change to the Senate's current role in approving constitutional amendments. Subject to the consensus, Senate powers and procedures should be parallel to those in the House of Commons.

The Senate should continue to have the capacity to initiate bills, except for money bills.

If any bill initiated and passed by the Senate is amended or rejected by the House of Commons, a joint sitting process should be triggered automatically.

The House of Commons should be obliged to dispose of legislation approved by the Senate within a reasonable time limit.

13. Revenue and Expenditure Bills

In order to preserve Canada's parliamentary traditions, the Senate should not be able to block the routine flow of legislation relating to taxation, borrowing and appropriation.

Revenue and expenditure bills ("supply bills") should be defined as only those matters involving borrowing, the raising of revenue and appropriation as well as matters subordinate to these issues. This definition should exclude fundamental policy changes to the tax system (such as the Goods and Services Tax and the National Energy Program).

14. Double Majority

The originator of a bill should be responsible for designating whether it materially affects French language or French culture. Each designation should be subject to appeal to the Speaker of the Senate under rules to be established by the Senate. These rules should be designed to provide adequate protection to Francophones.

On entering the Senate, Senators should be required to declare whether they are Francophones for the purpose of the double majority voting rule. Any process for challenging these declarations should be left to the rules of the Senate.

15. Ratification of Appointments

1. CANADA: A NATION IN LIMBO

The Constitution should specify that the Senate ratify the appointment of the Governor of the Bank of Canada.

The Constitution should also be amended to provide the Senate with a new power to ratify other key appointments made by the federal government.

The Senate should be obliged to deal with any proposed appointments within 30 sitting days of the House [of] Commons.

The appointments that would be subject to Senate ratification, including the heads of the national cultural institutions and the heads of federal regulatory boards and agencies, should be set out in the specific federal legislation rather than the Constitution. The federal government's commitment to table such legislation should be recorded in a political accord.(*)

An appointment submitted for ratification would be rejected if a majority of Senators voting cast their votes against it.

16. Eligibility for Cabinet

Senators should not be eligible for Cabinet posts.

B. THE SUPREME COURT

17. Entrenchment in the Constitution

The Supreme Court should be entrenched in the Constitution as the general court of appeal for Canada.

18. Composition

The Constitution should entrench the current provision of the Supreme Court Act, which specifies that the Supreme Court is to be composed of nine members, of whom three must have been admitted to the civil law bar of Quebec.

19. Nominations and Appointments

The Constitution should require the federal government to name judges from lists submitted by the governments of the provinces and territories. A provision should be made in the Constitution for the appointment of interim judges if a list is not submitted on a timely basis or no candidate is acceptable.

20. Aboriginal Peoples' Role

The structure of the Supreme Court should not be modified in this round of constitutional discussions. The role of Aboriginal peoples in relation to the Supreme Court should be recorded in a political accord and should be on the agenda of a future First Ministers' Conference on Aboriginal issues(*).

Provincial and territorial governments should develop a reasonable process for consulting representatives of the Aboriginal peoples of Canada in the preparation of lists of candidates to fill vacancies on the Supreme Court(*).

Aboriginal groups should retain the right to make representations to the federal government respecting candidates to fill vacancies on the Supreme Court(*).

The federal government should examine, in consultation with Aboriginal groups, the proposal that an Aboriginal Council of Elders be entitled to make submissions to the Supreme Court when the court considers Aboriginal issues(*).

C. HOUSE OF COMMONS

21. Composition of the House of Commons

The composition of the House of Commons should be adjusted to better reflect the principle of representation by population. The adjustment should include an initial increase in the size of the House of Commons to 337 seats, to be made at the time Senate reform comes into effect. Ontario and Quebec would each be assigned 18 additional seats, British Columbia four additional seats, and Alberta two additional seats, with boundaries to be developed using the 1991 census. An additional special Canada-wide redistribution of seats should be conducted following the 1996 census, aimed at ensuring that, in the first subsequent general election, no province will have fewer than 95 per cent of the House of Commons seats it would receive under strict representation-by-population. As a result of this special adjustment, no province or territory will lose seats, nor will a province or territory which has achieved full representation-by-population have a smaller share of House of Commons seats than its share of the total population in the 1996 census.

The redistribution based on the 1996 census and all future redistributions should be governed by the following constitutional provisions:

(a) A guarantee that Quebec would be assigned no fewer than 25 per cent of the seats in the House of Commons;

(b) The current Section 41(b) of the Constitution Act, 1982, the "fixed floor", would be retained;

(c) Section 51(a) of the Constitution Act, 1867, the "rising floor", would be repealed;

(d) A new provision that would ensure that no province could have fewer Commons seats than another province with a smaller population;

(e) The current provision that allocates two seats to the Northwest Territories and one seat to Yukon.

A permanent formula should be developed and Section 51 of the Constitution Act, 1867, should be adjusted to accommodate demographic change, taking into consideration the principles suggested by the Royal Commission on Electoral Reform and Party Financing.

22. Aboriginal Peoples' Representation

The issue of Aboriginal representation in the House of Commons should be pursued by Parliament, in consultation with representatives of the Aboriginal peoples of Canada, after it has received the final report of the House of Commons Committee studying the recommendations of the Royal Commission on Electoral Reform and Party Financing(*).

D. FIRST MINISTERS' CONFERENCES

23. Entrenchment

A provision should be added to the Constitution requiring the Prime Minister to convene a First Ministers' Conference at least once a year. The agendas for these conferences should not be specified in the Constitution.

The leaders of the territorial governments should be invited to participate in any First Ministers' Conference convened pursuant to this constitutional provision. Representatives of the Aboriginal peoples of Canada should be invited to participate in discussions on any item on the agenda of a First Ministers' Conference that directly affects the Aboriginal peoples. This should be embodied in a political accord(*).

The role and responsibilities of First Ministers with respect to the federal spending power is outlined at item 25 of this document.

E. THE BANK OF CANADA

24. The Bank of Canada

The Bank of Canada was discussed and the consensus was that this issue should not be pursued in this round, except for the consensus that the Senate should have a role in ratifying the appointment of its Governor.

III. ROLES AND RESPONSIBILITIES

25. Federal Spending Power

A provision should be added to the Constitution stipulating that the Government of Canada must provide reasonable compensation to the government of a province that chooses not to participate in a new Canada-wide shared-cost program that is established by the federal government in an area of exclusive provincial jurisdiction, if that province carries on a program or initiative that is compatible with the national objectives.

A framework should be developed to guide the use of the federal spending power in all areas of exclusive provincial jurisdiction. Once developed, the framework could become a multilateral agreement that would receive constitutional protection using the mechanism described in Item 26 of this report. The framework should ensure that when the federal spending power is used in areas of exclusive provincial jurisdiction, it should:

(a) contribute to the pursuit of national objectives;

(b) reduce overlap and duplication;

(c) not distort and should respect provincial priorities; and

(d) ensure equality of treatment of the provinces, while recognizing their different needs and circumstances.

The Constitution should commit First Ministers to establishing such a framework at a future conference of First Ministers. Once it is established, First Ministers would assume a role in annually reviewing progress in meeting the objectives set out in the framework.

A provision should be added (as Section 106(a)(3) that would ensure that nothing in the section that limits the federal spending power affects the commitments of Parliament and the Government of Canada that are set out in Section 36 of the Constitution Act, 1982.

26. Protection of Intergovernmental Agreements

The Constitution should be amended to provide a mechanism to ensure that designated agreements between governments are protected from unilateral change. This would occur when Parliament and the legislature(s) enact laws approving the agreement.

Each application of the mechanism should cease to have effect after a maximum of five years but could be renewed by a vote of Parliament and the legislature(s) readopting similar legislation. Governments of Aboriginal peoples should have access to this mechanism. The provision should be available to protect both bilateral and multilateral agreements among federal, provincial and territorial governments, and the governments of Aboriginal Peoples. A government negotiating an agreement should be accorded equality of treatment in relation to any government which has already concluded an agreement, taking into account different needs and circumstances.

It is the intention of governments to apply this mechanism to future agreements related to the Canada Assistance Plan(*).

27. Immigration

A new provision should be added to the Constitution committing the Government of Canada to negotiate agreements with the provinces relating to immigration.

The Constitution should oblige the federal government to negotiate and conclude within a reasonable time an immigration agreement at the request of any province. A government negotiating an agreement should be accorded equality of treatment in relation to any government which has already concluded an agreement, taking into account different needs and circumstances.

28. Labour Market Development and Training

Exclusive federal jurisdiction for unemployment insurance, as set out in Section 91(2)(a) of the Constitution Act, 1867, should not be altered. The federal government should retain exclusive jurisdiction for income support and its related services delivered through the Unemployment Insurance system. Federal spending on job-creation programs should be protected through a constitutional provision or a political accord(*).

Labour market development and training should be identified in Section 92 of the Constitution as a matter of exclusive provincial jurisdiction. Provincial legislatures should have the authority to constrain federal spending that is directly related to labour market development and training. This should be accomplished through justiciable intergovernmental agreements designed to meet the circumstances of each province.

At the request of a province, the federal government would be obligated to withdraw from any or all training activities and from any or all labour market development activities, except Unemployment Insurance. The federal government should be required to negotiate and conclude agreements to provide reasonable compensation to provinces requesting that the federal government withdraw.

The Government of Canada and the government of the province that requested the federal government to withdraw should conclude agreements within a reasonable time.

Provinces negotiating agreements should be accorded equality of treatment with respect to terms and conditions of agreements in relation to any other province that has already concluded an agreement, taking into account the different needs and circumstances of the provinces.

The federal, provincial and territorial governments should commit themselves in a political accord to enter into administrative arrangements to improve efficiency and client service and ensure effective co-ordination of federal Unemployment Insurance and provincial employment functions(*).

As a safeguard, the federal government should be required to negotiate and conclude an agreement within a reasonable time, at the request of any province not requesting the federal government to withdraw, to maintain its labour market development and training programs and activities in that province. A similar safeguard should be available to the Territories.

There should be a constitutional provision for an ongoing federal role in the establishment of national policy objectives for the national aspects of labour market development. National labour market policy objectives would be established through a process which could be set out in the Constitution including the obligation for presentation to Parliament for debate. Factors to be considered in the establishment of national policy objectives could include items such as national economic conditions, national labour market requirements, international labour market trends and changes in international economic conditions. In establishing national policy objectives, the federal government would take into account the different needs and circumstances of the provinces; and there would be a provision, in the Constitution or in a political accord, committing the federal, provincial and territorial governments to support the development of common occupational standards, in consultation with employer and employee groups(*).

Provinces that negotiated agreements to constrain the federal spending power should be obliged to ensure that their labour market development programs are compatible with the national policy objectives, in the context of different needs and circumstances.

Considerations of service to the public in both official languages should be included in a political accord and be discussed as part of the negotiation of bilateral agreements(*).

The concerns of Aboriginal peoples in this field will be dealt with through the mechanisms set out in item 40 below.

29. Culture

Provinces should have exclusive jurisdiction over cultural matters within the provinces. This should be recognized through an explicit constitutional amendment that also recognizes the continuing responsibility of the federal government in Canadian cultural matters. The fed-

eral government should retain responsibility for national cultural institutions, including grants and contributions delivered by these institutions. These changes should not alter the federal fiduciary responsibility for Aboriginal people. The non-derogation provisions for Aboriginal peoples set out in item 40 of this document will apply to culture.

30. Forestry

Exclusive provincial jurisdiction over forestry should be recognized and clarified through an explicit constitutional amendment.

Provincial legislatures should have the authority to constrain federal spending that is directly related to forestry.

This should be accomplished through justiciable intergovernmental agreements, designed to meet the specific circumstances of each province. The mechanism used would be the one set out in item 26 of this document, including a provision for equality of treatment with respect to terms and conditions. Considerations of service to the public in both official languages should be considered a possible part of such agreements(*).

Such an agreement should set the terms for federal withdrawal, including the level and form of financial resources to be transferred. In addition, a political accord could specify the form the compensation would take (i.e. cash transfers, tax points, or others). Alternatively, such an agreement could require the federal government to maintain its spending in that province. The federal government should be obliged to negotiate and conclude such an agreement within a reasonable time(*).

These changes and the ones set out in items 31, 32, 33, 34 and 35 should not alter the federal fiduciary responsibility for Aboriginal people. The provisions set out in item 40 would apply.

31. Mining

Exclusive provincial jurisdiction over mining should be recognized and clarified through an explicit constitutional amendment and the negotiation of federal-provincial agreements. This should be done in the same manner as set out above with respect to forestry(*).

32. Tourism

Exclusive provincial jurisdiction over tourism should be recognized and clarified through an explicit constitutional amendment and the negotiation of federal-provincial agreements. This should be done in the same manner as set out above with respect to forestry(*).

33. Housing

Exclusive provincial jurisdiction over housing should be recognized and clarified through an explicit constitutional amendment and the negotiation of federal-provincial agreements. This should be done in the same manner as set out above with respect to forestry(*).

34. Recreation

Exclusive provincial jurisdiction over recreation should be recognized and clarified through an explicit constitutional amendment and the negotiation of federal-provincial agreements. This should be done in the same manner as set out above with respect to forestry(*).

35. Municipal and Urban Affairs

Exclusive provincial jurisdiction over municipal and urban affairs should be recognized and clarified through an explicit constitutional amendment and the negotiation of federal-provincial agreements. This should be done in the same manner as set out above with respect to forestry(*).

36. Regional Development

In addition to the commitment to regional development to be added to Section 36 of the Constitution Act, 1982 (described in item 5 of this document), a provision should be added to the Constitution that would oblige the federal government to negotiate an agreement at the request of any province with respect to regional development. Such agreements could be protected under the provision set out in item 26 ("Protection of Intergovernmental Agreements"). Regional development should not become a separate head of power in the constitution.

37. Telecommunications

The federal government should be committed to negotiate agreements with the provincial governments to co-ordinate and harmonize the procedures of their respective regulatory agencies in this field. Such agreements could be protected under the provision set out in item 26 ("Protection of Intergovernmental Agreements").

38. Federal power of Disallowance and Reservation

This provision of the Constitution should be repealed. Repeal requires unanimity.

39. Federal Declaratory Power

Section 92(10)(c) of the Constitution Act, 1867, permits the federal government to declare a "work" to be for the general advantage of Canada and bring it under the legislative jurisdiction of Parliament. This provision should be amended to ensure that the declaratory power can only be applied to new works or rescinded with respect to past declarations with the explicit consent of the province(s) in which the work is situated. Existing declarations should be left undisturbed unless all of the legislatures affected wish to take action.

40. Aboriginal Peoples' Protection Mechanism

There should be a general non-derogation clause to ensure that division of powers amendments will not affect the rights of the Aboriginal peoples and the jurisdictions and powers of governments of Aboriginal peoples.

IV: FIRST PEOPLES

Note: References to the territories will be added to the legal text with respect to this section, except where clearly inappropriate. Nothing in the amendments would extend the powers of the territorial legislatures.

A. THE INHERENT RIGHT OF SELF-GOVERNMENT

41. The Inherent Right of Self-Government

The Constitution should be amended to recognize that the Aboriginal peoples of Canada have the inherent right of self-government within Canada. This right should be placed in a new section of the Constitution Act, 1982, Section 35.1(1).

The recognition of the inherent right of self-government should be interpreted in light of the recognition of Aboriginal governments as one of three orders of government in Canada.

A contextual statement should be inserted in the Constitution, as follows;

The exercise of the right of self-government includes the authority of the duly constituted legislative bodies of Aboriginal peoples, each within its own jurisdiction:

(a) to safeguard and develop their languages, cultures, economies, identities, institutions and traditions; and,

(b) to develop, maintain and strengthen their relationship with their lands, waters and environment

so as to determine and control their development as peoples according to their own values and priorities and ensure the integrity of their societies.

Before making any final determination of an issue arising from the inherent right of self-government, a court or tribunal should take into account the contextual statement referred to above and should enquire into the efforts that have been made to resolve the issue through negotiations and should be empowered to order the parties to take such steps as are appropriate in the circumstances to effect a negotiated resolution.

42. Delayed Justiciability

The inherent right of self-government should be entrenched in the Constitution. However, its justiciability should be delayed for a five-year period through constitutional language and a political accord(*).

Delaying the justiciability of the right should be coupled with a constitutional provision which would shield Aboriginal rights.

Delaying the justiciability of the right will not make the right contingent and will not affect existing Aboriginal and treaty rights.

The issue of special courts or tribunals should be on the agenda of the First Ministers' Conference on Aboriginal Constitutional Matters referred to in item 53(*).

43. Charter Issues

The Canadian Charter of Rights and Freedoms should apply immediately to governments of Aboriginal peoples.

A technical change should be made to the English text of Sections 3, 4 and 5 of the Canadian Charter of Rights and Freedoms to ensure that it corresponds to the French text.

The legislative bodies of Aboriginal peoples should have access to Section 33 of the Constitution Act, 1982 (the notwithstanding clause) under conditions that are similar to those applying to Parliament and the provincial legislatures but which are appropriate to the circumstances of Aboriginal peoples and their legislative bodies.

44. Land

Future principles scheduled for the first ministers' table

POLITICAL ACCORD(S)—POSSIBLE ELEMENTS

INSTITUTIONS

Item

6. The Canadian Common Market: The following principles will be reviewed by First Ministers at a future First Ministers' Conference:

(1) Canada is a social and economic union within which, to the extent provided below, persons, goods, services, and capital may move freely across provincial and territorial boundaries.

(2) The Parliament and Government of Canada, the provincial legislatures and governments and territorial legislative authorities and governments shall not erect interprovincial trade barriers by a law or practice that,

(a) arbitrarily discriminates on the basis of province or territory of residence, origin or destination, and

(b) impedes the efficient functioning of the Canadian economic union.

(3) The above would not apply to:

(a) a federal law or practice that furthers the principles of equalization or regional development;

(b) a provincial or territorial law or practice that is directed at reducing economic disparities between regions wholly within a province or territory;

(c) any law that restricts the acquisition of land by non-residents of a province or territory that has any such restrictions on the day this action comes into force;

(d) fish or agricultural products marketing or supply management systems.

(4) For greater certainty, the principles outlined in (1) and (2) would not invalidate a federal, provincial or territorial law or principles respecting the following if

its primary purpose is not to create a disguised restriction on trade:

(a) public security, safety or health, protection of the environment, consumer protection, fair trading practices, or laws and practices related to language protection;

(b) the provision of social services;

(c) the establishment and maintenance of monopolies;

(d) labour practices, including, but not limited to, pay equity or employment equity, affirmative action, plant closings, or minimum and fair wages;

(e) reasonable public-sector investment practices or a law or practice that relates to a subsidy or tax-incentive program established for the purpose of encouraging investment;

(f) explorations, development, conservation and management of natural resources.

Nothing in the above affects anything in s.6 of the Canadian Charter of Rights and Freedoms.

Nothing in the above affects anything in the Social and Economic Union provisions.

First Ministers will decide on the best approach to implement these principles at a future FMC on the Economy.

In this respect, First Ministers would have the authority to create an agency. If this agency were created, this agency would report to First Ministers, and, once established, would be independent. First Ministers would decide on the specific role, mandate and composition of this agency. It is envisaged that such an agency, if created, would be responsible for:

(a) mediation and conciliation;

(b) determination that a prima facie case exists (screening);

(c) final determination on a case;

(d) dispute resolution which would be binding. . . .

The specific constitutional provision on the inherent right and the specific constitutional provision on the commitment to negotiate land should not create new Aboriginal rights to land or derogate from existing aboriginal or treaty rights to land, except as provided for in self-government agreements.

B. METHOD OF EXERCISE OF THE RIGHT

45. Commitment to Negotiate

There should be a constitutional commitment by the federal and provincial governments and the Indian, Inuit and Métis peoples in the various regions and communities of Canada to negotiate in good faith with the objective of concluding agreements elaborating the rela-

tionship between Aboriginal governments and the other orders of government. The negotiations would focus on the implementation of the right of self-government including issues of jurisdiction, lands and resources, and economic and fiscal arrangements.

46. The Process of Negotiation

Political Accord on Negotiation and Implementation

A political accord should be developed to guide the process of self-government negotiations(*).

Equity of Access

All Aboriginal peoples of Canada should have equitable access to the process of negotiation.

Trigger for Negotiations

Self-government negotiations should be initiated by the representatives of Aboriginal peoples when they are prepared to do so.

Provision for Non-Ethnic Governments

Self-government agreements may provide for self-government institutions which are open to the participation of all residents in a region covered by the agreement.

Provision for Different Circumstances

Self-government negotiations should take into consideration the different circumstances of the various Aboriginal peoples.

Provision for Agreements

Self-government negotiations should be set out in future treaties, including land claims agreements or amendments to existing treaties, including land claims agreements. In addition, self-government agreements could be set out in other agreements which may contain a declaration that the rights of the Aboriginal peoples are treaty rights, within the meaning of Section 35(1) of the Constitution Act, 1982.

Ratification of Agreements

There should be an approval process for governments and Aboriginal peoples for self-government agreements, involving Parliament, the legislative assemblies of the relevant provinces, territories and the legislative bodies of the Aboriginal peoples. This principle should be expressed in the ratification procedures set out in the specific self-government agreements.

Non-Derogation Clause

There should be an explicit statement in the Constitution that the commitment to negotiate does not make the right of self-government contingent on negotiations or in any way affect the justiciability of the right of self-government.

Dispute Resolution Mechanism

To assist the negotiation process, a dispute resolution mechanism involving mediation and arbitration should be established. Details of this mechanism should be set out in a political accord(*).

47. Legal Transition

A constitutional provision should ensure that federal and provincial laws will continue to apply until they are displaced by laws passed by governments of Aboriginal peoples pursuant to their authority.

A law passed by a government of Aboriginal peoples, or an assertion of its authority based on the inherent right provision may not be inconsistent with those laws which are essential to the preservation of peace, order and good government in Canada.

48. Treaties

With respect to treaties with Aboriginal peoples, the Constitution should be amended as follows:

• Treaty rights should be interpreted in a just, broad and liberal manner taking into account the spirit and intent of the treaties and the context in which the specific treaties were negotiated;

• The Government of Canada should be committed to establishing and participating in good faith in a joint process to clarify or implement treaty rights, or to rectify terms of treaties when agreed to by the parties. The governments of the provinces should also be committed, to the extent that they have jurisdiction, to participation in the above treaty process when invited by the government of Canada and the Aboriginal peoples concerned or where specified in a treaty;

• Participants in this process should have regard, among other things and where appropriate, to the spirit and intent of the treaties as understood by Aboriginal peoples. It should be confirmed that all Aboriginal peoples that possess treaty rights shall have equitable access to this treaty process;

• It should be provided that these treaty amendments shall not extend the authority of any government or legislature, or affect the rights of Aboriginal peoples not party to the treaty concerned.

C. ISSUES RELATED TO THE EXERCISE OF THE RIGHT

49. Equity of Access to Section 35 Rights

The Constitution should provide that all of the Aboriginal peoples of Canada have access to those Aboriginal and treaty rights recognized and affirmed in Section 35 of the Constitution Act, 1982, that pertain to them.

50. Financing

Matters relating to the financing of governments of Aboriginal peoples should be dealt with in a political accord. The accord would commit the governments of Aboriginal peoples to:

• Promoting equal opportunities for the well-being of all Aboriginal peoples;

• Furthering economic, social and cultural development and employment opportunities to reduce disparities in opportunities among Aboriginal peoples and between Aboriginal peoples and other Canadians; and

• Providing essential public services at levels reasonably comparable to those available to other Canadians in the vicinity.

It would also commit federal and provincial governments to the principle of providing the governments of Aboriginal peoples with fiscal or other resources, such as land, to assist those governments to govern their own affairs and to meet the commitments listed above, taking into account the levels of services provided to other Canadians in the vicinity and the fiscal capacity of governments of Aboriginal peoples to raise revenues from their own sources.

The issues of financing and its possible inclusion in the Constitution should be on the agenda of the First Ministers' Conference on Aboriginal Constitutional Matters referred to in item 53(*).

51. Affirmative Action Programs

The Constitution should include a provision which authorizes governments of Aboriginal peoples to undertake affirmative action programs for socially and economically disadvantaged individuals or groups and programs for the advancement of Aboriginal languages and cultures.

52. Gender Equality

Section 35(4) of the Constitution Act, 1982, which guarantees existing Aboriginal and treaty rights equally to male and female persons, should be retained. The issue of gender equality should be on the agenda of the First Ministers' Conference on Aboriginal Constitutional Matters referred to under item 53(*).

53. Future Aboriginal Constitutional Process

The Constitution should be amended to provide for four future First Ministers' Conferences on Aboriginal Constitutional Matters beginning no later than 1996, and following every two years thereafter. These conferences would be in addition to any other First Ministers' Conferences required by the Constitution. The agendas of these conferences would include items identified in this report and items requested by Aboriginal peoples.

54. Section 91(24)

For greater certainty, a new provision should be added to the Constitution Act, 1867, to ensure that Section 91(24) applies to all Aboriginal peoples.

The new provision would not result in a reduction of existing expenditures on Indians and Inuit or alter the fiduciary and treaty obligations of the federal government for Aboriginal peoples. This would be reflected in a political accord(*).

55. Métis in Alberta/Section 91(24)

The Constitution should be amended to safeguard the legislative authority of the Government of Alberta for Métis and Métis Settlements lands. There was agreement to a proposed amendment to the Alberta Act that would constitutionally protect the status of the land held in fee simple by the Métis Settlements General Council under letters patent from Alberta.

56. Métis Nation Accord(*)

The federal government, the provinces of Ontario, Manitoba, Saskatchewan, Alberta, British Columbia and the Métis National Council have agreed to enter into a legally binding, justiciable and enforceable accord on Métis Nation issues. Technical drafting of the Accord is being completed. The Accord sets out the obligations of the federal and provincial governments and the Métis Nation.

The Accord commits governments to negotiate: self-government agreements; lands and resources; the transfer of the portion of Aboriginal programs and services available to Métis; and cost-sharing arrangements relating to Métis institutions, programs and services.

Provinces and the federal government agree not to reduce existing expenditures on Métis and other Aboriginal people as a result of the Accord or as a result of an amendment to Section 91(24). The Accord defines the Métis for the purposes of the Métis Nation Accord and commits governments to enumerate and register the Métis Nation.

V. THE AMENDING FORMULA

Note: All of the following changes to the amending formula require the unanimous agreement of Parliament and the provincial legislatures.

57. Changes to National Institutions

Amendments to provisions of the Constitution related to the Senate should require unanimous agreement of Parliament and the provincial legislatures, once the current set of amendments related to Senate reform has come into effect. Future amendments affecting the House of Commons which can now be made under s.42 should also require unanimity.

Sections 41 and 42 of the Constitution Act, 1982, should be amended so that the nomination and appointment process of Supreme Court judges would remain subject to the general (7/50) amending procedure. All other matters related to the Supreme Court, including its entrenchment, its role as the general court of appeal and its composition, would be matters requiring unanimity.

58. Establishment of New Provinces

The current provisions of the amending formula governing the creation of new provinces should be rescinded. They should be replaced by the pre-1982 provisions allowing the creation of new provinces through an Act of Parliament, following consultation with all of the existing provinces at a First Ministers' Conference. New provinces should not have a role in the amending formula without the unanimous consent of all of the provinces and the federal government, with the exception of purely bilateral or unilateral matters described in Sections 38(3), 40, 43, 45 and 46 as it relates to 43, of the Constitution Act, 1982. Any increase in the representation for new provinces in the Senate should also require the unanimous consent of all provinces and the federal government. Territories that become provinces could not lose Senators or members of the House of Commons.

The provision now contained in Section 42(1)(e) of the Constitution Act, 1982, with respect to the extension of provincial boundaries into the Territories should be repealed and replaced by the Constitution Act, 1871, modified in order to require the consent of the Territories.

59. Compensation for Amendments that Transfer Jurisdiction

Where an amendment is made under the general amending formula that transfers legislative powers from provincial legislatures to Parliament, Canada should provide reasonable compensation to any province that opts out of the amendment.

60. Aboriginal Consent

There should be Aboriginal consent to future constitutional amendments that directly refer to the Aboriginal peoples. Discussions are continuing on the mechanism by which this consent would be expressed with a view to agreeing on a mechanism prior to the introduction in Parliament of formal resolutions amending the Constitution.

VI. OTHER ISSUES

Other constitutional issues were discussed during the multilateral meetings.

The consensus was not to pursue the following issues:

- Personal bankruptcy and insolvency
- Intellectual property
- Interjurisdictional immunity
- Inland fisheries
- Marriage and divorce
- Residual power
- Telecommunications
- Legislative interdesignation
- Changes to the "notwithstanding clause"
- Section 96 (appointment of judges)
- Section 125 (taxation of federal and provincial governments)
- Section 92(a) (export of natural resources)
- Requiring notice for changes to federal legislation respecting equalization payments
- Property rights
- Implementation of international treaties

Other issues were discussed but were not finally resolved, among which were:

- Requiring notice for changes to federal legislation respecting Established Programs Financing
- Establishing in a political accord a formal federal-provincial consultation process with regard to the negotiation of international treaties and agreements
- Aboriginal participation in intergovernmental agreements respecting the division of powers
- Aboriginal participation in annual First Ministers' Conferences
- Equality of access to the mechanism for protecting intergovernmental agreements
- Establishing a framework for compensation issues with respect to labour market development and training
- Consequential amendments related to Senate reform, including by-elections, floors on House of Commons representation, time limits with respect to the reconciliation process and joint sittings with the House of Commons
- Any other consequential amendments required by changes recommended in this report.

(*) Asterisks in the text indicate where the consensus is to proceed with a political accord.

The Supreme Court of Canada and the Constitution

The members of the Supreme Courts in both Canada and the United States, in the last decade, have come under increasingly intense scrutiny both by those who nominate and appoint them and by the general public. This scrutiny now includes a close examination of their life-styles and personalities, as well as their ideologies and decisions.

Stephen Bindman's article profiles the nine justices of the Supreme Court of Canada who were serving in April 1992. Eight of the nine were appointed by Prime Minister Brian Mulroney. Each justice has areas of particular expertise such as privacy, criminal, corporate, and civil law. They also turn out to be very complex human persons.

It is also necessary to examine how the Canadian Charter of Rights and Freedoms (1982) has significantly changed the job descriptions for all levels of the court system. Prior to the charter, most judges "were trained, not to judge laws, but to apply them. . . ." While increasing the justices' social responsibility, the charter has, paradoxically, diminished the Court's role as a general court of appeal, due to severe constraints on their time.

The role of legislators has also been altered by requiring them to take into account the public's increasing awareness and assertion of their rights. Some critics and observers see this as an increase in the Americanization of the political process in Canada.

Al Strachan reports on the controversy started by two University of Calgary political science professors, who argue that a Court Party has emerged as "An inevitable outcome of the 'Charter Revolution' . . . a loose alliance of judges, bureaucrats, lawyers, activists . . . academics and media personalities who use 'a new playing field for the pursuit of politics—the courts.' "

All this rather sudden attention, focused on the Supreme Court, has resulted in an increase in criticism about the current process of nomination and confirmation. Professor Jacob Ziegel presents a detailed critique of the process, and then suggests some alternatives.

The next selection demonstrates how the Court can divide itself on decisions that affect fundamental rights such as freedom of speech and the publication of false news. It seems that one cannot easily predict how the justices will decide on any given case.

The final selection presents a detailed examination of the evolution of the Court's approach to the Charter. Professor Wayne MacKay of Dalhousie University's law school in Halifax "sees a major change in the court's interpretation of the Charter" from the previous decade, when it seemed to focus on protecting minorities. There now seems to be less willingness "to second-guess the legislatures." Some argue that "the Court may be evolving into a style similar to that of the U.S. Supreme Court. . . ." The article then analyzes 10 important cases from the last two years of Court decisions.

Looking Ahead: Challenge Questions

How useful is it to know the personal backgrounds of the justices of the Supreme Court? Can we predict their behaviour on the Court from this information?

How has the Charter of Rights and Freedoms breached the doctrine of legal positivism?

Is there a danger of politicizing the nomination process in the same way as it has been politicized in the United States?

Are citizens' rights strengthened or weakened by recent decisions of the Supreme Court of Canada?

Unit 2

AND JUSTICES FOR ALL

Stephen Bindman

Special to The Star
Southam News

OTTAWA

Claire L'Heureux-Dube can go bicycling in the summer in her T-shirt and shorts without being noticed on the streets of the capital.

Some lawyers still don't recognize Antonio Lamer as the country's chief justice, let alone the people at the local pound who retrieve his frequently absconding dog, Gaspard de Rapidieu.

And only rarely does someone come up to a stark naked John Sopinka in the locker room of his squash club and say, "Hello my Lord."

Despite the importance of the decisions made by the judges of the country's top court every day, life on the Supreme Court of Canada is still largely anonymous.

And that's just fine with them.

For Madam Justice Beverley McLachlin, anonymity means freedom.

"If you can't go into a bookstore and look for a book without worrying that somebody's going to be looking over your shoulder and making an assessment of your taste in literature. (If there's) an imposition on your freedom, you're going to be less likely to go to the bookstore, you're going to be very careful about which books you pick."

The nine judges are chosen by the prime minister on the advice of the justice minister. Except for Lamer, every justice of the current court was appointed by Brian Mulroney.

By law, three of the justices must be from Quebec and by tradition three others are from Ontario, one from Atlantic Canada and two from the West.

The recent Beaudoin-Dobbie constitutional committee recommended that the prime minister choose future judges from lists of candidates submitted by the provincial and territorial governments. The failed Meech Lake accord made a similar proposal.

Here is a rundown of Canada's top judges, in order of seniority:

■ **Antonio Lamer.** The mustachioed 59-year-old native of the streets of Montreal's brawling east end likes to compare his job as chief justice to the manager of a ballet troupe.

"I can't tell them how to dance. I can only tell them when we're going to perform and for how long and who's going to dance with whom. The actual ballet belongs to them."

A star criminal lawyer who once saved a man from the gallows, Lamer was appointed to the Quebec Superior Court when he was only 36. He was the first vice-chairman of the recently disbanded Law Reform Commission and later its chairman. He was named to the Supreme Court in 1980 by Pierre Trudeau and is now its longest-serving member.

While he was in boarding school studying Latin and Greek, Lamer says many of the neighborhood kids were helping their fathers bootleg and were well on their way to a life of crime.

As chief justice, Lamer is also head of the Canadian Judicial Council, National Judicial Institute and the committee that selects recipients of the Order of Canada.

There is a lot of ceremony attached to the job—he is Number 3 on the protocol list behind the prime minister and governor-general and every new ambassador pays him a personal visit and is supposed to throw a reception in his honor.

When he's not judging, Lamer likes to fish and hunt for partridge, read history, go for long walks with his wife Daniele, a lawyer with the federal justice department, and spend time on his 1939 classic cabin cruiser, Mahogany.

Fluently bilingual, he took up Russian a few years ago in order to converse with a visiting group from Moscow. He still practises greetings using a flip-chart placed in the shower of the private bathroom off his court office.

■ **Gerard La Forest.** It is fitting that La Forest should become the court's expert on privacy.

The 65-year-old native of Grand Falls, N.B., has written several rulings warning of the "grave threat" posed by modern technology such as wiretaps and other forms of electronic surveillance.

"A society which exposed us, at the whim of the state, to the risk of having a permanent electronic recording made of our words every time we opened our mouths might be superbly equipped to fight crime but would be one in which privacy no longer had any meaning," he wrote in 1990.

One of the most private members of the court, he frequently spurns the judges' private dining room to zip home for lunch with his wife of 40 years.

He was Brian Mulroney's first appointment to the top court in 1985 after four years on the New Brunswick Court of Appeal. Before that, the former Rhodes Scholar served with Lamer on the Law Reform Commission and taught law at the universities of Ottawa, Alberta and New Brunswick.

The bilingual La Forest is also a former senior bureaucrat in the federal justice department and was a constitutional adviser to the Trudeau government in the late 1960s. As a lawyer, he often argued constitutional cases before the Supreme Court.

He occasionally joins fellow judges Sopinka, Cory and Iacobucci for a game of tennis and often longs to return to the Maritimes.

"The Saint John River, the sea and the old houses in places like Fredericton. I'm from New Brunswick, my wife is from New Brunswick and even with an appointment of this magnitude, it still hurts to leave," he said after his selection.

■ **Claire L'Heureux-Dube.** Although she denies she's a workaholic, L'Heureux-Dube often stays in her office until two or three in the morning, reading cases or writing judgments.

The 64-year-old extrovert with an infectious laugh and blunt manner has been dubbed the "Great Dissenter" because she so frequently disagrees with her colleagues.

Since she was elevated from the Quebec Court of Appeal in 1987 to become the second woman on the top court, L'Heureux-Dube has penned more than 30 dissents.

She decided to go to law school while taking dictation in the office of a cod-liver oil processing plant in Rimouski, Que.

"The letter the guy was dictating was so stupid I thought: 'Why shouldn't I be on the other side of that desk?'" she said shortly after she was appointed.

An expert in family law, she co-authored a legal text with her good friend Rosalie Abella, who was recently named to the Ontario Court of Appeal.

A longtime widow, L'Heureux-Dube says she longs for the "joie de vivre" of her friends in Quebec.

■ **John Sopinka.** A former halfback with the Toronto Argonauts and the Montreal Alouettes and a would-be concert violinist, Sopinka's chambers resemble a trophy room more than a law office.

A squash and tennis fanatic, the 59-year-old Saskatchewan native likes to brag that since he took over his team hasn't lost the annual squash tournament with the Parliamentary Press Gallery.

The son of Ukrainian immigrants, the always-competitive Sopinka is a rare breed on the Supreme Court—he went straight from his lucrative Bay Street law practice to the top court and was never a judge before his 1988 appointment.

Among his high-profile clients were former Tory cabinet minister Sinclair Stevens and Susan Nelles, who was cleared of wrongdoing in a series of suspicious baby deaths at Toronto's Hospital for Sick Children.

Since his appointment, Sopinka has given dozen of speeches trying to demystify the judiciary, criticizing the use of royal commissions, pressure groups who demonstrate on the steps of courthouses and the "sea of commercialism" that has engulfed modern law firms.

He has caused a stink within the traditionally conservative judiciary by saying judges should be free to speak out on many controversial subjects.

"I don't think a judge has to be a monk."

■ **Peter Cory.** A remarkable double for the host of the TV children's show *Mr. Rogers' Neighborhood,* the World War II bomber pilot hands out cookies to his colleagues and their staffs every day at four p.m.

Lamer jokes that if he's ever reincarnated he'd like to come back as Peter Cory's dog, Dooley.

Known for his gentle sense of humor and love of puns, the Windsor-native was on the Ontario Court of Appeal for eight years before being named to the Supreme Court in 1989.

The 66-year-old Cory created a storm of controversy last summer when he told a legal conference at the University of Cambridge that the top court never intended its so-called Askov ruling to lead to tens of thousands of criminal charges being tossed out for unreasonable trial delays.

A father of three and doting grandfather of one, he still beats people half his age on the squash court though he usually apologizes after hitting a winning shot.

■ **Charles Gonthier.** The shyest and most low-key member of the court, Gonthier is also one of its least frequent writers.

Since he was appointed along with Cory in 1989, Gonthier has only penned 31 rulings, though almost all are unanimous, showing he can rally support among his colleagues. He has only written one dissenting opinion.

Gonthier, the father of five boys, shuns the spotlight and rarely gives public speeches. His wife is a Montreal gynecologist and although he keeps a *pied a terre* in Ottawa, he frequently spends weekends in Montreal or at the family cabin in the Laurentians.

When Gonthier, 63, was plucked from the Quebec Court of Appeal after only eight months, he wasn't the first family member to achieve high public office. His father was Canada's auditor-general from 1923 to 1939 and his maternal grandfather was justice minister in the Conservative governments of Robert Borden and Arthur Meighen.

2. THE SUPREME COURT OF CANADA AND THE CONSTITUTION

■ **Beverley McLachlin.** The youngest on the court at 48, some people joke that McLachlin has made it through the justice system quicker than some cases.

A self-described "farm girl" from Pincher Creek, Alta., she was first appointed to the county court of Vancouver in 1981 and made it to the Supreme Court just eight years later. Along the way she was the first woman on the B.C. Court of Appeal and the first female head of the province's trial courts.

Often touted as a likely candidate to become the country's first female chief justice after Lamer retires, McLachlin is the mother of a teenaged son.

She won praise last year from the Canadian Judicial Council for a speech in which she said criminal laws against abortion and prostitution are based on outdated stereotypes and attempts to solve social problems on the "backs of women." The conservative group REAL Women wanted her removed from the bench for her "feminist" bias.

She's a widow who recently remarried in the Supreme Court's dining room after receiving an unusual high-level proposal—over the intercom of an Air Canada flight to England.

■ **William Stevenson.** The 57-year-old Edmonton native once began a judgment with the words, "A bunch of the boys were whooping it up."

The case Stevenson heard as a lower court judge involved a man from the Klondike town of Dawson charged with causing a disturbance by riding a horse into every bar in town for a drink. The reveller claimed it was all just in good fun.

Stevenson, the son of Edmonton's former deputy police chief and the first Albertan appointed to the Supreme Court since 1958, is also the first who has served as a judge in the Northwest and Yukon territories.

A veteran of three levels of Alberta courts and a former law professor, he counted his current colleague Justice McLachlin among his many students at the University of Alberta.

Before he was appointed to the Supreme Court in 1990, he was a pioneer in continuing education for judges and authored a report which led to the establishment of the Canadian Judicial Centre, now the National Judicial Institute.

■ **Frank Iacobucci.** The son of Italian immigrants, the 54-year-old Iacobucci says the more different life experiences a person has had, the better a judge he or she is likely to be.

He should be a great judge.

Before being named to the Supreme Court in December, 1990, Iacobucci was chief justice of the Federal Court of Canada, federal deputy minister of justice, dean of law and vice-president at the University of Toronto.

At his swearing-in ceremony, he spoke in Italian to offer "a thousand thanks and a big hug" to his late mother, Rosina, and his ailing steel worker father, Gabriel, for their hard work.

A proud father of three, including a recent Rhodes Scholar, the tennis buff has only written a handful of judgments since his appointment and admits the Supreme Court really wasn't his first choice for a career change.

"My Walter Mitty dreams are managing or general managing the Blue Jays. I'd like to have one year as manager and one year as general manager and then say goodbye to it."

SOUTHAM NEWS

How the Charter changes justice

The Charter of Rights and Freedoms became part of the Constitution on April 17, 1982. As the 10th anniversary approached, Chief Justice Antonio Lamer of the Supreme Court of Canada discussed the significance of the Charter with Jeff Sallot of The Globe and Mail's Ottawa bureau.

What has happened to the role of the Supreme Court as a result of the Charter?

Not only to this court, but all courts and judges, the Charter has changed our job descriptions. Most judges were trained in the law prior to . . . the Charter, so we were trained, not to judge laws, but to apply them and, if they were open to interpretation, to interpret them.

But with the Charter we are commanded, when asked to do so, to sometimes judge the laws themselves. It is very different activity, especially when one has to look at Section 1 of the Charter [the passage that says laws must be consistent with the principles of a free and democratic society], which is asking us to make what is essentially what used to be a political call.

And so to many of us—to most of us, not all—this was a very drastic change in the judicial approach to law. We have done it. We had to adapt to this new role . . . We've had to change our libraries, and start reading a lot of American stuff that we weren't used to, and lots of European stuff . . . If you are talking about cruel and unusual punishment [prohibited under the Charter], the U.S. books could cover a wall . . . it would be ridiculous if we wanted to reinvent the wheel here [in Canada]. Though we don't necessarily have to follow American jurisprudence . . .

[This new role] has curtailed our regular work in two ways. One, it has cast upon us a social responsibility that is nothing comparable to what the court used to be. Secondly, it has diminished our role as a general court of appeal. Because there are just 24 hours in a day . . .

Mind you, we are hearing more cases than we used to hear. And we are handing down more judgments than we used to. In fact, we are doing it faster . . . I think it has forced us into being better-organized . . . This has a ripple effect throughout the system in the sense that [provincial] courts of appeal are, more often than they were in the past, the court of last resort. They've had to adjust. They also have the Charter . . . every judge is a constitutional judge in Canada . . .

The Charter has also had an effect on law schools. They've had to change their curriculum. And there is a demand for greater maturity on the part of lawyers. It is not sufficient to be a legal wizard. You have to be a socially and politically well-balanced person. Lawyers are having to develop expertise in fields other than strictly law. You don't go through a Section 1 analysis of law of the Charter just with law books.

How has the Charter affected Canadian society? Do you sense that Canadians have a greater appreciation of their fundamental rights, that there is greater confidence in the institutions of government knowing that there is a court that will be able to review the decisions of parliamentarians?

Well, much more has been done out of court than in court. In 1982 when the Charter came in, governments were watching the courts to see what we would do. I think now they realize we haven't gone berserk with the Charter and we aren't striking down laws right and left. They know how far we'll go and how far we're not going to go because we've said so . . . Knowing that—and they've known that for a few years— they have done lots of things. They've sifted through their law and any law that was suspect they have fixed it. The Department of Justice, and at the provincial level . . . there is somebody or some committee that passes on any bill that goes to the House to be sure that it does not attract Charter scrutiny. So the Charter has had a preventative effect . . .

On the part of the public it has created a demand on the court. The public now wants its rights. They've been told they have these rights and they want them. And they know if they are correct the court will give it to them . . .

From *The Globe and Mail*, April 17, 1992, p. A11. Reprinted by permission.

The Charter is a very active factor in the legal life of our country . . .

Nobody has really linked the Charter with other important events and this requires a little bit of knowledge of law . . . Legal positivism stifles the Charter and things like that. Legal positivism says that what is right is what the law says is right—and legal positivism was our system . . . Then you have the UN resolution on human rights in 1946, and that was the first breach of legal positivism.

And then Canada gradually, through various treaties and subscribing to various resolutions in the United Nations, started dismantling strict legal positivism. But the only country in the world that really acknowledged individual rights, the first country in the world, was Canada in 1982.

In 1982 we put an end to most legal positivism. Now that's a revolution. That's like introducing the metric system. It is like Pasteur's discoveries. Medicine was never the same after. Like the invention of penicillin, the laser. It was a great event.

'In 1982 we put an end to most legal positivism. Now that's a revolution. It is like the invention of penicillin, the laser. It was a great event'

What got lost—and academics didn't discuss this and our philosophers never discussed this—was to try to draw a continuum and to see what (former prime minister Pierre) Trudeau did in that perspective. Everybody was talking instead about patriation [of the Constitution] . . . There was no discussion at all about the Charter's historical significance. I think now Canadians are discovering . . . [that the Charter] is, from a philosophical and a sociological point of view, a tremendous event.

You think it has been positive in the way individual citizens view their relationship with the state?

Yes. It has reaffirmed a very fundamental point. You know, I don't think society is an end in itself. I think a person is the most important thing. Anything else is there to assist the person to fulfill one's life. That's why we have society to begin with. We congregate to be happier. If we were happier by not congregating we wouldn't congregate.

I'm very libertarian in that sense. And I think the Charter has had an educational value in making people aware that a person is a very important thing. Everything else is subordinate. Even collectivities.

There has been a lot of cynicism at times about government in general . . . Has the fact that courts have become involved and are seen as protectors of an individual's rights reduced the sense of cynicism about government?

I don't know. But one thing I do know is that society's attitude in general toward the courts has changed and that's quite natural. And we have to live with that. We have to accept that we will be more easily criticized and more aggressively criticized than in the past. Because we are fulfilling one of the functions that wasn't [previously] part of the job. We have to accept a greater amount of criticism . . .

I think Canadians appreciate that courts can be very useful when society gets into deadlocks. Look at patriation. That was a deadlock, and I think the court served well its purpose . . .

People are not always frank when they talk to us about what they think about us. Sometimes there are contradictions about us . . . There is an ambivalence out there on the powers of the court.

My bottom line on all that is that Canadian citizens and the government see we are not going beyond our power. We still think the ultimate highest court in the land is still Parliament and we keep that in mind.

What about the profile of judges? . . . There have been discussions in Canada

about the fact we don't know much about our judges.

I wish you had asked that 20 minutes ago because I have a 20-minute answer . . . I acknowledge that, if not [for] all judges, then judges of this court, there might be a different [appointment] process. I don't think the American process is a good one. It always is the senator who is from a different party than the president who asks the difficult questions, and the senator from the same party as the president who asks the easy question . . .

Furthermore, I don't think that [the U.S. adversarial] process is very helpful . . . If I had been asked at a [confirmation] hearing what was my position was on abortion, I would say personally I am against abortion. Yet I concurred with the reasons of [former chief justice Brian] Dickson . . . In fact I wrote reasons in Daigle [a case recognizing a woman's right to an abortion].

So what one thinks about things is not necessarily conclusive as to what one will do with a case. I so happen to think that my personal views as regards to abortion should not be imposed upon others. So that's a different shading. So I don't think it is very helpful to get into that kind of thing [at a confirmation hearing].

Obviously, the puritanism that is going on down there [in the United States], I mean, you are asking a person about what that person did 15 or 20 years ago when you wouldn't have appointed him 15 or 20 years ago, precisely because he was too young and precisely because he was doing those kinds of things. I'm not condoning what might have been done or not. What I'm saying is, what's the purpose of knowing what you were doing when you were 20 years old if you don't want to appoint somebody before the age of 50?

. . . But I don't shut the door on a different [judicial appointment] process. But I don't think Canadians realize the extent of the process that goes on [now] with appointments to this court. It is very thorough . . . When a person is picked for this court there is an extensive inquiry that is made within the profession. In most cases the person has been a judge . . . or has been a prominent lawyer. And everybody knows what he or she did right or wrong or better or worse.

All of this is canvassed with the local bar, the Canadian bar, the law society, the chief justice. Even the RCMP do a job . . . If there is a serious negative in all of that consultation there is a fat chance the appointment will not be made.

So what more do you want?

Maybe it is a question of the Canadian public not knowing . . . Maybe its a failing on the part of people in my business.

Maybe. But you can't ask somebody how they are going to decide a case in advance because it is in a vacuum. What we must be very careful not to do is to politicize the process. That's what the Americans have done. We've worked very hard to depoliticize the process. We started 25 or 30 years ago and I think we have succeeded. You know, I was appointed to this court by Mr. Trudeau. I was

appointed Chief Justice by Mr. Mulroney. I don't think there is any love lost between the two of them . . .

So I think we've attained a degree of maturity in Canada. We don't seek out, as the Americans do, for the spectacular. They are wonderful people. They have wonderful institutions. They command my admiration in many aspects. But I unfortunately don't think their best is in the way they choose their judiciary either by that [hearing] process or by electing them . . .

They can do what they want as long as they don't export it.

The hidden opposition

Forget Parliament. It's the judicial system that has emerged as the instrument of political change

Al Strachan

Alberta Bureau

Calgary

Western Canada has long been a spawning ground for political parties. The CCF, the forerunner of the NDP, was established here. So were Social Credit, the Reform Party and the Farmers' Party.

The latest addition is the Court Party.

But this political movement differs somewhat from its predecessors. It hasn't started in Western Canada so much as it has been *identified* here—by two University of Calgary political-science professors, to be precise.

They are F. L. (Ted) Morton and Rainer Knopff, and they have stirred up something of a storm in political circles through their recent papers and speeches putting the spotlight on what they call the Court Party.

An inevitable outcome of the "Charter Revolution," they see the Court Party as a loose alliance of judges, bureaucrats, lawyers, activists (who may also be bureaucrats and/or lawyers), academics and media personalities who use "a new playing field for the pursuit of politics—the courts."

The Canadian Charter of Rights and Freedoms, Dr. Morton said in a recent article expanding on the original views of the two professors, "is not so much the cause of the revolution as the means through which it is carried out. The Declaration of Independence did not 'cause' the American Revolution, nor the Declaration of the Rights of Man, the French Revolution."

However, the fact that judges "have become active players in the judicial process," a relatively recent phenomenon, has provided a new avenue for political activism.

The Bill of Rights had no great impact because judges displayed deference and self-restraint in 1960. But today, "The judges drive the Charter, not vice-versa" and the members of the Court Party have taken full advantage of these developments.

LEAF, the feminist Legal Education and Action Fund, is a prototypical example. Writes Dr. Morton: "After having heavily influenced the wording of the equality-rights sections (15 and 28) of the Charter, feminist groups then sought ways to take advantage of the broad wording.

"LEAF has gone on to become the most frequent non-government intervener in Charter cases before the Supreme Court.

"What is true of LEAF is true of a rapidly growing list of groups with a similar political genesis: The Canadian Disability Rights Council; the Charter Committee on Poverty Issues; The Canadian Prisoners' Rights Network; The Advocacy Group for the Environmentally Sensitive; the Equality Rights Committee of the Canadian Ethno-Cultural Council; EGALE (Equality for Gays and Lesbians Everywhere) to name just a few."

Most of these groups use taxpayers' money from two specific sources—the Secretary of State and the Court Challenges Program—to finance their actions. They rely heavily for support in other areas: Human-rights commissions and the courts, for example, provide them with personnel and an institutional playing field. They also have the support of the universities that provide constitutional experts and policy intellectuals.

"A common career path for a Court Party activist would include multiple migrations between government positions, university appointments and administrative or executive positions within his or her Charter-based group. At least from the taxpayers' perspective, this entire career path is within the public sector."

The media are also involved. When the Court Party wins a Charter challenge, it has only achieved part of its aim, say the Calgary professors. It must now make sure legislation is not re-enacted. This requires that public opinion be influenced—which the media do well, sometimes intentionally, sometimes unwittingly.

The intentional side is easily understood. But if media representatives don't understand a Charter decision, they seek help from "Charter experts" who, Dr. Morton says, "are usually law professors associated with the Charter groups involved in the case." They, naturally enough, "tend to provide 'interpretations' that reflect and thereby advance their political views."

From *The Globe and Mail*, January 11, 1992, p. D3. Reprinted by permission.

Dr. Morton says that, "You can't have a revolution without a revolutionary party. Nobody disputes that what has happened in Canada since 1982 is a mini-revolution."

In the fight for responsible government in Canada at the beginning of the 19th century, people who favoured executive power over elected assemblies were known as the Court Party.

At the end of the 20th century, nothing has changed.

The 'Court Party' in practice

Here are a few examples of how the Court Party works, as Calgary political scientists Ted Morton and Rainer Knopff see it:

■ In 1988, Canada's abortion law was overturned on procedural grounds (specifically, the lack of access and delays caused by hospital therapeutic-abortion committees). The new bill abolished the need for these committees, thereby eliminating the original legal objection. But "members" of the Court Party staged a public-relations battle on the ground that the abortion law violated the Charter, even though that was not the ruling. The implication that the government was ignoring the Charter was a powerful weapon in the pro-choice arsenal.

■ In the subsequent abortion debate, the media relied heavily on interviews with women lawyers and law professors, most of whom qualify as Court Party representatives. Madame Justice Bertha Wilson was quoted at length; the opinions of the four judges who agreed with her on procedural grounds were minimized; the two dissenting judges were virtually ignored. Studies have shown that Madame Justice Wilson is twice as likely to rule in favour of Charter claimants than is Mr. Justice William McIntyre.

■ Despite the fact that the United Nations said Canada's refugee-determination project is a model for the rest of the world, the Supreme Court held that it violated the Charter.

■ The Askov decision regarding the right to a speedy trial resulted in 40,000 cases being dismissed in Ontario.

■ In the Schecter case, the maternity-leave provision of the Unemployment Insurance Act was interpreted to provide some benefits for adoptive fathers but not for natural fathers. For the first time in Canadian history, the courts ordered the government to spend money, thereby assuming a right that has traditionally accrued only to elected representatives.

■ With the exception of two areas (feminists supporting censorship of obscenity and Quebec nationalists applauding the limitation of anglophone language rights) it is virtually impossible (since lawyers are in the front ranks of Court Party membership) to find a law-review article expounding judicial self-restraint or narrow Charter interpretations. In "Women's Organizations' Use of the Courts," Karen O'Connor advocates flooding the law reviews with articles supporting women's views.

■ Deborah Coyne, chairperson of the Canadian Coalition on the Constitution, virtually defined the Court Party when she said, "The Charter's appeal to our non-territorial identities—shared characteristics such as gender, ethnicity and disability—is finding concrete expression in an emerging new power structure in society. . . . This power structure involves new networks and coalitions among women, the disabled, aboriginal groups, social-reform activists, church groups, environmentalists, ethnocultural organizations, just to name a few. All these new groups have mobilized a broad range of interests that draw their inspiration from the Charter and the Constitution."

The coalition, the professors point out, then defeated the Meech Lake accord, a constitutional amendment that enjoyed the support of all 11 first ministers and the leaders of both opposition parties.

■ Elizabeth Shilton, who represents the feminist Legal Education and Action Fund, the most frequent non-government intervener in Charter cases before the Supreme Court, said at a conference in November on the impact of the Charter on public policy, "I am a feminist litigator and I am in the business of social change."

■ MaryLou McPhedran, another feminist lawyer associated with LEAF, told the same conference: "I represent the public and work against government, all governments." LEAF receives more money from the taxpayer-funded Challenges Program than any other organization.
—Al Strachan

Better Ways to Choose a Judge

Jacob S. Ziegel

Jacob Ziegel is a professor of law at the University of Toronto.

It is four months since Mr. Justice William Stevenson resigned unexpectedly from the Supreme Court of Canada. Astonishingly, despite the court's heavy caseload and the new judicial term about to start, a successor still has not been appointed.

This cannot be because of a lack of suitable candidates in the Prairie provinces, from which the appointee will almost certainly be drawn—each has many able judges and lawyers.

So why the unconscionable delay? We do not know, because the federal government does not deem it appropriate to tell us. Therein lies the first of many flaws in the system of appointments to the court.

There is no requirement for Ottawa to fill vacancies on the Supreme Court—or on any other court, for that matter—within a reasonable period. Delays of up to a year for lower-court appointments have not been uncommon.

Even if the new judge were appointed tomorrow, several more months would elapse before the appointee would be able to pull his or her full weight on the court. Meanwhile, the remaining eight judges carry the extra burden, and litigants are denied their entitlement to have important cases decided by the court's full complement of judges.

The delay would be bad enough if the Supreme Court were merely another slot in the judicial hierarchy, but it is much more than that. It is Canada's court of last resort on all constitutional questions and on all questions affecting the Charter of Rights and Freedoms, and much else.

It is Canada's third arm of government, and now wields as much power as Parliament and the federal cabinet. The Charlottetown accord has recognized this by agreeing to entrench the Supreme Court in the revised Constitution.

This prospect should be a challenge to put the appointment of judges to the court on a sound, democratic basis. We do not have that assurance now. We shall not have it if the new accord is approved in the Oct. 26 referendum.

Up to now, appointing members to the Supreme Court has been the prerogative of the prime minister. He is not obliged to consult anyone before making his decision. Usually he does, although he is entitled to ignore whatever suggestions are made. He is accountable to no one—not to Parliament, not to the provinces and not (Heaven forbid) to the people of Canada, whose daily lives are affected by the court's decisions.

Such an autocratic procedure is bound to lead to abuses, and in the past it frequently has. Up to Lester Pearson's day, judges were often appointed for partisan reasons as well as on their merits.

Purely partisan reasons have diminished significantly since then, but the unfettered discretion of prime ministers and lack of accountability has led to many unwise appointments. This is reflected in the number of judges who have resigned prematurely—at least five over the past 20 years, not counting resignations based on purely medical grounds.

Our system of appointing judges is borrowed from Britain. However, the Canadian circumstances are totally different and British precedents are no longer apt. The United Kingdom is not a federation; it has no written constitution and no entrenched Charter of Rights, and the British courts have no power to strike down legislation.

Significant changes are much overdue in the federal appointment of judges. In the case of the Supreme Court, the changes should encompass the following features.

First, when a vacancy arises, the federal government's nominee should be drawn from a short list of highly qualified candidates prepared by an advisory committee.

Second, the committee should be national in scope and include laypersons of national stature as well as representatives from the various branches of the legal profession.

Third, the committee should be wholly independent of governments. It should be free to conduct its inquiries as it sees fit and encouraged to interview candidates in person where appropriate.

Fourth, after the government has announced its nominee, a joint committee of the Senate and House of Commons should hold public hearings and then vote to ratify the nomination.

If the advisory committee has done its work well, the process should be straightforward. Still, it is important that the nominee be exposed to public scrutiny, to discourage executive abuses and ensure that interested citizens have an opportunity to express their views before the committee votes on the nomination.

These modest proposals have ample precedents, within and outside Canada. Nevertheless, they are sure to be branded as radical by myopic politicians maintaining that the existing system could not possibly be improved upon. Others will claim that scrutinizing a nominee publicly is demeaning and will deter good candidates from allowing their names to go forward.

The objections are not well grounded. If federal members of Parliament are required to seek voter approval at least once every five years, should we cavil at a system of screening and public scrutiny for an unelected group of men and women wielding vast powers who are entitled to remain in office until the age of 75?

Unhappily, it is clear that the Charlottetown accord envisages only modest changes in the system. The only important change is that the federal government must select the candidate from a list presented by a provincial government or, if it dislikes the list, start all over again. In case of a deadlock, the Chief Justice of Canada will apparently be authorized to make a temporary appointment.

There are many objections to this formula. It is right that the provinces should be involved in the appointment, but the compilation of short lists should not be the prerogative of provincial politicians. Nor should the involvement be restricted to politicians from a single province. Canadians from coast to coast have a profound stake in the appointment of every member of the Supreme Court and should participate directly or indirectly.

One weakness of the Charlottetown provisions is that Canadians will have no opportunity to comment on the provincial list or on Ottawa's selection from it; they will be faced with a *fait accompli*.

Another point of concern is the provision for temporary appointments. Surely critical court decisions should not turn, as well they may, on the swing vote of a judge who is not a permanent member of the court.

Little progress has been made to put appointments to the Supreme Court on a sound and democratic basis. If Canadians care—and they should—now is the time to speak up, before it is too late.

Wrestling in Court Over Charter Goals

Sean Fine

Justice Reporter

Toronto

It was a classic collision between free speech and minority rights—and free speech won.

The Supreme Court of Canada's decision last week to throw out the conviction against Holocaust-denial publisher Ernst Zundel for "publishing false news" underscored its political role in the era of the Charter of Rights and Freedoms.

The court, after nearly nine months of wrestling over fundamental but conflicting Charter goals, offered competing visions of what constitutes reasonable limits on freedoms in a democracy.

For the minority, the limit on free speech in the false-news law was minimal—it was a case of protecting society from the harm done by outright lies. They cited Nazi Germany as a lesson offered by history for guarding against racist propaganda.

For the majority, the limit was far too sweeping—they cited author Salman Rushdie as a lesson in the dangers of governments separating accepted fact from harmful opinion. Indeed, the two sides disagreed on nearly everything, from whether hate dissemination was even an issue to whether the law was vague or specific in its wording.

The 4–3 decision follows important cases in which the court upheld curbs on free expression—giving its stamp of approval in the past two years to laws against pornography

---

Points of Disagreement

History of the law

The Supreme Court majority said the false-news law was designed to protect the security of the state but had been used in pernicious ways—for example, in convicting an American immigrant in 1907 who put a sign in his shop window telling Americans to stay away from Alberta because they were not wanted there. The minority said the law was partly designed to prevent hostilities among social groups in society.

Concept of "mischief"

The majority said the concept of "mischief to the public interest," with its "undefined and virtually unlimited reach," was possibly the greatest danger of the false-news law. They said that the minority, in defining the public interest in light of Charter values, simply selected certain values, "values which do not include freedom of expression."

Lies and free speech

The minority said a lie, like violence, is not subject to the protection of the Charter. The majority said that satire or jokes could be subject to prosecution; it also said the law has no business trying to determine what is true or false in history.

(by a 9–0 vote) and hate propaganda (4 to 3), for example.

But it remains difficult to predict what limits to fundamental freedoms the court will accept on a particular case, according to court watchers such as Andrew Heard.

"To me it's become a real crapshoot," said Prof. Heard, who teaches political science at Simon Fraser University in Burnaby, B.C., and who has studied voting patterns on the court. "So much depends on which individual judges are chosen for that panel. Four–three one way or 4–3 the other way is going to make a tremendous difference."

Ultimately, the decision was swung by the unlikely figure of Madam Justice Claire L'Heureux-Dubé—unlikely, because she seldom votes to strike down laws and because she showed in supporting the hate-propaganda conviction of Alberta teacher James Keegstra that she is not an all-out free-speech advocate.

The result was a decision that leaves the parties back just about where they began in 1983, before the two sometimes bizarre trials of Mr. Zundel, in which the veracity of the Holocaust itself was debated.

Behind the debate over free speech was a split over how to interpret laws passed before the Charter of Rights and Freedoms took effect in 1982. The false-news law was put into the Canadian Criminal Code in 1892, and transferred to the code's nuisance section in 1955.

"They have no systematic framework for dealing with a law that was passed after the Charter and a law

From *The Globe and Mail*, September 1, 1992, p. A12. Reprinted by permission.

passed before the Charter," Prof. Heard said.

The majority took a conservative approach—ruling that it must be interpreted by considering what the legislators had in mind when they wrote it into the statutes.

The court "cannot assign new objectives nor invent new ones," Madam Justice Beverley McLachlin wrote, supported by Mr. Justice Gérard La Forest, Mr. Justice John Sopinka and Judge L'Heureux-Dubé.

The minority took a liberal approach—looking not only at the legislators' intentions but considering whether the law's use in this case was in line with values of equality, multiculturalism and "human dignity" promoted by the Charter of Rights.

This may have been one reason that the minority lost Judge L'Heureux-Dubé, the only member of the panel in the 1990 Keegstra free-speech/hate-incitement case to switch sides on the Zundel case.

"The majority just felt that that whole process was judges creating law, and they weren't prepared to do that," said a Toronto lawyer familiar with the decision.

How do the judges decide what is reasonable? In much the way legislators do—they must ask themselves if the law is needed, if its purpose is compelling, if the means are proportionate to the ends, said University of Toronto political science professor Peter Russell.

"It's making the policy of rights," he said in an interview.

Prof. Heard added, "The sort of process that judges go through is very individual. I don't see it as being an objective process at all. So the difficulty comes in balancing the personal values of the judges against what they see as the values of society in modern times."

Prof. Heard, in a study of the Supreme Court's first 121 Charter decisions, from 1982–89, found that the composition of the court panel chosen by the Chief Justice, which may vary from case to case, had a major effect on whether a law was struck down for violating the Charter.

"If you had a majority of judges who were pretty much pro-Charter, the chances of the case being decided in favour of the Charter were more than twice as high as if the majority of the panel were the less receptive judges," he said.

What's more, he found it difficult to identify a consistent voting pattern from the court's eight current judges (one spot on the nine-member court has been vacant since Mr. Justice William Stevenson resigned because of ill health in June.)

Of Judge L'Heureux-Dubé, he said: "She's the one I have the most difficulty trying to figure out. At least the first few years of her record, she was very skeptical of Charter claims. On the other hand, there are a number of decisions like this one where she comes out in favour of the Charter right in a context where I would have thought she wouldn't."

Supreme Court charts new direction for Canadian values

Sean Fine
Justice Reporter

With its leading liberals gone, the Supreme Court of Canada has become the fief of pragmatists—a group that is feeling its way, case-by-case, toward a new vision of rights and freedoms, court watchers say.

Led by an increasingly cautious Chief Justice, Antonio Lamer, the court is struggling to find consistency, as it grapples with its powerful role as final arbiter of the country's deepest values.

Legal observers say two key figures are emerging, along with Chief Justice Lamer, to steer the Charter of Rights and Freedoms through its second decade: Madam Justice Beverley McLachlin, a pro-Charter activist with

TRACKING THE COURT ON 10 RECENT

DO THESE LAWS VIOLATE THE CHARTER?	Pimp	Obscenity	Insanity	Hate incitement	Mandatory retirement	Extradite to face death	Rape shield	Seizure of tapes	Jury selection	False news
RULING	NO (4–3)	NO (9–0)	YES (6–1)	NO (4–3)	NO (5–2)	NO (4–3)	YES (7–2)	NO (6–1)	YES (4–3)	YES (4–3)
Antonio Lamer	–	No	Yes*	–	–	Yes	Yes	–	Yes	–
Beverley McLachlin	Yes	No	–	Yes	–	No	Yes*	Yes	No	Yes*
Claire L'Heureux-Dubé	No	No	No	No	Yes	No	No	No	–	Yes
Peter Cory	No*	No	Yes	–	No	Yes	Yes	No*	Yes*	No
Gérard La Forest	Yes	No	Yes	Yes	No*	No*	Yes	No	Yes	Yes
John Sopinka	No	No*	Yes	Yes	No	Yes	Yes	No	–	Yes
Charles Gonthier	No	No	Yes	No	No	No	No	No	No	No
Frank Iacobucci	Yes	No	–	–	–	–	Yes	–	No	No
Others who participated in decisions	–	Stevenson: NO	Wilson: YES	Wilson: NO Dickson: NO*	Wilson: YES Dickson: NO	–	Stevenson: YES	Stevenson: NO	Stevenson: YES	–

— Not on panel.   *Author of majority judgment.

From *The Globe and Mail*, September 19, 1992, pp. A1, A8. Reprinted by permission.

strong civil-libertarian instincts, appointed to the court in 1989; and Mr. Justice Gérard La Forest, appointed in 1985, more restrained, more likely to defer to legislatures—a "reluctant civil libertarian," in the words of University of Guelph political scientist Frederick Vaughan.

"I would say by far the front-runner is La Forest and the other two are McLachlin and the chief," said Dale Gibson of Edmonton.

The constitutional lawyer, who also teaches at the University of Alberta law school, added: "The other judges seem content to do the job as they see it, but I don't see any of them trying to become the voice of the court."

If that is true, the court may speak quite differently than it did when Madam Justice Bertha Wilson and Chief Justice Brian Dickson were leading it into uncharted territory—a strong defence of individual and minority rights, giving bold definition to Charter protections. Judge Wilson retired in 1991, Chief Justice Dickson in 1990.

Already, Professor Wayne MacKay of Dalhousie University's law school in Halifax sees a major change in the court's interpretation of the Charter from the Wilson and Dickson years. For him, the court's decision this month throwing out a conviction against Holocaust-denial publisher Ernst Zundel for publishing false

news is a signal of this change. "I think what's changed is the [past] focus on the Charter to protect minorities."

What is replacing it? Prof. MacKay said he finds it hard to discern a unified vision in its place, but like many legal observers he feels the court is generally less inclined to second-guess the legislatures.

Even so, the signals vary; court watchers differ in interpreting them. Roland Penner, law dean at the University of Manitoba, suggested the court may be evolving into a style similar to that of the U.S. Supreme Court—one where "different levels of scrutiny" are applied to different sorts of issues, where limits to freedom of speech receive possibly the most rigorous scrutiny.

A review by The Globe and Mail of 10 major rulings in the past two years suggests a court that is still soul-searching, still trying to decide where to defer to legislatures and where to challenge them—a court described by one Quebec academic as going "everywhere at the same time."

"They're at sea," said Frederick Vaughan, a political science professor at the University of Guelph.

"This is something so new to our court, for judges to be thrown into the vortex of so many competing social values. They have no clear compass."

The competition is played out over the Charter's first section, which both guarantees and limits the rights and freedoms set out in the rest of the document. If judges decide that a fundamental right is infringed, they must then decide whether the infringement is reasonable—that is, if it can be "demonstrably justified in a free and democratic society."

CHARTER DECISIONS

VIEWPOINT

Strong defender of rights of accused, libertarian but more restrained since becoming chief justice. Wrote ruling that struck down insanity law, saying "not everyone acquitted by reason of insanity has a personal history of violent conduct. . ."

Strong libertarian instincts, activist on Charter, though not easy to pin down, wrote judgments striking down rape-shield and false-news laws saying that the former law "misdefines the evil to be addressed as evidence of sexual activity, when in fact the evil to be addressed is the narrower evil of the misuse of evidence of sexual activity"

Tough on crime, liberal on social issues, identifies with women's concerns, "quite likely to do own thing" (Dalhousie University law professor Wayne MacKay). Wrote in rape-shield dissent that "absolutely pivotal. . . . is the realization of how widespread the stereotypes and myths about rape are, notwithstanding their inaccuracy."

Eloquent defender of liberal values, has cited retired justice Bertha Wilson as stressing "human dignity" in understanding the Charter and wrote in opposition to ruling on extradition to face death penalty that "the ceremonial washing of his hands by Pontius Pilate did not relieve him of responsibility for the death sentence imposed by others."

Influential, a moderate conservative libertarian, gives legislature benefit of doubt in close calls, no crusader, "clearly the strongest lawyer on that court (University of Alberta law professor Dale Gibson). Wrote ruling on mandatory retirement: "To open up all private and public action to judicial reviews could strangle the operation of society and impose an impossible burden on the courts."

Defender of due process rights, "pragmatic liberalism" (Prof. MacKay), more concerned with right result in case before him than long-range effect on the law (Prof. Gibson). Wrote in obscenity ruling: "Serious social problems such as violence against women require multi-pronged approaches by government."

Deferred to government on 9 of 10 decisions in Globe and Mail review, only judge to side with Judge L'Heureux-Dubé in defending rape-shield law, doesn't write many Charter judgments. Wrote in dissent on law favouring the Crown in jury selection: "The accused. . . has no right to a jury of his or her choice."

Newest member, concerned about court activism, sensitive to minority concerns, may emerge as "the great brain on that court" (Guelph University political science professor Frederick Vaughan). Co-wrote with Judge Cory dissent on false-news law: "It would be unfortunate if the Charter was used to strike down a provision that protects vulnerable groups."

The Globe's review of the 10 cases, all of which involved Section 1 arguments, shows the difficulty in making sweeping statements, either about the court's direction or individual judges. The usual labels—liberal or conservative, activist or restrained—do not always

THE CASES

- **Pimp:** Requires accused person who lives or consorts with prostitutes to prove he's not a pimp. Kenneth Downey, operator of an Edmonton escort service, argued law violates his right to be presumed innocent. He lost.
- **Obscenity:** Outlaws certain types of explicit sexual material. Donald Butler, owner of a Winnipeg video store, said law violates free expression. He lost.
- **Insanity:** Required that anyone found not guilty by reason of insanity be committed to a mental institution. Owen Swain of Toronto, confined after assaulting his family, said law violated right to liberty. He won.
- **Hate incitement:** Bans promotion of hate against identifiable groups. Alberta high-school teacher James Keegstra, who taught that the Holocaust is a lie created by Jews, said law violates free speech. He lost.
- **Mandatory retirement:** Permits private sector to force employees to retire at 65. Professors at several universities said this violates equal rights. They lost.
- **Extradite to face death penalty:** Charles Ng and Joseph Kindler, wanted for murder in the United States, said law violates guarantee against cruel and unusual punishment. They lost.
- **Rape shield:** Restricted circumstances in which sexual history of rape victim could be introduced in court. Steven Seaboyer and Nigel Gayme of Toronto argued it violated right to fair trial. They won.
- **Seizure of media material:** Permits police to search newsrooms for evidence of crimes. CBC, which had taken videotapes of violent labour disputes, said practice violates free speech. It lost.
- **Jury selection:** Permitted Crown four times as many chances as defence to rule out potential jurors. Craig Bain, accused of sex assault, said practice violated right to fair trial. He won.
- **False news:** Prohibited willful publication of lies that could harm public interest. Ernst Zundel, a Toronto publisher of anti-Semitic works, said law infringed on free speech. He won.

apply. If a judge chooses the rights of accused over women's protection, what tag fits? A simple count of the number of cases on which a judge sides with or against government may not tell much about how the member tends to choose.

Still, a few observations can be made about the court based on these 10 rulings.

- **It's hard to predict**—The court struck down a law protecting rape victims from being questioned about their sexual history, calling it a violation of an accused's rights. It later upheld a law that forces men living with prostitutes to prove they are not pimps—calling it a reasonable limit on an accused's right to be presumed innocent. On obscenity, it said the 1959 law was designed to prevent harm to society—a harm ini-

tially defined in terms of public morality, but today as harm to women. Later, in overturning the false-news conviction against Ernst Zundel, it said the law's original purpose could not now be seen through modern eyes. Mr. Justice John Sopinka, who wrote the court's judgment on obscenity, sided with the majority in the 4–3 Zundel decision.

- **Two women on the court exemplify its philosophical tensions**—They are both heirs to Bertha Wilson's tradition—Judge McLachlin the pro-Charter trendsetter; Madam Justice Claire L'Heureux-Dubé defending the rights of women and minorities. But Judge McLachlin tends to support striking down laws that are designed to protect vulnerable groups but infringe on civil liberties; Judge L'Heureux-Dubé tends

to support laws that seek to control criminals, but offers a critique of the justice system's treatment of women. "There's a fermentation on both sides taking place there," Prof Vaughan said. "Those are the ones to watch."

- **Small-1 coalition forming**—In the mid-1970s, a liberal troika dubbed LSD often came together—Bora Laskin, Wishart Spence and Brian Dickson. In the '90s, there may be LSC: Chief Justice Lamer, Judge Sopinka and Mr. Justice Peter Cory. The Chief Justice agreed with the two others in all four non-unanimous decisions in the Globe review in which all three took part. One example was the extradition of two fugitives to face the death penalty in the United States—which the threesome opposed. (They lost, 4–3. Judges McLachlin and L'Heureux-Dubé joined to swing a close vote, as they did later in the Zundel case, also 4–3). Judges Cory and Sopinka agreed in six non-unanimous cases and disagreed just once—on the Zundel case. Judge Cory, who seems to be carrying forward the liberal torch from Ms. Wilson, agreed just once in six non-unanimous judgments with Judge McLachlin—supporting her judgment in the rape-shield case.
- **Judge L'Heureux-Dubé the iconoclast**—She found just one judge with whom she agreed more often than she disagreed on these 10 decisions—Mr. Justice Charles Gonthier. Judge McLachlin had just two allies more often than not in non-unanimous rulings—Judge La Forest and Mr. Justice Frank Iacobucci. Over the past 100 Charter cases, Judge L'Heureux-Dubé is the most frequent dissenter, said political science professor Peter Russell of the University of Toronto.
- **On a split court, look for L'Heureux-Dubé**—On the four 4–3 judgments in which she was involved among those reviewed by The Globe, she sided with the majority all four times. Judge McLachlin was with the majority just twice in five 4–3 rulings; Judge La Forest three times out of five. Prof. Gibson said Judge Sopinka may play the role of "swing-vote pragmatist," as Mr. Justice Willard

Estey did in the 1980s. He was with the majority on two of four 4–3 rulings.

"I see [Judge La Forest's] influence as being the really powerful one on that court," Prof. Gibson said. "It's very much a more lawyerly, . . . less goal-oriented, if you know what I mean. He doesn't obviously take sides."

Robin Elliot, associate dean of law at the University of British Columbia, commented: "I don't see anybody on the court now that comes close to Wilson in terms of that willingness to stake out a position—a philosophical position, not just a pragmatic position.

"My sense is that you don't want a Supreme Court that is uniformly one way or the other, that it's good to see different approaches. I think it's unfortunate—with Wilson's retirement, there is less of a commitment to fundamental principle on the court."

Judges Wilson and Dickson could often count on the support of Antonio Lamer in the 1980s; for years he set the dominant position in criminal law, strongly in favour of the rights of the accused, said McGill University law professor Jeremy Webber. However, he has been moving to a more restrained position since he became Chief Justice in 1990, several observers said (though he took the pro-Charter position four out of five times in the cases reviewed by The Globe).

"I think he feels the weight of the office," Prof. Vaughan said. "He really feels he has got to be a quarterback and orchestrate the best possible judgments. I think he's trying to steer a very moderate course on the bench."

Prof. Elliott recalled a speech that the Chief Justice gave at UBC two years ago, telling of the court's difficulties in resolving issues in which many competing interests are at stake.

"He said, 'We just don't have the experience, we just don't have the tools to ensure that our view of how these issues should be resolved is the right view,' " and in those cases " 'we exercise restraint.' "

Prof. Elliot commented: "I found it hard to believe it was the same guy."

The Parliamentary System

There is an increasing criticism that the Canadian parliamentary system has been changed so fundamentally that it follows more and more an "executive" or "administrative" model. In the first unit article, David Kilgour, MP, argues that this has increased alienation among citizens. He believes that there is a "right package of parliamentary reforms . . . ," and he sees Canadians divided between Inner and Outer Canada. Inner Canadians live in Toronto, Ottawa, and Montreal—successors to Toronto's Family Compact and Montreal's Chateau Clique before the 1830s.

Kilgour contends that Canadian MPs "face the tightest party discipline in the entire democratic world." He reviews recent changes to the rules of the House of Commons to see whether they are likely to help or harm the occupational status of MPs. He would prefer free votes at all times except for budgets, in order to heed the legislative needs of constituents rather than party leaders and bureaucrats. Kilgour also strongly supports the adoption of the U.S. congressional committee system, and the Australian Triple-E Senate.

In "Cleaning House," Stevie Cameron investigates the internal administrative apparatus of the House of Commons, especially the powers of the "master fixer, the dispenser of favours," Gus Cloutier.

The next article looks at the way the chief of staff to the Canadian prime minister carries out his duties. The COS's job description would include "gatekeeper, chief adviser, confidant, administrator, and link to the outside world."

The outside world seems to be dominated by lobbyists. In "Lobby Horse," Charlotte Gray investigates how one firm, Government Policy Consultants, with 70 clients, has catapulted to the top spot among the profusion of lobbyists. This firm does not just peddle access to decision-makers, it also provides issue-monitoring services and strategic advice to all its clients. There is, however, mounting criticism of the activities of lobbyists, and efforts to open their activities to public and legislative scrutiny have increased.

Besides lobbyists, interest groups, such as women's, aboriginal, Greenpeace, and so on, seem to have become increasingly influential. Some experts believe that lobbyists and interest groups are making political parties much weaker, as they increasingly work outside of political parties and ignore them. While parties provide much less of an umbrella for myriad citizens' groups and regional interests, governments and bureaucrats find both groups useful, even if they are sometimes obnoxious.

The final article outlines the model of a Triple-E Senate that was closest to the thinking of most provincial premiers and the federal government during the latest round of constitutional negotiations, in the summer of 1992.

Looking Ahead: Challenge Questions

How useful is it to use the concept of "Inner" and "Outer" Canadians? Why?

Do recent changes to the rules of the House of Commons help or harm the status of Members of Parliament?

Does a prime minister need a chief of staff?

Is a government better served by the use of "in-house" think tanks, or by private lobbyists?

Are interest groups pushing aside traditional political parties?

Unit 3

THE PERILS OF EXECUTIVE DEMOCRACY

*A large wall chart in the PCO shows
how government really works.
Off to one side, joined by a
single line, is Parliament.*

David Kilgour, MP

David Kilgour is the member of Parliament for Edmonton Southeast and Liberal energy critic. He is author of *Inside Outer Canada* and *Uneasy Patriots—Western Canadians in Confederation.*

A NUMBER OF RECENT OPINION POLLS INDI-cate that most Canadians have little confidence in our system of government or in the ability of legislators to represent their constituents. Will some of them stop voting in national elections? Will we drop to the U.S. level, where half the population doesn't bother to vote? Will even more people vote for the Reform Party and Bloc Québécois? The present national unity/constitutional crisis on the bright side affords an opportunity to effect fundamental changes to our present model of "executive" or "administrative" democracy.

One of several consequences of the Al-Mashat affair is that a number of Ottawa's most senior mandarins, the people who outlast cabinets and MPs alike, stand revealed as being no more concerned with doing the correct thing for the correct reasons than the elected managers of what is probably the most ethically-weak government in Canadian history. A host of genies are now out of their urns; the times are clearly out of joint for defenders of the *status quo* in Ottawa and perhaps in our provincial capitals as well.

The right package of parliamentary reforms could reduce alienation among what I call Outer Canadians. Defined broadly, Inner Canadians are those who live in Toronto-Ottawa-Montreal; more narrowly, they are a few thousand people in these cities, successors to Toronto's Family Compact and Montreal's Chateau Clique before the 1830s, who have called most of the national policy shots before and since 1867, and possibly never more so than since 1984. Outer Canadians are the 18 million or so of us living across the remainder of the country. Time and time again over the decades "national" governments have favored Inner Canadians.

Reforming the role of MPs is vital to "nationalizing Ottawa" because there is a widespread public impression that we are brute voting machines, robots, or trained seals for our respective party whips. Experts say Canadian legislators face the tightest party discipline in the entire democratic world. Since I was elected in 1979, the members of the various parties have voted as uniform blocs in virtually every House vote. Why doesn't the Speaker simply ask all party leaders to vote on behalf of their entire caucuses?

In this sense, "caucus solidarity and my constituents be damned" might be the real oath of office for many honorable members. Our counterparts in the Senate, of course, have neither constituents nor elections to worry about.

I worry that even a Triple-E Senate would tend to assume the bad habits of our present House unless we can reform the House first in major ways. The recently-proposed changes in the present Senate's rules, most notably the one allowing closure at any stage of a bill after a two-hour debate, for the first time in its history, are not reassuring for those of us who seek a reformed upper house.

Let's look for a moment at whether the resent changes to the rules of the House are likely to help or harm the occupational status of MPs. Formalized pairing with whip approval should reduce the stigma of paired MP absences from votes. More private members' bills and motions might be voted upon and pass. There are 25 more days for private members business than before. The cutbacks in yearly sitting days for the House represent a setback for those of us who want to have more, not less, public input on government policy in Question Periods and sittings. The speed-up in the ability of a government to impose closure is a setback. So, too, in my view is the further reduction in the scope for independent MPs to deny unanimous consent. More than ever, if you're not a member of a recognized party, you're not on the "varsity."

Backbenchers in all parties will only become less robot-like when our voting practices change. Virtually anything

From *Policy Options*, Vol. 13, No. 5, June 1992, pp. 3-7. This article first appeared in *Policy Options*, Canada's Forum for Public Policy Debate.

today that MPs or their provincial counterparts vote on can, if lost to the government of the day, be deemed by a first minister retroactively to have been a vote of non-confidence. A former Clerk of the House told me that even a frivolous opposition motion to adjourn for the day can still so qualify.

Fear of a premature general election, of course, obliges government members to vote with their whips. If they waver on a matter, immense pressure is applied, usually in the form of implied threats. In the opposition parties, the pressure to conform often takes this form: "If we don't vote as a bloc, the media will say we're a divided party." Media habits of mind thus reinforce the almost comical *status quo* in both our provincial and federal assemblies.

In my view, this *status quo* has persisted so long because party leaders and policy mandarins obviously prefer it. Measures going into a House of Commons where one party has a majority usually emerge essentially unscathed. Everything follows a highly predictable script: obedient government members praise it; opposition parties rail against it; and plenty of bad measures become law essentially unamended.

Deep-seated discontent among both backbench MPs and the general public is giving new hope to those of us in all parties who want free votes at all times except for budgets, throne speeches, supply motions and opposition motions which specifically describe themselves as non-confidence motions as recommended by the McGrath Committee.

This would force conscientious MPs not in cabinet to consider carefully how they vote on most issues. The legislative needs of our constituents would replace party hierarchies in determining how we vote. Our fellow citizens would soon develop greater confidence in MPs, knowing that our final loyalty is to them whenever our loyalty to our party conflicts with our duty to our electorate. Cabinets and bureaucrats alike would also have to adjust quickly to a Canadian *perestroika*.

If, for example, proposed legislation were detrimental to, say, Atlantic Canada, Outer Canadian MPs from all parties could unite to block it.

To those who say that this smacks of "creeping congressionalism," we reformers say, "so what?" The system of government we assumed in the heyday of the British Empire, albeit, as the late Eugene Forsey stressed, almost entirely in the form Canadians wanted, is plainly no longer adequate to the needs of a sophisticated population at the end of the 20th century. If you prefer a European reform model, let's adopt the "constructive non-confidence motion" of the German *Bundestag*, which prescribes that no administration can be defeated unless members wishing to defeat one Chancellor simultaneously choose a new one who has the confidence of a majority of *Bundestag* members.

Another approach would be for the next government of Canada to specify at the start of its mandate which matters at the heart of its program will be confidence issues. The present government, for example, might have spelled out in late 1988 that the Canada-U.S. Free Trade Agreement and the GST would be confidence issues. In those situations, party discipline would be justifiable. Otherwise, its backbenchers would be free to vote for their constituents' interests at all times. This restored independence for legislators would lead to better representation for all regions of Canada.

Upgrading House Committees

A prominent feature of the U.S. Congress is its vigorous committee system. Committees and their investigative staffs use their oversight role in supervising the executive branch with an effectiveness that is almost unknown in Canada.

By choosing a federal system, did not Canadians reject the notion that a national majority must prevail?

Canadian parliamentary committees in practice are mostly still dominated by party whips. Committee chairmen, for example, are normally chosen for anticipated obedience rather than for any ability or special knowledge as independent policy-makers. Don't, please, cite Donald Blenkarn's Finance Committee to the contrary. Bluster from the chairman was tolerated in exchange for obedience on cabinet priorities like the GST.

Full regional representation is provided directly in the composition of congressional committees. On the House of Representatives side, almost 40 per cent of committee seats are reserved for members of specific states. In the discharge of their oversight role, congressmen and senators have numerous tools—some say too many—to promote regional and local causes, including large personal staffs and large numbers of investigative personnel who work directly for committees. American public officials can be and are summoned to committees on short notice and in practice must reply to questions.

Their federal counterparts in Canada can be called to committees through subpoena, but because of a host of practices, including the tradition of windy replies by ministers and officials on the government's estimates and short meetings, the oversight role on, say, public spending is effectively non-existent.

To the best of my knowledge, only one matter of proposed spending—a $20,000 CIDA item—has been voted down in committee since 1969. It turned out that the items in issue had already been spent when the committee voted to block it. An order-in-council, which I understand is still on the books, bars federal officials from revealing to parliamentarians anything learned in the course of their employment. If enforced literally, committees would be even more toothless than they are now, but it's available if push ever comes to shove.

The American congressional oversight function, which has opened up the national administration to territorial representation, is really only effective because individual congressmen have political clout in their own right. Some American analysts have therefore concluded that U.S. federal agencies are overly sensitive to Congress. Departments and other branches of government in Ottawa, on the other hand, are usually considered to regard Parliament as a once-a-year mosquito bite during which their estimates are sped through

Parliament. Indeed, I'm told that there is a large wall chart in the Privy Council Office showing how the government of Canada really works. Off to one side, joined by a single line, is Parliament.

One remedy for the legislative hollowness problem in this area might be fixed term parliaments for, say, four years. A reformed and elected Senate would be helpful here. Elected members from both chambers could attack and defend the government on grounds other than party loyalty if they were not under the thumbs of their party whips. An increasing number of observers and participants alike appear to be coming to the conclusion that Canada should adapt some variant of the congressional system of government, complete with its full panoply of checks and balances.

Another problem with our present House committees is that not enough of them do much substantive work. When they do produce a good report, their recommendations are often either ignored by the government or are only partially implemented. In a different political culture/system, committees could make substantive changes to policies, which could then at least be put to a vote in the House of Commons, where members will vote according to their conscience. Governments don't want committees to become too independent and effective because they might criticize government policy and overshadow ministers on issues.

Many Canadians appear to have lost faith in our system of government, but according to polls most prefer to see Canada rebuilt, rather than to fall apart. Ominously, however, a poll done only a week before the Quebec referendum on sovereignty-association in 1980 found 56 per cent of Quebeckers felt profoundly attached to Canada. According to a Southam survey, that figure has now dropped to 30 per cent.

And when asked whether Quebeckers feel more attached to Canada than their province, two thirds recently chose Quebec. Nor is this shift in loyalty exclusive to Quebec: Newfoundland also has a higher percentage of residents who feel more committed to their province than to Canada. Overall, nearly one third of Canadians living outside Quebec are less committed to the country than they were a few years ago, a finding attributed to the constitutional "trauma" since 1987.

Most believe that the problem is a basic flaw in the system of government, including the division of federal-provincial powers, and they want to change it. A major goal of constitutional reform should be to provide Canadians with better representation in their national and provincial governments. Giving people a bigger voice in the development of the laws and policy of Canada would help on both national unity and legislator credibility.

Discussions of regionalism in Canada invariably boil down to arguments over which should prevail: regional interests or "the national interest." By choosing a federal system of government, did not Canadians reject the notion that the national majority should always prevail?

Federalism means that on some issues the will of the popular majority will be frustrated. If the biggest battalions of voters are to prevail over smaller ones under any circumstances, we should drop the charade that we have a federal system of government that respects minorities in times of stress. The notion that the largest groups of Canadians, i.e., southern Ontarians and metropolitan Quebeckers, must be accommodated always, has resulted in discontent elsewhere and accompanying feelings of regional irrelevancy.

In an increasingly interdependent world, Canadians want new or altered institutions that will represent the interests of both Inner and Outer Canadians effectively. Unless we move

Canadian democracy would benefit if we put our present mind-numbing party discipline where it belongs—in the history books.

away from the notion that "the national interest" is merely a code-phrase for the most populous region dominating all corners of the country, frictions between Inner and Outer Canada are likely to worsen.

Political Parties and Regionalism

The Reform Party has modelled itself after the greatest protest movements which evolved out of my region near the turn of the century and in the middle of the Great Depression. Traditionally, to be successful as a new party, the leadership of that party must not only offer radical public policy alternatives, but must also have a program of institutional overhaul to implement those alternatives.

The final ingredient in the creation of a viable protest movement is a base of support. In a country like ours, there is no shortage of regional discontent to create such a base. Western Canada has understandably become famous as fertile ground for discontent. The leaders of the Reform Party have learned their history well. They have recognized that regionally-based discontent can translate into a potentially powerful bloc of decision makers on the floor of the House of Commons. If a "New Canada"—to use their term—is to emerge from this discontent, our national institutions and conventions must be overhauled.

The Reform Party presents a vision that has addressed the regional inequity many Outer Canadians have suffered. It has hit some of the right keys with the public. They have wonderful slogans—"The West Wants In," "Building a New Canada," etc. They have had the foresight and the energy to support their vision with a professional fundraising apparatus and an impressive communications strategy. The Reform Party may tout itself as a grassroots party, but it has to date avoided most of the problems traditionally afflicting grassroots political participation.

The Reform Party has established itself as the party of new ideas opposed to the traditional public policy options restricted in their scope and imagination by party discipline and bureaucratic entrenchment. For these ideas to take root, institutional overhaul is essential. Included in this Reform Party agenda is radical House reform that would include measures to impeach members and the restructuring of the Senate to be elected, effective and regionally equal.

All this would indicate that the main reason for the success of the Reform Party to date is the realization that Canada isn't working. However, it is probably more of a reflection on the failure of the other parties to represent the interests of Outer Canadians. Certainly there are some institutional changes that are essential to serve Canadians better, such as the Triple E Senate. But to say that the human frailties of those who have influenced the evolution of our current brand of parliamentary democracy means that Canada itself is flawed is not only irresponsible, it indicates a clear lack of understanding of the common values shared by all regions.

The ultimate flaw in the Reform Party's vision is that it fundamentally defies definition, and that worries me. The Reform Party platform brings policy making down to the level of sloganeering. As a regional movement, it will never be asked to come up with a governing agenda for all of Canada.

Instead, the vision panders to the fears of 7.5 million western Canadians wanting to acquire more political and economic strength. The slogans will probably translate into a healthy number of seats in the next election, but they simply won't translate into a government agenda unless they can be spelled out.

If any party is going to provide an alternative to the *status quo*, it will have to be a party which seeks to represent our nation as it stands now, a national family that includes Quebec. Ontario has always been a dominant economic and political force in Canada, yet for the most part Canadians don't mind that. They simply want to see the federal government maintain, improve and make fairer the partnership agreement known as Confederation.

It then becomes clear that parliamentary reform must originate from the traditional parties themselves if we are to create a more democratic institution.

American Example

In the United States, congressmen, representing single member geographical districts after 1842, became important vehicles for injecting local priorities into their national government in both its administrative and legislative branches. The first loyalty of every member of the House of Representatives is to the district, just as that of U.S. senators is to the state. In the words of one political analyst, "The first concern of every congressman seems to be how to get as much as he can out of the nation for his own state." Such an assertion could rarely be made of Canadian Members of Parliament—unless they are also members of the cabinet.

In turn, successful American presidents, being elected by voters everywhere, seek to reflect in their persons the diversity of their entire nation, by shaking off all personal regional coloration. Unfortunately, there is a serious question today in our own country whether a resident of other than our three officially favored cities, Toronto, Montreal and Ottawa, could lead any political party to a majority in a general election.

The constitutional separation of powers between the executive and legislative branches and the weakness of party discipline in congressional voting behavior greatly enhance effective regional representation in Washington. Presidents and congressmen are elected for fixed terms and none resign if a particular measure is voted down in the Senate or House of Representatives. The congressional system also provides the freedom for effective territorial representation when an issue has clear state implications.

Congressmen depart frequently from party lines to represent state interests; elected men and women in the American capital don't hesitate to place their state or district interests

No one of any vigor will want to be elected to a reformed Senate unless it has powers mainly co-equal with the House.

ahead of their respective party line when voting. In contrast, few Canadian MPs have any real opportunity to put their constituents' interests first in votes in the House of Commons. Real power is concentrated in the hands of the three party leaderships. Canadian democracy itself would thus benefit substantially if we put our present mind-numbing party discipline where it belongs: in the history books.

Another feature of the U.S. congressional system that fosters effective regional input in national policy making is territorial bloc-voting—something quite unknown in Canada's House of Commons. Weak party discipline in the Congress is one of several factors encouraging the formation of regional voting blocs that cross party lines. Legislation detrimental to regional interests can be opposed without fear of the government being defeated and an early election being called. Representatives from the two political parties of the Mountain states, Sun Belt states, New England states and others vote *en bloc* or work together in committees to advance common regional interests.

An example of how regional representatives can influence the geographic location of federal government procurement, which affects the geographic distribution of the manufacturing sector, is the southern congressional influence. It played a major role in the postwar concentration of federal military and space expenditures in the South and in the general economic revival and growth of the Sun Belt. If bloc-voting occurred in the Canadian House of Commons, possibly encouraged through the enactment of a fixed four-year term in office, we might see more measures detrimental to Outer Canadians voted down when MPs would cross party lines to put the interests of their regional constituents first.

Australian Triple-E Senate

The Australian Triple-E Senate provides an excellent model for Canada today partly because, like Canada, about two thirds of Australia's population live in two of its six states. We also share a tradition of parliamentary rather than representative democracy. The founding fathers from Australia's four smaller states refused during the 1890s any form of federal union, unless it included a second house representing all states equally. Initially in 1901, the Australian Senate had six senators from each state, all elected by statewide ballots. Since

1906, half of them take their seats on fixed dates every three years.

The Australian Senate still holds equal powers with the lower chamber, the House of Representatives, except for some limitations on money bills. Changes in its legislative authority, but not the numbers of senators from each state, can only be made by a referendum which produces an overall majority of votes cast nationally and majorities in any four of the six states.

I might add here as an Outer Canadian that federal Liberal delegates from across Alberta recently approved an amendment formula which for amendments affecting all of Canada would require support from the House of Commons, a reformed Senate and at least seven of the provincial legislatures provided the seven hold 85 per cent of the population of Canada.

There are numerous lessons for Senate reform in Canada. From Outer Canada's perspective, the first is the increased responsiveness coming from an institutional check on the present prime ministerial domination of our House of Commons.

Effectiveness in short is a central feature of reforming our upper house. Apologists for the *status quo* say that an effective Senate would collide with our long-established concept of responsible government, but we are not tiny, mostly illiterate and disenfranchised Britain in the earlier part of the 19th century. An effective Senate works well in Australia and we should adapt it as a hybrid to our own conditions in the interest of a more responsive democracy. No one of any vigor will want to be elected to a reformed Senate, in my view, unless its powers remain essentially co-equal with those of the House except for sharply limited confidence votes.

For the Senate to be effective and politically self-confident, there must be direct election of senators. A Canadian Senate based on equal representation from all provinces and elected through a proportional voting system would frequently have a majority different from that of the House. Two major obstacles to overcome here are our longstanding essentially imitative political culture, with its increasingly anomalous notion of letting governments govern without effective restraint, and the fear some have of an effective upper chamber.

Conclusion

We cannot build unity if as many as possible of the things that divide Canadians are not dealt with candidly as part of a genuine renewal process. Examining what Canada is all about must include what the country might become. Repeating worn-out clichés and appealing to a sentimental concept of Canada cannot replace serious attempts to address basic constitutional issues at the heart of the many problems facing our country.

Addressing head-on the inequalities resulting from the division of the country into Outer and Inner Canada is vital. Our outer regions contribute to the success of the centre, but for more than a century our role in Confederation has been reduced to little more than natural resource hinterlands. Our national Main Street must start to share opportunities.

The failure of numerous federal governments to deal with and reconcile divergent regional needs has compounded serious strains and cracks in the fabric of our country. Only once has Canada defined its overriding national goals. In 1879, the "National Policy" of Sir John A. Macdonald set these goals as populating the country, linking the common market with a national transportation network, and developing our industrial base. The two central provinces, more accurately the southern parts of them, were the beneficiaries of the industrial strategy with the consequent economic stability and political weight.

More than at any other time in our history, we now need to formulate a New National Policy. Central to it must be the principle of fairness and equality of opportunities for all, including the residents of the eight outer provinces, of the two territories, and of our aboriginal peoples. All have worked hard to strengthen Inner Canada during the earlier years, often at the expense of their own unrealized potential and aspirations.

Atlantic Canada, Northern Ontario, peripheral Quebec, Western Canada and the North—all need to be fully integrated into a national partnership. Their priorities and concerns must be addressed by elected and non-elected policy makers in Ottawa in a manner sensitive to the local needs of each of them.

We require national leaders capable of setting a clear agenda for the current political climate and of bringing us together. These must be men and women who have the respect and trust of Canadians generally, and ultimately people whose vision of our country includes regional fairness in all government policies, equal economic opportunity for Canadians everywhere, and personal integrity.

Above all, we need a higher sense of national purpose and a redefinition of our national objectives, policies and institutions which must better reflect our differences. The concerns of all of us, no matter where we live, must become a part of national policy making. Only in these terms can we find the nation and the unity the vast majority of Canadians are seeking.

CLEANING HOUSE

On the Hill, Gus Cloutier was the master fixer, the dispenser of favours, and the parliamentary guide to where to get stuff cheap. When he was finally reined in, the Hill became a colder, harsher place

Stevie Cameron

The brief printed notice from the Speaker's Office went off like a bomb in the House of Commons. Carefully wrapped in bureaucratic blah-blah, the message still made its point: Gus was defanged.

Gus, to everyone in the House.

To you, Major General M. Gaston Cloutier, Sergeant-at-Arms of the House of Commons, a tall, erect, charming soldier, the man with the tricorn hat and the mace who walks the Speaker into the Green Chamber of the House when Parliament is in session. In the House, Gus used to be the master fixer, the ultimate operator, the dispenser of favours. In a tight spot just the man to know. Parking spaces, a new sofa, a little French polish on an old credenza, a page's job for a bright young student, a splendid room for a private party . . . Gus would see to it. But after the Speaker's crisp command, issued on March 27, 1991, Gus could no longer see

to it. They'd brutally swept away the empire he'd commanded since he was appointed in 1978, an empire that had shrunk and calcified over the years, but was still not one to be taken lightly.

Certainly not one to destroy without the discreet consent of Prime Minister Brian Mulroney. The Speaker, John Fraser, did have a word and Mulroney quietly agreed. Surprising, perhaps, because Mulroney owed Gus. Back in 1983, when he was running for the Tory party leadership and his team was organizing hospitality suites in various Ottawa hotels, they were unsatisfied with the ambience they could create out of the standard hotel stacking chairs, folding tables, and ashtrays. Cloutier and Patrick MacAdam, who was then the legislative assistant to an Alberta Tory MP, Gordon Towers, arranged for sofas, armchairs, and coffee tables borrowed from the House of Commons sitting rooms to

be transferred to the hospitality suites for the duration of the leadership convention. When the bean-counters were adding up the cost of each campaign, one wonders whether they threw in the value of the House loans arranged by Cloutier. But maybe they didn't know.

Cloutier was appreciated for just that kind of favour. For him it was simple; he commanded armies of blue-collar workers—messengers, movers, cleaners—not to mention vans and drivers. To understand Cloutier's power, you need to know that the House of Commons is a small, gossip-driven city-state in which 3,500 people toil. Its annual budget is $230-million—more than twice the budget of ten years ago. Of the staff, 295 are MPs and another 1,100 or so are political personnel working for MPs. The rest ultimately report to the Speaker.

The Speaker delegates authority over his share of this incestuous, expensive little world to three senior managers: the Clerk, Robert Marleau, who sits at the head of the long table in the House and advises the Speaker during procedural wrangles; the Administrator, Ed Riedel, who is the money man; and the Sergeant-at-Arms. Cloutier's empire in his heyday, around 1984, included all the parliamentary restaurants, all the blue-collar workers, all the space allocation, and the distribution of most of the perks that grease the wheels. All that is left for him now is cleaning, maintenance, and traffic enforcement.

As stunned Hill bureaucrats read the Speaker's terse memo on their E-mail, and fax machines hummed and sliced the notice all over town, Cloutier reeled out of the House and into the friendly hands of the staff at the Ottawa Press Club. White-faced and shocked at the way his epaulettes had been stripped off, he told his tale to a friend. According to riveted bystanders, the friend's advice was excellent: "You've got a place in Florida; why not go there till this all dies down?" Fraser must have heard something similar. Soon after his statement was in the messengers' hands, the Speaker took off, buffered by the usual assortment of aides and their spouses, on an official visit to Hungary, too far away for reporters to hassle.

A tempest in a teapot? Far from it.

When the Speaker raised the price of a meal from $4.40 to $8, MPs howled in outrage. Apparently the House runs on its stomach

What people were watching so avidly was the final battle in a twelve-year struggle to reform the House of Commons. As one senior official said, "It took a long time but things have changed around here. There is a new work ethnic—there is work, there are ethics."

Of course, Gus Cloutier did a lot of work and he had ethics. It's just that he operated in a time warp. Cloutier's methods were from a different era at the House, a time when it was a gentlemen's club run with airy disregard for cost, run to suit only the convenience of the members. A time when the House offered a shining example of one set of rules for the people and another set for the lawmakers. A time when MPs argued passionately that efficiency, fairness, and professional management of a multimillion-dollar facility were not as important as gentlemanly traditions in a clubby atmosphere where the members themselves decided what was important and what was not.

The struggle for reform began in 1979, just a year after Cloutier arrived at the House. With financial affairs obviously out of control, James Jerome, then the Speaker, ordered the auditor general, James Macdonell, to conduct a first-ever audit of the House of Commons. For decades, House administration had been a sewer of patronage, corruption, bribery, and mismanagement. Macdonell's preliminary findings, which took a year to gather and were tabled in the House in September, 1979, could not have been worse. The personnel department was a farce—most jobs were doled out on a patronage basis. Cleaning women, some as old as eighty-five, were working just over two hours a day and being paid for three and a half at much higher than commercial rates. The Parliamentary Dining Room and cafeterias were losing $3.5-million a year thanks to fixable problems: workers were stealing food and liquor at an incredible rate because there was no inventory management; no competitive tenders were issued; and the food was so heavily subsidized that staff and MPs could buy meals at a fraction of their real cost.

Macdonell delivered his final report on April 29, 1980, and, though he wrote with bureaucratic understatement, he did not mince his words. "The quality of general and financial administration is significantly below a minimum acceptable standard. We found serious deficiencies in the House administrative organization and in budgeting, operational planning, human-resource management, performance measurement, and management reporting. As a result of these deficiencies, management control over provision of services is inadequate."

As if all this weren't enough there were other terrible problems at the House, problems that had been overlooked for years. For starters, sexual harassment was a fact of life for many women working on the Hill. In late 1984, the former speaker, Lloyd Francis, who was part of the team that began to clean up the House, told a CBC reporter taping an oral history for the National Archives about one secretary who had told him that a personnel officer had ordered her to attend a party and take off her clothes or she would be fired from her job. She refused, and *was* fired. Such incidents were common. Francis also spoke of senior staff who embezzled funds and of bugging devices put in place by other senior Hill employees who monitored sensitive meetings.

Macdonell agreed to lend his deputy, Rhéal Chatelain, to start the cleanup, and thus began the pitched battles between the House reformers and the traditionalists. Chatelain lasted less than a year, opposed at every turn by Gus Cloutier who—despite being a newcomer and in no way part of the cause of the problems—decided to become the old regime's spokesman on the senior management team. He was backed by a raucous crew of die-hard old boys led by Tory backbench MP Robert Coates; a former speaker, Marcel Lambert; and Liberal backbenchers such as Gérard Duquet and Marcel Roy. The irony here was that Coates, as chairman of the House management and members' services committee (the MMSC), was the one who had ordered the audit and accepted the final report.

Chatelain's job was almost impossible because of the political chaos of the times. Joe Clark's government was defeated on December 13, 1979, and Clark immediately began preparations for a February election. One of his last acts was to appoint Jerome to a judgeship in the federal court, so the House was without a Speaker. And without a Speaker to support him, Chatelain was at the mercy of rumours such as the ones that he was issuing used briefcases to members and forbidding members' spouses to use the Parliamentary Restaurant. "He was lied to, lied about, and made to look bad at every opportunity," reported Jason Moscovitz in a two-part CBC documentary about the reform battles. "He was perceived as a threat and he was a threat." Disheartened and discouraged, Chatelain gave up and retreated to Quebec City.

Chatelain's problems were just preliminary skirmishes. On April 14, 1980, Prime Minister Pierre Trudeau, in power once again, appointed a new Speaker, Jeanne Sauvé, who had been minister of communications in the last Liberal government. She would have much preferred a senior cabinet job and took the new position with great reluctance. So it was to Sauvé that Macdonell delivered his final report. Reforming the House was certainly not her idea of a good time but the Mcdonell audit gave her no choice.

Coates, who became defence minister in the 1984 Conservative cabinet before resigning over a sex scandal, continued to lead the fight against reform with Cloutier, who was a member of the MMSC along with the other senior House officers. They were fighting, for example, to keep the Sergeant-at-Arms' traditional right to hand out Commons jobs as patronage instead of through competition; they were also fighting on behalf of MPs who did not want to be accountable for their expenses. Lloyd Francis, who was deputy Speaker at the time, says he could get no cooperation at all from Coates's committee on the issue of unpaid bills from the Parliamentary Restaurant. The "deadbeats," as Francis called them, came from all parties and often owed as much as $1,000 each. As chairman of MMSC, Francis explained, "Coates had a predilection for in camera meetings and rarely permitted a public meeting of his committee. He wouldn't even let the minutes circulate—he'd grab the only copy."

Standing by Sauvé's side, along with Francis, were her new hand-picked administrator, Arthur Silverman, and her clerk, Beverley Koester, a gentle and scholarly man who had once been clerk of the Saskatchewan legislature and was dedicated to the professional training of procedural staff. They helped Sauvé implement changes from the sublime to the ridiculous—from installing word processors and modern accounting systems to using clear plastic garbage bags in the kitchens so that employees could not continue hauling home green garbage bags full of hams and roasts of beef and bottles of booze. One wonders why Cloutier would be so ferociously committed to the old ways when he himself had been at the House such a short time. Born in 1935 in Drummondville, Cloutier joined the RCAF at seventeen. In those days it was unusual for a francophone to attend an English-speaking university like Mount Allison in New Brunswick, but that's where he went while he was still a young air-force recruit. Later, he attended the University of Liège in Belgium. When he was only twenty he married a Prince Edward Islander, Joan Cahill of Summerside; they were later divorced. The couple had two children, Charles Michael and Nancy.

Little is known about Cloutier's airforce career until 1970 when, as a major, he was appointed executive assistant to Defence Minister Donald Macdonald. Four more Liberal defence ministers rolled through the department over the next eight years but Cloutier stayed, the indispensable aide to Edgar Benson, then "Bud" Drury, James Richardson, and Barnett Danson. Each time a new minister arrived, Cloutier got a military promotion. "As an executive assistant, he was locked into a certain level of the public service," explained one of his friends. "So the only way they could give Gus a raise was to give him a promotion." By the time Barnett Danson took over as minister in 1976, Cloutier was a major general and had learned how best to serve the mighty.

"What favours can a minister of defence hand out? And who hands them out?" asks a senior Ottawa civil servant who has known Cloutier for many years. "Every minister has someone in charge of giving away whatever is in the minister's right to give away, everything from the flag on the Peace Tower to a job for someone's kid to seats on a military aircraft."

Cloutier was perfect in this role, says one former defence minister, who did not want to be named even after all these years. "He ran the office as a personal fiefdom. He was really an operator, he controlled the whole scene. If you wanted something done, you contacted Gus." (It's not surprising that many people interviewed about Gus Cloutier do not want to be named; he has many friends in Ottawa and still wields power there. Cloutier himself did not respond to written requests for an interview for this piece, nor to an informal request through a friend.)

Another former defence official said that Cloutier's power reached its zenith in James Richardson's ministry, from 1972 to 1976. "Richardson delegated everything to him. In fact, here was this officer running the department, doing the minister's job. His office was the minister's office. He personally sat at the minister's desk." (Cloutier may have seemed to be running the department, but he was only sweating the small stuff; no-one has ever suggested he was handing out major government contracts.)

Things changed when Barney Danson arrived in 1976. Danson wanted another man as executive assistant and insisted on separation from his helpful aide. He also wanted his desk back. Danson noticed that Cloutier hardly seemed to be part of the military. "I knew he was an air-force officer," said Danson, "but didn't know he was a major general until I saw his uniform hanging in my office cupboard. I never saw him wear his uniform. He was an affable, hail-fellow-well-met type, but I don't think he was one of the military team."

When Danson put in his own executive assistant, Eric Acker, Cloutier started to lobby for the Sergeant-at-Arms position. In 1978, with support from senior Trudeau aides and from Danson, he was moved in to replace Lieutenant Colonel David Currie, a World War II Victoria Cross winner who was retiring at sixty-five after eighteen years in the job. Trudeau announced Cloutier's appointment on April 27. "Shortly after Gus became Sergeant-at-Arms," remembers the Thomson newspapers' Ottawa columnist, Stewart MacLeod, "he invited me to his office for a drink. I'd known Colonel Currie and he kept a skimpy room for himself with a simple wooden desk. Gus's office had three or four interconnected rooms, each progressively more expensive." By 1991, Cloutier had a valet to help him with his robing before entering the Chamber, a car, and the salary—about $140,000—and status of a deputy minister.

And so, back in 1978, began the parliamentary career of this interesting man, a man who loved to surround himself with cronies, a man who is, by all accounts, a merry companion. "He has every social grace," says a former colleague. "He looks good and sounds good. He has charisma and he fills the room."

"He said to me once, 'You've never been to one of my lunches,'" recalls a Hill journalist. "This is where he entertained political chiefs and judges and other important people. Gus told me he held the lunches in a private dining room and if I came I should plan to spend all afternoon." The journalist thought it prudent not to accept.

Cloutier quickly made it his business to take care of cabinet ministers and MPs just as he had his defence ministers. Nothing was too good for his friend Bob Coates, the back-bench right-winger from Amherst, Nova Scotia. For him, Cloutier turned over a splendid suite of offices in the historic East Block and saw to it the rooms were furnished in an appropriate style.

Cloutier also befriended the late Keith Martin, then John Diefenbaker's executive assistant; no-one was surprised in 1979 when the Sergeant-at-Arms was named one of fifty-nine honorary pallbearers at Diefenbaker's funeral. "I was one, too," jokes Stew MacLeod. "I was never surrounded by such a pack of rogues in my life." After Diefenbaker's death Cloutier hired Martin to run the members' services office.

Another of Cloutier's closest pals is Peter Fleming, who was brought into the House in the mid-1970s by James Jerome. Jerome liked Fleming because he was a wonderful piano player and no-one at the House enjoyed a party more than Jerome. Fleming's skills were best deployed in planning entertainments and musicals and working with reporters on the annual Press Gallery Dinner. "Peter was like Gus's social secretary," said one senior Hill staffer. "He's a very nice man. Peter is in charge of accommodation; he moves people in and out of offices." For many years, Fleming has been Cloutier's steady lunch date, either at the same table in the corner of the Parliamentary Dining Room or in another reserved corner of Hy's Steakhouse.

3. THE PARLIAMENTARY SYSTEM

Given Cloutier's style, the clash with Sauvé's reformers was inevitable and the newspapers ate it up. As Silverman trimmed staff, ordered inventories, set up a competition system for jobs and a merit system for promotions, clashing armies battled it out through leaks to favourite reporters. The *Ottawa Citizen's* Frank Howard, who covers the bureaucracy, and *The Toronto Sun's* Doug Fisher, himself a former MP, strongly supported the Cloutier faction and the old guard. In one column in August, 1985, Howard made fun of Lloyd Francis's "self-serving ruminations" about the "Bad Old Days" when sexual harassment was so common. Howard went on to dismiss "all the talk about beleaguered reformers" who were, he claimed, actually in the business of building their own bureaucratic empires of "patronage and privilege." *Citizen* editorials admitted a cleanup might be overdue but tut-tutted about Sauvé's and Silverman's lack of respect for "Hill tradition." (Read old boys' club.)

Cloutier and Coates did not win everyone over. *The Globe and Mail's* John Gray and Michael Valpy, both then based in Ottawa, and CBC's Jason Moscovitz appeared to stand behind the reformers. But whatever side you were on, House reform was a hot topic. On one occasion, the then CTV bureau chief, Bruce Phillips, was having lunch with Cloutier and taking the side of the reform group. "After a lot of wine," remembers someone who was at the table, "Bruce was defending Silverman while Gus and his entourage were defending his side saying things like 'Parliament was never meant to be efficient, it was meant to serve MPs.' Bruce said, 'Well, it's time they started to crack down on all those thefts.' Gus's reaction was that 'on an operation this size, you're bound to have some leakage...'

"Bruce said, 'Leakage! Paper and pencils are one thing – but grand pianos?'

"Cloutier was indignant: 'There was only one.'"

Cloutier drove Sauvé wild. Just when she thought she had made some gains, she would find him behind another project that she had to fight. One dilly occurred in the fall of 1980, when she discovered that Cloutier had ordered $10,000 worth of riot gear for Commons guards without telling her. When she ordered the twelve-gauge shotguns and handcuffs and bullet-proof vests returned,

the supplier complained and was paid his money – leaving Commons staff to scurry around trying to find buyers for all of it. Sauvé reprimanded Cloutier for taking this action without consulting her or other Commons officials and, what was more unusual, let it be known that he'd been reprimanded. As Hill entrails are read, this was a defeat for the old guard.

Another dust-up occurred when, without Sauvé's knowledge, he set up a restaurant for senior employees of the House, one not open even to MPs. It offered a luxurious five-course meal for $2.75, which meant taxpayers were subsidizing each meal by $12.14. Furious, Sauvé waited until she could prove it had only a twenty-per-cent occupancy rate (except for Friday nights when it rose to fifty-two per cent) and that it was losing money. She closed it down in July, 1981, announcing losses of nearly $140,000.

That was just the beginning. In an effort to improve services to members, the House asked Cloutier to give them bar fridges for the offices. Instead of ordering 300 at a discount, he ordered them one or two at a time from a retail outlet and doled them out as favours to members. House purchasing officials, trying to set up a competitive purchasing system, tore their hair out. Then there was the warehouse he rented without authorization. His friend Keith Martin (who died a few years ago) had been talked into buying a year's worth of toilet paper and dispensers for washrooms on the Hill. The only problem with the bulk order was storage. Cloutier had to rent a warehouse from an Ottawa firm, Boyd's Moving and Storage, to hold the paper and the dispensers.

One Ottawa mandarin who once worked with Cloutier described Cloutier's management style: "He goes to every meeting he's ever invited to, shows up on time, listens attentively, agrees to majority decisions. Then he goes away and does whatever he wants." But, said the observer, everything was always handled with enormous civility. "Silverman, for example, never had an argument with Gus. Ask anyone – Gus and Art never had an argument, no harsh words. But it was a legendary war because it was a war of values.

"Gus would rent a warehouse and Art would dispose of it. Gus would open a restaurant and Art would close it. "Gus is one of the most likable people the city has ever met. But what are the values? The clash of values is much more difficult

to reconcile than a clash of personalities."

The House had worked as an old boys' club for a hundred years because no-one ever challenged the underlying values. It was a culture that bred a James Jerome, who said he couldn't see anything wrong with the way the House was run. It bred a James McGrath, the Conservative backbencher appointed by Mulroney to study the House in 1985, who had a chance to stamp out the old ways. But McGrath only suggested developing more committees to keep backbenchers busy. McGrath also recommended making the Board of Internal Economy, which runs the House, an all-party board instead of a board filled by government members. It seemed like a good idea at the time but the net result was that it institutionalized the House as a club: the board of directors is all of us, therefore none of us can be criticized.

The clash of values went on even after Trudeau appointed Sauvé governor general. The new Speaker, Lloyd Francis, had been Sauvé's deputy and was a determined reformer; so was John Bosley, the Tory Speaker appointed in 1984 much to the disappointment of those who had hoped for a speedy return to the glorious old ways. Bosley signalled his direction early in 1985 when he agreed to more realistic charges in the Parliamentary Dining Room and raised the price of a formal dinner from $4.40 to $8. When MPs screamed he hastily produced a $5 "light lunch" for the dining room, one that ran a mere three courses and could include fresh salmon or jumbo shrimp or rare roast beef. But the damage was done. Bosley was the enemy, too. His opponents were men like Patrick MacAdam, then the prime minister's liaison to the caucus, and Coates. Leaks about Bosley's extravagant style began to appear in the press and before long the Prime Minister's Office, thanks to Cloutier, had the weapon it needed – furniture.

Although Cloutier had lost control of the restaurants in 1985, he had hung on to a few little treasures. One of these was the decorating fief of fifty-odd carpenters, upholsterers, picture-framers, painters, furniture-refinishers, and cabinet-makers that fell under the administrative wing of a military crony, Colonel J.A.J. Spénard. The operation doesn't stint; as Ottawa reporters Bob Fife and John Warren note in their new book, *A Capital Scandal,* "between 1980 and 1985 the Commons spent $4.6-million on office furniture, $1.6-million for carpets, drapes, and upholstery and $6.1-million on office renovations. In 1990-91 it spent $2-million on office furniture and equipment. In the two previous years the Commons spent nearly half a million dollars on carpets, drapes, and upholstery." Cloutier took great interest in these services; after all, some members tired quickly of colours and fabrics and liked redecorating as often as they could get away with it.

In 1985 John Bosley made the fatal mistake of not watching closely enough to keep the shop from spending 750 hours refinishing antique furniture acquired for Kingsmere, the newly renovated Speaker's Farm in the Gatineau Hills. In 1986 Mulroney, persuaded by the complaints of Coates, MacAdam, and other die-hard traditionalists, as well as by Tories who believed Bosley was doing a poor job controlling the Opposition during Question Period, decided Bosley had to go. Joe Clark was given the dirty job of getting rid of Bosley and one of the whips used to beat a resignation out of him was the extravagance of the 750 hours.

Cloutier was nearly caught in a similar trap himself. In 1984 it was discovered that he'd ordered a massive walnut bookcase built by Wolf Bartsch, the talented cabinet-maker who produces all the custom-built furniture for the Speaker's Office, the Prime Minister's Office, and for senior cabinet ministers. With two assistants, the job took Bartsch three weeks; when the bookcase was done it was between five and six feet wide and about seven feet high. It boasted a built-in bar and space for a television and stereo. Senior House staff were convinced the piece was for Cloutier's home and made an unusual expedition to the workrooms to see it. "Gus said it was for his office," said three witnesses to the affair. But where this would fit into his office was another mystery. According to one workman who had laboured on the piece, it stayed in a storeroom for two months. "We came in one Monday and it was gone. It disappeared over the weekend." To this day no-one admits to knowing where the piece went, but it didn't go to Cloutier's office.

When John Fraser was elected Speaker on October 1, 1986, he too supported the administrative reforms, though with less zeal than his predecessors; after Fraser took over, Cloutier still exercised a

great deal of power. One victory that flew in the face of the reformed House's strict rules about hiring only by open competition was the employment of a close friend who had been a waitress at Hy's; Cloutier was able to have her first given a job with the defence department and then briskly transferred into the House. Before long she was managing the dining room; the corridor gossip burbled over his coup. Today she works for House administration.

An appointment like this is, admittedly, a rare event in the House. On the whole, competition and merit have become the ways people get hired and promoted. But some things never change no matter what systems are put in place – and this brings us back to furniture. According to staff in the furniture shops, filling special orders for custom-made furniture or refinished antiques was one of the favours Cloutier was still able to provide politicians.

Luciano Boselli frequently refinishes pieces that belong to politicians personally; he takes them home and works on them out of view of the rest of the workers. "When a personal piece comes in," explained one of the Commons staff, "they [the supervisors] use Boselli to do the work and he takes it home. They never use work orders for personal pieces. Luciano does a special piece every month or two, owned by some MP or other, but it is always a secret."

Workshop sources say they don't have many options about doing the "private" work if they want to hang on to their jobs. What upsets the workmen most, however, is not special work done secretly for special people, it is their own working conditions. For years, complaining of nausea, headaches, and other illnesses, they have railed against the fumes from the lacquers, sealers, strippers, and thinners they use in their cramped second-basement shops in the House's Wellington Building. Dust from the sanders adds to the noxious mix and the workers say the air-exchange system cannot function in such a small space. The men have repeatedly gone public with demands to improve their ventilation systems, the House sends in experts who say everything is fine, the union health-and-safety people yelp in protest, and then it starts all over again.

With life's unerring instinct for the absurd, it was just such a tedious health-

and-safety issue that finally defanged Gus Cloutier. Asbestos did the trick. Ever since 1980, when electricians started drilling holes through historic old walls and ceilings to install cables for a massive communications system and asbestos began dribbling through, employees have known they had a problem. For years there have been studies and even some serious attempts to tear the asbestos out of some areas. But estimates of up to $40-million to remove it from the West Block (where the problem is the worst) have blocked a final decision. After all, employees were assured, the asbestos is just sitting there, not moving around.

In 1988, after more pressure from worried employees, the Department of Public Works hired Trevor Harris & Associates, a company with offices in Toronto and Ottawa, to study it again. In a 225-page report James Sutherland and Richard Nelligan concluded that "large amounts of loose debris evident in every range" of the attics could travel through the ventilation systems to other parts of the building. Asbestos levels were seven or eight times higher than acceptable levels for buildings, the report said. And the firm even made a six-hour video showing how asbestos fibres moved along through ventilation pipes and into the building's air. It showed the fibres floating around in the attics. The report recommended immediate action to protect workers who had to do maintenance work in the hazardous attic areas but it also recommended getting cracking on removing the asbestos. The reports warned strongly of the real possibility of "future litigation."

Pretty alarming news. And who received it? The man in charge was Gus Cloutier, and apparently he sat on it. Or rather, he took part in what one union representative described as "a circle sit" – many House officials say that the powerful Board of Internal Economy would also have known about the report. But for two years the report stayed a secret and officials claimed that tests had proved there was no asbestos in the West Block air.

Finally someone leaked the Trevor Harris report to Stan Gray, a Toronto asbestos expert and Greenpeace activist hired as a consultant by the Unions' Workplace Environment Committee. Gray held a press conference in Ottawa on December 12, 1990, and all hell broke loose.

The workers weren't the only ones who were furious. MPs also said they knew nothing of the report. The Board of Internal Economy hastily called for a new independent study and that made everyone even angrier because they saw it as another stonewalling tactic. The new study, conducted by Pinchin and Associates and released in January 1991, found that the asbestos levels were acceptable. Union spokesmen retorted that the study was inadequate.

Why was the original report hushed up? It wasn't just the expense of a cleanup, say many Hill staffers; asbestos is also a sensitive political issue. It's the major industry in Defence Minister Marcel Masse's Frontenac riding and the stakes are enormous. Canada used to supply ninety-four per cent of the asbestos used by American companies and most of that came from Quebec. After the U.S. Environmental Protection Agency banned most uses of the material in 1989, Canadian producers launched a court action in Louisiana in 1990 to overturn the ban.

"Masse sent one of his people to talk to us about how wonderful asbestos was," said Debbie Broad, a spokesperson for the workplace environment committee, adding that one asbestos-industry employee told a committee member that the House of Commons situation could affect the U.S. court action.

As the flak flew Gus maintained a low profile. "We were directing questions to Fraser, telling him he had to do something," said Broad, "but he handed it all over to Edna MacKenzie, the director of human resources in the House." Eventually, however, the easy-going Speaker got fed up. John Fraser was not interested in taking any blame himself; he'd already suffered through one horrendous scandal when he was fired as fisheries minister over his decision to release tainted tuna.

Cloutier, in the end, looked like the best person to carry the can because he'd already upset the Board of Internal Economy that year. The board had been pondering ways to keep the noisy anti-corruption demonstrator Glen Kealey from

shouting at Mulroney and other cabinet ministers on their way into the House each day. At one meeting the board decided to ask the department of public works for ideas. The next thing they knew, an order in council was passed making it illegal to stand closer than fifty metres to Hill entrances; when Kealey and another demonstrator objected, they were arrested by the RCMP and spent several days in jail. The ruling backfired in a blaze of publicity; MPs were once again angry at the restrictions on freedom of expression, the RCMP decided not to make any more arrests, and the board, to its fury, was blamed. It was Cloutier, said one member of the board, who had engineered the order in council.

Enough was enough. Cloutier was quietly fingered for the asbestos debacle and stripped of most of his authority.

But Cloutier was only doing what many MPs wanted him to do, what members had been doing for a hundred years – and, despite the reforms, what they are still doing. Just this past year MPs passed Bill C-79, which gives them legal privileges enjoyed by no other Canadians; it gives the Board of Internal Economy "exclusive authority" to decide whether an MP has misused his or her office budget. And when the RCMP is investigating an MP, it must also consult the board before seeking a search warrant or a wiretap. The bill was ushered into law by four cabinet ministers on May 7, 1991 – the day before Tory MP Maurice Tremblay was due to appear in court on charges of fraud and breach of trust. It also claims for the board *retroactive* jurisdiction over whether members misappropriated funds in the past. Within hours Tremblay used the new act to delay his trial; another Tory MP, Gabriel Fontaine, also used the act to postpone legal proceedings he was facing for misuse of his office budget. (The board also decided that the House should pay the legal fees of all MPs under investigation until such time as charges are laid.)

Last year the House passed a law giving members up to $6,000 more in tax-free housing allowances; they already receive $21,300 in tax-free allowances originally designed to cover housing and other

costs. "The House covers travel, family travel, everything we can think of," said one longtime manager. "Then we said, 'Here's another $21,300 to cover things we haven't thought of.' Now we've added another $6,000."

Though the Mulroney government has adopted a tough "user pay" attitude towards government services, MPs don't want that philosophy applied to themselves. MPs and House employees do not pay for parking on the Hill, for example, and neither do Press Gallery members. It's a benefit worth at least $1,300 a year. "You keep people in line with little things," said one former House employee, "and you make sure you give spaces to the press to keep them in line too. And when a House employee sees MPs trying not to pay their restaurant bills or giving themselves raises and not calling them raises— they see it as normal behaviour. So why should they be any different?"

It all comes back to the issue of culture. The question is not why are there still fumes in the furniture shop – the question is why do they still have a furniture shop at all? The answer is obvious. It's nice to have your own furniture shop because that way you don't have to attribute costs to anyone – just some people you pay by the year. The government finds it cheaper to contract out printing, food, and cleaning operations – everywhere except on the Hill. The problem with contracting out furniture-making or upholstering means that there would be a bill to say who ordered it.

The culture of Parliament for so many years has been that of a secretive, institutionalized club. It does not fall within the Access to Information law, so that members and staff do not have to produce records for public scrutiny. The whole organization, even today, operates in a climate of intrigue and double-dealing. "Then we expect the civil servants who serve these people to be better?" asks one senior manager. "They are no better. They take on the characteristics of the family that adopts them." This is not just a story about who Gus Cloutier is and what he did – it's a story about how Gus Cloutier came to be.

A NEW TOP GUN

*HUGH SEGAL
BRINGS A BUOYANT
OPTIMISM TO HIS
JOB AS THE PM'S
CHIEF OF STAFF*

The early-afternoon telephone call from Prime Minister Brian Mulroney came as Hugh Segal was relaxing at home in Toronto with his wife and daughter on Sunday, Jan. 5. Mulroney, who was leaving for a Florida vacation the next day, asked Segal, a senior adviser, if he could fly to Ottawa for a meeting that night at the Prime Minister's residence. Said Segal: "I presumed he just wanted to discuss a couple of policy decisions before he left." But after Segal arrived for his 7:45 p.m. meeting in Mulroney's study at 24 Sussex Drive, the Prime Minister surprised him. Recalled Segal: "He told me that the position of chief of staff in his office was now open—and he wanted me to take it." Earlier that day, Mulroney had notified his chief of staff of 16 months, Norman Spector, that he was moving him from the top job in the Prime Minister's Office to become Canada's ambassador to Israel. Recalled Segal: "When you are offered a job, you usually just say at first that you will think about it." But presented with Mulroney's invitation, he said, "There was nothing to think about: I said yes at once."

With that decision, the 41-year-old Segal accepted a position that is one of the most critical and personally consuming in the federal power structure—at a time when the country and its governing party have seldom seemed more divided or insecure. As chief of staff to Mulroney, Segal takes over a position that one of his predecessors describes as the Prime Minister's "gatekeeper, chief adviser, confi-dant, administrator and link to the outside world." In fact, both his legion of friends and his political opponents say that the heavy-set, jovial Segal, who is often referred to as "Hughie the Happy Warrior," is exceptionally well suited to those tasks. Declared Senator Michael Kirby, a Liberal and former adviser to prime minister Pierre Trudeau; "Beyond any measure, his qualifications are the best in the country. I do not know why Mulroney did not do this years ago."

Still, Segal, a longtime Conservative activist who has been on the PMO payroll as an adviser since last summer, faces a daunting task in the weeks ahead. Mulroney will turn immediately to his new chief of staff to draw up for his consideration the policies and actions that have so far eluded him in his search for a constitutional settlement and, coincidentally, for a revival in the fortunes of the Conservative party. Indeed, despite the unelected and traditionally low-profile nature of the chief of staff's position, many senior Tories say that Segal carries much of their hopes for restoring the public's confidence in the deeply unpopular Mulroney government. Declared one close friend and senior party adviser last week: "Basically, it is up to Hughie to save the Prime Minister's ass—and maybe the country's."

Challenge: The scale of that challenge is underscored by another more sombre expectation that also resides with Segal. If he cannot restore Mulroney's standing in public opinion polls before the next election campaign, likely in mid-1993, said one Mulroney insider, "There are a lot of people in the party who think it will have to be Hughie who gives the Prime Minister the message that he should then leave." For his part, Segal, in a 75-minute interview last week with *Maclean's*, buoyantly dismissed the likelihood of his ever offering such grim advice. "There are all kinds of people prepared to offer all sorts of reasons why we cannot succeed," he acknowledged. But he added: "I obviously would not be here if I did not believe in our chances—and in this Prime Minister."

Still, Segal's appointment takes place at a time when even the most devout and optimistic Tories are struggling to find reasons for hope. Nationally, the economy is reeling through one of the worst recessions in Canadian history. On the constitutional front, the government last week suffered a potentially devastating setback when Alberta Premier Donald Getty—a fellow Tory who had been a strong supporter of the Meech Lake accord—unexpectedly attacked the federal government's policies of official bilingualism and multiculturalism (see box).

Getty made his comments at a time when both public support for the federal Conservatives is languishing in the mid-teens in public opinion polls and there are continuing defections of grassroots Tories to the right-wing reform party. But it was not the only blow that the government's constitutional initiative has suffered recently. In Ottawa, senior officials acknowledged that infighting among Constitutional Affairs Minister Joe Clark, Clerk of the Privy Council Paul Tellier, Spector and other key Mulroney advisers has severely hampered the government's attempts to move the constitutional debate forward.

Blood: Mulroney may be hoping that much of that bad blood among his advisers will dissipate with Spector's departure. A career public servant, Spector commands wide respect for his grasp of constitutional details. But his reserved and cerebral personality presents a chilly exterior that did little to foster confidence among fellow Tories. Indeed, he acknowledged last week that he first began contemplating his departure from Mulroney's staff during the summer, when it became clear that senior Tories were applying unrelenting pressure on Mulroney to replace him. Spector told *Maclean's:* "The Prime Minister was very eager to have me stay in the office as a senior constitutional affairs adviser. It became clear in the last few days that his efforts for that idea were not succeeding."

In his choice of Segal to replace Spector, Mulroney has plainly signalled his desire for less rarefied advice in the run-up to the election. One immediate result is likely to be a substantial change of course in the government's approach to constitutional reform. Repeated polls have shown that many Canadians believe that the government is spending too much time and effort on constitutional reform—at the expense of other issues. As well, the annual *Maclean's* poll, released in the Jan 6 issue, showed that 82 per cent of respondents have at best only a "vague" knowledge of the government's unwieldy 28-item package for constitutional reform. With the departure of Spector, who drafted much of the reform package, senior officials predict that the proposals will be sharply redrawn and reduced in scope, probably by the end of March.

Still, the most striking changes may result from the difference in style and personality that Segal brings to the office formerly occupied by Spector—despite the two men's remarkably similar backgrounds. Just one year apart in age—Spector is 42—they grew up as members of Montreal's Jewish community, where they attended the same Jewish parochial elementary and high schools. Both speak fluent French: Segal studied history at the University of Ottawa while Spector took political science at McGill. Later, both men worked at various times for the Ontario provincial government. But Segal's affability and Spector's reserve made for a personal relationship that was sometimes cool and that improved only after Segal arrived in Ottawa last summer.

Expertise: Within Ottawa and provincial government circles, Spector was widely respected and sometimes feared for his formidable intellect, rigorous personal discipline and expertise. Said L. Ian MacDonald, Mulroney's former speech writer and a friend of Spector: "Norman is a brilliant man, and that sometimes intimidates people." As well, Spector, who is single, is a reclusive figure with little interest in party politics. He can be a witty and engaging conversationalist when he chooses. But his blunt and sometimes bitingly sarcastic manner tended to alienate more casual acquaintances. As a result, some critics said that under Spector, the PMO had fallen out of touch with the concerns of the caucus and party members. As well, Spector was not always kept informed about the partisan consequences of political changes. In one case, when Mulroney named former Nova Scotia premier John Buchanan to the Senate while Buchanan's government was under investigation by the RCMP over allegations of patronage and corruption, Spector learned about the appointment in the newspapers.

With the arrival of Segal, that situation is likely to change dramatically. Few people in political circles in Canada are liked more. Said William Fox, a former press secretary to Mulroney and a close friend of both men: "Hugh has the intellectual capacity to make a substantive contribution in policy areas and the communication skills to get that policy across to people." As well, Segal is renowned for his

A JOVIAL FORMER AD EXECUTIVE REPLACES AN AUSTERE INTELLECTUAL

near-photographic memory: one friend who bumped into him recently at an airport and began reminiscing about a political organizer of their acquaintance then stood by in astonishment as Segal recited the precise dates and complete results of more than a dozen campaigns that their friend had organized.

In fact, Segal acknowledges that he has been captivated by politics in general and the Tory party in particular since he was 12, when he heard then-Prime Minister John Diefenbaker make a speech at his high school extolling his Canadian Bill of Rights. Like three of his four predecessors under Mulroney, Segal is a native Montrealer. But he is best known in political circles for his network of contacts outside of Quebec. After university, he worked as a self-described "junior, junior, junior" aide to then-Tory Leader Robert Stanfield in the early 1970s. An unsuccessful candidate in both the 1972 and 1974 elections, he later became principal secretary to then-Ontario Premier William Davis in 1975. He worked for Davis on and off for the next seven years—with two interruptions to work as an advertising executive in the private sector—and tried unsuccessfully to persuade Davis to run in the 1983 leadership campaign that eventually brought Mulroney to the leadership.

Segal has known Mulroney for about 20 years. He now says: "I have always admired him and his devotion to our party." In fact, Segal put aside a lucrative advertising business in Toronto, as well as a high-profile position appearing as a weekly commentator on CTV's *Canada AM*, last August when Mulroney invited him to Ottawa as an adviser. Friends say that he now earns only a fraction of the income that he had in private business. At the same time, Segal, a devoted family man whose wife, Donna, is a provincial civil servant in Toronto, now commutes from there to spend four nights a week in Ottawa. There, he shares an apartment with three Tory senators, including Manitoba's Nathan Nurgitz and Montreal's Michael Meighen.

Segal, who is renowned for his quick wit and irreverence, is particularly disdainful of the perpetually solemn manner in which official government life unfolds in the capital. Said Segal: "Ottawa takes itself very seriously. I do not know why so many people feel it is important to look unhappy all the time in their jobs." Despite that complaint, friends say, Segal felt unable to refuse Mulroney's offer. Said Harry Near, a friend and former business associate of Segal: "The thing about Hugh is that beneath all the jokes he makes about himself, he has a belief that public service is the most noble thing you can do."

Loyalty: At the same time, friends and former colleagues say that even if Segal privately did not approve of Mulroney or another Tory leader, his loyalty to the party would compel him to serve. Former Ontario premier Frank Miller, who replaced Davis briefly after his retirement in 1985, recalls that before he won the leadership, Segal "sure did not support me." But after he became leader, said Miller, "I never had cause to distrust him. He is very loyal to the party."

In fact, Segal, a self-described "Red Tory" whose strongest party ties are in Toronto circles, is often viewed with suspicion by more right-wing Tories from outside the city. Some Ontario Tories say that his reputation as a master strategist is largely undeserved, and they blame him for the disastrous 1985 campaign that saw the Tories driven from power for the first time in more than 40 years. Said Kimble Ainslie, a provincial Tory organizer who owns a London, Ont.-based polling firm: "We have not had a lot of great experiences with Mr. Segal. We resent this notion that he is a thoroughgoing winner."

At the same time, both friends and many political opponents say that Segal's open and often exuberant manner disguises an intense determination to compete—and win—on his own terms. Indeed, Segal recalls that as a chubby nine-year-old hockey player, he used to tire more easily than other smaller boys. In order to avoid criticism of his size if he came off the ice before others on his shift, he said, "I used to deliberately get a penalty so that I could get a rest. And if I wanted an even longer rest, I just cursed the referee" to get a 10-minute misconduct penalty.

Incident: Some critics argue that the adult Segal applies the same techniques to politics. The most frequently cited example is an incident in 1987, when Segal was one of the key advisers to then-Ontario Tory Leader Larry Grossman during a provincial election. Despite the fact that he is a strong personal supporter of bilingualism—to the point that his nine-year-old daughter, Jacqueline, attends a French immersion school in Toronto—the party's campaign strategy focused in part on fear that the opposition Liberals would declare the province officially bilingual. Said one former Liberal strategist sarcastically: "Hugh was part of a wonderful campaign which had the tinge of racism about francophones." Added the Liberal: "It was not that he was ideological—but rather that he was quite the pragmatist."

Despite that, Segal is widely respected and liked among counterparts in all parties for his overall decency, strength of character and charm. Hershell Ezrin, who served as principal secretary to former Ontario Liberal premier David Peterson, cites Segal's "big heart." Declared Ezrin of Segal's appointment: "There is absolutely nothing better than someone with some credibility who is a bit of a cheerleader to bring up everyone else's spirits." And, said Ezrin, "He has a very creative mind, and he is very good on tactics as well as strategy."

For his part, Segal said that he is already looking forward to the day when he leaves the PMO and his new job. That time will come, he said last week, "The day after they swear in the new Tory cabinet after we win the next election." But many insiders say that Segal may fulfil another ambition before that. He recently bought a house in Kingston, Ont., and

some friends and political opponents say that he has already discussed plans to run there as a candidate in the next election. Declared one friend and Tory adviser: "He is just itching to run." And Peter Milliken, the Liberal MP for that area, said rumors of Segal's intentions as a candidate were "the only thing people talked about at Christmas."

Joyless: But for now, many Tories are clearly happy that Segal is in his present position. That includes current and former members of the PMO, who often decry its draining and joyless atmosphere. Said Fox: "He has an infectious personality, and I think it will really improve the moral right through the system." Former speech writer

MacDonald, in fact, describes the office where Segal is taking charge as being "like some kind of gloomy sorority most of the time: you cannot imagine the pressure until you have been there." He added: "If anyone can bring spirits back up, it is Hughie and his politics of joy." But faced with a despondent party and an often angry populace, even someone renowned as a happy warrior may find that to be the most difficult battle of all.

ANTHONY WILSON-SMITH and **E. KAYE FULTON** with NANCY WOOD, GLEN ALLEN and LUKE FISHER in Ottawa and PAUL KAIHLA in Toronto

TURNING BACK BILINGUALISM

Even as the federal Conservatives desperately attempt to broaden their national appeal, the Constitution remains Ottawa's most pressing preoccupation. That was strikingly clear last week when Alberta Premier Donald Getty sent shock waves through political circles with his call to abolish official bilingualism. In a speech to the Edmonton Downtown Rotary Club, Getty said that bilingualism should be a matter of individual choice rather than "a punitive, unwelcome law." Said Getty, a strong supporter of the Meech Lake constitutional accord: "We need to find new ways to remove the irritants among us, and enforced bilingualism has become such a symbol all across the country."

It was a political bombshell in official Ottawa. In fact, the federal government

briefly considered re-examining Canada's constitutionally entrenched language policy in the fall—but dropped the issue in order to avoid opening old wounds.

Reaction across Canada to Getty's speech indicated that the government's concern was justified. Prime Minister Brian Mulroney's Quebec lieutenant, Benoît Bouchard, said that such remarks threatened to derail the delicate constitutional negotiations. Declared Bouchard: "I hope we will be able to avoid including a topic as inflammatory as language in the constitutional debate. We do not need that." Other responses ranged from dismay among minority groups—such as the English-rights organization Alliance Quebec and francophones in New Brunswick—to delight among anti-bilingualism activists in both Quebec and the rest of the country. Said Ronald Leitch, president of the Toronto-based Alliance for the Preservation of English in Canada, of Getty's remarks: "It puts us right back in the ball game again."

But there were also charges that Getty's comments were part of a strategy to save his

faltering Alberta Tories from defeat in the next election. Getty recently lost a senior minister, Raymond Speaker, to the archconservative federal Reform party, whose members have attacked both legislated bilingualism and multiculturalism—another of Getty's targets last week. For his part, Liberal Leader Jean Chrétien accused Getty of "indulging in desperate politics" by adopting a major Reform party plank. Said University of Alberta political scientist Edmund Aunger: "It seems to be a statement that panders to people's prejudices."

But for Getty, political circumstances may have dictated his actions—even at the risk of inflaming the national debate. Still, when the parliamentary committee on constitutional reform visits Alberta later this month, it will not be able to talk to Getty. He will be in Palm Springs, Calif., on his annual winter golf vacation.

E. KAYE FULTON in Ottawa with JOHN HOWSE in Calgary

OTTAWA

Lobby Horse

**Now that the government thinktanks
have been shut down, the feds are starting
to let private lobbyists like Jon Johnson
do their thinking for them**

Charlotte Gray

If you want to see where the lobbying industry in Ottawa is going, look at Jon Johnson. The founder and sole owner of GPC Government Policy Consultants, Johnson is generally recognized as the sharpest-clawed cat in the lobbying jungle. A tall, athletic thirty-eight-year-old with a penchant for expensive suits and crisp monogrammed white shirts, he hustles for business like a Salomon Brothers broker. He is determined to be, in the felicitous jargon of Wall Street traders, one big swinging dick.

Most people who arrive at Ottawa Airport quickly learn about Johnson's ambitions. They walk beneath a billboard that proclaims GPC as "The Experts in Government Relations." Founded as a one-man office in 1986, GPC had revenues of $5-million last year and now has seventeen consultants on payroll. With seventy clients (including Power Corp. and General Electric Capital Canada Inc.), it has already catapulted up the lobby-industry ladder to take top spot from Hill and Knowlton. GPC opened a Toronto office two years ago, an Edmonton office last January, and aims to be in Brussels and perhaps London with-

in a year. And Jon (pronounced Yoan) isn't the kind of guy to hide his chutzpah. His sales pitch portrays his firm as a multinational-in-the-making and his competitors as nickel-and-dime artists.

"We're not interested in the kind of stuff that most firms around town do," Johnson insists, sitting in GPC's plush boardroom, a stone's throw from Parliament Hill. "Some firms are just escort agencies, who peddle access to decision-makers. Other firms are boilerplate outfits, providing the same issue-monitoring service and strategic advice to all their clients. The majority of people in this business can't even read a balance sheet." Johnson's ice-blue eyes glitter as he leans forward to explain his prowess. "Our value-added is the quality of our analysis. My people have more degrees than a thermometer. We get involved in our clients' corporate planning."

Johnson unfolds his lanky frame from the pastel-upholstered chair towards a blackboard. As he scribbles MBA jargon on it, I realize the blackboard itself is the latest bit of office swank: an automatic, self-cleaning electronic board that can print out anything written on it. The Canadian government, let alone John-

son's rivals, doesn't boast such toys.

The government of Canada doesn't boast a lot of things these days. A shrinking public service has meant fewer policy analysts and more functions farmed out to the private sector. Last February, Finance Minister Mazankowski took a meataxe to some of the few remaining sources of independent advice that once fed into government. With the demise of the Economic Council, the Science Council, and various other government-funded arm's-length institutions, Ottawa's ability to analyse, interpret, and forecast these days is approaching the level of a hardware-store manager's. So where can it turn for advice? Why, the private sector, of course! Lobbying firms are now competing to provide the kind of service and policy advice that once came exclusively from the bureaucracy. "Contrary to most commentary," says Mark Daniels, president of the Canadian Life and Health Insurance Association Inc., who has also been a senior mandarin and a lobbyist, "the lobbying industry is demand, not supply driven. As government down-sizes, the industry can only grow."

That's where Johnson is taking GPC.

His firm's forte, he likes to boast, is business-government project management. Recently GPC helped Hudson Bay Mining and Smelting Co. put together a $120-million project, involving federal and provincial government loans, for a smelter in the Manitoba town of Flin Flon. "We provided the secretariat," says Johnson. "We prepared the documents, the meetings, the loan applications – there are very few people in this business who could put that together." GPC has been involved in similar projects in Saskatchewan and in Alberta. Fifteen years ago, such projects would have been run and financed entirely by government.

There's no doubt that Johnson is pursuing this type of business more aggressively than his competitors. But GPC owes much of its success to the same factors that grease the wheels of other thriving firms. Connections, connections, connections – and results.

Ottawa's lobbying industry is peopled by "used to be's": former senior officials, premiers, ministers, ministerial staffers, and party presidents. Sometimes, the "used-to-be" label is employed as a door-opener. The most notorious flogger of this type is Fred Doucet, a used-to-be senior adviser to the prime minister until 1987. Even today, Doucet is rumoured to occasionally route his phone messages through the Prime Minister's Office. The approach pays off: Fred Doucet has sixty-two registered clients, all eager for a Doucet quick fix. "It's the eighth wonder of the world," snarls Johnson.

More often, the used-to-be label signals that the holder understands the tortuous processes of government and has expertise in a particular area. General Ramsey Wither, a used-to-be deputy minister of transport, is now GCI Government Consultants International Inc.'s expert on Canada's transportation and defence industries.

Johnson himself has gold-plated Tory used-to-be credentials – essential with a government that has always been more comfortable with its friends than with its officials. He was a senior policy adviser to Brian Mulroney in 1983 and 1984, and helped shape Conservative economic policies while the party was in opposition. His father is a former Tory minister in Manitoba and now the province's lieutenant governor: his sister

Janis is one of the Mulroney appointments to the Senate.

Among the other arrows in Johnson's quiver: a doctorate in political economy from the London School of Economics and two years' banking experience, which gives him the analytical skills and intellectual framework for discourse with the mandarin elite. He learned the lobbying ropes as a vice president of Public Affairs International (PAI), now part of Hill and Knowlton. Moreover, he has been smart enough to know that GPC needs bureaucratic, as well as political, used-to-be credibility. So when he decided to focus his firm on financial institutions, he recruited William Kennett, former inspector general of banks, to advise clients on the new banking legislation. Trade policy, pharmaceuticals, procurement, and telecommunications – all growth areas in the GPC empire – each has a competent used-to-be on the file.

Johnson has even taken on board some used-to-be's who don't share his intensely Tory world-view to ensure that, if Mulroney falls, GPC's healthy profits won't vaporize. Former Trudeau minister David Collenette is a senior consultant, and Sharon Vance, former chief of staff to NDP leader Audrey McLaughlin, is also payroll.

GPC's rivals bristle at Johnson's hard-sell tactics. They resent the way he bad-mouths the competition. They claim he inflates his client numbers by registering individual members of associations he represents. They credit him only with carving out a neat market niche for himself in government-business projects, which is to say they sell him short.

GPC represents the latest stage in the evolution of Ottawa's lobbying game. Before Johnson, the handful of firms dominating the industry fell into two categories: factories and boutiques. The factories are public-relations multinationals Burson-Marsteller, and Hill and Knowlton. They offer soup-to-nuts service: polling information, policy analysis, a worldwide network, but they share a sort of faceless, bill-by-the-hour corporatism alien to Ottawa's back-slapping insider culture. The boutiques are smaller operations, low on overhead, strong on contacts and prestige, and high in price. The acknowledged front-runners here are the Neville Group,

Tory back-roomers *sans pareil*, and the Earnscliffe Group, which includes Harry Near, an expert on energy issues who helped run the last Tory campaign. Johnson's innovation has been to marry boutique quality with a factory-style range of services. That leaves him better poised than anyone to assume the policy, planning, and deal-making functions Ottawa is increasingly incapable of performing. Johnson has carefully honed his pitch so that he even *sounds* a bit like an official, as he describes how GPC acts more "in a merchant-banker capacity than simply as a representative of our client's interests."

Lobbyists in one form or another have been around as long as the Peace Tower, but the phenomenon of paid lobbyists took off in 1968, the year two young Liberal executive assistants decided that the private sector needed advice on how to make its case to government. Bill Lee and Bill Neville founded Executive Consultants Ltd. – or ECL, as it was quickly known. However, they carefully avoided the kind of brass-knuckle tactics that Capitol Hill lobbyists use in Washington. ECL guys were scrupulous: they never buttonholed legislators in corridors, slipped government officials cheques for bogus "expenses," or swept decision-makers off on Florida freebies, during which clients could press their case. Neville and Lee were successful enough to spawn a slew of imitators, notably Public Affairs International.

"What changed in 1984 was that a new bunch of people arrived in the industry," explains Sean Moore, a PAI alumnus who edits *The Lobby Monitor*, a biweekly newsletter. "They argued that a new government required new lobbyists, with access to the political players. They themselves had access to the prime minister, the new ministers, and the caucus – and that's what they sold."

This stage in the industry's growth didn't just consist of a bunch of Tory cronies setting up shop. There was also an abrupt change of gears. The newcomers embraced U.S. practices such as direct representation (they talked to their pals in government on behalf of clients), contingency fees (success was rewarded with fat bonuses), and more power name-dropping than *Vanity Fair*.

Horror stories began to circulate.

GCI Government Consultants International Inc., headed by Frank Moores, former premier of Newfoundland and a friend of Mulroney's, quickly became notorious. Among GCI's more gauche acts was the $3,000 it charged to fix an interview between the minister of fisheries and a fisherman who wanted a licence. (GCI insists the meeting was about other matters.) A month after that story broke, Moores was in trouble again. He was representing the European company that wanted to sell Airbuses to Air Canada, despite being on the board of directors of the airline. Moores resigned from the board, but mutterings about the way his firm did business (and the size of its contingency fees) continued. The tut-tutting just swelled GCI's client list with companies eager for a Moores fix.

Before long, the tut-tutting reached the predictable climax – a demand for regulation of lobbyists. The prime minister, dripping with new-found concern about morality in public life, announced he would introduce legislation to control the lobbying process "by providing a reliable and accurate source of information on the activities of lobbyists."

The lobbyists were furious. Powerful connections were important to all of them. Now Moores's carpetbaggery had tarnished their image and threatened to saddle them with rules that could only complicate their lives. "They resented being listed in a central registry," says John Sawatsky, author of *The Insiders: Government, Business, and the Lobbyists.* "They disliked even more having to reveal the identity of their clients, and absolutely bristled at the prospect of divulging their fees."

Their fears proved groundless. The act that was finally passed in 1989 was quickly tagged "the business-card bill" by its critics, because it demanded so little information. So-called Tier One lobbyists – hired guns (including lawyers) on contract to clients – are required to register their clients, and all the parent companies of their clients, and the areas in which they are lobbying on their behalf (procurement, for instance, or trade policy). Tier Two lobbyists, a category including over 2,000 representatives of associations, corporations, public-interest groups, and unions who regularly talk to government, are simply required to register themselves.

The truth is the 1989 legislation trailed behind events. In the interest of long-term survival, most Ottawa lobbying firms were cleaning up their acts before the registry was even established. S.A. Murray Consulting Inc., for example, a highly successful firm of eager young Tories, always worked with a strict code of ethics. From mid-1986, Government Consultants Inc. worked hard to shed its tacky reputation, while Moores himself faded from the picture (though not out of its ownership).

Ineffective or not, the federal registry gives a tantalizing glimpse of how large the industry has become. As of December, 1991, 773 active lobbyists were on file, a sixty-five per cent increase from the first registry report less than two years previous. And as the industry grows, competition intensifies. The registry, ironically, is now appreciated by lobbyists for allowing them to see what their competitors are doing. *The Lobby Monitor* publishes information on new registrations, and a league table of firms with the most clients. "If Firm A sees that Firm B has registered to lobby on particular issues for a new client," grins editor Moore, "you can bet that Firm A gets right on the phone to that client's competitor, suggesting they need someone to do the same for them."

The competition isn't limited to rival consulting groups. In the early days, seventy per cent of most lobbying firms' revenues came from retainer fees averaging $7,500 a month. The rest came from projects focused on a single objective, such as a government contract. But the private sector has since come to appreciate that it can't afford to ignore Ottawa. Many firms now have their own government-relations VP, rather than a hired gun, to provide a watching brief on the feds. Lobbying firms are having to market themselves relentlessly. "That's a much tougher way to cover your overhead than schmoozing through a retainer relationship," says Moore. "Today's clients are more demanding."

Another reason lobbyists now like the registry is that it officially acknowledges what has fast become apparent on the social scene – that their profession is a necessary part of life in the capital. Lobbyists throw Ottawa's smartest parties, sponsor the best good-cause galas, boast the biggest expense accounts. Each lunch

hour, lobbyists can be seen scurrying along Sparks Street, the broad pedestrian mall that links the government's office towers with their own, greeting their numerous connections with a cheery, "How ya doin'? What'ya hearin'?" They are affable, ubiquitous – and very, very affluent. Harvie Andre, a Tory minister who has spent twenty years in the trenches of public life, gazed around him in amazement when he arrived for a reception at the opulent Rockcliffe mansion of the Earnscliffe Group's Harry Near. "Why is it better to know Harvie Andre," Andre asked another guest, as he stood at the foot of a Southforks-style staircase, "than to be Harvie Andre?"

The 1989 act comes up for review in the fall. Critics who regard lobbyists as parasites on government are already sharpening their arguments: this time, they want disclosure of fees and contingency billings. That goes *too* far, retort the lobbyists. "Fee disclosure would breach client confidentiality," insists Jon Johnson. "Opposition members just raise the fee issue for partisan purposes."

If we're lucky, discussion of the act will move beyond fee disclosure to the more crucial question of how large a role the likes of Jon Johnson should play in Ottawa. The federally funded agencies cut by the Tories last winter could be counted on to provide the government with reasonably independent advice and information on an array of policy items. Can the private sector really be expected to provide the same service? And how many public functions do we want to hand over to people who aren't publicly accountable? Can taxpayers really trust a lobbyist to balance public and corporate interests in his submissions to clients and government? As Mark Daniels of the Canadian Life and Health Insurance Association says, lobbyists are assuming "the delicate role of trying to define, understand, and accommodate the public interest while credibly pursuing their self-interest." When Johnson orchestrates some business-government deal, where do his loyalties lie – with his Tory chums now looking for re-election, or with the corporation that pays his bills this year, and, if he is successful, maybe next year too? These are the questions that arise as demand for Jon Johnson's services grows.

Interest groups the new power in Ottawa

Val Sears

Special to The Star. *Val Sears is a former political editor of* The Star *who now lives in Ottawa.*

OTTAWA

Party politics is no longer the way to make a difference.

In the hurly-burly world of the '90s, if you really want to grab the national agenda to save the planet, control guns, take back the night for women, build wheelchair ramps or just get a little respect, the way to go is public interest groups.

These narrowly focused collections of like-minded men and women now number in the thousands and, experts say, are gradually taking over the role of political parties in determining policy and creating legislation in Canada.

Besides, as former external affairs minister Flora Mac-Donald says. "It's often more fun to be part of an advocacy group than a political party."

Public interest groups, as opposed to professional lobbyists for business or industry, have become such a vital part of government decision-making that in 1991-92, even with cutbacks, more than 3,000 organizations received a total of $130 million in funding from Ottawa.

And for those such as the environmental group Greenpeace, shunned by the government, the take from private door-to-door canvassing was still impressive: $10.4 million from 300,000 supporters.

They were effective as well. Some notable triumphs:

■ Women's interest groups succeeded in getting federal funding restored for 76 women's centres, a rare instance of cabinet backing down on a fiscal decision.

■ Women's groups again were successful in tightening up gun control legislation and in revising terms of sexual consent with their "no-means-no" lobby.

■ A Burlington mother, Priscilla de Villiers, formed an interest group, Caveat, after the murder of her daughter. Her campaign for tougher parole laws coincided with new federal regulations restricting prisoner release.

■ Aboriginal groups guaranteed themselves recognition in the new Constitution.

■ Greenpeace claims credit for bringing international attention—and domestic controversy—to the killing of seal pups, the snaring of dolphins in fish nets and fur trapping.

■ Dozens of pieces of legislation, from the Communications Act to the Bank Act, were substantially formed as a result of interest group testimony before parliamentary committees.

So influential have interest groups become in an era when polls show institutions such as Parliament are losing credibility, that some believe political parties have become hollow shells.

'SEETHING COUNTENANCES'

"There is a tendency of individual Canadians to move toward affiliating themselves with special-interest groups and to take less interest in political parties because they perceive they can achieve their goals more quickly by other means," says MacDonald, who is now involved with refugee organizations.

"Political parties are diminishing and becoming, more or less, vehicles for choosing leaders and not vehicles for policy discussions."

Political scientist Susan Phillips of Carleton University says flatly: "Interest groups are the most important way to make a difference. Some are starting to bypass government altogether."

Steve Shallhorn, legislative director of Greenpeace, is even more direct: "The parliamentary option is a dead end. Parliament is an outdated institution."

But those parliamentarians directly involved with the process of legislative policy, such as Don Valley North MP Barbara Greene, chairperson of the Health and Welfare Committee, thinks this is far too extreme.

"The interest groups may suggest, but we recommend," she says. "And we have a good many more sources than interest groups, including our own research."

While they have had some victories, citizens' lobbies have been unsuccessful in getting a tough environmental "green plan" from the government. Nor have day-care advocates been able to win government support for more public day-care centres.

Not everyone is enthusiastic about how interest groups perform.

From *The Toronto Star,* April 28, 1992, p. A17. Reprinted with permission from The Toronto Star Syndicate.

Essayist Wib Everett, wrote recently about interest groups in *The Idler:* "Their seething countenances leap from the television on public affairs shows, daytime talkfests and community cable forums. The radio waves are filled with their indignant cries. Newspapers are crammed with heavily edited quotations of their jumbled sentences. Their numbers and their influence grow with each passing day. . . .

"They are the interest groups . . . these thousand points of darkness suck enlightened debate into the vacuum of their single-minded, self-righteous, self-interest . . . They have reduced the functions of government to a scramble to get in step with the endless tattoo of their demands."

Government, nonetheless, finds the rat-a-tat-tat valuable, indeed, essential.

For civil servants, who have neither the time nor enough money for thorough research, interest groups offer expertise that good legislation requires.

"Put in simplest terms," writes political scientist Robert Jackson, "interest groups collect information, predigest it and process it so that coherent demands can be made on political actors."

Carleton's Phillips argues, however, that civil servants, who "naturally tend to be risk-averse, find it much easier to deal individually with polite, professional lobbyists . . . than with 'amateur' sometimes angry, representatives of citizen groups."

A task force on civil service dealings with the public recently recommended the creation of a deputy secretary of consultation in the Privy Council Office to deal with input from interest groups.

Backbenchers, as well, crave the attention of advocacy groups that offer them valuable insights into the possible reaction of their constituents to certain political behavior. A recent survey shows that 75 per cent of MPs of all parties had frequent or occasional contact with interest groups.

More controversial is the favorite weapon of the minority and low-income interest groups: the demonstration on Parliament Hill.

The crowd of placard-waving enthusiasts, spurred on by chants ("What do we want? . . . When do we want it? Now.") and bullhorn blasts, makes good television but its effectiveness, argues Jackson, is doubtful.

"On the whole, groups which use this strategy are likely to be ignored, discredited or placated with purely symbolic action," he says.

But direct action, whether by demonstration or occupation of government offices, does work, says Greenpeace's Shallhorn. "It raises the profile and gets media attention."

Women's groups' "Weiner Roasts" of Secretary of State Gerry Weiner and the occupation of Secretary of State offices in St. John's and Ottawa are credited with getting the government to restore grants to women's organizations.

But there are those who say that established interest groups are run by an elite.

Christie Jefferson of the Women's Legal Education and Action Foundation (LEAF) acknowledges the problem.

LEAF, a charitable organization that received government funding to assist in promoting legislation on women's issues, tries to deal with this by reaching out to lower-income and immigrant groups with education programs.

But an impression remains that some women's groups are more concerned with the pinched legal secretary than the sexually harassed single immigrant mother working in a garment factory.

SELECTIVE CUTS

The Conservative government has become more dependent on interest group input, particularly in the committee stage of legislation.

The favorites, of course, were industry or business representatives anxious to guard or expand their turf.

At the same time the Conservatives don't want opponents too well-armed. As one Tory backbencher said, "Why give them the bullets to shoot us with?"

So funding cuts to interest groups have been more and more selective.

Money has shrunk for aboriginal and women's groups, but has been rising for official-language minority associations and multicultural groups.

In 1991–92, the $28.4 million distributed by 337 language groups was almost three times greater than the amount provided to women's groups and eight times as much as that given to organizations for the disabled.

"Support for all sorts of advocacy groups representing women, the disabled, visible minorities, etc., is being dismantled without any public debate," says LEAF's Jefferson.

Premiers design new Senate

Deal being forged for a whole new way for Parliament to work

Susan Delacourt

Parliamentary Bureau

OTTAWA—A new Senate has finally been designed by Canada's first ministers.

It is billed as a blend of two different ideas of Canada—one in which all provinces are equal and one which respects the country's delicate balance between French and English.

Moreover, it paves the way for a whole new way for Parliament to work in Canada. A bigger House of Commons will be expanded by 42 more MPs from Quebec, Ontario, British Columbia and Alberta, and Quebec gets a guarantee of 25 per cent representation in the House. The new Senate will be filled with 62 senators, six from each province and one each from the two territories. When the House and this new Senate clash on a bill, they will get together to solve their disputes in a joint vote.

Achieving this agreement required an arduous, long session of political arithmetic. And it is only a provisional part of the entire national-unity deal that is far from finished or certain. The meeting continues today and the Senate deal still has to stand up against some tough bargaining over economic and power arrangements, and the question of native self-government.

"It's a change to a central institution of Parliament, and it requires reflection and prudence," a cautious Prime Minister Brian Mulroney told reporters as he announced the provisional Senate deal.

"We'll have to see tomorrow if we're able to transform an interim agreement into a permanent agreement."

But he also said the deal on the Senate is the key piece in the national-unity puzzle. It may be only part of the deal, but it's a cornerstone, he said.

"I've long believed that unless and until we were able to resolve the matter of the Senate . . . then we couldn't move on very well or very successfully to other questions. That has been done, on a provisional basis."

Premiers such as Alberta's Donald Getty and Newfoundland's Clyde Wells declared that a bridge had indeed been built between the ideas of equality of the provinces and the two languages.

It meant tempering the idea of pure equality by bowing to Quebec's interests, Mr. Wells said. "In the end, this was a compromise that we had to make. . . . That principle had to be moderated if we were to give effect to the social, historical and cultural fact in Canada."

The two big moderating factors are the guaranteed 25 per cent for Quebec and the deal to give francophone senators special additional clout over language and culture bills.

Mr. Getty also is convinced that this deal is a successful mix of the two Canadas.

"I don't think we have conferred special status," the Alberta Premier said, using the two words "special status" that proved to be so provocative in the West during the Meech Lake years. He is convinced that this deal

can be sold as a win for Alberta and a win for Quebec.

Quebec Premier Robert Bourassa said he would be telling his province—where equality of provinces is a hard sell—that he had carefully managed to dilute that principle in this deal.

"Those who were insisting to have an equal Senate will say clearly that there are elements in that agreement which are not equal," Mr. Bourassa said.

Quebec has won an important goal with a guarantee of 25 per cent of the Commons seats, he said.

The province also won the right to send its senators to this Senate through a vote from the National Assembly, not from the Quebec people. In this way, Mr. Bourassa can argue that there may be fewer senators, but they are a direct extension of the power centre in Quebec City.

Political peril and public opinion were also on the mind of Ontario Premier Bob Rae, who believes that he, too, can portray this as a gain for Canada's biggest province.

In an impassioned address, he said Ontario and everyone had to act for the sake of Canada as a whole. "People say why did you go along with the principle of the equal Senate, with respect to Western Canada? My answer is, what the hell is the point of building a country by standing on somebody else's neck, and I've won my principle at your expense."

And Mr. Rae took pains to point out why it was so important to bow to the idea of Quebec's special interest as the French province in this new Senate,

From *The Globe and Mail*, August 20, 1992, pp. A1, A4. Reprinted by permission.

3. THE PARLIAMENTARY SYSTEM

House of Commons

Province	Number of seats		% of total	
	Proposed	Current	Proposed	Current
Quebec	93	75	27.6	25.4
Ontario	117	99	34.7	33.6
Alberta	28	26	8.3	8.8
British Columbia	36	32	10.7	10.8
Saskatchewan	14	14	4.2	4.7
Manitoba	14	14	4.2	4.7
Nova Scotia	11	11	3.3	3.7
New Brunswick	10	10	3.0	3.4
PEI	4	4	1.2	1.4
Newfoundland	7	7	2.1	2.4
Yukon	1	1	0.3	0.3
NWT	2	2	0.6	0.7
TOTAL	337	295	100	100

Parliament (House plus Senate)

Province	Number of seats		% of total	
	Proposed	Current	Proposed	Current
Quebec	99	99	24.8	24.8
Ontario	123	123	30.8	30.8
Alberta	34	32	8.5	8.0
British Columbia	42	38	10.5	9.5
Saskatchewan	20	20	5.0	5.0
Manitoba	20	20	5.0	5.0
Nova Scotia	17	21	4.3	5.3
New Brunswick	16	20	4.0	5.0
PEI	10	8	2.5	2.0
Newfoundland	13	13	3.3	3.3
Yukon	2	2	0.5	0.5
NWT	3	3	0.8	0.8
TOTAL	399	399	100	100

Senate

Province	Number of seats		% of total	
	Proposed	Current	Proposed	Current
Quebec	6	24	9.7	23.1
Ontario	6	24	9.7	23.1
Alberta	6	6	9.7	5.8
British Columbia	6	6	9.7	5.8
Saskatchewan	6	6	9.7	5.8
Manitoba	6	6	9.7	5.8
Nova Scotia	6	10	9.7	9.6
New Brunswick	6	10	9.7	9.6
PEI	6	4	9.7	3.8
Newfoundland	6	6	9.7	5.8
Yukon	1	1	1.6	1.0
NWT	1	1	1.6	1.0
TOTAL	62	104	100	100

Premiers achieve breakthrough on proposd changes to Parliament

Population per seat in House and Parliament

	Population	% of population	Population per seat in House of Commons		Population per seat in Parliament	
			Proposed	Current	Proposed	Current
Quebec	6,912,300	25.3	74,326	92,164	69,821	69,821
Ontario	10,062,000	36.8	86,000	101,636	81,805	81,805
Alberta	2,558,200	9.4	91,364	98,392	75,241	79,944
British Columbia	3,290,500	12.0	91,403	102,828	78,345	86,592
Saskatchewan	992,900	3.6	70,921	70,921	49,645	49,645
Manitoba	1,095,000	4.0	78,214	78,214	54,750	54,750
Nova Scotia	906,800	3.3	82,436	82,436	53,341	43,181
New Brunswick	727,700	2.7	72,770	72,770	45,481	36,385
PEI	130,100	0.5	32,525	32,525	13,010	16,263
Newfoundland	575,100	2.1	82,157	82,157	44,238	44,238
Yukon	27,600	0.1	27,600	27,600	13,800	13,800
NWT	55,900	0.2	27,950	27,950	18,633	18,633
TOTAL	27,334,100	100				

DIANA CLIFFORD AND BERNARD BENNELL/The Globe and Mail

even as Canada now acknowledges the idea of equality of the provinces.

"What has been a unique feature of Canadian life has been the partnership between French and English," he said. "It's something that's distinct not only about Quebec, it's something that's distinct about Canada."

The new Senate is not exactly the equal, elected and effective Senate that was a cause for the West and for New-foundland. It is equal, but Quebec has its own kind of influence. It is elected, but "election" will be a loose term in the federal law that sets up this body. Senators will be elected by the people or by the legislatures. And it is only effective in a limited way.

Only one kind of bill can be absolutely killed by this Senate—natural resources legislation. Mr. Mulroney called this the "NEP-proof" Senate.

He was saying that Alberta would be able to block a future National Energy Program, such as the one introduced by the former Liberal government in the 1980s—the same program that galvanized the crusade for a Triple-E Senate.

For the rest of the legislation that comes before Parliament, this Senate can only object, not obliterate. If more than half of the senators vote against this bill, it triggers a brand-new event in Canadian political culture—the joint sitting of the Commons and equal Senate. Together, these two houses solve their differences through a combined vote.

Every premier knows, though, that this new Senate will not be in place by 1997 or 1998 as planned if they do not achieve the whole national-unity deal. As Saskatchewan Premier Roy Romanow said last night, "The deal is the whole deal."

The Senate was the biggest problem to solve at this first ministers gathering, but it was not the only thorny issue.

Native self-government is an entirely separate controversy, with its own political land mines and fights among the provinces. Now, the attention turns to this debate.

While the spotlight was on the Senate feud on Tuesday night, a small army of officials worked until late into the night merely to list all the problems that lie within the web of complicated arrangements surrounding native self-government.

Four separate sets of problems with self-government have been laid at the first ministers' feet. They include:
• How self-government will be defined and how it will be enforced in the courts;
• How self-government could be used in relation to land rights in Canada. This is the so-called "territorial integrity" issue;
• How the right of self-government is exercised on and off native people's land base;
• How the "third order of government" for aboriginal people will actually work with other governments.

The first ministers were expected to get into some detailed wrangling to solve these problems. Some debates may be settled by simply adding a word here and there to the July 7 agreement. Others revolve around more philosophical debates.

Newfoundland, for instance, has insisted that the financing of aboriginal governments be chiefly the responsibility of the federal government. But this is slightly at odds with the July 7 accord that asks all levels of government—federal, provincial and aboriginal—to work out a shared agreement to pay for self-government.

In addition, the Assembly of First Nations is still looking for guarantees that native rights inside Quebec will not be harmed by the recognition in the Constitution of that province as a distinct society.

None of these problems are likely to be resolved quickly or easily, and the discussion could force the first ministers to continue their meetings beyond today.

Participation and Elections

The last federal general election in Canada returned a Progressive Conservative majority government. The main issue in the election was free trade with the United States. The next federal election will likely center on whether Mexico should be included in the free trade zone of North America.

Since the last election, the North American economy has fallen deeply into recession. U.S. President Bush was likely the first casualty of that recession when he was defeated in the November 1992 elections. It may be that Brian Mulroney's government may also fall. The first unit article notes that in Canada "there is a fury in the land against the prime minister."

Much of the blame for the economic recession is laid at the door of the Free Trade Agreement (FTA). Yet, it is misleading to personalize politics. A graph shows that the

popularity rating of all recent Canadian prime ministers "forms a consistent pattern—downhill all the way." Do Canadians place an excessive faith in their leaders, only to face excessive disappointment later? It may be a paradox that "prime ministers who head majority governments may wield too much power for their own or the country's good." It can be argued that a "Canadian prime minister who commands a majority in the House of Commons . . . exercises more power, vis-à-vis the legislature, than other democratically elected leaders." The heavy price to be paid for this power is that the prime minister will be blamed when things go wrong. And, in 1992, the health of the economy was still wrong.

Some of the excessive power of the Canadian prime minister over a party and parliamentary caucus may come from the fact that there are virtually no controls over the process by which party leaders are selected. The "present Canadian practice allows contributors to give unlimited amounts to leadership candidates with no requirement that the contributions ever be disclosed to the public."

The Lortie Royal Commission on Electoral Reform and Party Financing made numerous recommendations that would attempt to control and limit the financing of leadership races. Bill Cross's paper examines some of the key recommendations, and he compares a few of them in light of the U.S. experience. Cross favours adopting the U.S. practice of matching contributions, and presents two case studies: the 1990 race to succeed John Turner as leader of the Liberal Party of Canada, and the 1989 New Democratic Party's replacement of Ed Broadbent. He concludes that "party leadership campaigns are too consequential a part of Canadian politics to continue operating completely outside of the purview of campaign financing laws."

Even if a party has substantial funds, it may have severe difficulty in getting its message across to the voters, because the Canada Elections Act allocates each party's media exposure on the basis of the number of seats it had won in the previous election. Broadcasters must make available 390 minutes of prime time advertis-

ing space that parties can buy. This grossly distorts the television broadcasting among the parties.

Party leaders control the party's advertising budgets and the content of the message that goes out. They also can intervene in the candidate selection process at the grass-roots of the party, that is, at the constituency/riding level. This power to veto local selection of party candidates was granted to the Liberal party leader only recently, and Jean Chretien's intervention in some half-dozen ridings caused an uproar in these ridings. William Walker describes how this happened in several Ontario ridings.

The Lortie Commission avoided the issue of constituency autonomy in its recommendations, and it did not address another perennial of Canadian electoral politics—the single-member plurality or "first-past-the-post" system. The *Globe and Mail* examines the SMP system in "A Better Way to Count the Votes," and it suggests some alternatives.

Another electoral device is receiving widespread enthusiasm, although the defeat of the Charlottetown Agreement provides a second sober thought. David Pond reviews the history of referenda and plebiscites in Canada, the United States, and Switzerland, and he draws some tentative conclusions about their use. The next article asks whether referendum results should be legally and morally binding. This unit ends with a detailed discussion of 17 basic differences between Canadian and U.S. election systems.

Looking Ahead: Challenge Questions

Can the Progressive Conservative Party of Canada win the next federal election?

How can one create a more responsive government? Is the problem one of leadership or too-rigid party discipline?

Is the Canadian prime minister more powerful than the president of the United States?

How and why should the financing of leadership campaigns be reformed?

Is the newfound enthusiasm for direct democracy wise?

Anger at the System Sources of Discontent

Anger at the system in Canada seems not to be a function of who is in power at any one time. It instead appears to be a deep-rooted concern on the part of ordinary Canadians towards the way they are governed. The closed door meetings of executive federalism are no longer sufficient for the most educated and politically aware Canadians ever: they want truly responsive government.

Peter Dobell
and Byron Berry

While opinions differ as to whether Canadians are as angry as they were during the turbulent interwar period, no one contests that political discontent is now widespread in Canada. Our survey of polling results is conclusive. Nor does anyone doubt that it is focused to an extraordinary degree on the Prime Minister. Keith Spicer's eloquent foreword to the *Citizens' Forum*, "there is a fury in the land against the prime minister," conveys it all.

This personalization of our political problems is misleading. At the simplest level, it implies that Canada's difficulties can be resolved by changing the leader and the government he heads. In the pages that follow we intend to analyze several sources of discontent, and then suggest some changes in the way the political system functions that could alleviate the situation.

The State of the Nation

A prime minister's public image is to a substantial degree hostage to the state of the nation's economy and to the mood of the country. Close to 20 years ago, it was possible to have as an election slogan: "The land is strong." In those days the economy was buoyant, commodity exports were surging, inflation was not yet rampant, and

the confidence of Canadians in the country's future was still untroubled. None of these conditions prevails today. Not surprisingly, the changed situation and soured public mood impact on the government's popularity.

To a very substantial degree, the root of today's political problems is financial. In 1983-84, the annual deficit of the federal government amounted to $33 billion. With debt service costs of $18 billion, $15 billion was available to supplement government revenues. For every dollar of revenue collected, this meant that government was spending $1.23 on delivering programs. By 1991-92, debt servicing costs actually exceeded the deficit by $13 billion, so that tax revenue has been diverted to repay the debt. As a result, for every dollar of tax paid, program expenditure on behalf of Canadians now amounts to only 90 cents. In eight years the Canadian public has suffered a loss in government services of 36 per cent relative to the taxes they pay. Provincial governments are facing similar restraints.

A change of this magnitude inevitably causes substantial difficulties for governments. Previously they could, in effect, buy their way out of political problems by establishing new programs without having to

touch established services. Gone are those days. Now, in the face of this huge decline in available revenues, governments have had to start cutting existing programs.

To find funds needed to rescue grain farmers or to finance welfare payments, governments in Canada have had to claw back old-age pensions, to close post offices and land registry offices and to legislate wage freezes. No wonder there is discontent in the land and governments are in trouble. For an indefinite period, this is a situation that all governments, federal, provincial and municipal, will confront. It may get worse. This underlines the need to seek ways to open up the process of consultation. Such an approach will not eliminate distress when programs are cut back, but if the public feels that their views are being taken into account, experience confirms that there will be a greater acceptance of the decisions that a government takes.

Pursuing Unpopular Policies

A truly remarkable feature of the current political scene in Canada is the determination that Prime Minister Mulroney and the Conservative government have shown in persisting with highly controversial and

From *Parliamentary Government*, Vol. 11, No. 1, January 1992, pp. 12-17. Copyright © 1992 by Parliamentary Centre for Foreign Affairs and Foreign Trade. Reprinted by permission.

even extremely unpopular policies in spite of their standing in the polls. As has been noted earlier, a perceived quality of the Canadian system of government has been the strong leadership it makes possible. The Mulroney government has exploited that potential to the fullest. But this capacity to drive legislation through the system has been achieved at a substantial cost in terms of political discontent.

Prime Minister Trudeau was often criticized for his strong, even autocratic leadership. The comment is just, but it refers primarily to his style of leadership. When it came to legislation, the several governments he headed were surprisingly cautious. An exception often cited was the National Energy Policy. True, in western Canada it was an anathema, but not so in Ontario, Quebec and the Atlantic provinces, all of which benefited from lower oil prices. So while the NEP generated anger in western Canada directed equally at Trudeau personally, the Liberal government and at Ottawa as the symbol of federal power, the effect in the rest of Canada was probably to increase support for the government.

By contrast, the two Mulroney governments have pressed policies through Parliament with a determination that is awesome, in the face of strong and popular country-wide opposition. The task was substantially complicated in each instance by the resistance mounted by the Liberal majority within the Senate. But rather than compromising, which might have been unavoidable had there been an elected Senate, the government held on like a pit bull terrier. On the three most controversial policies, ultimately they got their way.

The first of these was free trade with the United States. The legislative instrument that provoked the parliamentary battle was the need to pass enabling legislation to put the Free Trade Agreement into effect. In this instance, amendments by Parliament were out of the question once the Agreement—actually a treaty—had been negotiated with the United States. Congress and Parliament had to work from identical texts. With time running out on the term of the first Mulroney government, the

Liberal majority in the Senate stood pat, neither approving nor rejecting the enabling legislation. Ultimately, the government called an election on the issue and won, whereupon the Senate quickly passed the necessary bill. While the policy was and remains controversial, the election legitimized the government's action.

The Meech Lake debacle had a different outcome. The Accord actually involved numerous compromises. The deal was cut, however, behind closed doors, so that the public could not participate in the give and take.

The public's impression, once the legislation was introduced into Parliament, was of relentless movement toward its passage. In practice the hearing process within the House of Commons was extensive. In the confrontational atmosphere of the House, however, there was no room for give and take. Even so, on a number of points of detail, including the rate of the tax, advice from the Conservative members of the Finance Committee resulted in modifications to the legislation. Of this the public had no awareness.

The paradox illustrated by Mr. Pearson's experience is that Canadian prime ministers who head majority governments may wield too much power for their own or the country's good.

In no way did they have a chance to feel a part of the process. What is more important is that the Accord was flawed: it either failed to address some matters of public concern or sections had been drafted in ways that raised anxiety about their possible implications. Unfortunately, once the deal was struck, the government insisted that it was "a seamless web" that could not be touched. In retrospect, a process that provided for public responses and allowed for mutually agreed amendments might have saved the Accord. As it was, it reinforced the image of unresponsive governments.

With revenues stagnant and increased competition for a piece of an economic pie that is no longer growing, governments have looked for new remedies. For Canada's current ailments the present government has prescribed strong medicine—the GST and free trade with the United States. No one likes strong medicine, especially when it has serious side effects. It is not surprising that both the diagnosis and the remedies prescribed have been challenged.

Introducing the GST has generated substantial political resistance. Although part of the Conservative platform in the 1988 election, the election focused on free trade. Besides, Canadians do not normally pay much attention to party platforms.

The political process was complicated by the resistance of Liberal Senators, who were still in a majority in the Upper House. The decision to proceed to appoint eight additional Senators so as to achieve a government majority and then to modify the rules of procedure in order to prevent a filibuster provided dramatic television material. In the process, however, it reinforced the public's impression both of a government ready to override all opposition, and of the need for Senate reform.

In fact, each of these controversial policies was drawn up following extensive consultation. In this process, all kinds of battles were fought and many reasonable compromises reached. From the public's perspective, however, these battles were fought and the compromises reached in secret—within the bureaucracy, within cabinet, in caucus or, in the case of Meech, in closed federal-provincial meetings.

This is a major deficiency of the Canadian political system. It permits a closed approach to policy-making and implementation. In other democracies, where power is not as concentrated as it is in Canada, compromises more often than not are confirmed in public. Confrontation between conflicting views is resolved in votes in which different combinations of legislators form part of fluctuating majorities. From the public perspective, the system is seen to be responsive and responsibility for each decision is shared between the head of government and many other actors.

Prime Ministers on Toboggan Slides

The widespread public anger against Prime Minister Mulroney is palpable. Polling results only confirm the obvious. The Prime Minister has at this stage in his second mandate the lowest approval rating—15 per cent—since polling began.

With the passage of time, there is a tendency to forget that former Prime Minister Trudeau experienced a decline in popularity that was no less precipitous. It had upturns, such as during the FLQ crisis of 1970, but the overall direction was steadily downward. Although his personal popularity never reached the same murky depths as Mulroney's, the drop was just as dramatic because Trudeau began his first term of office with a level of popularity that was without precedent. Mr. Trudeau's personality attracted support of a kind that Mr. Mulroney has never been able to generate.

Plotted on a graph, the popularity rating over time of Canadian political leaders forms a consistent pattern—downhill all the way. In *Absent Mandate*, published in 1991, four academic researchers documented the popularity profile during the past 20 years, measured from election to election. The striking fact is that all Canadian leaders save Broadbent have steadily lost popularity. Broadbent was exceptional in that he peaked several years after being elected NDP leader, but the drop in his popularity was ultimately decisive (see figure).

Compared to other peoples, Canadians seem to place excessive faith in new leaders. Disappointment inevitably follows when they fail to achieve the unreasonably high expectations.

In this cycle the media play a substantial part. From the moment of the political convention at which a party chooses a leader, and particularly at election time, the media and party organizers—each for their own reasons—play up the personality of the leaders. With the arrival of television, this emphasis on the leader has been further exaggerated. Al-

Figure

Thermometer Scale Readings of Party Leaders, 1968-1988

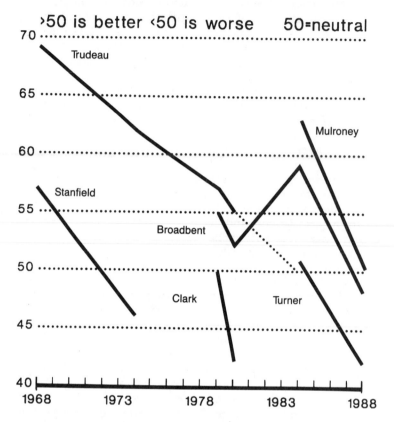

›50 is better ‹50 is worse   50=neutral

source: *Absent Mandate*. It should be noted that Pierre Trudeau was not PM when the poll was taken in 1984.

though politics is pre-eminently a team sport, the modern media focus most of their attention on the captain.

Most Canadians are taught in school that the merit of our system of responsible government is that it concentrates power in the hands of the prime minister, thereby permitting strong government—which Canada needs. This perception is accurate. But there is a price: the prime minister is saddled with responsibility for all the important decisions of government. And, since every decision involves compromises in which various interest groups are adversely affected, the prime minister attracts the anger of the losers. The process is cumulative and ultimately fatal.

The experience of Prime Minister Pearson forms an interesting contrast with those of Mr. Trudeau and

Mr. Mulroney. In neither of his governments did he gain a majority, so that he never had the power to drive legislation through Parliament. On controversial questions, such as the creation of the Canadian flag, he was forced to undertake exhaustive public consultations. In Parliament itself, he had to craft legislation in order to attract enough support from one of the opposition partners to get a majority. He also had the benefit of a buoyant economy, sufficient to finance popular new social programs. Although Mr. Pearson never achieved the levels of popularity of his two major successors, neither did he experience the same precipitous decline. In the public's eye, he was not seen as a strong leader, but he was responsive.

The paradox illustrated by Mr.

Pearson's experience is that Canadian prime ministers who head majority governments may wield too much power for their own or the country's good. Because the capacity of such governments to move legislation through Parliament is great, they are not obliged to take the case to the people or to accommodate pressure for amendments. Although their legislation will be passed, the public may feel ignored and even angry. One of the features of minority government that the Canadian electorate seems to like is that it forces governments to consult and to make their compromises publicly.

Comparisons with the way other political systems operate clarifies the point. Canadians follow developments in the United States closely and they think of the American President as being uniquely powerful. But his independent power within the federal government is substantially circumscribed. While a president has the standing that comes from being the directly elected head of the executive branch, he must constantly enter into public battle with the Congress. This forces him, on major matters, to appeal over the head of Congress to the American people. Ultimately the approval of each piece of legislation results from a series of compromises that are publicly debated and concluded with a vote that is "free." In terms of public image, what matters is that responsibility for each outcome is spread among a large number of actors. And since each major decision involves a different coalition, responsibility is not only shared but is constantly changing.

The changing fortunes of President Mitterand of France throw light on the issue from a different angle. Under the Fifth Republic, power is concentrated in the hands of the President: he is directly elected for a seven-year term and he names and can dismiss the prime minister. During most of President Mitterand's first term, his Socialist Party had a majority in the National Assembly. Coincidentally his approval rating declined. The 1986 elections produced a majority coalition of Gaullists, forcing the President to nominate a Gaullist prime minister and to share power with him. It is interesting to note that during this period President

Mitterand's popularity increased again. He was seen as being willing to share power and, hence, escaped being made solely responsible for all decisions. Along with the fact that the other candidates lacked popular appeal, this was sufficient to bring Mitterand a second term in the presidential election of 1988.

The conclusion to which these comparisons point is that the public prefers a political process that is transparent. They place their trust more readily in leaders who take their case into the public forum and who are willing to modify their policies in response to popular concerns.

This process will occur naturally if power is diffused; in the Canadian context this happens naturally during minority governments. But when a prime minister has a majority of seats in the House of Commons, a government that has made up its mind what it wants to do is in a position to press ahead without compromise. Governments sometimes back off, as in 1985 on de-indexing old-age pensions, when they have badly assessed the public mood, but this has not been characteristic behaviour.

The personality, style and ability of Canadian political leaders, equally at the federal and at the provincial levels, affect the public's perception of them and of the achievements of their governments. This is self-evident. To a substantial extent, however, the public image of Canadian political leaders may suffer if they head majority governments because the political system allows them to push their legislation through the legislatures regardless of the criticism. From the public's perspective, such behaviour confirms the impression that governments rarely listen to them.

This conclusion points to a dilemma. While the public is affronted by what it regards as excessive party

discipline, it also looks to political parties to recruit and develop leaders, to help focus attention on policy choices, and to integrate different elements in society. From the party perspective, a party that wins an election in which it has forthrightly announced its commitment to introduce a certain program, can hardly be faulted for proceeding to do what it said it would do. That having been said, a government must not forget that people have many reasons for casting their vote and the present electoral system can return governments with substantial majorities, which receive the support of only a minority of those who vote. The message that this seemingly contradictory behaviour conveys is that the public appreciate the contribution that political parties can make, but it expects a party that forms a government to consult the public extensively, even when carrying out its mandate.

Comparing Canadian Prime Ministers to Other Leaders

Since Canadian prime ministers share power with provincial premiers, they are constrained in a way that the heads of unitary states are not. However, within the federal government, a Canadian prime minister who commands a majority in the House of Commons—and this is the appropriate verb—exercises more power vis-à-vis the legislature than other democratically elected leaders. Of course, under a minority government a totally different situation prevails, requiring a very different style of leadership. The same concentration of power applies equally at the provincial level.

Margaret Thatcher was a dominant figure in British politics. Yet a number of practices and conventions of the British Parliament that constrained her power do not exist in Canada. What is most notable is that Mrs. Thatcher and her predecessor,

> *Canadian opposition leaders have usurped the daily question period, thereby making it almost impossible for backbench members to use this instrument to pursue important regional and local issues.*

4. PARTICIPATION AND ELECTIONS

Ted Heath, were both driven from the Conservative party leadership in a matter of weeks by their own party supporters in the British House of Commons. Their fate constrains the independent exercise of power by her successors. Electing party leaders in a convention, as we do in Canada, gives them an independent base and renders them independent of their party supporters in the House of Commons.

British political parties also tolerate a limited amount of cross-voting in the House and the defeat of a piece of ordinary legislation is not normally regarded by the opposition as a defeat of the government. Nor do party caucuses as we know them in Canada meet to adopt a party position. Instead, the party platform serves as a unifying force and whips keep tabs on the views of party members in Parliament. Finally, a substantial number of candidates occupy "safe" seats, making them relatively impervious to party control.

Nor does the British Parliament provide for the automatic substitution of members of standing committees, a Canadian practice that effectively places control over the work of committees in the hands of party leaders. Chairmen of British committees, once elected, normally continue in office for some time and acquire some personal authority. The membership of committees is relatively stable, even from parliament to parliament. In these ways, committees in the British parliament develop an independent authority that Canadian committees lack—even after the reforms of 1985. Finally, Canadian opposition leaders have usurped the daily question period, thereby making it almost impossible for backbench members to use this instrument to pursue important regional and local issues. In the British House, backbenchers of all parties have a recognized place in question time.

Taken together these several differences in the way the British House of Commons functions constrain the power of the prime minister and of the leaders of the opposition parties. With backbenchers of all parties showing greater independence, British voters seem more satisfied than their Canadian counterparts that their MPs are responsive.

Only two other advanced democracies—Australia and New Zealand—adopted the British parliamentary system in its entirety. They too have developed practices, unknown in Canada, that limit the power of their political leaders. In both countries the sitting Members of the Labour Party elect the members of the Cabinet. Although the prime minister allocates the portfolios, his power relative to his colleagues in Cabinet is constrained by the fact of their election by caucus. Furthermore, the party caucuses can and do replace their leaders if the Members feel that they are exercising too much power. The rejection of the Australian Prime Minister, Bob Hawke, in the middle of a parliamentary term, is only the most recent manifestation of this practice.

New Zealand has for over a hundred years held elections to the House of Commons every three years on a fixed term, thereby removing from the prime minister the substantial disciplinary power that comes with the right to call an election. In spite of this constraint on the prime minister's power relative to his supporters in the House, the New Zealand Parliament, during the 1980s, introduced a number of reforms that enhanced the role of backbenchers. Much of the impetus for these changes came from a Labour Party minister, Geoffrey Palmer, who became prime minister briefly in 1989. In a book entitled *Unbridled Power?* published in 1979, he wrote of the prospects for reducing executive power.

Under the domination of a two party system where party discipline is exceedingly strict as it has been in New Zealand since 1935, this possibility is remote and theoretical. And that fact has robbed Parliament of far too much power and a great amount of its prestige.

The concentration of power in the hands of a Canadian prime minister who leads a majority government is understandable. Canada is not an easy country to govern. The sheer size, the cultural and linguistic differences among regions, and the varied regional economic interests create conflicts that cause huge problems for any government, even at the best

of times. The growth during the second half of the century of the power of government to intervene in the life of the country has increased public expectations—and the likelihood of disappointment. Higher education and improved communications have multiplied the numbers of people who expect to participate in the larger political process.

The sense of community that used to prevail and which facilitated political communication seems also to have diminished, as single-interest politics has taken hold. The single-minded pursuit of a multitude of goals by organizations committed to a specific cause has contributed to what Sheldon Wolin has called "the chopping up of political man". In the process, they have vastly complicated the taks of governing.

Looked at from this perspective, it is hardly surprising that Canadian leaders have used whatever powers were at hand. But there is a heavy price that comes with this power, a price paid equally by the prime minister and by the country. The more power a leader exercises, the more he will be blamed when things go wrong. The risk is especially great in Canada. The size of the country and the diversity of interests ensure that rarely does any action by government produce general satisfaction. Even the relative winners may be unhappy at what they fail to get. Given the prime minister's pre-eminence, he is normally seen as responsible for whatever decisions are reached. With no one sharing power, the prime minister becomes the lightning rod for all political dissatisfaction.

The style of leadership naturally affects the public image and can hasten or retard the decline in public support for Canadian prime ministers. But the primary cause is the system, because it allows the prime minister and the cabinet, once they have composed their differences, to get their way in Parliament, often without further compromise. Even where public resistance is stronger than anticipated, the necessary adjustments are generally worked out privately. With the whole process of accommodation worked out largely behind the scenes, it is no wonder that the public regard government as being unresponsive.

Financing Leadership Campaigns in Canada

In recognition of campaign financing's potential impact on the political process, Canadian governments have enacted campaign finance legislation. From the 1874 Dominion Elections Act various regulations have, among other things, required disclosure of campaign receipts and expenditures, imposed spending limitations on parties and candidates, and provided public funds for the financing of campaigns. One domain of electoral politics has, however, consistently remained outside the jurisdiction of these regulatory schemes. The financing of federal party leadership campaigns has never been regulated by parliament. In February 1992 the Royal Commission on Electoral Reform (Lortie Commission) included in its findings a recommendation that leadership campaign financing be included in any renewed effort at campaign finance legislation. The purpose of this paper is to outline these recommendations and to consider the impact they would have had on the two most recent federal leadership campaigns.

Bill Cross

Bill Cross worked previously as legal counsel to the Democratic National Committee in Washington D.C. He is presently doing graduate work at the University of Western Ontario. This is a revised version of a paper presented to the Canadian Political Science Association Meetings in Charlottetown, Prince Edward Island on May 31.

There appears no sufficient justification for excluding party leadership races from the regulatory scheme governing campaign financing in Canada. Leadership races are one of the most consequential components of Canadian politics. The rationale that resulted in Canada regulating the financing of political parties and general election candidates applies even more conclusively to leadership races. Because Canada practices a parliamentary system of government, legislative power is concentrated in the hands of the Prime Minister and his cabinet. Those wishing to influence Canadian public policy will center their efforts around these elected leaders. The present Canadian practice allows contributors to give unlimited amounts to leadership candidates with no requirement that the contributions ever be disclosed to the public. It is the relationship between elected leaders and moneyed interests that any system of campaign finance rules must

monitor and regulate. The Lortie Commission made the following recommendations: Leadership candidates be required to provide full disclosure of financial activities, including size and source of contributions of $250 or more; Spending limits of no more than 15% of the election expenses permitted the party under the *Canada Elections Act* for the most recent federal general election (currently $1,890,000 for the three major parties). This spending limit is to be effective as of the time the party chooses the date for election of the leader; A preliminary financial report be required from leadership candidates on the day preceding the election of the leader. A final report to be due within three months of selection of the leader; and contributions to leadership candidates be eligible for inclusion in the tax credit system available to parties.

Given that leadership campaign financing should be regulated, the first question raised is whether candidates should be required to disclose the sources and amounts

From *Canadian Parliamentary Review*, Summer 1992, pp. 16-23. Reprinted by permission.

87

of their contributions. Disclosure of campaign contributions is the most fundamental tenet of any effective system of campaign finance regulation. Disclosure serves three principle objectives:

- Identification of contribution sources allows voters to know who their candidates have chosen to ally themselves with. Delegates to a leadership convention have a right to know who has bankrolled the various candidates' campaigns. This is important information as it likely foretells what constituent groups will have easy access to the candidate should he become leader. Equally, voters in a general election have a right to know who contributed to the party leaders' leadership campaigns.

- Disclosure requirements provide the political system with protection from those candidates and donors who may be tempted to make a quid pro quo deal during a campaign. A tempted leadership candidate will likely think twice before accepting a contribution with legislative strings attached if he must publicly disclose the contribution.

- Disclosure requirements make possible the enforcement of other restrictions and prohibitions. For instance, if the scheme of leadership finance regulation includes limits on the amounts one may contribute, disclosure of all contributions and their amounts is necessary to detect any violations.

The Lortie Commission recommended that leadership candidates be required to disclose all contributions of $250.00 or more. The Commission further suggested that candidates be required to file preliminary reports the day before leadership voting and that final reports be due no more than three months following the voting.

For the reasons listed above leadership candidates should be required to disclose their sources and amounts of contributions. In order for disclosure requirements to be effective they must encompass certain provisions. The first question is what must be disclosed. The current Canadian practice of requiring parties and general election candidates to report all receipts in excess of $100 should be applied to leadership races. There is no magic to the $100 mark, but some minimal threshold amount should be set above which all contributions are disclosed. Given the change in the value of the dollar since the inception of the $100 mark in 1974, the Lortie Commission's suggestion of $250 seems reasonable. The disclosure requirements, however, must be broadened to include more than merely the contributor's name and contribution amount. The information presently disclosed by parties does not allow for certain identification of contributors. Disclosed information should include a contributors's home city, province, and occupation. This information will allow interested parties to accurately identify contributors. The

Commission does recommend a broadening of the disclosed information to allow for more accurate donor identification. Some argue that such disclosure will put contributors at risk of receiving unwanted solicitations from other sources. This concern is easily addressed by including a provision in the regulations that the information disclosed cannot be used for solicitation purposes of any sort.

The second question concerning disclosure requirements is when such information should be required. The current practice in Canada, for parties and general election candidates, is to require such information after the election. The United States system of campaign finance provides a helpful example in this area. The U.S. law requires periodic reports right up to the week before the election. This system of regular pre-election reporting seems better suited to meeting the objective that voters and party delegates have this information in hand when choosing their leaders. Leadership candidates should be required to file periodic reports showing receipts and expenditures right up to the week of the convention. In the United States' 1988 Democratic primaries, Governor Dukakis successfully attacked Congressman Gephardt for accepting significant contributions from political action committees. Using Gephardt's disclosure reports Dukakis was able to produce a most effective television advertisement that listed all the special interest groups contributing to the Gephardt campaign. Requiring these reports prior to the choosing of a party leader will ensure that any violations are known before the balloting and will allow delegates to assess the appropriateness of each candidate's funding before casting their votes. The Lortie Commission's call for a preliminary report to be due the day before the balloting is a step in the right direction in this regard. What is not clear, however, is what will be required in this preliminary report. The day before the balloting is also very late to allow for the contents of the report to be assessed and considered by the media and delegates before balloting begins.

The second issue to be considered in fashioning a regulatory system for party leadership financing is whether there is too much money in the process. The question here is whether there should be a limit on the amount a candidate may spend on his leadership campaign. While we do not know how much money was spent by 1984 Progressive Conservative candidates chasing their party's leadership, the amounts spent by NDP and Liberals in their most recent contests do not seem overly high. The NDP imposed an extremely low limit of $150,000 on their candidates while the effective Liberal limit appears to have been approximately $2,500,000. Party leadership races are extremely important events in Canadian politics. Many of the participants in these contests go on to serve in leading parliamentary positions with many serving in cabinet and a fortunate few becoming Prime Minister. These campaigns very much narrow the field of options available to Canadians when choosing their Prime Minister. Any regulation of the financing of these races must not be so strict so as to make it difficult for candidates to communicate with party members and the full Canadian electorate.

Leadership races provide voters an opportunity to assess the talent in a party and to begin to learn about the party's future candidate for Prime Minister. These races also can provide for intelligent and lively discussion of issues facing the country. For all of these reasons it is important that an artificially low limit not be placed on the campaigns resulting in a lack of public interest due to an inability on the candidates' part to have their message heard. While we should guard against too low a limit, it seems there should be some limit to prevent extremely well heeled candidates from drowning out the messages of their opponents. The adopted, though not enforced, Liberal limit of $1,700,000 (supported by the Lortie Commission) would seem like a fair amount. The 1990 Liberal race generated a good deal of debate among the candidates on various issues; received a good amount of press coverage, both nationally and regionally as the candidates travelled; generated public interest in the race; and, resulted in a good many party members involving themselves in the delegate selection process.

The real problem in the amount of money spent in leadership races is not the amount of expenditures but rather the lack of sufficient receipts. As will be seen in the following case studies, candidates in the 1990 Liberal race did not have any trouble spending funds. The problem was that several of the candidates were not able to raise sufficient funds to compete effectively. Another goal of regulating leadership financing must be to ensure that all serious candidates are able to raise sufficient funds to compete. As will be shown in the second case study, the most recent NDP leadership race addressed this issue through the $5,000 cash grant, and various subsidies provided to candidates. The party also guaranteed that all serious candidates would at least be able to send literature to every riding and participate in a cross country tour. One other way to accomplish this goal, and to lessen the intense fundraising pressures facing leadership candidates, is to institute a system of public financing. Parties and general election candidates receive public treasury funds after a general election to offset a portion of their expenses. However, funds received after the nominating convention will not encourage greater participation and competition in the race. In the case of leadership candidates the funds should be made available to candidates for use during the campaign.

The reason party and general election candidates receive their public funds after the election is to ensure that their candidacies enjoyed some degree of public support and that public funds are not going to frivolous candidates. In the case of leadership races this concern can be addressed by eligibility requirements similar to those used in the public financing of U.S. presidential primary candidates. After receiving contributions of $250 or less in twenty states, totalling at least $5,000 in each state, candidates are entitled to have the first $250 of each contribution matched with public funds. Canadian legislation could require that leadership hopefuls raise $15,000 in four provinces in contributions of $500 or less in order to be eligible to receive public financing. This would require a candidate be able to raise $60,000 and show support in different parts of the country before qualifying for public funds. There is no science to these numbers, but, a requirement of this type will ensure that candidates receiving public funds enjoy some degree of support across the country.

The second threshold requirement utilized in the U.S. system, that candidates achieve success in the primary process in order to continue receiving public funding, would be difficult to apply to a Canadian leadership race. The Canadian process operates differently in that our leadership races tend to operate in a shorter time frame with most delegates being selected in a period no longer than six to eight weeks long. Also, the results of riding elections are not as easily tracked and converted into candidate delegate support as are U.S. primary results. The Canadian system also differs in that Canadian leadership conventions are almost always contested affairs, with all candidates who entered the race remaining in until at least the first round of convention balloting. In the United States contested conventions are becoming very rare. The majority of U.S. presidential candidates drop out of the race well before the convention. The requirement that contestants receive 10% of the primary votes to retain eligibility for public financing merely reflects the reality that hopefuls cease to be active candidates once falling below this threshold.

It does not appear that a second eligibility requirement need be placed on Canadian leadership hopefuls. However, if legislators thought such a requirement necessary, they could require that candidates receiving public funds, in order to retain their eligibility, submit the names and signatures of a certain number of elected delegates who are supporting their candidacies prior to a set date.

The U.S. system of matching contributions seems well suited to Canadian leadership races. As the following example illustrates, such a system will provide candidates with a significant amount of campaign funds while also encouraging solicitation of moderate and small contributions.

> A candidate who solicits one contribution of $3,000 from a wealthy friend will realize a net contribution of $3,500 – the original $3,000 plus $500 in public funds. Another candidate who solicits six smaller contributions of $500 will net $6,000 – the original $3,000 plus $3,000 in public funds.

By only matching contributions received from individuals we are also discouraging candidates from concentrating their fundraising efforts on the traditional big contributors – law and accounting firms, and corporate and union donors.

The third issue to be considered in developing a regulatory scheme is whether a limit should be placed upon the amount any one contributor may give to a candidate. The Lortie Commission recommends no limit be placed on the amount any contributor may give to leadership candidates.[1]

Two Case Studies

We can now look at how Canadian leadership races operate in the absence of the kind of reforms proposed by the Lortie Commission. We look first at the 1990 race to succeed John Turner as leader of the Liberal Party of Canada. We then turn to the 1989 race to succeed Ed Broadbent as Leader of the New Democratic Party.

The 1990 Liberal Leadership Race

The race that culminated in the convention of June 23, 1990 really began on the evening of Prime Minister Mulroney's re-election with a majority government in November 1988. Mr. Turner would not officially resign for several months, and the national executive would not issue the call for the leadership campaign until the following summer, but all involved knew that Mr. Turner's days as leader were over and that he would not lead the party into the next election. Mr. Chrétien, who had never really stopped campaigning for the party leadership since his second place finish in 1984, was the immediate front runner. Chrétien was thought to face tough challenges from new Montreal MP Paul Martin and potentially from veteran MP Lloyd Axworthy of Manitoba. Both Chrétien and Martin spent months following the November election putting together a campaign organization, developing a fundraising plan, and travelling the country to build support for their coming candidacies. For others, like Axworthy, Quebec MNA Clifford Lincoln, Ontario MP Sheila Copps, and Quebec MP Jean Lapierre these months were spent assessing their chances of raising the necessary funds and putting together an organization capable of sustaining them through a successful campaign.

In the summer of 1989, the national executive announced the date of the leadership convention. In accordance with Articles 17(3) and (4) of the Constitution of the Liberal Party of Canada, the party established a twenty-two person "Leadership Expenses Committee". The Committee was co-chaired by Senator Dan Hays and Margo Brousseau. The mandate of the Committee was to establish regulations governing the financing of the leadership candidates' campaigns.

Before the Committee completed its work, the Liberal parliamentary caucus took the initiative with MPs and Senators endorsing a spending limit of $500,000. On September 1, 1989 the Committee released the regulations it had drafted. The Committee's draft, subject to approval by the national executive, included the following provisions:

- A $1,700,000 expenditure ceiling.
- A requirement that the party disclose the total spending reported by each candidate as well as a master list identifying all contributors who give an aggregate of more than $100. The regulations provided no disclosure of what candidate(s) identified contributors supported.
- A requirement that candidates file quarterly expenditure reports with the party. Contributions, however, need not be reported to the party until four months following the closing of the nominating convention.
- Exempt from the spending ceiling are expenditures for the candidate, the candidate's spouse, and one aide's travel and accommodations, as well as all fundraising costs and any funds paid to the candidate as a salary. There are no limits on these expenditures.
- Contributions may be funnelled through the party to a designated candidate in order to avail the contributor of the tax credit allowed party contributors.
- If candidates are found in serious breach of these rules the regulations provide that the party will consider one or both of the following sanctions: 1. publication of the transgression, and, 2. curtailment of the tax receipt privilege for contributors to the candidate found to be in violation.[2]

At the press conference announcing these regulations, Senator Hays stated that he believed the party should disclose which candidate contributors donated to but that he was overruled on this point.[3] Committee members also admitted that the party has few sanctions available to apply if the rules are broken.

Reaction to the announced regulations was swift and harsh. Lloyd Axworthy, himself a potential leadership candidate, immediately called for an emergency national caucus meeting to discuss the proposed regulations and to demand that the national executive overturn the rules.[4] He was particularly concerned with what he believed to be an overly high spending ceiling and a lack of policing provisions and effective sanctions. He charged that "the regulations serve to undermine the credibility of the rule-making exercise and the party itself."[5] Critics contended that the Committee ignored the express wishes of the parliamentary caucus and many grassroots Liberals for a lower spending ceiling. In opposing the rules Axworthy cited a "...clear sense of feeling among Canadians that the power of big money should not be the dominant factor in determining the outcome of any political decision the party makes."[6]

Supporters of the leading candidates, Chrétien and Martin, did not voice objection to the proposed rules.

Chrétien's national campaign manager would, however, later object to the $1,700,000 spending limit as being too low. John Ray claimed that the limit is just not enough for a professional year-long campaign.[7]

Upon reviewing the suggested regulations, the party's national executive approved the spending limit, but objected to the disclosure requirements. On September 16, 1989 the national executive sent the rules back to the Committee, with national president Michel Robert saying the proposed rules "do not seem to meet" the requirement in the party constitution for "full and complete disclosure of contributions to leadership campaigns."[8] On September 29, 1990 the Committee released what would be the operative rules for the campaign. These regulations differ from the earlier draft in that they require the party to release a list by candidate of all contributions of more than $100 to that candidate for which the party issues a tax receipt. Thus, any contributions not resulting in issuance of a tax receipt would not be publicly disclosed. This list would be made public only after the conclusion of the leadership convention.

Shortly after the promulgation of the final rules, three potential candidates - Lloyd Axworthy, Jean Lapierre and Clifford Lincoln announced that they would not become candidates at least to some degree because of their inability to raise the necessary funds.[9] Mr. Lapierre did not, however, criticize the set spending limit saying: "All those who have been closely involved in a leadership campaign know it is enormously expensive and I think that if we're going into the major leagues we can't wear pee-wee skates."[10]

As the campaign progressed it became clear that campaign funding was creating two tiers of candidates. Mr. Chrétien and Mr. Martin were raising significantly more funds than the remaining candidates. Candidate John Nunziata complained that "Money is dictating this leadership convention" and that "This is not a battle of ideas, it is a battle of organization and money."[11] It also became clear that the regulations were not effective in holding spending even to the prescribed level of $1,700,000. Senator Pietro Rizzuto, a key Chrétien backer, stated of the Chrétien campaign "If we used all the loopholes we could effectively double the budget."[12] Mr. Nunziata complained that: "The rules are being broken left and right. They are very difficult to enforce and there does not appear to be the will to enforce them.[13]

The leading candidates were able to evade spending limits in two ways. The first practice was to have contributors give their money directly to a supportive delegate in order to defray the delegate's costs of attending the convention. While the campaign would arrange these transactions, the funds never passed through the candidate's coffers and thus did not appear on either the candidate's reports of expenditures or receipts. Senator Rizzuto confirmed that the Chrétien campaign engaged in this practice and Anthony

Housefather, an organizer for Sheila Copps' campaign, "said the practice of diverting campaign contributions to youth delegates is wide spread."[14] This practice also violated a party rule explicitly prohibiting candidates from paying delegates expenses. Senator Hays stated that he believed these practices were not permissible, yet, no actions were taken against any campaign for engaging in this diversion of campaign funds.

The second common violation of the rules concerns a regulation exempting from the definition of campaign expenditures service provided by a volunteer. This provision exempts such volunteer services provided: "such individual provides, outside of his or her working hours, or on unpaid leave of absence, and free of charge, service to a candidate."

Mr. Martin's campaign manager, Michel Robinson, said his campaign was interpreting this rule to mean: "workers are volunteer as long as they were not hired by a company for the sole purpose of working on Martin's campaign, and continue performing any function for their employer."[15] Mr. Axworthy summed up the effectiveness of the party regulations stating "If they can raise it they can spend it, the sky's the limit."[16]

Five months after the leadership convention, on November 7, 1990, the Committee would release the numbers showing the total amounts the candidates reported having spent on their leadership campaigns. The following are the reported expenditures for the various candidates:[17]

Candidate	Expenses subject to limit	Excluded & pre call expenses	Total Expenses
Chretien	$1,671,768	$774,268	$2,446,036
Copps	$481,838	$324,226	$806,604
Martin	$1,637,147	$737,543	$2,371,690
Nunziata	$166,076	-	$166,076
Wappel	$143,186	-	$143,186

No definition was provided of "pre call expenses." Presumably, this refers to expenses made in support of one's candidacy before the official calling of the convention. However, without a clear definition these numbers are not very meaningful as Chrétien, for example, spent several years prior to the convention travelling the country and keeping his organization in place for the coming leadership race. It is doubtful that the reported numbers include the expenses of all of these activities.

The party also released a list of each candidate's donors of more than $100 who received tax receipts from the party. These lists merely show the name of the contributor and the amount of his contribution. No other identifying information is provided. No totals or analysis of any type are provided with the numbers. After examining the more than fifty pages of listed contributors, questions are raised as to the accuracy of these reports. Chrétien's list totals approximately

$875,000. This represents approximately one third of Chrétien's claimed total expenditures. Martin's disclosed contributions total approximately only $390,000 – about one seventh of his claimed total expenditures. Both of these numbers seem low. It does not seem likely that Chrétien raised two thirds of his campaign funds ($1,600,000) in contributions of one hundred dollars or less. Even more unlikely is Martin's having raised $2,000,000 in contributions of one hundred dollars or less. There is also no apparent reason why Martin should have such a large base of small contributors compared to Chrétien. What is likely the case is that either these reports are incomplete or both candidates did not submit a significant percentage of their contributions to the party for purposes of procuring a tax receipt. There is no apparent reason why a contributor would not want a tax receipt – other than the accompanying public disclosure of the fact that the contribution was made. Without any evidence to the contrary, it appears that both Chrétien and Martin, though Martin to a more significant extent, did not submit a substantial portion of their contributions to the party for issuance of a tax receipt in order to prevent public disclosure of the contributions.

The 1989 NDP Leadership Race

The New Democratic Party took a very different approach to controlling spending in their December 1989 leadership race. The Montreal *Gazette*, in commenting on the NDP approach, said "the federal NDP is about to launch a noble experiment. It is going to try to prove to Canadians that a modern political party can run a fair and frugal leadership campaign when it comes to choosing a successor to Ed Broadbent."[18] The NDP limited spending during the leadership race to $150,000. There was no internal dissent from party members or candidates to this low limit. Convention Co-Chairman Sue Hart explained the low limit was established in order "...to make the job available to everybody not just those with money."[19] The party executive believed the $150,000 limit to be "...low enough to prevent anyone from dazzling the delegates with expensive gadgetry, while at the same time within the reach of any serious contender."[20] The NDP spending limit, unlike its Liberal counterpart, was also made retroactive to the day following Broadbent's announcement of retirement. The NDP also placed a strict limit on the amount any one source could contribute to a candidate at $1,000. Final financial reports, disclosing the source and amount of all contributions of $100 or more were required by July 31, 1990.

The NDP attempted to create a lively campaign while keeping the candidate's costs down by having the Party pay for some of the campaign costs. The NDP headquarters paid for two mailings from each candidate to all 295 riding associations. The party also made available a travel allowance to all delegates travelling more than 480 kms. to the convention. Most significantly,

however, the Party organized and paid the costs of a fifteen city speaking tour through all ten provinces and the Yukon. While newspaper reports vary greatly as to the actual amount, the NDP clearly spent a considerable amount organizing and promoting these all candidate meetings in Halifax, Charlottetown, Regina, Whitehorse, Edmonton, Vancouver, Nanaimo, Saskatoon, Sudbury, Winnipeg, Montreal, St. John's, Fredericton, Ottawa and Toronto. In addition, the Party paid each candidate $5,000 to ensure that they would be able to travel and attend these meetings. It was the Party's hope that these meetings, held between August and November 1989, would be the centerpiece of the campaign.

The Party also established rules to ensure that sitting MPs did not have an advantage over other contenders. In an effort to "...prevent MPs from using commons privileges in the campaign"[21] the rules prohibited House of Commons staff from working on leadership bids during regular office hours and prohibited use of government material such as stationary, facsimiles and photocopy machines on the leadership race.

Unlike the Liberal race, there are no news stories about any NDP candidates or potential candidates complaining about the Party spending rules or about being wildly outspent by their opponents. The numbers reported by the candidates to the Party illustrate that while none of the candidates raised even eighty percent of the spending limit, there was a significant variance in the amounts raised by different candidates. The five major candidates reported the following financial activity:[22]

Candidate	Receipts	Expenditures	Balance
Barrett	94,505	113,986	-19,481
DeJong	17,516	42,516	-25,000
Langdon	57,426	52,461	4,965
McCurdy	73,364	72,891	473
McLaughlin	116,051	128,575	-12,524

One obvious question raised from examination of these two races is how did the NDP candidates manage to run a leadership campaign on approximately 4% of the funds available to the leading Liberal candidates. There are several apparent reasons why the NDP race should have been less expensive than the Liberal campaign:

- Labour unions select approximately one-third of all NDP convention delegates. Candidates traditionally campaign for these delegates by meeting with the leadership of organized labour. The result of this is that approximately 1,000 delegates are campaigned for through a limited series of meetings with labour leadership – there is no reason to travel the country meeting these delegates one on one in their home constituencies.
- The NDP national headquarters made available travel grants to offset delegate travel to the convention. In the Liberal campaign the leading candidates admitted spending significant funds

paying for the travel of their delegates to Calgary.

- The NDP national headquarters paid for the cost of two candidate mailings and for a fifteen city candidate tour. The Party's arranging of the tour saved candidates the expense of arranging meetings in each of these cities on their own.

- There was virtually no campaign in the province of Quebec. It is estimated that only sixty to seventy five delegates from Quebec attended the NDP convention. This saved candidates the expense of competing for delegates in Quebec's many ridings.

- The NDP campaign was significantly shorter in duration than was the Liberal's. The NDP convention was held ten months after Mr. Broadbent's resignation announcement as opposed to the Liberal's being held almost two years later.

It does also appear that the NDP candidates did not run as precise a campaign in competing for and then identifying and tracking delegates at the riding level. The NDP campaign appears to have been more wide open with candidates appealing to broad categories of delegates. This is illustrated in poll results showing a large percentage of undecided delegates shortly before the convention, and in newspaper reports that "...organizers for the candidates were unable to provide firm figures on levels of support"[23] shortly before the convention.

Conclusion

Party leadership campaigns are too consequential a part of Canadian politics to continue operating completely outside of the purview of campaign financing laws. Leadership races determine the options available to Canadians when choosing their prime ministers, and, leadership hopefuls tend to progress to key roles in cabinet and opposition. A system that allows candidates to take unlimited contributions from corporations and other special interests without having to disclose these transactions is simply unacceptable. Canadian voters have a right to a system that at least attempts to protect them from elected leaders being bought by well heeled special interests. And, while there is a question of cause and effect, it does seem that ability to raise substantial financial resources is having a significant impact on the outcome of party leadership races. Alternative sources of funding, such as a system of public matching funds, must be considered to ensure that all serious candidates have access to necessary funds. Public funding will also lessen the reliance of candidates on private contributions.

The Lortie Commission's recommendations that legislation be enacted imposing spending limits of approximately $1,890,000 and requiring disclosure of contributions in excess of $250.00 are sound suggestions. However, while these recommendations are a step in the right direction they fall short of the needed change discussed in this paper. While these suggestions nibble at the edges of the fairness question by requiring disclosure and imposing a spending ceiling, they fall short of their target. A spending ceiling will only work towards increasing competitiveness if coupled with some sort of public financing, and, disclosure requirements are only effective if disclosure is made early enough to have an impact on the election and if enough information is disclosed to allow for full identification of contributors.

While an electoral system may never achieve complete "fairness", the Canadian system of choosing its party leaders is only beginning to move in such a direction. The recommendations of the Lortie Commission begin to move towards fairness, but must be more comprehensive to meet the fairness objective they set for themselves.

Notes

1. While the NDP limited contributions to $1,000, Liberal candidates, Mr. Chrétien and Mr. Martin both reported receiving several contributions of $10,000 or more with Mr. Chrétien reporting one gift of $20,000. These very large contributions are troubling. It is these large contributions that raise questions concerning whether the contributors are buying access or some other legislative favour from the candidates.

    It is almost impossible to discern a contributor's motives in giving a candidate a large donation. However, because we cannot definitively conclude the contributor's motives, we should give the benefit of the doubt to the political process and prohibit such large contributions. The implementation of a public matching fund scheme should more than offset the loss of revenue from these large contributions. It is, also, only the leading candidates that appear to receive such large contributions. At a minimum, very large contributions raise an appearance of impropriety, and, if for no other reason than to remove this cloud of suspicion, large contributions should be prohibited. There is no easy definition of an overly large contribution. U.S. law limits presidential primary candidate contributions to $1,000 from individuals and $5,000 from political committees. Many object to the $1,000 limit, which has not been adjusted since 1974, as being too low. I would suggest that Canadian leadership candidates be limited to accepting contributions no larger than $3,000.

2. Liberal Party Release of September 1, 1989.
3. *Globe & Mail*, September 1, 1989, p. A4.
4. *Toronto Star*, September 2, 1989, p. A9.
5. *Ibid*.
6. *Ibid*.
7. *Montreal Gazette*, March 31, 1990, p. B6.
8. *Toronto Star*, September 17, 1989, p. A7.
9. *Montreal Gazette*, March 31, 1990, p. B6. It should be noted that Mr. Lincoln's funding dried up after losing the Chambly by-election.
10. *Toronto Star*, September 17, 1989, p. B6.
11. *Montreal Gazette*, March 31, 1990, p. B6.
12. *Ibid*.
13. *Ibid*.
14. *Ibid*.
15. *Ibid*.
16. *Ibid*.
17. Liberal Party Release, November 7, 1990.
18. *Montreal Gazette*, "NDP Leadership Race to be Lesson in Frugality," March 17, 1989, p. B3.
19. *Ibid*.
20. *Ibid*.
21. *Calgary Herald*, "NDP Sets Rules to Ensure Clean Leadership Race," June 11, 1989, p. D16.
22. Financial statements of candidates as reported to the NDP National Headquarters.
23. *Vancouver Sun*, October 12, 1989, p. 8.

TV advertising limits handicap Reform

William Walker

Toronto Star

CALGARY—Canadians will see all kinds of political television ads during the next election campaign—but little of the Reform party logo or leader Preston Manning.

It's not because Reform cannot afford to buy the ads.

But under an antiquated formula, the Canada Elections Act allocates each party television advertising minutes based on the number of seats a party won in the previous election.

Critics mock the rule, saying it provides a built-in advantage to the winner of the previous election.

The infant Reform party was shut out in the 1988 election. It now has one MP, Deborah Grey, who won a later Alberta by-election.

So while the other parties get hundreds of minutes of advertising time, Reform is virtually shut out. It will be allowed to buy only 10 minutes of television time, despite placing higher than the governing Tories in most recent public opinion polls.

The Elections Act requires television broadcasters to make available for sale 6 1/2 hours, or 390 minutes, of prime time advertising space for parties to buy.

An arbitrator recently decided—using the formula based on seats and popular vote in the past election—to award 173 minutes to the Progressive Conservatives, 110 minutes to the Liberals, 71 minutes to the New Democratic Party, 10 minutes to Reform, 7 minutes each to the Christian

Heritage, Rhino and Green parties and 5 minutes to the Commonwealth party.

Each party may purchase as much prime time advertising, within these limits, as it can afford.

As the party's Calgary headquarters gears up its election readiness, the television issue is by far the No. 1 concern.

"You can just imagine the money the Conservatives will be spending on advertising in the next election. We just won't be able to compete with that," says party chief administrator Cliff Fryers.

A mammoth report by the Royal Commission on Election Reform and Party Financing in February called for an end to the television restriction. The Tory government is unlikely to adopt any of the proposed changes before the next election, however, so Reform has gone to court to have the advertising rules overturned.

The case won't be decided before the election, expected next year.

"We think a lot of irate voters will see the unfairness of it," says Virgil Anderson, who works on election readiness at the party's Calgary headquarters.

The act prohibits broadcasters from selling or giving more air time to parties, so the biggest, richest parties can't buy unlimited air time.

Yet there are no restrictions on political ads by special interest groups, such as the pro-free trade lobby which helped the Conservatives win the 1988 election.

That means Reform could still benefit from such ads, even if they must not mention the party name, its leader, or show its logo.

So friends of Reform would likely have to advertise such key party issues as the benefits of debt reduction or ending universality of social programs—or, perhaps, portray incumbent MPs as tired old hacks and urge their defeat.

Oddly enough, the donation-rich Reform party could afford to buy as much prime time space as the Conservatives.

Reform fundraiser Don Leier says the money continues to pour in.

He said 1991 revenues were projected at $3.3 million, but were actually $5.5 million. Projected revenues for this year are $6 million to $7 million. The party already has a cash reserve of about $700,000.

"We have very generous members," said Leier, who expects that in June, when the Elections Canada list of party fundraising is released, Reform will lead all parties in individual contributions.

Anderson says Reform will spend the maximum allowable under the Elections Act during the campaign, about $6 million. He said it will go toward more print ads, billboards, lawn signs, automobile caravans, special rallies and door-to-door blitzes—since television will be out of the picture.

Another Reform strategy will be to blitz the airwaves in the weeks prior to the Prime Minister calling the election—because there are no rules until the campaign begins.

What Reformers will be saying in those ads has much to do with Stephen Harper, the 32-year-old policy chief in the Calgary office and a candidate in the riding of Calgary West.

Harper has been the main architect of party policy. No election platform will be decided—in Reform's so-called grass-roots fashion—until a party convention in October, but Harper's views will be close to the finished product.

The party has asked ridings to state their policy priorities and send them back to Calgary for tabulation.

That allows Manning to tell members what policy directions the party already prefers—making it difficult to disagree.

For instance, during his recent Ontario tour, Manning repeatedly told audiences that other Reform members favor, by a 2–1 margin, keeping the goods and services tax in place. Surprise—Harper says that's likely to be adopted at the fall convention.

Yet two years ago, Manning attracted many Albertans to his party because of his absolute outrage against the GST. Albertans, who did not pay

any provincial sales tax, loathed the new federal sales levy.

The new party position to keep the GST will likely include a guarantee the party would not increase the rate of the tax. But Harper admitted the party may favor broadening the base of the GST so it would be charged more widely on items now exempt.

Harper says the campaign platform priorities are likely to be:

- A balanced budget.
- Reducing the federal debt.
- Tax law reform.
- Policies on fishing, agriculture and trade.
- Resolution of the constitutional question.
- A so-called Triple E (elected, equal and effective) senate.
- Use of binding referendums, recall votes for MPs and more free votes by the House of Commons.

For a party that continually emphasizes its grass-roots tendencies, the platform will be tightly controlled.

"There will be a high degree of expectation that candidates will not buck the line on those issues, but there will be more freedom on other issues at the riding level," Harper said.

There'll be less specifics on what kind of programs—social benefits of environmental protection, for example—would be cut under Reform's restraint plans.

"That's the thrust we'll try to preserve in the middle of all the flak about what's your position on X-Y-Z and of that," Manning said.

"A lot of people say it doesn't matter. The country falls apart and what difference does it make what your position is in the sugar beet industry? There'll be a lot more things to worry about than that."

Nomination rules rile some grass-roots Liberals

Powers given leader and campaign chiefs add up to a certain ruthlessness

William Walker

Toronto Star

OTTAWA—Out in the Ottawa Valley, just about everybody around Pembroke knows Art Jamieson. His house doesn't have an address. People just know it.

Some people know him as the principal of the school their children attended. Or as the master of ceremonies at local auctions. Or as the local reeve and one-time warden of Renfrew.

And for 35 years, Jamieson served the Liberal party in this federal and provincial Grit stronghold. At one time or another, he has held every position on the Renfrew-Nipissing-Pembroke Liberal riding executive—except MP.

For a long time, Jamieson dreamed that one day he'd get his chance to sit in the House of Commons; that all his work in the community and his loyalty to the Liberal party would pay off.

Two years from retirement, Jamieson decided the time was now. The incumbent Liberal MP, Len Hopkins, had held the seat for 27 years. The 22-member riding executive voted. It was time for Hopkins to retire and give someone else a chance.

But due to strict new nomination rules adopted by the Liberal party, Jamieson's dream was shattered because the party protected Hopkins. Jamieson won't even get the chance to run.

"It just seems the whole concept of Liberalism that we grew up with—Liberalism that was grass-roots decisions and people from the grass roots up sending the messages—has been replaced under these new rules," says a bitter Jamieson.

"Now it's right from (leader Jean) Chretien down that decisions are coming and they don't give a damn about the local people."

Chretien's new rules seem to have cleaned up the messy, publicly embarrassing way his Liberal party selects candidates to run for the House of Commons, but at what cost?

At the cost of alienating a 35-year party supporter like Jamieson and many more like him?

Prior to the 1988 election there were several chaotic, even ugly, nomination fights—many in Metro—that involved blocks of "instant Liberals" and one-issue lobby groups, such as pro-lifers, determining the outcome.

In one riding, Eglinton-Lawrence, the incumbent Liberal MP, Roland de Corneille, lost the nomination to Joe Volpe, who sold a massive number of new riding memberships to people who voted him the party nominee.

Under Chretien, the party was determined to avoid such embarrassment in this pre-election period, but some say the new rules go too far.

Under new nomination rules, Chretien has unprecedented powers to refuse to allow candidates he deems unsuitable. And he has already used those powers in two ridings, one of them Toronto's Davenport riding, where incumbent Charles Caccia was assured he could seek nomination without being challenged.

Also, provincial campaign chairpersons have absolute power to orchestrate the timing of nomination meetings, often to suit the candidate privately tagged as the "party choice," whether it be an incumbent or hand-picked "star candidate."

It all adds up to a certain ruthlessness in the air as Liberal nominations begin across the country.

Grass-roots Liberals, hoping to breathe some fresh air into the party by running in the next federal election, have in some cases been squeezed out.

Now some of them are simply walking away from the federal Liberal party, saying it amounts to a Chretien old boys' club with undemocratic rules guaranteeing that nominations are preordained.

Three candidates who sought to challenge Hopkins say the nominations for the Liberal candidacy were opened and closed on June 1 by the Toronto-based provincial campaign chairperson, David Smith.

That infuriated Michel Chartrand, who is president of the Young Liberals of Canada and also comes from Hopkins' riding.

"Mr. Hopkins has failed his executive, many of his closest and longtime campaign workers and the people of the valley," Chartrand wrote in a letter to the Pembroke Observer. "Has Mr. Hopkins not become the Renfrew-Nipissing-Pembroke single-interest group these rules aim to freeze out?"

Even Earl Lindsay, Hopkins' campaign manager in 1988 and past president of the riding executive, told The Star he asked Hopkins to step aside and let the challengers fairly seek the nomination.

"There is certainly what I'd call widespread dissatisfaction among long-time Liberal supporters," Lindsay says.

Hopkins says the prospective challengers simply failed to make themselves aware of the new rules. He says Jamieson would have made a "credible candidate . . . if he knew what the rules were and got his papers in."

Jamieson attracted 800 Liberals to a meeting to announce his candidacy had been thwarted.

"I can tell you there's a tremendous amount of bitterness in this riding and I have a great fear right now that the Liberals are going to lose this riding," Jamieson says.

"People (at the meeting) were furious, saying they'd cast their last vote for Hopkins and they'd vote any other party other than the Liberal party. I don't like to hear that.

"I'm not going to switch political parties. You don't do that after 35 years. But if a credible Reform party candidate ran in this riding, I believe he or she would stand a good chance."

Hopkins admits there was "an initial shock" among local Liberals, but he says that is changing gradually as they begin to understand the new rules.

"The rules have been such a massive change and people around here were really not on top of them," he says.

Both Smith, the tough-talking Bay St. lawyer and Ontario campaign chairperson, and Sheila Gervais, executive director of the Liberal Party of Canada, says there's no reason to overturn Hopkins' nomination and start over.

How was the Renfrew nomination run? Jamieson says Smith informed the riding executive on a Friday that he wanted to have a conference call the following Monday, which was June 1. It took place at 6:30 p.m.

Smith informed the executive during the conference call that nominations in the riding had closed. They had opened earlier that day. Only Hopkins had filed the necessary papers, since nobody else knew about the deadline, Jamieson says.

"When Smith came on the line from Toronto, the cold hard facts of life came through. He told us he had the right to consult but not necessarily agree with the riding executive," Jamieson says. "You'd have to be pretty naive not to smell a rat there."

"I don't buy that, frankly," says Gervais. "I know there was a mailing done to all Ontario riding presidents to explain the rules. The rules say that in the case of an incumbent, nominations can open and close the same day."

Smith also points out that members of Hopkins' riding executive did not attend the party's national convention in Hull last February when the rules were adopted; nor a subsequent provincial meeting in Sudbury, where Smith explained how they would be implemented.

"But I think it's fair to say we're not encouraging people to challenge incumbents," Smith says. "We're not ruling it out, but we're not encouraging it, either. We're discouraging it."

He says the party wanted to assure members of caucus they wouldn't have to worry about securing renomination. Smith says that is a key factor if the party wants MPs to have good attendance in the House of Commons and in committees.

"You can't expect these people to show up in the House of Commons when there's someone back in the riding working full-time to take their nomination away," Smith says.

Yet, safeguarding nominations for incumbents and star candidates does nothing to solve the problem of a lack of women and ethnic minorities representing the Liberal party.

To date, only one incumbent MP is being challenged in Metro. Derek Lee (Scarborough-Rouge River) is being challenged by Gobinder Randhawa. Party officials are privately angry about this, even though Randhawa would give the party a much-needed boost in terms of ethnic representation.

The key question may be what effect the nomination process is having on Liberal party workers who will be much needed when an election occurs. Only 20 nominations have been scheduled so far in Ontario's 99 ridings.

"There is a feeling in some quarters that local democracy has been quashed," says former Ontario education minister Sean Conway, who has held the Renfrew seat at Queen's Park since 1975.

"That tends to leave a very bad taste with people. Certainly all is not well with the application of these rules, there's no question about that."

"The feeling is deep and it's bitter," Jamieson says. "In the Ottawa Valley . . . one thing they sure as hell don't like is anybody from Toronto or Ottawa telling us how to run our politics."

A better way to count the votes

Canada has spent five years in intense discussion of the basic tenets of its political system, through two constitutional rounds. It has just heard from a Royal Commission on Electoral Reform that spent three years poking into nearly every aspect of the electoral process. Yet through all this, the key question in any democratic system—how people choose their representatives—has remained largely unaddressed. This is curious, since Canada's system of voting is in such obvious and pressing need of repair.

In common with Britain, the United States, and a handful of other countries, Canada elects Members of Parliament and the provincial legislatures by the plurality, or "first-past-the-post" system: whoever has the most votes in a riding wins, whether that means 51 per cent of the vote or 21 per cent. The results are well known. Governments are routinely elected with heavy majorities based on the support of 40 per cent or less of the electorate. Parties have taken power that won a smaller percentage of the vote than their opponents, or than they themselves obtained in losing the previous election. Smaller parties with a wide following but no concentrated geographic base are shut out.

At the federal level, exaggerated national majorities are reproduced in regional ghettos: a party may win all the seats in one region with half the votes, while a quarter of the vote in another is worth next to none. Though a party's support may be drawn from across the country, it will naturally listen most closely to the region that gives it the largest presence in Parliament, while across from it sits a party with an equally heavy regional rump. Not only does the system imperil the legitimacy of government, but it exacerbates regional divisions—as if they needed it.

Mention the obvious alternative, proportional representation, and many people think of one word: Italy, perhaps, or Israel. Certainly, a system in which seats are allocated strictly according to the proportion of the popular vote risks creating a series of unstable coalition governments, hostage to the demands of single-issue splinter parties. Israel has not had a majority government since its founding. The life expectancy of an Italian government is less than a year. The same instability marks other countries where pure proportionality is the rule. Poland's recent elections were contested by more than 140 registered parties, of which 29 found their way into the Sejm.

But proportional representation does not always lead to such debilitation. Indeed, some form of PR is in place in nearly every country in Europe, including stable-to-a-fault Sweden and Germany. Local circumstances explain part of the discrepancy: votes in the Italian parliament until recently were by secret ballot, making party discipline impossible. But where PR works the critical factor seems to be the imposition of a "hurdle" for entry to the legislature. Parties in Germany, for example, must gain at least 5 per cent of the vote nationally to take a seat in the Bundestag. Stable two- or three-party coalitions are the result. In Israel, by contrast, less than 1 per cent of the ballot, or just 22,000 votes scattered across the country are enough to win a seat, and perhaps the balance of power.

The other major criticism of PR concerns the loss of a direct link between the voters and individual candidates. In pure PR, parties draw up ranked lists of candidates; if a party wins 12 seats, the top 12 names get in. This can make an election seem a formality: if a party can be fairly expected to win 20 per cent of the vote, the names of its Members of Parliament are known well in advance, regardless of whether these would find favour with the electorate on their own. This might sometimes be a good thing—candidates with much to offer but little skill at campaigning could still enter Parliament—but in any case, there are less extreme varieties that preserve an element of constituency representation.

One such model is the hybrid form of PR used in Germany, Sweden, and Japan, among others. Half the German lower house is elected directly, while half is drawn from party lists. A similar "topping-up" was proposed for the Commons by the Pépin-Robarts commission in 1979, which recommended adding 60 seats

From *The Globe and Mail*, March 6, 1992, p. A12. Reprinted by permission.

allocated proportionally from provincial lists. This would achieve a better regional distribution without leading to electoral deadlock: research for the commission indicated such a system would not have changed any majority government since 1950 into a minority.

The alternative is to elect representatives from multi-member constituencies, with parties offering competing slates of candidates. The Beaudoin-Dobbie committee's proposal for a Senate elected by proportional representation suggests each electoral district be given four seats or more. This *would* affect the party standings: of the last eight federal elections, according to a study by former MP Michael Cassidy released this week, only one would have produced a majority in a Senate elected under PR (assuming the same voting patterns held as for the Commons).

This raises a new difficulty, however. The point of having an upper house is to counter regional majorities in the Commons with different regional majorities in the Senate. If the Commons is left unreformed, while proportional representation dissipates regional power blocs in the Senate, then central Canada could still assure its domination by voting solidly for one party in the Commons. Any move away from first-past-the-post in the Senate must be matched in the lower house.

If proportional representation is too radical a reform for the Commons, perhaps a milder medicine might go down easier: the transferable ballot, in use in Australia and Ireland. Voters rank the candidates; the candidate with the fewest first-place votes drops out; his votes are divided among the others on the basis of second-preferences; and so on through third- and fourth-preferences, until one candidate has a majority of the vote. (Some version of

this is envisaged for the Senate under Beaudoin-Dobbie).

This would at least ensure a majority government in fact commanded the support of a majority of the electorate, giving voice to millions of voters whose choices are ignored under the plurality system. And it would go some way to correcting distended regional majorities: many times the early frontrunner under a transferable ballot lacks enough second- and third-preference votes, as party leadership races attest.

The constitutional wagon is admittedly already groaning under the weight of various items for reform. But the present electoral system is one of the chief contributors to the regional resentments that so inflame our constitutional difficulties. And Senate reform on the basis of proportional representation, as proposed, might be worse than no reform at all, unless similar measures are undertaken in the Commons. The issue cannot be avoided.

Direct Democracy: The Wave of the Future?

A newfound enthusiasm for direct democracy, in the form of referenda and plebiscites, is spreading across Canada. In June 1991 the Quebec National Assembly passed a bill which empowers the Quebec government to hold a referendum on the constitutional future of the province in 1992. In the October 1991 elections held in Saskatchewan and British Columbia, referendum and plebiscite questions were on the ballot. (In Saskatchewan the voters agreed that the provincial government should be required to introduce balanced budget legislation, and that the public should have the right to approve through a referendum any proposed constitutional amendments; they also voted no to a question asking them whether the government should pay for abortions. In B.C., the voters voted yes to questions asking them whether they should have the right to recall their MLAs, and to propose referendum questions). This paper explains how referenda and plebiscites work, and assesses their impact in two of those democracies which have experimented with them.

David Pond

David Pond is a Research Officer in the Legislative Research Service, Ontario Legislative Library. This is an amended version of a paper which was prepared for the Ontario Delegation to the 16th Canadian Regional Seminar of the Commonwealth Parliamentary Association held in Whitehorse in November 1991. The views expressed in this paper are those of the author and not those of the Legislative Research Service.

A referendum is a vote of all eligible voters in a jurisdiction on a proposed policy or law. The wording will be in the form of a question, which the voters will be required to answer with a yes or a no. Referenda can be binding on the government which conducts them, or merely advisory.

Historically, the terms plebiscite and referendum have been used interchangeably. The former is the older term, dating back to 4th century B.C. Rome. The plebiscite has tended to be the term used to describe references to the people of a specific question entailing the approval of a leader, regime, or a change in national boundaries. Plebiscites have been employed in Europe to sanction the unification of disparate city-states (into modern Italy), the creation of new nations (Norway's separation from Sweden in 1905), and the resolution of boundary disputes (Schleswig's with France and Germany in the 1920s). Napoleon used plebiscites to demonstrate popular support for annexations by France of other countries, and revisions of the French constitution.

In recent decades the term referendum has replaced plebiscite in common usage. For example, Denmark, Ireland, France, Norway and the United Kingdom held referenda, not plebiscites, on the question of membership in the European Economic Community in the early 1970s.

Saskatchewan's recent *Referendum and Plebiscite Act* revives the use of the term plebiscite, to describe a referendum held under its provisions whose result is not binding on the government. Under the Saskatchewan Act, a plebiscite must be held once a petition calling for one on a particular question is signed by at least 15% of the electorate. This kind of referendum or plebiscite is more commonly known as the initiative. The initiative is most used today in the United States and Switzerland. It is a device which enables the citizenry to vote on a measure before it becomes law. It differs from the referendum in that the decision to hold a vote originates with the electorate, not the government. The initiative procedure is attractive to enthusiasts of direct democracy because it

From *Canadian Parliamentary Review*, Winter 1991-1992, pp. 11-14. Reprinted by permission.

empowers the voters to bypass a government reluctant to introduce a policy which enjoys popular support.

The initiative enables citizens to compel the government to hold a referendum on a measure supported by a specified percentage of the voters who have signed a petition indicating their support. Once the petition attracts the requisite number of signatures, a national vote is automatically triggered. When a majority votes yes in the vote, then the measure in question becomes law whether the government agree with it or not, or (as in the case of the Saskatchewan legislation) the government is compelled to take whatever steps are necessary to implement the result of the referendum, such as introducing a bill into the legislature.

THE UNITED STATES

The referendum and the initiative have a long history in the United States, reflecting the country's populist traditions and distrust of government. The referendum was introduced in the Massachusetts Bay Colony as early as 1640 and the initiative in 1715. Today, 25 states and the District of Columbia use the referendum; 23 states and the District use the initiative. Twelve states allow municipalities to use the initiative. Congress has never adopted either the referendum or the initiative, though it has debated the possibility on a number of occasions. In the November 1988 elections in the U.S., there were more than 200 referendum questions and initiatives on the ballot in 41 states. In California alone there were 29 initiatives.

Perhaps the most famous initiative was Proposition 13 in California whose passage in 1978 slashed property taxes by half and compelled painful cuts in public services. Examples of initiative questions and referendum voted in recent US elections include:

- in Massachusetts, whether to shut down two nuclear power plants with poor safety records, and whether to cut state taxes;
- in Michigan and Arkansas, whether to continue public funding of abortions;
- in California, whether to require an HIV test for anyone charged with assault or sex crimes; and
- in Colorado, whether all proposed tax increases should be put to a public vote.

One of the most striking developments in the use of the initiative in recent years is the number of petitions aimed at modifying the operation of the state legislatures. The following are examples of initiative questions of this nature circulated among the voters in the last three elections.

- in Alaska and Oregon, whether to reduce the salaries of state legislators;

- in California and Kansas, whether to reapportion the state legislature; and
- in Colorado, California and Oklahoma, whether to set limits on how many terms a state legislator can serve.

Until 1990 few of these initiatives passed. In 1990, however, the voters of Colorado and Oklahoma overwhelmingly approved an initiative proposal to limit the term of state legislators to eight years. In California the voters approved Proposition 140, which set strict limits on the number of years any statewide office-holder could serve, from governor to the superintendent of education. Under this Proposition, state senators, who serve a four-year term, are limited to two terms; and members of the state assembly, who serve a two-year term, are limited to a maximum of three. In addition, Proposition 140 cut by a third all legislators' salaries and their office budgets, and eliminated legislators' pensions. Students of Californian politics suggest that Proposition 140 has eliminated full-time professional politicians from state politics. Critics argue that a legislature composed of part-time, inexperienced legislators will be more vulnerable to lobbyists.[1]

Another feature of contemporary "initiative politics" which is worth pointing out is the significant number of initiatives introduced by politicians themselves. For example in California 15% of all initiatives circulated for signatures since 1970 have been authored by state politicians. Moreover, they have been the proponents of more than one-third of the initiatives which actually qualified for the ballot.[2]

A number of reasons have been offered for why politicians might want to start initiatives:

- he or she can draft the measure to read exactly as desired; a bill, in contrast, will often have to be amended to attract the support of other legislators;
- the initiative campaign, regardless of whether it is successful, can be used by a politician to raise his or her profile in the community and the media; and
- members of a minority party in the legislature can use the initiative process to introduce measures the majority party is blocking in the legislature.[3]

There is a long-running debate among students of initiatives over whether the process favours left- or right-wing causes. One study found that between 1977 and 1986, 43 out of 96 initiatives qualifying for the ballot across the country which were introduced by liberal, environmentalist or left-leaning groups passed, for a success rate of 43%, while 41 out of 91 initiatives introduced by right-wing groups passed, for a success rate of 45%.[4] This suggests that the initiative is a politically neutral instrument which activists on both the left and the right can wield with roughly equal chances of success. However, critics point to the high costs of circulating a petition for signatures and the subsequent campaign, and argue that well-heeled business lobbying groups can afford to spend the money necessary to defeat measures proposed by reform and progressive groups.

A study of initiatives which qualified for the ballot in California shows that between 1980 and 1987, the side spending the most money 16 times won. Total spending by both sides in the 29 campaigns amounted to $130 million.[5] On the other hand, in recent years there have been a number of high-profile campaigns in which the big spenders lost. For example, in 1986 in California Proposition 65, the Clean Water–Get Tough on Toxics Initiative, passed though its opponents outspent its supporters by a margin of more than three-to-one. In 1988, Proposition 99, a 25-cent tax increase on cigarettes passed despite a massive spending campaign against it by business. It remains true, however, that critics of the initiative will always be able to cite campaigns in which it appears that money made the difference. A recent prominent example occurred in November 1990 when a recycling initiative in Oregon was defeated in a campaign which saw the oil and chemical industry outspend environmentalists by a margin of eight-to-one, which included a $2.5 million television advertising campaign. The "yes" campaign was ahead in the polls before its opponents' negative television ads were aired.

SWITZERLAND

Direct democracy also has deep historical roots in Switzerland. As early as the 13th century some Swiss cantons (the equivalent of provinces in Canada) regularly made decisions by popular assent in citizen assemblies. As the population grew and such assemblies became impractical (today they survive only in the more thinly populated mountain cantons), the referendum was adopted as a means of continuing this tradition of direct democracy.

All amendments to the Swiss constitution which are approved by the federal parliament must be submitted to a popular referendum. As well, 100,000 citizens (just under 3% of the electorate) can trigger a referendum on a proposed amendment by signing a petition containing its text within 18 months of its publication. This is known as a constitutional initiative. The Swiss National Assembly cannot change the text proposed in a constitutional initiative, but it can present a counter-proposal, which sometimes results in the withdrawal of the initiative by its sponsors. All constitutional amendments proposed in a referendum (including a counter-proposal) must win the support of a majority of those voting nationally, and a majority of the cantons. This latter requirement makes it impossible for the large urban cantons to impose an amendment on the smaller rural ones.

An ordinary law passed by the federal parliament is not subject to a referendum, unless this is demanded by 50,000 citizens (in the form of a petition) or eight cantonal governments within 90 days of its publication. If a referendum is held, only a simple majority of those voting is necessary for the law to carry. Certain categories of legislation, such as the budget, are exempt from the referendum process.

The use of referenda and initiatives by the cantons varies. In some cantons, including the populous ones of Zurich, Berne and Argau, a referendum is obligatory for all laws passed by the cantonal parliament, excluding certain kinds of financial legislation. (The legislative output of the cantonal legislatures is considerably smaller than that of Canadian provincial legislatures). In other cantons, a referendum can be triggered by a petition: the number of signatures required varies considerably from canton to canton. In addition, all cantons employ the legislative initiative whereby the signatures of specified numbers of citizens on a petition can trigger a vote on a law passed by the cantonal parliament.

The only comprehensive statistical study in English on direct democracy in Switzerland was published in 1979, and it focused exclusively on federal politics. It found that between 1848 and 1978, 212 referenda on constitutional questions were held. In 199, the majority of the population and a majority of the cantons voted the same way (107 yes, and 92 no). In each of the five cases in which an over-all majority voted yes, but the cantons voted no and prevented the proposal from becoming law, the proposal would have given new powers to the federal government. In 18 cases the federal parliament put forward a counter-proposal: in seven out of the 18 the original initiative was then withdrawn.[6]

Another study, also published in 1979, found that between 1945 and 1977, 55% of all constitutional initiatives were started by political parties, mostly by the smaller ones which had little hope of forming the government.[7] As in the U.S., therefore, direct democracy enables politicians excluded from power to circumvent the control exercised over the legislative agenda by the dominant political forces.

CONCLUSION

It is difficult to make generalizations about how political institutions developed in another society would work in one's own. However, the experience of the U.S. and Switzerland with the referendum and initiative do suggest that while these devices may well enable popular sentiment to be brought directly to bear on the political process, they will be utilized by those already involved in political activity—interest groups and the politicians themselves.

Critics of direct democracy suggest that in a parliamentary democracy the ready use of the referendum or initiative would undermine the legitimacy of representative government and downgrade that status of the individual Member. Whether or not this is likely can only be a matter of speculation. It is important to point out that under our system of government public policies can only be transformed into legislation by means of bills approved by the legislature and the government remains responsible for the administration of legislation. Under the British Columbia and Saskatchewan statutes providing for referenda, a referendum result in favour of a particular policy simply requires the government to do whatever *it deems* "necessary or advisable" to abide by the referendum result, such as changing existing policies, or introducing new legislation into the legislature. Thus, the final arbiters of public policy remain the elected legislators.

NOTES

1. See Ronald Grover, "The Little Word Heard Coast to Coast: No," *Business Week* 88:3 (19 November 1990): 47; and "Out You Go," *The Economist* (24 November 1990): 22–23.

2. Charles Bell and Charles Price, "Are ballot measures the magic ride to success?" *California Journal* 19 (1988): 380.

3. David B. Magleby, "Legislatures and the Initiative: The Politics of Direct Democracy," *Journal of State Government* 59:1 (1986): 32–33; Sandra Singer, "Should We All Vote On It?," *State Legislatures* (October 1988): 26; and Kenneth Reich, "The 64-Million Dollar Question," *Campaigns and Elections* (March–April 1989): 15.

4. Congressional Quarterly, "Initiatives: The Democracy or Bad Lawmaking?" *Editorial Research Reports* 30:1 (17 August 1990): 463.

5. Charles Price, "Afloat on a Sea of Cash," *California Law Journal* 19 (1988): 481.

6. Jean-François Aubert, "Switzerland," in *Referendums: A Comparative Study of Practice and Theory*, eds. David Butler and Austin Ranney (Washington, D.C.: American Enterprise for Public Policy Research, 1978), pp. 43–46.

7. Marjorie Mowlam, "Popular Access to the Decision-making Process in Switzerland: The Role of Direct Democracy," *Government and Opposition* 14:2 (1979): 185–187.

Plebiscites common in Canada, abroad

Ross Howard

Parliamentary Bureau, Ottawa

The federal government's decision to hold a referendum on the Constitution if necessary, but not necessarily to hold a referendum, echoes the last such national sounding 50 years ago.

As in 1942, the proposition will be advisory rather than binding upon the government—if Ottawa decides to proceed.

Government House Leader Harvie Andre emphasized that the legislation unveiled Friday is "just a precaution, a case of being prepared" if current federal-provincial negotiations on the Constitution fail to achieve consensus.

Provincial and territorial governments have resorted at least 47 times to this type of vote. Only three Western nations—the United States, the Netherlands and Israel—have not held a national referendum.

Aside from 1942, Ottawa has followed that route only one other time, a 1898 plebiscite on liquor prohibition. In 1942, the Liberal government of Mackenzie King conducted a national vote on the heated issue of imposing military conscription if it were necessary. Just what "necessary" meant was not spelled out.

In the vote, Quebec strongly differed from the rest of the county's acceptance of conscription, and King kept his cabinet intact by waiting two years before making military service compulsory.

Any campaign resulting from Mr. Andre's legislation would rely on public-interest groups, just as in 1942, when the pro-conscription side was partly financed by liquor companies and distilleries.

Mr. Andre's legislation does not prohibit the federal government—or the provinces—from spending any amount of money to advocate a posi-

---

Just asking . . .

Before asking voters to answer any referendum questions on the Constitution, Canada's politicians should first answer a question of their own making: What will the vote results add up to when the ballots are counted?

Technically, the term "referendum" is a misnomer. The referendum law says the vote will merely be advisory in nature—which makes it, strictly speaking, a plebiscite.

That's because the current formula for amending the Constitution requires ratification only by Parliament and the provincial legislatures—with no provision for popular consent. Now, after five years of constitutional discord, it's understandable, indeed desirable, that politicians would want input from the people before enacting changes of such magnitude.

But they can't have it both ways. If they want the people's advice, they can't ignore the results after the fact.

Legally binding or not, the results should be morally binding on the politicians in power—in all provinces.

Since ratification requires the unanimous consent of all legislatures and Parliament, it follows that the package be approved by a majority of voters in each and every province. If one province should find itself the odd man out on Oct. 26, its premier ought not to override the result. Far better for him to try to resolve the conflict by calling a snap election on the issue.

Otherwise, the referendum risks being not just advisory, but illusory. Before they pose the question, the Prime Minister and the premiers should tell Canadians how they intend to interpret the people's verdict.

Toronto Star, September 10, 1992, p. A26.

tion in the referendum.

Mr. Andre did not rule out the possibility of cabinet ministers campaigning vigorously at public expense. He said he hopes opposition Liberal and New Democrat MPs "will all be on the same side," but he would not say whether the government will cover the cost of having them on board.

"It will be fairly much of a free-for-all" if spending limits and other amendments are not made to the legislation, Conservative MP Patrick Boyer predicted.

Mr. Boyer's proposed legislation to define referendum procedures in detail has been sidelined by the government.

Bloc Québécois Leader Lucien Bouchard complained that Ottawa's legislation is so wide open on financing that "even foreign companies, foreign countries, too," will be allowed to spend unlimited funds in the referendum.

By contrast, referendums conducted in Quebec in 1980 and Britain in 1975 were conducted through two umbrella organizations each. These had primary responsibility for the Yes and No sides of the questions. Each side initially received public funds to mobilize voters.

In Quebec, strict limits on total funds were applied. Rules governing other expenses and procedures followed conventional election-campaign limitations. The referendum was managed by a council composed of three provincial court judges.

Referendum procedures in other jurisdictions also differ from the noncommittal style adopted this time by Ottawa. At its discretion, the Saskatchewan government may submit referendum questions to the public. If more than half the eligible voters cast ballots and more than 60 per cent of those voting adopt one position, the result is binding.

In British Columbia, results are considered binding on the government if more than 50 per cent of the voters favour one position. New Brunswick is the only province that has not held a referendum.

Farther afield, some legislatures are required to hold referendums. For example, in Australia, Austria, Japan and Ireland, constitutional amendments must be ratified by voters.

Canada Versus the United States

A review of which country has the most effective political and election system

John Redekop

John Redekop teaches political science at Wilfred Laurier University in Kitchener-Waterloo.

The results of the American national election . . . provide an excellent opportunity to compare the Canadian and U.S. election process.

What are the basic differences? What strengths and weaknesses can be identified? Which system works best?

This evaluation, obviously somewhat subjective, will look at 17 individual points to determine whether the American or the Canadian system gets the nod.

1. Americans schedule their national elections in advance. The early November date can be calculated far into the future. The president knows he has four years in office and can plan his legislative program accordingly. Neither lawmakers nor voters in the U.S. need to fear any sudden or unnecessary election.

One disadvantage in such an arrangement is that with the election date known the campaign begins more than a year in advance.

In Canada, the prime minister announces an election at any time during his five-year mandate, though there are some customary restraints. This leeway gives him inordinate power. However, the campaign itself lasts only 50 days.

Here, the strengths and weaknesses cancel each other. It's a tie.

2. In the United States, the government does not conduct a general voter enumeration or registration. Parties and interest groups on their own, do the best they can to get potential voters to register. Many never do register. In Canada, the government canvasses all households at its own expense.

Chalk this one up for Canada.

3. Months before the November election virtually all U.S. states conduct primary elections to choose party candidates for congressional and other offices. About half the states also use the primaries to select delegates for the presidential nominating conventions.

While the American system is much more democratic than the Canadian practice of having non-primary national leadership conventions and nomination meetings in each parliamentary constituency, it has serious disadvantages. The primary system has proven to be costly, very divisive for the political parties and time-consuming. Also, a few states with early primaries wield undue power.

Call this one a draw.

4. In Canada, the voters in only one constituency actually vote for the national party leader. Each leader runs in one of the 295 constituencies. In the U.S. all voters get to vote for the presidential candidate of their choice. Though the archaic Electoral College, with its "winner takes all by state" arrangement, distorts the outcome, national involvement in presidential selection has many advantages. The leaders campaign nationally, are elected nationally, and don't have to "service" their own local riding.

Give this one to the U.S.

5. In the U.S., a president is limited to two, four-year terms or to ten years if, because of his predecessor's incapacitation or death, he comes into office during a term. Thus even a very popular president like Ronald Reagan may have a "lame duck" second term.

The Canadian arrangement sets no limits. The parties keep or replace leaders as they see fit and voters have the last word.

Give Canada this point for a more democratic system.

6. In the American system, when voters elect a head of government they also elect the official head of state; the president holds both offices. In Canada, the monarch and her Canadian representative, the governor-general, continue in office. They're above partisan bickering.

The U.S. arrangement combines partisanship with the key symbol of patriotism, the head of state. In Canada, they're separated, a practice which has major advantages.

This one goes in the Canadian column.

7. When Americans elect a president they also elect a vice-president. That's a sensible and democratic way of choosing the alternate president. In Canada, the prime minister, accountable to no one, selects any MP he wishes to be his deputy prime minister.

The Yanks get this one because here their system is more responsible and democratic.

 From *The Hamilton Spectator,* November 8, 1988, pp. A7. Reprinted by permission of John Redekop.

8. In the U.S. the voters vote separately for the presidential ticket and for their representatives in Congress. They are not forced, as in Canada, to vote for the local candidate if they want to vote for that candidate's national leader.

The American system reflects voter preferences more accurately; the Americans win this round.

9. Many Canadians have had their fill of an appointed Senate, with terms to age 75, and yearn for an elected Senate. The Americans have an elected Senate which is fully accountable to the voters.

On the specific criterion of Senate accountability and responsiveness to voters, the American system comes out ahead.

10. Aside from its non-democratic nature, the Canadian Senate is woefully misrepresentative. Newfoundland, with half a million people, has six seats, as do each of the four western provinces although their populations range between one and three million each. Ontario and Quebec each have 24. The whole arrangement no longer makes much sense.

On the question of reasonable Senate representation, the U.S. with two senators for each state, wins easily.

11. In the United States, the Senate and House of Representatives, both elected, have roughly equal powers. Such a truly bicameral legislature makes much democratic sense but it also produces much deadlock when the two chambers disagree, as they often do.

In Canada, the House of Commons prevails over the appointed Senate on all important issues. It's less democratic but more efficient.

This one's a tie.

12. While the members of the U.S. national legislature, in both houses, get selected democratically and according to fair apportionment, the system may produce a serious problem. Sometimes, one party controls the Senate while a different party controls the House of Representatives. That produces a party-based reason for additional squabbling and even deadlock. In both houses the dominant party can claim a democratic mandate.

Such a democratic deadlock cannot occur in Canada. The Senate may be dominated by a different party but that party can never claim a democratic mandate.

Canada wins this one.

13. American voters, when they wish to express their electoral wrath, don't know whom to blame. Not only may different parties control the executive and legislative branches, but it's often impossible to ascertain which branch is actually responsible for some action or inaction. Each branch blames the other. In Canada, the executive and legislative branches are fuses; the cabinet controls the House of Commons. The government party must take responsibility for everything. Thus, it's easy to know which party to blame at election time. Canada handily wins this one.

14. In the U.S., only one-third of the Senate is elected in a presidential election; every two years one-third are elected for a six-year term. That allows for continuity. All members of the House of Representatives are elected every two years. With the staggered terms and different parties controlling various parts, rarely can a president claim a national mandate to carry out a set of policies, let alone have a Congress that will support him.

The Canadian system of giving the prime minister a mandate by giving him the necessary votes in parliament makes more sense. Give this one to Canada.

15. In an American election, no one ends up as leader of the opposition. The losing candidates for the presidency have no national status and they generally fade away. Nor is there a shadow cabinet leading the opposition.

The Canadian system of having a "government in waiting" to criticize the government and to present itself as an alternative, makes sense. This arrangement keeps the government on its toes.

Another one for Canada.

16. In the American system the national cabinet, other than the president, is not elected. Subject to Senate confirmation, the president can appoint whomever he wants. The American cabinet is not accountable directly to Congress. The elected Canadian cabinet, aside from one or two Senators, is politically accountable both to the particular constituency voters and to parliament, through the question period and nonconfidence votes.

The Canadian system provides better control of the cabinet. Give Canada this one.

17. When Canadians elect a prime minister, they elect a virtual dictator, at least in certain respects. He has incredible power. He selects the cabinet. He controls the legislative process. He decides who will become speaker. He can muster automatic majority support (unless he heads a minority government). He controls the budget. He controls all senior appointments. And he can decide when to call the next election.

Concerning the question of concentration versus distribution of power, the Americans win.

So, what has our survey produced? Canada received eight wins, the U.S. six. Three items were deemed a draw.

Clearly, both systems have many strengths. For generations, both have produced stable, free societies with government of at least passable quality.

Can we combine the best of both? No, that doesn't work. In their essentials, a responsible parliamentary system and a "checks and balances" presidential system don't mix. They rest on different sets of assumptions. We can't have it both ways.

The Canadian and American electoral systems are both excellent models on the world scene. Both have stood the test of time and both deserve high marks.

The Politics of Culture

It has been said that no sooner had Canada moved out from under British political, economic, and cultural domination, than it quickly fell under equally friendly but possessive U.S. influence. In the first unit article, Bernard Ostry insists that not only Canada and the U.S., but all national cultures are part of the global village, where "trade and communications are now almost universal, the great corporations are transnational. . . ." He argues that "public broadcasting is the most powerful medium to deliver effective remedies" for the contemporary crises in culture, education, literacy, and multiculturalism. Ostry cites a *Report* of the standing committee on communications and culture of the House of Commons of Canada, which concluded that "culture and communications are fundamental investments that will help to achieve renewal of our sense of pride and unity as a nation." A resolution of the constitutional crisis will then permit culture and communications to bind Canada together.

While Ostry focused his attention on the world stage, there remain many others who focus on the internal (seemingly eternal) struggle for control over culture within Canada. Allan Gotlieb, a former Canadian ambassador to the U.S., claims that rather than devolving powers over culture to the provinces, and especially Quebec, only federal intervention and control can create true centers of excellence, the equivalent of Harvard or Yale Universities. He deplores the creation of provincial bureaucracies devoted to culture. "It isn't the Quebec nationalists or the U.S. film lobby that pose the biggest threat to a strong federal system of culture. The real enemy is within."

Part of the deep cultural division between the two official language groups is reflected in the increasing use of English outside Quebec, which is mirrored by the increasing use of French only in Quebec. In "Language in Canada," Luc Albert finds some small ray of hope, because bilingualism is also increasing across Canada.

Carol Martin focuses on Canadian publishing. She thinks that the federal government has abandoned its commitment to protect, and even encourage, the development of a domestically controlled publishing industry. She points to a Canadian paradox in book publishing: that "the more profitable a segment of the industry, the more likely it is to be foreign-controlled; the less profitable, the more likely it will remain Canadian."

Pierre Berton, next, provides a textbook example of how the *Reader's Digest*, an American publication, came to masquerade itself as a Canadian publication. He asks, Why is "Revenue Canada giving it a favored status over all similar (American) magazines?"

Looking Ahead: Challenge Questions

Is the challenge to Canada's cultural independence primarily internal, from the United States, or global?

Is strengthening public broadcasting the most important means of protecting cultural sovereignty?

What is the situation with respect to the official status of French and English in Canada? Is French threatened?

Is the Canadian book publishing industry in need of government support?

Unit 5

How can Canada maintain its cultural independence?

Bernard Ostry

Bernard Ostry is the former chairman of TVOntario. This article is adapted from The Survival of Canada Through Broadcasting, his recent Alan B. Plaunt Memorial Lecture presented at Carleton University.

Ottawa

The demand for cultural sovereignty, to be masters in the house of our spirit, reflects anxieties that are now all but universal. All national cultures tend to show a certain built-in defensiveness in the forms of conservatism and xenophobia. It may be that racial bigotries and jokes are part of this defensiveness, a kind of fence-building or marking of psychic territory.

The paradox of culture is that like a great tree it is rooted and nourished in a particular soil, yet spreads its branches into the universal air, from which it also draws nutrients. But trade and communications are now almost universal, the great corporations are transnational, the signals of news and commerce are lightning flashes from the stratosphere. And in our new world such lightning can strike and kill one's own tree.

Those lightnings and comets at present strike in the form of denatured productions from multinational broadcasters whose object is to sell goods and services. There is nothing wrong with that, it's part of life, but it has to be balanced by less self-interested communication.

We have to understand that these seemingly immaterial matters are as real as the ground we walk upon. The Irish poet, W. B. Yeats, put it like this:

Civilization is hooped together, brought
under a rule, under the semblance of peace
by manifold illusion; but man's life is thought.

There must be room for that life of thought, as for the images of which we construct our community and society, and for the knowledge and discovery and imagination that amount to civilization. We need to be able to find that life of thought within our own culture. We should not allow ourselves to be distracted by the chatter of advertising.

There are urgent reasons why we and the governments we elect should rediscover the principles of public broadcasting. There is a crisis in education, a crisis in literacy, a crisis in training for jobs. Public broadcasting is the most powerful medium to deliver effective remedies. There is a cultural crisis. Public broadcasting can once more lead a cultural renewal, a multicultural regeneration. There is a crisis of nationalism. Public broadcasting can create the rituals by which we create and share our identities. There can be no isolation of culture or nation. The two are one.

There's no safe place, no Himalayan refuge or Shangri-la where a culture can immure itself in cloistered and fugitive virtue. We have seen in the Soviet bloc how the ruthless idealism that sought to create heaven made for itself a hell on earth. In a single generation, as we saw, Shangri-la became Albania, a country whose citizens abandoned it in despair. Utopia became Vietnam, casting its children on the waters.

It seems that whatever we do in cultural development we must, and indeed should, do together with other cultures, other nations. In a time when the costs of transnational communication are as high as the satellites themselves, we Canadians cannot only do what the sky barons and skypans and skycoons have done and collaborate with other nations on a massive scale but outdo them in imaginative uses of the new technologies. Only by joining and trying to lead the crowd, the satellite set, can we assure our solitude, our unique way of becoming what we are and what we ought to be.

Deep in our collective memories is the notion that plurality of languages and cultures is nothing less than babel, a divine curse on human pride. Yet when we look at the biological world, what we see is an extraordinary multiplication of living forms, of genera and species and mutants pullulating and seething and adapting to a myriad of ecological niches.

It seems a cruel and a wasteful world, the food chain in which species preys on species, devours its own young and its own mates. And yet without this miraculous propensity of life to differentiate into infinite variety it could never have evolved or have generated the creatures that survive in every sort of environment. Even on the glaciers of high mountains you find the humble algae and their predators. Even in the ocean abyss where the sun never penetrates, life has found the way, taking its energy from Earth's internal fires.

Without differentiation the Earth would be naked and sterile. We could do without blackflie, we could do without mosquitoes and the gypsy moth, but we're stuck with them, and maybe for the best.

It is not so different with human cultures. Variety of cultures is the most striking fact in ethnology. Never static, cultures grow and change, adapting to new environments and technologies.

The tendency of systems, of machines, of rationality is towards uniformity and a kind of static order. The tendency of cultures is to grow and differentiate and boil over. In a world whose communications increasingly dissolve borders and differences, it is vital that room should be made for national and local cultures to survive and develop. It is natural that Quebeckers would be deeply occupied with this problem.

There's a relation between culture and communication, as there is between political economy and communication. But human society is not merely a creation of communication. James W. Carey, in his book *A Cultural Approach to Communication* suggests that a narrow view of communication as transmission or transportation is a legacy of 19th-century imperialism. Instead of seeing communication as transmission, Carey offers what he calls a ritual view, a process through which a shared culture is created, modified and transformed. Here is a human use for television.

Spring is upon us. Ottawa looks to its tulips. The ice is breaking up, the rivers are unlocked. This is a time of hope.

In parliament, the standing committee on communications and culture has submitted its first report. And in all modesty I can't help noticing that its recommendations and arguments are more or less those that I offered myself in my book *The Cultural Connection*, written in the mid-70s. After 15 years, a committee of eight members of parliament finally agrees with me. Not bad at all for an aging mandarin.

So it's natural that I should be happy with the report in almost every respect. The title is The Ties That Bind. The committee concludes that, "culture and communications are fundamental investments that will help to achieve renewal of our sense of pride and unity as a nation. We sincerely believe that, in both resolving the constitutional crisis which now confronts us and fulfilling the distinctive constitutional promise that lies before us, culture and communications will truly prove to be the ties that bind."

It's promising that the difficulties with Quebec nationalism have at last been recognized as cultural ones. And as I suggested earlier, the CBC long ago began the task of developing cultural sovereignty in both Canadian language groups, and still offers the best hope for continuing the work. But even if Quebec chooses political independence it will still have to collaborate to conserve and develop its culture, not only with English-speaking Canada but with other countries facing similar challenges.

The committee is also to be commended for not being content with pious verbiage, long the curse of any deliberation on culture.

Recommendation No. 5 reads: "As an investment in the future of our Canadian society and in support of the growth potential of cultural industries, both domestically and internationally, the government of Canada target an increase in its current budget investments in culture and communications in the order of five per cent annually over the next five years."

No. 6 asks, "That the government of Canada initiate a comprehensive strategy of incentives to encourage and motivate high levels of philanthropy and voluntarism in support of cultural activities in Canada." Other recommendations are to strengthen the Canada Council, compensate artists, improve Canadian film distribution and provide the CBC with a stable and predictable five-year funding program revolving annually, and take measures to haul Radio Canada International out of the Slough of Despond.

All this is admirable and a step forward in clarity and courage. In the matter of public broadcasting it brings us almost to the original principles on which our Canadian broadcasting system is founded: freedom of opinion, accessibility, cultural development and its connection with the emerging nation, independence from party-political and plutocratic control alike.

My only cavil, as usual, is that the recommendations don't go quite far enough. They don't take account of the heavy expense which is going to be imposed by the need to compete with the sky barons and the DBS challenge, and the consequent need to collaborate with other countries in similar straits. And by the way, when it comes to collaboration, we should certainly not go into a huddle with the neighbourhood strongboy and try to work out a bilateral deal, in which we would surely be worsted. That is not the table on which to place culture. We should go to the GATT with the problem, and settle it in company with others who share our anxieties and aspirations.

One more thing. If we are to survive at all, we are going to have to treat the matter as seriously as we would a material threat to our security. We are going to have to spend the kind of money we would not grudge if some enemy were bombarding our cities. There is no cultural defence against direct satellite broadcasts. The only defence is to attack, as it were, by putting up our own satellites in alliance with friends and fellow-broadcasters, and by generating our own excellent productions.

More than ever before, our survival depends on being able to compete with our trade partners in education, information, research and cultural development. At present we are losing our competitive edge. Singapore, for example, a tiny country which only yesterday was Third World, spends four times as much as we do per capita on education. They are also spending very heavily on culture, with the excuse that it will be good for tourism—but here they are missing the point. They spend a lot more per capita than we do on R & D. This is only one example of the competition we are facing in the global market.

But I have to say that the standing committee on communications and culture has given an excellent example of how the dangers and difficulties may be seized as opportunities. At last a group of parliamentarians has understood the kind of world we're living in, the poet's world of shadows, of manifold illusion which nevertheless is real and palpable, a world where ideas and images, values and aspirations are as potent as substantial things. Only by developing the mind and imagination of Canadians can we survive with influence over our life and community. Only by that influence can we come together, even if only in the old way we know so well, the way of agreeing to differ, of live and let live.

One thing only remains. We have to act. The chairpersons of the standing committee—Conservative, Liberal, nationalist—have work before them. Bud Bird, Sheila Finestone and Jean-Pierre Hogue have to rise from their chairs and get on the road across Canada with their NDP committee colleagues. First they have to talk to their caucuses to teach them, if necessary, the ABC of survival in the information age, to secure their enthusiastic support for strong action. In the provinces they have to win support from the governments and drum up grassroots support for cultural development through public broadcasting the way Alan Plaunt and Graham Spry did in the 1930s.

There is work, above all, for the government of Can-

ada. We have seen that in this age no one can go it alone: Canada must go the arenas where we have friends and collaborators. First to the OECD, a body that includes the Europeans as well as the United States and Japan, because we need a lot more first-rate analysis of cultural and broadcasting issues and the OECD has the human and financial resources to provide it.

Next, to the GATT where we have so many friends to make strong representations that the cultural and service matters be tabled and agreements reached that will guarantee everyone a place at the cultural feast. And finally to UNESCO, where Canada chairs the powerful executive committee.

There is urgent need to discuss and agree on measures to develop and distribute the images of our cultures. Here again, the government of Canada should instruct our representatives that the matter is urgent, not just something to be put on a list and dropped in exchange for free importation of canary birds. We need world services fully funded by international sources and governed by universally agreed rules. I am calling for action, backed by faith.

In conclusion, let me tell you a story. There's a Hassidic tale of a rabbi whom God showed the burning pit, full of fire and hideous demons, stinking of brimstone and smoke. God told the rabbi to jump in, and such was his faith (the story says) when he was launched in midair the demons turned into beautiful angels, the stench of brimstone became a sweet perfume of roses, the fire turned into delicate air that let him down gently on a grassy bank.

You'd never get me to jump, yet I see the point of the story—which is, if you believe that good must prevail, maybe it will.

Gotlieb Warns the Real Enemy Lies Within

Stephen Godfrey

Senior Features Writer

Is the federal government about to get out of paying for the culture business on the domestic front, and fork over all the rest to the United States in the current free trade talks? Over a long, hot summer, those have been the questions posed by the arts community, but Allan Gotlieb, who knows the workings of government and, increasingly, the arts, has concluded there is nothing to worry about. Or rather, that the worry should be directed closer to home.

Gotlieb, a civil servant and senior diplomat for most of his working life and, since 1989, occupant of a variety of positions including publisher of Saturday Night and chairman of the Canada Council, is busy these days plugging his book, *"I'll be with you in a minute, Mr. Ambassador,"* an expanded version of a series of lectures on his years as Canadian ambassador to Washington. But he feels he has talked to enough of the players involved in federal funding of culture and free trade, including Communications Minister Perrin Beatty and Trade Minister Michael Wilson, to come to a few conclusions on these issues. Not quickly or provocatively—he wasn't a diplomat for nothing—but with a hesitant thoughtfulness, as if he is pulling mental strings in his mind, sifting through what he knows of people, power, and the trade-offs that would make the tampering with culture by the powers that be worthwhile.

Since last spring, Quebec has been openly demanding that all authority and money for culture be transferred to the province from the federal government. It is a process which both Beatty and his predecessor Marcel Masse have hinted could be extended to all provinces, according to the Canadian Conference of the Arts, among others. But cultural issues are only part of the upcoming package, which Gotlieb refers to as "the mother of all Meeches."

Obviously, ever since the failure of Meech Lake, the federal government has been putting together a comprehensive constitutional package," he says. "It would address some of the legitimate demands of Quebec, and might involve the weakening of some national institutions."

"But in the cultural field, I don't believe the federal government will go ahead with devolution. It would be vastly unpopular, and a huge mistake. I've spoken to Perrin Beatty, and I think he is a strong supporter of national institutions, whereas his predecessor, Mr. Masse, didn't even like to use the term 'national institutions.' I think the federal government will choose another area to make concessions."

Reflecting his Ottawa-based experience, Gotlieb is convinced that true centres of excellence are impossible without federal intervention. "I happen to think that one of the reasons we have no Harvard or Yale is because there is no federal involvement in universities." And in the cultural field, he is no fan of the provincial bureaucracies he has seen springing up in the past 25 years.

Gotlieb recalls that he was made the first deputy minister of the federal Department of Communications, which was created in 1969. "By the next year, both Ontario and Quebec felt they had to have a deputy minister in that field, and the other provinces soon followed. I think they did it partly because it was trendy—if the federal government has one, we should have one—and because there is a bureaucratic will to power. Now, you can hardly distinguish between the federal and provincial bureaucracies in terms of competence, but none of the growth has been a necessity."

This doesn't mean Gotlieb thinks the provinces should get out of culture altogether. It's just that the reasons are more financial than anything else. "It is simply better to have more than one source of money, because it produces a kind of diversity, and in overall terms, more money produces the excitement, energy and magic that comes with cultural creativity," he says. "That is why Quebec artists shouldn't favor devolution, because it is absolutely clear that on a per capita basis they receive far more money under the current system."

On Canada's current free trade talks with the United States and Mexico, he is even more confident, partly because he was instrumental in negotiating the Canada-U.S. free trade agreement—a role for which many cultural nationalists have never forgiven him. He finds it ironic that many observers are afraid

From *The Globe and Mail*, September 14, 1991, p. C7. Reprinted by permission.

the federal government will cede to U.S. demands that protectionism be removed in cultural industries such as publishing and film, since many of the same critics felt that was what happened in the first round. "It is as if they are saying we've already given it up once, and now we're in danger of giving up the same thing twice," says Gotlieb. "In any case, I just can't imagine the federal government giving a wooden nickel in this area. There is no possible advantage to them in making any concessions."

Gotlieb risks sounding like an apologist for the federal government which has been his employer most of his working life, except that he has become increasingly critical of its cutbacks in funds to the Canada Council, which he feels has become "nobody's child. Because it is not a child of government—being at arm's length from government—there is no political advantage in any Member of Parliament to fight for it. As a result, we saw how Marcel Masse channelled a lot of spending on arts through the Department of Communications, rather than the Canada Council."

The result is that the council has 20 per cent less to spend in real terms than it did in 1985. It is not a determined policy to kill institutions like the council, or for that matter, the CBC. It is simply a process of what Gotlieb calls "death by decrement."

The implication is clear. It isn't the Quebec nationalists or the U.S. film lobby that pose the biggest threat to a strong federal system of culture. The real enemy is within.

The bell tolls for Canadian culture

Paul Audley

Paul Audley is president of Paul Audley & Associates Ltd., Toronto.

As any half-decent con man knows, the key when playing the shell game is to trick the victim into focusing on the wrong object. With the North American free-trade talks entering a critical stage, Canadians must be careful not to fall into the trap.

News stories in the past six months have focused on the conflict between U.S. Trade Representative Carla Hills and Canada's International Trade Minister, Michael Wilson, over exempting cultural industries from the agreement. Mrs. Hills has been pressing hard to eliminate the exemption incorporated in the 1988 deal between Canada and the United States, while Mr. Wilson has said that protection for Canada's broadcasting, recording and publishing industries will not be on the bargaining table.

The obvious thing to do is watch the talks and see what happens, but experience suggests that to do so will be to miss the real action. The important discussions are more likely to go on away from the negotiating table and to involve Canadian concessions on individual "irritants."

A look back to the last set of negotiations shows how the process really works. In film policy, for example, Canada's chief negotiator, Simon Riesman, was able to say that "film and television were never the subject of negotiations at my table."

That may well have been true, but it was largely irrelevant. Why? Because at other tables, officials from both countries met to bargain away the substance of a proposed law that would have strengthened Canada's domestic movie distribution.

The need for such a law had been argued forcefully in a 1985 federal task force report; drafting instructions had been approved by cabinet in 1986; a draft bill had been prepared by the Justice Department and in February, 1987, the communications minister had announced the government's intention to introduce the legislation quickly.

At that point, however, push came to shove and, in the context of the trade negotiations, the bill was never tabled. Instead, in a process separate from the trade talks but not unrelated to them, all provisions favouring Canadian-owned film-distribution companies were removed from the bill.

The same process also led to the rejection of guidelines recommended by the 1985 task force for screening new foreign investment in film distribution. Despite explicit recommendations to the contrary, U.S. investors were given the right to set up new businesses in Canada, and to sell their existing businesses here to the highest bidder.

So Canada is being treated increasingly as part of the domestic U.S. market, and Canadian distributors' share of the theatrical film market continues to slip—to a mere 14 per cent in 1990, compared with 27 per cent a decade earlier.

Thus, while Mr. Riesman could claim that film policy was not negotiated at the free-trade table, in reality, the bill and its proposed foreign-investment guidelines had been gutted. However, he was straightforward enough to say that he and the lawyers on his negotiating team considered the revised bill "fully consistent with the FTA."

A broader review of Ottawa's actions since 1987 demonstrates how maintaining a trade exemption for Canada's culture provides no assurances that it is actually being protected.

Before the 1988 federal election, the Conservatives maintained that existing support measures for culture were fully protected and that new ones would be easier to implement because the trade deal set limits to the countermeasures the Americans could take in response.

Yet the exemption has not been used even once to create any new measure to strengthen Canada's fragile cultural industries. Policies viewed as irritants by the United States, however, have continued to be eliminated or modified. For example:

• In June, 1987, the government announced that the Capital Cost Allowance incentive for investment in

5. THE POLITICS OF CULTURE

Canadian films and television programs would be reduced from 100 per cent to 30 per cent. This virtually ended its effectiveness and resulted in a substantial drop in Canadian production.

• Concessionary postal rates for Canadian publications are being eliminated, despite an explicit promise before the 1988 election there would be no reduction for at least five years. The direct-subsidy program to replace the special rates will have $110-million less money each year.

• In March, 1988, the government declined, for the first time, to apply its policy restricting new foreign investment in the book industry. While the policy has never been changed, it seems that no one has been required to comply with it since the trade deal was signed.

• It is also significant that simple legislative amendments required to make the Investment Canada Act effective have never been made. For three or four years it has been obvious, particularly from cases in the book industry, that the existing process of review is unworkable and that new foreign investors can comply technically with the Canadian ownership requirement while retaining effective control. This fundamental flaw renders illusory any protection of Canada's cultural industries that relies on the Investment Canada Act.

These and other measures have further weakened Canada's already fragile cultural industries, damaging our ability to finance cultural works and to distribute and market them effectively from coast to coast.

In an important 1987 policy paper entitled Vital Links: Canadian Cultural Industries, the government recognized that "the fundamental structural dilemma affecting Canada's cultural industries has worsened" and that if nothing is done, they "would erode further." But it has responded by making even more concessions to the Americans that are making this dilemma worse.

The North American free-trade talks have turned up the heat again, but it's unlikely that the cultural "exemption" will be lost. Rather, a new round of concessions elsewhere will simply weaken federal policies further.

For instance, the 1985 policy on screening new foreign investment in the book industry could be amended to exempt U.S. and other foreign owners of publishing and distribution businesses from having to seek a Canadian buyer should they decide to sell. Then only the financially fragile, Canadian-owned part of the industry would have to sell to Canadians.

Equally high on the list of irritants is Bill C-58, which limits the success of U.S. broadcasting and publishing services in reselling their U.S. content to Canadian advertisers. There will also be U.S. pressure to allow new American direct-to-home satel-

lite services such as Skypix into Canada—although the 1991 Broadcasting Act was deliberately drafted to prevent this and foster the creation of a Canadian service.

It is also possible that the investment provisions will be changed, perhaps to eliminate the screening of indirect acquisitions in the cultural industries. The government may even decide not to proceed with the pathetically watered-down film bill that the U.S. movie industry agreed to let us have in 1988.

The great advantage for the government of making step-by-step concessions is that it doesn't have to fight a big battle on the issue. But the results are the same for Canada's capacity to survive as an independent, unified and distinct nation.

Of course, it's possible there will be no more concessions—and even that something concrete will be done to strengthen Canada's cultural and communications systems. Recent statements by Michael Wilson show he understands that what's at stake is not so much protecting these industries as maintaining the links necessary to hold the different regions of Canada together. Communications Minister Perrin Beatty has also stated clearly that the problems facing cultural industries are systemic and structural, and can't be solved with financial Band-aids.

Unfortunately, the government's record since the free-trade deal offers little basis for optimism.

Language In Canada

Luc Albert

Luc Albert is a senior analyst with the Household, Family, and Social Statistics Division, Statistics Canada.

Census data indicate that there have been several distinct trends in the linguistic make-up of Canada since 1971. Both the proportion of the population in provinces other than Quebec with English mother tongue,[1] and that with French mother tongue in Quebec have risen. As well, bilingualism has become more common, as a growing percentage of Canadians report they are able to conduct a conversation in both official languages.

English increasing outside Quebec

In the last decade and a half, the proportion of Canadians living outside Quebec with English mother tongue has increased. In 1986, 80.0% of people living in provinces other than Quebec reported English as their mother tongue; this was up from 78.4% in 1971 and 79.4% in 1981. During the same period, the proportion of this population with French mother tongue fell from 6.0% in 1971 to 5.0% in 1986.

Other than Quebec, New Brunswick has by far the largest share of its population with French mother tongue. In 1986, 33.5% of residents of this province had French as their mother tongue, down slightly from 34.0% in 1971.

The proportion of people with French mother tongue was much lower in the remaining provinces. The figure was around 5% in Ontario, Manitoba, and Prince Edward Island; 4% in Nova Scotia; 2% in Saskatchewan, Alberta, and British Columbia; and just 0.5% in Newfoundland. As well, the percentage of the population with French mother tongue fell in these provinces between 1971 and 1986.

The proportion of Canadians outside Quebec whose mother tongue was neither English nor French has also declined. In 1986, 14.9% of this population had a mother tongue other than an official language, down from 15.6% in 1971.

There is considerable provincial variation in the percentage of people with a mother tongue other than English or French. In 1986, 22% of Manitoba residents, along with between 15% and 17% of those in Ontario, British Columbia, Saskatchewan, and Alberta, had a mother tongue other

than English or French. In comparison, only 2% of people in Nova Scotia and around 1% of those in the other Atlantic provinces had a mother tongue other than one of the official languages.

Francophone population increasing in Quebec

The proportion of Quebec residents with French as their mother tongue has increased steadily in the last decade and a half. In 1986, French was the mother tongue of 82.8% of the people living in this province, up from 80.7% in 1971 and 82.4% in 1981.

There has also been a slight increase in the proportion of Quebec residents reporting a mother tongue other than English or French, from 6.2% in 1971 to 6.8% in 1986.

The actual number of people in Quebec with English mother tongue also continued to decrease between 1981 and 1986, although the decline was smaller than in the previous five-year period. The number of anglophones in Quebec fell 4% between 1981 and 1986, compared with a 12% decline between 1976 and 1981.

Much of the decline in Quebec's anglophone population is attributable to the fact that the number of these peo-

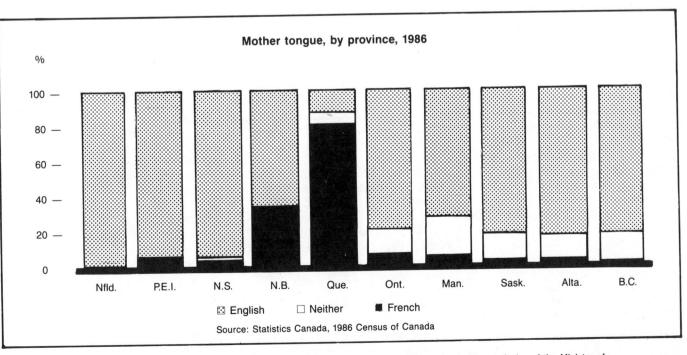

Mother tongue, by province, 1986

Source: Statistics Canada, 1986 Census of Canada

From *Canadian Social Trends*, Statistics Canada, Spring 1989, pp. 9-12. Reproduced with permission of the Minister of Supply and Services Canada, 1989.

5. POLITICAL CULTURE

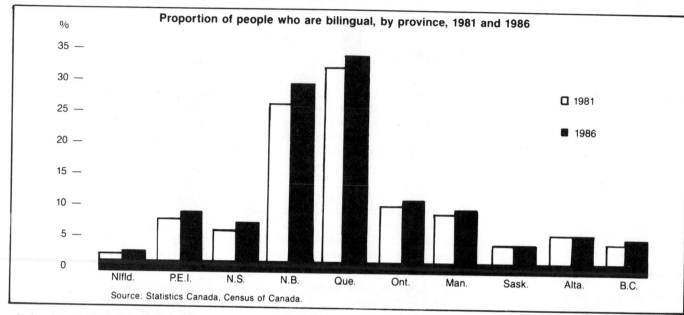

Proportion of people who are bilingual, by province, 1981 and 1986

□ 1981

■ 1986

Nlfld.   P.E.I.   N.S.   N.B.   Que.   Ont.   Man.   Sask.   Alta.   B.C.

Source: Statistics Canada, Census of Canada.

ple leaving Quebec for elsewhere in Canada far exceeds the number entering the province from other regions. Between 1981 and 1986, 41,000 more anglophones left Quebec for other parts of Canada than came to Quebec from other provinces. This was down significantly from a net loss of 106,000 during the 1976–1981 period.

English increasing, French declining across Canada

When figures from Quebec and the other provinces are combined, the results show that the proportion of all Canadians with English mother tongue has risen, while the percentage whose mother tongue is French has fallen. Between 1971 and 1986, the percentage of people with English mother tongue rose from 60.2% to 62.1%, while the proportion with French mother tongue declined from 26.9% to 25.1%.

Several factors have contributed to the overall decline in the proportion of Canadians whose mother tongue is French. These factors include low fertility in immigrants who speak French, as well as the linguistic assimilation of French-speaking minorities outside Quebec, and the tendency of people with mother tongues other than English or French to adopt the English language.

On the other hand, there has been little overall change in the proportion of Canadians with a mother tongue other than French or English. In the 1971-1986 period, the share of people with another mother tongue remained stable at around 13%.

However, there were changes in the proportion of people with different mother tongues. There was strong growth in the number of people reporting languages associated with the birthplaces of recent immigrants, notably Spanish, and Asiatic languages such as Chinese, Vietnamese, Persian (Farsi), and Tamil. On the other hand, the proportion of people with mother tongues such as German and Ukrainian has fallen.

More Canadians bilingual

In 1986, more than four million Canadians reported they could conduct a conversation in both English and French. That year 16.2% of the population was bilingual, up from 13.4% in 1971 and 15.3% in 1981.

Quebec has the highest proportion of population which is bilingual. In fact, slightly over half of all Canada's bilingual population in 1986 lived in this province. That year, 34.5% of Quebec residents reported they could conduct a conversation in either official language.

The most bilingual group within Quebec was anglophone. In 1986, more than half (54%) of these people were bilingual, as were almost half (47%) of Quebec residents whose mother tongue was neither English nor French. At the same time, about a third (30%) of Quebec francophones were bilingual.

In contrast, fewer than 6% of people residing outside Quebec with English, or a language other than English or

French, as their mother tongue reported they were bilingual in 1986. However, the vast majority of people outside Quebec with French mother tongue were bilingual. In 1986, almost four of every five (79%) of them were able to conduct a conversation in both official languages.

Outside Quebec, the most bilingual province was New Brunswick, where 29.1% of the population reported themselves as able to conduct a conversation in both official languages. In the remaining provinces, the proportion of the population which was bilingual ranged from around 12% in Ontario to less than 3% in Newfoundland.

Between 1981 and 1986, bilingualism increased in all provinces except Alberta, where the proportion reporting they were able to converse in both official languages was unchanged.

Youth more bilingual

Young Canadians are generally more likely than other people to be bilingual. In 1986, 20.5% of the population aged 15-24 could conduct a conversation in either English or French; this compared with 19.9% of those aged 25-44, 16.8% of those aged 45-64, and 12.4% of people aged 65 and over. This suggests that French immersion programs in Canadian schools have contributed to the growth of bilingualism.

NOTES

1. Mother tongue is the language first learned and still understood.

Writing Off Canadian Publishing

The Tories' good-news announcement on the book industry conceals more than it reveals about their attitude toward Canadian culture.

Carol Martin

Carol Martin is a member of the Forum's *editorial board and a former book publisher and Canada Council officer.*

On January 28 of this year, the federal government announced a change of policy that could kill the cherished Canadian dream of a domestically controlled publishing industry.

Ever since U.S. publishing giant McGraw-Hill purchased Ryerson Press from the United Church in 1970, Canadians have understood that, as in the newspaper, magazine and broadcasting industries, Canadian control of the book industry is crucial to our cultural sovereignty. For the most part, government ministers and bureaucrats have concurred with public opinion on this objective. The need to have book publishing in Canadian hands is based on a simple fact: most of the books written by Canadians are published by indigenously owned firms.

But when Perrin Beatty, Minister of Communications in the Conservative government, announced that multinational book publishers operating in Canada will no longer be required to divest control to Canadians when the parent company changes hands, the chances of achieving this objective were seriously undermined. Not only will the slow move to Canadianize the industry cease, but Canadian-owned firms in book publishing and distribution can now be sold, under certain "extraordinary circumstances" of financial distress, to foreign investors. For the first time since the early '70s, the country's slow, stumbling and sometimes ineffective moves toward legislating a Canadian-owned book industry have been halted.

To comprehend the ownership issue in book publishing, it is necessary to understand one basic principle: the more profitable a segment of the industry, the more likely it is to be foreign-controlled; the less profitable, the more likely it will remain Canadian. Thus the lucrative areas of educational publishing and distributing imported books are dominated by foreign-owned companies, while originating Canadian scholarly works and books of fiction, poetry and non-fiction for the general public (known as trade publishing) is undertaken principally by Canadian-owned publishers. Statistics Canada figures consistently show that Canadian-owned firms publish 80 per cent of Canadian-authored titles, but account for substantially less than half of the total sales of the industry.

The capacity to publish Canadian books across a wide range of subject matter requires a continuous financial investment. Generally speaking, it is not an investment that produces a high return, or any return at all, yet it is highly valued by the country as essential to its political and cultural survival.

But supporting the principle of Canadian control in book publishing, and actually adopting the policies required to achieve it, have been two vastly different things. Successive federal governments have been leery of taking measures that would inevitably be unpopular with foreign, particularly American, publishers and governments. Although the objective of greater Canadian control has remained a high priority for the industry since the '70s, the federal response, first under the Liberals and then under the Conservatives, has been to offer Canadian-owned publishers crisis funding in the form of grants, instead of making the tough policy decisions that would produce structural change. This has happened even though it is clear from other cultural industries—for example, the regulations on advertising in Canadian magazines and on Canadian content in broadcasting—that structural measures *do* work.

The so-called Baie Comeau Policy, adopted by the Conservative government in 1985 to increase Canadian ownership in book publishing, was just such a structural measure. Honoured far more in the breach than the observance, it was finally buried by Beatty's announcement on January 28. Its history is instructive for an understanding of Canadian cultural policy.

From FIRA to Baie Comeau

Over the past 20 years there has been slow movement in the direction of legislated change. In 1974, the Trudeau Liberals passed the Foreign Investment Review Act (FIRA). Under FIRA, all sales of Canadian companies to foreign interests, whatever their previous ownership, were to be

From *The Canadian Forum*, Vol. 70, No. 809, March 1992, pp. 18-21. Copyright © 1992 by Carol Martin. Reprinted by permission.

scrutinized for the benefits to Canadians, before the sale could take place. In the book sector, this scrutiny included bookstores, wholesalers and distributors, as well as publishers.

Some valuable changes resulted from this process: U.S.-owned Simon and Schuster agreed to distribute its books in Canada through Canadian-owned General Publishing, rather than undertaking distribution on its own; and a new mass-market paperback house, Seal Books, was created through a joint venture between McClelland and Stewart, which owned 51 per cent, and Bantam Books (Seal has now become 75 per cent Canadian-owned). But there were justified complaints from investors that they were in the dark about what position FIRA might take on any given transaction; decisions could be irritatingly slow; and there was no consistent monitoring or follow-up action regarding the "net benefits" to Canada of the transactions that were allowed to go through.

General disillusionment with FIRA was replaced by outright depression in 1984, when the first Mulroney government replaced FIRA with the Investment Canada Act, and declared the country "open for business". It therefore came as some surprise when, just one year later, Minister of Communications Marcel Masse announced a new, tougher policy regarding foreign investment in book publishing. It was called the Baie Comeau Policy after the place where it was announced in July of 1985.

Masse's appointment as minister had been greeted negatively by English-Canadian publishers. He had a more hands-on attitude toward culture than is popular in English Canada, and had little sympathy for the arms-length policies so dear to the heart of most Canadian artists and cultural organizations. But the publishing community soon came to respect his conviction that culture *is* important—perhaps the most important thing that governments can support—and when Masse persuaded Cabinet to adopt a policy that might, if consistently enforced, gradually transfer the book industry into Canadian hands, he won the support of the writing and publishing community.

Under Baie Comeau, Canada took the position that, as long as multinational publishers operating here remained under the same ownership, it would be unfair to require them to divest control. However, if at any time the parent company changed hands, the new owner would have to sell at least 51 per cent of the Canadian operation to Canadian citizens.

Potentially, the policy could have expanded Canadian ownership in educational publishing and import distribution, to the point where these profitable areas would have become significantly Canadian-owned. Unfortunately, there were serious obstacles to making the policy work. At 51 per cent, the level set by the Investment Canada Act, the definition of Canadian ownership was not sufficiently high, nor accompanied by other guarantees of actual, as opposed to apparent, Canadian control. The cash-strapped Canadian industry had little ability to generate the investment capital required to purchase a controlling interest in branch publishers that came up for sale; no loan assistance for this purpose was created. No mechanism was created to establish a fair price for the companies to be sold. And companies were allowed to change hands before divestiture was required by Investment Canada (theoretically, the sale was to be completed within two years).

In sum, neither the federal cabinet nor the bureaucrats at Investment Canada were sufficiently determined to implement Masse's policy by creating the conditions for its success.

On January 28 of this year, the federal government announced a change of policy that could kill the cherished Canadian dream of a domestically controlled publishing industry.

Moreover, the powerful multinationals that own much of Canada's publishing industry were furious with the policy and promised, through the American government, severe reprisals (such as the famous "scorched earth" threat of Gulf + Western, now Paramount Corporation). This meant that when hard decisions had to be made, the Canadian government backed down.

Backing Down

Few companies whose acquisition came under Baie Comeau actually divested 51 per cent to Canadian owners. When they did so, they often became Canadian-owned in name only—the big decisions were still being made by the multinational owner. Then, as of January 1, 1989, the Free Trade Agreement stipulated that the Canadian government would be required to be the buyer of last resort when divestiture was required (Article 1607), and Baie Comeau became unworkable.

In the only case where Article 1607 was implemented, the federal government purchased 51 per cent of the combined assets of two educational publishers, Ginn and GLC, from Paramount, after the latter had been allowed to retain its acquisition of Prentice-Hall of Canada. The purchase of Ginn/GLC by the Canada Development Investment Corporation (CDIC) cost the Canadian taxpayer some $9 million. To date it has produced little discernible benefit to Canada or Canadian-owned publishing, since the CDIC has not seen fit to resell its shares to Canadian investors.

Meanwhile, HarperCollins, controlled by Rupert Murdoch, has sought to exploit an apparent loophole in the Baie Comeau Policy. After Murdoch acquired the company in 1989, it formed a new Canadian-controlled company, HarperCollins Publishers Ltd., to publish Canadian titles, while keeping its more profitable distribution business within the foreign-controlled HarperCollins Canada Ltd. The Murdoch interests ended up with complete control of the profitable distribution rights previously held by Canadian-owned Fitzhenry & Whiteside. The HarperCollins case, the Maxwell Macmillan case, and several other multinational subsidiaries whose parent companies have changed hands in the past three years have remained under review by Investment Canada, which has displayed no urgency or resolve in enforcing Baie Comeau.

Instead of meeting the problems presented by Baie Comeau head-on—none is impossible to solve—the Conservative government has now backed off the policy completely.

The New Publishing Policy

In outlining his government's new policy for book publishing in January, Perrin Beatty, Minister of Communications, announced the following changes:

- *Definition of "Canadian" for funding purposes.* Only companies at least 75 per cent owned by Canadians will be eligible for federal programs of financial support. This is an improvement over the previous requirement of only 51 per cent Canadian ownership, and will help to ensure that government support goes to companies that are genuinely Canadian-controlled. An amendment to the Investment Canada Act will also empower the government to investigate cases where partial foreign ownership of book publishers may mean that control in fact does not reside with Canadian shareholders.

- *Increased funding.* Over the next five years, new funding of $102 million for the Canadian-owned industry will be provided, in addition to existing Department of Communications commitments of $38 million during the same period. Total funding for the first year of the program, 1992-93, will be $25.6 million, to be supplemented in 1993-94 by an additional $25 million per year for book distribution and marketing purposes, to replace the current postal subsidy.

This is a big direct-funding increase and has been welcomed by Canadian-owned publishers, but it is not nearly as generous as it might sound. The distribution and marketing program next year takes the place of the traditional government subsidy to Canada Post to reduce the cost of mailing books (Book Rate). The old postal subsidy was in the amount of $60 million. So, in fact, the change will save the government $35 million. On the positive side, the remaining $25 million will be earmarked entirely for Canadian-owned firms, whereas the $60 million was open to foreign-owned companies as well. At this stage, it is unknown exactly how the new funding will be used when the two programs come into effect.

The $25.6 million to be made available this year should improve the financial health of beleaguered publishers substantially, but even it pales in comparison with the GST collected from all book sales in Canada. Some estimates place that figure as high as $150 million annually, in addition to the book industry's loss of its exemption under the former federal manufacturing sales tax—an "invisible" mode of support that was probably worth at least $50 million to the industry.

Although Beatty has promised to consult the publishers on how the funds will be used, and even offered to turn administration of the program over to them, the basis on which the new money will be distributed remains unclear.

- *Copyright changes.* The Copyright Act will be amended to require Canadian libraries, school boards, bookstores and wholesalers to buy imported books from the Canadian publishers holding distribution rights to them. Booksellers and librarians will be unhappy with this strengthening of protection for Canadian rights-holders and will complain—frequently with justification—that they get quicker, easier and sometimes cheaper service from American wholesalers. Nonetheless, this amendment will serve to strengthen the Canadian-based publishing and distribution industry by keeping business (and jobs) in Canada. It should also put pressure on publishers and government to ensure that the postal-subsidy replacement funds mentioned above ensure that customer service by Canadian distributors improves.

- *Changes to the Investment Canada Act.* The revised guidelines state that foreign investment in new book-related businesses will be limited to Canadian-controlled joint ventures. Foreign acquisition of a Canadian-owned company will not *generally* be permitted, except in "exceptional circumstances" of dire financial need, when Canadian investors have had an opportunity to bid for the company. Indirect acquisitions (purchase of a Canadian branch plant through purchase of its parent company outside Canada) will no longer require that the majority of the Canadian operation be sold to Canadians, but will be reviewed by Investment Canada, to ensure that the new foreign owner provides "undertakings" that will benefit Canada and the Canadian-controlled sector of the industry. However, since the Baie Comeau Policy didn't work, and Investment Canada was unable or unwilling to regulate the behaviour of branch plants when it had the stick of enforced divestiture, what chance is there that they will be more successful under this weakened policy?

Perrin Beatty seems to believe that by strengthening Canadian-owned publishing companies with grants, he will somehow make it possible for them to buy back their industry. But the new money going into Canadian publishing, as welcome as it may be, is not significant enough to accomplish a turnaround of this magnitude.

The transactions under review at Investment Canada will be resolved under the new regulations. Worse, the government has opened the door to the sale of Canadian-owned companies to foreign interests. Although "foreign acquisition of a Canadian-controlled business will not generally be permitted", according to Perrin Beatty's news release, the Minister acknowledged, in a CBC *Morningside* interview with Peter Gzowski, that "if no available Canadian buyer is available and the consequences to the company would be closure", such a sale *would* be allowed. With Canadian-owned publishers frequently in a deficit position, this situation might arise at any time.

Once more, instead of continuing to work toward desirable structural changes in the book industry, the government has increased its direct financial support to Canadian-owned companies. (See "The New Publishing

Policy," for details of the announcement.) And who can argue with that? If substantial new money hadn't become available this year, from federal and in some cases provincial sources, the loss of some of the country's most culturally important publishers would have continued at an accelerated rate.

But the question remains: why did the government feel that it must, at the same time, negate the only measure adopted in Canada's history to restore this cultural industry to Canadian hands? It is easy to feel paranoid about this decision, as it is about so much else that has gone wrong in the country lately, and to believe that it was based solely on a wish to placate the American government, and on arrangements that were "understood" under the Free Trade Agreement. Recent revelations by Val Ross, publishing reporter for *The Globe and Mail*, that the policy was at least discussed with, and at worst agreed to, by American officials before being announced, is no doubt an indication of that. But it may simply be that in this, as in so many areas, the present government is without the commitment or courage required to continue a serious thrust toward strengthening Canadian ownership.

A Personal Postscript

My husband Peter and I were among the few, small Canadian publishers who came together for the first time when the sale of Ryerson Press was announced in 1970. There was no organization small publishers could afford to belong to at that time and we had never before met to share information and to discuss our problems. We immediately formed The Emergency Committee of Canadian Publishers and within a few days held a press conference to present a statement calling on the government to take steps to help publishers. One of these was to "Prohibit sales of Canadian companies to foreign owners".

This small group went on over the next 20 years to become the Association of Canadian Publishers (ACP), the politically powerful organization to which more than 90 per cent of Canadian-owned publishers now belong. Throughout that time the ACP has continued to press for the Canadianization of the industry, whether by calling for its designation as "a key industry" in the '70s, or by urging the government to strengthen "FIRA with the objective of a gradual repatriation of the publishing industry" in the '80s.

This year, when the dream of a Canadian publishing industry is so severely threatened, the Canadian publishers, and the ACP, have been strangely silent. It is hard to blame them, given the urgency of the financial problems many of them face. But in private, publishers are gravely concerned about the loss of Baie Comeau, and seem demoralised on the ownership issue.

It is important, now, for other groups who support the idea of Canadian ownership of publishing to speak out. Although no improvement can be hoped for under the current government, other parties may be willing to listen, and to prepare to take new steps to regulate ownership in the future. It is possible that the long-term result of this setback will be a stronger resolve to work toward repatriating Canadian publishing. When writers, publishers, most of those involved in the industry, and a majority of interested Canadians are essentially in agreement about the importance of Canadian publishing, finding the courage to ensure Canadian control should not be impossible.

Perrin Beatty and the Conservative cabinet may have been successful, for the moment, in their latest move to harmonize the country with American interests, but it seems unlikely that the dream of a Canadian-owned industry will die so quietly.

How come the Digest qualifies as Canadian?

Pierre Berton

In the continuing debate over the erosion of Canadian culture, everybody seems to have forgotten about the *Reader's Digest*, an American publication masquerading as a Canadian publication.

The *Digest* enjoys a very special advantage over other American magazines in this country. Its advertisers are allowed to claim their costs as an untaxable business expense.

That's because the *Digest* is pretending to be a Canadian magazine and no one at Revenue Canada has bothered to find out just how Canadian it is.

Last spring the *Digest* eliminated the core of its Canadian operation in Montreal. Five senior editors—who dealt primarily with Canadian writers and condensations from Canadian magazines and books—were dropped, along with two Canadian researchers, and three Canadian contributing editors (one of whom resigned and was not replaced).

It closed both its Toronto and Ottawa editorial offices on the ground that they were no longer needed. The magazine doesn't see itself as a Canadian magazine any more, but as an international publication.

That wouldn't matter if the *Digest* hadn't made some specific promises in order to keep the tax benefits for its advertisers. In the past couple of years, these promises have been forgotten.

Back in the mid-'70s, following the media report by Keith Davey's Senate committee, a great fuss was made over the special status accorded to the Canadian editions of *Time* and the *Digest*. At a time when Canadian magazines were foundering financially, both were enjoying a substantial tax break and an unfair advantage. *Time* eventually closed its Canadian operation, but the *Digest* dug in its heels and mounted a strong campaign

to justify its position as a national publication, supporting both Canadian writers and Canadian magazines from whom it purchased articles.

In October, 1974, the then president of the Canadian *Digest*, Paul Zimmerman, announced that "every word" of the contents of the two editions (French and English) "is edited by a Canadian editorial team for its relevance to Canadian readers." In a letter to the then secretary of state, Hugh Faulkner, Zimmerman pledged that the *Digest* would run a minimum 35 per cent of genuine Canadian content—articles assigned to Canadian writers on specific Canadian subjects.

For years, the magazine made a real effort to hold to this formula. But now, under a new regime, the number of original articles by Canadian writers has been cut in half and so has the number of articles condensed from Canadian magazines.

The *Digest*'s intense two-year campaign for the right to tax exemption for its advertisers also resulted in the passing of Bill C-58. That specifies that the magazine has a legal commitment to run an average of 80 per cent Canadian content. The ratio is supposed to be monitored by Revenue Canada.

The *Digest* seems to believe that C-58 nullified the Zimmerman pledge. It doesn't. Its definition of "Canadian content" is so broad it's a joke.

C-58 allows the magazine to count its "adaptations" as Canadian content—articles supposedly re-edited or re-condensed from articles that also ran in the American edition. By using this loophole, the *Digest* has tried to wriggle out of the Zimmerman pledge.

How much creative work and editorial expertise goes into these so-

called adaptations? To what extent are they revised to give them a Canadian spin? How much new material is added? Precious little. By merely changing a word or two, the magazine can now claim that an article written in the United States by an American on an American subject with American examples, can be designated, for tax purposes, as Canadian content!

Let us look at last March's American edition, which carried 10 articles that were "adapted" for Canada. Nine were virtually unchanged. "Mid-January" became "January 15"; "every day" became "daily." "America" became "North America," though the relevant statistics weren't adjusted. In one case, the final paragraph was changed.

This is Canadian content? For this does the *Digest* get special consideration? There was a time when the *Digest*'s Canadian editors made a real effort to add Canadian statistics and Canadian examples to articles taken from the parent magazine. Now they're being discouraged from making costly changes by the American head office.

There was a time when pressure from the United States was resisted, as in the biography of Norman Bethune, *The Scalpel, The Sword*, which the Americans tried unsuccessfully to suppress. Now the Americans call the tune.

There was a time when Canadian stories were almost always assigned to Canadian writers. But when the Hercules crash in the Canadian Arctic made headlines, the *Digest* preferred to send an American.

Nobody wants to bar the *Digest* from this country. But why, oh why, is Revenue Canada giving it a favored status over all similar magazines?

From *The Toronto Star,* August 29, 1992, p. G3. Reprinted with permission from The Toronto Star Syndicate.

The Regionalism of Federalism

While regionalism is a political phenomenon in all large nations —and indeed in many small nations, too—it is especially politically important in Canada. The fact that Canada's population is spread out like a 300-mile-wide ribbon across the continent—over 90 percent of Canada's population lives within 300 miles of its southern border— puts a strain on Canadian political unity that might not be so intensely felt if the population were distributed in a different fashion. When this is combined with a number of important issues that are regionally focused, such as the concentration of French Canadians in Quebec and the importance of language-related issues in Quebec, the importance of energy and energy-related issues in Alberta, the importance of natural resources and resource-related issues in British Columbia, fisheries and related issues in the Maritimes, and so on, it is easy to see how regionalism can be a politically significant factor.

This section begins with two general articles that discuss questions of federal powers, economic policy-making, and regional federalism. Nate Laurie and David Kilgour discuss economic federalism and regional disparity and whether federalism can solve more problems than it creates. Issues related to Canada's "have" and "have not" provinces are raised, and the sensitive question of whether executive federalism has created one Canada or two is addressed.

The next series of articles focuses on Canada's Atlantic region. Andrew Cornwall asks what would happen to the Atlantic provinces if Quebec pulled out of Canada and whether the Atlantic region might eventually be forced to join the United States. John DeMont focuses on the issue of fish and how the collapse of cod fisheries is affecting Newfoundland—especially Newfoundland's social structures.

Following this, the Canadian Midwest is examined. Richard Gwyn offers a stark examination of the difficult economic times facing Saskatchewan's farmers. Ultimately, Gwyn seeks to determine whether Saskatchewan's farms can survive the current hard times and what policy changes need to be made to ensure their survival.

The final group of articles in this section focuses on the Canadian west and north. The neoconservative right and the democratic left are the subjects of an article focusing on British Columbia. The impact of increasing trade with and immigration from Asia on British Columbia politics is discussed. Finally, two articles dealing with the Arctic territories and the native peoples conclude with discussion about aboriginal relations with the federal government and how aboriginal self-government might work.

Looking Ahead: Challenge Questions

How does Canadian federalism make coordinated policy-making more difficult for the federal government in Ottawa? What role should provincial governments play in providing more social services? How active should the federal government be in ensuring that all Canadians have similar standards of living?

While the federal government cannot prevent all regional disparities, what should the role of the federal government be in helping provinces to deal with natural problems such as the decline in fisheries or hard times for Canada's farmers?

Is Canadian ideology changing? Now that the New Democratic Party is in control in Ontario, is it changing its agenda? Is it no longer a truly social democratic party? How do ideologies differ between the Canadian West and the Canadian Midwest and East?

What role will Canada's aboriginal peoples end up playing in their own government? Can they reach an agreement with the federal government that will permit both sides to be satisfied with a power-sharing arrangement?

Unit 6

If we are ever to get this country going again, we will have to begin by:

ENDING REGIONAL FAVORITISM

David Kilgour, MP

David Kilgour is the Member of Parliament for Edmonton Southeast and Liberal energy critic. He is author of *Inside Outer Canada* and *Uneasy Patriots—Western Canadians in Confederation*.

ROMOTED BY OUR PARTICULAR brand of executive federalism and elitist executive democracy inherited from abroad in the heyday of British colonialism, we have created two Canadas: one economically diverse, stable, populous and prosperous—Inner Canada; the other characterized by small populations, resource-dependent economies, high unemployment, low political clout and varying degrees of regional discontent—Outer Canada.

Inner Canada at different periods was identified with Ontario, Quebec or both. It is, in fact, a narrow southern band of each, 300 kilometres wide and 1,000 long, extending from Windsor to Quebec City. Its epicentre today is clearly Metropolitan Toronto and, to a lesser extent, Greater Montreal.

Early Inner Canadians, with good incomes derived from a rich agricultural economy and foreign trade in staples, used the tariff, railway-building and other features of John A. Macdonald's 1879 National Policy to establish their regional dominance in manufacturing, transportation and financial spheres everywhere.

As a result, for example, farm producers in Prairie Canada found themselves able to buy tractors and other machinery from the Canadian core only.

Ottawa's Bank Act of 1871, by opting for branch banking rather than the American model of state-regulated and usually locally-owned banks, resulted in the rapid rise of large banks controlled in Montreal and Toronto.

Another Ottawa policy, low postal rates, allowed Inner Canada retailers with catalogues (such as Eaton's) to challenge local retailers and regional wholesalers throughout Outer Canada. Very weak-wristed federal anti-trust laws (which persist today) encouraged heartland companies in numerous sectors to absorb their competition, initially in Atlantic Canada, but later throughout Western Canada as well.

Entering the 20th century, Inner Canadians held the additional advantage of large local markets, ready access to prosperous and large American markets, proximity of transportation routes, and above all, the political and administrative muscle in Ottawa necessary to enhance the heartland role of Central Canada. In short, residents of Toronto-Montreal-Ottawa, with major assistance from the "national" government, eventually came to control most wholesale and retail prices, insurance rates, electronic communications, trading and investment policies from St. John's to Nanaimo to Yellowknife.

From *Policy Options,* Vol. 12, No. 9, November 1991, pp. 3-7. This article first appeared in *Policy Options,* Canada's Forum for Public Policy Debate.

Figure 1
Who Benefited Most from Confederation
Opinions in a Gallup Poll 1989

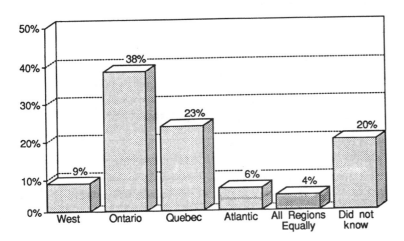

Greater Toronto is the dominant metropolis of not only our heartland but also the rest of the country. It is our national business capital, accounting for a quarter of our country's gross national product and half of our national exports. Forty-four per cent of the sales of Canada's top 100 industrial companies take place in Toronto.

The Toronto Stock Exchange now accounts for about three-fourths of the activity on all Canadian stock exchanges. Equally significant, the Greater Toronto area now provides half of all income taxes paid by Ontarians to our federal and provincial governments.

Per capita income within the city during 1987, the most recent year available, was $21,905 compared with $12,541 in one district in northeastern Ontario, $12,400 in Newfoundland.

The city houses half of Canada's largest 500 companies, whereas Manhattan holds only about one tenth of America's Fortune 500 Companies.

Sixty per cent of our computer firms and four out of five foreign banks operating in Canada are there.

The metropolis-hinterland pattern of economic geography exists in other nations, but the two-tier model is deeper and more enduring in Canada than in most other countries. Australia, for example, a vast land, sparsely settled with just over 15 million inhabitants, is often portrayed as a "region-less" nation.

From data assembled by the Australian Bureau of Industry Economics in the early 1980s, it is evident that disparities in unemployment by state and regional income differentials in Australia were smaller than in the United Kingdom, Canada or the United States.

Regional problems do exist in Australia; policies designed to divert population and economic activity away from the major centres have not worked as expected. Nonetheless, regional fairness appears to be constantly on the agenda of Australian cabinets unlike Canada. Section 99 of the Australian constitution orders the federal government to favor no state, or any part of one, over another state or its components. Another section bars favoritism on tax matters either between states or within regions of them.

In Canada, the lack of a balanced economic growth policy in Ottawa has aggravated regional alienation at a time when national unity is clearly under major strain for constitutional and other reasons. Consider the following examples of disparities in regional economic performance further exacerbated by an evident bias of federal government policies.

Between the 1984 election and January 1990, approximately 1.6 million jobs were created across Canada. About 8 per cent of them were created in Atlantic Canada, 24 per cent in Western Canada and fully 65 per cent, or more than one million, in Ontario and Quebec.

During the same time, the unemployment rates in parts of the country outside southern Ontario and Quebec often were twice and three times those in our industrial heartland.

Recent unemployment rates document the growing gap in employment opportunities between the regions. For example, while districts in southern Ontario until the recent advent of our present very serious recession—itself worsened, and to some mostly caused by Ottawa's prolonged high interest rate and high dollar policy—enjoyed unemployment rates of 4.7, 4.8 and 5.1 per cent, there are economic regions in Newfoundland with unemployment rates of 26.3 per cent; Nova Scotia, 18.0 per cent, New Brunswick, 16.1 per cent, and peripheral Quebec, 23 per cent.

Despite such unevenness in employment opportunities across the country, the money expected to stimulate regional economic growth flows mostly to Central Canada. As an illustration of this point, the figures for 1986-87 and 1987-88 indicate that our largest, most diversified and industrialized provinces, Quebec and Ontario, received the major portion of regional grants; 60 per cent of the total for both of the provinces in 1986-87 and fully 71.5 per cent during fiscal 1987-88.

Regional development programs have largely failed to spread economic growth into the outer regions. Most growth has occurred in Central Canada. According to Statistics Canada data on provincial economic performance, Ontario and Quebec accounted for 65.1 per cent of Canada's gross domestic product in 1989—the four Atlantic provinces 6.0 per cent and Western Canada 28.9 per cent.

In contrast, the United States has been far more successful in stimulating balanced economic growth. During 1989, Florida led all 50 states in growth, and Orlando ranked fourth nationally during the same year in attracting new business facilities and expanding existing ones. The top five metropolitan areas in new plants and expansions: Dallas, Portland, Atlanta, Orlando and Los Angeles, are located in five different American states and the best-performing ten states under the same criteria were Florida, California, Alabama, North Carolina, Texas, Ohio, Pennsylvania, New York, Virginia and Georgia.

Though not all regions are represented, the more balanced economic growth pattern is obvious.

Our private and public sector companies usually establish their head offices in Toronto-Ottawa-Montreal. According to the Financial Post's 1989 ranking by sales or operating revenues, fully 265 of our largest 500 companies—73 per cent—have their head offices in Ontario or Quebec.

6. THE REGIONALISM OF FEDERALISM

An even greater percentage of our largest financial institutions—four-fifths—are based in Ontario and Quebec, leaving 18 per cent for the West and 2 per cent only for Atlantic Canada. The head offices of all six of the major chartered banks are located in Toronto or Montreal. A few thousand powerful people in the two cities continue to call most of the economic shots across the country.

Numerous Ottawa agencies, departments and Crown corporations follow the high concentration in the centre. Only five out of 40 of our largest and best-known national Crown corporations have their head offices outside Central Canada. Not one of the five is in Atlantic Canada. They are all located in either Ottawa or Montreal. Some call it Ottawa's Kremlin complex.

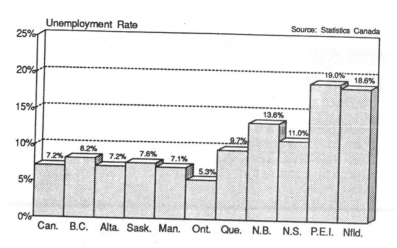

Figure 2
Unemployment Rates by Province
April 1990

Ottawa Practices

Our national government is a highly centralized organization with a disproportionate number of its key decision makers originating in Inner Canada. In consequence, the organizational capacity of Ottawa to represent regional circumstances is inadequate.

Federal officials play, of course, key roles in shaping policies and government decision-making processes. Major decisions are normally made at the middle and senior levels of departments.

Cabinet ministers rarely have much influence on the first draft of a policy position paper or cabinet documents. The aphorism in Ottawa, "He who controls the first draft, controls policy," carries considerable and probably increasing weight.

It is therefore useful to look at the federal bureaucracy from a regional perspective in order to see who are the usually faceless personalities behind policies which affect Canadians in every part of the country.

Data on the regional or provincial composition of federal public officials are difficult to find because, unlike linguistic and gender data, they are rarely recorded. My own survey of the 220 most senior individuals in 28 federal departments and agencies in mid-1989 indicated that only about 10 per cent were born and educated in Western Canada, which holds approximately 30 per cent of our national population.

Four per cent were from Atlantic Canada (which has almost 10 per cent) in both education and birth. Senior executives who were both born in and educated in either Ontario or Quebec

held 70 per cent of the highest posts. Eight per cent of the top job holders were born outside Canada, but all of these had received at least part of their education in Ontario or Quebec.

None of these high-achiever newcomers to Canada had completed any post-graduate education outside Inner Canada. None of the officials surveyed was born or educated in the Yukon or Northwest Territories. The remainder were persons born in Outer Canada who later either moved to Ontario or Quebec or completed their education there.

There are 11 senior executives in the prime minister's office. My research as of 1989 showed that by place of birth and place of post-secondary education used as a criterion of regional origin, the following breakdown applied to the PMO: Of the 11 members, 9, or 82 per cent, were both born and educated in Central Canada. The same basic regional pattern of the PMO applied to the 25 senior executives in the Privy Council Office.

Spending Cutbacks

It is usually at the level of national policy making that Outer Canadians lose to politically powerful Inner Canada. Some recently introduced measures and deficit-reducing programs have demonstrated a disproportionately stronger negative impact on Outer Canada.

For example, northern residents were hit with the impact of new mail rates effective last November for northern commercial shipping. The average increase in postal rates is roughly 30 per cent for the entire North—one of the

immediate consequences—$300 more on a family's monthly grocery bill.

Atlantic Canadians, who were the largest per capita users of VIA Rail services, suffered most from the recent cutbacks. Overall, over three-fourths of the inter-Maritime routes were eliminated and the frequency of all others reduced by over 50 per cent.

In the estimate of the Atlantic Provinces Economic Council, about half of the 1989 budget cuts, as measured by employment, were in Atlantic Canada. The closing of the Summerside military base is expected to result in the disappearance of 1,300 direct jobs and even more in indirect ones.

In Premier Joe Ghiz's view, it was the equivalent of 100,000 Ontarians being thrown out of work. The local impact of additional base closings at Barrington and Sydney, Nova Scotia, Moncton, New Brunswick and scaledowns at Gander, Newfoundland and Chatham, New Brunswick will also be disproportionately heavy. Similarly, the most recent cuts to CBC television have hit Outer Canadians very hard and essentially left the Toronto-based television network alone.

Goods and Services Tax

The Goods and Services Tax is hitting most severely the residents of outer provinces. Atlantic Canada contains more low-income Canadians than most parts of the country, so the inherently regressive nature of consumption taxes will hit residents there harder than most Canadians.

Credits, which are not fully inflation-

Postal rate hikes cost northern families an average of $300 more each month on their grocery bills.

indexed, are unlikely to overcome this overall regional impact.

Regional consumers will be affected most severely because the GST would tax for the first time transportation services. Most consumer products are made in southern Ontario and the cost of moving a refrigerator from there to, say, Nanaimo or St. John's would be taxed on the distance involved.

The farther you live from Toronto, the more such tax one pays. The new levy on transportation also hits producers hardest according to how far they live from the population centres in Ontario and Quebec where most products are consumed.

The GST will probably contribute to the worsening of existing regional disparities and its impact will be most harmful in the provinces with the highest provincial tax rates. For example, in Prince Edward Island, there will be a total of 17 per cent charged through the GST and the provincial tax system as the 10 per cent provincial tax will be added to the cost of the item plus the cost of the GST. A farmer in PEI will pay more for farm equipment than a farmer in Ontario because of the increased costs in transportation.

Federal Institutions

A major reason for the political impotence of the outer regions to influence the process of national policy making is the fact that the institutions of our centralized federal government, most notably the House of Commons, Senate and public service, have proven profoundly insensitive at providing effective regional representation to Outer Canadians.

The Canadian practice allows all three party leaders in Ottawa to have their followers vote as trained seals virtually always. There is thus little incentive for any of them to reform the confidence vote which lies at the heart of the problem.

Unlike the practice in other Commonwealth parliamentary systems, including Westminster, virtually every vote in our Canadian Parliament is considered potentially one of non-confidence. Even a frivolous opposition motion to adjourn the House for a day can be deemed by a prime minister, if lost, to have been one of non-confidence.

The whips of government parties in Ottawa for decades have used the possibility of an early election to brow-beat their members into voting the party line on virtually every issue which arises.

One way of reducing party discipline in the interest of greater fairness for every province would be to write into our constitution, as the West Germans have done in their Basic Law, that MPs and senators shall "not (be) bound by orders and instructions and shall be subject only to their conscience."

Party discipline has certainly diluted this principle in West Germany, but when combined with another feature of their constitution—that no chancellor can be defeated in their equivalent of our House of Commons unless a majority of the members simultaneously agree on a new person to become chancellor—there appears to be a more independent role for members of West Germany's Budestag than for Canadian Members of Parliament.

A similar rule, if adopted by the House of Commons, would inevitably weaken our party discipline significantly because MPs from all parties could then vote on the merits of issues, knowing that defeat would bring down only the measure and not the government.

At present, few government and opposition MPs have any real opportunity to put their constituents first in votes in the House of Commons. Real power is concentrated in the hands of the three party leaderships. Canadian democracy itself would benefit substantially if we put our present mind-numbing party discipline where it belongs—in the history books.

Australia

The Australian Triple-E Senate provides an excellent model for Canada partly because, like ourselves, about two thirds of Australia's population live in two of its six states. We also share a tradition of parliamentary rather than representative democracy.

The founding fathers of Australia's four smaller states refused during the 1890s any form of federal union unless it included a second house representing all states equally. Accordingly, the Australian Senate initially in 1901 had six senators from each state with all elected by state-wide votes and half being elected to take effect on fixed dates every three years.

The key role of the Australian Senate is to balance the executive branch. As in Canada, the party discipline has subordinated most activities in the Australian lower house to the wishes of the cabinet of the day.

The Australian Senate, however, being powerful in its own right, can effectively check a cabinet when it is not controlled by the party then in office.

Even more important is the close scrutiny it gives to proposed legislation and the public hearings it provides for groups often ignored by the clubby relationships which tend to exist between governments and their favored interest groups.

If a ministry of the day cannot convince some senators of a different political complexion of the merits of its proposals, assuming the Senate is not controlled by the same political party which forms the government, they simply do not become law.

Another area of key Senate activity is free-wheeling investigations of issues of public interest, often on matters which cabinets would prefer to be ignored, in a manner free of government manipulation or control.

Australia's national government and democratic spirit have, I gather, both improved significantly because of this interplay.

Our unloved Canadian Senate was fatally flawed from Confederation on because senators were both appointed for life rather than elected and named by the prime minister, a double defect completely incompatible with producing effective regional voices in the Canadian Senate.

Few, if any, Senate clashes with the House of Commons have in consequence been based on regional conflicts.

More than century of appointments of mostly tired party war-horses, hacks and fund raisers by prime ministers of both major political parties have cumulatively delivered a mortal blow to our Senate as an institution.

National Purpose

I believe that a major impetus to reforming our federal institution is the independence movement in Quebec which has finally convinced decision makers in Toronto and Ottawa that the *status quo* can no longer be maintained. What we need badly today as well is a higher sense of national purpose. Greater unity is essential for us to survive as a single great country.

The failure of the successive federal governments to deal with and reconcile divergent regional concerns and needs has obviously produced serious strains.

Since birth, Canada has defined its national purpose only once. The "National Policy" of 1879 set our objectives to populate the country, to link the common market with a national transportation network, and to develop an industrial base.

The two central provinces, or more accurately, parts of them and a small number of families, were the beneficiaries of the industrial strategy with ensuing economic stability and political clout.

Our Atlantic provinces declined in relative importance after the 1880s and became more and more dependent on Ottawa's assistance over the years. This spawned a bitter sense of regional grievance, one that Western Canadians have shared fully and is now in my region for various reasons probably at an all-time high since the Depression.

Some opinion polls suggest that Brian Mulroney's government is more disapproved of across Outer Canada today than was Pierre Trudeau in his bleakest 1981-82 period. Now, as the country is going through a perilous time, we need more than at any other time during our history to formulate a New National Policy.

The late Robert Kennedy used to say: "Some men see things as they are and

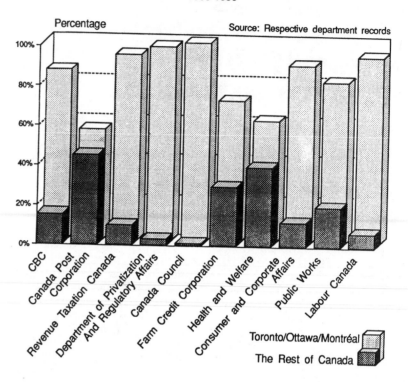

Figure 3
Spending on Goods and Services
1988-1989

Percentage

Source: Respective department records

100%
80%
60%
40%
20%
0%

CBC · Canada Post Corporation · Revenue Taxation Canada · Department of Privatization And Regulatory Affairs · Canada Council · Farm Credit Corporation · Health and Welfare · Consumer and Corporate Affairs · Public Works · Labour Canada

Toronto/Ottawa/Montréal
The Rest of Canada

say 'Why?' I dream things that never were and say 'Why not?'."

Canadians of good will must today not hesitate to think things that never were. The vision for the future of Canada I hold is one where the principles of regional equality and fairness will not only be reflected in national institutions, but serve as eminent precepts for the conduct of decision and policy makers.

Should the legitimate concerns of the disadvantaged outer parts of our country not be integral parts of national interest and addressed accordingly? In short, we need to renew our entire national government apparatus from top to bottom.

To meet the demands of our time, we also need political leaders who will rise to the occasion. Disillusionment with our current government probably makes

it impossible for Canadians not only to trust its members again, but also to believe they can reconcile our differences and bring about healing.

The intellectual vacuum that now permeates Ottawa seems incapable of reconciling the contradictory forces at play. Nor can it deal effectively with regional demands and at the same time rekindle a national spirit of unity.

We need national leaders capable of setting a clear agenda for the current political climate and bringing us together. The concerns of all of us, no matter where we live, must become a part of national policy making. Only in these terms can we find the nation and unity the vast majority of Canadians are seeking.

SHARING CANADA'S POWER
AT WHAT COST?

Nate Laurie

Deputy Editorial Page editor, Toronto Star

For months, a constitutional cry has been raised from several influential corners for Ottawa to hand over many of its economic powers to the provinces.

The rationale, often unspoken, is that the provinces couldn't be any worse at running the economy and that somehow the debt crisis would be resolved.

Is that possible?

The short answer is that constitutional change can't cure Canada's fiscal problems. In fact, it could make matters much worse.

If, for example, Ottawa agreed to give the provinces significantly more power, it would virtually collapse under the weight of its own massive debt.

Today, Ottawa spends nearly 36 cents of every dollar of revenue in interest payments on the national debt. If the more radical proposals for decentralization were put into force, Ottawa could end up spending 75 cents of every revenue dollar just to carry its debt.

Furthermore, the federal government would lose effective control over many of the levers it uses to run the Canadian economy, such as interest rate policy and the raising of taxes.

The province of Ontario, for example, could easily end up with as much fiscal clout as the central government.

Such dramatic changes would undoubtedly bring about a very different and decentralized Canada. But could the country function successfully?

According to three major groups, the answer is yes:

■ The Quebec Liberal party, in the Allaire report, has urged Ottawa to vacate no fewer than 22 jurisdictional fields, and give each province enough money to run its own show.

■ A blue-ribbon panel of 22 prominent Canadians has also recommended that Ottawa turn over half its spending to the provinces, but keep its troublesome $30 billion deficit as well as its mammoth debt.

(Among its members, the Group of 22 counted former Ontario premier Bill Davis, former Saskatchewan premier Allan Blakeney, New Brunswick frozen food king Harrison McCain, Alberta oilman Bob Blair, economist Sylvia Ostry, and former federal cabinet ministers Jean-Luc Pepin, Maurice Sauve and John Roberts.)

■ Finally, the Business Council on National Issues, the voice of big business, sees decentralization as the best way to eliminate costly duplication and give Canadians "more efficient and accountable" government.

The common thread running through these reform proposals is the belief that Ottawa is so choked by debt it has lost its capacity to meet the country's needs.

There is little doubt that most Canadians don't see the federal government as much of a bargain any more. With the cancer of compound interest on the debt eating away at federal revenues, a tax dollar now buys only 90 cents in federal programs and services, compared with $1.33 a decade ago at the height of Ottawa's borrowing spree.

Not surprisingly, Prime Minister Brian Mulroney's popularity has vanished along with services that Ottawa used to provide.

If Ottawa is no longer capable of delivering a dollar of services for a dollar in taxes, then, as the decentralists see it, it should stop over-extending its reach into areas outside its jurisdiction, and stick to its own constitutional turf.

As the Group of 22 put it: "It is imperative, and in the interests of all Canadians, that (Ottawa) act aggressively and well within its own jurisdiction. . . . The federal government ought not to try to be all things to all people. Ottawa will derive its legitimacy and respect from doing its own job well, not from doing the job of the other level of government."

A detailed economic analysis of such wholesale decentralization, however, shows that it could leave the federal government too weak to break the bonds of its crippling $420 billion debt.

Instead of helping to improve Ottawa's fiscal position, decentralization would keep the federal deficit at present levels, and enshrine it in a virtual constitutional guarantee.

Consequently, by treating Ottawa's deficit as if it were a federal problem—and not a national one—both Allaire

From *The Toronto Star,* September 22, 1991, pp. B1, B7. Reprinted with permission from The Toronto Star Syndicate.

and the Group of 22 would make our fiscal predicament even more intractable than it now seems to be.

To see why, consider what Ottawa's current budget would look like if it were redrawn along the lines of these two decentralization schemes.

TRANSFERS TO PERSONS

The biggest part of Ottawa's program budget ($35.8 billion) is spent on cheques for the elderly, family allowances, unemployment insurance benefits and veterans' pensions.

Leaving Ottawa with only veterans' pensions, the Allaire report would shift responsibility for the other 95 per cent of these transfers to the provinces.

For its part, the Group of 22 would also make the federal government jointly responsible for the pure insurance component of unemployment insurance, while turning the remaining 70 per cent of transfers to persons over to the provinces.

Under both schemes, Ottawa would, of course, also have to give the provinces enough revenue to allow them to pay these additional bills.

TRANSFERS TO OTHER LEVELS OF GOVERNMENT

As Ottawa's second-largest program expenditure ($23.3 billion), these cash transfers are paid to the provinces for health, post-secondary education and welfare.

They also include equalization payments to the have-not provinces to ensure that Canadians in all provinces enjoy reasonably comparable levels of services for reasonably comparable taxes.

In the reconfiguration of Canada that they envision, both the Group of 22 and Allaire would wipe out all these dedicated federal transfers except for equalization. To make up for the loss to the provinces, Ottawa would relinquish enough money to enable them to fund health, education and welfare themselves.

OTHER MAJOR TRANSFERS

The federal government spent $11.6 billion last year to help business, natives, farmers, and to pay for job creation and student loans.

Since the provinces would take over many of these responsibilities under both the Allaire and Group of 22 schemes, Ottawa would have to give up roughly another $8 billion.

OTHER GOVERNMENT OPERATIONS

Last year the federal government spent $18 billion, mostly for labor and capital, to run its various departments.

Spending Canada's cash

$ billions	Today	Under Allaire	Under Group of 22
Major transfers to people (Old age security, family allowance, U.I., etc.)	$ 35.8	$1.7	$10.7
Major transfers to provinces (Include equalization payments.)	23.3	9.0	9.0
Other major transfers (to business, farmers, natives, etc.)	11.6	2.5	4.0
Ottawa's operating costs	18.0	12.0	14.0
Payments to major crown corp.	4.9	4.9	4.9
Defence	12.1	12.1	12.1
Foreign aid	2.6	2.6	2.6
TOTAL	**108.3**	**44.8**	**57.3**
Public Debt charges	43.0	43.0	43.0
TOTAL	**151.3**	**87.8**	**100.3**
Federal revenues	120.8	57.3	69.8
Federal budgetary deficit	30.5	30.5	30.5

Source: 1991 Federal budget and Toronto Star calculations

The leaner, meaner central government pictured by the Group of 22 and the Allaire report would require fewer departments, offices and workers to play its more limited role.

Of course, the provinces would need more. So Ottawa would hand over roughly $6 billion to the provinces under the Quebec Liberal party recommendations, or $4 billion under the proposals of the Group of 22.

PAYMENTS TO CROWN CORPORATIONS, DEFENCE AND FOREIGN AID

In both of the decentralist schemes, these three areas (and their combined $19.6 billion budget) would remain under exclusive federal control.

The impact of all of these changes on federal finances would depend on whether Ottawa ceded tax room to the provinces or created a new federal general-purpose transfer for giving them more funds.

Under the first option (illustrated in the chart), Ottawa's over-all program budget would shrink by 50 per cent under the Group of 22 formula, and by 60 per cent under Allaire's disentanglement scheme.

Federal revenues would also drop—by 40 to 50 per cent.

But out of those reduced revenues, Ottawa would still have to make annual interest payments of $43 billion to service the federal debt.

The implications for federal finances would be grim.

Ottawa now pays 35.6 cents out of every tax dollar in interest on its mammoth debt. That's 35.6 cents out of every dollar that can't be used for programs Canadians want.

To prevent even further erosion of its programs, the government says it must wipe out the deficits that drive the federal debt.

But if you think 35.6 cents is excessive, how would you feel about paying 61.6 cents out of every federal tax dollar to service the national debt? That's how much Ottawa would have to pay if it followed the suggestions of the Group of 22, because interest payments would come out of a much smaller kitty.

That figure would rise to an astounding 75 cents out of every tax dollar if Canada were reshaped along the lines of the Allaire report.

And the situation would grow even worse with time because both Allaire and the Group of 22 would leave a shrunken federal government with the same massive deficit that it's saddled with today.

In other words, disentanglement would leave Ottawa in the untenable position of financing 53 to 68 per cent of its program budget with borrowed money, compared to 28 per cent today.

An already diminished federal government would thus be compelled to cut its deficit deeply and quickly—but that would be easier said than done.

For starters, it would be virtually impossible for Ottawa to raise taxes. In such a highly decentralized Canada, the federal government would be so far removed from the daily lives of people that it wouldn't have a shred of political authority to impose a significant tax hike.

So Ottawa would have to cut spending even more.

But where? To cut the deficit in half, Ottawa would have to pare the few programs it had left by another 25 to 30 per cent.

To wipe out the deficit entirely, it would have to transform itself into a $15 billion to $30 billion operation—not counting the $43 billion it would still have to pay in interest on the public debt.

It could do that, for example, by eliminating defence, closing down virtually every other department, and cutting off all foreign aid.

To wipe out the federal deficit would be to wipe Ottawa off the map.

The Group of 22 would reject that scenario, claiming that its proposals wouldn't strip down Ottawa's tax base quite so far.

In one of the ironies of its scheme for disentangling federal and provincial finances, the Group of 22 would have Ottawa pay a new general-purpose transfer to help the provinces out.

The only difference between the new transfer and, say, the one Ottawa now pays for health, is that the provinces would get the money with no strings attached. Ottawa would lose its right to set national standards, but would pay all the same.

And that leads to a second irony. Instead of delivering the increased political accountability it promises, the Group of 22's version of disentanglement would lead to less.

But the ironies don't end there. The popular appeal of decentralization stems in part from Ottawa's attempt to enlist the provinces in its battle with the deficit. In its effort to restrain spending, the federal government has cut back transfers to the provinces for health, post-secondary education and even welfare.

The provinces call that buck-passing. They say Ottawa is jeopardizing programs that are outside its sphere.

But if the jurisdictional overlap in areas such as health is one of the weaknesses of our current constitutional arrangements, it is paradoxically also one of their strengths.

That's because shared responsibility has given Ottawa considerable leverage to force the provinces to share in restraint.

The federal deficit is a *national* problem that requires a national solution. Pretending otherwise won't accomplish anything.

The shrunken federal government envisaged by the Group of 22 would have no choice but to rein in transfer payments to get the deficit under control.

Knowing that, the provinces would inevitably seek to protect any new transfer arrangement with a constitutional guarantee.

They would be especially wary after last month's Supreme Court ruling that Ottawa has no legal obligation to share their welfare costs.

After all, why would the provinces accept total responsibility for health, welfare, pensions, family benefits and post-secondary education without a binding constitutional commitment from Ottawa to give them the requisite funds? But if it were to give that assurance, the federal government would put itself in an even tighter strait-jacket, with only a few spending areas left in which it could make cuts.

This analysis suggests Canadians should be careful not to confuse the pain of a fiscal crisis with the need for constitutional change.

If it makes no sense to transfer the deficit directly on to the provinces, it makes even less sense to hamstring Ottawa in its efforts to get Canada out of this mess.

The fatal flaw of both the Allaire report and that of the Group of 22 is that they pretend there is a constitutional detour around the painful necessity of continued fiscal restraint.

O ATLANTICA, WE STAND ON GUARD FOR THEE?

If Quebec separates, the Atlantic region will be isolated.
What would it look like as an independent nation?

Andrew Cornwall

Andrew Cornwall is a resident of Nova Scotia. An economist by trade, he has 14 years experience carrying out a variety of economics research assignments for provincial governments.

Nova Scotians and other Atlantic Canadians are trying to come to terms with the possibility of Quebec's separation from Canada. Without Quebec, Canada would be divided into two parts with a large hole isolating the Atlantic region from the remainder of the country. In this situation, it is not hard to imagine the eventual division of the Atlantic region from the western remnant of Canada. This prospect, even if it is remote, heightens the feeling of uncertainty about where the future of Canada will lead.

Sometimes it is suggested that the Atlantic provinces would join the United States. The idea of union with the United States has been part of the Canadian subconscious throughout our country's history. Nevertheless, the view that any of the separated Atlantic provinces should undergo annexation by the United States has not been carefully thought out.

There is an alternative outcome to the separation scenario, however; that is, Nova Scotia and at least some of the other Atlantic provinces could join together to form a new, independent country. Initially, the idea of being an independent country is intimidating. If this option is to be considered rationally, Atlantic Canadians must overcome the sense of insecurity which pervades the region.

One way to do this is to examine how the new nation would compare with other countries of the world. Additionally, it is important to assess the ability of countries similar to the new nation to achieve a high standard of living. Finally, examples of successful comparable countries should be identified that could serve as models for understanding how a new nation might develop.

The Canadian World Almanac and Book of Facts 1991 (Global Press, Toronto) contains summary information on 170 nations. In particular, the *Almanac* chronicles data on population, geographic, and economic size. Indicators of personal prosperity reported in the *Almanac* are infant mortality at birth and life expectancy. GNP per capita, another important indicator of personal prosperity, can be estimated by dividing a nation's GNP by the size of its population.

The *Almanac* provides a similar profile of information for the provinces of Canada. Not all of the data in the *Almanac* pertain to the same years, which makes it difficult to precisely rank countries by their non-geographic characteristics, however, the data is reasonably current and refer to periods within the previous few years. Information for a representative sample of 43 of the 170 countries is listed alphabetically in Tables I and II.

It is impossible to predict the composition of a new nation containing Nova Scotia and conceivably some of her sister Atlantic provinces. For a comparison with existing countries, a new nation can be contemplated consisting of either Nova Scotia alone, the Maritime provinces, or the Atlantic provinces. For purposes of discussion, a nation comprising each of these combinations may be called Nova Scotia, (the) Maritimes, and Atlantica.

Compared to Canada as it is now, Nova Scotia, the Maritimes, and Atlantica would be small countries. In terms of geographical area, population, and economic size the new nation would have the dimensions indicated in Table III.

Generally, Canadians consider themselves to be residents of a geographically large and wealthy, albeit relatively underpopulated, country. Residents of the new nation could no longer think of themselves as living in a country whose area is the second largest in the world. Instead, the new country's area would rank either 47th (Atlantica), 89th (the Maritimes), or 113th (Nova Scotia). Similarly, population ranking would drop from the top fifth (Canada's rank of 31 out of 170) to the bottom third (a rank ranging from 117 to 131). An independent country would not be one of the world's economic leaders (Canada's position is 8th); even so, it would rank in the vicinity of the top third of the world's largest economies.

Although Nova Scotia, the Mari-

From *Policy Options*, Vol. 13, No. 3, April 1992, pp. 13-16. This article first appeared in *Policy Options*, Canada's Forum for Public Policy Debate.

times, or Atlantica would be among·the smaller-sized nations, this is not necessarily a handicap in providing a high standard of living. As illustrated in Table II relating information on GNP per capita, life expectancy (average of male and female), and infant mortality, there is not a consistent relationship between standard of living and country size. Indeed, amongst the countries of the world, many of the poorest have the largest populations (e.g., China, India, Indonesia). Alternatively, the standard of living is sometimes highest in countries having relatively small populations (Sweden, Norway, and Iceland). There is an approximate consistency, however, in the association of the indicators of standard of living. That is, countries with a high GNP per capita tend to have a longer life expectancy and a lower infant mortality rate.

Although a country's size is not a good predictor of the standard of living of its residents, it is true that there are a number of small, poor countries. For example, of the 72 countries worldwide with populations of under five million, only eight have an annual GNP per capita greater than $10,000; they are Finland, Iceland, Liechtenstein, Luxembourg, Nauru, New Zealand, Norway, and Qatar. (GNP is not reported for another five, mostly poor, countries.) Except for Albania, Cyprus, and Ireland, however, the small and comparatively poorer countries are mainly in Central and South America and Africa. With regard to geography, heritage, or political development these countries are generally distinctly different from the Atlantic provinces.

Because of common regional characteristics, the Nordic countries of Denmark, Finland, Iceland, Norway, and Sweden are particularly interesting regarding the prospects for success of an independent nation situated in Atlantic Canada. The Nordic countries are relatively small, maritime-based, and agriculturally handicapped by a cold climate. Further, they are located on the fringe of the substantial European market, just as the Atlantic provinces are on the edge of the North American market.

The size and standard of living indicators of the Nordic countries are shown in Tables IV and V. To help put these indicators into perspective, figures are also shown for the United States and Canada. As well, available standard of living indicators are reported for Nova Scotia, the Maritimes, and Atlantica.

Residents of all the Nordic countries enjoy a very high standard of living. As

Table I
Indicators of Country Size

Country	Population Millions	Rank	Area sq.km.	Rank	GNP Billion U.S. $	Rank
Albania	3.3	(108)	28,749	(123)	2.8	(105)
Australia	16.6	(49)	7,682,422	(6)	220.0	(15)
Bangladesh	118.0	(9)	143,998	(88)	18.1	(61)
Benin	4.8	(95)	112,620	(96)	1.4	(124)
Brazil	153.8	(6)	8,511,918	(5)	313.0	(10)
Burundi	5.6	(89)	27,866	(125)	1.2	(129)
Cape Verde	0.4	(140)	4,033	(145)	0.1	(156)
China	1,130.1	(1)	9,596,916	(3)	350.0	(9)
Costa Rica	3.0	(110)	50,699	(113)	4.2	(95)
Cyprus	0.7	(135)	9,251	(142)	3.5	(100)
Czechoslovakia	15.7	(51)	127,855	(91)	158.0	(19)
Dominican Republic	7.3	(84)	48,733	(114)	5.5	(79)
El Salvador	5.2	(91)	21,393	(131)	4.1	(97)
Guatemala	9.3	(69)	108,888	(98)	9.6	(67)
Haiti	6.4	(88)	27,749	(126)	2.2	(110)
India	850.1	(2)	3,280,466	(7)	246.0	(13)
Indonesia	191.3	(5)	1,904,335	(15)	75.0	(34)
Ireland	3.5	(105)	70,285	(110)	28.6	(51)
Japan	123.8	(7)	377,765	(57)	1,800.0	(3)
Kuwait	2.1	(120)	17,819	(134)	19.1	(60)
Liberia	2.6	(114)	99,067	(101)	1.0	(134)
Madagascar	11.8	(59)	586,996	(44)	2.1	(112)
Mali	9.2	(70)	1,239,993	(23)	1.6	(119)
Mexico	88.3	(11)	1,972,545	(14)	126.0	(23)
Mozambique	14.7	(55)	786,758	(35)	4.7	(87)
Nepal	19.2	(43)	145,392	(87)	3.1	(102)
Niger	7.7	(80)	1,266,994	(21)	2.2	(110)
Oman	1.3	(125)	212,457	(80)	7.5	(74)
Paraguay	4.7	(96)	406,750	(55)	7.4	(75)
Portugal	10.5	(64)	92,075	(105)	33.5	(50)
Saint Lucia	0.2	(153)	616	(155)	0.2	(150)
Saudi Arabia	16.8	(48)	2,175,580	(13)	70.0	(36)
Singapore	2.7	(113)	580	(156)	23.7	(54)
South Korea	43.9	(23)	98,484	(102)	171.0	(18)
Sudan	25.2	(36)	2,503,889	(9)	8.5	(71)
Switzerland	6.6	(87)	41,287	(117)	111.0	(26)
Thailand	54.9	(20)	513,999	(48)	52.2	(40)
Trinidad and Tobago	1.3	(126)	5,128	(144)	4.5	(91)
Uganda	17.6	(45)	241,786	(75)	3.6	(98)
United Kingdom	57.1	(16)	244,044	(74)	758.0	(7)
Uruguay	3.0	(111)	176,215	(84)	7.5	(74)
West Germany	61.0	(14)	248,188	(72)	1,208.0	(4)
Zaire	35.3	(28)	2,345,397	(11)	5.0	(84)

Note: ranking is from largest (1) to smallest (170) world-wide.

a region, their performance is unparalleled. For example, the Nordic group includes the first, second and third highest GNP per capita. Life expectancy and infant mortality are, likewise, among the most favourable in the world. The GNP per capita of every Nordic country is higher than those of the United States and of Canada. Further, Nordic country infant mortality is about the same as in Canada, but lower than in the United States.

Based on comparable situations of other small countries, it would appear hopeful that a new nation of Nova Scotia, the Maritimes, or Atlantica would not be doomed to poverty because of its small size or northern location. Statistics for the Nordic countries, in particular, suggest that a world-leading standard of living can flourish in conditions similar to those of the potential new nation.

Indeed, the Nordic countries may be worthy models for the nation of Nova

The fragmentation of Canada need not be a terrifying proposition.

Scotia, the Maritimes, or Atlantica to study and follow. In addition to having a high standard of living, the Nordic countries are noted for their internal civility and international integrity.

The experience of the Nordic and other successful small countries does not suggest, however, that Nova Scotia, the Maritimes, or Atlantica would be better off being separated from Canada if given an opportunity to remain in this country. Among other attachments, Atlantic Canadians have a deep emotional investment in being part of Canada.

Compared to Canada, the domain of a new nation would be dramatically smaller. Further, forming a new nation would involve political, economic, and institutional adjustments that many Atlantic Canadians would not want to endure. Nevertheless, based on the situations of other countries, the separation of Quebec and the further fragmentation of Canada need not be a terrifying prospect.

Table II
Indicators of Country Standard of Living

Country (Population Rank)	GNP per Capita* U.S. $	Rank	Life Expectancy in Years	Rank	Infant Mortality Deaths/ 1000	Rank
Albania (108)	857	(96)	72.0	(38)	59	(88)
Australia (49)	13,216	(20)	76.5	(9)	8	(12)
Bangladesh (9)	153	(160)	53.5	(118)	138	(154)
Benin (95)	289	(139)	49.5	(134)	124	(144)
Brazil (6)	2,035	(62)	66.5	(73)	67	(97)
Burundi (89)	213	(147)	51.5	(124)	114	(136)
Cape Verde (140)	363	(125)	61.0	(94)	66	(95)
China (1)	310	(136)	69.0	(63)	33	(63)
Costa Rica (110)	1,385	(76)	76.0	(14)	17	(39)
Cyprus (135)	4,944	(44)	77.0	(7)	8	(12)
Czechoslovakia (51)	10,067	(24)	71.5	(41)	13	(32)
Dominican Republic (84)	758	(100)	62.6	(90)	64	(93)
El Salvador (91)	785	(99)	64.5	(86)	62	(90)
Guatemala (69)	1,028	(89)	61.0	(94)	66	(95)
Haiti (88)	343	(130)	55.5	(110)	92	(118)
India (2)	289	(138)	57.5	(105)	91	(116)
Indonesia (5)	392	(120)	59.0	(103)	58	(87)
Ireland (105)	8,086	(34)	75.0	(21)	6	(3)
Japan (7)	14,542	(16)	79.0	(1)	5	(1)
Kuwait (120)	9,183	(27)	74.0	(30)	14	(33)
Liberia (114)	368	(123)	54.5	(115)	119	(138)
Madagascar (59)	178	(153)	51.5	(124)	99	(123)
Mali (70)	174	(155)	45.5	(149)	173	(162)
Mexico (11)	1,426	(72)	70.0	(49)	42	(75)
Mozambique (55)	319	(133)	46.5	(145)	200	(165)
Nepal (43)	162	(156)	49.5	(134)	101	(126)
Niger (80)	286	(140)	49.0	(137)	137	(152)
Oman (125)	5,747	(42)	56.5	(107)	107	(128)
Paraguay (96)	1,588	(70)	69.5	(57)	49	(79)
Portugal (64)	3,182	(52)	74.5	(28)	15	(35)
Saint Lucia (153)	1,085	(88)	70.5	(47)	18	(43)
Saudi Arabia (48)	4,177	(48)	65.5	(81)	74	(107)
Singapore (113)	8,768	(29)	74.0	(30)	9	(20)
South Korea (23)	3,894	(49)	69.5	(57)	25	(51)
Sudan (36)	338	(131)	53.0	(120)	98	(122)
Switzerland (87)	16,747	(11)	78.0	(2)	7	(8)
Thailand (20)	951	(92)	65.0	(83)	40	(69)
Trinidad and Tobago (126)	3,543	(50)	70.0	(49)	15	(35)
Uganda (45)	205	(148)	50.0	(131)	99	(123)
United Kingdom (16)	13,270	(19)	75.5	(16)	10	(23)
Uruguay (111)	2,498	(56)	71.5	(41)	34	(66)
West Germany (14)	19,811	(5)	74.8	(25)	8	(12)
Zaire (28)	142	(162)	52.5	(122)	107	(128)

Note: a ranking of "1" out of a possible 170 countries indicates the highest GNP per capita, longest life expectancy, or lowest infant mortality.

* GNP per capita is derived from data in Table I by dividing GNP by population. This calculation tends to marginally underestimate GNP per capita for poorer countries where data on population is often more up-to-date than that for GNP.

Table III

A Size Comparison: Canada

	Area		Population		GNP *	
	Square Kilometres	World Rank	1990 Estimated	World Rank	Billion U.S. $	World Rank
Canada	9,970,610	2	26,440,000	31	468.0	8
Nova Scotia	55,490	113	889,000	131	12.3	65
Maritimes	134,590	89	1,792,000	122	23.6	55
Atlantica	540,310	47	2,365,000	117	30.2	51

Note: a world rank of "1" would indicate the largest respective area, population, or GNP.

* Figures for Nova Scotia and the other Atlantic regions are Gross Domestic Product for 1988.

Table IV

A Size Comparison: World

	Area		Population		GNP	
	Square Kilometres	World Rank	1990 Estimated	World Rank	Billion U.S. $	World Rank
Denmark	43,079	116	5,134,000	92	101.3	27
Finland	337,007	59	4,977,000	94	96.9	28
Iceland	103,001	100	251,000	148	5.3	82
Norway	324,217	62	4,214,000	99	89.0	31
Sweden	449,961	52	8,407,000	76	179.0	17
United States	9,372,570	4	250,372,000	4	4,800.0	1
Canada	9,970,610	2	26,440,000	31	468.0	8

Table V

Standards of Living: Key Areas

	GNP per Capita U.S. $	World Rank	Life Expectancy in Years	World Rank	Infant Mortality Deaths/ 1,000	World Rank
Denmark	19,731	6	75.5	16	8	12
Finland	19,470	7	75.0	21	6	3
Iceland	21,116	3	78.0	2	6	3
Norway	21,120	2	76.3	13	7	8
Sweden	21,292	1	77.5	4	6	3
United States	19,171	8	75.5	16	10	23
Canada	17,700	9	76.5	9	7	8
Nova Scotia	13,859*	17	75.5	21	not available	
Maritimes	13,620*	17	75.8	15	not available	
Atlantica	13,114*	20	75.8	15	not available	

Note: for standard of living indicators a world ranking of "1" indicates the highest GNP per capita, longest life expectancy, or lowest infant mortality.

* Figures for Nova Scotia and the other Atlantic regions are based on Gross Domestic Product for 1988.

Bitter on the Rock

Newfoundlanders fight to break the cycle of povert

As he sits in the kitchen of his white clapboard house in Pouch Cove, a fishing village 30 km north of St. John's, Nfld., retired fisherman William Noseworthy casts his mind back half a century, to a bygone era of abundance. "Back then, the cod were so thick that you could just look over the side and see them swimming in the water," says the ruddy-faced Noseworthy, 69, between puffs on a hand-rolled cigarette. But those days are long past. Noseworthy's 34-year-old son, Barry, now has to drop four times as many cod traps to pull in half the number of fish that his father once caught in a day. "I don't think there's much of a future in fishing anymore," the younger man says. It is a common complaint among the 28,000 men and women who work in the northern cod fishery. And unfortunately for Newfoundlanders, the outlook for the rest of the provincial economy appears no less bleak.

Recent events have focused new attention on the province's perennially desperate economy. In February, Newfoundlanders learned that a massive $5.2-billion plan to develop the Hibernia oilfield, 220 miles southeast of St. John's, had been shelved because low oil prices have made the megaproject less attractive. That decision put 800 people immediately out of work and dashed, perhaps for all time, the province's dreams of offshore riches. Then, last week, federal Fisheries Minister John Crosbie dealt a near knockout punch to the province's economy. Crosbie announced a 35-per-cent rollback in the total allowable catch of northern cod—Atlantic Canada's most important fishery. Inevitably, the reduced quota will force thousands of fishermen and fish-plant workers onto the unemployment rolls—a severe blow to a province where the jobless rate already stands at 19.2 per cent, eight points above the national average.

Yet the immediate consequences of those announcements were overshadowed by a deeper fear—that the already beleaguered prov-

ince has entered a downward economic spiral that could continue for years, perhaps even decades. According to some analysts, Newfoundland's future can now be secured only by adopting painful economic policies aimed at weaning the province from its reliance on government supports—a strategy that could threaten the island's social fabric. Declared Newfoundlander Harry Steele, president of Newfoundland Capital Corp., a Dartmouth, N.S.-based transport and communications company with many interests in the province: "Tough medicine is needed. The question is whether the patient can stand the treatment."

Already, the province is reeling. In slashing the total allowable catch to 120,000 tons from 180,000 tons, Crosbie left fishermen with a quota that was one-third the size of their 1988 allowable catch. By most accounts, the Newfoundland-born fisheries minister had little choice. Earlier this month, a federal scientific advisory panel urged Crosbie to slash the quota even more, by 50 per cent. The panel warned that the cod stock, which first drew European fishermen to the Grand Banks nearly 500 years ago, could be wiped out if fishing continues at current levels. Declared Cabot Martin, president of the Newfoundland Inshore Fisheries Association, which represents the province's 10,000 small-boat fishermen: "What has occurred on the Grand Banks is an ecological disaster."

The fact that Crosbie stopped short of the panel's requested 50-per-cent reduction was cold comfort to the thousands of Newfoundlanders already suffering from the fishery crisis. The province's biggest fishing company, St. John's-based Fishery Products International Ltd., has already tied up 11 trawlers and closed shut several Newfoundland fish plants due to declining catches. Only two weeks ago, the company mothballed its state-of-the-art cod plant in Catalina, 300 km north of St. John's, putting 890 plant workers and 150 trawlermen out of work—including about 70 employees who are particularly vulnerable because they have not worked enough this year to qualify for unemployment insurance benefits. "It was a shock," recalls Ambrose Butt, 34, a former cutter at the Catalina plant who now supports his wife and 18-month-old son on UI

benefits of $320 a week. "If we don't reopen in the spring, I'll have to think about looking elsewhere for work."

Variations on that theme can be heard throughout Newfoundland—in devastated fishing outports as well as in inland communities that have been hit by layoffs in the province's severely depressed mining and forestry industries. Nowhere, perhaps, is the concern greater than in Arnold's Cove, a tiny fishing village nestled on the rugged shoreline of Placentia Bay. Last month, the village's 1,400 inhabitants were rocked by the news that the Hibernia project had been put on hold and that work had been halted on a $1.2-billion offshore platform being built only five kilometres away. But the cod cuts were an even bigger blow. Last week, the village's main employer, Halifax-based National Sea Products Ltd., announced the temporary closure of its Arnold's Cove plant, which employs 500 people. Declared Thomas Osburne, the village's mayor and a supervisor at the National Sea plant: "We've made it through tough times before. Hopefully, this time won't be any different."

In fact, many Newfoundlanders say that they fear the province may never recover from the latest economic setbacks. Among economists, politicians and business leaders, there is widespread agreement that many years of dependence on government handouts and regional development programs have spawned a welfare mentality among some Newfoundlanders. That attitude is likely to become even more pervasive as the fishery layoffs exacerbate the cycle of government-sponsored make-work projects and short-term employment that marks life in many outports. Said Karl Kenney, vice-president of product development for Matrix Technologies Inc., a St. John's-based electronics company: "Decades on the government dole have made us docile and dulled our edge."

Although successive federal and provincial governments have attempted to break the cycle of dependence, none of them has succeeded. Most economists and businessmen agree that the UI system—which allows fishermen to become eligible for 42 weeks of payouts after as little as 10 weeks of work—has left recipients with little motivation to retrain or to search for work elsewhere. "The UI system is a disincentive to work," says Craig Dobbin, chairman of St. John's-based Canadian Helicopters Ltd., North America's second-largest helicopter operating company.

But simply cutting off income supports now, in the midst of a recession, would only cause more pain in the outports. And there is no consensus on an alternative to the UI system. Donald Savoie, an expert in regional development and an economics professor at New Brunswick's University of Moncton, says that unemployment benefits should be paid only to people who are actively trying to upgrade their skills by enrolling in job-training programs. Other analysts, such as Wade Locke, an economics professor at Memorial University in St. John's, have called on Ottawa to introduce some sort of mobility incentive to assist people in moving from the outports to jobs in urban areas elsewhere in Newfoundland and on the mainland.

Ultimately, an exodus from the outports may be unavoidable. "There has to be a rationalization of some of these outlying communities," says Christopher Collingwood, president of Baine, Johnston & Co. Ltd., a St. John's-based real estate and insurance firm that is one of the oldest companies in the province. Adds Steele, a native of Musgrave Harbour: "Newfoundlanders cannot stay put in the province if the opportunities are not there."

Whether the future will be any brighter may well depend on the results of several recent initiatives. Among the most prominent is the province's Economic Recovery Commission, which Premier Clyde Wells created three years ago. Its objective: to help diversify the provincial economy and reduce its reliance on fishing, forestry, mining, energy megaprojects and federal transfer payments. The commission, led by

Memorial University economist Douglas House, has provided advice to struggling small businesses and has even acted directly to arrange business deals between outside investors and local companies. Next month, a group of industry leaders appointed by the commission will report on ways to create jobs in 11 different business sectors, including non-resource manufacturing, tourism and high technology. Declared House: "We need to widen the scope of industry in the province."

But for now, and perhaps forever, the depleted fishery remains the province's major industry. And for Newfoundlanders like Barry Noseworthy, that means a future that is as unpredictable as the weather over the North Atlantic fishing grounds where he makes his meagre living.

JOHN DeMONT *in St. John's*

Slow death
of a nation's heartland

Richard Gwyn

TORONTO STAR

*"A town dies slowly
like an old pioneer.
The heart goes
the eyes go
but the mind stays clear.
It remembers how it was a long time ago
a few little houses against the blowing snow"*
        —Lyrics from a song by Connie Kaldor, quoted
        in Sharon Butala's novel, *The Fourth Archangel*

EASTEND, Sask.—Stop your car at any height of land along Highway 13 in southwestern Saskatchewan. Get out and swivel 360 degrees. Count all the farms you can spot out to the horizon perhaps 30 kilometres away.

Probably, your tally will be six. Maybe you'll get up to 8 or 10, in all that vast circle.

In fact, the real number will be lower. If you drove up to some of those farmhouses sheltered behind rows of poplar trees, you'd find them shuttered.

In their own district, radiating outwards from the town of Eastend that's cupped into a valley created by the Frenchman's River, Peter and Sharon Butala believe they know of—certainty in such matters is impossible until after it happens—seven families who are being foreclosed or who are leaving their land.

Peter, 57, raises 200 head of Herefords on the rolling hills south of Eastend. He's big, strong, soft-spoken, reflective. He drives a visiting reporter around his land, worries that two bulls have wandered too close to each other, stops carefully to pick up a strand of rusted barbed wire, points out excitedly—"That's what this country alone has"—four antelope who raise their heads at the sound of the truck.

Sharon, 52, is small, intense, passionate, voluble. She's become a kind of bard of prairie peoples' sense of loss, of dispossession, of defeat.

She did it first in an extraordinary article, Field of Broken Dreams, that she wrote two years ago for *West* magazine (itself now closed). In it she uttered the ultimate prairie heresy.

Maybe, she wrote then, John Palliser was right when he said the triangle of semi-desert flatland that he surveyed in 1859 and that thrusts up from the U.S. border to above Regina and out into Alberta and Manitoba, ought never to be broken—it was too dry to be cultivated. "Perhaps it is finally time to admit that the settling of farms on the dry, southern plain was a mistake," Butala wrote.

Much of this vast wheat field, she continued, "could be turned into a national park."

As true bards do, she then turned from analysis to keening angst. If this happened, she wrote, it would mean "the death of the heart of a nation."

In her recently published novel *The Fourth Archangel*, Butala returns to this theme. As their small town of Ordeal shrinks and as they age, the townspeople succumb to apocalyptic religious visions, hear grain trains roaring along abandoned tracks at midnight, stage frantic, futile political rallies, and then accept that what has to be, will be.

"Maybe it will all go back to the wild—be full and animals and the grass will grow again and people will come to see it and walk on it because it's so beautiful," says the novel's hero, Val.

By no means everyone agrees with Sharon Butala. In Ottawa, Grains Minister Charles Mayer says forthrightly, "Anyone who says that Palliser was right is talking through their hat." The problem, says Mayer, "isn't with them or with their land, it's entirely that of the goofy (international) subsidies."

Indeed, the amount of prairie land seeded for grain will actually set a new record this year, at 14.4 million hectares (35.6 million acres). Exports are up, thanks to new sales to India and Russia. If a new international agreement to liberalize trade is ever agreed on, Europe's subsidized grain mountains will shrink.

Sooner or later, though, Russia and Ukraine are bound to become again huge grain exporters. Beyond that, there's bio-technology and genetics to improve everyone's productivity and therefore to lower everyone's prices.

This is why, where Butala was once a lone voice, she now is part of a chorus.

For prairie farmers, that moment of future truth has arrived already. In real terms, adjusted for inflation, today's $2.50 a bushel price for wheat is actually lower than it was during the Depression. The only grain producers now making a profit—after repayment of principal and interest on their loans for land and equipment—are those who own farmland outright, usually because they inherited it debt-free.

Among the 150 farmers in the Whitewood region, where his son now farms and where he once did, Saskatchewan Wheat Pool president Garf Stevenson reckons he can "count on the fingers of two hands the number who are economically viable." A provincial civil servant, himself a farmer, recounts a neighbor breaking down, explaining that he was having to use his equipment loan to buy groceries.

A solution does exist. It's "consolidation." Today's grain farms average about 400 hectares (1,000 acres). With four-wheel-drive tractors, and 20-metre (70-foot), now even 30-metre (100-foot)combines, a single farmer can seed and harvest 800 hectares (2,000 acres). Corporate farms could be even bigger.

"Within five years, we're going to lose half of our farms," predicts Doug Elliott, editor of the weekly, *Saskatchewan Trends Monitor*.

That solution would mean profitable grain being produced by almost no people.

This process isn't new in itself. There were 90,000 farmers in Saskatchewan in 1961. Today, there are fewer than 60,000.

Saskatchewan's population has slipped below the 1 million mark. Some long-term projections put its stable population at around 750,000, notwithstanding the rapid increase of its native population. (By the year 2000, it's been estimated, one in two new entrants to the provincial labor force will be Indian or Metis.)

Prairie people are among the country's toughest, as they have to be to survive the ferocious winters, the short, blistering summers, the intimidating distances, and that awareness of human insignificance imposed on everyone there by the immense arch of the sky.

They are as distinct a society as is Quebec, or Newfoundland, bonded together by the commonality of their intimacy with the land, and with nature, and by their ethic of egalitarianism and collectivism. History here may be short—from ox-carts and sod huts to the dust storms of the 1930s—but there's a passionate pride in it because it was, uniquely on the prairies, that a part of Canada was created out of, quite literally, nothing.

It was a Manitoban who made me understand this, as she described the agonizing choice she faces. Sandi McNabb's great-grandfather homesteaded in Minnedosa in 1878. She still owns—rents out, in fact—324 hectares (800 acres) there. Each year, her costs, on principal and interest, are $34 an acre, while her rental income is $20 an acre.

"So I've reached two conclusions," recounted McNabb. "That I can never turn my back on that history and will at any cost maintain that farm. That if I could get out, I'd be gone in a flash and never look back."

In Saskatchewan, tens of thousands of farmers and small-town people now are confronting that same appalling choice.

After Sharon Butala first said the unsayable—in effect, exposing the wounds of her tribe for outsiders to gaze at—it came as a surprise to her that no one in the province attacked her for her heresy.

Butala thinks she now understands why. It was the silence, not so much of consent as of defeat.

"Everyone is too demoralized to fight. Many know the land should never have been broken up, but they have nowhere to go and they have to eat. Others may disagree, but they are no less scared. Every rural conversation turns into a chronicle of who may be leaving, of who is still struggling, of what if anything there will be for our kids. Everyone is just so desperate and so afraid."

Butala now accepts that there's enough local moisture in parts of the Palliser Triangle for wheat always to be grown there. The rest she believes should be returned to a pastureland of native grasses, for cattle, buffalo, antelope, as it was before people like Sandi McNabb's great-grandfather struck out west. Afterward, she hopes that city dwellers will come out to the flatlands, not just to visit it but to live on it "as stewards of nature."

It's hard to believe this will happen. Yet it is impossible to accompany Peter and Sharon Butala around their ranch and among their cattle and the antelope and not be moved by the beauty of the land, and, even more, to be moved by their love of its beauty.

Which is why it is so hard to watch, in Butala's words, "the death of the heart of a nation."

ACTION AND HIGH ENERGY

BRITISH COLUMBIANS CONFRONT RADICAL CHANGE

British Columbia, by any measure, occupies the most spectacular wedge of Canada's real estate. But it is its people who have constructed for their province a unique role in Canada. They have created an outdoors lifestyle that mixes high-energy work in forestry, fisheries, mining and shipping with high-action play. They nurture ancient aboriginal arts, and experiment in new forms. Their politics has made the province a combat zone for the neoconservative right and the democratic left, leaving little middle ground. British Columbians look as much westward to Asia as to the south and the east for clues to their future prosperity. Now, with mainstays of their well-being menaced by a changing global economy and a recession that struck the Pacific coast later than elsewhere, British Columbians are coping with radical change. **Hal Quinn,** *Maclean's* Vancouver *bureau chief since 1988, chronicles the changes taking place through the eyes and in the words of a sampling of citizens from various walks of life. His report:*

As he has in most recent summers, logger **Ronald Corbeil,** 36, registered at the Unemployment Insurance Commission office in the Vancouver Island community of Port Alberni last month. But unlike the thousands of forestry workers whose jobs have disappeared over the past 10 years in British Columbia's leading industry, Corbeil will likely have a job to go back to, probably in September. "Every year, in late July and August, it gets too dry to work in the forest," he said in an interview. "It's just too dangerous. We get our holiday pay at the beginning of the summer, then we always get laid off, so no one ever actually takes a holiday. And, of course, by the time the UIC kicks in—I usually get about one cheque—then it's back to work. It's a crazy system."

There is much that is even more disturbing in the industry that has traditionally been British Columbia's economic powerhouse. It was the lure of work that brought Ron Corbeil's father, Maurice, to Port Alberni in the 1930s from near Granby, Que., to work as a logger, then as a mill hand and as an executive with the International Woodworkers of America. Ron Corbeil, born and raised in the inland island town (population now about 18,000), started working during the summers in the local sawmill while he was attending high school. And after two years studying recreation administration at Malaspina College in nearby Nanaimo, he returned home in 1977. But even then there were signs of change in the community.

Corbeil, who lives in a four-bedroom home with his wife, Jill, and their three children, recalls that in the early 1970s, "they would list the two leading places in Canada in per-capita income as Oakville, Ont., and Port Alberni." In those years, he notes, "you would put your applications in at the mills around town and that night you'd get four or five calls." The mill where he worked while he was in high school then employed 1,300 people. Now that mill provides about 400 jobs.

The last recession a decade ago damaged the forest industry in general and Port Alberni in particular. After mass layoffs in 1982, Corbeil himself got a logging job in Lillooet on the B.C. mainland, returning home when a job finally opened in Port Alberni. For the past 18 months, he has worked as a scaler, measuring the volume and grade of wood in cut trees. Other jobs have disappeared for men with as much as 20 years' experience. Last year, a local plywood mill closed, leaving the town with two sawmills and a pulp mill. "In the past four years, about 1,000 people in town have lost their jobs," he says. Like others in the industry, Corbeil says that the slower pace of logging is dictated not only by economic conditions but by environmental concerns, and activists. And he has harsh words for outsiders who seem to be disrupting life in Port Alberni, where "you can still buy a decent house for $70,000, and nobody I know wants to join the rat race in Vancouver." Says Corbeil: "It is really frustrating that the decisions affecting our future are made by some committee in Victoria or Vancouver, by some environmentalist, or in some bloody boardroom in Toronto."

He questions whether environmental activists even know that "we've logged second growth in forest that was logged in the 1920s and 1930s, and that in another 60 years it will probably be logged again." People criticize the clear-cutting of entire forests, Corbeil notes, "but on the slopes we work—some 80-per-cent grades—you can't cut selectively, it's impossible." The protesters "play on the dramatics, hang themselves from a bridge or climb a tree and smear themselves with excrement, and it never fails—they are always on TV."

Environmental concerns, along with mechanization, changes in technology and recession, have contributed to a 14-per-cent reduction in the allowable cut in the forests of the Port Alberni region. The pressure on jobs will only increase, Corbeil predicts. "These preservationists will go off and save the seals, or the whales, or whatever's next, and those of us without jobs will be gone." He says that his son Matthew is unlikely to follow him and his father into forestry: "The days of just putting your name in and getting a handful of phone calls that evening are long gone."

Deborah Doss bounces her 10-month-old son, Vance, on her knee in her home adjacent to the Department of Fisheries office in Lillooet, four hours of serpentine and scenic driving northeast of Vancouver. Contemplating the little bundle she holds, the earlier maternity leave, the training, and the recent ceremony applauded by provincial and federal politicians, Doss, 25, concedes that it has been "a very busy time" in her life. It has also been a historic one for Doss, and for British Columbia's native peoples generally. Near the end of July, she and four colleagues were sworn in to the province's first police service administered by an aboriginal community. The new officers have the same authority as police forces in other British Columbia municipalities, and their jurisdiction covers seven of the Stl'Atl'Imx Nation communities surrounding Lillooet.

For Doss, her first official day on the job, Aug. 10, was the successful conclusion of four years of determined effort. Doss and her three sisters were born in Lillooet, but are members of the 500-strong Fountain Band, whose reserve is 15 km from the town of 1,500. Her life, she says, "has not always been that great." Although she completed high school and a year at Capilano College in Vancouver, by 1988, a single mother with a son, Steven, then 3, Doss was working as a clerk and cashier in a corner store in her home town. Then, an older sister suggested that she should apply to become a tribal peacekeeper, a security officer on the reserves. "I wasn't convinced, but I was curious," Doss recalls. But finally, after longer consideration, she says, "I applied and was accepted."

After taking eight weeks of police training in Lillooet, "we ended up having to go through the training twice," said Doss. "We had completed the course, but we weren't recognized by the province. There was a lot of political stuff involved." She then went on to six months of police academy training at the Justice Institute of British Columbia at Westbank, in the Okanagan Valley. "It was the same course, the same training," she said. But that finally qualified her and her fellow native candidates to serve as the equivalents of municipal police officers. And now, after completing 10 weeks of field training with the RCMP, Doss is finally on the beat.

The primary responsibility of Doss and the other new officers is policing the area reserves at Pavilion, Cayoosh, Seton Portage, Mount Currie, Anderson Lake, Fountain and Lillooet, where Doss is stationed. Even off the reserves, Doss and her four male colleagues, like other municipal police officers throughout the province, possess the full power to enforce the law.

With pride, Doss explains the shoulder crest on her tribal police uniform, an eagle inside a circle of four arrows above a cluster of feathers. Said Doss: "Native peoples have a lot of respect for an eagle, and it is in the centre of the arrows. They point in the four different directions and also represent the four races—red, yellow, black and white—combined to sit in harmony. Feathers below the circle stand for the 11 bands who live in the Stl'Atl'Imx territory."

Doss is under no delusions that the nonnative community totally supports the native officers. "Some are opposed," she said quietly. "My life has not always been the easiest, but I've decided to not let that hold me back. I am the only one that can change it and make it better, and that's what I've done. It's been rough, but it has been worth it."

The wind had an edge to it, but at 9 a.m. on Nov. 27, 1986, at least it was not raining, which is unusual for Vancouver at that time of year. **Daniel Sitnam,** a helicopter pilot barely 30 years old, watched from the tarmac of Vancouver Harbour Heliport as another pilot lifted off on the inaugural flight of Helijet Airways. Sitnam, born in England, a resident of Vancouver since he was 15, recalls that he envied the pilot. Helijet, with the first licence ever granted in Canada to operate helicopters on a scheduled passenger service, was largely his brainchild, and he was president of the new company. He also remembers a sobering thought: "When that helicopter took off for Victoria, I figure we were about $1.5 million in the hole."

For three "hand-to-mouth" years, says Sitnam, Helijet struggled financially, running eight return trips a day across the Strait of Georgia between Vancouver and Victoria. But now, with about three times as many daily flights on that route, the helicopter commuter company is expanding into British Columbia's fastest-growing business, tourism. On June 29, Helijet began operating three flights a day, seven days a week, to the all-seasons Whistler mountain resort, expanding a one-a-day service launched at the end of last year to and from the playground community, 120 km north of Vancouver.

The genesis of Sitnam's project had its beginning almost 20 years ago. After bouncing around from England to Brazil, Quebec and Ontario as his father pursued a career in the aerospace industry, Sitnam was working as a chef at a restaurant on Burnaby Mountain, west of downtown Vancouver. One day, a helicopter landed in a nearby park. The pilot, explaining that his client had failed to show up, offered Sitnam a ride. "After that little spin, I thought it would be interesting to do that for a living," he recalls. Four years later, Sitnam earned his commercial helicopter pilot's licence and began flying for forestry and mining companies in the north.

Then, in 1983, Sitnam and two partners bought a four-passenger Gazelle light helicopter for $150,000 and tried, with limited success, "to develop a corporate clientele, affluent people who wanted to move around." Facing financial failure, they hatched the plan for the Victoria commuter service, obtained a licence in Ottawa in 1985, and leased a 13-passenger Bell 412 helicopter. They rented a hangar and office at the airport, hired a staff of 16, and launched their service that November morning in 1986. Six years later, Helijet has a staff of 100 and runs six 12-passenger Sikorsky S-76A helicopters on more than 20 daily Vancouver-Victoria return flights, the highest-frequency scheduled service between two points in North America. At $230 (plus tax) per return ticket, Helijet, now a public company, records annual sales of over $10 million.

In marketing the newly expanded Whistler schedule, "we promote the destination, not just our service," says Sitnam. Helijet is building links with Cathay Pacific and Japan Air Lines, because "our studies show that a large percentage of the people going up to Whistler are from offshore, particularly the Pacific Rim."

Life is more secure now for the president of Helijet Airways. He and his wife, Laura, a native of Odessa, Tex., and their 2 1/2-year-old daughter, Corra-Rose, await the arrival of a son. But just as he did on a windy morning almost six years ago, Sitnam has his eye on the future. From his vantage point, and with a strong outlook for tourism in British Columbia, it looks like clear skies ahead.

When **Viggo Elvevoll** went to work as a rookie cop in 1971, life in Vancouver was simpler and cleaner. And he had ambitions to match. "You think you're going to go out there and save the world and get rid of crime," he recalls. Now, at 42, as a detective in the Vancouver police department's Asian crime section, he says that "of course, that all falls apart in a few years and you realize that you are not the white knight in shining armor." And it is becoming even more difficult, and dangerous, to hold on to youthful hopes, especially on the gangland beat where crime has become a growth industry. "When I started, there was very little fear of a guy carrying a gun or a knife, but now guns and knives are commonplace," says Elvevoll. "What we find now from our informants, and prove by our seizures, is that organized gangs have access now to fully automatic weapons—both handguns and rifles—which is the really scary part."

Vancouver now is Canada's murder capital in per capita terms, with 4.15 homicides per 100,000 of population last year, compared to Montreal's 3.49 and Toronto's 2.70.

Police list the gang names—Big Circle, Lotus, Red Eagle, Viet Ching, Fly Dragons—that have made a business out of drug trafficking, credit card and cheque fraud, counterfeiting, prostitution, extortion, kidnapping and home invasions, when gangsters terrorize victims to extract cash and other valuables. "There is certainly a lot more violence," says Elvevoll. "Whether that be the ultimate, murder, or assaults, they have greatly increased over the years."

As a Vancouver boy in the 1950s, an immigrant with his family from sub-Arctic Norway to what his seaman father Leif, called "the land of opportunity where you get treated well and make lots of money," Elvevoll remembers quite a few fistfights at first. Not knowing a word of English, young Viggo often interpreted the other boys' comments as taunts or jokes. After finishing high school, he went to Norway and worked for a year, but then returned to Vancouver and joined the force.

Elvevoll has walked beats from downtown to skid row; worked as a plainclothes officer in a special strike force; served in the serious assaults, intelligence, and drug sections; worked undercover alongside the RCMP; and for 10 years, along with other duties, was a member of the emergency response team. In October, 1989, he joined the Asian crime section. During that time, he and his wife, Margaret, have raised their two children, Jennifer, 16, and Kristopher, 15. Over the years, much else has changed. For members of the Asian crime section, the changes have been dramatic.

Vancouver police first became aware of the presence of an Asian gang in 1965, one that they said was involved in extortion. But in the past 10 years, Asian gangs have become a major criminal force in North America, particularly in port cities. The kidnapping for ransom and the murder of restaurant manager James Ming and his wife, Lily, in 1985, a case that remains unsolved, led to the formation of the Asian crime section. The gang members, says Elvevoll, are mainly recent immigrants. He says that "a lot of the gang members that are using the violence came from mainland China, Vietnam, or Korea, where things were violent to begin with. Most of them were criminals before they came over here, or learned how to become criminals in the refugee camps. Those are the people who are the most violent, not your homegrown hoods." Elvevoll says that only tougher immigration screening and harsher sentences for violent crimes can help solve the problem.

Even now that the Vancouver force maintains contacts with Asian crime police units across North America, Elvevoll says that "I don't think we can ever win, but we can keep it in check. We're not going to win unless there is a hard stance taken by immigration and the courts." Frustrations are frequent, the victories few, but Elvevoll says that he is going to stick with his job. "I guess there is still a little bit of that white knight left in me," he says. "When you do get one deported, or even just a lousy sentence, it makes it all kind of worth it."

There was that starlit night in 1987 when the 50-foot Princess Cherie ran aground off the Queen Charlotte Islands, sank in less than a minute, and **Cayt McGuire** and four fellow crew members found themselves cold and wet in a skiff staring in wonder as the glow of the Cherie's lights slowly disappeared into the icy black water. And there was a windy day the following season when the boom broke and smashed into her head, splattering blood across the deck, before sliding down to almost slice off her right arm as it inflicted compound fractures. And there were the two years of sexist verbal harassment from a crewman—"I kept thinking up the most cutting responses, only making him worse, until I finally just completely ignored him and he, well, stopped." But with a laugh that comes easily and heartily, Cayt ("Mom's Welsh") McGuire, 37, says that she loves her life as a mate on a salmon seiner out of Prince Rupert, and would not trade it for her old one, or many others.

McGuire is accustomed to being at the helm of her life, and now of a seiner whenever she is called upon to take over from the skipper. Born and raised in Calgary with six sisters and two brothers, McGuire sums up one period of her life by saying, "I got married at 17, had a child at 18, and a divorce at 19." While caring for her son, "always called Willie" (now 18 after a year at the University of Victoria), she earned a communications degree at the University of Idaho in 1979. Later, back in Calgary, she worked as a freelance writer in film, magazines and TV. But in 1983, during the last recession, "the bottom fell out of everything, so in 1984, I cashed in my pension plan, walked away from the house, and Willie and I moved to Saltspring Island."

On that scenic patch between Vancouver Island and the B.C. mainland, McGuire found work as a carpenter's helper and the following year "got a chance to go fishing." After a friend's recommendation, a long-distance call and a hurried flight north, McGuire signed on as a cook and deckhand with former Montrealer Michel Jutras, the skipper of a salmon seiner, a boat that uses a net that tightens like a purse around the catch, in Prince Rupert. "I'd never seen a seiner, had no idea how it worked," McGuire says. "The first instruction I got from the skipper was, 'When in doubt, grab a rope and pull like a bastard.' "

Now, after taking navigation and other marine courses in her off seasons (the seiners usually work from July to November), McGuire is Jutras's mate, responsible in his absence for their new boat, the Heather Isle. When the salmon are running, the crew members regularly work 20-hour days, cramming more than 2,000 hours of labor into the annual norm of 15 weeks of fishing. They share in the income from the sale of the catch to processors. "The year we sank the boat, I made $10,000," says McGuire. "But last year was a good one and I made $25,000."

For all her love of her job, McGuire says that she does not see a bright future for the fishery. "There is the fresh salt air, the most gorgeous scenery this country has, and the tremendous immediacy to the job," says McGuire. "What you're doing, and the value of what you're doing doesn't depend on anyone else's opinion, or whim."

But the opportunities to enter that satisfying life are shrinking. Boats are getting more efficient, but costs are rising. "The industry is tied up tightly in terms of boats and licences, and is shrinking dramatically in terms of its labor force," McGuire says. "There will be fewer boats and fewer people to catch the same amount of fish."

But with her eye on wider horizons, McGuire plans more studies in hopes of crewing on a deep-sea vessel. And with her hearty laugh, she said that when Willie recently indicated an interest in fishing, "I told him it was too dangerous. He's going to get his degree and wear a suit."

Dwight Chan works in a business that has helped British Columbia defy the recession—real estate. The housing industry has spared the province, especially the Lower Mainland area, where more than half of British Columbians live, from the worst consequences of the recession now gripping the country. A price index for new housing issued last week by Statistics Canada shows that in Vancouver prices rose by 8.9 per cent in the year to June, and by 4.1 per cent in Victoria. For Chan, and other British Columbians in the housing business, that indication of sustained demand for new homes represents a slowdown from a hot market in the late 1980s. But it is stronger than in most of the rest of the country, where prices generally remained flat or, particularly in southern Ontario, declined. And Chan, 42, is among a growing number of entrepreneurs in British Columbia who maintain trans-Pacific links that enable them, and the province generally, to benefit from keeping their business eggs in more than one basket.

Chan owns and operates a Re/Max real estate franchise in Vancouver that employs 25 to 30 sales agents. In 1990, just as the local market began to cool after two years of soaring prices, he opened a branch in his native Hong Kong. While awaiting an economic recovery in Canada, Chan says, "the opportunities right now are back there." But, newly married and planning to buy a home himself, Chan adds that he has no intention of moving back to Hong Kong.

He says that he felt differently after he first arrived in Vancouver on a date burned into his memory, Feb. 22, 1974, with his parents, his brother and twin sisters. Their move fulfilled a dream by Chan's businessman father, Lionel, ever since he had been captivated by Vancouver during a mid-1950s visit. But for Dwight Chan, "My first thought was, 'I want to go back.' " Chan said that he had been prepared for a city that would surpass Hong Kong, with its modern skyscrapers. "Here, we were looking at one- and two-story buildings," he says. "Instead of 50 years ahead, Vancouver looked 50 years behind."

Chan, who had earned a Bachelor of Science degree

from Hong Kong's Chuhai College, began his new life in hotel jobs, from busboy to shift manager, turned to selling insurance and then, in 1980, to real estate, opening his present firm in 1986. His business has been helped by Asian property investment. Although that is a relatively small part of the total, he says, "it represents a strong injection of confidence, and acts like a motivation sometimes for the local market to keep going."

On frequent visits to Hong Kong, its frenetic pace and its business opportunities remain fascinating for Chan, but he says that he no longer has a desire to live there. Referring to his March bride, Miranda, 28, also Hong Kong-born and whose maiden name also happened to be Chan (they met four years ago while she was attending Simon Fraser University), Dwight Chan says that "we have no second thoughts about living here: the people are nice, it is beautiful, cosmopolitan, a good mixture of East and West. I personally regard it as paradise."

THE DEATH OF DENENDEH

The eastern Arctic, soon to become Nunavut, represents a victory for the region's 17,500 Inuit. The Dene of the western Arctic once dreamed of a distinct territory, too. But squabbling and fragmentation have all but destroyed that hope

Miro Cernetig

The Globe and Mail, Yellowknife

Twenty years ago, as America's natives mobilized themselves under the banner of the Red Pride movement, a similar but more peaceful uprising was taking hold along the length of Canada's Mackenzie River.

A new generation of Canadian Indian was rapidly coalescing into a united political front to fight the Mackenzie Valley pipeline. Their goal was simple: to stop the inevitable cultural assimilation that would follow if the likes of Exxon, Gulf and Trans-Canada Pipelines moved into the North searching for oil and gas.

The Indians, most of them in their twenties and early thirties, took to wearing their hair long and braided, a protest against the brush-cuts and perms their parents had adopted during their years in residential schools. Some, influenced by the militant American Indian Movement, called themselves warriors, wore caribou-skin jackets and sewed the Canadian flag upside down on the backside of their jeans.

Emboldened, many went into bush camps in the western Arctic's barrens with their elders to relearn the old ways and dream of a new and sovereign Indian nation in Canada's north. They called it Denendeh—the People's Land. Some even hoped outsiders would eventually need passports to enter this new country.

In 1977, they celebrated victory when former B.C. Supreme Court Justice Thomas Berger recommended the pipeline be delayed a decade, pending settlement of native land claims. Ottawa listened.

The following year, the Dene Nation, a federation of the peoples of the Mackenzie Valley, replaced the old Indian Brotherhood of the Northwest Territories.

And the dream of Denendeh seemed on the verge of coming true.

Today, the bright dreams have dimmed.

Instead of working together, the 10,000 Dene Indians are bickering among themselves, allowing others to play them against each other. They have reverted to the same pattern that the fur traders used against them centuries ago to ensure the North's riches passed into the hands of business. The tactic is making it possible for the federal government to settle aboriginal land claims across the North in a piecemeal fashion.

"People are beginning to lose their vision, I suppose," laments Bill Erasmus, the chief of the Dene Nation, which has its headquarters in Yellowknife. "What's happened is there's a turnover in leadership. The young leaders are taking a different view than we did back then."

Indeed, a large part of Denendeh's undoing has been the growing acceptance among northern natives of the federal government's comprehensive land-claims policy; natives are offered millions of dollars for turning the bulk of their traditional

land over to the Crown. The natives get clear title to thousands of square kilometres of land (including the minerals beneath it) but are signing away the rest forever. Once the claims are settled (possibly in just a few years), there will hardly be a land base left for Denendeh.

Chief Erasmus, a 37-year-old former activist who admits he still clings to the dream of Denendeh, tells northern natives the federal government is engaging in a divide-and-conquer strategy. The land claims—called modern-day treaties by Ottawa—require native leaders to extinguish aboriginal title to their ancestors' land. It is a clause, he says, that could come back to haunt northern natives who may be giving up more than they realize, like the natives who signed treaties during Canada's settlement only to discover later they were sentencing their children to a life on reserves.

But Chief Erasmus is becoming a lonely voice in the North.

This week, 54 per cent of northerners voted in favour of a boundary that will split the Northwest Territories in half. Nunavut—meaning Our Land—will be the homeland of Canada's 17,500 Inuit as well as the base for their $580-million land claim, which was reached in 1991 and is expected to be ratified this year.

The Inuit took their lead from the Inuvialuit, the Inuit of the western Arctic who in 1984 settled what is probably the most lucrative land-claim deal in Canadian history. The

From *The Globe and Mail*, May 9, 1992, p. D4. Reprinted by permission.

147

2,500 Inuvialuit, who live along the coast of the Beaufort Sea and the Mackenzie Delta, received $169.5-million and title to 91,000 square kilometres of land, including 11,000 square kilometres of sub-surface rights—that is, oil.

Watching the Inuvialuit prosper has greatly divided the Dene Nation. Last month, the delta's 2,200 Gwich'in Indians, the Inuvialuit's southern neighbours, settled a $75-million land claim with Ottawa. The Sahtu Indians, the southern neighbours of the Gwich'in, are expected to follow soon.

These recent agreements in the Mackenzie Delta are largely a reaction to the decision of the Dene leadership in 1991 to pull out of a $500-million settlement that would have covered all of the Dene-Métis in the western Arctic. The Gwich'in walked out of the meeting in disgust and almost immediately split away to negotiate their own deal with the federal government.

Their decision is understandable. With unemployment high and poverty higher still, the feeling in many native communities is that future generations must be given something to build a future with. Says one official for the Assembly of First Nations: "The people are just getting tired of waiting." An Inuvialuit leader was blunter: "We are open for business."

Even long-time Dene leaders who are happy that the settlements are going ahead agree the Dene nation has been hurt. "Because we don't have our act together it leads to a lot of fear and tribalism," says Stephen Kakfwi, the Northwest Territories constitutional and aboriginal affairs minister. "Everybody is afraid for themselves. We don't have a plan. It's a serious situation, but in my mind it's not serious enough to say we should put a stop to every other [land-claim] process that's going on."

The acceleration of land-claims settlements also promises a troubling period of heightened racial tension in the North, where almost everything is increasingly being defined along race lines.

When Nunavut is created, for example, whites will suddenly be in the majority in the western Arctic.

But they will be without the benefit of the eastern Arctic's Inuit who have generally taken a pragmatic approach to government, forming a buffer that alleviated tensions between whites and the Dene, many of whom hold that neither the territorial nor federal government has any right to direct their lives.

Relations between the Dene and the Inuit are likely to be increasingly turbulent, too. The Dene overwhelmingly rejected the new boundary for Nunavut in last week's vote because it cuts through their traditional hunting and burial grounds. (The Inuit were even accused in the days before the boundary vote of casting a spell on a Dene leader who had fallen ill with an ailment doctors weren't able to diagnose. It was an unusual flash of enmity.)

The cost of setting up a new territorial government in Nunavut is likely to be a major source of tension for years between the Inuit and citizens of the western Arctic, who will be fighting to preserve their piece of a shrinking federal pie. One study has suggested the creation of a new seat of government in Nunavut could cost more than $600-million and cause hundreds of job losses in Yellowknife. The federal government has yet to reveal its estimate.

What Indian Affairs Minister Tom Siddon has no qualms revealing, though, is his belief that a sovereign nation called Denendeh is dead. In interviews, he indicated that he supports a revamping of the western Arctic's government when Nunavut is created. This may allow the creation of native-controlled regional governments akin to city states (though still within the normal framework of government in Canada).

"Somehow, some interests have kept alive the notion of almost a free-standing nation, Denendeh, which would have virtually sovereign powers," acknowledges Mr. Siddon. "That doesn't take into account the need for investment, that there are a large number of non-native people living in the North, [or that] the North is part of Canada."

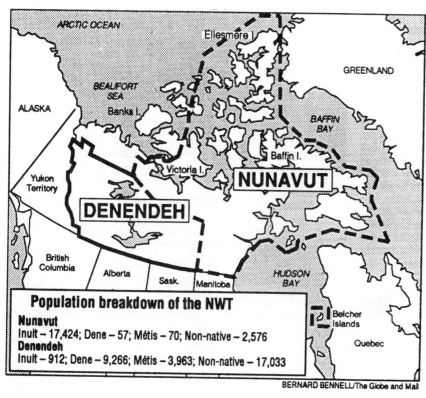

Population breakdown of the NWT

Nunavut
Inuit – 17,424; Dene – 57; Métis – 70; Non-native – 2,576
Denendeh
Inuit – 912; Dene – 9,266; Métis – 3,963; Non-native – 17,033

BERNARD BENNELL/The Globe and Mail

Too little, too late to save N.W.T.?

Darcy Henton

Darcy Henton is The Star*'s native affairs reporter.*

YELLOWKNIFE—On the shores of picturesque Frame Lake rises the $12 million edifice of a government that may not exist in seven years.

The Northwest Territories' 24-member legislative assembly is moving into its own 40,000-square-foot Taj Mahal next summer after 25 years of running the government out of school gymnasiums and, lately, a downtown hotel.

But a boundary plebiscite earlier this month, which sets the stage for division of the N.W.T. in 1999, has some residents of the western Arctic wondering what, if anything, will be left to govern after that split occurs.

They fear the end of strong, central government in the western Arctic and wonder what kind of clout a fragmented region will have with Ottawa, which provides 70 per cent of the $1 billion N.W.T. budget.

Already three-quarters of the pie has been divvied up among the Inuit, Inuvialuit and Gwich'in and there's every indication that all claims in the North could be settled before the end of the decade.

The eastern half of present-day N.W.T. and its 22,000 mostly Inuit residents will split off to govern themselves in 1999. The new territory, to be known as Nunavut, will feature a publicly elected government. The remaining 35,000 residents in the west—including 17,000 non-natives—are now grappling to determine what kind of government to build with what's left.

"Now that the east is going ahead with public government, some fear the west will be stuck with a bunch of fiefdoms all fighting with each other," observes Mike Scott, general manager of Northern News Services, which publishes newspapers in Yellowknife and Inuvik. It's a very real possibility.

The Inuvialuit (western Arctic Inuit) and Gwich'in Indians (formerly known as the Loucheux) have signed land claim agreements that entitle them to huge chunks of the west. The Sahtu Indians are expected to sign an agreement soon and the pressure is on other Dene-Metis groups to the south to negotiate a deal or risk losing out on a possible mining and oil bonanza.

Some groups have already said they will bypass the Yellowknife-based N.W.T. government and deal directly with Ottawa. Out in the hinterland there is no love lost for Yellowknife politicians and 6,200 bureaucrats and 800 boards and agencies, which, from a distance, have pulled the strings in 62 N.W.T. communities since 1967. The sprawling urban centre, which is one of the few spots in the North where non-natives outnumber natives, is about as popular as Toronto is to rural Ontarians and western Canadians.

Willard Hagen, Gwich'in Tribal Council president, makes no effort to hide the animosity between his people and the government of the day.

"It's not that we don't like them— we *despise* them," he says. "That's the word.

"They bettered some people's lives, but it sure wasn't the native people."

Yellowknife, with its four-lane highways, office towers and movie theatres, was built "on the backs of the poor in the settlements," says Hagen.

Natives continue to live in squalor, he complains.

When the Gwich'in got into tough bargaining with Ottawa over their recently signed land claim, they didn't find any help in Yellowknife.

"The territorial government was totally against our claim," says Hagen. "They fought us all the way.

"They weren't ready for it. They didn't have a plan in place and they were scared of all the power they would lose."

During its visit to Inuvik and Fort McPherson, the Royal Commission on Aboriginal People was astonished to hear such complaints.

Commission co-chair Rene Dussault says he assumed that native self-government would be much more easily achieved in the N.W.T. than in the southern provinces since 18 of the 24 members of its legislature are native.

N.W.T. politicians concede they have not done a great job of looking after regional interests. A major decentralization plan is in the works to put more power and development in other communities. But plans to decentralize may be too little too late.

Yellowknife MLA Michael Ballantyne says that the May 4 plebiscite which set the stage for division has forever changed the N.W.T.

"The status quo is gone," he says. "Once you break the egg, you can't put it together again."

Yellowknife MLA Charles Dent says it will be tough to convince native groups that territorial government offers them a better future than they could achieve through their own self-governing regions.

"It will take some pretty fancy footwork to get them back. The biggest advantage we've got is time to work out some kind of accommodation."

From *The Toronto Star,* May 28, 1992, p. A23. Reprinted with permission from The Toronto Star Syndicate.

Quebec

The tempo and temper of Quebec nationalism has fluctuated over the last few years with the ebb and flow of public opinion, specific policy issues, political personalities, miscalculations in electoral strategies and fortunes, the rise and fall of "Meech Lake," and, most recently, the question of the new constitutional arrangement that was rejected by voters nationwide as well as in Quebec.

The first article in this section asks the question, "What if Quebec Separates?" and offers a historical examination of Quebec's boundaries, resources, and culture. The high stakes of the question are emphasized by an examination of possible reactions to separation by Anglophone and aboriginal groups. A presentation of several maps demonstrates that there have been many "Quebecs" over the years, and the precise borders of a newly independent Quebec might be the subject of yet further tension between Quebec City and Ottawa.

In an article on the French language sign law, David Baugh describes the importance of French culture to Quebec and why the symbolic importance of signs in French has been a focus of policy for the government of Quebec. He suggests that the Supreme Court of Canada's rulings on Quebec sign laws have not resolved the situation, and that we will be seeing this subject come up again in future years.

An economic perspective on Quebec independence is presented in the next article, which surveys business leaders on their views concerning the future of Quebec. The study reveals mixed opinions on the desirability of sovereignty-association and a wide range of concerns dealing with the effect of independence on Quebec's economy. The author concludes that the issue is "too important to be left only to the politicians." He suggests that more direct negotiations between the government of Quebec and the federal government are needed.

The final article in this section also focuses on Quebec's economy, as it specifically examines the relationship between Quebec's economic recession and the constitutional debate regularly taking place in Quebec. Sandro Contenta suggests that Quebec's economy can survive any constitutional reform, if there is cooperation among the various sectors of the economy.

Looking Ahead: Challenge Questions

What is the likelihood that Quebec will decide to separate from the rest of Canada? If it does make such a decision, what will the new Quebec look like? Which argument related to Quebec's "true" borders is most compelling, and why?

Why is Quebec so sensitive about the role of French in a province in which the majority of the population speaks French? Should Quebec be more concerned about the language rights of the English-speaking minority within its borders than the rest of Canada is with the language rights of the French-speaking minority elsewhere? What is the "proper" balance of language rights? Should provinces become involved in legislating language at all?

What is the relationship between independence, or sovereignty-association, and Quebec's economy? What would the effect of sovereignty be on Quebec's economy? Is there any way that Quebec could have *both* sovereignty and continued economic prosperity?

Unit 7

WHAT IF QUEBEC SEPARATES?

POLITICIANS ARE SHYING AWAY FROM A BIG ISSUE: THE POTENTIAL BATTLE OVER DIVIDING UP QUEBEC

In polite political circles, it is the topic that dare not speak its name. In federal and provincial capitals, most politicians simply refuse to consider what the boundaries of a seceding Quebec should be. At issue is the ownership of a glorious swath of land, stretching from fogbound Hudson Strait to the Eastern Townships, where the barns are often round because legend holds that the devil hides in barn corners; from the Spartan Cree settlements of James Bay to the wild North Atlantic where the 16th-century mariner Sir Martin Frobisher once looked for a passage to the riches of Asia. At stake is the wealth of that land and its resources, the future of its disparate peoples and its priceless tradition of strained but enduring civility. Perhaps Canada's silent leaders assumed that the very mention of the topic breaks the bounds of that civility. But their silence has largely left the explosive issue to the consideration of the threatened and the threatening.

The few leaders who have the courage to confront the issue believe that the eerie silence should end—for the sake of the nation. Across Southern and Eastern Europe and in the former Soviet Union, ethnic hatreds are shredding the social fabric and blurring official boundaries. In Yugoslavia, ethnic rivalries have fired a vicious civil war, killing hundreds of people and devastating the medieval port of Dubrovnik. Such hatreds do not run as high in Canada. But there are many people—aboriginals, French-Canadians, anglophone Quebecers and those outside of the province—who have a stake in the landmass of Quebec (see "Drawing Lines in the Sand"). University of Saskatchewan law professor Donna Greschner, for one, questions what would happen if Quebec seceded—and its native people did not choose to stay with Quebec. "With whose sovereignty do we side?" she asked. "We cannot blindly pretend that force is not part of the Canadian tradition."

In coolly rational terms, Canadians should discuss who owns what if Quebec separates. A historical examination will help to understand why boundaries were drawn and why peoples grieved (see "The Roots of the Struggle"). It may throw light on why claims are made and why positions clash. That process could heal the nation, or it might at least ensure that future boundaries are drawn—and claims are settled—in peace. There are those who dispute that approach: Parti Québécois Leader Jacques Parizeau, for one, assured U.S. officials last week that separation would occur inevitably—and painlessly. Countered University of Toronto history professor Desmond Morton: "It is a misreading of history to believe that countries are torn up easily or without a tremendous risk of tragic conflict. Concealing that fact because we do not want 'to alarm the children' is both deceptive—and contemptuous to the people of this country."

The first lesson of history is that its mistakes are easily repeated. The second is that *threatening* people are also often the *threatened.* Like other aboriginal groups across Canada, Quebec's nine aboriginal nations have fought hard for recognition of their rights. In 1990, the Supreme Court of Canada ruled that a 230-year-old agreement between the Hurons and the Crown constituted a treaty between nations—and that aboriginals in the Lorette Indian reserve near Quebec City still held the right to camp and to make fires in Jacques Cartier provincial park. In light of their troubled past, it is only natural for natives to ask if an independent Quebec would also recognize such aboriginal and treaty rights. It is only a small step further to the native peoples' assertion that they have outstanding claims, throughout the province, to two-thirds of the landmass.

French-Canadians, in turn, have sadly observed the erosion of their cultural status. In 1867, they viewed themselves as a founding nation of Canada. Quebec generously extended constitutionally guaranteed rights to its English-language minority. But throughout the ensuing decades, comparable minority rights were callously withdrawn or withheld from bewildered French-speaking, Roman Catholic peoples in other provinces. As a result, many Quebecers feel that the boundaries of their province represent the boundaries of French Canada. From that belief, it is only a small step to the assertion that an independent Quebec should ensure its viability—and reclaim its rich heritage of Labrador from Newfoundland.

English-Canadians, including anglophone Quebecers, also have grievances. When Parliament added the territory of northern Ungava to Quebec in 1912, it was partly to compensate for the erosion of minority francophone rights in Western Canada. That doubled the landmass of the province; it added rich minerals and rushing rivers. It is only natural that many English-Canadians ask why many Quebecers assume that an independent Quebec would still own Ungava. It is only a small step from that question to the assertion that Parliament must take back Ungava from a seceding Quebec. Together, those small steps could lead into an abyss.

But if the past gives a cause for rancor, it also gives reason for comfort. Throughout Canadian history, it is compromisers who have always saved the nation. Perhaps today's partisan politicians are incapable of fitting the explosive issue of boundaries into their already crowded agenda. But it is exactly for that reason that many Canadians might wish to refer the issue to a constituent assembly, or an academic conference, or a public-interest group. Whatever the forum, another historical lesson holds: when people talk to each other, tension abates. The topic that dare not speak its name would then speak—in a rational, generous and understanding exchange.

MARY JANIGAN

From *Maclean's*, November 25, 1991, pp. 20-24, 26-29. Copyright © 1991 by Maclean Hunter Ltd. Reprinted by permission.

WHAT IF QUEBEC SEPARATES?

••

DRAWING LINES IN THE SAND

SEPARATION CARRIES HIGH STAKES

The meeting was private, a two-day strategy session organized to give the leaders of the Parti Québécois an opportunity to roll up their sleeves and get down to the serious business of planning a sovereign state. But even the 80 sovereigntists gathered in suburban Beauport, on the outskirts of Quebec City, were taken aback by the proposal advanced by an avuncular professor of political science from the University of Montreal. Edouard Cloutier, invited to the conclave to provide expert advice, urged the assembled party officials to consider establishing a military force to counter possible acts of sabotage and disorder from equally secessionist-minded groups—natives and anglophones in particular. "It's a touchy subject," Cloutier acknowledged last week. "But we cannot afford to do nothing in the face of threats to take away from an independent Quebec territory that rightly belongs to it."

PQ officials quickly dissociated themselves from the proposition, especially when accounts of the incident, which occurred early this fall, reached reporters. Natives and anglophones just as swiftly expressed outrage. But neither the denials nor the denunciations could disguise the fact that the mild-mannered professor had clearly exposed a raw nerve in the debate over Quebec's future. What cannot be denied is the existence of a small but swelling chorus aimed at the separatist credo that the borders of an independent Quebec would match its current provincial boundaries. It comes from native groups, who even today are challenging Quebec's authority over vast reaches of the province. And it comes from sectors of the English-speaking population, both inside and outside Quebec, who argue that an independent Quebec could not lay claim to all of the province's territory. Complained Cloutier: "What is being discussed is nothing less than the fate of the land that is the soul of the entire ideal of Quebec sovereignty."

In raising the prospect of armed force to defend that ideal, the professor also touched on another explosive issue. To most Canadians, English and French alike, an armed conflict over Quebec's future borders seems a remote possibility. But not everyone shares that as-

sumption. In early November, historian Desmond Morton sounded a warning when he spoke at a Toronto conference staged by the Canadian Institute for Strategic Studies to debate the military implications of Quebec separation. "I don't believe—and here I disagree with PQ Leader Jacques Parizeau—that countries break up easily or in a civilized way," the University of Toronto professor said as he urged Canadians "to look into this abyss of violence—and step back from it."

Others, though, say that there may be no stepping back. "Not only is armed conflict possible, it is highly probable," predicts University of Calgary political scientist Barry Cooper, co-author of the recently published *Deconfederation: Canada Without Quebec*, a study recommending the speedy departure from the Canadian Confederation of a radically truncated Quebec. Added Bill Wilson, political secretary of the Assembly of First Nations: "People who are told that they are Quebecers without having their decision-making respected are going to protest. If we don't sit down and talk now, the confrontation will be 100 times as bad as it needs to be."

Anger: Recent events have already presaged potential confrontations to come. In the summer of 1990, armed Mohawks at Oka, Que., angered over a local decision to expand a golf course onto land claimed by the natives, engaged in a tense 78-day standoff with the authorities that began when a Quebec provincial police officer was killed in circumstances still under investigation. In fact, it is Quebec's Indians who mount what is perhaps the most compelling challenge to the view that the province's borders are inviolable. "One hundred per cent of the province is the traditional hereditary territory of the aboriginal nations," declares James O'Reilly, a Montreal lawyer who specializes in representing Indians in land-claim battles. "Almost every one of those nations has a good case in law to title."

Quebec's 10,000 Cree have been at the centre of much of the debate over the territorial integrity of an independent Quebec—largely because they inhabit the lands where Quebec's massive James Bay hydroelectric project is located. Quebec now plans an expansion of that

project. But a month ago, Ovide Mercredi, grand chief of the Assembly of First Nations, ignited a furious debate when he suggested that the Cree might withdraw from Quebec should the province secede from Canada.

At the core of that particular dispute is the widely held conviction in official Quebec circles that the Cree have no legal claim on Quebec territory as a result of the 1975 James Bay and Northern Quebec Agreement. According to the Quebec government, under that agreement the Cree and Inuit ceded their historical rights to the land for $225 million. Parizeau has insisted that all Cree claims to northern Quebec are "false, illegal and unconstitutional." PQ vice-president Bernard Landry reiterated that opinion last week. "Both the Cree and the Inuit agreed in writing to yield, renounce, dedicate and transfer all their rights—and we paid them in return," he told *Maclean's*.

Spokesmen for the Cree, however, have a different view. "The agreement was entered into with Quebec in Canada," says Billy Diamond, chief of the Waskaganish Cree and a member of the Quebec Cree Grand Council's constitutional committee. "We did not sign an agreement with an *independent* Quebec. If that happens, the agreement would become null and void—and that would certainly jeopardize the boundaries of Quebec."

Other Quebec natives are also exploring the legal ramifications of Quebec independence—including the possibility of declaring their own independence. "We are all seriously looking at it," says Jean-Yves Assiniwi, a mixed-blood native of Quebec and an adviser to the Native Council of Canada. The underlying motivation, he points out, is native reluctance to sever long-standing ties with Ottawa. Said Assiniwi: "I don't think too many aboriginal groups want to entertain the possibility of letting go of their relationship to the federal Crown."

Much the same kind of sentiment is driving some members of Quebec's anglophone minority to contemplate a rearrangement of the provincial frontiers. The strength of those currents is not easy to gauge—largely because the subject's delicate nature has precluded an open discussion. And for some Quebec politicians, suggestions that an independent Quebec's borders could be readjusted amount to a "scare tactic," as Parizeau has said, to weaken support for independence. Added the PQ's Landry: "All of these attempts to fracture or fragment or dislocate Quebec are transparently illegal and bound to fail."

Questionable: But legality or illegality are questionable concepts when applied to uncharted waters. In *Deconfederation*, Cooper and his colleague, historian David Bercuson, argue that because Quebec's present borders are largely a direct result of its being a part of Canada, an independent Quebec would not be entitled to much more than the original French colonial territory scattered along the shores of the St. Lawrence River before the fall of New France in 1763. A similar argument has been advanced by B.C. lawyer and constitutional expert David L. Varty in his study *Who Gets Ungava?*—Ungava being the northern hinterland ceded by Ottawa to the province after Confederation. Varty argues that an independent Quebec would have no claim to that territory.

Both books draw heavily on the material contained in *Partition: The Price of Quebec's Independence*, first published in 1980 by Montreal authors William Shaw and Lionel Albert. Shaw, a dentist who at the time served as an MNA, and Albert, a businessman, argued that Quebec could not afford to separate because it would lose too much territory. Together, those studies raise the issue: if Canada is divisible, Quebec should be as well. Said McGill University constitutional law professor Stephen Scott in an interview: "What's sauce for the goose is sauce for the gander. It is sheer effrontery on Quebec's part to demand the northern two-

thirds of the province. Those territories were added to Quebec—to be governed as part of a Canadian province."

Diverse: Challenging Quebec's claim to some of its territory appears to be gathering steam among Quebec anglophones. Earlier this year, 38-year-old Montreal financial consultant Gregory Gogan almost single-handedly founded a Quebec anglophone separatist movement called Option Canada. Gogan proposes to transform Option Canada into a federal political party dedicated to carving a new province out of southwestern Quebec—including the western half of the island of Montreal—where most of the province's non-French-speaking population resides. "There are 1.5 million people in that region," says Gogan. "They are ethnically diverse and bilingual. I am convinced that the overwhelming majority will support the creation of a new bilingual and economically stable province that is progressive in attitude and tolerant in spirit."

Gogan clearly has a steep road to climb. Still, during the past seven months he has been tirelessly addressing small gatherings—and claims that he has convinced 2,000 Quebecers to join his organization. And in a sense, Gogan's idea is merely the logical extension of another, less ambitious program. Reed Scowen, chairman of the anglophone-rights organization Alliance Quebec, has proposed the creation of what he calls "English territories" within Quebec. These so-called territories, all with either anglophone majorities or hefty minorities, would seek exemption from Quebec's restrictive language laws. Declared Scowen: "The idea is to give some kind of political expression to those regions of Quebec, scattered largely

along the southern and western borders, who voted 'no' in the 1980 referendum on sovereignty and are likely to vote the same way if another referendum on the same issue is held."

In the same vein, Quebec's tiny English-rights Equality party recently published a study by McGill Unversity economist William Watson that advances the argument that electoral ridings voting against sovereignty in any future referendum should be allowed to form new provinces or join neighboring ones. "The political life of a post-independence Quebec would be much more peaceful if dissident regions were permitted to opt out of the secession," Watson wrote.

Few of those propositions have been treated with anything but a passing remark from either the PQ or Robert Bourassa's ruling Liberals. Parizeau, in fact, has cavalierly dismissed the proposals by noting that "there will never be an independent republic of Sept-Iles." Such an attitude may well reflect an accurate assessment that the threat of separation from within an independent Quebec is, indeed, a minor one. But it may also mirror wishful thinking. There is reason for worry, particularly over the possibility of anglophone dissent coupled with the far more dangerous prospect of repeated aboriginal unrest, should Quebec follow the path to independence. If that were not the case, the University of Montreal's Cloutier would not have thought it necessary to raise the need for a new military force to counter it.

BARRY CAME *in Montreal with*
E. KAYE FULTON in Ottawa and
BRIAN BERGMAN in Toronto

THE ANGLOPHILE SEPARATIST

Jacques Parizeau is an unlikely hero. The 61-year-old leader of the Parti Québécois makes no secret of the fact that he is an admirer of most things English. He is a graduate of the London School of Economics, speaks English with a British clip, chainsmokes English cigarettes, confesses to harboring a "soft spot" for the Queen and is inordinately fond of that most English of French wines—claret. Parizeau even dresses in the image of a modern English banker—or at least used to, until his advisers recently persuaded him to abandon his trademark three-piece English pinstripe. Still, Parizeau remains resolutely committed to the goal of Quebec sovereignty.

It is a conviction that he has held since 1968, when, after a lengthy period of

uncertainty, he reached the conclusion that independence was the best course for Quebec. He made his decision during a long train ride across Canada. "I got on the train in Montreal a federalist—but I got off the train in Banff a separatist," he has remarked on more than one occasion. The belief is deeply held. He walked out of René Lévesque's cabinet in 1984, resigning his post as finance minister, after the former Quebec premier decided to steer the PQ away from separatism and towards the goal of working to achieve the province's nationalist goals within the framework of Confederation.

During his years out of politics, Parizeau, an economist by training and a former university professor, did not waver from his *indépendantiste* goals. And he has remained loyal to his ideals since wresting control of the PQ in 1988 from the moderates who ran the party after Lévesque. At the moment, Parizeau is riding high. If a provincial election were

held now, all the polls point to a PQ victory. And if that were to happen, he openly pledges to immediately begin moves to take Quebec out of Canada. He reiterated that view last week in Washington, when he told three U.S. senators, all members of the senate foreign relations committee, that he would stage a referendum on the issue eight to 10 months after taking office.

Parizeau has no doubts about the outcome of a popular vote, despite the fact that the tide of nationalist sentiment that swept over Quebec after the failure of the Meech Lake accord now appears to be gradually receding. But even if he does finally manage to reach his goal and lead Quebec out of Canada, it is not likely to alter his fondness for the English. When he was asked in Washington last week whether an independent Quebec would remain in the British Commonwealth, he replied: "It may well be that we will remain in this—for old time's sake."

B.C.

WHAT IF QUEBEC SEPARATES?

●●●

THE ROOTS OF THE STRUGGLE

A TURBULENT PAST HAUNTS QUEBEC

It is perhaps fitting that the history of French-speaking Quebec began with an acrimonious territorial dispute. In 1534, seeking gold and passage to the fabled Asia, navigator Jacques Cartier and his crew of 61 fishermen anchored their two ships in a Gaspé harbor, where the St. Lawrence River spills into the Atlantic Ocean. On July 24, after several days of tentative contact with the Iroquois, Cartier ordered his men to assemble an enormous wooden cross. In the centre was a shield with three fleur-de-lys, the heraldic emblem of the French crown; above the shield, a wooden board proclaimed, "Long live the king of France." In the name of his monarch, Francis I, Cartier raised his cross—and thus staked his claim—to a rich land teeming with fish and furs. The Iroquois chief, Donnacona, reacted with fury. Clad in a black bearskin, he paddled his canoe up to the interloper's vessel. As Cartier recorded in his journal, "He pointed to the land all around about, as if he wished to say that all this region belonged to him, and that we ought not to have set up this cross without his permission."

That bitter episode epitomizes the tangled and troubled history of the Quebec landmass. First settled after 9,000 BC, as the glaciers of the ice age retreated northward, the sprawling province that today covers 600,000 square miles has been the home of great peoples and the hostage of proud empires. The Quebec of Cartier's time was home to aboriginal peoples as varied as those of Europe: Cree, Micmac, Inuit, Naskapi, Montagnais, Algonquin, Iroquois. Oblivious to the territorial claims of those peoples, the French pushed their empire across the heart of the continent, from Labrador to the Gulf of Mexico.

Struggle: But the frequent wars between Britain and France, which spilled across the high seas into their new world, interfered with French expansionism. Eventually, in 1763, France lost its continental North American possessions; New France went to Britain. The victorious English promptly divided their winnings: they carved out "Quebec," a rectangular

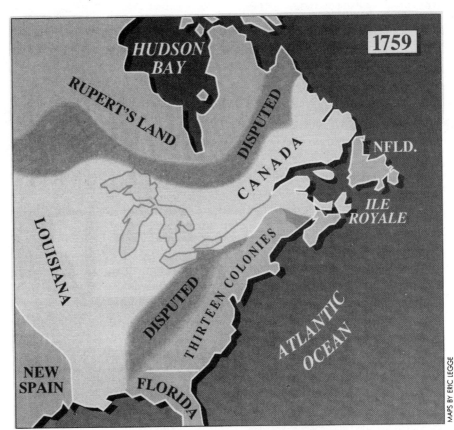

■ *The fall of Quebec City to Britain leads to the rapid loss of France's vast North American territories, stretching from Labrador to the Gulf of Mexico*

slice of land along the shores of the St. Lawrence. For the next 164 years, from 1763 to 1927, as French Canada struggled for cultural survival, and as Canada evolved into a nation, the boundaries of Quebec repeatedly grew and shrank in response to political forces or judicial decisions. With the flourish of a pen or the pounding of a gavel, boundary lines shifted hundreds of kilometres across territory rich in forests and minerals and rivers and peoples.

Those dizzying boundary shifts are now the focus of modern-day tension sparked by the possibility of Quebec's separating from Canada. Most Quebec separatists, for one, maintain that an independent Quebec should lay claim to Labrador: they reject a 1927 British Privy Council decision which confirmed Newfoundland's ownership of territory traditionally claimed by Quebec. In response, prominent Toronto lawyer James Arnett, who has extensively researched the issue, counters that Ottawa should have a contingency plan: if Quebec attempts to secede, the federal government should pass legislation to take control over the administration of Ungava, the huge northern territory stretching from Hudson Bay to Labrador that Ottawa deeded to Quebec in 1912. Finally, many aboriginal peoples, such as the Montagnais and the Labrador Naskapi, claim huge swaths of Quebec territory, insisting that they never relinquished title to their land.

Wrenching: Those vehement positions rest upon differing interpretations of Quebec's past. The story of its boundaries is, in fact, an essential theme in the dramatic, tumultuous and often wrenching history of Quebec. As the authoritative geographer Norman Nicholson, who died in 1984, noted, "In a growing country like Canada, boundaries have frequently changed in accordance with new situations and needs. Therefore, their development is an indication of the development of the country."

That development actually began thousands of years before the Europeans discovered their new worlds. Most scholars believe that aboriginal peoples first streamed into uninhabited North America from Asia between 12,000 and 30,000 years ago, across a strip of land, now called the Bering Strait Land Bridge, that then joined the two continents. The movement into modern Quebec probably began around 11,000 years ago. Over the next millennium, different aboriginal peoples—with differing ways of life—settled.

Their values and institutions evolved; peoples moved or perished. When Cartier, for one, reached North America, the so-called St. Lawrence Iroquois dominated the area around the St. Lawrence River from the Gaspé to Lake Ontario. More than seven decades later, in 1608, when the explorer Samuel de Champlain founded his settlement at Quebec City, all traces of that tribe had disappeared—probably because of warfare with other aboriginal nations. Instead, the explorer usually encountered Algonquin peoples with whom he forged alliances and fought battles, incurring the lasting enmity of the Iroquois peoples.

With the guidance of its native allies, the French pushed into the heart of the continent, expanding the boundaries of New France. Their motives were mixed: to expand the French empire; to discover a passage to the elusive East; to secure a rich supply of furs; and to convert the natives to the Roman Catholic faith. Throughout the 17th century, through the zeal of its missionaries and the greed of its traders, New France expanded from the shores of Labrador and Acadia through southern and central Quebec and Ontario, southward along the Mississippi River.

But that empire, magnificent on early maps, was fragile. The British empire, equally anxious for furs and glory, was also forging alliances with natives, especially the anti-French Iroquois—and staking its rival territorial claims. In 1670, the English monarch Charles II granted the entire Hudson Bay watershed, named Rupert's Land after the king's cousin Prince Rupert, to the Hudson's Bay Co.—with the exception of lands "possessed by the Sub-

■ *Britain creates 'Quebec' from the densely inhabited portion of New France*

■ *The Quebec Act restores New France's western borders as far as the Mississippi River*

■ *After the American Revolution, land south of the Great Lakes goes to the United States*

■ *Quebec is partitioned into Lower Canada and English-speaking Upper Canada in the west*

jectes of any other Christian Prince or State." But the notion of possession was ill-defined and, as a result, the territorial claims of England and France overlapped in a broad band across the north of New France. And to the south and east of New France, in a semicircle around Britain's American colonies, British claims also overlapped those of the French.

Those territorial rivalries sparked bitter clashes in the ferocious wars that France and Britain waged between 1689 and 1763. With each new peace treaty, whole chunks of North America changed hands: in 1713, under the Treaty of Utrecht, France ceded Newfoundland and Acadia to Britain. Those French losses were merely a taste of the disaster ahead. In 1759, British troops defeated a French army at Quebec City. In 1760, the British took Montreal. Three years later, with the Treaty of Paris, France lost the rest of its mainland North American empire.

The resulting peace was uneasy for both the losers and the winners. The losers, 70,000 French-speaking people, desperately clung to their distinct language, culture, religion and legal system amid two million British North Americans. The winners held a huge empire—but their security was largely dependent upon the goodwill of France's former native allies.

That goodwill was strained. As University of Ottawa historian Susan Mann Trofimenkoff noted in *The Dream of Nation*, "Numerous groups of [Western] Indians were unhappy. The war had not only cut the flow of trade, it had raised prices of trade goods."

Throughout the summer of 1763, irate natives attacked British forts to the south of the Great Lakes. A nervous Great Britain issued the Royal Proclamation of 1763—primarily to contain that unrest. The rich hinterland across the north and the west of the former French colony was reserved for the natives. The Labrador coast went to Newfoundland—a separate British colony. As well, England drew the boundaries of French-speaking "Quebec"—a rectangular chunk of land around the St. Lawrence River. This drastic alteration in the boundaries of French Canada was accompanied by the imposition of English laws and English courts. And the British further angered their new subjects by decreeing that Quebec would be governed by a non-elected council and an elected assembly whose members would have to take anti-Catholic oaths.

Loyalty: A decade later, England backed

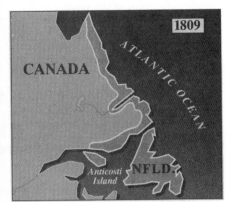

■ *Britain transfers the 'coasts of Labrador' from Quebec to its colony of Newfoundland*

■ *Part of the Labrador coast (now Quebec's North Shore) is returned to Lower Canada*

■ *At Confederation, most maps show Quebec's northern boundary at the Hudson Bay watershed*

away from its hard line in the face of new threats to its empire. Alarmed at the increasing restiveness of its American colonies, Britain took steps to secure the loyalty of its unwilling subjects to the north. The Quebec Act of 1774 guaranteed the rights of Quebecers to the Catholic faith and French civil law. As well, to boost the colony's economy and to placate western natives who preferred to trade with the French, Britain expanded

Quebec's boundaries. Quebec now stretched north to Rupert's Land, eastward over all of Labrador, westward over the Great Lakes and southward to the junction of the Mississippi and Ohio rivers.

The repercussions were extraordinary: French Quebec survived. But those concessions only increased the tensions between Britain and its American colonies, who were infuriated because the expansion of Quebec blocked their dreams of western growth. Two years later, those colonies revolted. When peace was concluded in 1783, Quebec's boundaries were again truncated: land to the south and west of the Great Lakes had suddenly, with the slash of signatures on a treaty, become part of the United States.

Other concessions to the new United States eventually resulted in further boundary changes. The 1783 peace treaty allowed U.S. fishermen to dry their catch on the unsettled shores of Labrador. As a result, American fishermen thronged to the fish-rich seacoast. But the government of Quebec could scarcely administer a coastal area that was thousands of kilometres from its Quebec City capital. In 1809, the British Parliament transferred to Newfoundland the "coasts of Labrador" from the Saint-Jean River to Hudson Strait. Quebec fishermen in their traditional fishing grounds off southern Labrador were suddenly subject to Newfoundland's laws. In response to their complaints, the British Parliament restored a portion of the coast of southwest Labrador to Quebec in 1825. It moved the Labrador boundary to the east, specifying that it stretched from Ance Sablon on the coast to the 52nd parallel.

Estranged: Meanwhile, to the west, peace had another profound effect on geography. In the wake of the American War of Independence, thousands of United Empire Loyalists flowed over the new international boundary into Britain's northern colonies. Some settled in Nova Scotia and New Brunswick. But others chose to carve out homes in Quebec's Eastern Townships and the wilderness of the interior stretching southwest between Montreal and the Detroit River. Those English-speaking colonists of the interior felt estranged from the customs and laws of the Quebec government. In response, Britain divided Quebec into Upper Canada (Ontario) and Lower Canada (Quebec). A British cabinet order drew a boundary that ran largely along today's boundary between the two provinces. As well, the British Parliament provided each colony with a British governor, an elected assembly and appointed legislative and executive councils.

But the new arrangement sowed the seeds of its own destruction. For the next 46 years, each colony's elected assembly battled the government for control of the public purse strings—and over demands for real representative government. In 1837, those democratic stirrings erupted into rebellion in both Upper and Lower Canada. Although military forces quickly extinguished both protests, the alarmed British government hastily appointed Lord Durham to investigate the uproar. His infamous 1839 report damned the French-Canadians as "an old and stationary society in a new and progressive world"—and he recommended the assimilation of French-speaking Quebec through political union with Upper Canada. A year later, the British Parliament united the two colonies into the Province of Canada, governed by a governor general, an appointed legislative council and an elected English-language assembly containing 42 representatives from each colony.

The history of 19th-century French Canada is a story of survival. French-Canadians overcame the assimilating tendencies of the Province of Canada—in spite of Lord Durham—largely because of an alliance forged by reformers in French Canada and English Canada. The two groups eventually ensured that the members of the governing council were largely drawn from the elected parliamentary majority: in effect, they won responsible government. Elected French-Canadians could now govern in their voters' interests.

By the 1860s, however, the Province of Canada had become a troubled colony saddled with an enormous debt—the result of ambitious railroad and canal construction programs. Events south of the border contributed to the unease: Canada feared that the victorious North in the bloody U.S. Civil War would retaliate for Britain's support of the southern Confederacy. And ultimately, Canadians were tired of political instability after a dizzying series of coalition governments among the competing parties.

In 1867, in a bid for prosperity, security and stability through unity, the Province of Canada united with Nova Scotia and New Brunswick to form the Dominion of Canada. With Confederation, the Province of Canada devolved into its two components, now called Ontario and Quebec. But Confederation did not mark an end to domestic turmoil. For the next 30 years, Quebec and Ontario challenged Ottawa's constitutional powers in the courts. That struggle for provincial rights became particularly poignant in Quebec, however, as other provinces rescinded rights held by their French-Canadian minorities. Many Quebec nationalists uneasily concluded that the boundaries of Quebec were becoming the boundaries of French Canada.

It was against this turbulent backdrop that Quebec's northern boundary was defined—and redefined. In 1870, the Hudson's Bay Co. transferred Rupert's Land to Canada. Under the Quebec Act of 1774, the southern boundary of Rupert's Land was also the northern boundary of the colony of Quebec (which then included much of present-day Ontario). But no one knew precisely where that boundary lay. The new province of Ontario insisted that its northern boundary ran along the Albany River, 250 km north of Lake Superior—well into the Hudson Bay watershed. The federal government countered that the boundary of Rupert's Land fell much further to the south, a mere 25 to 80 km north of the shores of Lake Superior and Lake Nipigon. In 1878, an arbitration panel supported Ontario's claims. But Ottawa refused to implement that decision. Finally, in 1884, Canada sent the question to its highest court, the British Privy Council. Without giving any reasons, the Privy Council favored Ontario's claims, but defined only a portion of Ontario's northern boundary. In 1889, Ottawa accepted the implications of the council's ruling: it drew Ontario's boundary along the Albany River.

Quebec had followed that dispute with fascination. The province argued that the Privy Council had, in effect, set the southern boundary of Rupert's Land. As a result, Quebec contended, its northern boundary also extended well into the Hudson Bay watershed; it argued that its growth should, in fairness, match Ontario's growth. The province suggested that its boundary should run along the Eastmain and Hamilton rivers to the "coasts" of Labrador (which belonged to Newfoundland). That line ran roughly along the same latitude as the Albany River. Ottawa did not rule upon the legal merits of Quebec's arguments. But, in 1898, it officially endorsed that line as the northern boundary of Quebec.

Complex: Still, complex boundary problems remain unsolved. Because the British Privy Council did not give its reasons when setting Ontario's boundaries, the extent of Rupert's Land is still open to debate. Some English-Canadians, such as McGill University law professor Stephen Scott, say that if Quebec secedes, it should receive only the territory that it possessed at the time of Confederation. But the location of Quebec's northern boundary in 1867 remains a hotly contested question. Many scholars maintain that when Ottawa set Quebec's boundaries

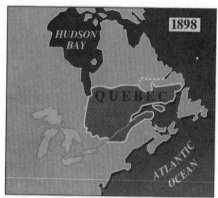

■ *Quebec and Canada agree upon a northern boundary including part of modern Labrador*

■ *Quebec expands to Hudson Strait and claims Labrador as far as the Atlantic coastal area*

■ *Quebec assumes its present shape after the Privy Council defines the Labrador border*

in 1898, it was expanding the province. Others suggest that Ottawa may have merely recognized an already existing boundary. Osgoode Hall law professor Kent McNeil argues that issue is too complex for pat answers: "In 1884, the Privy Council simply decided where the *northwest* boundary of the colony of Quebec was as a result of the Quebec Act of 1774."

There was more turmoil in the first six decades of the 20th century. Quebec's indus-

trial base expanded from light manufacturing to natural-resource-based industries such as hydroelectricity and pulp and paper. Its population poured from the farms into the cities. Confronted with social and economic upheaval, the province's nationalists worried about the preservation of Quebec's distinct identity. They resisted English Canada's attachment to Great Britain—Quebecers bitterly denounced conscription in the two world wars. And they resisted Ottawa's centralizing impulses. Premier Maurice Duplessis, for one, refused to accept federal tax transfers from 1947 to 1954, arguing that the province should collect its own personal and corporate taxes.

In this climate of anxious nationalism, two other boundary changes aroused intense interest. In 1908, Parliament granted a large chunk of Rupert's Land, the Territory of Keewatin, to Manitoba. Despite impassioned French-Canadian pleas, that legislation provided no guaranteed right to Roman Catholic schools for the Keewatin French-Canadian minority. Quebecers reacted with hurt—and anger. Partly to soothe that dismay, the federal government endorsed the province's requests for a further northward extension. In 1912, federal legislation authorized Quebec's annexation of Ungava, a northern territory that also once formed part of Rupert's Land.

Meanwhile, another territorial dispute simmered—this time over Labrador. In 1902, the Newfoundland government granted leases to a pulp company to cut timber on 297 square miles of land along the Hamilton River, 100 km north of the 52nd parallel. Quebec protested vehemently. According to the 1809 and 1825 acts of the British Parliament, it argued, Newfoundland governed merely "the coast" north of the 52nd—and "the coast" did not run along the Hamilton River. The argument festered. In 1922, both sides turned to the British Privy Council. Quebec contended that "the coast" was a 1.6-km-wide strip along the water. Newfoundland—which did not join Canada until 1949—countered that "the coast" followed the watershed of the rivers flowing into the Atlantic Ocean north of the 52nd parallel. In 1927, the council ruled for Newfoundland: in a complex decision, it reasoned that under international law, occupation of a seacoast included the right to the territory around the rivers that drained into that coast. That controversial boundary, which gave 112,000 square miles of rich land to Newfoundland, was confirmed in the Terms of Union when Newfoundland joined Canada. And that document, in turn, is part of the Constitution of Canada.

The final chapter in the story of Quebec's boundaries is perhaps the most ironic. In 1960, Quebec Premier Jean Lesage began the so-called Quiet Revolution, modernizing the province's social and economic institutions. Over the ensuing 31 years, the changes have been massive: the province has mobilized its own savings to invest in Quebec-based companies; its once antiquated school system has produced a formidable technological sector. In that climate, Quebec nationalism has proudly flourished.

But Quebec nationalism has also clashed with the increasing assertiveness of aboriginal peoples. In 1975, Quebec experienced a small taste of what the future may bring when it was forced to negotiate a land-claims settlement with the Cree of northern Quebec. Now, the Cree are again mobilizing their forces against the Quebec government's planned Great Whale expansion of the James Bay project, claiming it violates the terms of their earlier settlement. Other aboriginal groups, such as the Labrador Naskapi or Innu, have extensive claims to large areas of Quebec. And most refuse to relinquish title in exchange for a small land base.

Those sentiments may be setting the stage for the next act in the history of Quebec's boundaries. The tale of the landmass is rich; the claims of its competing groups are tangled. After centuries of struggle to preserve and enlarge its own boundaries, Quebec now faces the same wrenching dilemma that once confronted Cartier and Donnacona.

MARY JANIGAN

AFFIRMATIVE ACTION AND THE SIGN LAW

If linguistic harmony is to be reached, the rest of Canada must accept the unique needs of Quebec. But Quebeckers must also change.

David J. Baugh

David Baugh teaches Canadian politics and political theory at Red Deer College, and previously taught at St. Francis Xavier.

SINCE THE 1960s, QUEBEC POLITICS HAS CENtered around three forces: 1) centralizing federalists for a strong Ottawa; 2) separatists; 3) decentralizing federalists expanding the Quebec state. Among the latter are the authors of "distinct society": Bourassa's provincial Liberals and some of the Quebec wing of the federal Progressive Conservatives.

Quebec is protective of her majority language in the North American milieu. Fearing minority status in a country dominated by a strong Ottawa, many Quebeckers want strong provincial powers. Anglophones claiming to support bilingualism, while hostile to even minimal extra protections for the hearth of French, help fuel Quebec isolationism. The rest of the story is Quebec nationalism, and the aggression and ambition of politicians in promoting their own turf.

Decentralists portrayed the demise of Meech as a rejection of Quebec, by denying minimum demands. Centralizing federalists were driven from the field and Quebec's state-building agenda was accelerated. The Allaire Report proposed a decentralization so massive that, in the words of Jeffrey Stevens, it was "dead on arrival" in the rest of Canada.

Separatists claim Quebec's demands for more powers are insatiable. Either the separatists win in the short term, unless Ottawa makes concessions, or separatists win in the long run as the powers of Ottawa are lost. One interpretation of the Allaire Report is that decentralizing federalists, having reached despair in their unstable loyalty to Canada, were expelling themselves, by backing into a corner with an untenable negotiating position.

That interpretation should be rejected; Quebec does not need to leave. With no centrist counterpoint at the ministerial level to Quebec's province-first stance, the current crisis unfolded from the Meech process with implacable logic. Quebec's decentralizers pushed for what they could get, leaving others to worry about the Canadian whole; none did. Allaire pushed harder.

When the proverbial wolf was sensed under the sheep's clothing of "distinct society" the clause died with Meech. Skeptics were rewarded when Allaire's lengthy wish list soon followed, backed by separatist warnings.

While Allaire foresaw other provinces having the same expanded powers, the more common version of "distinct society" is that the rest of Canada should also have a national government. The distinct society would have major powers denied other provinces.

Parliamentary government, however, is group government, based on the majority principle and the confidence vote. A government with strong cabinet representation from Quebec, or a Prime Minister, would lack legitimacy were Quebeckers to dictate policies for the rest of Canada that did not apply in Quebec. But if Quebeckers abstained from voting in matters sovereign to Quebec, majority government could collapse.

With Allaire also sinking, one possibility is the lesser ceding of powers and another try at "distinct society," enacted by the minimum seven provinces, followed by more entreaties that Quebec not leave and more booty. Were Quebec to call itself a society distinct from the Canadian, it should only be a matter of time and logic before popular sovereignty, residing in society, makes sovereign institutions.

The new package defines "distinct society" as "civil code" (a redundancy, it's already in the Constitution), "French-speaking majority" and "culture." With no culture to be shared with Canada, future talks would target federal control of Radio-Canada, the National Film Board and so on, and expand the meaning of distinct society. But, judging by the fate of Meech, son-of-Meech is not likely to be much loved either.

The progress of Canadian federalism is blocked—and the

From *Policy Options*, Vol. 13, No. 4, May 1992, pp. 15-18. This article first appeared in *Policy Options*, Canada's Forum for Public Policy Debate.

decision of committing to Canada is deferred—by imprecise words. Decentralizing federalists sit on the fence between separatism and federalism through a well crafted ambiguity: "distinct society." The price tag for the political cleverness is the inability to resolve practical problems.

The greatest poverty of Meech was the use of "distinct society" to mask disagreements over the Quebec sign law. Most of the signatories attacked the sign law; Premier Bourassa defended it. Each read whatever he wanted into the distinct society clause and pretended they were in agreement. Had it passed it would have been the source of fruitless court battles on language and a host of issues. Even asking the Supreme Court to interpret something so vague would have exposed the high court to reproach. Meech would have bought delay but no solutions; left unrepaired, it failed its own deadline.

The new clause would allow Quebec to override minority anglophone rights in order to "promote" the French-speaking majority. However, it is one thing to over-ride minority rights in perpetuity, by saying that Quebec is a distinct society and minority rights count less. It is quite another to limit as few minority rights as necessary when the majority is under a real threat, and to restore them as much as possible as the threat subsides. The latter is the affirmative action approach; it also repudiates the separatist agenda in distinct society.

Quebec is not an easy province to govern. Unfortunately, the ambiguous federal face of the Bourassa Liberals has been too ignored by Meech opponents.

When the Meech Accord failed its deadline for ratification, it was Quebec that first dropped the secrecy and first-ministerial elitism of the Meech process. Quebec created the Belanger-Campeau commission. Ottawa, British Columbia, Manitoba, Ontario, New Brunswick and Alberta reciprocated with broadly-based commissions and public hearings.

Despite overwhelming support for separation by the majority of witnesses before Belanger-Campeau, the report proposed a two-track strategy, with separatism in the background as a bargaining chip. One committee has been created to consider the reform ideas of the rest of Canada.

This is reasonable, since a criticism of Meech was that it was unbalanced: major revisions were shaped by demands of a single province. The second committee is to consider the costs of separation—also conciliatory, for it puts separation as much on the defensive as federalism. The potential now exists for an agreement more thorough-going and more acceptable than Meech.

Quebec opposes a constituent assembly. The populist demand for an elected, one-shot constitutional assembly was born of a rejection of the last 25 years of compromises, and the seemingly endless constitutional wrangle. Quebec knows that the 1982 patriation, with entrenchments of French language rights, marked progress—but at the expense of a new disequilibrium.

Critics of the 1982 Charter, as well as strong supporters such as Prime Minister Pierre Trudeau, saw in it a centralist triumph. Provincial power, which got next to nothing, would have to compete with Canada-wide rights issues. Also, rights individualism in the Charter was feared by Quebec to be insensitive to the collective needs of the francophone majority. Threats to the French stronghold from the *force majeure* of the Charter would be aggravated by the collapse of Meech. On the other hand, critics of Meech interpreted it as one-sided decentralization and revenge for 1982.

The point is to return to a sense of balance: by resolving issues that were being whittled down to size, rather than launching off on tangents to write a new constitution. Language problems are nearing resolution: even a compromise on the sign law is in reach. The remaining issues—Senate reform, the division of powers—are first of all political disputes about province-building and state-building that constitution-writing in the abstract will not resolve.

Better political accommodation, with clarification of economic priorities after the trade deal with the U.S., should be ironed out first, before constitutional change, or an untried, less efficient system could be entrenched out of the political imbalance.

Strong centralizers and decentralists both subscribe to the humdrum view that organization demands centralization: either by Ottawa, or else at the provincial level (often at the expense of municipalities) under the rubric of decentralization. But Canada, unlike most countries, has modernized with significant development at subnational as well as federal levels.

If traditions are any indication, Canadians want *both* strong provincial government and strong central government. Renewed federalism boils down to finding a way to ensure strength at one level without creating debilitating weaknesses at the other. Quebec demonstrated this very Canadian demand in a series of historic votes.

After nearly a decade of Pierre Trudeau in Ottawa to strengthen the centre and the French-speaking presence, Quebeckers voted René Lévesque to power on a reform platform, with separatism in the background as a bargaining tool. In February of 1980 a new Trudeau majority swept 74 of 75 Quebec seats.

That May the PQ Referendum on sovereignty-association was defeated, but by a narrow margin to enhance the negotiating position. In 1981, Lévesque was re-elected. These conflicting votes were no "accident of the heart." Again and again Quebec summoned, face to face, its strongest advocate of central power and its most dynamic proponent of Quebec power to find a reconciliation.

On language issues each accomplished much. Full federal government service in the official language of one's choice, legislated by Trudeau in 1969, was entrenched in 1982. Lévesque passed Bill 101 in 1977 to keep the hearth of the language strong. Also in 1977, Lévesque set wheels in motion on the schools issue. English instruction would be offered only if the parents had received it in Quebec, but he proposed added bilateral agreements. Quebec would offer English instruction to children of parents educated in provinces offering instruction in French for families from Quebec.

In 1982, nine provinces with anglophone majorities joined Trudeau in creating minority language education rights in all provinces. When the courts struck down the restrictive education provisions of Bill 101, the country had delivered on Lévesque's own proposition. On the amending formula, Lévesque was even more federalist than Trudeau, endorsing equality of provinces when he accepted the "Gang of Eight's" formula.

While bilingualism has not yet succeeded, it has not failed. The courts have upheld Bill 101 sections with French as Quebec's language of work, and the language education rights of francophones outside Quebec and of anglophones within. There are now 230,000 anglophone children enrolled in French immersion. Quebec anglophones also enjoy a wide range of minority rights and services in English.

The remaining issue is the sign law. What is this law which constitutional conferences cannot talk about if they are to conclude, smiles and backslapping, with excessively fragile

Quebec must stop putting Canadian unity at risk with "semi-hemi-demi separatism."

agreements? The new law, Bill 178, is a modification of part of the old Bill 101. Using the notwithstanding clause it continues the practice, struck down by the courts, of French-only external signs but expands use of both official languages inside businesses.

Recent reports, especially testimony by demographers Marc Termote and Jacques Henripin before Belanger-Campeau, indicate French is now much stronger. Some conclude that the sign law should be abolished altogether, or never have been invoked. While improvements should be made, views that the law was unnecessary are short-sighted.

Constitutions are not made for conditions of the moment, to be changed with public policy. In the early 1970s, Henripin showed French Quebec was in danger of losing Montreal by the integration of immigrants into the anglophone stream. Were the sign law to be relaxed tomorrow, it remains inexcusable that Quebec would have had to override the Constitution, or separate, to preserve the French face of Montreal when it was under duress. While the law now could be made more lenient for small business, it should not be repealed.

If linguistic harmony is to be reached, the rest of Canada must accept the unique needs of Quebec. But Quebeckers must also change. They must climb off the fence from what Eugene Forsey has called "semi-hemi-demi-separatism." Quebec must stop putting Canadian unity at risk through the questionable federalism of "distinct society" and the impracticality of "sovereignty-association," and stop using the separatist threat as a tool of public policy objectives.

The status quo has already backfired. The constitutional vulnerability on language, in which Canada has left Quebec, has meant a retreat inwards. The "distinct society" was forced to override the Charter of Rights—a key symbol of citizenship for the rest of Canada which Quebec refuses to sign. Retreat inward creates vulnerability externally. Job losses in manufacturing to the U.S. are the most immediate example.

In recommending a Free Trade Agreement with the U.S., the 1985 Macdonald Commission warned that an FTA would only be feasible were it accompanied by concerted action in economic restructuring and productivity improvement. Canada got the trade deal without the needed federal-provincial cooperation, and major job losses (exacerbated by high interest rates and a high dollar). Today, the needed collaboration is displaced by abstract quarrels about distinct society and division of powers.

Before the FTA was signed, Jacques Parizeau warned that it would make separation more likely. It would become harder to keep Quebec in a position of linguistic vulnerability through economic threats of lost access to Canadian markets. But there was also a warning about the way Canada was proceeding. Continentalism poses a greater threat to national break-up if the smaller country, already at a disadvantage, has major unresolved constitutional divisions that frustrate cohesive action.

In 1965, Parizeau called for an "empirical balance" between federal and provincial powers before attempting constitutional change. This also rings true today. A country under the duress imposed by free trade and big deficits is no longer permitted the luxury of inefficiencies in governance. It ought to determine, empirically and without delay, which matters are best left to provinces and which to Ottawa.

Because of the national impact of major regional policies, often ignored, as well as regional fallout from national activities and the current general default, empirical balance takes on added meaning. More important than rewriting the division of powers may be the creation of an intergovernmental body, eventually a reformed second chamber, to better manage overlaps. Initially, no amendment is needed, but the best solution would look like Ottawa's proposed Federal Council.

The Ontario Premier's Council on Technology has identified four areas that cannot be well managed by Ontario alone, or by any province left to itself if it is to become fully competitive: science and technology; training; taxation; economic development spending. Until Quebec and the rest of Canada cross the language divide to make better use of the Canadian market as a springboard to the world market, continental and global free trade will keep the country in retreat.

If Canadians are serious about settling the language issue, and facing common problems from a shared regime of justiciable human rights, both languages must be treated fairly.

The Supreme Court ruling that struck down the old sign law and the prior Quebec Appeal Court ruling both found Bill 101 to violate the Quebec Charter and the Canadian Charter as well. Lévesque had not exempted his sign law from the Quebec Charter by using its override. He remained a voice for human rights but insisted on the embarrassing need, at least in the short term, for a sign law. The Constitution, however, has yet to reflect this sensibility.

The addition of official language affirmative action clauses to the Charter was suggested by Claude Ryan in November, 1981. That would remedy the feeling of vulnerability for francophone Quebec. Unlike laws that use an override they would be reviewable by the courts, ending the anglophone minority's sense of vulnerability.

Minority language affirmative action clauses could be added by amending Section 59 of the *Constitution Act, 1982*. The current Section is:

(1) Paragraph 23(1)(a) shall come into force in respect of Quebec on a day fixed by proclamation issued by the Queen or the Governor General under the Great Seal of Canada.

(2) A proclamation under subsection (1) shall be issued only where authorized by the legislative assembly or government of Quebec.

(3) This Section may be repealed on the day paragraph 23(1)(a) comes into force in respect of Quebec and this Act amended and renumbered . . . .

The articles of Section 23 to which Section 59 refers are:
(1) citizens of Canada
   (a) whose first language learned and still understood is that of the English or French linguistic minority population of the province in which they reside, or
   (b) who have received their primary school instruction in Canada in English or French and reside in a province where the language in which they received that instruction is the language of the English or French linguistic minority population of that prov-

A distinct society clause would poison the desired future economic association.

ince, have the right to have their children receive primary and secondary school instruction in that language in that province . . . where numbers warrant.

Section 59 is in danger of becoming permanently inoperative. There has been no proclamation and is not likely to be. Education rights limited exclusively to Section 23 1(a), by the terms of Section 59, would offer no flexibility were demographic conditions to change.

The proposed amendment would leave Sections 59(1) and 59(2) unchanged, and Section 59(3) would be repealed. A new 59(3) would allow reversion from 23(1)(a) back to 23(1)(b) if the integration of immigrants to the majority language stream becomes sharply reduced, notwithstanding a proclamation under 59(1) and 59(2).

A new 59(4) would state that "the constitutional equality of Canada's two official languages does not preclude any law, program or activity that has as its object the amelioration of either official language, where numbers warrant, when that official language is in decline." A new 59(5) would specify that laws enacted under 59(3) and 59(4) be subject to regular monitoring and review.

Section 59(4) mentions both official languages: affirmative action for one language must not endanger the other. Justifiable actions to maintain the French face of Montreal should not diminish the already hard-pressed English-speaking presence in the Eastern Townships. "When in decline," the courts would have to give this substance, as they have been doing with "where numbers warrant," but it would not preclude other types of official language programs that do not disadvantage the other language. Those that do must be within limits, and only when the other is in decline.

Ottawa and the provinces should complete the work of 1982, when only two affirmative action clauses were included: in Section 6, for local hiring where there is high unemployment; in Section 15, for women, aboriginals, visible minorities. Section 59(5) would be similar to the limits placed on local hiring under Section 6: equality must prevail when employment reaches the national average. Section 15 was left highly ambiguous, and might be re-examined later.

Affirmative action, thus limited and judicially reviewable,

is a better option than distinct society. Moreover, a distinct society clause (DSC) elicits opposing demands for an elected, equal Senate. The DSC would penalize Quebec anglophones, the Senate would retaliate against Quebec and Ontario. Each demand represents one of the agendas that played through Meech, and that are now out into the open as mature resentments. Neither proposal would be good for Canada, or for its most ardent supporters.

A DSC that made Quebec anglophones second class might be accepted reluctantly if it would keep the country together, but only if Quebec gained no extra legislative powers to make MPs from the rest of Canada second class. Entrenchment of second class status for English in one province would, with equality of provinces, mean abandonment of equal rights for francophones in nine provinces.

First the legislative enactments and broadcasting system would disappear, later the minority language education guarantees. DSC would poison the desired future economic association. And an elected, equal Senate, to enable outer Canada to punish Quebec and Ontario, would automatically be equal: as a third regional voice it would exclude all provincial governments equally.

The demand for an elected Senate looks backward to old resentments about tariffs and energy policies which the trade deal with the U.S. now prohibits. It would distract from where real power resides, and the continuing default of Canadian political will: overdue inter-provincial and federal-provincial cooperation in restructuring and job creation through the proposed Federal Council. There the sought after equality of provinces has already been proposed.

Provincialization of language, as both Allaire and the Reform Party demand, would lead to the dismantling of Canada; a strengthened Charter would mean equal rights. The proposed intergovernmental forum would help both levels of government to coordinate their actions in the most efficient, effective way.

National standards could be set for social programs, for example, with more provincial flexibility in implementation. The Federal Council is also the best site for overdue adjustment programs, and a public/private mix to restructure for continental and global trade, harnessing strengths of the regions and of both levels of government.

But Quebec also must be given more assurances. The Supreme Court Act with its guarantee of three civil code judges should be entrenched—a housekeeping amendment left from 1982, when the Court's composition was placed in Section 41 without constitutionalizing the Court.

Canada is working out a balance among French and English, Ottawa and the provinces, majority and minority rights. Greater balance would develop were anglophone provinces to recognize the minority status in North America of the Quebec francophone majority, and were Quebec to join the Canadian majority under the Charter by no longer exempting from effective judicial review an all-important language law.

DUELLING
IN THE DARK

Our exclusive survey reveals deep divisions and dangerous misunderstandings between the business solitudes of Quebec and Canada over the future of a foundering federation

CHARLES MACLI

86% of English-Canadian business leaders prefer anything but sovereignty-association. **72%** of Quebec business leaders would choose sovereignty-association; **63%** of English-Canadian business leaders believe Quebec *won't* opt for independence; **72%** of Quebec business leaders say sovereignty would *help* Quebec's long-term economy; **73%** of English-Canadian business leaders say sovereignty would hurt Quebec's long-term economy.

THESE ARE THE REMARKABLE HIGHLIGHTS of a *Report on Business Magazine* survey of business leaders to determine their views on the future of Quebec in–or outside of– Canada. The results reveal that the business communities of Quebec and English Canada already appear to be living in two different countries. They agree on almost nothing, and are most sharply divided on the desirability of sovereignty-association, the likelihood that it will occur, and the economic consequences for

Quebec and Canada. If there is common ground, it is a sense of shared doubt that the federal government can (or even should) manage a reconciliation.

Our survey was conducted as a joint venture with *Magazine Affaires Plus* of Montreal and carried out by the polling firm Léger et Léger. We sought the views of 6,000 business leaders, 3,000 in Quebec and 3,000 in the rest of Canada, on the chances for renewed federalism, the likelihood of Quebec sovereignty, and the eco-

nomic consequences of Quebec's going it alone: 1,711 of them responded to our questionnaire, and hundreds added detailed and thoughtful comments. The divisions between French and English are marked and, for those who dream of a renewed federalism, distressing. English Canada and Quebec are at the moment speaking two different constitutional languages. Even so, the responses may offer important clues for ways around the impasse in the Quebec-Canada dialogue.

Reprinted from *Report on Business Magazine*, April 1991, pp. 29-31, 33, 35, 38.

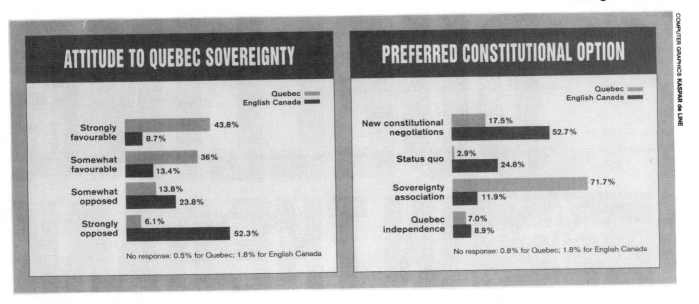

ATTITUDE TO QUEBEC SOVEREIGNTY

Quebec
English Canada

Strongly favourable	43.8% / 8.7%
Somewhat favourable	36% / 13.4%
Somewhat opposed	13.8% / 23.8%
Strongly opposed	6.1% / 52.3%

No response: 0.5% for Quebec; 1.8% for English Canada

PREFERRED CONSTITUTIONAL OPTION

Quebec
English Canada

New constitutional negotiations	17.5% / 52.7%
Status quo	2.9% / 24.8%
Sovereignty association	71.7% / 11.9%
Quebec independence	7.0% / 8.9%

No response: 0.8% for Quebec; 1.8% for English Canada

COMPUTER GRAPHICS **KASPAR de LINE**

REQUIEM FOR RENEWED FEDERALISM
One key question in our survey was:
Which constitutional option do you prefer?

Of Quebec respondents, 71.7% prefer sovereignty-association for Quebec. Only 17.5% want to open new constitutional negotiations. But even fewer–7%–want full Quebec independence, without economic ties. English-Canadian respondents

"If Quebec is determined to be a second Louisiana, then let's get on with it."

A RESPONDENT FROM ONTARIO

are hostile by a margin of three to one to the notion of sovereignty. They opted overwhelmingly for new constitutional negotiations (52.7%) or the status quo (24.8%). In fact, there was more preference expressed for the status quo than for both sovereignty-association and full independence combined (11.9% and 8.9%).

Support for federalism has been eroding steadily among Quebec business people. In February, 1990, a CROP-*Revue Commerce* poll showed only 57% of Quebec business respondents in favour of sovereignty-association. In our poll, even big business leaders, whose firms' revenues exceed $200 million, now give strong support to sovereignty (70%).

In addition to asking our respondents what they *want* to happen, we asked them what they *thought* would happen. Three out of four Quebec respondents believe their province *will* become a sovereign state (75.9%) and will do quite well economically in the long run (72.1%). Once

again the English-Canadian response is almost a reverse image; nearly two out of three (63.4%) don't believe Quebec will end up by leaving Canada. If Quebec does leave, English-Canadian business leaders see short-term pain for both parties and nearly three-quarters (72.8%) see long-term economic problems for Quebec.

THE POWER-SHIFT RIFT Our Quebec respondents confirm that the Quebec Liberals' recent Allaire Report (which appeared in January, after our survey was done) speaks for them on at least one important point: It endorses a major transfer of federal powers to the province, and so do they. Asked if Ottawa should agree to transferring powers in nine major areas, Quebec business said "yes" to eight of them. Affirmative responses ranged from a high of 92.6% for regional development down to 72.4% for the environment. They felt Ottawa could keep international relations.

The opposite case held in the rest of Canada, even though respondents were given a third choice of transferring federal powers to all provinces. Only 30.1% believed that Quebec should have exclusive jurisdiction over its own culture and communications, although another 42.5% would agree to transfer these powers if other provinces got the same. A similar pattern, narrowly supporting power transfers to *all* provinces, held for health and welfare, employment and regional development. A clear majority of respondents opposed any transfer of federal powers in the following areas: international relations (81.5% said no), immigration (63.6%), taxation (63.1%), energy (54.6%) and the environment (53.9%). The re-

sponses are a clear rejection by English respondents of any form of special status for Quebec.

These and other recent polling results suggest that there is no vestige of enthusiasm anywhere for more last-chance negotiations with the attendant panoply of pressure tactics, political posturing and phony deadlines. English Canada seems to be insisting: "We'll talk but we aren't giving anything away." Quebec's response: "Then why bother?" A Jan. 24 Gallup poll also seemed to confirm the futility of discussions centred on an expanded Quebec agenda. In that survey, 62% of Canadians opposed meeting Quebec's demands, even if to do so would result in Quebec independence.

ON THE DOCK OR ON THE BOAT In English Canada, Quebec sovereignty is both unpopular and judged unlikely to occur. In Quebec, a majority of respondents favour sovereignty and think it will happen.

"No other country would put up with individual provincial agendas as we do. We are fed up with the continuing saga of what Quebec wants."

BRITISH COLUMBIA

Nonetheless, pollster Marcel Léger, who was once a PQ cabinet minister, finds room for optimism in results showing English Canada's accepting independence if it occurred. Our survey asked, "If the majority of Quebec citizens vote yes in a referendum on sovereignty, should Cana-

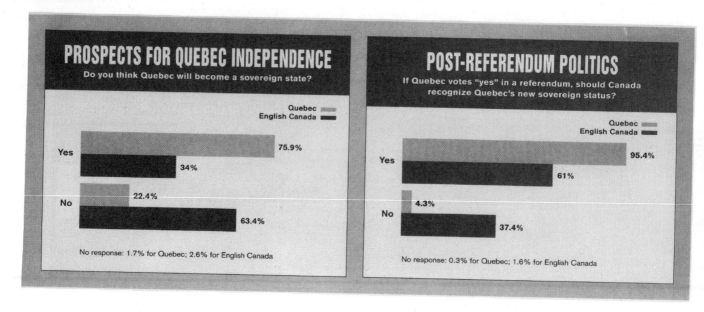

PROSPECTS FOR QUEBEC INDEPENDENCE
Do you think Quebec will become a sovereign state?

Quebec
English Canada

Yes
75.9%
34%

No
22.4%
63.4%

No response: 1.7% for Quebec; 2.6% for English Canada

POST-REFERENDUM POLITICS
If Quebec votes "yes" in a referendum, should Canada recognize Quebec's new sovereign status?

Quebec
English Canada

Yes
95.4%
61%

No
4.3%
37.4%

No response: 0.3% for Quebec; 1.6% for English Canada

da recognize Quebec's new political status?" We also asked, "Following a yes vote on sovereignty, should Canada and Quebec negotiate economic association?" Most English-Canadian business leaders say yes to both questions; 61% are for recognition and slightly fewer, 55.4%, are for negotiating economic association. They are specifically in favour of a free trade deal. "I think this shows the future is very positive," says Léger. "It will give both sides a chance to direct their own destinies, and come together and make agreements on the things we have in common."

Perhaps. But first English Canadians and Québécois will have to get closer on what their new relationship will be. Asked what items should be covered by sovereignty-association, French and English respondents agreed only that they want a free trade pact (Quebec: 84.5%; the rest of Canada: 78.7%) and don't want the supranational parliament proposed by

"I favour the Swiss model. The cantons are responsible for almost everything except monetary policy, defence and international relations."

ONTARIO

Quebec Premier Robert Bourassa. Quebec respondents desire a common currency, shared defence and a common central bank. English-Canadian business leaders oppose a deal on these items.

The gap between each party's assumptions about sovereignty may narrow in time. After all, Québécois have had more

than 20 years to refine the concept of sovereignty-association. English Canadians have had barely nine months to consider their post-Meech options. But the current attitudes, reflected by this survey, suggest that there is still a long distance to cover before the two sides meet. Québécois view "sovereignty" as independence with a safety net. For English Canada, the only alternative to federalism is independence. Period. Writes one Alberta businessman: "French Canada is either on the dock or on the boat." Without a shift in English Canada's view of sovereignty, Québécois may find that the dock has far fewer planks than they expect.

WHAT PRICE SOVEREIGNTY? If each side hews to a very different idea of the terms of Quebec sovereignty, both also have diametrically opposed views on the economic consequences. Business leaders in both Quebec and the rest of Canada foresee short-term negative consequences all around. But as time goes on, each thinks that the impact will be far more harmful to their ex-partner in Confederation.

English Canadians don't see sovereignty helping either country's economy. More than a third (39.3%) say sovereignty would have a negative effect on Canada's long-term economic health; roughly one in four (27.1%) predict no change. The prognosis for Quebec is much worse, however. Nearly three-quarters of English respondents (72.8%) say Quebec's economy would suffer in the long run, affecting virtually every area from unemployment (83.9% say it would increase) to Quebec's ability to handle its debt (90.2% say it would worsen).

Unlike their English confrères, Quebec respondents are buoyant about their own long-term prospects: 72.1% predicted that sovereignty would have a positive impact on Quebec's economy. Only 22.9% saw favourable long-term consequences for Canada's economy. Comments from Quebec reflect the hard-won confidence in Quebec's own economy. "With recent

"Not to divorce would mean devoting even more energy to fighting political battles rather than improving the economy."

QUEBEC

improvements in Quebec's business milieu," writes one, "sovereignty is no longer a question of nationalism but of logic." Many of the comments ring with disdain for Ottawa's fumbling of the economy. "The federal government has proven its budgetary incompetence," writes one. "It couldn't get much worse in a sovereign Quebec – only better." In 1991, in sharp contrast to the past, the economic arguments appear to be on the sovereignist side of the ledger.

Some of our survey results, not surprisingly, raise as many questions as they seem to answer. Just what assumptions lie behind our respondents' economic predictions? If the prognosis for Canada's economy is so negative, why would Quebec want an economic association that ties it to our currency and our central bank? And why, if economic association is so helpful to Quebec, won't it also help Canada?

For English Canada, do the negative

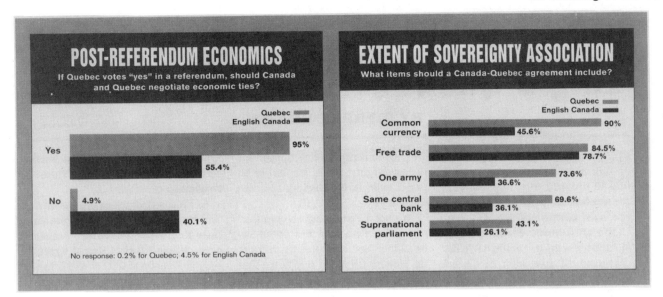

POST-REFERENDUM ECONOMICS
If Quebec votes "yes" in a referendum, should Canada and Quebec negotiate economic ties?

Quebec ■
English Canada ■

Yes — Quebec 95%
Yes — English Canada 55.4%

No — Quebec 4.9%
No — English Canada 40.1%

No response: 0.2% for Quebec; 4.5% for English Canada

EXTENT OF SOVEREIGNTY ASSOCIATION
What items should a Canada-Quebec agreement include?

Quebec ■
English Canada ■

Item	Quebec	English Canada
Common currency	90%	45.6%
Free trade	84.5%	78.7%
One army	73.6%	36.6%
Same central bank	69.6%	36.1%
Supranational parliament	43.1%	26.1%

predictions for Quebec's economy assume there will be no economic association beyond a free trade deal between Quebec and Canada, and a new state beset by the problems of having to back its own currency and establishing its international credit? To what extent do these contradictory economic predictions take into account, or ignore, Canada and Quebec's different views of economic association?

And to what extent do they reflect a more pessimistic view in English Canada of Quebec-Canada trade after sovereignty? In our poll, 47.6% of English respondents, who currently have business relations with Quebec, thought the volume of that business would decrease to some degree after sovereignty. Only 30.4% of Quebec business people, who had business ties with English Canada, foresaw either a slight or a significant decrease.

THE UNCERTAINTY FACTOR On Jan. 29, Quebec's Liberal Party published the Allaire report which called for a massive transfer of federal powers to Quebec. Among other things, the report opens the way to 18 more months of constitutional haggling. One can imagine groans rising from both the English and French business communities. About the only real point of convergence in this poll was agreement that Ottawa give precedence to economic problems over constitutional ones. The figures were nearly identical: 79.7% of English respondents and 76.5% of Quebec respondents said the economy, not constitutional reform, should be the first priority of the federal government. These numbers may just reflect exhaustion after so much

constitutional bickering. One western writer sums up the frustration of many anglophones: "If Quebec does separate it has my blessing on one condition—it takes Ottawa with it." Or they may be business's way of telling government to stop using the constitutional issue to deflect attention from a deteriorating economic situation. ("With an annual deficit of $30 billion, we cannot afford the luxury/stupidity of constitutional talks," remarked a respondent

from British Columbia.) A common thread running through the comments was a sense of exasperation—not so much with the other side in the dispute as with politicians, past and present. Marcel Léger observes that Québécois are especially worried about the current state of uncertainty— uncertainty largely attributable to political posturing. For Léger, "the future of Quebec is too important to be left only to the politicians."

WILL QUEBEC SOVEREIGNTY HAVE A POSITIVE OR NEGATIVE IMPACT ON THE ECONOMY, OR NO EFFECT?

QUEBEC	POSITIVE %	NEGATIVE %	NONE %	N/R %*
EFFECTS IN QUEBEC				
Long-term economy	72.1	15.3	11.0	1.6
Short-term economy	13.7	68.7	16.1	1.5
Unemployment	45.5	31.8	20.2	2.5
Standard of living	33.9	34.6	29.4	2.2
Trade	51.6	25.0	21.0	2.4
Fiscal position/debt	58.1	27.7	12.1	2.1
EFFECTS IN CANADA				
Long-term economy	22.9	46.2	28.0	2.8
Short-term economy	6.3	73.5	18.2	2.0
Unemployment	9.9	30.3	56.4	3.4
Standard of living	9.5	41.1	46.4	2.9
Trade	15.3	34.6	49.0	3.1
Fiscal position/debt	10.8	55.0	31.3	2.8

ENGLISH CANADA	POSITIVE %	NEGATIVE %	NONE %	N/R %*
EFFECTS IN QUEBEC				
Long-term economy	10.5	72.8	15.5	1.3
Short-term economy	4.2	88.1	6.4	1.3
Unemployment	5.0	83.9	9.3	1.8
Standard of living	2.4	86.2	9.7	1.8
Trade	9.3	71.7	15.5	3.5
Fiscal position/debt	3.4	90.2	3.5	2.9
EFFECTS IN CANADA				
Long-term economy	31.4	39.3	27.1	2.3
Short-term economy	8.1	78.3	11.8	1.9
Unemployment	26.4	31.1	40.6	1.9
Standard of living	22.7	32.4	43.0	1.9
Trade	13.8	51.7	30.6	3.9
Fiscal position/debt	40.4	38.5	18.2	2.9

* N/R = No Response

CANADA-QUEBEC BUSINESS TIES

Does your firm currently have clients, suppliers or operations in Quebec? (Quebec respondents: "In Canada?")

English Canada in Quebec
Yes 62.3%
No 35.7%

Quebec in English Canada
Yes 51.7%
No 47.8%

No response: 0.5% for Quebec; 1.9% for English Canada

TRADE WITH A SOVEREIGN QUEBEC

How would sovereignty affect the amount of business you do with Quebec? (Quebec respondents: "With Canada?")

Quebec
English Canada

Greatly increase — 1.9% / 0.5%
Slightly increase — 6.2% / 2.8%
No effect — 56.8% / 44.6%
Slightly decrease — 20.7% / 30.8%
Greatly decrease — 9.7% / 16.8%

No response: 4.7% for Quebec; 4.5% for English Canada

A VIEW FROM THE BRINK To comment on the significance of the *Report on Business Magazine* poll, we sought the opinions of four Canadian academics: George Perlin, professor of political studies at Queen's University; Charles Taylor, political science professor at McGill University; Michael Bliss, professor of history at the University of Toronto; and David Bercuson, history professor at the University of Calgary.

For Perlin, the most significant survey finding is the divergence in viewpoints of French and English business elites. "It's a measure of how serious the problem is, if the elites are divided in this way," says Perlin, who recalls that during the 1980 Quebec referendum contest both business

> **"I believe Quebeckers will handle their own economy and cultural development better when they don't have to contend with federal interference."**
>
> **ALBERTA**

communities were basically on the same federalist side.

The defiant tone of some of the comments also concerns Perlin. "It's not the dispassionate response you'd expect from business. There's something raw in them, reflecting popular emotions. That too underscores the seriousness of the problem."

Says David Bercuson, "It sounds as if one party is on Mars and the other is on Venus. If they *were*, at least these results would be logical. What we have instead are two different groups looking

at exactly the same circumstances and data, and coming up with totally different conclusions." Bercuson says Quebec business people are operating on the assumption that they've already obtained what they want. "They start with the premise that 'independence is a fine thing' and then work their way back to explain away the difficulties."

This explains the apparent gulf in

> **"How can a legitimate referendum be held on independence, if the financial impact is not defined?"**
>
> **NOVA SCOTIA**

responses to the outlines of a post-sovereignty agreement. "Someone should tell Quebec that we'll be discussing a free trade agreement as two sovereign nations," Bercuson says, "and that the Canada-U.S. deal is not transferable to them. They may be in for a rude shock when they sit down to negotiate with the States." Other parts of the Quebec wishlist come in for criticism. Example: the desire for a common currency and central bank. "Why would Canada with a gross domestic product four times as large as Quebec's, give it an equal say in monetary matters?" asks Bercuson. "We should be talking about these things now, but the politicians won't do it. And anyone else who does is going to be accused of economic terrorism."

Charles Taylor also focuses on that wide gulf in how the two sides define sovereignty, calling it the "joker in the

deck." In Quebec, says Taylor, sovereignty is an acceptable word for having autonomy, for flexing one's muscles. It doesn't necessarily mean that people who call for "sovereignty" actually want a sovereign state. He also worries that English Canada is still not taking Quebec seriously, and that this ratchets up the rhetoric. "Québécois are desperate to be believed. But how do you prove you're serious? By doing things that get people angry." Hence the "gun to the

> **"The majority of citizens are not ready to accept the sacrifices that separation will require."**
>
> **QUEBEC**

head" imagery, and radical constitutional demands.

At the same time, Taylor worries that the current nationalist euphoria has tended to put real dangers in the shade. And in the end, what Quebec sees as a way to obtain recognition and respect may backfire. Confesses Taylor, "I'm afraid of the reaction that says to Quebec, 'Just go away.'" He adds, "A real possibility for negotiation may be lost in this zone of misunderstanding."

Michael Bliss has some criticisms of the structure of the survey. "It's a badly drawn up poll," he comments. "People should have been asked a follow-up to the economy versus the Constitution question, namely, if they agreed that the constitutional issue be put on the back burner while we take care of our economic problems. It doesn't elicit a sense of how urgent business feels the problem is. What the survey does show is that business is as divided as the rest of the country."

Bliss is also concerned about Quebec business leaders' easy assumptions regarding sovereignty-association. And he's bothered by the failure to define "sovereignty" in the survey. "Polls have shown that Quebec support for out-and-out independence is much smaller. And this poll doesn't test for different degrees of sovereignty.... How many support it if they have to turn in their Canadian passports, for example?" Although Bliss concludes 55.4% of English business support for economic association does reflect a residual good will towards Quebec, he warns that separation would dissipate such feelings. "I doubt that a free trade proposal could stand up to the bitterness created by Quebec's departure. I think the divorce

metaphor is wrong. . . . Separation would be an amputation without anesthetic."

One thing is clear: The issue *is* too important to be left only to the politicians. What we haven't had in this country is direct Quebec-to-Canada talks without the mediation of partisan messengers. If the poll shows one thing it's that potentially **fatal misconceptions continue to go unchallenged. Perhaps it's time for English Canada and Quebec to confront the clear disagreements over the shape of**

"Top business people should speak out. The vast majority of English Canadians want a united Canada with full participation by Quebec."

ONTARIO

Quebec independence and both parties' "post-sovereign" economic prospects. A

business-to-business dialogue might also achieve what politically directed discourse has failed to do: to expose and defuse some of the potent symbolic imagery surrounding the debate. Quebec may not realize that the rest of Canada has already felt the gun barrel to its temple during the Meech Lake hysteria. Or that English Canada's skepticism about Quebec independence serves as a warning growl rather than a sigh of self-satisfaction. The rest of Canada might try harder to understand the depth of Quebec's exasperation, and recognize to what extent emasculating Ottawa will or won't attenuate the Québécois sense of grievance and rejection.

"There's no politician who has as yet come forward to take the lead," says Charles Taylor. "People linked by common interests ought to get together. It would dispel some of the misunderstandings that create a lack of desire to negotiate. And we need a national negotiation."

Hard Times and Quebec

Sandro Contenta

Toronto Star

MONTREAL—After 31 years of labor at the same plant, Marcel Leboeuf will be out of a job in six months.

By then, the Dominion Textile factory in Valleyfield, Que., will be shut down, throwing Leboeuf and 224 other workers out on the unemployment lines.

"It feels like I lost my future," said Leboeuf, a 50-year-old quality control inspector at the plant west of Montreal.

Leboeuf and his co-workers are victims of a Quebec economy described by Industry Minister Gerald Tremblay as being in a "state of emergency."

Newspaper headlines tell the story: "In Montreal, one of every two adults is without work," La Presse reported recently.

"I think politicians don't care about workers at all. All they know how to do is talk about the Constitution," said Leboeuf, who wonders how he'll meet the mortgage payments on his home.

The backdrop to Quebec's heated constitutional debate is a recession that has scarred the province with a 12 per cent unemployment rate and left some 635,000 people on welfare.

Predictably, federalist and sovereignist forces in Quebec have made the province's economic misery a central theme in the early stages of the referendum campaign.

Last month, Premier Robert Bourassa stressed in two major speeches that breaking up the country would be costly. Worried foreign lenders, Bourassa said, could unload Canadian bonds and send the dollar tumbling to 75 cents.

Parti Quebecois Leader Jacques Parizeau scoffs at what he terms federalist scaremongering. He blames Quebec's economic woes on federalism and continues to talk of a clean and painless break.

Even federalist observers concede that the doomsday scenarios used to frighten many Quebecers during the 1980 referendum on sovereignty-association, won't be as effective this time around.

Still, it's no mystery why Quebecers are far more concerned about the economic than the Constitution—gloomy statistics and forecasts are as easy to find as boarded up stores or Montreal panhandlers:

■ In January alone—while Ontario gained 3,000 jobs—4,000 Quebec workers joined the unemployment lines.

■ The labor ministry's own economists say the Montreal region, which pumps out half of what Quebec produces, will experience a state of "quasi stagnation" in employment levels. The rate of job creation won't increase until 1995.

■ Private investment in 1991 is estimated at $27.5 billion, $1.2 billion less than the year before.

■ More than 400,000 people are out of work, some 180,000 of them in the Montreal region.

■ By the end of 1991, 635,000 Quebecers were on welfare—a 12 per cent increase from the previous year. Of these, more than 330,000 were adults considered employable.

In Ontario, 1,131,300 were on short and long term welfare in January, a 33 per cent increase from last year. (Ontario's estimated population in 1991 was 9.7 million, compared with Quebec's 6.8 million.)

■ In February, 20 per cent of Quebecers aged 15 to 24 were without jobs. In Ontario, 18.7 per cent of young people were unemployed that month.

The Conseil du Patronat, which represents firms that employ 70 per cent of Quebec workers, estimates that 80,000 jobs are going begging because of a lack of skilled workers.

■ The forestry industry—Quebec's largest, accounting for 22 per cent of the province's exports—laid off 10 per cent of its 65,000 workers last year.

■ One in five people lives below the poverty line in Montreal and almost 40 per cent of Quebec high school students drop out.

Quebec business leaders complain of poor productivity, high interest rates, a high dollar and the recession in general. In this sense, their woes are no different from those of Ontario.

Indeed, when Dominion Textile announced the closing of its plant near Montreal, it also announced the closure of its weaving plant in Long Sault, Ont.

Quebec analysts are quick to note that the recession hit Toronto much harder than Montreal.

Statistics Canada reports that while the Montreal area lost 34,000 jobs last year, Metro Toronto was clobbered with a loss of 17,000 jobs. Metro's loss, however, came after almost a decade of economic growth—a sharp contrast to Montreal's slow decline during the same period.

Added to Quebec's economic woes is a political uncertainty that has been blamed for a flight of labor and capital.

The Montreal-based Canadian Bond Rating Service, the largest credit-rating service in the country, holds regular information meetings for Japanese, German and Swiss investors concerned about Canada's political stability.

"When it's time to renew or buy Quebec bonds, some ask for higher interest rates, some decide not to participate in the bond issue and some, when their bonds mature, take their cash and do not reinvest it in Quebec," said Thor Kots, managing director of the rating service.

Citing Quebec's uncertain future, the rating service put Quebec on a credit watch last year.

Kots adds, however, that Ontario is no more attractive than Quebec to investors because of its high deficit and its poor economic performance during the recession.

A growing amount of investment money, Kots said, is making its way to Alberta, British Columbia or leaving the country completely.

Some 200,000 anglophones have left Quebec since 1976—an exodus largely responsible for Montreal's economic decline, says a Quebec government report released last December.

The report, written by eight cabinet ministers, said Montreal's loss was Toronto's gain.

In 1953 the Montreal region had 20 per cent more head offices of financial institutions than Toronto. By 1988, Montreal had 80 per cent fewer financial head offices than Toronto.

The departure of anglophones diminished Montreal's attraction to foreign investors and turned the city into a far more parochial centre, said the report, which coincided with a $415 million government plan to invigorate the city's economy.

Francophone businesses were unable to keep the foreign markets held by the anglophones who left, the report said.

The anglophone exodus occurred at a time when the traditional sectors that had made Montreal the economic hub of Canada—transportation and manufacturing—were dying a slow death.

In short, as Montreal struggled to transform its economy into an information-based, service sector one, it also had to replace its business elite.

"When your economy is in transition, it's certainly not the time to have a changing of the guard," said Marcel Cote, founder of the influential SECOR consulting firm and a former adviser to Premier Robert Bourassa and Prime Minister Brian Mulroney.

Despite the concerns many anglophones still have over the province's future, Cote believes it's only a matter of time before language tensions subside and Montreal is transformed

into a vibrant cultural centre where Canada's anglophone and francophone communities meet.

Economist Pierre Fortin is even more optimistic.

"By the year 2000, Quebec will experience an economic boom. It's almost inevitable," says Fortin, who wrote a study on the viability of Quebec independence for the Belanger-Campeau commission on the province's future.

With half of Canada's fastest growing companies based in Quebec, Fortin believes the province is well positioned to come out of the recession.

Quebec's economy should also get a big boost from the industrial strategy recently announced by Industry Minister Tremblay, Fortin says. The plan is to create industrial "clusters"—companies in the same sector working together to become more efficient and competitive.

As Quebec's economy improves, Fortin says, the economic costs of getting out of Canada will also diminish.

Over the next decade, Quebec will likely stop getting equalization payments and the Canadian trade barriers that now protect Quebec's dairy and textile industry will likely be eliminated by GATT, the international treaty on trade.

In short, Fortin believes Canadians had better strike a lasting constitutional deal this time around or they'll face an economically confident Quebec in future negotiations.

'Quebec Inc.' cushions recession's blow

Sandro Contenta

Toronto Star

MONTREAL—Richard Robitaille says he owes his job to "Quebec Inc."—an economic model that resembles the all-in-the-family approach

of Japan rather than the dog-eat-dog credo of North American business.

With their company on the verge of bankruptcy, Robitaille and 124 other workers at the Bourguinon printing factory faced the gloomy prospect of unemployment at the height of the recession last year.

Their jobs were saved when the Fonds de solidarite, a union investment fund unique in Canada, helped a rival printing company buy out the struggling Bourguinon plant with a $1.5 million investment.

The relieved workers then accepted a one-year wage freeze to help the new owners, Groupe Wilco, get their expanded operation off the ground.

"With the hard times we have today, the bosses and the workers have to walk hand in hand. If we keep fighting each other, everyone's going to lose," said Robitaille, the 30-year-old father of a young child and a seven-year employee at the plant.

"The deal saved jobs and it allowed us to grow. . . . It's the kind of co-operation between unions and employers that could make Quebec the Japan of North America," said Serge Roger, co-owner of Groupe Wilco.

For about a decade, business leaders in Canada watched with great interest as Quebec pieced together an economic formula that many have dubbed "Quebec Inc."—a synthesis of labor, government and business working together.

It also combines an old-boys' network with unique development tools, like the Fonds de solidarite, to create a solid economic base for the province.

With 12 per cent unemployment and some 635,000 people on welfare, it's clear that Quebec's economy is in pain.

But even federalists reject talk that Quebec's homemade economic engine—which helped fuel the sovereignist movement—is sputtering out.

Analysts both within and outside the province believe "Quebec Inc." not only helped cushion the blow of e current recession, but serves as a blueprint for doing business in an increasingly competitive, global economy.

"Business, labor and government seem to be working together in Quebec, developing a common strategy to advance the provincial economy," said Michael Porter, the Harvard economist who recently wrote an analysis of the Canadian economy for the federal government.

"Frankly, Quebec Inc. is a model the rest of Canada would do well to follow," Porter recently told a business group in Montreal.

Behind this co-operative model is an old-boys' network that tran-

scends political ideologies and blurs the line between government and business.

Two recent examples stand out: A farewell bash for Louis Laberge, the retiring leader of the Quebec Federation of Labour, and the operation to salvage 4,000 jobs threatened by the demise of engineering giant Lavalin Inc.

Laberge's party last October was a who's who of "Quebec Inc." that saw sovereignist labor leaders break bread with federalist bosses.

Premier Robert Bourassa and Prime Minister Brian Mulroney were on hand to praise Laberge, although both were singing a different tune in the 1970s.

Bourassa threw Laberge in jail for four months in 1972 when he urged striking public service employees to defy a back-to-work order. And Mulroney rose to prominence in the 1970s as a member of the Cliche provincial inquiry, which alleged Laberge tolerated corruption in construction unions.

"One of them put me in jail, and the other one tried to," Laberge said that night.

But they were all smiles, handshakes and good cheer for the party.

Mulroney recalled his days as a labor lawyer when he and Laberge would celebrate agreement on each clause of a contract with a shot of cognac. It's the kind of old-boys' camaraderie that helps let bygones be bygones.

This camaraderie was put to work last summer when Quebecers were jolted by the Lavalin collapse. Lavalin was Canada's largest engineering firm and one of the crown jewels of Quebec's homegrown economy.

The company, with sales of $415 million, had got into trouble by diversifying into areas that had nothing to do with engineering. With less than two weeks to meet its payroll, negotiations began on a complicated deal to merge Lavalin with its engineering rival, the smaller SNC Groupe Inc.

The head of Lavalin was Bernard Lamarre, a tough executive with ex-

tensive government contacts. On his payroll were former PQ cabinet ministers Clement Richard and Yves Berube.

The head of SNC is Guy Saint-Pierre, a former minister of industry with the Liberal governments of the 1970s. When Saint-Pierre lost his seat in the 1976 election, Lamarre, his old classmate, offered him a job, which he declined.

Representing the government was industry minister and former management consultant Gerald Tremblay. The middlemen in the deal were Serge Saucier, head of the largest accounting firm in Quebec, and Marcel Cote, founder of the influential SECOR consulting firm and former adviser to both Bourassa and Mulroney.

SNC bought the assets and contracts of Lavalin Inc. in a $90 million deal that included loans from eight banks, Ottawa and Quebec.

Cote says it's unlikely such a complicated deal could be struck so quickly in provinces where government and business aren't as closely linked as in Quebec.

"We all knew each other on a first name basis; it was very much Quebec Inc. in action," Cote said in an interview.

The merged company is run by Guy Saint-Pierre, a key player in the group of top Quebec corporations working to keep the country united. The company's vice president is former PQ minister and sovereignist, Yves Berube.

Sovereignists and federalists strongly disagree on the viability of an independent Quebec. But no one doubts that the coalition of strange bedfellows that makes up "Quebec Inc." will continue even if Quebec separates.

The family ties of "Quebec Inc." go way back.

"The workers and the owners are almost relatives. The Tremblays come from the same original Tremblay family and the Blanchets in Quebec come from the Blanchet that arrived in 1636," said Claude Blanchet, head of the Fonds de solidarite.

But much of "Quebec Inc." has a more recent history.

Massive educational and economic reforms in the early 1960s produced a close-knit group of francophone professionals and entrepreneurs eager to take on the task of becoming *maitres chez nous* (masters in our own house).

Business, labor and government join forces

"From the moment we entered university, the message was 'You have a country to build,'" said Pierre Parent, a self-described child of the Quiet Revolution and head of the Groupe Promexpo Inc. which organizes major exhibits.

It's the kind of nationalist talk that makes federalists uneasy.

"We have never used the word "Quebec Inc." and we will never use it," says Ghislain Dufour, head of the Conseil du Patronat, which represents firms employing 70 per cent of Quebec's workers.

Dufour says the term is either used by "ultra-nationalists" to exaggerate Quebec's economic gains or by anglophones trying to denigrate them.

Instead, Dufour talks about Quebec's "unique economic tools"—a mix of homegrown financial institutions and crown corporations used to develop a local economy.

Chief among those is the Caisse de depot et placement, set up in 1966 and now the largest stockmarket player in Canada with assets of $41 billion. Its promotion of homegrown companies has created some of Quebec's economic stars, such as Pierre Peladeau of Quebecor and Bertin Nadeau of Provigo Inc.

Ontario's NDP government is thinking of setting up a smaller version of the Caisse, to be called the Ontario Investment Fund.

Accounting professor Leo-Paul Lauzon charges that the Caisse has propped up francophone business people with little experience in running a company.

"Quebec Inc. is a myth, it's a wet firecracker," says Lauzon, a professor at the University of Quebec in Montreal.

The Societe de Developpement Industriel du Quebec, a government investment agency that acts as a lender of last resort, was recently criticized by the province's auditor-general for investing millions of taxpayers' dollars in companies it knows little about and fails to follow up on.

In his report last December, provincial auditor-general Guy Breton said the investment agency lost $16.7 million for the year ending March 31, 1991.

A more recent tool of economic development is the Quebec Federation of Labour's Fonds de solidarite, created by an act of the National Assembly in 1983. (The Ontario government has introduced legislation to set up a more modest version of the Fonds.)

The Fonds has net assets of $425 million and its investments have created or saved 20,000 jobs in small- and medium-sized companies, its last annual report said.

The Fonds' investment money comes from 115,000 stockholders who receive a 40 per cent tax credit for their investment. A company must have more than 50 per cent of its jobs in Quebec to receive the Fonds' support.

Once involved in a company, the Fonds holds regular seminars with workers to explain the financial state of the company—a strategy that often leads to better labor relations and higher productivity, Blanchet said.

"Workers aren't stupid. When they see that their jobs are vulnerable they inevitably say, 'Hey, we've got a problem. Let's roll up our sleeves and work together.'"

It's an attitude that has helped build the co-operative aspects of

"Quebec Inc." praised by Michael Porter and others.

The latest example is Industry Minister Gerald Tremblay's plan to create industrial "clusters"—companies in the same sector working together to become more efficient and competitive.

Tremblay has so far identified 13 clusters across the province including the aerospace, pharmaceutical and forestry sectors.

Labor and business leaders—involved in the design and implementation of the plan—were on hand to enthusiastically support Tremblay when he unveiled the scheme last December.

"Once again, these invited guests left the impression that confrontations between employers and employees no longer exist in Quebec," the daily newspaper Le Devoir commented at the time.

Of course, that isn't quite the case. The city of Montreal's striking blue-collar workers, for instance, were accused of vandalizing municipal offices and setting off homemade bombs in front of the homes of management personnel in January.

These kinds of excesses, however, are largely a thing of the past.

Labor relations are generally going so smoothly that the Conseil du Patronat, recently dropped its court battle against Quebec's 14-year-old "anti-scab" law, which bans the hiring of replacement workers during strikes.

"After the big strikes of the 1970s, we realized that confrontation did not bring results," said Pierre Paquette, an economist and general secretary of the Confederation of National Trade Unions, which represents 224,000 workers in a wide range of jobs.

Two recessions in a decade have made both sides realize that co-operation is a better route than strikes to job protection and profits, Paquette said. There are still strains, however. He notes that attempts to give workers more say in how companies are run have so far met with limited success.

Aboriginal Issues

As it has on many occasions in Canadian history, the question of aboriginal rights has surfaced as a highly visible issue in Canadian politics in recent years. Since the Meech Lake agreement, when aboriginal issues were specifically put on the agenda of social problems needing to be resolved, aboriginal leaders have continued to press their agenda on Canadian political leaders and the Canadian media. This section includes five articles covering several different important dimensions of aboriginal issues.

In an article focusing upon the question of culture, Jerry Diakiw shows that a number of "European" cultural patterns can actually be traced to Canada's native societies. He shows that Iroquois' ideas influenced a number of Western philosophers and political leaders, from Karl Marx and Friedrich Engels to Lester Pearson. This article suggests that while we may know that the Canadian "tapestry" is composed of a wide range of different "threads," we do not always appreciate that Canada's European heritage may have aboriginal roots.

An important dimension of aboriginal problems deals with the extent to which aboriginal rights must be honoured by the Crown. Thomas Isaac studies decisions of the Supreme Court of Canada related to aboriginal groups, and he concludes that the Court has recognized the "existing aboriginal and treaty rights" of the aboriginal peoples of Canada. The interesting question is, what are the *policy* implications of these rights? He suggests that the Crown must honour its relationship with aboriginal peoples, despite the fact that conflicts will inevitably arise with the interests of other groups of Canadians.

Two articles follow that focus on the political structures of aboriginal peoples. In an article dealing with the Assembly of First Nations, E. Kaye Fulton discusses the political structures developed by "status Indians" in Canada today. Increasingly, demands for self-government,

sovereignty, and financial resources have been the focus of agendas of meetings between native leaders and federal officials. The question of self-government for the native peoples is the subject of an article by Jack Aubry. These groups want the same kind of "distinct society" status as that demanded by Quebec, and they have argued that because of historical relations between their leaders and the government of Canada, they have an "inherent right" to self-government.

Finally, an article by André Picard focuses on the Inuit people and their quest for recognition by Ottawa of a special status in Canada's north. Although Parliament has held hearings on the subject, and has made recommendations to the government, no decision has been made as yet.

Looking Ahead: Challenge Questions

In how many different ways can we see the impact of native societies on contemporary Canadian society? Are the linkages visible in many different areas, or only a few?

Has the government of Canada lived up to its obligations to the aboriginal peoples of Canada? In what areas must more effort be made to ensure that the aboriginal peoples are treated as they *should* be treated?

Should the government of Canada support the claims of aboriginal leaders for native self-government? Are there any areas in which self-government should not be granted? What would be the financial obligations of Canada toward such a self-governing entity?

Do Canada's aboriginal peoples have the same type of claim to "distinct society" status as the people of Quebec? Are their claims stronger or weaker? Is there such a thing as an "inherent" right to self-government? Should there be a separate legal system for Canada's aboriginal peoples?

Our culture's native roots

Iroquois ideas influenced philosophers like Montaigne, who helped lay the groundwork for modern democracy

Jerry Diakiw

Jerry Diakiw is an educator who has written extensively on multicultural and anti-racism issues.

The origins of Canadian culture and identity are tangled and knotted, but if you dig deeply, some surprising roots are revealed.

Revisionist authors as widely divergent as McGill's Bruce Trigger, (*Children of Aataenisic*), feminist Paula Gunn Allen (*Who is Your Mother? The Red Roots of White Feminism*), and popular writers like Ronald Wright (*Stolen Continents*), are revealing the extent to which the genesis of our culture is grounded in native society.

We have always been led to believe that the richness of our culture is a product of the glory and achievement of Western civilization. It is humbling to realize that it is not as simple as that.

Our social safety net, our ability and reputation as mediators, conciliators and peacekeepers and our democratic freedoms enshrined in our federal system of government, are three of the many conceptions of our cultural identity that intertwine and overlap to create a whole greater than the sum of the parts.

While these are considered sophisticated products of a European heritage, it is instructive to consider that they may also be deeply rooted in native societies.

The Hurons, for example, like other Iroquoian tribes, looked after their own from the cradle to the grave in a manner that smacks of our Canadian safety net.

When Etienne Brulé wintered with the Hurons on the shores of Georgian Bay in 1610, Champlain guaranteed his safety by sending a Huron chief's son to Paris for the winter. When the young man returned and was asked what Paris was like, he explained to his disbelieving tribesman that people in Paris begged for food on the streets. That a society allowed this to happen was incomprehensible to the Hurons.

He also described the appalling manner in which children were harnessed, spanked and beaten publicly, and the way citizens were punished or executed in public squares in the early 1600s. To the Hurons, the Europeans were savages.

Montaigne, the French philosopher whose writings strongly influenced the struggle for liberty, justice and equality in Europe and elsewhere, acknowledged the commentaries of other Iroquoian visitors during the colonial era, who were shocked at the gross inequities they observed between the rich and the poor in Europe.

An ethnology of Iroquoian society written by Lewis Henry Morgan in 1851 was a popular treatise in Europe at the time. It outlined in some detail the workings of a matricentral society with an egalitarian distribution of goods and power, a peaceful ordering of society and the right of every member to participate in the work and benefits of the society.

Freidrich Engels reacted excitedly to this text: "This gentile constitution is wonderful! There can be no poor . . . All are free and equal—including women."

Certainly Karl Marx and other socialist thinkers at the time were similarly profoundly influenced by Morgan's ethnology. Marx's evolving ideas of female equality and women's liberation for example, though never achieved in practice, were fundamental to his socialist theories and can be clearly traced to the impact of his reading of Morgan's ethnology about the role of women in Iroquois society.

How these values informed Canadian identity is evident to this day. One of our most enduring qualities is our historic ability to mediate disparate points of view. Canada's evolution is a wonder of nation building. This immense land, with a divisive geography and a harsh climate, was united without military revolution, civil war or a war of independence.

This skills to achieve this remarkable feat have stood us in good stead internationally. Canada has long had a reputation as a peacekeeper for the world and we perceive ourselves that way. Canada's leadership and commitment to the United Nations, exemplified by Lester B. Pearson's Nobel Peace Prize, and our undiminished involvement as a peacekeeping force, are evidence of our conciliatory skills honed in nation building at home.

Confederation, itself, epitomizes our ability to unify a wide variety of disparate interests. We normally attribute this to the evolution of democracy and the parliamentary system, a crowning achievement of Western civilization.

But the Iroquoian Confederacy, a political organization comprised of five distinct native societies, (later six), had a profound influence on both the American and Canadian systems of government. Paula Gunn Allen reminds us that we inherited slavery and vote by male property owners from the European democracies.

At the Treaty of Lancaster in 1744, Canasatego, an Iroquois chief, spoke for the Iroquois, "We are a powerful confederacy; and by your observing the same methods our forefathers have taken, you will acquire fresh strength and power."

In the audience was a young Benjamin Franklin, later a co-author of the American constitution. He acknowledged in his writings the influence of this confederacy: "It would be a very strange thing if Six Nations of ignorant savages should be capable of forming a scheme for such a union . . ."

But such a union they formed. The symbol of the Iroquois Confederacy was an eagle clutching five arrows in its claw—one for each of the Iroquois nations. The symbol of American independence was an eagle clutching 13 arrows—one for each of the 13 colonies.

The American confederacy adopted the Iroquois system of distinct executive, legislative, and judicial branches of government and both Canada and the U.S. instituted the unique Iroquois system of three levels of government—local or municipal, state or provincial, and federal.

Through adopting this Iroquoian model, Canada was able to reconcile the many conflicting and divergent regional and cultural interests and bring about and maintain a confederation that more democratically represented the Canadian people. The fusion of the federal system and the parliamentary system is a unique Canadian approach to democracy.

The roots of our identity are indeed tangled and knotted but it is reassuring to realize the extent to which the First Nations have contributed to our uniquely Canadian culture. But it is less significant to untangle all the roots to ascertain their precise origins than it is to realize they are part of an integrated whole.

THE HONOR OF THE CROWN

In the Sparrow *case, the Supreme Court made it clear that aboriginal rights are here to stay, and they must be dealt with.*

Thomas Isaac

Thomas Isaac lectures in the Department of Political Science at St. Thomas University in Fredericton. He received his MA from Dalhousie and his LLB from the University of New Brunswick.

ON MAY 31, 1990 THE SUPREME COURT OF CANada rendered one of the most important decisions concerning aboriginal rights in Canada. In *R. v. Sparrow* the Supreme Court provides an analysis with which Section 35(1) of the *Constitution Act, 1982* should be examined. Section 35(1) guarantees that the "existing aboriginal and treaty rights of the Aboriginal peoples of Canada are hereby recognized and affirmed." Ronald Sparrow, a member of the Musqueam Indian Band of British Columbia, was charged with an offence under the *Fisheries Act* for fishing with a drift net that was longer than that permitted in the Band's fishing licence. Sparrow admitted that the facts constituted an offence. However, he defended his action by asserting that he was exercising an existing aboriginal right to fish and that the drift net length restriction in the Band's licence was contrary to section 35(1) of the *Constitution Act, 1982* and ought therefore to be declared invalid. Sparrow·was convicted at trial and through appeal and cross-appeal, the case came before the Supreme Court. The question posed to the Court was whether the restrictions on the net length in the Band's licence were inconsistent with section 35(1) of the *Constitution Act, 1982*.

On examining the word "existing" in section 35(1), the Supreme Court concluded that the section applies to those rights that were in existence when the *Constitution Act, 1982* came into effect. Rights which were extinguished prior to 1982 are not revived. An "existing" aboriginal right is not static and, therefore, it should be given a flexible interpretation and ought not to be restricted to its content before 1982. The Supreme Court stated that aboriginal rights are not extinguished by being controlled or regulated, but rather, there must exist a clear intention of extinguishment by the government.

In this case, the Crown failed to prove that the aboriginal right to fish of the Musqueam Band had been extinguished. The mere fact that it was controlled by the *Fisheries Act* was not *prima facie* evidence of extinguishment. While governmental policy can regulate a section 35(1) aboriginal right, it cannot extinguish it.

The Court then turned to the question of the meaning of the words "recognized and affirmed." The decision recognizes that section 35(1) is the result of a "long and difficult struggle in both the political forum and the courts for constitutional recognition of aboriginal rights." The nature of section 35(1) suggests that it ought to be interpreted in a "purposive way." When the purpose of the promotion of aboriginal rights is considered, a "generous, liberal interpretation of the words . . . is demanded." The Court noted that since section 35(1) is not part of the Charter, it is not subject to the Charter's section 1 limitation clause.

Although the Court stated that section 35(1) is substantive in nature, it made clear the fact that the rights contained therein are not absolute. Federal legislative powers continue pursuant to the division of powers in section 91 of the *Constitution Act, 1867*. In effect, the federal government's legislative power must be reconciled with the rights enunciated by way of section 35(1).

In order to justify a federal or provincial government infringement of a section 35(1) right, the legislative objective must "uphold the honor of the Crown and must be in keeping with the unique contemporary relationship . . . between the Crown and Canada's aboriginal peoples." Therefore, the Crown bears the burden of justifying legislation that threatens the enjoyment of a section 35(1) right.

The Court provides an analysis of section 35(1) that is to be applied and, in this case, it was applied to the *Fisheries Act*. The first point to be asked is whether the legislation interferes with an "existing aboriginal right." If legislation interferes with section 35(1), then it is a *prima facie* infringement of the section. The second part of the analysis concerns the issue of justification.

The justification analysis has two parts to it. First, is there a valid legislative objective? Here the court examines whether or not the interference with the right is valid. While it was determined that a public interest analysis was too vague, in light of the case at hand, the justification of conserving and managing the fisheries resource was deemed to be "surely uncontroversial."

The second part of the justification analysis deals with the honor of the Crown. The fiduciary responsibility of the Crown to aboriginal people is to be the first consideration in terms of deciding whether or not legislation limiting the use of

From *Policy Options*, Vol. 13, No. 1, January/February 1992, pp. 22-24. This article first appeared in *Policy Options*, Canada's Forum for Public Policy Debate.

section 35(1) can be justified. In honoring the relationship that the Crown has with aboriginal people, certain conflicts are sure to arise, in that the interests of aboriginal people may conflict with the interests of others. In the case of fisheries, after valid conservation measures have been implemented, priority must be given to the aboriginal right to fish. Although the justificatory standard imposes a heavy burden on the Crown, it nevertheless may already be supported by statute. For example, the *Fisheries Act* allows for priority of Indian food fishing over other users so long as the conservation measures are respected.

The justificatory standard includes a list of other considerations depending on the circumstances. For example, whether the infringement has been as little as possible to achieve the desired result; whether the aboriginal group has been consulted in the particular conservation measure under review; and whether, with respect to expropriation, there would be compensation offered. This list is not exhaustive.

The Supreme Court directed that the *Sparrow* case be sent back for a new trial with the outlined analysis to be applied.

The decision is significant for a number of reasons. Although a number of provincial Courts of Appeal and academics have suggested that section 35(1) is substantive, the Supreme Court has affirmed their conclusions. The decision recognizes that aboriginal rights mean "something" in the Canadian legal system. Although these rights are not absolute, they do, nevertheless, exist and there is a heavy burden on the Crown to justify the limitation of or interference with section 35(1) rights. In this way, when one speaks of aboriginal rights in Canada, section 35(1) allows for some understanding or meaning of the concept to be ascertained.

The Supreme Court indicates that section 35(1) provides a "constitutional base upon which subsequent negotiations can take place," between aboriginal people and the governments of Canada. As well, the section affirms that aboriginal people have constitutional protection against the use of provincial and federal legislative powers in that they must be "justified" and not arbitrary.

The result of this may be that when aboriginal people and the government of Canada negotiate a settlement, that there are certain minimum standards under which all parties must operate. The decision may give to aboriginal people a "level playing field" on which to operate when negotiating.

The insight of the Supreme Court on the nature of aboriginal rights, *vis-à-vis* section 35(1), in the decision is notable. Indeed, the Supreme Court showed an awareness of the aboriginal situation in Canada that many thought was barely alive. The fact that the Court can speak of the "honor of the Crown" is interesting. There is no strict *legal* character to the word "honor," and yet, it is used and thus infuses a sensitivity towards aboriginal people by making a connection between their rights and the duties of the Crown. As well, since the Court indicates that the justificatory analysis involves many questions, the need for a holistic approach of analysis is underscored:

> The aboriginal peoples, with their history of conservation-consciousness and interdependence with natural resources, would surely be expected, at the least, to be informed regarding the determination of an appropriate scheme for the regulation of the fisheries. . . . Suffice it to say that recognition and affirmation requires sensitivity to and respect for the rights of aboriginal peoples on behalf of the government, courts and indeed all Canadians.

This type of language is significant for the maintenance, recognition and promotion of aboriginal rights in Canada. The above excerpt illustrates precisely the tone of the judgment.

All Canadians can take some pride in what this judgment says to us.

It is one of understanding and indeed, the excerpt should be read with pride by aboriginal and non-aboriginal people. Aboriginal people ought to be proud because of the recognition given as regards their rich culture and unique lifestyle. Non-aboriginal people should be proud because the Supreme Court has made the most comprehensive statement to date on the nature of the relationship between the Constitution and aboriginal rights.

This is not to suggest that the *Sparrow* case is to be or should be seen as the last word on aboriginal rights in Canada. Merely because the Supreme Court has given significant meaning to the words in section 35(1) does not mean that life on the reserves will improve or that the standard of living for aboriginal people will increase. Note that *Sparrow* is not the first example of the Supreme Court deciding a major aboriginal issue. In 1973, the Supreme Court held in the *Nishga* decision that aboriginal rights could be shown to exist prior to European contact and these rights existed without acknowledgment by the government of Canada.

The analysis set out by the Supreme Court in *Sparrow* may be likened to the analysis that the Court outlined in the 1986 decision of *R.* v. *Oakes*. In the *Oakes* decision, the Supreme Court stated that in order for a Charter right to be limited by section 1 of the Charter, it must meet two central criteria. First, the statute in question must be of sufficient importance to override a constitutionally protected right. Second, the limitation must be "reasonably and demonstrably justified." In order to determine whether a limitation is "reasonably and demonstrably justified," a three-part proportionality test must be applied:

1. The measures must be designed to achieve the objective in question.
2. The measures must impair rights as little as possible.
3. The proportionality between the effects of the measures and the objective desired must be of sufficient importance.

Although section 35(1) is not subject to section 1 of the Charter, there is, nevertheless, a striking similarity between the *Oakes* test and that outlined in *Sparrow*. Under the justificatory analysis of *Sparrow*, there must be a valid legislative objective in order to override an aboriginal right. This is similar to the first criteria in *Oakes* in that a statute must be of "sufficient importance" to warrant an override of a Charter right.

The fact that in the *Sparrow* decision the "honor of the Crown" must be maintained in that aboriginal people must be the first consideration in determining whether legislation or an action can be justified, means that even if a valid legislative reason is ascertained, aboriginal rights maintain their strength. In this way the remaining analysis in *Sparrow* is like that of the proportionality test in *Oakes*. For example, *Sparrow* indicates that as little infringement as possible of aboriginal rights is desirable. This is similar to point number two of the proportionality test in *Oakes*, in that a Charter infringement should impair rights as little as possible. As well, the Supreme Court notes that the list of questions it provided concerning an inquiry into the justification of overriding an aboriginal right is not exhaustive.

However, the use of a Charter-section 1 analysis in a non-Charter clause, namely section 35, should raise some concerns. First, section 35 is not part of the Charter. It is in a distinctly separate of the *Constitution Act, 1982* and ought, therefore, to be handled as such. Although there may be merit in imposing some sort of limitation scheme on section 35 rights, such a scheme should be separate and apart from the Charter-section 1 analysis. Section 1 of the Charter is to apply exclusively to the Charter and, therefore, it is difficult to determine why such an analysis would be applicable to that which is a non-Charter item.

Second, the last segment of the justificatory analysis allows for the use of subjective queries to be posed in ascertaining the proper limitation on a section 35 right. By leaving such an important part of the analysis open to a varying degree of subjectivity, the Supreme Court may have undermined the original intent behind the justificatory analysis. That is, to provide a fair rationale to balance the interests of Canadian society in general with the interests of aboriginal people in particular.

Indeed, the section 1 analysis in *Oakes* is not the only example of where the Supreme Court appears to be drawing on Charter jurisprudence to help it define section 35(1). In stating that there is a heavy burden on the Crown to prove the need to override aboriginal rights, it is following the same reasoning for the two-part analysis outlined in *Oakes* which places an onerous duty on the Crown to justify the limitation of a Charter right.

Finally, by stating in *Sparrow* that section 35(1) is to be construed in a "purposive" way and that it demands a "liberal" interpretation, the Supreme Court is following the reasoning it set out in the 1985 decision of *Big M Drug Mart*. There the Court outlined the technique involved in the purposive approach to the Charter. Essentially, the approach demands a liberal and open understanding to Charter interpretation. In this way, the interpretation of section 35(1) does not have to remain static.

The significance of the decision is not confined to the substantive meaning given to section 35(1). For example, section 35(3) of the *Constitution Act, 1982* reads:

(3) For greater certainty in subsection (1) "treaty rights" includes rights that now exist by way of land claims agreements or may be so acquired.

As a result, land claims agreements under section 35(3) are "constitutionalized" to the extent that they are now included

in the substantive clause; section 35(1). The scope of this argument is too broad to be discussed here, however, it is enough to say that land claims agreements, such as the 1975 *James Bay and Northern Quebec Agreement* have been given additional meaning and increased status by their inclusion in section 35(1) and the substantive meaning given to it by the *Sparrow* decision.

As well, the decision may have an effect on section 25 of the *Canadian Charter of Rights and Freedoms*. Section 25 reads:

The guarantee in this Charter of certain rights and freedoms shall not be construed so as to abrogate or derogate from any aboriginal rights or freedoms that pertain to the aboriginal peoples in Canada, including (a) any rights or freedoms that have been recognized by the Royal Proclamation of October 7, 1763; and (b) any rights or freedoms that now exist by way of land claims agreements or may be so acquired.

Section 25 states that Charter rights shall not abrogate or derogate from any aboriginal rights, including those recognized by the *Royal Proclamation* and land claims agreements. It has been suggested and is maintained by this writer that section 25 places aboriginal rights above Charter rights in that the Charter cannot have a negative effect on aboriginal rights.

If "aboriginal rights" in section 25 refers to those rights in section 35, and indeed it appears as though they do, then section 25 rights receive the meaning given to section 35 rights as outlined in the *Sparrow* decision. Important to note is that section 25 does not grant rights *per se*. Rather, it is to be used as an interpretive tool.

It is submitted that if the above argument is accurate, then section 25 has been affected indirectly by the *Sparrow* decision and thus, additional meaning has been given to section 25.

The decision offers a broader message than the mere words themselves. It could be seen as an ushering in of a new era in the relationship between the majority Canadian community and the minority aboriginal community. Although there have been a number of setbacks in the area of aboriginal rights, most noticeably with the Oka standoff during the summer and fall of 1990, there is reason to hope. The Supreme Court may be the messenger of that hope and through its words might send a strong message to the Canadian government and to the Canadian people that aboriginal rights are here to stay and that they must be dealt with.

In recognizing this fact, it must also be remembered that the degree of success that aboriginal people have in ascertaining their rights will depend on the Canadian government's willingness to obey not only the letter of the law, but also its spirit.

DRUMBEATS OF RAGE

CONFLICTS WILL INTENSIFY AS NATIVES INCREASE DEMANDS FOR SELF-GOVERNMENT

Across rural Ontario, the surging clash over rights has provoked bitter feuds, pitting neighbor against neighbor. It began in May, 1991, when Ontario Premier Bob Rae announced that natives would be allowed to hunt and fish for food, or for ceremonial purposes, ignoring provincial wildlife laws. In the view of the province's 117,000 natives, Rae's action was a long-overdue recognition of their traditional right to harvest the land. But many Ontarians claim that the decision has recklessly endangered the province's fragile wildlife resources. Among other things, they accuse natives of netting as much as a million pounds of spawning walleye from the Thames River near London, Ont., and selling the catch to nearby restaurants. Declared Matthew Murphy, a spokesman for the Ontario Federation of Anglers and Hunters: "A minority of natives are abusing the system, creating absolute biological anarchy. They say, 'Don't give me white man's conservation.' But science knows no race or cultural background. It is not 1492: you cannot hunt and fish with abandon." Those conflicts are sure to intensify as natives across Canada escalate their demand to govern themselves—in some cases, beyond the reach of existing federal and provincial laws.

The natives point out that their ancestors controlled their own lives for thousands of years—and that they have never relinquished that right. Indeed, at a constitutional conference in Ottawa this week, native representatives will examine in detail the practical implications of native self-government. Leaders from four organizations representing Canada's one million Indians, Métis, Inuit and non-status Indians plan to debate how they would run their own governments—and how they would pay for them. The outcome of that conference will likely reinforce unwavering native demands for the constitutional recognition of their inherent right to self-government.

But that strong native campaign faces tough and skeptical opposition from many federal leaders and most of Canada's 10 premiers. Although most of the first ministers appear willing in principle to entrench the "inherent native right to self-government" in the Constitution, they are seeking to define and to limit that right before they recognize it. As Quebec Conservative MP Jean-Pierre Blackburn has repeatedly insisted, "We do not want to give them a blank cheque."

It is almost impossible for Canada's disparate natives to put forward a tidy and detailed proposal. The 512,000 status Indians and 32,000 Inuit across Canada have far different demands and expectations than Canada's 500,000 Métis and non-status Indians, who have no land base and who often live inner-city lives of desperate poverty. Those differences make it difficult to spell out in practical terms how natives would exercise jurisdiction over health care, education, justice, the environment and resource development.

Instead, natives are asking Canadians to make a massive leap of faith. The Assembly of First Nations (AFN), for one, which represents status Indians, asserts that native governments should have the right to choose their own laws and to replace specific Criminal Code provisions with their own decrees. In addition, the AFN says that natives should have the right to tax themselves—but that they should remain exempt from the taxes that other Canadians pay. Confirming the worst fears of self-government opponents, many members insist that natives should also have sovereignty over their land. In that case, individual bands would be empowered to run revenue-raising operations, such as casinos, that are outlawed in the rest of Canada. As AFN National Chief Ovide Mercredi told *Maclean's*, "Forms of self-government may not necessarily be identical with those of the dominant society. There is nothing compelling us to make them similar."

The charismatic Mercredi has emerged as the central figure in the controversy over self-government, a lightning rod for both its supporters and its fiercest opponents. A 46-year-old Cree from northern Manitoba, he is the son of a Roman Catholic non-status Indian who worked as a night watchman for Manitoba Hydro. In the nine months since his election as national chief, the University of Manitoba-educated lawyer has enraged Quebecers with his demands that natives be recognized as a distinct society, while inspiring many natives with his success in pushing aboriginal concerns to the forefront of the national agenda.

But Mercredi has to straddle the yawning gulf between moderates and radicals in his own organization, which represents 633 widely diverse bands. The executive of the 14-band Nuu-chah-nulth Tribal Council on the west coast of Vancouver Island has urged natives across the country to approach self-government with caution, examining the costs carefully before accepting the responsibilities. By contrast, the Cree of northern Quebec have appealed to the UN Commission on Human Rights to assert their long-standing claim to outright sovereignty over a huge swath of sparsely populated land that includes the lucrative James Bay hydroelectric project.

As well, Mercredi will have to sit at the negotiating table alongside three national native organizations whose priorities often differ widely: the Inuit Tapirisat of Canada, the Native Council of Canada, which represents non-status Indians, and the Métis National Council.

He and other native leaders will also have to retain the goodwill of a Canadian public increasingly wary of demands for special status—and not just from natives. Said Mercredi: "People look for any excuse to jump on the denial of rights for other people. The phobia related to natives is, 'How can you trust these savages to run their own affairs?' "

In general, Canadians appear sympathetic to the natives' aims. But many also say that the right to self-government should be clearly defined and limited. In an Angus Reid Group poll released last month, 58 per cent of the respondents favored the entrenchment of native self-government in the Constitution. But 76 per cent of the 1,500 adults who took part in the survey agreed with Ottawa's position that the concept must first be firmly defined. A mere nine per cent agreed that natives should be allowed to act "with complete sovereignty like a separate nation."

Native leaders say that they are hesitant to respond to those demands because they do not want to limit their options at the bargaining table. Indeed, the Inuit Tapirisat and the AFN have insisted that they should be treated as the representatives of a third founding nation, alongside the French and English. That would give natives the power to deal on a government-to-government basis with the prime minister and the premiers. Last month, Mercredi went even further by claiming that the right of natives to self-government had no limits: natives themselves, he said, would voluntarily cede control over monetary policy and defence to Ottawa.

Despite Mercredi's desire to avoid discussing specifics, some models do exist for native self-government. In 1986, the 817-member Sechelt band of British Columbia negotiated a self-government agreement with Ottawa. Ignoring the objections of many native leaders, the band settled for a restricted form of self-government with municipal powers. For their part, 17,500 Inuit in the eastern Arctic have agreed to abandon their claim to 800,000 square miles of land in exchange for title to 140,000 square miles and $580 million to be paid over 14 years, with interest. As well, the Inuit would receive the right to administer a territorial-style government over the entire eastern Arctic—one-fifth of Canada's landmass. That agreement has to be ratified this year by an Inuit plebiscite.

Another model exists in the United States, where the Supreme Court ruled in the 1830s that Indian tribes constituted "dependent sovereign nations." In 1934, in recognition of that approach, Congress passed the Indian Reorganization Act, which permitted self-government on Indian reservations. Since then, Indian tribes have had full power to license and control businesses on native land, assess taxes, determine their own membership and enact their own laws in areas such as divorce and traffic offences. Still, there are limits on Indian power. Indian governments and tribal courts

THE CONCEPT OF SELF-GOVERNMENT REMAINS A MINEFIELD OF PROBLEMS

must respect an Indian civil rights code, established by Congress in 1968, that guarantees equal protection before the law, the right to a lawyer and freedom of speech and religion.

Even with those models, the concept of self-government remains a minefield of questions and challenges:

Land: Natives with existing land bases want Ottawa to transfer to their reserves or communities specific powers—among them the right to develop resources. But that creates complications. The Dene nation in Saskatchewan, for one, is locked in a dispute with the Inuit over their land settlement with Ottawa. The Dene claim that the Inuit land, known as Nunavut, overlaps their ancestral hunting grounds. As a result, they refuse to recognize the Inuit boundaries. Similar disputes exist across the country. That presents a serious dilemma: should native communities assume self-government before the thorny issue of their boundaries—and the ownership of resources—is settled?

Urban self-government: The fate of urban natives is perhaps the most difficult issue to resolve with self-government. At the core of the problem is which level of government—and native organization—is responsible for the hundreds of thousands of Indians scattered across the country without a land base. In Metro Toronto alone, there are an estimated 65,000 natives from nearly 60 U.S. and Canadian bands. Rodney Bobiwash, the urban self-government co-ordinator for Toronto's Native Canadian Centre, told *Maclean's* that urban natives need their own representatives at the constitutional table—and their own governing entity. Bobiwash's demands include a House of Commons seat for Toronto's natives; a land base for Indians on Toronto Island or in the expensive downtown core; full application of native rights so that native laws apply to Indians on city streets; and full tax-exempt status. Those demands are certain to fuel controversy and anger among Canadians.

The justice system: Native leaders have demanded the right to craft their own code of law, reflecting native needs. But such a document might overrule the Criminal Code, the Charter of Rights and Freedoms or provincial codes that govern worker safety, the regulation of the environment and labor relations. There are precedents: most provinces now recognize that the existing justice systems can do little to rehabilitate native offenders without the in-

volvement of native communities. As a result, the Alberta government has worked with the Blood band of southern Alberta to establish a native-run police force and a minimum-security prison.

Still, many Canadians reject the proposals that individual bands should be allowed arbitrarily to select their own laws, creating a patchwork of zones across Canada in which different rules would apply. And some native women have launched a vocal campaign to retain the supremacy of the Charter of Rights and Freedoms—contrary to suggestions by a male-dominated native leadership that natives should write their own charter and perhaps their own constitution. Said Winnie Giesbrecht, the president of the Indigenous Women's Collective of Manitoba: "My biggest fear is that native women are not going to have any rights whatsoever. They will be controlled by the male powers in the native hierarchy."

Health and welfare: Many native communities are racked by chronic unemployment, a persistent cycle of welfare dependency and a staggering array of emotional and physical problems. Indeed, Ottawa spends six times as much on native health and welfare as it does on native economic-development programs: $613 million compared with $102 million in 1991-1992. Those who support local autonomy point out that spiritual healing is a powerful tradition in native culture. But some native leaders maintain that the quality and range of services would suffer if tribal councils or bands had control over health and social programs. Ottawa counters that natives must accept the additional responsibilities of self-government along with its benefits. As a result, health and welfare programs are certain to be on the constitutional bargaining table.

Revenue: Native leaders argue that entrenching the right to self-government in the Constitution means little unless natives have the money to implement it. Collectively, natives now own less than one per cent of Canada's land. Because they can cede title to their lands only to the Crown, they are unable to mortgage their property to raise bank financing for economic development. Said Mercredi: "Land rights are part of the answer to the question of who will pay for Indian self-government. Land is the basis of wealth in Canada."

Along with clear ownership of their land, most natives want the right to generate income on that land. Under existing laws, they do not have to pay income tax as long as they live and work on the reserve. Nor can the various levels of government assess taxes on band property

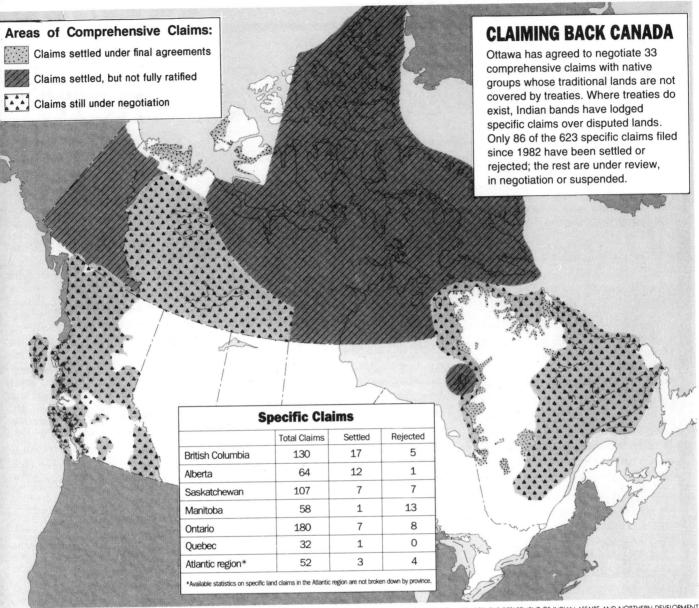

Areas of Comprehensive Claims:

- Claims settled under final agreements
- Claims settled, but not fully ratified
- Claims still under negotiation

CLAIMING BACK CANADA

Ottawa has agreed to negotiate 33 comprehensive claims with native groups whose traditional lands are not covered by treaties. Where treaties do exist, Indian bands have lodged specific claims over disputed lands. Only 86 of the 623 specific claims filed since 1982 have been settled or rejected; the rest are under review, in negotiation or suspended.

Specific Claims

	Total Claims	Settled	Rejected
British Columbia	130	17	5
Alberta	64	12	1
Saskatchewan	107	7	7
Manitoba	58	1	13
Ontario	180	7	8
Quebec	32	1	0
Atlantic region*	52	3	4

*Available statistics on specific land claims in the Atlantic region are not broken down by province.

MARK MCGUIRE   SOURCE: THE DEPARTMENT OF INDIAN AFFAIRS AND NORTHERN DEVELOPMENT

on a reserve. With self-government, natives want the right to tax their own people to pay for their own government. They also want to establish their own tax rules in order to attract business to reserves. As well, Mercredi says that native groups want to establish a fish marketing corporation to find international markets for the natives' inland fisheries. Because that corporation would negotiate its own prices, it would compete with provincial and federal governments in international markets.

Still, native leaders concede that there will be a gap between the money they generate and the cost of the services they provide. To cover the shortfall, they want the government to provide transfer payments, in the same way that it now distributes money among poorer provinces. There is no reliable estimate of the additional costs of self-government.

For natives, many of the benefits of self-government are clear. After centuries of repression, Canada's Indians, Inuit and Métis appear determined to regain their pride and right to self-determination. Said Manitoba MLA Elijah Harper: "The land and its resources do not belong to any one person; they should benefit everyone. We are no different from anyone else. We want to have a good life and a good home." Those are basic and defensible desires. But they entail a massive shift in the nature of the country. And they will severely test the tolerance and understanding of Canadians during one of the nation's stormiest eras.

E. KAYE FULTON in Ottawa

What is self-government?

Jack Aubry
For Southam News

Jack Aubry is native affairs reporter with the Ottawa Citizen.

OTTAWA — Native self-government. Most Canadians don't know what it is, or what it will cost, but they like the concept.

It's not a new idea. It was batted around the 1980s when the premiers and prime minister met three times to discuss aboriginal constitutional issues. Those attempts to clarify the issues ended in failure in 1987 and it wasn't until 1990 that the country really sat up and noticed.

Elijah Harper's bold stand against the Meech Lake accord, and the Oka crisis a few weeks later, carried natives to the top of the public agenda.

An Angus Reid poll in September 1990, as the armed standoff of Mohawks drew to a close, showed that aboriginal issues had become the No. 1 concern for Canadians. Only three months earlier, native issues had languished at the bottom of the heap, identified by only 2 per cent as subjects of national importance.

A poll released today and a recent survey of provincial government positions on constitutional reform show solid support for native self-government. Preliminary results from an $11-million cross-country native consultation show it has grassroots support.

Despite this support, the debate hit a sour note this week when Constitutional Affairs Minister Joe Clark threatened to pull aboriginal issues off the table. The disagreement isn't over self-government, however, but the Assembly of First Nations' insistence that natives be given distinct society status along with Quebec.

Federal proposal

In its constitutional reform package, the federal government proposes constitutional recognition of the native right to self-government, subject to Canadian laws and the Charter of Rights and Freedoms. If deals on self-government aren't reached within 10 years, the courts would decide what it means.

Native leaders say it is essential that the "inherent" right to self-government be recognized, that Canadians accept that natives were self-governing before they had contact with Europeans and that they never gave up their rights. They believe the 10-year delay is too long and reject the Charter, saying they will develop one of their own.

Mr. Clark says he has no trouble tacking on the term "inherent" as long as it does not lead to the formation of separate nations.

Native leaders stress that they do not envisage sovereignty for their communities. But they balk at committing themselves to a definition of self-government.

Many Canadians believe that whatever self-government means it will lead to federal budget savings, that in return for quasi-independence, native communities will give up annual federal funding.

That is far from certain.

Mr. Clark says fiscal arrangements will be on the table for discussion as

Pending comprehensive native land claims

Area	Population	Land claim	Money claimed
Yukon Territory	8,000 Indians	40,000 sq. km	$250 million
Mackenzie Delta	2,000 Gwich'in	60,000 sq. km	$75 million
Sahtu Region (north of Great Slave Lake in N.W.T.)	2,500 Sahtu Dene/Metis	282,000 sq. km	$205 million
N.W.T. (Tungavik Federation of Nunavut)	17,500 Inuit	2 million sq. km in central and eastern Arctic	$580 million
Northern B.C.	5,000 Nisga'a	23,750 sq. km	————
Quebec and Labrador	15,000 Montagnais	700,000 sq. km	————
Northern Labrador	3,800 Inuit	Coastline, interior and offshore of northern Labrador	————
Labrador	1,250 Naskapi and Montagnais	Labrador	————

Southam News Graphics

 From *The Hamilton Spectator,* February 15, 1992, p. A9. Reprinted by permission of *Southam News.*

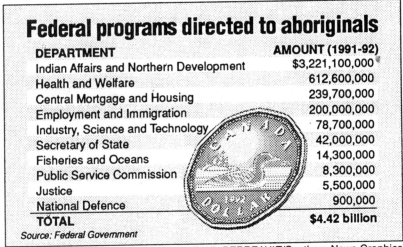

Federal programs directed to aboriginals

DEPARTMENT	AMOUNT (1991-92)
Indian Affairs and Northern Development	$3,221,100,000
Health and Welfare	612,600,000
Central Mortgage and Housing	239,700,000
Employment and Immigration	200,000,000
Industry, Science and Technology	78,700,000
Secretary of State	42,000,000
Fisheries and Oceans	14,300,000
Public Service Commission	8,300,000
Justice	5,500,000
National Defence	900,000
TOTAL	**$4.42 billion**

Source: Federal Government

PAUL PERREAULT/Southam News Graphics

part of reforms to bring about native self-government.

"We're talking here about a change in the way aboriginal people govern themselves and that is bound to have an effect upon the degree of freedom . . . (status Indian) tribes have from federal regulation.

"But also it would mean that some of the financial support that has been in place through the Department of Indian Affairs . . . would not be available under a self-government regime," says Mr. Clark.

Native leaders such as Assembly of First Nations national chief Ovide Mercredi, however, maintain that the $4.4-billion annual budget for federal programs for aboriginal people will increase after self-government is put in the Constitution.

Mr. Mercredi makes no apologies for that. "It is going to cost more. Of course. But the cost of carrying on with the status quo would be higher."

What would native self-government look like? That depends on who you ask.

Some say it would lead to a country dotted with hundreds of tiny independent native nations not subject to Canadian laws or programs. Others say it would result in municipal-type governments with limited powers in the federal scheme of things.

Likely, it would be something in the middle—a new third order of government with a blend of municipal, provincial and federal powers.

And the mix could differ from community to community.

But one thing is certain. Self-government would free natives from the oppressive weight of the Indian Act.

The Indian Act, passed in 1876, gives the federal government sweeping powers over about 600,000 "status" Indians in Canada and their reserves. Reserve land is held in trust by the government. Under the act Indians are allowed only to "use" it.

The act bars bands from mortgaging their lands since it guarantees the lands cannot be seized as collateral for loans. Because the avenues used by non-natives to raise money are closed, natives are completely dependent on the government for financing.

As well, the act allows the federal government to limit hunting and fishing on reserves and the federal minister has a veto over any bylaw passed by a band council.

And while constitutional talk about self-government heats up, the Department of Indian Affairs continues to quietly carry on its six-year-old program of "community based" negotiations with individual bands on self-government arrangements aimed at allowing them to get out from under sections of the Indian Act.

The ministry says about 150 bands are participating in negotiations despite harsh Assembly of First Nations' criticism of the process.

If the resolution of native issues took on a new urgency after Oka and Meech Lake, the political fallout has rendered debate one-sided. Tough questions are seldom asked.

Bryan Schwartz, law professor at the University of Manitoba, says the country's guilt over its shabby treatment of natives shouldn't prevent hard questions from being asked before native self-government is entrenched.

Otherwise, it will result later in further confrontation and misunderstanding between native and non-native leaders, he says.

For instance, how would recognition of self-government affect the land claims currently before the courts?

Huge claims

It is estimated that aboriginal people have laid claim to about half the country and are asking for between $100 billion and $200 billion to settle these claims.

Resolving those claims would bring the cost to taxpayers to about $30 billion if you use a conservative $50,000-a-person estimate from previous settlements.

And some believe that entrenching the "inherent" right would give native land claims a boost in the courts.

To establish aboriginal title to land, lawyers representing native bands have to show that the community resided on the land prior to contact with settlers and that it was an organized entity. Proving a community's pre-European existence is difficult, expensive and time consuming.

If the federal government entrenches self-government, in effect it will be recognizing that native bands were nations before the arrival of non-native settlers and natives will likely no longer be required to prove it.

Donald Worme, president of the Indigenous Bar Association, goes one step further, saying a new "threshold" test may be introduced in court cases requiring the federal Crown to justify infringement of that inherent right.

The Internal Exiles of Canada

Inuit of Northern Quebec who 'volunteered' to be relocated in the 1950s want more than an apology from a government that denies they were dropped into the North to protect national sovereignty

André Picard

Quebec Bureau, Inukjuak, Que.

Markoosie Patsauq clearly remembers the fateful day in the fall of 1953 when he boarded the supply ship C. D. Howe along with 32 other Inukjuak residents and their dog teams. Despite the promises of a Garden of Eden at the end of the journey, nine-year-old Markoosie cried, tears that foreshadowed the hardship and loneliness that lay ahead in his new home, a place 1,900 kilometres north that his father would call Ausuitoq—the place where the snow never melts.

Today, the tears have given way to anger, and Mr. Patsauq's fists clench when he recalls the Cold War "experiment" in which Inuit families—14 from Inukjuak and three from Pond Inlet—were moved from Northern Quebec to Resolute Bay and Grise Fiord, far above the Arctic Circle. The object of the relocation, conducted over three years, was the assertion of Canadian sovereignty over islands where only foxes, polar bears and walruses roamed, and where a few natives from nearby Greenland ventured to hunt for food.

"What the Canadian government did to us was wrong," says Mr. Patsauq. "Our human rights were violated, and we think we deserve an apology and compensation for our suffering. Until this matter is resolved, we can't consider ourselves real Canadians, because we have never been entitled to the same justice as others."

The "Internal Exiles," as they call themselves, are seeking an apology from the Prime Minister of Canada, formal recognition of their role as defenders of the country's Arctic borders, and a $10-million trust fund to ensure the economic well-being of their descendants, who number about 250. The package is similar to that granted Japanese Canadians interned by the federal government during the Second World War.

To date, Ottawa has steadfastly rejected the Inuit demands but has offered to pay moving expenses and said

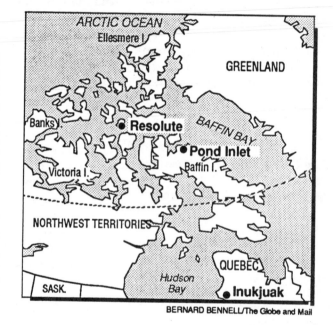

BERNARD BENNELL/The Globe and Mail

Quebec will assume the housing costs of any Inuit who wants to leave Canada's most northerly communities to return to Northern Quebec, a decision that has cost about $1-million to date.

In a recent letter to News North, a Yellowknife newspaper, Indian Affairs Minister Thomas Siddon restated the government position, saying the "relocation of the Inuit people of Inukjuak to the High Arctic was motivated by humane concerns. It was not . . . an experiment designed to assert sovereignty in the Arctic."

He also quoted a report prepared for the government last year by Hickling Corp. that concluded that "to apologize for a wrongdoing it did not commit would constitute deception on the part of the government. It would imply that the project had not been reasonably successful whereas this has not been the case."

 From *The Globe and Mail*, September 7, 1991, p. D3. Reprinted by permission.

In Grise Fiord, there were only five types of animal, no plants and no lakes. There was also perpetual darkness from October to February, and no soapstone for carving, which added to the Inuits' acute homesickness

But John Amagoalik, ex-president of the Inuit Tapirisat of Canada and an Internal Exile who left Inukjuak for Resolute Bay as a five-year-old boy, says the contempt and racism that characterized the treatment of the Inuit is a "wound on Canada's human-rights record that needs to be healed." The situation is being compounded by the government's obstinate refusal to admit any wrongdoing.

"Any sensible person looking at the facts will realize there was a travesty of justice. I don't know why Indian Affairs still defends their actions. They were wrong."

Mr. Amagoalik says that after a decade of battling for compensation and an apology, he has been buoyed by recent developments. The most significant is the appointment of Daniel Soberman, a Queen's University law professor, as a "special reporter" to the Canadian Human Rights Commission. The Inuit and Ottawa have agreed, in writing, to let Mr. Soberman conduct a no-holds-barred investigation and make recommendations on how the issue can be resolved. He has already visited Inukjuak, Pond Inlet, Grise Fiord and Resolute Bay and conducted in-depth interviews with two dozen of the deportees and their descendants.

There was no doubt the resettlement was motivated primarily by a fear of losing sovereignty. It was compounded by bureaucrats who thought moving the Inuit to more remote locations would do them good

His report should be completed before the end of the year, and while the recommendations are not binding, Mr. Soberman says the parties have a "moral obligation" to accept his conclusions.

Yet, other influential bodies have not swayed the Conservative government. Last spring, the Tory-dominated Parliamentary Standing Committee on Aboriginal Affairs, after holding the first public hearings ever on the matter, recommended that the government officially recognize the role of the relocated Inuit in defending Canadian sovereignty. The committee said a formal apology and compensation should be paid for their service to Canada and the "wrongdoing inflicted upon them."

The report, issued at the height of the Meech Lake debate, went virtually unnoticed, and Mr. Siddon answered the committee by commissioning the Hickling report. The minister said the independent study, which had the approval of the Inuit group Makivik Corp., clearly established there was no wrongdoing and vindicated the government.

This summer, Northern Perspectives, the policy journal of the Canadian Arctic Resources Committee, published an academic study that dismissed the Hickling report as a "grievously inaccurate" political whitewash.

Shelagh Grant, a Trent University historian who studied government documents from the time, said there was no doubt the resettlement was motivated primarily by a fear of losing sovereignty over the Arctic. It was compounded by a "paternalistic, right-wing, macho attitude" of bureaucrats who thought moving the Inuit to more remote locations would do them good.

"Ottawa's refusal to accept the facts of the past as truth will stand out as hypocrisy in its finest hour," Ms. Grant wrote. "So far, the present government appears to have compounded errors made 37 years ago by attempting to rewrite history and thus avoid granting rightful respect and honour to those who most deserve it."

The government response to the historian's work was a stinging rebuke from Mr. Siddon, who leapt to the defence of his departmental officials and political consultants and accused her of shoddy research.

Ms. Grant, currently doing research aboard the HMS Polaris off Greenland, says "Mr. Siddon should be ashamed of the lengths he has gone to save-face for a few bureaucrats instead of holding out an olive branch to defenders of Canadian sovereignty.

"There is no doubt that an injustice was done to the Inuit, and that sovereignty was at the root of that injustice," says the author of the book, *Sovereignty or Security*. "The facts speak for themselves."

Sovereignty concerns were expressed as far back as 1880 when the Arctic islands were transferred from Great Britain to Canada, ostensibly to keep the United States from claiming them. Wintering U.S. whalers and frequent incursions by Danish explorers and Greenland Inuit caused on-going concern, prompting a series of bureaucratic measures: creating the Eastern Arctic Patrol, raising the flag on remote Arctic islands, establishing remote RCMP posts, issuing licences to explorers and enforcing game laws.

The first formal challenge to Canada's title over the archipelago was settled in 1930, when the Norwegian explorer Otto Sverdrup was paid $67,000 for his discovery of three major islands. Four years later, 22 Inuit from Cape Dorset were relocated to Dundas Harbour, an "experiment in acclimatization" that ended in failure.

During the Second World War, U.S. military and civilians greatly outnumbered Canadians in the North. In 1946, confidential U.S. Air Force reports suggested the

'One Sled, Six Dogs . . .'

A "report on selected families and status of their equipment" shows how sparse the possessions were of the Inuit to be resettled:

FROM INUKJUAK:

Family F: three hunters (including two sons), wife, daughter, step-daughter; one sled, six dogs, two rifles, two shotguns, one tent, no traps, one kayak

Family J: one hunter, wife and child (to use equipment of above family)

Family P: one hunter, wife and two children; one sled, four dogs, two rifles, one shotgun, 50 traps, one tent, one kayak

Family S: one hunter, wife, one son, two daughters; one sled, five dogs, two rifles, one tent, one kayak

Family S2: two hunters (brothers), one wife, one grandmother; one sled, seven dogs, two rifles, one tent, one kayak

Family T: one hunter, wife, three sons; *no sled*, three dogs, one rifle, 15 traps, one tent, one kayak

Family A: one hunter, wife, three sons and one daughter; one sled, five dogs, one rifle, 20 traps, one tent, one kayak

FROM POND INLET:

Family A1: one hunter, wife and three children; one sled, 11 dogs, one rifle, 40 traps, one seal net, one fish net, one tent

Family A2: one hunter, wife and three children; one sled, 14 dogs, three rifles, 40 traps, one tent

Family A3: one hunter, wife and four children; one sled, 13 dogs, three rifles, 90 traps, 1 seal net, one tent
Source: Telegram from RCMP Inspector Henry Larsen to the director of northern administration, May 23, 1953

U.S. claim an undiscovered island in order to construct an Arctic weather station. The Air Force also recommended sovereignty be claimed over uninhabited Arctic islands if Canada refused to co-operate in a time of crisis.

In addition to Cold War paranoia about a Soviet attack over the North Pole, the Canadian government feared new claims by explorers. The opening in 1950 of a trading post close to the border in Etah, Greenland, heightened concern. The next year, Greenlanders were reported to have wintered on the archipelago and the Danes requested permission to set up a geodetic station on the island for mapping purposes.

Noting these alarming developments, RCMP Inspector Henry Larsen suggested that new RCMP posts be established and that Canadian Inuit be urged to settle nearby.

At a meeting in 1953, Secretary to the Cabinet Jack Pickersgill said the most important issue to be addressed was a "seeming encroachment upon Canadian sovereignty." He said steps must be taken "to ensure that civilian activities in the North were predominantly Canadian."

Four days later, RCMP officers in remote detachments were asked to co-operate with a resettlement plan involving three northern communities. Formal plans for the "human experiment" were submitted in March, 1953, and formally approved a month later, at which time RCMP officers were ordered to round up "volunteers" in Pond Inlet, Inukjuak and Kuujjuaq (the last community was later dropped).

By fall, most of the "willing volunteers" were aboard ships, though there were trickles of new arrivals over

three years. In total, 87 Inuit were moved to communities some 3,200 kilometres north of Montreal.

"Once the Inuit set foot on the boat, they were locked in a controlled experiment over which they had no means of escape," Ms. Grant wrote. The hardships that would mark many lives began aboard the C. D. Howe, where special "native quarters" were set up for the Inuit and their dogs. While non-natives were fed full-course meals in the dining room, the Inuit were fed four "hard-tack biscuits" and a cup of tea, for which they paid 40 cents.

"The Inukjuak Inuit on arrival were described as dispirited and in poor health, inadequately clothed, their tents and equipment in poor repair, their dogs too few in number and weak," Ms. Grant wrote in Northern Perspectives. The only reason they survived was that the local RCMP constable spoke Inuktitut and gave them meat from his personal cache until they could get enough equipment and knowledge to hunt.

Alex Stevenson, the Eastern Arctic Patrol official who hatched the resettlement plan, said of the arrival of one group of Exiles in a telegram: "Sovereignty now is a cinch."

Mr. Patsauq said his family spent the first seven years living in an igloo built over a ripped tent because there were no other building materials. A combination church and school was built with packing crates that carried their belongings. Back home in Inukjuak, where the Inuit had lived off the land, there were 55 species of game and plenty of lakes. In Grise Fiord, there were only five types of animal, no plants and no lakes. There was also perpetual darkness from October to February, and no soapstone for carving, which added to their acute homesickness.

In its bureaucratic zeal to deny the Inuit material comforts in a misguided effort to get them to return to the old ways, the government ordered natives not be paid wages for labour (such as unloading cargo from supply ships and acting as guides), imposed exorbitant markups on goods sold at trading posts and paid a fixed price for pelts that was far below market price. In 1958, for example, the government paid hunters $6,000 for fox pelts it then sold to the Hudson's Bay Company for almost $18,000. The result was acute poverty and needless suffering.

The men left to hunt for long periods of time, sometimes leaving women and children without food and supplies. It is alleged by Mr. Patsauq and others that, during those outings, RCMP officers "traded food for sex, abused children and sometimes raped the women."

Robert Pilot, a former RCMP constable in Grise Fiord who went on to become a senior civil servant in the Northwest Territories, says he heard of no allegations of sexual abuse until a few years ago.

Sergeant Pierre Bélanger, a spokesman for the RCMP, said the allegations are being investigated.

Mr. Pilot, now retired and living in Pembroke, Ont., has become a key ally for the Inuit. "There is no question we [the RCMP] were there to raise the flag, and there is no doubt in my mind that the Inuit were there for sovereignty purposes."

By March, 1954, virtually all references to the relocation experiment disappeared, abruptly and without explanation, Ms. Grant found in her research. Plans for further relocations were scrapped.

In the mid-70s, when the Inuit of Northern Quebec signed the James Bay and Northern Quebec Agreement, a land-claims settlement that paid the Inuit $90-million, some of the Exiles returned home to their newly prosperous communities. In 1982, a group led by Mr. Patsauq and Mr. Amagoalik made the formal request for an apology and compensation.

Today, virtually all residents of Resolute Bay (166) and Grise Fiord (76) want to stay, because the villages are home. To force them to leave would be an act as unjust as the one that sent their families north in the first place, the Exiles say.

But almost four decades after he and his fellow villagers went to the place they called Kaujuitoq, the place where the sun never shines, Mr. Amagoalik wants the government to brighten the future of the remaining defenders of sovereignty by recognizing the role of their forebears in protecting Canada's territorial integrity.

"Our pain is real. Our tears are real," Mr. Amagoalik says. "We want the healing to begin but, for that to happen, the government snowjob has to stop."

Free Trade

In recent years, one of the most problematic issues in Canadian foreign policy has been the relationship between Canada and the United States. This has been articulated along a number of different policy dimensions, including foreign policy, military policy, and economic policy. Canada has wanted to be seen as an independent state, one that makes its own foreign policy decisions and one that does not make decisions according to the desires of the United States.

It is clear that among the many policy areas that could have become subjects of tension, the single biggest issue involving Canadian-American relations has been the Free Trade Agreement between the two actors. Free trade was seen by many to have significant implications for cultural nationalism and the maintenance of a distinctly Canadian existence in Canada when it came into force in 1989, and it has continued to be seen in this way since that time. Many critics argued that with free trade the borders would be swept away and a continental (read: American) character would take over the entire North American marketplace. While this "worst case" scenario has not come to pass, there have been some areas of the economy in which free trade has had a deleterious effect.

This section contains nine articles that discuss Canadian-American economic relations. Such subjects as global trade, the Free Trade Agreement with the United States, and the recently negotiated North American Free Trade Agreement among Canada, the United States, and Mexico are among the subjects covered in the reading.

In the first unit selection, the arguments of the federal government for the proposed North American Free Trade Agreement are put forward. This selection from the Ministry of Industry, Science, and Technology, and the Ministry for International Trade claims that the 1989 Free Trade Agreement was strategically good for Canada, and it suggests that an expansion of the North American free trade marketplace would be consistent with this experience, despite (or perhaps because of) a variety of trade challenges in the global marketplace today.

The second article suggests that it is still too soon to determine whether the Free Trade Agreement was a good idea for Canada. There are a number of variables that have affected the Canadian economy, and it is not easy to determine exactly how the Free Trade Agreement would have affected the Canadian economy without the fluctuations in interests rates, the value of the dollar, and the international recession that have existed since the Free Trade Agreement came into effect.

The next four articles offer more of a debate over the success of the 1989 Free Trade Agreement and the wisdom of extending that pact with the 1992 North American Free Trade Agreement (NAFTA). Léo-Paul Dana suggests that free trade agreements are common, and he provides some historical background for appraising the effectiveness of the Canada-United States Free Trade Agreement.

An article by Keith Bradsher looks at the position of Richard Gephardt, the majority leader of the U.S. House of Representatives, who has suggested that NAFTA is flawed from the perspective of the United States and that it will result in a loss of jobs and destruction of the environment. Gephardt argued that NAFTA should be renegotiated before the United States agrees to participate in the new association.

In an examination of the 1989 Free Trade Agreement from the Canadian perspective, Mel Hurtig suggests that the agreement was "a horrendous deal" for Canada. The United States won access to Canada's natural resources and domination of Canada's markets, and in return Canada received very little.

The position of the United States is defended by its ambassador to Canada, Edward Ney. He suggests that the Free Trade Agreement was never expected—nor intended—to eliminate all trade disputes, only to establish a framework within which future trade conflicts could be amicably resolved. Thus, he suggests, recent American actions in relation to softwood and automobiles are not signs of protectionism, but instead they are normal responses to market pressures.

The final three selections in this section focus on the North American Free Trade Agreement and the specific implications that Mexican participation will have for the Canadian and American economies. In the first of these three articles, David Olive suggests that free trade will benefit all three partners in the agreement and that NAFTA is more progressive in terms of environmental concerns than any international trade pact has been in the past. The next selection suggests that in 1988 little atten-

tion was paid in the United States to the issue of free trade, but this time around is quite different. Ian Austen indicates that "a trilateral deal has spawned a trilateral network of opponents" and that there may be real problems in store for NAFTA. Finally, Gordon Ritchie, Canada's chief negotiator for the Free Trade Agreement, argues that while Mexico is likely to benefit most from NAFTA, in the long run a more prosperous North America will be the result of the agreement.

Looking Ahead: Challenge Questions

What are the major arguments of those who argue for increasingly free trade in the international marketplace? What arguments can be made against this kind of free trade?

Has Canada's experience with the Free Trade Agreement with the United States confirmed or refuted the arguments of those who predicted in 1988 and 1989 that the agreement would be disastrous for both the Canadian economy and Canadian culture?

How is the North American Free Trade Agreement different from the 1989 Free Trade Agreement with the United States? Are these differences significant in terms of whether Canada should support the new agreement?

Confronting the global trade challenge - Canada gets ready to take on the world and win.

Today, nothing affects the lives of people in countries throughout the world to a greater extent than international trade. And nowhere is this more true than in Canada.

Canada's commitment to being a major player in a stable international trading environment has a long history. As far back as 1947, we were present and participating in the foundation of the GATT (the General Agreement on Tariffs and Trade) in Geneva.

66 *We have received an increasing number of inquiries from Mexico. Economic improvements, coupled with the proposed NAFTA, have made the Mexican market more promising.* 99

John R. Downie, Marketing Manager, Dy-Core Systems Inc., Vancouver

Since 1947, the GATT has conducted an ongoing series of meetings, called "rounds", to progressively expand and define the areas and rules governing international trade. Currently, the "Uruguay Round" is nearing completion heralding significant possible changes to areas such as agriculture and trade in services. Canada has played and continues to play an active role in these negotiations.

While the GATT , and Canada's role in it, remains extremely important to our future, other international trading developments have caused us to pursue additional options as well. The most significant of these have been regional free trade agreements.

The evolution of the European Economic Community, for example, with a population of 360 million people, effectively rendered Canada an outsider. So we faced the prospect of becoming an isolated market of 27 million people caught between the massive European,

American and Asian markets. Hardly the place to be in a trading environment that is becoming increasingly global in scale.

66 *Mexico is the fastest growing North American economy so we may as well start looking at the possibilities. The Mexicans are for real.* 99

Stephen Van Houten, President, Canada Manufacturers' Association, Southam News, July 14, 1992

At the same time a rising tide of protectionism was taking place in the United States and Canada was getting caught in the crossfire. In just two years - 1985 and 1986 - the U.S. initiated 14 trade actions against Canadian exports.

The Canada/U.S. Free Trade Agreement (FTA) was negotiated partly in response to this rising tide of U.S. protectionism. Its intent was not to prevent all bilateral trade disputes - but to provide Canada with a mechanism to ensure that those disputes which inevitably arise are handled in a fair and expeditious manner. This goal has been achieved.

66 *Competition is your best friend. If there's no competition, then you become fat and lazy.* 99

Len VanderLugt, President, Aldershot Greenhouses, Burlington, quoted in Canadian Business, August, 1992

Experts consider the FTA dispute settlement mechanisms to be better than those of the GATT. Not only is FTA dispute settlement faster, but Chapter 19 FTA panel decisions are binding on both governments. This prevents the U.S. from blocking decisions it doesn't like - a major weakness of the GATT. Indeed - the FTA has been suggested as a model for improving the GATT.

The success of the Canada/U.S. Free Trade Agreement has now led to the

proposed North American Free Trade Agreement (NAFTA), and the creation of an additional market for Canadian goods and services of some 85 million people, 20 million of whom are well off by Canadian standards.

Will a North American Free Trade Agreement be a panacea for Canada? No. Not any more than Canada/U.S. free trade has been.

66 *As we approach a new millennium the attitude is beginning to change. Issues such as free trade have forced Canadian business to break out of its isolation and search for global opportunities.* 99

Farrell Campbell, Vice President and General Manager, Mercair Inc. Aerospace Industries, St-Laurent

But in today's global trade challenge, there is no free lunch. NAFTA will provide challenges and opportunities. Some day it could lead to a Western Hemisphere Free Trade Agreement linking both North and South America. And along with our continued role in the GATT and further trade negotiations in the Asia/Pacific region, it represents a significant aspect of how Canada is preparing to take on the world and win.

UNDER THE GATT, CANADA'S

AVERAGE PROTECTIVE TARIFF

HAS DECLINED FROM ABOUT

30% IN 1947 TO JUST 3.3% TODAY.

THROUGH ALL THIS TRADE

LIBERALIZATION, CANADA

HAS GROWN MORE PROSPEROUS.

Reprinted from *Canada*, September 1992, pp. 1-6. Reprinted by permission.

Free Trade A Winner!

THE NUMBERS START TO ROLL IN – FREE TRADE BOOSTED EXPORTS, CREATED JOBS AND HELPED CUSHION THE RECESSION.

As Canada emerges from a global recession, bruised but less battered than many countries, evidence is mounting that free trade has indeed been working to our benefit.

In the period 1989-1991, Canadian merchandise exports to the U.S. grew by almost 11% to $323.8 billion. Up from $292.5 billion in the period 1986-1988.

Last year, Canada sold $13.9 billion more to the U.S. than they sold to us. In fact, 1991 exports were up $5.0 billion over 1988. That's worth remembering when you consider that every billion dollars worth of exports creates 15,000 Canadian jobs.

Free trade is helping create the kinds of jobs Canadians need to compete in today's global marketplace. The range as well as the quantity of Canadian exports is growing. And the numbers are impressive. Consider these growth statistics from 1988 to 1991:

PHARMACEUTICAL EXPORTS
are up 90%
to $133 million

CHEMICAL PRODUCTS
are up 33%
to $232 million

PLASTICS
are up 16%
to $1.8 billion

MAN-MADE FILAMENT FIBRES
are up 133%
to $200 million

CLOTHING (NOT KNITTED)
is up 89%
to $179 million

ELECTRICAL MACHINERY
is up 74%
to $5.7 billion

RAILWAY EQUIPMENT
is up 126%
to $482 million

AEROSPACE PRODUCTS
and parts up 77%
to $2.3 billion

FURNITURE
is up 28%
to $1.3 billion

The fact is, Canada's export performance has been setting records. In May, U.S.-bound exports were $9.9 billion, and total exports to the world increased for the sixth month in a row, hitting a record monthly high of $12.9 billion. As a result, an all-time export record of $75.5 billion was set in the first half of 1992, up 7.6% over 1991. Commenting on the export figures in the first four months of 1992, Earl Sweet, Assistant Chief Economist at the Royal Bank says, "the restructuring is starting to show results in our ability to export more, which helped bring an increase in manufacturing employment."

Since the FTA, **no** country has been able to take a larger share of the U.S. market for manufactured goods than Canada. According to Statistics Canada data, 19 of 22 Canadian industries gained share in their respective U.S. markets since the FTA.

The benefits of free trade have spread widely across the country. Most provinces have seen their exports to the United States increase since 1988.

ALBERTA
exports have increased
30% to $11.8 billion

SASKATCHEWAN
exports have increased
18% to $2.3 billion

QUEBEC
exports have increased
2.0% to $17.7 billion

MANITOBA
exports have increased
2.4% to $1.9 billion

ONTARIO
exports have increased
5.6% to $58.8 billion and are up 18% so far in 1992 over 1991

Exports are also up for **P.E.I.** and **Nova Scotia** exports are up a strong 11% so far in 1992 over 1991.

In **British Columbia**, dramatic gains have been made in sectors such as tool exports (up 180%); vehicles and parts (up 69%); and optical equipment (up 44%). And B.C. exports are up 18% so far in 1992 over 1991.

With the largest two-way trading relationship in the world, it should be no surprise that disputes arise between Canada and the U.S. What is surprising is that such disputes affect less than 5% of all the trade conducted. Even within that 5%, Canada has benefitted from the dispute resolution mechanisms of the FTA. Of 12 completed cases involving Canadian challenges of U.S. trade actions against Canada, 7 of 12 have resulted in positive results for Canada. If there had been no FTA, all these cases would have gone against Canada.

Perhaps the final comment on free trade should be left to Professor Peter Pauley of the University of Toronto. After extensive study, he concluded that the FTA has stimulated growth and lowered the unemployment and inflation rates, therefore lessening the severity of the recent recession.

The Free Trade

RECORD EXPORTS TO U.S.

In April 1992, Canada's exports to the U.S. hit an all-time monthly high of $10 billion. In June, U.S.-bound exports were $9.9 billion. And Canada set an all-time high for exports to the world during the first half of 1992.

FTA BRINGS HOME THE BACON

Early last year the highest trade authority in the U.S. was required by an FTA panel to reverse its finding that imports of Canadian pork threatened to injure the American industry. The result: duties against Canadian pork producers were revoked, collection of further duties stopped and $17 million in duties paid were refunded to Canadian exporters.

BETWEEN FRIENDS

In at least 10 instances, the FTA has been used successfully by Canada to head off and protect us from new and potentially damaging U.S. trade legislation.

ADVANTAGE CANADA

Last year, Canada sold $13.9 billion more to the U.S. than came north. U.S.-bound exports were up $5.0 billion in 1991 over 1988. And Canada's merchandise trade surplus with the U.S. in the first six months of 1992 is running at an annual rate of $17 billion.

EXPORTS CREATE NEW JOBS

Every $1 billion in exports generates 15,000 jobs, and Canada's exports to the U.S. are up $31 billion in 1989-91 compared to 1986-1988. Given that, the FTA has played a positive role in the maintenance or generation of up to 500,000 jobs that have depended upon increased exports to the U.S.

JUSTICE FOR ALL. FASTER

In the past, when a Canadian company appealed a U.S. government decision to the U.S. Court of International Trade, it had to wait an average of 26 months, and in some cases as long as 53 months, for a decision. By contrast, the average time for FTA panel decisions has been 10.5 months.

ON THE REBOUND

With increasing exports, manufacturing employment is rebounding: hitting 1,803,000 in July - up 113,000 from the March low.

SERVICING THE U.S. MARKET

Thanks to the FTA, for the first time Canadians can enter the U.S. for short periods to sell their services and earn income. 8,971 did just that in 1991 - up 145% since 1989.

SHARING PROSPERITY

According to Statistics Canada data, 19 of 22 Canadian industries gained share in their respective U.S. markets since the FTA.

Scoreboard

REVERSAL OF FORTUNES

Canada's share of the U.S. market fell off in the mid-eighties. According to Statistics Canada data, that trend reversed after the introduction of the FTA. Meanwhile, the U.S. share of Canadian market has decreased from 28.3% in 1986 to 27.5% in 1991.

OFF WITH THEIR TARIFFS

Almost a thousand Canadian companies have demonstrated their belief in free trade by pushing for accelerated tariff removal. To date, tariffs have been removed faster than called for in the FTA on $8 billion in two-way trade.

A MATERIAL WORLD

Since FTA, our apparel exports to the U.S. have increased by 60%, yarn exports have more than doubled, fibre exports are up 50% and fabric exports by 15%. Under NAFTA there is now room for even more growth.

INVESTING IN PEOPLE

Last year the government spent $3.1 billion to provide training and adjustment programs for approximately 630,000 Canadians. This year we will spend $3.55 billion to do the same for another 650,000 workers. Canada spends 35 times more per capita on adjustment programming than the U.S.

CONSUMERS SAVE BIG

Statistics Canada data shows that lower duties on imports from the U.S. have resulted in savings to Canadian consumers of some $167 million in 1991 alone, with total savings to Canadian business and consumers in 1991 of some $700 million.

DUTY-FREE CANOLA OIL

On January 1st, 1992, the U.S. tariff on canola oil was eliminated. This saves Alberta canola growers as much as $3 million a year in U.S. duties. So how much would that be in, say, 20 years?

YES, WE CAN!

In part due to increased investment in plant and equipment to be competitive under the FTA, Canada is becoming dramatically more productive. Wood Gundy forecasts call for manufacturing productivity to be up as much as 8% in 1992 and 12% in 1993.

INVESTING IN CANADA

The FTA has helped attract offshore investment and create jobs in Canada. Several examples:

Hitachi Canadian Industries Ltd., Saskatoon, Saskatchewan
Nikon Optical Canada, Montreal, PQ
YHS Pacific Fruit Concentrate, Chilliwack, B.C.

NAFTA.

Our North American market expands to 360 million people.

Initial agreement has just been reached to create the world's biggest and richest free trade market. The proposed NAFTA (the North American Free Trade Agreement) brings Canada, the United States and Mexico together into a free trade area even larger than the European Economic Community. And Canada stands to be a big beneficiary.

By being part of NAFTA, Canada protects its ability to attract off-shore investment to serve the North American market. Had a separate agreement been signed between Mexico and the United States, only a company located in the United States would have had free access to the entire North American market, negatively affecting Canada's competitive position.

With a booming economy and 85 million consumers, Mexico represents a massive market opportunity for Canadian business. As demonstrated by the $500 million contract recently awarded to SHL Systemhouse of Ottawa to redesign, implement and manage a new computer system for the Mexican government's finance department, Canadian firms have the specialized skills and knowledge to complement Mexico's economic development efforts.

Mexico is already Canada's largest trading partner in Latin America, with two-way trade exceeding $3 billion in 1991. That figure is expected to double by the end of the decade. And, by eliminating Mexican import tariffs and other barriers to trade, NAFTA will rectify the present situation which has 80% of Mexican goods already entering Canada duty-free, while most Canadian goods and services face barriers entering Mexico (in effect, one-way free trade in Mexico's favour).

Canadian firms are already working hard to develop new export opportunities in the Mexican market, and the vast majority - over 80% - are small and medium-sized businesses.

In January of this year, Canada mounted its largest ever trade show in Latin America. Canada Expo 92 attracted more than 200 Canadian companies to Monterey, Mexico.

The results: over $3 million in on-site sales and more than $80 million in projected sales. In addition, 2,113 Canadian exporters visited our Embassy in Mexico in 1991 while 2,921 have visited in the first six months of 1992, all actively pursuing local market opportunities. These efforts are starting to generate results: **Canada's exports to Mexico rose 105% to $316 million in the period January through May 1992 over the year earlier period.**

Canada needs NAFTA. We're a trading nation. Over 25% of our GDP comes from trade. One in every four Canadian jobs is directly related to trade. And given our small home market, trade is the only way to maintain our high standard of living.

CANADIAN EXPORT OPPORTUNITIES IN MEXICO

- By 1994, the total North American auto parts market will be worth $12.8 billion.
- Computer software is a Canadian strength. That market alone could be worth $1.4 billion in Mexico.
- Mexico is the world's 13th largest market for machine tools and imports 90% of its needs.
- The oil and gas equipment market in Mexico is worth over $2 billion.
- Mexico will buy over $600 million worth of plastics and resins this year.
- Mexico's market for pollution control equipment and technology is worth $280 million and growing.
- Mexico will be updating and improving its telecommunications system to the tune of $30 billion over the next 10 years.
- NAFTA will grant immediate access into Mexico for Canadian-made medium and heavy duty trucks and buses, and immediate, significant improvements in access for automobiles. Domestic auto, truck and bus manufacturers believe NAFTA will lead to more production and jobs in Canada.

Canadians can compete.

The rapid growth in Canadian exports to such low-wage countries as Malaysia (up 61% to $296 million in 1991 over 1988) and Thailand (up 33% to $357 million), speaks volumes about the capabilities of Canadian men and women and the reputation Canadian products and services command in international markets. And this year's surge in Canadian exports to Mexico confirms that we have what it takes to boost our share of that expanding market.

The GATT. Where Canada stands on worldwide trade talks.

Right now, representatives of 108 countries are in Geneva trying to hammer out new rules for international trade.

Called the "Uruguay Round", the current series of negotiations has been ongoing for six years. Canada, as a founding member of the GATT, has been at the table all the way and, like the other nations, hopes to see a successful conclusion before year end.

Among the difficult issues being addressed at the GATT negotiations are rules on services, intellectual property and agricultural subsidies. As a major player in all three sectors and as the world's 8th largest economy, Canada has a lot at stake. That's why GATT membership has been, and remains, a cornerstone of Canada's international trade policy.

HOW CANADA TRADES WITH THE REST OF THE WORLD

Yes, we can! Canadian exporters prove it.

Canada is coming out of the recession and exports are leading the recovery. For the first six months of 1992, Canada's exports hit an all-time high!

Canada/U.S. free trade has played a major role in this export success story. Since 1988, our cumulative exports to the U.S. are up almost 11%. In April of this year, our exports to the United States hit an all-time high of $10 billion. And our current merchandise trade surplus with the U.S. is running at an annual rate of $17 billion.

Can Canada compete? Yes, we can. And our exporters are proving it.

Note the strong upsurge in exports following the Canada/U.S. Free Trade Agreement signed in 1988. This year, exports are setting all-time records.

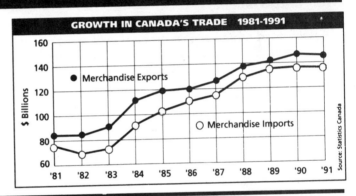

Canada is changing from a raw materials exporter to an exporter of job-creating, high value-added manufactured goods.

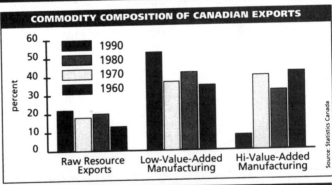

High technology products are becoming an increasingly important component of Canada's export mix.

Look Again at the Free Trade Deal

Well before the FTA, it was hard to find a Canadian economy distinct from the U.S. economy. It may shortly become impossible.

Mel Watkins

Mel Watkins is Professor of Economics and Political Science at the University of Toronto and a long-time political activist. In 1987-88 he was a special advisor to the Canadian Labour Congress on free trade.

Some may feel that after three years of life under the Free Trade Agreement, and more like five years of bickering between proponents and opponents, we ought to strive for a consensus as to what the deal has meant for Canada, and we ought all to try to work together for the benefit of Canadians. I agree, though both are much easier said than done. If a consensus could be arrived at with respect to the economic impact of the FTA, it seems to me it would have to go something like this: We don't know for sure; we can't really tell. Two reasons would be cited for that uncertain state of affairs.

Firstly, it's too early. It will be five years, 10 years—I heard top government negotiator Michael Hart say recently perhaps as many as 15—before we can tell. This agreement, after all, is about restructuring over the long pull.

Secondly, there are too many other things going on to have any hope of isolating the effects of the FTA, like high real interest rates, an overvalued dollar, a wounding recession. The necessary *ceteris paribus* assumption is shot to hell.

The consensus verdict on the FTA, then, would be the famous Scottish verdict of "not proven."

Now if I were of the pro-FTA persuasion, I would agree to this because it is the best I could hope for under present material circumstances. And, in fact, that is what many of them are mostly saying. For my part though, while I think there's a hard core of truth to that verdict, I have some problems, intellectual and otherwise, with such a nihilistic position.

For starters, why weren't we (meaning the Canadian public) told ahead of time that we wouldn't be able to tell 'till God knows when what the FTA was doing to us? Instead, promises were made, about jobs and a higher standard of living, and not just by the politicians who specialize in such behavior and should never be believed, but also by economists and business people. I recall no mention then of how there might have to be short-run pain for long-run gain. Certainly not, as the same Michael Hart asserts, how job loss might be proof the agreement is working—truly an incredible argument if you think about it, since it simply means that, no matter what happens, free trade is a good thing.

The public was apparently sold a hyped-up bill of goods. Perhaps that is why, as the polls show, the Canadian people have become highly suspicious of this agreement and have turned against the Tory government which pushed it.

I make this point not to refight old wars but because the same people who misled us on Canada-U.S. free trade are now using the same arguments to try to sell us on free trade with Mexico. Once bitten, however, is surely, rationally, to be twice shy.

What is at issue here, too, is not only the behavior of some economists who took the public podium to oversell the FTA, but troubling questions about the usefulness of economics, a matter about which, as an economist, I have a professional interest. How come orthodox, mainstream economics enables you to predict, before it happens, with absolute certainty what will happen, but then is unable to figure out after the event what has happened? Specifically, why can it confidently claim ahead of time that there will be benefits, but then is unable to find them two years later? Is this seriously to be thought how a real science—even a real social science—would perform?

The eminent political scientist Richard Simeon, who was one of the research directors for the Macdonald

 From *Policy Options*, Vol. 13, No. 2, March 1992, pp. 3-5. This article first appeared in *Policy Options*, Canada's Forum for Public Policy Debate.

Commission which played such an important role in legitimizing free trade, has described how the economists on the staff made the argument for free trade much more convincingly than did the business groups who presented briefs. Then the economists said, in effect, that political scientists and such like who might have doubts didn't need to be listened to because free trade was an economic issue in which they alone had expertise. What, pray tell, was that vaunted expertise?

What about the assertion that we can't tell because of all the other things that are wrong with the economy? This is news? This is a surprise? I am even tempted to say, on the basis of evidence available to anyone willing to look, that the pro-market neo-conservative mindset that brings you free trade is perfectly capable of bringing you these other things. Why were these possibilities not factored into the forecasts?

Why wasn't the government clearly told ahead of time that if it created a lousy macro-environment that would lessen the potential benefits from the FTA? In fact, however, didn't some economists imply, even explicitly assert, that the FTA was sufficient unto itself, thereby inviting the kind of wash-our-hands-of-any-responsibility-for-positive-economic-policy that the government is now pursuing?

Richard Lipsey, perhaps this country's most preeminent orthodox economist, liked to clobber critics who hadn't taken Economics 100 by insisting, during the great free trade debate, that an economy couldn't help but benefit from free trade because if there were problems in trade, the exchange rate would fall and equilibrium would be restored—as if exchange rates in today's world were, in any immediate or reliable sense, solely or even primarily determined by trade. Now the economy's having all these problems, but the exchange rate stays merrily up there. It is part of the problem, not part of the solution, and Lipsey is off studying something else—tech change, I think—with the help of big bucks from a government that can't afford to help workers who have lost their jobs because of free trade.

An important point in all this is that the benefits from free trade are potential rather than automatic. They don't just necessarily happen. Can you imagine, say, the Japanese believing otherwise? The greatest single failure of Canadian economists is not their advocacy of free trade—that was to be expected: it is a universal bias of the profession—but their disinterest in making the FTA work in a manner beneficial to most Canadians. It is they who threaten to give trade a bad name and feed isolationist forces. Statements of faith—exhortations to business to shape up or macho calls for action, which fall so easily from the lips of those economists in the employ of faculties of management—are substitutes for thought and for policy, not policy itself.

As the evidence accumulates that the FTA is not working, or is not working well enough, yet nothing is done, the public may decide it wants this agreement abrogated,

and it will deserve to be abrogated. Everyone can perhaps agree that will be a real mess.

But maybe we have to take mainstream economics, warts and worse, seriously because it's the only intellectual game in town. Wrong. Another paradigm informed the critics like myself: the political economy paradigm. It is an intellectually respectable and scholarly discipline, with its own publications, much of them from university presses, and its own learned journal *Studies in Political Economy;* it has the same right to be listened to as does orthodox economics.

Unlike orthodox economics, political economy has a sense of history, an understanding of how even in the longest of runs things that look good in the abstract don't always actually work out for the good. A relevant case in point is the theorizing of David Ricardo about the Law of Comparative Advantage and the mutual benefits from trade.

The task now is to make this damned deal work.

The story is spun out in terms of two countries and two commodities: for Ricardo they were England and Portugal trading cloth and wine. Two centuries later, do we not have a notion of who benefitted more from that exchange? Did England not go on to become the industrial workshop of the world while Portugal still struggles to industrialize? Or consider the fate of the Maritimes within Canada as a common market. Maritimers thought their manufacturing would flourish; orthodoxy says it should have, but it didn't. How do we know that Ontario won't now—isn't now—experiencing the same fate within North America? Political economy tells us that whole regions and countries can underdevelop rather than develop, be losers rather than winners.

Political economy, too, has a sense of the specificity of the Canadian economy, of its resource or staples bias and its underdeveloped manufacturing sector. With that in mind, political economists worried that the FTA was mostly about our getting access to the U.S. market for resources and about the U.S. getting access to our resources, particularly energy (a resource so critical that countries will go to war for it). What if the market forces unleashed by the FTA worked, in the nature of things, to weaken weak sectors and strengthen only the already strong? It would follow that the winner would simply be the resource sector, and all other sectors—manufacturing, services, even much of agriculture—would be losers.

Let us recall the Bank of Nova Scotia study that got leaked before the 1988 election, and so warned. Look now at the emasculation of the National Energy Board, unable any longer to conserve natural gas reserves in Canada for Canadian use. Most revealing, and frightening of all, witness the deindustrialization of Ontario. Free trade, the alleged instrument to make the Canadian economy mature, seems rather to be entrenching its truncated character.

As well, political economy has a sense that trade isn't just an economic phenomenon: that it has political consequences, that they can be highly problematic, and that they can play back on the economic effects. Take the critical issue of national unity. The Macdonald Commission said getting rid of tariffs would remove the prime cause of regional alienation and thereby promote national unity. Economists—Richard Lipsey, John Crispo, Tom Courchene—said that, just as the Law of Comparative Advantage guaranteed that Canada would be better off, so it guaranteed that every region would be better off. We would all necessarily end up feeling better about each other.

If the economic forecasts were dubious, these political forecasts were naive and dangerously wrong and may yet cost us this country. The free trade election exposed a basic cleavage between Quebec and English Canada which was evident for all who cared to listen. Jacques Parizeau said repeatedly that the FTA would facilitate Quebec's independence and that was why he and the PQ liked it. The late Donald Smiley, that most distinguished scholar of Canadian federalism, warned us that Canada was a loosly-linked political community that could fracture in the face of the major change in the rules, from east-west ties to north-south pulls, that would flow from the FTA. He took Parizeau's point seriously. Though a political conservative, he opposed the FTA on these political grounds. But not being an economist, he was ignored.

Consider also the matter of Canadian-American relations and of the relative autonomy of the Canadian economy within North America. Canadian ownership of the Canadian economy had been growing throughout the 1970s and 1980s relative to foreign and American ownership and there was increasing Canadian investment abroad, particularly in the U.S., and these were widely cited as evidence of the increasing maturity of the Canadian business class. With the FTA, there is at least anecdotal evidence that both American and Canadian capital are fleeing Canada. What sense is there in claiming we have a mature business class if the result is to lessen the prospects for our own economic development?

Well before the FTA, it was hard to find a Canadian economy distinct from the American economy. It may shortly become impossible. Anyone who believes this has no political consequences may qualify for a PhD in economics but should not be allowed out alone.

I note that the Americans are willing to admit us to the trade talks with Mexico in the light of our unstinting support for them in the Gulf War. That should be called political linkage, or political fallout, from the FTA.

Orthodox economics predicted pie in the sky, political economists doom and disaster. As a committed Canadian who wants this country to flourish economically and politically, I derive no satisfaction from the fact that so far my side seems to have made the better forecast.

The best that can be said, in my view, is that the economic consequences of the FTA have been problematic and the political consequences highly adverse, with the additional point that the latter are likely to play back adversely on the former. A question mark and a cost sum to a cost.

Let that gloomy observation be my penultimate point. My final position is to reiterate, as an economist and as a citizen, that the task now is to make this damned deal work. Here there is mostly bad news but a glimmer of hope.

We are stuck for a while longer with this useless government in Ottawa wreaking havoc on the country. We have, however, a government in Ontario, where so much of the manufacturing is, that seems prepared to sit down with business and labor and anyone else and talk, not about what can't be done, but what can, and should, be done to turn the Ontario economy around and revive its industrial base. I most earnestly hope that happens.

WHY WE MUST JOIN NAFTA

In a three-way free trade deal with Mexico and the United States, Canada will pick up more in high-wage jobs than it will lose in low-wage jobs.

Léo-Paul Dana

Léo-Paul Dana recently returned to Canada from doing ethnographic field research in the United States and Mexico. His most recent work specialized on international and cross-cultural aspects of management, and he has published several articles on the Canada-United States Free Trade Agreement including contributions to the *Journal of Small Business Management* and the *Journal of Small Business and Entrepreneurship*. He is now teaching graduate classes at McGill University.

IN JUNE 1990, THE UNITED STATES AND MEXICO announced intentions to negotiate a bilateral free-trade agreement. In September 1990, the Canadian government announced its own desire: to be included too. Less than a year later, in May 1991, the United States accepted to launch free-trade negotiations with Canada as well as Mexico.

A three-party North American Free Trade Agreement (NAFTA) would result in a market of 360 million consumers and a combined output of $7 trillion ($6 trillion U.S.). Yet some Canadians are not convinced that this would help Canada. After all, it does seem difficult to compete with a *maquiladora* plant which pays its employees the Mexican equivalent of approximately $1 per hour!

Will jobs go south leaving Canadians unemployed? Actually, wages are not the primary determinant for selecting manufacturing sites, but only one of many factors affecting final product cost. If low-wage countries were a veritable threat, then Haiti, India and Zaire would be prosperous.

In fact, free trade is a major force in encouraging free markets and private initiative; it is a means to cope with revolutionary changes in markets and technology. By the opening of borders, people are faced with unprecedented opportunities made possible by enlarged markets and economies of scale.

International Cooperation

Free trade agreements are nothing new. When Nuremberg was a city-state in the Roman Empire, it set up free-trade agreements with 70 other cities; although it lacked a good waterway, arable land and natural resources, its free-trade agreements enabled it to become a cosmopolitan business centre.

Five centuries later, the following are among the significant trade agreements of modern times:

1. Belgium, the Netherlands and Luxembourg participated in a customs union dating back to 1921;
2. The Treaty of Rome, which came into effect on January 1, 1958, established the European Economic Community (EEC), which has been increasing its size and scope, with the target date of 1992 for a united Europe;
3. The Stockholm convention of 1959 established the European Free Trade Association, which allows Austria, Iceland, Norway, Sweden and Switzerland to maintain different external tariffs while eliminating internal tariffs on industrial products originating within the free trade area;
4. In 1960 the European Free Trade Area came into effect.
5. The Latin American Free Trade Association linked Argentina, Bolivia, Brazil, Chile, Columbia, Ecuador, Mexico, Paraguay, Peru, Uruguay and Venezuela in February 1960, and the 1980 Treaty of Montevideo restructured these into the Latin American Integration Association (Associacion Latino-Americana de Integracion);
6. Also in 1960, the Central American Common Market (Mercado Comun Centro Americano) was born, with a general treaty between Costa Rica, Guatemala, El Salvador, Honduras and Nicaragua;
7. From 1965 until its integration into the EEC, the United Kingdom-Ireland Free Trade Agreement was in effect;
8. The Organisation Commune Africaine et Mauricienne was founded in 1965, with proposed objectives including customs reform possibly leading to the establishment of an African Common Market between Benin (Dahomey, at the time), Central African Republic, Ivory Coast, Mauritius, Niger, Rwanda, Senegal, Togo and Burkina Faso (formerly Upper Volta);
9. CARICOM, the Caribbean Community and Common Market was formed in 1973 as a movement towards unity among Antigua, Barbados, Belize, Dominica, Grenada, Guyana, Jamaica, Montserrat, St. Christopher and Nevis, St. Lucia, St. Vincent, the Grenadines and Trinidad and Tobago;
10. Also in 1973, Venezuela joined Bolivia, Chile, Columbia and Ecuador in the Andean Common Market, with plans to phase out foreign ownership of enterprises;
11. ASEAN, the Association of South East Asian Nations, originally established in Bangkok in 1967, resulted in an economic association between Indonesia, Malaysia, the Philippines, Singapore and Thailand, having its first summit meeting in Bali during February 1976;
12. In 1983, the Australia-New Zealand Closer Economic Relations Agreement came into effect;
13. In 1985, the United States-Israel Agreement came into effect;
14. The Canada-United States Free Trade Agreement (FTA) is

From *Policy Options*, Vol. 13, No. 2, March 1992, pp. 6-8. This article first appeared in *Policy Options*, Canada's Forum for Public Policy Debate.

broader in scope than most other free trade agreements. The initiative began in 1985. The agreement came into effect on January 1, 1989, with the intent of eliminating tariffs by January 1, 1998.

Whereas the Canada-United States agreement provides for liberalization in all sectors of the economy, even agriculture, none other includes binding commitments on trade in services, business, travel or investment. Given the concentration of small business in service industries, and in consideration of the entrepreneur's need to travel, this is of particular interest to small business.

Free trade is Darwinian. In the absence of tariff protection, the inefficient expect to be weeded out if incapable of competing. Many industries were expecting to suffer in Canada because of the Canada-United States Free Trade Agreement. However, the global picture for Canadians is far from gloomy. Trade between the two nations is growing rapidly, and in Canada's favor, despite the depreciation of the U.S. dollar: Canada's merchandise trade surplus with the United States in 1990 was more than $17 billion (U.S.), up from $14 billion (U.S.) in 1988, the last year prior to the agreement.

Furthermore, investment in Canada has been strongly stimulated by new opportunities arising from free trade. The average investment in textiles and clothing manufacture during 1988-1990 is up 24 per cent and 17 per cent respectively from 1985 to 1987.

United States-Mexico Trade

Up to the mid-1980s, Mexico's trade policy was based on an import substitution strategy, and international trade was discouraged. Import licenses controlled import levels, and regulated all imports up to 1983; up to 1986 applied tariffs were as high as 100 per cent.

Then policy shifted towards one of export growth. In August 1986, Mexico joined the General Agreement on Tariffs and Trade (GATT). Five years later import licenses covered less than 4 per cent of the categories in the Mexican tariff schedule; tariffs had been reduced such that the maximum rate was 20 per cent.

Such extensive liberalization in trade and investment helped bilateral trade between Mexico and the United States to increase by over 100 per cent from 1986 to 1991. By 1991 two-thirds of Mexican imports came from the U.S., and four-fifths of Mexico's manufactured goods were exported to the United States.

Numerous U.S. manufacturers, including Ford Motor Co. and Kodak, opened *maquiladoras* to assemble components in Mexico; these created jobs in Mexico as an alternative to assembling in other low-wage countries further away. For manufacturers, this meant efficiency; the alternative would have been increased transportation costs to plants overseas. The result of low-cost production is a more competitive product, increased sales and a net increase in jobs in the U.S..

Total bilateral trade in 1990 was $60 million (U.S.). U.S. exports to Mexico were growing faster than Mexican exports to the United States. While Mexico was selling auto parts, cars, cattle, coffee, oil, silver, televisions and tomatoes, the United States sold other auto parts, electronic parts, grain, oil products and plastic products to Mexico.

As United States-Mexico trade flourished, Canada had to choose between (a) staying left out and watching the United States and Mexico prosper bilaterally, or (b) entering tri-party negotiations.

Staying out of free trade with Mexico, Canada might in the short-term avoid job losses in certain industries and painful restructuring of some sectors. The inherent danger, however, would be a loss of competitiveness at the international level: almost 25 per cent of Canadian imports are used in the manufacture of Canadian exports. If the United States were to sign its own bilateral free trade agreement with Mexico, then U.S. manufacturers would obtain low-cost components, duty-free from Mexico.

If Canadian manufacturers could not obtain the same low-cost components duty-free, costs of goods sold would be relatively higher for the Canadian manufacturer. The result would be a less competitive Canadian product, and a decline in exports. Such a drop in demand for Canadian exports would then cost Canadian jobs.

Meanwhile, U.S. manufacturers with access to lower cost Mexican components would also have greater ease of exporting to Mexico, a market of 86 million people. This would allow the Americans (but not the Canadians) to increase economies of scale, and become even more competitive, even in Canada, squeezing the Canadian manufacturers out, and costing Canada even more jobs!

Then entering trilateral negotiations was the only feasible option for Canada. The alternative would run the risk of pricing Canadians out of U.S. markets, and because of the FTA, out of Canadian markets too—if U.S. manufacturers were to lower costs thanks to Mexico but Canadian competitors could not.

Furthermore, if Canada were not included in the agreement, investors would find Canada less attractive because the United States would be the only country from which they could serve Canada, the United States and Mexico.

What Canada Could Gain from NAFTA

I. Competitiveness: A reduction of barriers arising from such an agreement would stimulate increased trade and investments, allowing producers to achieve economies of scale, thus improving the international competitiveness of producers in each of the participating countries. Although Mexico has a comparative advantage when it comes to wages for unskilled positions, Canadian firms with better educated employees would have the advantage in high-tech sectors. Access to cheaper labor and components from Mexico would improve Canada's advantage further.

II. New Market: The new Mexican middle class has been on a binge for consumer items. Yet Canada-Mexico trade was only $2 billion (U.S.) in 1990. NAFTA would give Canadians improved access to a market of 86 million people. This would also allow companies in the service sector (including banking, engineering, architecture, law, insurance and telecommunications) in Canada to expand into Mexico. Also, increased manufacturing in Mexico would increase Mexican demand for machinery and transportation equipment which Canada could provide.

III. Energy and Raw Materials: Closer ties with Mexico may lead to a more reliable source of petroleum in a stable country within close geographical proximity. This would protect Canada from a possible dependence on Middle East sources. Apart from abundant oil supplies, Mexico could provide much silver, coffee beans, vegetables and meat, at lower prices.

IV. Penetration into Latin America: NAFTA may prove to be a logical stepping stone towards free trade across the Americas. Even in the event that it is not, once Canadians are familiar with doing business in Mexico, it will be easier to expand into other Latin American markets. Mexico already has established marketing channels with its southern neighbours, and this could be valuable to Canadians in the future.

Recommendations

The above discourse attempts to justify Canada's participation in NAFTA. Yet negotiators should not enter such a deal blindly. The author presents a few recommendations:

1. The agenda should include non-tariff barriers as well as tariffs. Even in the European Economic Community (EEC) non-tariff barriers have been impediments to trade. Belgian law, for example, requires a garment labelled as "pure wool" to contain at least 97 per cent wool. A "pure wool" garment which comes from France contains only 85 per cent wool despite the label "pure wool." This technical standard restricts French wool from entering Belgium. Dairy industry regulations in France prohibit importation of cheese produced from milk powder. This prevents some Dutch cheeses from being imported into France. Dairy industry regulations in Italy require a health certificate of inspection at the time of milking. This requirement necessitates Italian customs inspection on location, making it costly for Bavarian milk producers to export to nearby Italy. In order to prevent such problems in NAFTA, non-tariff barriers should be discussed up front.

2. The agenda should include the environment. Differences in standards among EEC countries has caused difficulties there. West Germany, for example, prohibits importing of fuel with a high lead content. This deters the imports of some French and Italian cars; however, the justifiable domestic purpose for this barrier is that West Germany is concerned about the air pollution caused by the exhaust of automobiles using high lead content gasoline.

3. The agenda should include agriculture. More avocados grow in Mexico than in any other country in the world; yet protective rules prevent the U.S. from buying them, because of allegations that Mexican avocados may hurt the California industry. Special clauses may be inspired by the FTA. Although Articles 401 and 702 call for the elimination of all tariffs over a period of 10 years, Chapter Seven (of Part Two) allows Canada to restore temporarily tariffs on fresh fruits and vegetables for a 20-year period under depressed price conditions. This could help Canada's horticultural industry by allowing it an opportunity to adjust to more open trading conditions, and a similar measure could protect U.S. agriculture from Mexico.

4. The agenda should include health standards. From February 1984 to December 1988, Mexican meat was banned from the United States as a result of noncompliance with U.S. standards for toxic residue detection and control. Common health standards would reduce such problems in the future.

5. The agenda should include paperwork requirements. Although free trade, in theory, simplifies trade, in the case of the FTA, considerable paperwork is necessary to obtain certificates of origin, which are required in order to be exempted from the payment of duty! During the FTA debates, the Canadian Federation of Independent Business (CFIB) strongly supported the initiative, based on the majority view of its small business membership. (The CFIB regularly surveys its thousands of members from coast to coast.) More recently, however, the CFIB reports a major complaint concerning excessive paperwork.

6. The agenda should include a "rules of origin" clause. The FTA has a "rules of origin" clause which benefits U.S. apparel manufacturers because it allows clothing to qualify for tariff reduction when the garment is made from domestically-produced fabric. While U.S. manufacturers tend to use U.S.-made fabric, much Canadian-made apparel is made from imported material.

Gephardt Criticizes Trade Pact

Urges Renegotiation On Jobs, Pollution

Keith Bradsher

Special to The New York Times

WASHINGTON, Sept. 9—Dealing a blow to Congressional prospects for the North American Free Trade Agreement, the House majority leader, Richard A. Gephardt, said today that the labor and environmental provisions were so badly flawed that the pact should be renegotiated.

Mr. Gephardt, one of the most influential House Democrats on trade issues, ran for President in 1988 on a platform that emphasized restrictions on imports from Japan. His last-moment support last year was crucial to the narrow approval of the measure giving President Bush the authority to negotiate the agreement among the United States, Mexico and Canada. Mexico and Canada do not want to renegotiate the pact.

Worried that support for the pact could hurt them among constituents anxious about job losses to Mexico, not even the Republicans at a Senate Finance Committee meeting on Tuesday and at a House Ways and Means Committee hearing today made any commitments to back it.

Easy Target for Criticism

But neither house will vote on the issue until next year, making it easy to criticize now and to support later. "Almost everybody who is carping to you now will vote for it," predicted Representative Bill Thomas, a California Republican on the trade subcommittee.

Mr. Gephardt's call for renegotiation followed a chorus of complaints from Senator Lloyd Bentsen, the Texas Democrat who heads the Finance Committee, and Representative Dan Rostenkowski, the Illinois Democrat who heads the Ways and Means Committee, about White House attacks on Gov. Bill Clinton for not taking a position on the pact. Mr. Bentsen and Mr. Rostenkowski said the election-year attacks had threatened the bipartisan consensus for free trade and the accord's prospects for eventual passage.

Protecting Their Candidate

The complaints reflected Congressional sensitivity to Mr. Clinton's possible vulnerability on the issue. "They're lining up to provide some cover for their Presidential candidate," said Thomas E. Mann, the director of governmental studies at the Brookings Institution in Washington.

But George C. Shipley, a Democratic consultant based in Austin, Tex., said he doubted that the issue would affect Mr. Clinton much at the polls because not enough voters were paying close attention to it.

Robert T. Matsui, a California Democrat and strong free trader on the Ways and Means Committee's trade subcommittee, said his constituents in Sacramento are ignoring the pact. "There's really no smart reason politically for a Democrat to support the fast-track or the Nafta," he said. "Those of us who have supported Nafta for policy reasons get no thanks."

But Mr. Gephardt said he had found the agreement deeply unpopular as he toured the Middle West. "The American people get it, this issue resonates with them, and the Nafta agreement is rapidly becoming, substantively and symbolically, representative of everything that is wrong in their lives economically," Mr. Gephardt said.

The consensus for free trade appears to be wavering.

Mr. Gephardt had said, before the agreement was finished, that shortcomings in it probably could be repaired by the legislation needed to put its provisions into American law. Today, he attributed his shift in position to his reading of the text of the agreement and conversations with voters.

President Bush announced the agreement on Aug. 12, and released its voluminous text in two installments on Friday and Tuesday. All drafts had been classified on the ground that public debate might limit the flexibility of the American negotiating team during the 14 months of talks. Though members of Congress were allowed to look at the drafts, many staff members lacked the necessary security clearances.

Areas That Raise Objections

Speaking at a conference here sponsored by the A.F.L.-C.I.O. and four other environmental, labor and consumer groups, Mr. Gephardt said the agreement failed to address specific pollution and workers' rights issues in Mexico and should have done so. "I call upon the Bush Administration to cease further efforts to win Congressional approval of the current North American Free Trade Agreement," he said, urging President Bush to renegotiate the pact or leave it until next year.

Asked afterward whether Mr. Clinton should renegotiate the pact if it is left until next year, Mr. Gephardt replied, "A lot of it can be done through the implementing legislation—I think some of it has to be done through renegotiation."

Mr. Gephardt's criticisms drew a sharp response from the Administration. "The Nafta will generate more jobs, provide more environmental protection and make America more competitive than has any other trade agreement, including trade agreements for which Mr. Gephardt has voted in the past," said Kathleen Lydon, the White House's chief spokeswoman on trade issues.

What Gephardt Wants

Mr. Gephardt said the agreement should include worker protection rules for Mexico and a special commission to issue bonds for environmental cleanup along the border. He called, as he had in July, for a tax on trade to help pay for the cleanup and to pay for retraining workers who lose their jobs to Mexico.

This tax should be "far lower than the current levy" on imports from Mexico, which averages about 4 percent, he said in the speech. But later he said when talking to reporters, "It may be 2 percent; it may be 3 percent."

In her testimony today before the Ways and Means Committee, Carla A. Hills, the United States trade representative, dismissed the idea of a border tax. "The whole purpose of the North American Free Trade Agreement is to lower barriers, not to raise taxes, and to do so would defeat the very purpose of the agreement," she said.

Mrs. Hills also identified for the first time those sectors of the economy that she thought would be most vulnerable to import competition from Mexico as a result of the free trade pact: glass and some farm products during certain seasons. The American household glass and fruit and vegetable industries are labor-intensive and are already having trouble in competing with imports from Mexico.

CANADA
LOVE IT OR LEASE IT

*In his latest book, The Betrayal of Canada,
economic nationalist Mel Hurtig lambastes
the Tory government over free trade and
the damage it, and other federal policies,
have wrought on Canada's economy*

Mel Hurtig

Special to The Globe and Mail
Edmonton

Shortly after the free-trade agreement went into effect, I spoke at a service-club dinner in a small Ontario city. The person who drove me from my hotel in Toronto and back was a senior executive with a Canadian manufacturing firm that owned plants in four Canadian provinces. He said that soon after the free-trade agreement was signed, his company purchased a large factory in the southern United States. In Canada, the firm paid an average of $16 an hour, plus benefits. In the U.S., they paid $6.50 an hour, with no benefits—no medicare, no pension plan, inferior unemployment protection and no pregnancy leave. As well, working hours were longer, safety practices were almost nonexistent and there was no air-conditioning in the factory. He said that if you saw how dreadful the conditions were in the washrooms, you simply wouldn't believe it. He then said, "Guess where all our new investment will be

taking place? And guess where we'll be closing plants in the future?"

My overriding concern with free trade before the deal was signed was about where new investment would take place. I was also worried about the basic theory of free trade, which assumes that benefits will accrue if both countries are enjoying almost full employment. Canada has had consistently high unemployment because it is a branch-plant country. Third, I wondered how free trade could possibly have any relevance when two-thirds to three-quarters of the two-way trade in many industries is conducted between parent companies and their subsidiaries or affiliates. And finally, I and others worried that Canada had weakened its bargaining power by its repeated assertions that free trade was necessary for its economic future.

There were other reasons to be apprehensive. But none of us, in our worst nightmares, ever dreamed the government would sign as horrendously bad a deal as it did. The Americans got what they wanted,

GRAPHICS BY BERNARD BENNELL

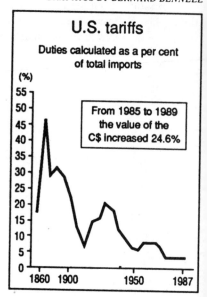

U.S. tariffs

Duties calculated as a per cent
of total imports

From 1985 to 1989
the value of the
C$ increased 24.6%

(%)

55 50 45 40 35 30 25 20 15 10 5 0

1860 1900   1950   1987

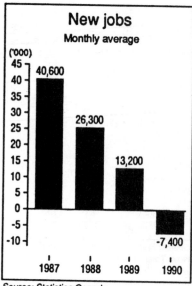

New jobs

Monthly average

('000)

45 — 40,600
40
35
30
25 — 26,300
20
15
10 — 13,200
5
0
-5
-10 — -7,400

1987   1988   1989   1990

Source: Statistics Canada.

From *The Globe and Mail*, October 5, 1991, pp. D1, D4. Reprinted by permission.

principally Canada's natural resources and the unimpeded right to buy up much of the rest of the country. Canadians got guaranteed access to integration with the U.S.

Whatever faults Americans may have, they are not stupid. If Canada had to have an agreement, Canadians would have to pay. And pay we did. The U.S. obtained almost everything it wanted, including vital concessions that most Canadians

knew nothing about, or which they had little reason to believe would be part of an agreement that most thought to be essentially about tariffs.

The trade agreement wasn't about tariffs. Over the past 40 years, tariffs have been progressively reduced throughout the world (see U.S. tariffs chart). For years, Canada has sold substantially more merchandise in the U.S. than it has bought.

Even if Canada had made an infinitely better deal with the U.S., the trade deal still had a crucial, fatal flaw. It seems incomprehensible that the supposedly capable people who negotiated the deal were oblivious to

the potentially disastrous impact of a large increase in the value of the Canadian dollar vis-à-vis the U.S. dollar. Incredibly, we allowed the value of the Canadian dollar to appreciate almost 25 per cent from the time free trade became an issue in Canada to the time it went into effect in 1989.

Astonishing! We give away control of our country to abolish tariffs of 2 or 3 per cent and then, at the same time, we adopted a strategy that put a 25-per-cent penalty on all Canadian exports to the U.S. The high value of the Canadian dollar both hinders exports and encourages imports.

How could Canada have been so stupid as to enter into a level-play-

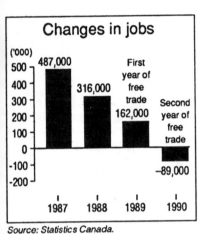

Changes in jobs

Source: Statistics Canada.

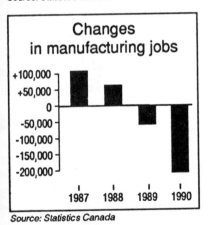

Changes in manufacturing jobs

Source: Statistics Canada

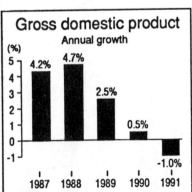

Gross domestic product
Annual growth

Source: Bank of Canada & Dept. of Finance
Note: Total value of goods and services produced by residents and non-residents of Canada, after inflation is removed.

Every one cent rise in the value of the Canadian dollar decreases our exports by $1.3-billion, says the Canadian Exporters Association.

◆

From 1987 to 1990, car trips from Canada to the U.S. doubled from three million to some six million, and cross-border spending jumped from $800-million to $2-billion.

◆

In the last 10 years for which figures are available (1978-'87), foreign-controlled firms received some 40 per cent of the profits in all of Canada's non-financial industries.

Business investment
Annual growth

Source: Statistics Canada
Note: Includes new investment in plants, machinery, equipment and inventory.

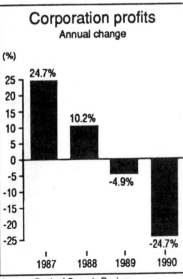

Corporation profits
Annual change

Source: Bank of Canada Review
Note: Before taxes.

In the first year of free trade, Canada's unemployment rate was 1.3 per cent higher than the OECD average; in the second year, 2 per cent higher. This year, it will be almost 4 per cent higher.

◆

In 1984, Canada's share of total world exports was 5.1 per cent. By 1990, it was 3.8 per cent.

◆

Of the 500 largest companies in Canada, 54 per cent are 100 per cent foreign-owned. Another 88 companies are partially foreign-owned.

ing-field agreement and then send our team out onto the field with the heavy iron balls and thick chains of high interest rates and an artificially high dollar?

There has been much rumour and speculation about whether there was a secret deal to guarantee a higher Canadian dollar. Without the behind-closed-doors scenario, it is impossible to explain how even the obsequious Mulroney government could have been so incredibly inept.

The trade agreement came with a promise of hundreds of thousands of new jobs—one Ottawa study predicted 370,000. This did not happen (see *New jobs* and *Changes in jobs*). Some 803,000 new jobs were created during the two years before the agreement, while only 73,000 new jobs were created in 1989 and 1990. By any measure, this is a staggering comparison.

The trend is reflected in today's unemployment figures. From January, 1989 (the first month of the agreement), to the end of June, 1991, the increase in the number of unemployed Canadians exceeded 452,000. By the end of June, there were 1,453,000 Canadians unemployed.

Even after the recession ends, there will be high unemployment, poor quality jobs, vastly underutilized capacity and a lower standard of living over all. It is safe to say that at least twice as many job layoffs in the current recession will be permanent compared with the recession of 1981–82. Some 60 to 70 per cent of the jobs recently lost in manufacturing and processing in Ontario and Quebec will be lost forever. In the last recession, only one-quarter of the job losses were permanent.

For the first time in Canadian history, more than two million Canadians are receiving welfare and more than 600,000 rely on food banks. Federal spending on job creation and training has been cut. Unemployment benefits have been reduced, and transfer payments from Ottawa to the provinces have been sharply cut back.

In the first two years of free trade, Canada lost 264,000 manufacturing jobs (see *Changes in manufacturing jobs*). Before the free-trade agreement, manufacturing jobs of member nations in the Organization for Economic Co-operation and Development accounted for, on average, 23.5 per cent of gross domestic product; in branch-plant Canada, it was only 19 per cent in 1988. By 1991, this had declined to 16 per cent. In terms of manufacturing as a share of

GDP, Canada is now nowhere near the top 20 nations.

The bottom line of a country's economic performance is the growth or decline of its GDP after inflation is removed (see *Gross domestic product*). Even the Department of Finance is predicting a decline of 1 per cent in real GDP for 1991 and a decline of 1.7 per cent in overall domestic economic activity. One brokerage house described the last quarter of 1990 and the first quarter of 1991 as "probably

Have we reached the

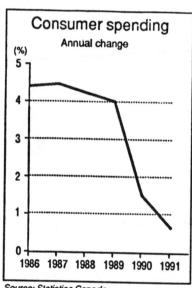

Consumer spending
Annual change

Source: Statistics Canada

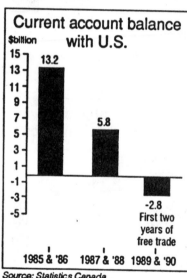

Current account balance with U.S.

Source: Statistics Canada

Merchandise trade surpluses with U.S.

Source: Statistics Canada

Foreign ownership
Comparative levels in non-financial industries (1989)

Source: Statistics Canada

the worst half-year for the Canadian economy since the Second World War." Before implementation of the agreement, from 1980 to 1988 inclusive, Canada's average annual real GDP increase was more than 3.5 per cent.

The OECD predicts that, of its 24 industrialized members, 21 will produce a better performance than Canada this year.

Canadians were repeatedly told that the free-trade agreement would produce bountiful amounts of new investment, leading to increased economic activity (*see Business investment*). The decline in business investment began shortly after the agreement went into effect, and investment has dropped drastically ever since. The estimated figure for 1991 is a further decline of 6 to 10 per cent. It is fascinating to note the comments of Simon Reisman, chief free-trade negotiator for Canada, in relation to investment. He has said that the true measure of the impact of the agreement on Canada's economy was not the number of jobs lost but the investment climate created—ironic words when one looks at both the actual investment figures and the job losses.

And what of the future? Vancouver entrepreneur Jimmy Pattison minces no words: "We're taking everything we've got and pushing into the U.S. . . . I keep telling our people to forget the border—it doesn't exist any more." Or the words of another

point of no return?

Foreign profits
1985

Mineral fuels	68%
Total mining	68%
Food processing & packaging	53%
Tobacco products	100%
Rubber products	84%
Textile mills	45%
Paper & allied industries	39%
Primary metals	46%
Machinery	63%
Transportation equipment	94%
Electrical products	67%
Non-metallic mineral products	71%
Petroleum & coal products	47%
Chemicals & chemical products	87%

Source: Corporations and Labour Unions Returns Act Report (1985).

Note: Represents the share of profits that foreign corporations took in Canadian industries.

Foreign-controlled firms buy 80 per cent of their business services from their parent companies or affiliates.

•

In 1985, research and development was 1.42 per cent of gross domestic product; now it is down to 1.36 per cent.

U.S. direct investment in Canada
1946–1990

	($bill.)
Net flow of U.S. direct investment into Canada	6.631
Dividend payments from Canada to the U.S.	69.460
Growth in the book value of U.S. direct investment in Canada	76.710

From 1985 to 1990, foreign-investment activity amounted to almost $88-billion; 92 per cent was for the takeover of businesses in Canada; only 8 per cent was in the form of new foreign business investment.

•

99 per cent of all Canadian corporate enterprises own just 14 per cent of assets and make just 25 per cent of profits

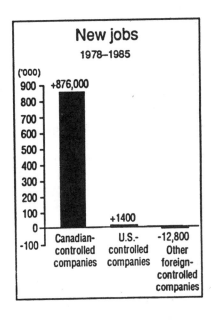

New jobs
1978–1985

('000)
- Canadian-controlled companies: +876,000
- U.S.-controlled companies: +1400
- Other foreign-controlled companies: -12,800

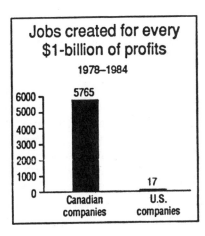

Jobs created for every $1-billion of profits
1978–1984

- Canadian companies: 5765
- U.S. companies: 17

Canadian patriot, Adam Zimmerman, chairman of Noranda Forest Inc.: "If you are in a business that can move, why bother with the hassle of staying in Canada?"

Looking back at the blind, bandwagon endorsement of the free-trade agreement by Canadian business, one can only be dismayed by how vacuous and naive much of their ideological rhetoric was (see Corporation profits). Now, the dismal profit figures are creating three reactions. Many businesses are simply moving to the U.S. or Mexico. Others are saying they cannot afford the taxes required to pay for social programs. The third reaction is an increasingly widespread understanding of how disastrous the agreement is for Canada.

During the trade debate, there were lavish promises about lower prices, consumer savings, reduced inflation and the abundant good life that would be certain to come. Canadian inflation rates for the two years before free trade and the two years after tell a different story (see Consumer spending).

People who are unemployed do not spend much. People with lowered standards of living tend to be careful spenders. People with little extra money do not buy a lot. People who are worried about their future are cautious. The same economic geniuses who brought us free trade also brought us high interest rates and the goods and services tax. A high school student entering first-year economics could have predicted the impact on the cost of living.

Canada has to sell more merchandise to the U.S. than it brings in to help offset the enormous costs of foreign investment in the country. Today's declining merchandise surpluses are ominous (see Merchandise trade surpluses with U.S.). In 1984, when Brian Mulroney became prime minister, Canada's share of total world exports was 5.1 per cent. By 1990, it was down to 3.8 per cent.

A far more important measurement of the real situation would include not only imports and exports but also local sales by U.S. com-panies located in Canada and by Canadian companies located in the U.S. Such a "product presence" merchandise-trade-balance measurement would substantially erode or completely wipe out our supposed trade surpluses with the U.S.

Two-way trade between Canada and the U.S. should also be measured in terms of jobs created and jobs lost. Our large trade surplus in crude products that produce comparatively few jobs—and our large deficit in labour-intensive finished products—substantially reduce our apparent trade benefits.

The real comprehensive bottom line of trade is the current account balance (see Current account balance with U.S.). That figure includes all the merchandise that is bought and sold plus "invisibles," such as money and service transactions flowing in and out of the country.

Canada had current account surpluses, not deficits, the year Mr. Mulroney became prime minister and in the two previous years. By contrast, our total current-account deficit for the first two years of free trade has been Canada's worst-ever two-year performance by far. The year Mr. Mulroney became prime minister, Canada had a $6.7-billion current-account surplus with the U.S.; but in the first two years of free trade, we had our first consecutive current-account deficit with the U.S. since the 1981–'82 recession.

The $42.759-billion current-account deficit for the past two years trans-lates into more than one million jobs. It means high interest rates, more reliance on foreign capital and more control of Canada by non-Canadians.

For each of the past five years, during the Conservatives' tenure, Canada's current-account deficits have exceeded the deficits for any previous years in the nation's history.

Whenever foreign takeovers threatened in Europe, the Europeans spoke of "the Canadian disease." Canada has consistently had rates of foreign ownership and control that would simply not be tolerated in other developed nations—or, increasingly, in any of the developing nations (see Foreign profits and Foreign ownership).

Bear in mind that 1990 saw a record growth in direct foreign investment in Canada, almost all of it for the takeover of businesses. It will be some time in 1993 (after the next federal election) before we shall learn exactly what the level of foreign ownership, control and profits was in 1990. We do know that large increases will appear in each industrial category.

I have yet to show the figures in the chart headed U.S. direct investment in Canada to a single person who has not found them astonishing, because they so directly fly in the face of the taken-for-granted, long-standing conventional wisdom in Canada about how "dependent" we are on U.S. investment. What it boils down to is that for every $1-billion of U.S. direct investment that comes into Canada, we sent back more than $10-billion to the U.S. in dividends. At the same time, the growth in the book value—that is, the balance-sheet value—of U.S. ownership of Canada was almost $77-billion. The real market value increase of U.S. control in Canada is probably closer to some $130-billion.

Who created all the new jobs in Canada in recent years? While foreign corporations in Canada were taking about one-third of all profits in this country—and doing so during a period when they managed to double their profits here—they actually reduced their employment in Canada (see New jobs).

Some Canadians who recognized the huge costs involved in foreign investment reluctantly still defend it because "at least it creates jobs." But, usually, when U.S. companies come into Canada to take over Canadian firms, they begin to transfer research and development back to the U.S., as well as much of their advertising and design (see Jobs created for every $1-billion of profit). When times get tough, more jobs end up back at head office or in a plant in the U.S. that is operating at less than capacity.

The truth is, foreign ownership

and foreign control, most of which is American, do not provide Canadians with jobs.

Since the signing of the free-trade agreement, Canada has been led steadfastly toward the point of no return. There are now in place legal constraints, severe restrictions and huge obstacles preventing any future elected government from carrying out the will of the people. As long as the agreement is in place, it binds the hands of the democratic process. In American ownership and control of our country, in energy, culture, social programs, fiscal and monetary powers, public ownership, resource policies and in dozens of other areas, the elected representatives of the people of Canada are unable to act in the best interests of their constituents.

As every day goes by, as more and more factories close forever, as more production in Canada is "rationalized," as more and more of Canada is bought up by non-Canadians, and as more Canadian standards and policies are harmonized with those in the U.S., the process becomes more irreversible. The integration and harmonization become accepted fact. The vulnerability grows to the point where future independence is inconceivable.

Recently, the chancellor of a major Canadian university and the former leader of an important provincial political party agreed over dinner in my home that it was now too late: Canada had no choice but to join the U.S. The June, 1991 issue of The Economist is direct and to the point: "Sooner or later, Canadians are going to become Americans. Too bad." Increasingly, young Canadians take the integration for granted. Increasingly, Canadians despair at the political vacuum they perceive.

Never before in my lifetime have I encountered a situation that so threatens the existence of our country. And never before have I felt so strongly that our nation and its people have been betrayed.

Adapted from The Betrayal of Canada, *by Mel Hurtig, published by Stoddart.*

'We're no protectionist bully'

Edward N. Ney

Edward N. Ney was the U.S. Ambassador to Canada, 1989–1992.

OTTAWA

A word from the bully to the boy scout:

By now, it is virtually an article of faith in this country that the United States, in denying duty-free status to Canadian-made Hondas and challenging the fairness of your softwood exports, is beating up on Canada for no good reason.

To some, this way of thinking is no doubt satisfying. It is also wrong.

Since these disputes jumped onto the front page, pundits and politicians across Canada have written off U.S. behavior as election-year bluster. It's not quite so simple.

In the first place, the United States has federal elections too often (in one form or another, every two years) for Canadians to attribute the current difficulties simply to political posturing. Second, both cases have long histories, complicating efforts to write them off as just an election-year phenomenon. Also, both issues are complex enough that reasonable people might disagree about them. And finally, Canada shares some of the responsibility for what is happening.

Let's look at the two issues currently generating heat.

First, softwood lumber. If Canada had not chosen last September to terminate the Memorandum of Understanding negotiated in 1986 to govern the softwood lumber trade, we would have no dispute on our hands. Canada's decision forced us to re-examine the status of softwood lumber imports, and take actions we felt were appropriate in defence of our own industry. The process is orderly and well-defined and it affords the Canadian government, the provinces and the lumber industry ample opportunity to present all pertinent evidence before a final determination is rendered.

Then there is the U.S. Customs audit of Honda Civics. Under the auto pact and the free-trade agreement, the United States and Canada agreed that the benefits of free trade should go to American and Canadian businesses. For this reason, rules of origin were conceived.

Within this context, the United States has an absolute right—as does Canada—to audit companies that claim the benefits of the FTA, to ensure they are in compliance with its provisions.

This process provides Honda with the opportunity to appeal Customs' preliminary finding and present additional evidence. Canada also has the right, which it has exercised, to seek consultations and resolution of the rules of origin issue.

Still, damage has been done. We must, therefore, take steps to defuse the anger and suspicion on both sides of the border, and restore the sense of common purpose that has long been the strength of our relationship.

This will not happen through talk of retaliation and trade wars, but through thoughtful and serious negotiation and consultation. We need to reach agreement on subsidies and the rules of origin, the complex, technical issues central to the softwood lumber and Honda cases.

We already have made progress on the subsidies question in the Uruguay Round of the General Agreement on Tariffs and Trade, and the trilateral North American free-trade talks provide an excellent opportunity to address rules of origin and North American content.

Nevertheless, at the moment, the perception in Canada is that the United States is in a bullying mood and playing a protectionist game. I might point out that Canada is no stranger to a tough style of play, having been known to fight for every advantage in its trading relationships. Here are just a few examples:

Canada continues to deny many U.S. service firms access to its market by levying customs duty on their specialized equipment, even though it will be returned to the United States after use.

Provincial marketing rules impede the sale of American beer and wine. Both the European Community and the United States have won GATT cases against Canadian practices.

Canada allows its food processors, but not those of other countries, to sell their products in large, non-standard package sizes, denying U.S. firms access to a significant portion of the Canadian market.

Most Canadians, I suspect, will look at these examples and chalk them up to legitimate self-defence. The same tactics employed by us would be called arrogant and protectionist.

All this talk of a protectionist America ignores the fact that the United States remains, by far, the world's biggest importing nation. We are the largest single market for foreign investment and, of all the major industrialized countries, we absorb the greatest share of exports from the developing world.

Last year, Canada sold more than $107-billion (Canadian) worth of merchandise to the United States; during that same period, we sent Canada goods worth more than $91-billion (Canadian). Realistically, in a relationship of this size, trade disputes are virtually unavoidable. In fact, given the immensity of our trade, maybe what's remarkable is how few disputes we have.

Which is not to diminish the seriousness of what is happening at the moment, or the damage it can cause.

One potential casualty is Canadian public support for the free-trade agreement, which seems to shoulder the blame every time something goes wrong in our trading relationship. If you were to believe some of the fantastic allegations lodged against the FTA, you might conclude that it is probably the single biggest threat to Western civilization.

What a surprise, then, to discover that, in fact, every serious, independent analysis of the FTA has found that it has softened the effects of the recession and contributed modestly to Canada's economic growth.

These are not my conclusions. They are the conclusions of studies undertaken by the Royal Bank of Canada and the University of Toronto's Institute for Policy Analysis.

What about Canada's trade performance with the United States under the agreement? According to Statistics Canada, during the last three years, while Canada's trade with the United States was growing by more than 4 per cent, Canadian exports to the rest of the world were shrinking by nearly the same amount.

And Trade Minister Michael Wilson noted recently that Canada's overall trade balance with the United States in the first two years of the FTA went from $14.2-billion to $17.5-billion—in Canada's favour.

Still, polls suggest that the trade deal continues to lose support in Canada. The latest criticism is that it has done nothing to prevent these current dustups.

This is a bum rap. The FTA was never expected to eliminate trade disputes. What it promised to do, and what it has done, is provide a framework to deal effectively with problems which, given human nature, will probably always be with us. These dispute-settlement procedures enable us to manage these problems and resolve them fairly and expeditiously.

I can't think of a single trading partner of the United States that would not welcome the access to U.S. markets—and the dispute-settlement mechanism when that access is threatened—that the FTA provides Canada.

Lately, I seem to hear a lot of people referring to the old adage that "a nation has no friends, only interest," to explain U.S. behaviour. I would argue that the strength of Canada–U.S. relations has always rested on our mutual ability to neither ignore our interest nor forget our friends. The time has come to draw upon this skill, to lower the volume, improve the reception and use this moment of adversity to usher in a new era of co-operation.

Fact, Fiction and
MEXICO

Alarmists are busily attacking the NAFTA deal, but free trade

among Canada, the United States and Mexico

will benefit all three countries

David Olive

Editor

HERE WE GO AGAIN. Four years after the outpouring of half-truths and accusations of traitorous motives that poisoned the debate on the Canada-U.S. free trade agreement (FTA), the coalition of economic nationalists, organized labour and New Democrats that attacked the FTA is girding up to refight that lost battle in the guise of opposing the North American free trade agreement (NAFTA) which replaces the FTA. NAFTA seeks to enlarge the trading area created by the FTA by embracing the 85 million people of Mexico, thereby establishing a trading bloc with 360 million people and some $6 trillion (U.S.) in output.

Make no mistake: The efforts to kill NAFTA before it can be ratified by Parliament next year aren't intended as an attack on Mexico, a country that barely registers on the Canadian consciousness. The anti-NAFTA campaign mounted by Bob White, Bob Rae, Maude Barlow and their compatriots is designed to drive the Mulroney government from power and force the Liberals to commit themselves to ripping up the deal. And if the victims of this endeavour are facts, the prosperity of Mexican and Canadian workers, and prog-ress toward a more unified community of nations shorn of destructive trade barriers, so be it.

Three specious anti-NAFTA arguments will be advanced:

ARGUMENT ONE: *The original FTA, which came into effect on Jan. 1, 1989, has been harmful to Canada.*

The anti-free trade gang has done its best to identify the FTA as the culprit behind every dismaying piece of economic news during the past three years.

Now Bob White, in his new role as president of the Canadian Labour Congress, promises that NAFTA will ignite "a debate not about what will happen to us, but what already has happened under the Canada-U.S. free trade agreement. By whatever yardstick, it has been a disaster for all sections of the country except perhaps for some of the corporate elite."

Let's look at the grim fallout of the FTA. By some estimates, Canada has lost as many as 330,000 manufacturing jobs since the FTA was signed—a suspect figure since it varies from one alarmist to the next, and does not take into account the high-wage jobs that have been *created* during this period by the likes of Siemens, Goodyear, Ericsson and other foreign-based firms seeking to exploit the U.S. market from a Canadian base. The period in question also coincides with a world-wide recession and a Bank of Canada policy designed to crush inflation at the expense of growth.

Despite these factors, which aren't related to the FTA, Canadian exports to the United States slipped just 0.3% last year, at a time when overall U.S. imports dropped by 1.7%—a successful effort by the U.S. to improve its trade position with most countries, Canada being a notable exception. The FTA's role in securing continued access to American markets suggests that Canada's recession would have been worse without the FTA.

ARGUMENT TWO: *The Americans are trade bullies, and they got the better of us in negotiating the NAFTA.*

No argument on the first score. Most notoriously on the issues of softwood lumber and Honda Civics, U.S. special-interest lobbies and zealous U.S. Customs Service agents have a penchant for tying up Canadian exporters by seizing their goods at the border, applying a fine, and letting the international arbitration process determine months later whether the action was justified. Congress can impose more than 8,000 different taxes on imports, with tariffs as high as 458%.

Reprinted from *Report on Business Magazine*, October 1992, pp. 11-12.

Canadians, however, give as good as they get, with our efforts to price U.S. and other foreign beer out of the market, and our persistence in propping up an inefficient farm economy by means of marketing boards and supply management programs. Until recently, Mexico was no less an offender, boasting some of the highest tariff walls in the world and strict limits on foreign investment.

The point of the FTA, and now of NAFTA, is to bring some order and equity to the chaotic, capricious sphere of trade. Under NAFTA's provisions, disagreements over the application of antidumping and countervail rules are no longer settled according to the biased judgment of trade commissars in Mexico, the United States and Canada, but instead are referred to an international dispute-settlement panel. This doesn't stop the trading partners from harassing one another, but it does block them from winning unfair victories – as a string of recent trade rulings in Canada's favour shows.

As for the supposed pushover status of Canada and Mexico, each dwarfed in power by the United States, anti-free traders forget that it was Canada, not the United States, that pushed for the FTA, fearing that protectionist forces in the United States would close the American market to exports of Canadian products. Similarly, it was Mexico which launched the NAFTA initiative. The United States entered both sets of negotiations seeking to gain the upper hand, but came away with surprisingly little. During the 14 months of NAFTA negotiations, Canada wound up with an even wider set of exemptions on culture than was provided by the FTA. Washington started out with a goal of requiring 65% to 70% North American content on autos, up from the FTA's 50%; it won only a 62.5% level, phased in over eight years, and automakers can now allocate more of their costs toward that limit than under the FTA. Mexico has been no less stubborn, clinging to constitutional rules forbidding foreign ownership of Mexican crude oil, and limiting foreign ownership of its financial services sector. All three countries benefit from an expedited dispute settlement process, which should eventually curb the arbitrary actions by customs officials which figured prominently in the Honda Civic dispute.

ARGUMENT THREE: *NAFTA means a further loss of Canadian jobs.*

In the absence of NAFTA, Canada and the United States have been losing low-wage, low-skill jobs to the Pacific Rim and Mexico for decades. Logic dictates that if low wages were the crucial factor in determining economic supremacy, countries such as Thailand and Ecuador would by now be ruling the world. Instead, as Quebec International Affairs Minister John Ciaccia points out, "The biggest problem we have in terms of competition and in terms of exports is with countries that have the highest wages in the world, namely Japan and Germany." The downside of losing additional jobs to Mexico is more than made up for by Canada's new access to the Mexican market for sophisticated products and services in which Canada specializes, including telecommunications, mass transit and aviation. Says Ciaccia: "We are opening a new market of 85 million people. Just the service sector alone for Canadian industries represents $8 billion."

Many liberal economists, including John Kenneth Galbraith, endorse NAFTA. But if the bitter anti-free trade campaign of 1988 is any guide, in the months to come we can anticipate ugly outbursts of both paternalism and primitive protectionism. Already there is much handwringing over Mexico's abysmal standards of environmental protection and working conditions. This ignores Mexico's outsize financial commitment to rehabilitating the polluted Mexico-U.S. border region, which exceeds that of the Bush administration. And the NAFTA deal includes more provisions for environmental upgrading than any international trade pact in history. As for working conditions, the salary and safety standards for Mexican workers can only improve as the economy becomes more prosperous with increased access to northern markets. Nothing about the current conditions in Mexico suggests that Mexicans will see an improvement in their standard of living with a continuation of the status quo. Neither, for that matter, will Canadians in a global economy where the workers and nations are becoming unavoidably interdependent.

This time, anti-free traders aren't alone

Groups in U.S. and Mexico are joining forces with Canadians opposed to continental trade deal

Ian Austen

Special to The Star

OTTAWA—At least they can joke about it.

Relatively short of financial resources, one of the three key U.S. groups opposed to the Canada–U.S.–Mexico trade pact uses the acronym MODTLE, pronounced "motley."

"One of our critics called us a motley collection of interest groups, so we took the name," said Karen Hansen-Kuhn of the Washington-based Mobilization On Development, Trade, Labor and the Environment.

But the appearance of U.S. opposition groups is a significant switch from four years ago. Then, most Americans didn't know about the Canada–U.S. free-trade deal, let alone debate its merits.

But this time Canadian critics like the Action Canada Network won't have to go it alone. The trilateral deal has brought with it a trilateral network of opponents.

"Opposition to NAFTA is becoming a movement in the United States," says Don Wiener of the Chicago-based Fair Trade Campaign. "Trade is becoming a central issue for a lot of constituent groups in the United States."

The lack of reliable polls makes assessing broad public opinion in the U.S. difficult. But there's no question the new deal—which has some U.S. workers worried about job losses to Mexico—has a much higher profile.

The trilateral deal and the ongoing global trade talks known as the GATT are the subject of a cover story in the current issue of the New York–based *Harper's* magazine.

Its author, Walter Russell Mead, calls for "progressive internationalism"—global trade efforts by labor, environmental, consumer and human rights groups to counter international corporate power.

With the NAFTA, something like that has come about. But Tony Clarke of the Action Canada Network, while a proponent of international co-operation, says that national trade opposition groups will always be necessary.

"The political context of each country make national groups paramount. Each network will have to focus in on its own agenda," he says.

Action Canada and Toronto-based Common Frontiers have been in regular touch for the past 18 months with groups in Mexico and the U.S.

The informal coalition formed early in the talks when critics from the three countries met while observing one of the regular trade ministers' sessions. Since then contact has been maintained by phone and fax.

In addition to MODTLE—a coalition of church, women's, human rights and union groups—and The Fair Trade Campaign, which has 20 organizers throughout the U.S. coordinating state and local opposition, there's a third major American opposition force affiliated with Ralph Nader's Public Citizen organization.

Mexico, Clarke admits, is a bit of a weak link. The country's political system stymies the growth of effective opposition on most topics, not just trade.

But efforts are being made by two active anti-NAFTA groups—Accion Mexicana and Equipo PUEBLO—and the Authentic Labor Front, one of the few union groups not connected to the government.

Despite their small size, the Mexican groups did win the right to meet this week with their government for a detailed briefing on the pact.

Clarke predicts Canadian groups will be of more help to the Americans and Mexicans than the other way around.

"We have not felt in our country that we desperately need allies in the U.S. and Mexico," he says.

Hansen-Kuhn says all U.S. opponents plan to focus on Canadian job losses and factory closings that groups like Action Canada blame on the current free-trade pact.

Already groups in the three countries have set up teams to analyze the complete text of the new plan.

When their work's done, Hansen-Kuhn says it will be consolidated into a trilateral critique.

While the Fair Trade Campaign will use Canada as an example, it's focusing its attention more directly on next fall's U.S. elections.

Its organizers—whose salaries have been met largely by donations from private foundations—have concentrated their efforts to help support or defeat Congressional candidates depending on their trade views.

While the deal was rushed through for presentation at last month's Republican convention, it wasn't given much attention at the gathering outside of a dry speech by trade representative Carla Hills.

But Wiener anticipates that will change and Bush will push the deal.

That could prove troublesome for the unions in the U.S. anti-free trade campaign.

By and large they back Democrat Bill Clinton who so far has tried to avoid supporting or denouncing NAFTA.

"There's a perception among his campaign staff that it's a no-win issue for him. For every vote Clinton picks up in the Midwest by being more protectionist, he loses one in Texas," Wiener says.

But whatever stance Clinton ultimately takes, it's clear that Canada won't be the only home of free-trade opposition in the upcoming debate.

SOUTHAM NEWS

The bottom line: a more prosperous North America

Gordon Ritchie

Gordon Ritchie, chief executive officer of Strategico, Inc., an Ottawa-based consulting firm, was Canada's deputy chief negotiator for the Canadian–U.S. Free Trade Agreement.

Ottawa

Once the United States and Mexico determined to negotiate a free-trade agreement, opinion polls indicated most Canadians agreed with the government that it was in our interest to be at the table—not because of Canada's trade with Mexico, but because of the need to play a role in the shaping of economic arrangements in this hemisphere around the hub of the giant U.S. market. Against these objectives, how have our negotiators fared?

Unquestionably, North American free trade (NAFTA) will stimulate Canadian-Mexican economic relations. This will be achieved directly through the phased reduction of tariffs and the reduction or elimination of many other barriers to trade and investment. Indirectly, it will be achieved through the improvement of Mexican living standards.

Initially, the most obvious gains will accrue to Mexico through increased exports to and investment from its NAFTA partners. The immediate effect on Canada will not be dramatic, given that two-way trade is relatively modest and likely to remain so. This is despite the best efforts of NAFTA promoters to boost the export and investment potential, and of NAFTA critics to prophesy a flood of low-cost imports from plants that will migrate to Mexico from Canada and the United States. Over the longer run, however, Canada clearly stands to benefit from a stronger, more prosperous Mexico.

What about our arrangements with the United States, once NAFTA replaces the Canadian–U.S. Free Trade Agreement (FTA)? This is difficult to assess in the absence of the full legal text and, indeed, the implementing legislation in both countries. From the information available, however, it would appear that the overall impact has been to stabilize without materially eroding the Canadian–U.S. arrangement. The adjustments are generally minor, with a few important exceptions.

In the automotive sector, the Americans sought to restrict shipments from the Japanese-owned companies in Canada. They have succeeded in raising the level of content required to qualify for duty-free entry to the United States. In return, we are assured by the government that the content definition has been clarified in such a way as to offset this higher rate and to reduce the scope for mischief by U.S. Customs. This reflects a difficult balance between the interests of the unions, the parts-makers, the Big Three car companies and the Japanese-owned firms in Canada.

In the apparel sector, the Americans sought to restrict imports of fabric and garments made in Canada from overseas materials. They have succeeded in imposing the restrictive standards their textile industry demanded. On the other hand, the Canadian negotiators obtained significantly greater quotas for products not meeting these tests—up 5 per cent over the next five years for woollen apparel, double the FTA quota for non-woollen apparel, triple for fabrics, quadruple 1991 export levels for yarn, and so on. The apparel lobbyists may not be pleased—they rarely are—but the result appears reasonable.

Furthermore, NAFTA gives Canada an additional two years (through to 1996) to allow exporters to "draw back" the tariffs on imported materials in products re-exported to the United States. This will make an important contribution to the cash flow of both the automotive and apparel sectors.

The other area of great sensitivity is dispute settlement. When a middle power makes a deal with the superpower, it must have some assurances that the deal will be respected. The Trade Minister assures us that NAFTA not only preserves intact the FTA machinery but significantly strengthens it and makes it more permanent: "The rule of law, not power, will prevail in settling trade disputes."

Allowing for political hyperbole, this may arguably be true for the general dispute-settlement procedures under NAFTA. If consultation and negotiation fail and retaliation results, Canada would have the formal right to a ruling on whether the retaliation is excessive. Furthermore, in disputes with private American investors, government decisions would now be subject to international

From *The Globe and Mail*, August 21, 1992, p. A15. Reprinted by permission.

arbitration. These measures do appear to bring more discipline into the process.

The same cannot be said for disputes over the application of countervailing and antidumping duties—the crucial issue of the FTA negotiations. Even under FTA, the United States has continued unilaterally to impose its own interests on Canadian exporters through hyperaggressive use of so-called "fair trade" laws. When the FTA panel system has attempted to curb these excesses, the Americans have reacted badly, stretching out the process as long as possible, taking extraordinary steps to challenge the panel decisions and, in some cases, threatening not to accept FTA jurisdiction.

I fail to see how the NAFTA provisions represent a step forward from the FTA. The Americans have achieved much, but not all, they sought:

• They have escaped making any further commitment not to take unilateral action (à la Section 301) without the sanction of a NAFTA or GATT panel decision.

• They have succeeded in strengthening the role of the "extraordinary challenge committee" and thereby added time, expense and uncertainty to the process.

• The proposed NAFTA system has been declared to be permanent, rather than a temporary stopgap, and the effort under FTA to reach a more satisfactory arrangement has been left to further "consultations" without a deadline.

• A new "special committee" has been created to ensure that Mexico plays by the new rules, but this will have little or no application to Canadian–U.S. relations.

In my view, we have still not reached an arrangement that would establish a basis for truly free and fair trade within North America.

The fact remains that the FTA system, even with some watering down under NAFTA, leaves us better placed than we would be without it.

The public debate is likely to turn on a series of issues that have little or nothing to do with the trade aspects of the NAFTA. These include the following:

• The herd of Canadian sacred cows is protected under this agreement. It completely exempts our cultural industries, leaves untouched our health and social programs, preserves our supply-management regimes for dairy, eggs and poultry, and does not require the large-scale export of water—all of which were in the pantheon of phony arguments against FTA.

• Mexico has declined to match the commitments Canada made to the United States on energy. These were designed to increase security of supply from Canada in the event of a shortage in exchange for our increased security of access to the U.S. market. FTA also foreclosed the use of export taxes, two-price systems or similar controls—much to the satisfaction of the energy-producing regions of Canada.

• Environmental impacts are only marginally addressed in NAFTA. Labour standards are entirely absent. This is as it should be with issues that are simply too important to be managed through a commercial agreement.

My bottom line is simply this. NAFTA represents a long-term investment in a more prosperous North America. There will inevitably be adjustments and hardship for some individuals and firms, and these should be reflected in national policies. For most Canadians, the overall impact, over the longer term, will be modest, but it should be positive.

Defence and Foreign Policy

Canada's foreign policy has traditionally emphasized Canada's role as a peacekeeping nation and its support for the United Nations and other international bodies committed to the maintenance of international peace. Just as is true for other nations, however, Canada has developed a military defence policy, and it is a member of several defence-related organizations, such as the North Atlantic Treaty Organization. Seven selections examine questions related to defence and foreign policy issues in contemporary Canadian politics. Many of these focus on a post–cold war world and the implications of this new geopolitical situation for the Canadian armed forces.

The first selection is an essay by Donald Wells that examines the impact of the end of the cold war on the size of Canadian armed forces and the implication of that for the Canadian economy. Because defence spending and arms expenditures will be cut, significant portions of the Canadian economy will shrink, resulting in a loss of jobs for many Canadians. Wells argues that the government must begin to plan now for ways to control the impact of these military cuts on the domestic economy.

Continuing the perspective of an examination looking toward the future, the next two articles suggest that Canada's defence planners need to think about the kind of identity that Canadian military forces will have in the years to come, as well as the best defence structure for Canada's military.

Despite the fact that military spending is being cut and will continue to be cut in the future, Tim Harper suggests that military procurements are still going to involve significant sums of money in the future. Harper examines a wide range of "big-ticket items," such as frigates, helicopters, and surveillance systems, and he concludes that military spending is not going to disappear as a significant impact on the economy.

The next selection is a fascinating interview with Canada's top soldier, General John de Chastelain. This article discusses his military career, his role in the standoff in Oka, Quebec, with the Mohawk Indians, and his concern about Canada's peacekeeping resources being stretched too thin, among other interesting topics.

The last two articles in this section examine Canada as an arms exporter and may serve to challenge some conventional images about Canada's role in the international arms race. Dorothy Goldin Rosenberg shows that Canadian scientists played a major role in the bombing of Hiroshima and that Canada is the world's largest exporter of uranium. Tim Harper points out that although Prime Minister Brian Mulroney wants Canada to lead the world in curbing trade in armaments, his goals have not been put into policy since the Persian Gulf War in 1991.

Looking Ahead: Challenge Questions

Is the problem of unemployment resulting from an "outbreak of peace" a significant one? Is it likely to have an important impact upon the Canadian economy? What options exist for the government of Canada to respond to the problem?

What changes are likely to take place in the structure and identity of the Canadian military forces as a result of the end of the cold war? What will Canadian defence structures look like in the future?

Can Canada continue to play the role of international peacekeeper that it has so successfully developed in the past? With the ever-increasing demands for international peacekeeping forces in today's world, what is likely to happen to Canada's armed forces?

A Jobs Policy for Peace

*Demilitarization means defence spending cuts—
borne, in the main, by a few communities. We need
a public policy to fund the economic conversion of
military spending.*

Donald M. Wells

Donald Wells is a political economist who teaches in the Labor Studies Programme and the Political Science Department of McMaster University in Hamilton, Ont.

W E ARE NOW INTO THE SECOND YEAR of the new spending policy for the Department of National Defence (DND), which was announced in April, 1989. At that time, the department scrapped previous commitments to funding increases; the defence budget would continue to grow, but not by nearly the amount that had been previously promised. While the DND's budget will still increase by 4.4% annually, the shortfall will come to $2.74 billion over a five-year period. When translated into defence spending programs, these cutbacks led to the immediate cancellation of several contentious and large capital acquisitions programs, including nuclear-propelled submarines, long-range patrol aircraft, and CF-18 fighter aircraft. Certain other capital items have been scaled back, stretched out, or postponed.

While these cuts in the DND's capital expenditures (the nuclear-powered submarines in particular) have been the focus of considerable public debate, the most politically controversial cuts have been in the operations and maintenance part of the DND's budget: the decision to shut down or reduce 14 military bases.

From the point of view of the social and economic impact of the cutbacks on workers and communities, it is the base closures which are currently the more significant. The reduction of the bases constitutes, on the whole, a more labor-intensive cutback. Furthermore, the local economies affected by these latter cuts are generally weaker than local economies directly affected by the cuts in the capital items: many capital cuts have their most direct economic impact on the manufacturing heartland, the cities of the Montreal-Windsor corridor, which tend to have relatively strong capacities to absorb unemployment. The opposite is true with regard to the base closures.

Six of the 14 bases are in Atlantic provinces that are at once the most dependent (on a per capita basis) on military spending and at the same time the least able to absorb these job losses. The DND estimates the costs to these six communities to be upwards of $73 million per year, due to lost wages and to the losses of other expenditures for goods and services. The hardest hit will be Summerside, Prince Edward Island, but serious damage is also in store for Sydney and Barrington, Nova Scotia, and for Moncton and Chatham, New Brunswick. Five other bases outside the Maritimes are also located in small towns which lack diversified economies.

Beyond the social and economic impact of these cuts, these base closures are significant because they provide an opportunity to assess the proper role of public policy in making a transition toward a less militarized economy. Of course, this does not mean that the cutbacks signify Ottawa's intention to demilitarize the Canadian economy. (The cutbacks reflect, rather, the Mulroney government's priorities in relation to inflation, deficits, and international competitiveness, as well as a sensitivity to public opinion: it would be far more difficult to "sell" the Goods and Services Tax and the cuts in VIA Rail, Unemployment Insurance, the CBC and day-care—without making *some* cuts in what are in any case unpopular defence expenditures.)

Nevertheless, the defence cuts have resulted in the *de facto* demilitarization of Prince Edward Island and parts of Nova Scotia and New Brunswick. They thereby raise the question of what kinds of public policies are needed in the event that more general demilitarization takes place in the future.

Consider, first, the kinds of policy responses that are now taking place in regard to the base closures. Unlike the military personnel who will be transferred to other jobs, an untold

Reprinted by permission from *Policy Options*, Vol. 11, No. 7, September 1990, pp. 8-10, published by The Institute for Research on Public Policy, Halifax, Nova Scotia, B3J 3K6, Canada.

number of the civilians at these bases will not be transferred. Besides losing the civilian and military jobs and the pay and allowances that went with them, the communities will also lose the military contracts for goods and services which previously went to local suppliers. Yet beyond estimating direct economic losses, the DND has made no detailed analysis of the broader social and economic impacts that the closures will have on these communities.

And despite a promise in Parliament to provide "an extremely generous package" to help workers at these bases find other jobs, Ottawa has thus far offered only minimal aid. Most important, there is no long-range plan to deal with the ensuing economic and social dislocations. Nor is it the government's intention to provide one.

"We try to get local groups involved in finding jobs for people who have been laid off," the DND's director of planning, infrastructure and coordination has explained. "We help find another use for the building we are leaving. But we don't do redevelopment."

Ottawa's current policy with respect to the base closures, albeit disguised as one of market-oriented self-reliance, is in effect a policy of forced labor mobility.

Ottawa has taken the same position in respect to cutbacks in the capital items in the DND budget. Here, however, adjustments to the cuts thus far appear to be less harmful, on the whole, to the workers and communities directly affected. This area of *relative* success in using market forces to effect a transition from dependency on defence spending may lead to drawing the wrong conclusions. The relative success of market adjustments in respect to cutbacks in capital expenditures is occurring under conditions which are not likely to obtain in the event of significant demilitarization.

In the first place, unlike the base closures (and unlike a policy of genuine demilitarization more broadly) many of the capital cuts are "paper cuts," i.e., cuts in *anticipated* expenditures based on the 1987 Defence White Paper. Moreover, and again in contrast to the bases, many of the cutbacks in capital items are taking place in local economies that are growing and well-diversified. It is especially fortuitous that the aerospace industry, a very large sector of the military economy, has been able to shift so much of its production to civilian aircraft, thanks largely to burgeoning global demand.

Given these unusually fortuitous conditions, it would not be correct, therefore, to conclude from this experience that markets are likely to be adequate, more or less by themselves, in coping with a larger-scale contraction in the military economy.

The emerging large-scale contraction of the Canadian military economy will not only stem from reduced Canadian government spending, it will also stem from shrinking foreign demand for Canadian military hardware. In the wake of rapidly diminishing East-West tensions, Canadian military exports are already falling. Since Canada's 300-odd military contractors sell more than two-thirds of their products to buyers outside the country, this is becoming a critical issue. Until recently, about three quarters of these exports went to the U.S., but that source of demand is drying up now that Pentagon spending has been cut to the point that there is no real increase (i.e., beyond the rate of inflation) in the U.S. military budget.

Canadian sales to Europe are also unlikely to be sustained at current levels. The fall-off in demand will probably continue as long as super-power antagonisms continue to abate. There are likely to be more declines in the demand for Canadian goods as the U.S. and Europe cut back on foreign

Canada's policy with regard to base closures is, in effect, a policy of forced labor mobility.

military procurement in response to domestic protectionist pressures and as long as low-cost contractors in countries such as Brazil, South Korea and Singapore continue to increase their shares of the global market in weaponry.

The decline in foreign demand for Canadian military goods, together with pressures within the political system for deeper cuts in the DND budget, are likely to highlight the kinds of inadequacies appearing in public policies related to the base closures. The problems go beyond the weaknesses already noted in Ottawa's *laisser faire* approach to restructuring through market forces. Problems appear as well in the strategies advocated by many peace activists who espouse the need to develop a planning process focussed almost exclusively at the *local* level.

Many peace activists envision a planning process which would prepare for and carry through the conversion of one military base or a single production site to civilian production. The key mechanism would be an "Alternate Use Planning Committee" made up of representatives from labor, management and community and peace groups. At the core to this vision of a local-centred transition from dependency on military spending is a set of participatory values in which there is often a deep disdain for the elitist, top-down nature of parliamentary politics. Instead, these peace activists have stressed that the planning process would be under the control of those whose lives would be most directly affected by these changes.

In situations such as the base closures, both this peace movement strategy and the Mulroney government's market-oriented strategy leave local economies to adapt to major changes without adequate assistance by the federal government. In the context of weak local economies, the chances for successful adjustment are confounded by the accelerating integration of Canada's economy not only into the North American continental economy but also into Pacific Rim and other world-wide financial and production networks.

This integration, combined with growing competition for investment and trade, means that weak local economies and peripheral regions become increasingly marginalized. Under such circumstances, initiatives which rely largely on local resources to convert military goods and services cannot but be ineffective.

As the prospects for a more comprehensive demilitarization of the economy increase, there is thus a need for a new vision of Ottawa's role in such a process. Activists in the peace movement need to evaluate the strengths and weaknesses of strategies which have focussed primarily at the local level. The main strength is the emphasis many activists have placed on broad participation in policy-making by those whose lives will be most affected by these changes.

At the same time, a successful transition will require national and even international planning, and this means that the peace movement, together with affected employees and communities, will need to focus on participating in pressure-group politics at the federal level. Furthermore, this planning will need to base itself on a meshing of defence and economic development policies—an area of policy coordination that is largely within federal jurisdiction.

Greater levels of funding and coordination will be required in those areas where workers and communities have become most dependent on military spending and where the local economies are the least diversified.

Finally, if the peace movement slogan "Jobs and Peace" is to be a genuine basis for an alliance between the peace movement and the labor movement, it cannot simply be assumed that increases in non-military public expenditures will emerge from the cuts in military spending: there is no automatic shift from one kind of public expenditure to another, especially given the emergence of the neo-conservative agenda at the federal level. Such shifts in expenditures can only reflect a political will that has yet to be articulated and mobilized.

A new vision of what a more effective transition to a more demilitarized economy might look like is already emerging. New Democratic Party M.P. Dan Heap is sponsoring a private member's bill, the Nuclear Weapons Economic Conversion Act, which would help communities, managers and workers plan the termination of contracts involving components of nuclear weapons by encouraging the conversion of their skills and the production technology to civilian uses.

Funds (based on 2.5 per cent of the gross revenue for each contract year) would be used to pay any laid-off workers at 90 per cent of their annual pay (more than normal unemployment insurance rates), to pay for retraining, and to implement these conversion plans. This approach is a welcome departure from the conventional planning models, in which politicians impose policies devised almost exclusively by bureaucrats in government offices. The Heap bill envisages heavy reliance upon planning by workers, managers and others at the local level with government providing the necessary funding, expertise and coordination at the federal level.

While the Heap bill has no chance of gaining passage in the current Parliament, it is this model of federally facilitated planning, combined with important local participation, which will be needed if the communities that have become deeply dependent on military spending are to make a successful transition to a more demilitarized economy.

Current DND budget cutbacks are a stimulus for a serious rethinking not only of Canadian defence policy but also of economic development policy. As hopes for serious demilitarization mount, it would be unfortunate if these cutbacks were to continue to be made in ways that leave whole communities to rely on their own resources—in effect, leaving them at the mercy of market forces. There is an alternative: a nationally coordinated, nationally funded economic conversion plan based on local participation.

In the context of the current dramatic decrease in East-West tensions, this type of public policy could shape the transition to a more demilitarized economy in such a way that those who have become the dependents of military expenditures do not become the principal victims of this extraordinary opening toward peace.

An Army for the 21st Century

*We ought to begin with an independent
Canadian Security Institute to plan and
recommend national policy initiatives.*

Rychard A. Brûlé

Rychard Brûlé presently works as a consultant in Ottawa, after a long and distinguished military career. Among other things, he served with the U.N. Forces in Cyprus and was also a member of the Strategic Policy Planning Board. Mr. Brûlé is a recent graduate of the Canadian National Defence College and has been with the Canadian Institute for International Peace and Security for the past three years.

IN 1987, THE CANADIAN GOVERNMENT PUBLISHED its long awaited White Paper on Defence. It promised to re-equip and modernize our forces including the provision of 10 to 12 nuclear-powered submarines for our Navy. In May 1989, the budget from the same government slashed heavily into the Department of National Defence envelope and cancelled the plan to acquire nuclear-powered submarines.

Notwithstanding more than 25 drafts of the White Paper and as many hours spent on it by the Cabinet, the government did not get it right. The proposal to obtain nuclear-powered submarines backfired. The Cabinet's will and commitment wavered when budget time came along. Why? What underlay the preparation of the Defence White Paper? Do the armed forces understand their future role, are they ready to accept it and to make the necessary adjustments in the national interest?

I would contend that the unfortunate imbroglio in which the Department of National Defence finds itself is directly linked to its unwillingness to use a global strategic forecasting or policy framework in the preparation of the White Paper, to some difficulties internal to the department and to its inability to explain to the Canadian public, and by extension, to their elected representatives the role of armed forces in the security policy of Canada.

Gaps such as the lack of an articulate general staff, strategic planning and enlightened policy discussion, will need to be addressed if the armed forces are to find their niche in the Canadian society, avoid a defence policy that is budget-driven and have the necessary funds and capabilities to match the needs of the future.

The International Environment

Faced by the challenges of the 21st century, Canada cannot afford the luxury of traditionally structured armed forces equipped for the last World War. Peace and security are political matters, not strictly within the realm of the military and weaponry.

Notwithstanding recent changes such as the crumbling down of the Berlin Wall, the fall of most Communist regimes in eastern Europe, the forthcoming German re-unification and, therefore, the emergence of a new international security system, the international environment of the next 15 years will likely remain over-armed, under-fed, economically unstable and dangerously polluted. These inequities, along with possible large population shifts and an uneven distribution of wealth compounded by questions of sustainable and equitable economic development, will surely be the main threats to global security in the coming decades.

A few still perceive the threats to Canadian security in the traditional order of superpower nuclear war; regional or local wars; other threats to Canada and Canadians; and finally domestic turmoil. Others contend that this perception is *passé* and unrelated to the realities of the 1990s, and definitely of limited use for the 21st century. The traditional threats are based on such assumptions as: the immutability of the existing world state system within a bi-polar structure; a restrictive definition of sovereignty and the absence of an effective international organization to deal with destabilizing developments such as the rising demands for economic development and the problems of demography and poverty. These assumptions are presently being invalidated.

Moreover, the long-standing exclusion of the Soviet Union and half of Europe from the OECD economy is likely to end

Reprinted by permission from *Policy Options,* Vol. 11, No. 7, September 1990, pp. 11-14, published by The Institute for Research on Public Policy, Halifax, Nova Scotia, B3J 3K6, Canada.

soon, as the newly-emerging nations of eastern Europe move towards full participation in an integrated industrial-world economy. On the political front, as a result of the forthcoming German re-unification, continued improving relations between the United States and the Soviet Union, military consolidation by the United States, the creation of "Europe 1992" and greater European military cooperation—NATO will become an anachronism.

If it survives as a political entity, NATO will be a shell of a military alliance within which the United States could continue to provide a nuclear guarantee to western Europe. But European integration [or pan-European nationalism] may decide otherwise and ensure its own defence without the U.S. umbrella. Meanwhile, Canadians will increasingly question the usefulness of continuing their postwar military activities in Europe and are likely to reduce or end their military role in Europe by the year 2000.

It is clear that, as a communique from the Canadian Institute for International Peace and Security put it, "In the face of increasing global interdependence, the threat of environmental catastrophe, serious strain in the global economy, deepening underdevelopment in much of the world and the potential for dramatic change in East-West relations, Canadians would be justified in asking serious questions about how much, and what kind, of military spending is necessary for our security." Especially since the Department of National Defence does not appear to have done so!

In view of the growing regime of mutual security, of the minuscule Canadian contribution to deterrence and of the fact that threats of direct military intervention in Canada and NATO countries remain improbable, it is obvious that it is in our national interest to direct our energies in the direction whence the real challenges to a peaceful world and the preservation of Canadian values and interest are likely to come.

National Challenges

On the national scene, the road to the 21st century will see population shifts within Canada compounded by its increasing multi-ethnicity, both will become cause for concern. A restructuring of Canadian society and of its political ethos will take place within the constraints that Canada will remain a trading nation with no direct enemy but with such obstacles as its natural/geographical dimension and its limited purse for strictly defence related matters; both within the context of large infrastructure costs, a universalist social welfare society and an aging population.

Global environmental effects may also necessitate increased Canadian Forces participation in disaster relief works, search and rescue operations, fighting forest fires, etc. While global population movement and entries of large migrant population, especially into the bigger Canadian cities, could induce an increase in terrorist activities on Canadian soil.

Within these demographic shifts, any attempt to increase the size of the reserve forces vastly and to integrate it completely with the regular forces will not be as easy as the White Paper had made it appear to be.

Finally, in military terms, the continentalization of Canadian defence will challenge our traditional role within NATO except, perhaps, in its utility as a training base and as a pool of resources and men in case of a prolonged conflict. But, more importantly, what is left for us to do, militarily, in America in the face of no obvious enemy, i.e., what structure for the armed forces?

It is clear that what we need is a strategy to face changes in the future, not solely a war plan for an unlikely European conflict. The choice really is whether we lead this inevitable change or resist it. In this search for new flexible and responsive structure, the Canadian Army and Air Force prepared two different answers; for example, and regrettably, Army 2002, the land-based forces' contribution to the exercise, in contrast to the Air Force's Project 2010, was prepared without having attempted to forecast what the world would be like in the year 2002, what the international and regional contexts would be and what Canada's national strategy could be by then. It concentrated solely on what the Army wanted to do to be ready for the next war which would, in their mind, be like the last one. Is it safe and legitimate to allow the Army to plan for its future without any contribution from the Canadian government?

We should restructure our forces in order to enhance our security, all within the context of our national interest, recognizing that social stability and economic development are crucial, basic components of security. It is time to rethink our national defence. What should we defend? Against whom or what? And what military forces are required to defend it?

Of course the Canadian Armed Forces have a duty to prepare as best as they can, and as professionally as they can, for the worst-case scenario, but the State also has the duty to make judicious choices based not only on an appreciation of the world of the future but also on its vision of a preferred world for Canada and Canadians to live in.

Politics is not only the art of the possible, but the allocation of scarce resources, in this case within the perception of the threat and its probability of happening. The choice of the appropriate response to a threat (by whatever means available to a State to express its will and pursue its goals in the international arena) is also a political choice that requires wise advice and professional guidance.

It is clear that the roles of the Canadian Armed Forces will change drastically to meet the new challenges of the year 2004 discussed earlier by, for example, increasing its military contribution to new alliances and modification of the contribution to older ones, an increase in various new peacekeeping activities and endeavours, and in their participation in relief programs linked to floods, famines, refugees' evacuation etc., an expansion of the Canadian presence in the Arctic, in fisheries patrols, in forest fire suppression, in search and rescue operations, in space development, etc.

In addition, the Defence Department plans for the future should include a requirement to expand and develop new techniques for:

a. assisting the police forces in detection and identification of potentially terrorist groups;

b. providing in-country assistance to friendly nations prior to the outbreak of hostilities;

c. diagnostic and consultative services to enable emerging nations to develop methods of preserving their sovereignty; and

d. training and equipping military or paramilitary forces to oppose terrorism and become a legitimate, peaceful and stabilizing factor in their region.

All of these are roles for which I believe Canada is eminently suited and by which it could make an additional contribution to international peace and security.

The Air Force

Severely short of long-range patrol aircraft, troops and cargo transport planes, the Air Force needs new additional equipment. Recently the Canadian Air Force could not airlift the 500 Canadian Peacekeepers required for the Iran-Iraq border. The U.S. Air Force was called in to carry the peacekeepers and their equipment to the Gulf. Yet, this is the same Canadian army that was supposed to be able to double the size of its forces in Europe—to more than 10,000—on similarly short notice.

As pointed out by Colonel Dobson and Rowbottom, not only will women play a larger role in the forces of the future but: "With a population of nearly 20 per cent of Canadians over 65 by 2010, the taxpayer pressure upon the Air Force to play a job-sharing in future role will be considerable. . . . The Air Force could be involved in the international scene as part of new alliances, increased peacekeeping activities, relief programs or refugee transfers. At home, the Air Force could be asked to relocate resources to northern regions, to increase fisheries patrols, and to participate more frequently in forest fire suppression and flood relief activities."

Tensions will undoubtedly arise within the service in this possible move from an "alliance" air force to a "national" or a "Defence of Canada" air force:

"Its continuing mission is to protect the national infrastructure; it does not need to postulate an 'enemy' that is a nation-state. Poverty, unemployment, technological layoffs, inequity of distribution of social goods and services, and all manner of man-made or natural disasters are its enemies insofar as they are the 'enemies' of the state and have a propensity to disturb the peace."

But, in order to fulfill these new roles and meet these challenges and commitments, the Air Force will need additional aircraft.

The Army

I believe that we should rethink Army 2002 in the light of what is probable (for the 21st century) and possible (for the 1990s) while increasing the size of the reserves as a national pool of trained, motivated, and qualified Canadians but outside of the total force concept as planned in Army 2002.

We should concentrate on defensive equipment that could be of use in Canada. The easiest case in point would be the replacement of tanks by other anti-tank platforms (light and medium helicopters, mines, multiple rocket launchers, digging equipment, anti-tank guns, etc.) and the parallel disbandment of tank units to be replaced by an augmentation of the anti-tank capabilities of infantry, artillery and engineer units.

The acquisition of tanks makes sense only if Canada is to retain its European commitment of ground troops in a divisional—traditional—battlefield organization for at least the next 25 years. Can we assume at this moment that such will be the need? Can we spare the money? Would it be cost effective?

Peacekeeping represents a real contribution to global security. This role creates needs for communications, light defensive protective equipment and airlift, especially if by necessity peacekeeping activities were, one day, to be transformed into real peace-making or peace-enforcing interventions—likely because the world community might someday decide that a certain conflict must be stopped, by force if necessary, in the interest of all. We may wish to consider the acquisition of defensive equipment alongside additional helicopters for observation, troop transport and the anti-tank role.

Finally, when the international community is ready, it would be in Canada's interest to set up an international training school for peacekeepers, observers and mediators,

It would be in Canada's interest to set up an international training school for peace-keepers.

fields in which Canada has unsurpassed, but under-exploited, experience and resources.

The forces should concentrate on the development of capabilities for electronic warfare and the use of artificial intelligence not only for its peacekeeping forces but also as a real contribution to forthcoming international monitoring agencies and verification agreements. As a side benefit any research and development in these fields will have a high utility return in the civilian sector.

The Navy

Today the issue of Canadian sovereignty centres on the Arctic and Canada's oceans. If any threat to the Canadian sovereignty exists, it still comes in a non-military fashion from the U.S.A. In that vein, and for other general purposes (such as drug and fisheries control) the navy—barring an increase in Canada's Coast Guard and its transformation into a para-military force—should at least be equipped with more minesweepers and be provided with additional patrol aircraft, long-range but also medium-range aircraft such as the DASH 8, sonar buoys and other fixed or movable listening devices, etc.

Yes, Canada has a three-ocean coast and with new technologies in listening devices and medium- and long-range patrol aircraft and the forthcoming developments in space-radar detection and tracking we should be able to address that situation. Of course, there is the sovereignty issue, but no sovereignty is lost simply because an intruder appears in one's space. Moreover, that is why we have allies, and maritime cooperation could ensure the peaceful use of the North West Passage or it could simply be closed, in time of danger, at choke points to all traffic.

In general, the role of the armed forces as a regional economic stimulus is unlikely to diminish; on the contrary, the taxpayer is likely to insist on more return, in services, for the defence dollar. The same can be said of the integrative role of the armed forces (especially such ventures as the Katimavik project, such para-military organizations as the Cadet Corps and the reserve forces in general) not only for women and the French-Canadians but for immigrants and natives in order to "socialize" and "Canadianize" them.

The responsibility of the forces as the prime example of a "national" institution in such fields as bilingualism and equal opportunities, reflecting the strength and commitment of

Canada and Canadians' values and aspirations, will remain a government priority whatever the cost.

The armed forces will be called upon more and more often to play a role in the protection of the state against such disrupting forces such as drugs and terrorism, a role that the Canadian Armed Forces will not be able to dodge and for which it must be equipped and trained. This role will require small units with light and maneuverable equipment and air, sea and land transport.

As pointed out in the White Paper on Defence, Canada should build longer airstrips in the Arctic (not necessarily or even primarily for military purposes) and even triple (if she can) the size of its reserve for the three elements (including the Canadian Rangers). Much of the training of the forces, and its expenses, could be civilianized. New equipment need not be built to military specifications but could be acquired from the upper scale of civilian standards.

There is no doubt that Canada needs to achieve a consensus around the need for defence and the shape of this defence, if only to depoliticize the defence allocation process and provide a stable environment in which, with clear objectives and a clear view of what needs to be protected, and how, the Canadian Armed Forces can get on with their job and have the long process of equipment acquisition proceed.

We need a national strategic planning group, a new "think tank" organization, publicly funded and accountable to Parliament but not to the Government of the day. An organization acceptable to all parliamentary parties which, like the Economic Council of Canada or the C.D. Howe Institute, would provide expert and unbiased views on questions of national security present and future and assist in the formation of a Canadian consensus on matters of security. Its responsibilities might be augmented by, or incorporate, a National Intelligence Assessment Unit that would assemble and digest "intelligence" from all Canadian government departments, agencies and private sources.

It could also take over responsibility for the little-known Interdepartmental Committee on Futures and Futures Forecasting which has been relegated to the back-burner and is stifled by bureaucratic weight. We need a new *stratégie d'intégration des structures décisionnelles canadiennes* that will coordinate and somewhat integrate all components of national security which consists of not only military, but also political, economic, social, ecological, and humanitarian and human rights aspects.

We should also pursue arms control objectives and possibly the demilitarization of the High Arctic, not only as a zone of peace *per se* but for the preservation of this sensitive ecosystem for the benefit of all of mankind. The need for patrol frigate and minesweepers is recognized for border patrol, protection of fisheries, supervision of off-shore exploration, training of our naval forces, drug enforcement and supervision of the 200 mile economic zone. As with the need for space-based listening posts, there is a similar need for ocean floor listening devices.

The Air Force needs more transport airplanes (for cargo and personnel), more long- and medium-range patrol aircraft, and more helicopters. However, the helicopters do not necessarily need to belong to the Air Force nor need to be piloted by officers only.

Finally, it is imperative that National Defence Headquarters contain an articulate, experienced and semi-permanent military staff which can be called upon to address national issues with knowledge of all national factors at play and with a good grasp of national and strategic planning. Such a staff could explain, and defend if necessary, military decisions and imperatives in whatever fora appropriate.

This staff cannot but be a general staff, which has been sadly lacking so far. The constant rotation of officers at headquarters and the penalty that most corps inflict on these officers for staying too long at the head office is wasteful, intolerable and counter-productive.

Conclusions

The armed services must strive to be more efficient in their existing activities, even as they re-organize to cope with change; good intelligence and staff work are still inexpensive weapon systems of the future and the forces of the future must be exquisitely sensitive to the art of the possible. Socially as well as technologically Canada's military forces are, in the final analysis, a reflection of local and national self-perceptions and of a national economic well being, whether manifested in the work done in overseas alliances, in job creation projects at home, or industry support and cooperation.

Change will come. We can either anticipate and guide it or become its victim. *Futuribles,* as an attempt to find one's way in the tempest of change, are like holding a candle in the eye of the storm. One cannot see much of the way (or ways) ahead but without it there is only darkness. One man can only do so much, as one candle can only light so much space. I, for one, would be content to let the members of a Canadian Security Institute light many a candle to find the proper route. In the meantime, the Department of National Defence would do well to resist the acquisition of any major equipment and immediately freeze the process of restructuring into divisions.

Closing down Canadian bases marks end of era

What kind of armed forces will we have in a new world?

Gerald Utting

Toronto Star

Ottawa's decision to close down the big Canadian military bases in western Germany, at Lahr and Baden-Soellingen, marks the end of an extraordinary 40-year-long commitment to the defence of Western Europe.

Canada has been the only non-European nation, apart from the superpower United States, to send troops to Europe for the long and thankless task of helping to provide a North American commitment that the European nations would not fight alone if the Soviet army suddenly marched westward.

The idea has become somewhat laughable in the 1990s, now that the Soviet Union has been exposed as a troubled nation, riven by internal strife, seeking even food from its former rivals.

The Soviet army, once feared as the enormously over-armed, monolithically organized military wing of a Soviet Communist party leadership out to subject the world, by force if need be, refused to back that blundering coup of the hardliners against Mikhail Gorbachev.

Gorbachev, restored to leadership by anti-Communist Boris Yeltsin, is after all the man who permitted Eastern Europe to wrest its freedom from Communist rule without a protest.

By allowing the reunification of Germany, Moscow abolished virtually the entire rationale for the North Atlantic Treaty Organization.

But 1991 is not 1949, when the NATO pact was signed.

Then, the Western Europeans were terrified at the prospect of facing the mighty Soviet army. They wanted a commitment by the United States that its troops would remain stationed in Western Europe.

We have grown used to the idea of NATO in the past four decades—as the most effective and perhaps the longest-lived military alliance in world history.

It provided virtual assurance that a Soviet push would turn into a nuclear world war—an essential ingredient in the strategy of "mutually assured destruction," otherwise known as nuclear deterrence.

Fortunately, this idea has never been put to the test. As has emerged in recent years, Soviet huffing and puffing and sabre-rattling in the post-Stalin era was as much to terrorize the historically turbulent Soviet people as to terrify Moscow's Western rivals.

The Soviet Communist party needed a bogeyman in the West to justify its oppression of hundreds of millions of abused subjects on the grounds of security.

But the Soviet Union, during World War II and after, was never a paper tiger.

Nor, for that matter, was Canada. In World War II, the Canadian armed forces grew from 7,945 in 1939 to 787,475 at the end of 1944. Altogether, more than a million Canadian men and women served in the armed forces; 46,542 of them were killed.

In 1946, Canadian troops garrisoning part of West Germany were withdrawn to Canada.

Canada wanted no part of a permanent occupation of Germany unless Ottawa fully controlled its own troops there, a privilege denied by Britain and the United States.

The Canadian armed forces were reduced to fewer than 50,000. The army, just on 500,000 strong in 1945, was cut down to 25,000.

Canada saw itself as a "middle power" in the immediate postwar era, a strong backer of the United Nations, often adopting neutral positions in disputes between the great powers.

Stalin's policies alarmed Western Europe and the United States.

The Soviets maintained a massive force in East Germany, organized a Communist government there, and refused to allow the nations it had defeated in the war to participate in the Marshall Plan.

From *The Toronto Star*, September 20, 1991, p. A19. Reprinted with permission from The Toronto Star Syndicate.

10. DEFENCE AND FOREIGN POLICY

In 1948, a Communist coup overthrew the democratic government of Czechoslovakia.

Western Allied influence was pushed out of the Balkans.

Finally, the Soviets blockaded West Berlin—a blockade defeated only by U.S. and British airlifts. Canada took no part in these airlifts.

By 1949 the Iron Curtain had fallen. It was known that the Soviets were working on their own atomic bombs. The Chinese Nationalists had been driven out of mainland China. The French were losing their war in Indochina.

Germany seemed permanently split. The western zones were united and declared to be the Federal Republic of Germany. The Russian zone became the German Democratic Republic.

The European nations, the United States and Canada signed the NATO pact. It provided for a defensive alliance which would see large North American contingents stationed in Western Europe with the new German republic having its own army, and troops from Britain, France, the Netherlands, and Belgium based in West Germany.

Canada began a troop buildup to meet this new commitment. The Korean War erupted in June, 1950, and Ottawa found itself having to deploy troops and aircraft and ships to Korea and Europe. The Canadian forces grew from under 50,000 in 1950 to more than 95,000 in 1952.

The Canadian government's target was to send 12 squadrons of fighters and the 27th Infantry Brigade, with 5,500 troops, to Europe.

The first Canadian troops sailed from Canada on Oct. 20, 1951, and were welcomed by Gen. Dwight Eisenhower, NATO supreme commander, at a parade in front of the Dutch parliament in Rotterdam on Nov. 21. The whole brigade had arrived and was stationed near Hanover, West Germany, by the end of the year.

The Royal Canadian Air Force squadrons arrived in Europe early in 1952 and were dispersed to air bases at North Luffenham, England, Grostenquin, France, and Zweibrucken, West Germany, by the spring of 1953.

At the same time, ships based in Halifax were assigned responsibility for anti-submarine operations in the North Atlantic, to protect convoys to Europe in the event of war.

Canadians also began a program of training European pilots and navigators.

So Canada became a military power again in Europe, a continent whose battlefields were liberally bedewed with Canadian blood in World Wars I and II. Not a major military power, by any means, but a token of increased resistance to a Soviet attack, and of Canada's determination to play a major part should such a war ever come.

The 1950s marked the peak of the Cold War, even though Stalin died in 1953.

The Soviet economy was in a period of high growth. The Soviets detonated an atomic bomb in 1950 and pressed on to develop their own hydrogen bombs and long-range bombers, then medium-range missiles, and finally long-range intercontinental ballistic warheads.

The Canadian forces in Europe became sure nuclear targets in the event of war, since NATO's announced policy was to escalate to nuclear weapons quickly to compensate for its lower troop strength. By 1960, Canada's armed forces totalled 120,000.

The cost of this was getting out of hand, as Sabre jets were replaced by fewer and far more expensive CF-100s, capable of striking with nuclear weapons supplied by the United States.

Canada was finding difficulty in paying for refits of the aging aircraft carrier Bonaventure, keeping its squadrons running and in finding meaningful roles for ground troops, who were not equipped to the standard of their NATO partners.

In 1969, the government of Pierre Trudeau decided on a policy that was to bring criticism from the NATO partners. The forces in Europe were cut in half; the Bonaventure was scrapped. Many of the new CF-5 fighters were stored.

The deployment of 10,000 troops in Quebec after October, 1970, saw the federal government begin to push a policy of bilingualizing the armed forces. There was a constant debate on just what Canada's posture should be in the nuclear world.

The armed forces were cut back to about 80,000—a reduction of one-third from the height of the Cold War.

The equipment of the armed forces was upgraded as the '70s progressed into the '80s. The battle group based at Lahr got Leopard tanks, made in West Germany and the world's best at the time.

They were constantly praised for their performance by NATO commanders while the European politicians chided the Canadian government for spending less on defence than virtually any other member of the alliance.

The fighter squadrons, now reduced to two, were nevertheless formidable, having been equipped with the CF-18 aircraft, which can serve either as a fighter or a bomber.

The Canadian squadrons no longer have a nuclear role.

The end of the Cold War raised serious questions about the future of the Canadian commitment to Europe.

Now armed with considerable striking power, they are designed to fight as part of an alliance in a war that is not likely ever to happen.

They now have more "teeth" probably than ever before, even with manpower only half of that seen by Europeans 30 years ago.

The Persian Gulf war saw CF-18s moved from Germany to the gulf, where they did not get into actual combat with Iraqi fighters. This did prove, however, that Canadian squadrons could be deployed rapidly.

The tanks, with their batteries of anti-aircraft missiles, their screens of lighter armored vehicles, and their massive repair and fuel vehicles, could not move to the gulf. Canada does not have the ships to move them and must rely on chartering foreign ships.

The navy did send ships to the gulf, but had to hurriedly make them seaworthy.

Now Prime Minister Brian Mulroney's government has revealed some of its plans for the future.

The armored base at Lahr and the jet base at Baden-Soellingen are to be phased out. The forces will come home, except for a smaller contingent that will become part of a Rapid Deployment Force being created by NATO for gulf-type wars.

The remaining question is: what kind of armed forces will Canada decide to have at home for the post–Cold War era?

Experience has shown that, at the start of World War I, World War II and the Korean War, Canada had tiny armed forces that took years to build up to the large size they eventually attained.

But in an age when Third World tyrannies struggle to make their own hydrogen bombs with long-range missiles to deliver them, will armed forces based on traditional ideas about overseas threats be of any value?

'Peace dividend' costly

Military budget puts billions into weaponry

Tim Harper

Toronto Star

OTTAWA—With typical theatrical flourish, Defence Minister Marcel Masse swooped down by helicopter in Mirabel, Que., this month to award a $1 billion contract to a local manufacturer.

The Bell Helicopter employees cheered, Masse took his bows, but defence critics and analysts grimaced.

It not only caught analysts off guard, it again raised questions about where Canada's defence policy is headed—and where the contracts are going.

In recent weeks, Masse and his defence department have begun what appears to be a reshaping of the Canadian military.

Yet at the same time, still on their shopping list are a number of big-ticket items which belie any realization at headquarters that the world has undergone remarkable change in recent years.

With the Cold War consigned to history books, Canada's defence budget will be $12.2 billion this year, up from last year when the government spent just under $12 billion on defence.

Big-ticket items like a $1.1 billion surveillance system to protect Canadian forces in Europe—troops who are coming home—and $9.3 billion for patrol frigates remain in the budget down the road, leaving little sign that a so-called "peace dividend" is at hand.

For Masse, the question is how to reallocate, not how to cut.

Now a debate has begun over defence spin-offs that Masse is earmarking for Quebec. Critics point to a minister who is an avowed Quebec nationalist, a man who has publicly stated that, even as a federal minister of the crown, his priority is the greater good for Quebec.

"He has a lack of interest in defence, but an all-consuming interest in doing what he can for Quebec," says Nicholas Stethem of Toronto's Strategic Analysis Group. "That is the defining credo of his tenure."

There is criticism that others could not bid on the Bell deal, shutting out Eurocopters Ltd. of Fort Erie, Ont., which would have had a chance at the windfall.

The engines for the helicopters will also be made in Quebec.

Metro Liberal MPs Robert Kaplan and Sergio Marchi were outspoken in their criticism of Masse's closing of a Downsview military depot and the opening of a new $100 million Montreal facility.

That criticism deepened when it was revealed Masse ignored his own consultant's recommendation to establish a new facility in Kingston. It ranked Masse's choice as the least attractive.

Now there are persistent reports in the defence community that Masse is poised to strike again, closing an armed forces staff school on Avenue Rd. and moving it to St. Jean, Que.

Kaplan wondered whether Masse was trying to put away a military nest-egg for an independent Quebec.

"I know Montreal is in dire economic straits, but you don't build up one part of the country by tearing down another," Marchi said. "I'm asking Toronto not be written off because the Tories don't think it counts politically any longer."

New Democrat defence critic John Brewin says he is hesitant to criticize Quebec contracts because of the fragility of the national unity debate.

"Nevertheless, I have concerns about the distribution of our defence contracts," Brewin says.

The overall result of the Masse defence regime so far is confusion and very little progress toward the government's stated goal of dramatically increasing the share of its budget to replace the country's rapidly aging equipment.

Time and again, defence analysts have called for an overall strategy to deal with a world in which the former Soviet Union is no longer considered a threat.

"Canada's navy, army and air force will be provided with the modern equipment they need to remain both capable and flexible," said Masse as he announced the purchase of 100 "utility" helicopters from Bell Helicopter of Mirabel.

Others say instead of a defence plan, there is only a vague idea defence contracts can be used as tiny boosts to industry in different regions of the country.

"Military morale is at an all-time low," Stethem said.

"The finance department still controls defence policy so you're left with something that is not shaped by any strategic analysis of the world situation."

Brewin said the government is merely "lurching" from one project to another.

"There's no consultation, no transparency, no accountability to Parliament or the public. There is only confusion."

While Masse was announcing the helicopter project, the junior defence minister, Mary Collins, was trumpeting a $800 million contract awarded to General Motors to build light combat vehicles for Canada's ground troops.

The helicopters do fit the new military profile. They're described as "off-the-shelf" helicopters, suited for environmental cleanup, medical evacuations or Oka-style domestic disputes.

The helicopter purchase will allow the department to retire four other helicopter types, all of which were incurring heavy maintenance costs because they are 20 years old.

But this game of sleight-of-hand, critics say, is important for what was more quietly announced.

A $2.8 billion program for more heavily armored vehicles, which had been on the defence shopping list, is gone, replaced by the lighter combat vehicles.

Savings—$2 billion.

A program to purchase three replacements for Canada's aged conventional submarine fleet was also deferred until after the next federal election.

The saving there would run into billions of dollars, but there is no precise figure because they are not in the government's spending estimates.

Still to be decided by federal cabinet this summer is another helicopter purchase which could be anywhere from $2 billion to $4 billion, depending on the details of the buy.

Masse would like to see 35 choppers placed on Canadian frigates and another 15 for search-and-rescue missions.

In addition, in recent weeks the government has:

• Announced a $20–$25 million purchase of 15,000 C-7 combat rifles from Diameco of Kitchener.
• Spent $200 million for 2,750 new trucks from West Star Truck of Kelowna, B.C.
• Awarded a $165 million contract to Bombardier to establish a pilot training centre in Portage la Prairie, Man.
• Announced it will spend $902,000 for renovations to Canadian Forces Base Goose Bay.
• Awarded a $360,000 contract to Employee Relocation Services of Toronto to help forces employees who will lose their jobs as part of the cutbacks.
• Begun considering an investment—which could run into the hundreds of millions, if not billions—in the new, revamped Star Wars program, named GPALS by the Pentagon.
• Decided to continue spending on the $1.1 billion air defence system known as LLAD, which is designed to protect Canadian troops in Europe, even though those troops are coming home.
• Sprinkled in smaller projects such as an underwater surveillance technology program in British Columbia and a new tactical command centre in Calgary.

The defence department maintains it wants to be spending 26 per cent of its budget on new equipment within five years, with a longer-term goal of 30 per cent on capital spending.

Most don't believe that figure will ever be approached.

Right now, the Canadian military uses about 23 per cent of its budget to buy new equipment.

Ed Healey, an Ottawa consultant who set the 30 per cent goal while deputy minister of defence, says unless the department works toward it, "you're going to have people standing around with broom handles instead of rifles.

"But it's not attainable without a lot of political will. We have to cut bases, cut people and cut deeper."

CANADA'S INVISIBLE GENERAL

Our top soldier is in charge of the greatest number of Canadian peacekeepers since the Korean War. And although he works at keeping a low profile, his achievements are gaining more recognition for the man in charge of the nation's defence

Tim Harper

Toronto Star

OTTAWA

He oversaw the first Canadian war effort in four decades, even as he was catching his breath from defusing the time bomb at Oka.

He's in charge of the largest number of Canadian peacekeepers in more parts of the world than at any time since the Korean War.

And he's steered the armed forces through major cutbacks while a new potential flashpoint, demanding Canadian help, seems to jump off the pages of the atlas daily.

Yet John de Chastelain remains Canada's invisible general.

The country's top soldier has so far pushed all the right buttons during a period of unparalleled post–World War II activity at the national defence department.

And he could probably walk through the Eaton Centre and not have a head turn his way in curiosity.

Even if he was wearing his four gold maple leaves, identifying him as the man to whom the country's 84,000-strong active forces, 29,000 reservists and 33,000 civilian defence employees ultimately answer.

That's not a bad trick for a man born in Romania to British spies and educated in Scotland, who began his armed forces career as a piper and never leaves those bagpipes far behind.

Maybe it's because he never—*never*—drops that private school veneer, a manner that strikes some as aristocratic, but others as unfailingly polite.

"If you find something beneath that veneer, please let me know," says a longtime associate of the general.

Maybe it's because, unlike his more celebrated underling, Maj.-Gen. Lewis MacKenzie, the hero of Sarajevo, he doesn't drive race cars but instead plays the bagpipes and builds furniture.

He jumps out of airplanes, likes to don his kilt for a good Scottish country dance on a Saturday night and can still probably, at age 55, play some decent rugby, a sport sometimes described as a ruffian's game played by gentlemen.

He was a fair country boxer in his time. But he's also a grandfather who laments that he doesn't spend enough time with his granddaughter, even if he's a bit defensive about being a grandfather.

"There's a lot of people younger than me who are grandfathers, you know," he says.

He doesn't make bold statements, he understates with a modesty that is perhaps a bit too thick.

More likely his lack of profile stems from the old adage that says a successful general, in Canada at least, is like a good baseball umpire. You only notice him if he does something wrong.

Sitting with de Chastelain in his office at defence headquarters is to imagine him born there; a central casting invention that appears a shade too perfect to be credible.

But his 1989 appointment was, in fact, the culmination of a 34-year military career that began as a piper in the militia with the Calgary Highlanders.

It's hard to think of him dragging his gear on dusty trails. He looks more at home sipping an aperitif at Government House.

"He got sweaty and he got sunburned and his crotch rotted just like the rest of us," recalls a former colleague, Vancouver consultant William Hutchinson.

And behind the demeanor—"When he's talking to you, there's no one else in the world," says former colleague and defence analyst Alex Morrison—is a pretty tough guy with some pretty clear ideas of how things should be run in the armed forces.

"If somebody needs the back of my hand, I'll give it to them," he says.

"If people give me bad advice and continually do so—keeping in mind that bad intelligence is worse than no

From *The Toronto Star*, September 6, 1992, p. B5. Reprinted with permission from The Toronto Star Syndicate.

intelligence—then I have to let them know that they and I have to part ways."

Part of that is the perfectionist in the man. He doesn't just build furniture, friends say, he builds elaborate, perfect furniture.

He doesn't just make homemade wine. He designs meticulous labels and christens his creation Le Choix de Chastelain.

Says Hutchinson: "He could tear a strip off someone with the best of them."

De Chastelain puts it differently.

"You have to insist on the right of people to make mistakes," he says. "Certainly once, maybe twice, never three times.

"But you don't have to be brutal about it."

It's more important that the rank be respected, he says, because "that's what makes the system work."

If that leads to a parting of the ways, so be it, he says—and he's had his share of parting of ways.

None was more public, or more notorious, than the resignation of his vice-chief of defence staff, the naval head, Charles (Chuck) Thomas.

They exchanged a pair of letters debating the future of the armed forces that were so public, so detailed and such signature statements of philosophy that they are expected to be studied by defence scholars in the future.

Today, there is no bad blood between the two.

"We parted friends," de Chastelain says.

"His concern wasn't entirely with me, but it was partly with me.

"His argument centred around a country he thought was disarming at a time that he felt was inappropriate. You could argue that to the extent we've been involved militarily since then, there's something to that."

Although de Chastelain's precise, disciplinarian style was nurtured in the private schools of Scotland, it was honed in his early military days in Western Canada.

He reveals little about life before that, although both parents worked for British intelligence. His father spent time in a prisoner-of-war camp; his mother worked for Sir William Stephenson, the man known as Intrepid.

Neither of the next generation of de Chastelains has anything to do with espionage or defence, although the general says that is not by design.

Son Duncan is articling for a Toronto law firm, daughter Amanda will be a Kingston physiotherapist. Wife MaryAnn is a guide at the National Gallery.

When de Chastelain landed as a brash piper in Western Canada, one former colleague says in retrospect, he was ushering in the era of the new breed of Canadian soldier.

De Chastelain arrived, the former colleague remembers, at a point when a number of middle-level military men were heavy drinkers.

"They set a horrible example," he says. "It's a real eye-opener if you're 24 or 25 years old and you see your superiors at 34 or 35 boozing it up every night.

"John wanted no part of that."

Anyone who recalls a first meeting with de Chastelain remembers a man who was destined to head the armed forces.

"He was a winner," recalls Hutchinson of that first meeting some 30 years ago. "He was bright and bilingual, energetic and gregarious.

"That's a pretty good recipe."

Even in 1964, as a 27-year-old commander of a Canadian battalion in Germany, he showed how persuasive he could be.

During a visit to Belgium as part of a 50-year anniversary commemoration of World War I, a Canadian soldier was jailed for stealing a bicycle in Ypres.

"You've got to remember, that's a pretty serious offence in Belgium in 1964," recalls Maj. Robert Burns of Halifax, who was with de Chastelain that night.

"The Belgians were adamant. This guy wasn't going to be released.

"Well, John went to work, and he negotiated for hours, well into the night.

"The next thing I know, not only does John have this guy released, but the Belgians are pleading with us not to punish him once we got our hands on him."

Later in his career, Ian Fraser, who runs the Nova Scotia military tattoo, told de Chastelain he was destined to become chief of defence staff.

Typically, de Chastelain demurred, playing down his chances.

"If you become chief," Fraser said, "you have to come to Halifax and perform as the lone piper in the tattoo."

De Chastelain agreed and that's how the chief of the defence staff, taking orders from a private, played solo at the Nova Scotia show last summer.

In Germany, as a captain, he would bring the bagpipes with him, serenading the rest of the company as they went on their weekly 40-kilometre (25-mile) marches.

He was apparently good enough that no one objected to the ordeal being put to music.

Besides, he was de Chastelain. He wasn't questioned.

He never flinched during the standoff at Oka, even though he admits having to deploy his troops on Canadian soil tore him apart.

"Inasmuch as it was important to maintain law and order, I didn't have any concerns about that," he says.

"But when you had that many people with that many weapons facing each other, the possibilities of something going wrong are great."

That past, he then lurched into the Persian Gulf war.

His political masters and the Canadian military had never had to deal with the crisis management brought on by war, he says, but that worked to his advantage.

He was also dealing with a cabinet that could boast no military expertise.

Typically diplomatic, de Chastelain agrees with that observation, but adds: "I have found a great willingness on the part of politicians to listen to military advice, to follow it if they figure it meets their requirements, but not to question it.

"My greater concern is to ensure the troops understand that we're looking after interests, that we're not giving politicians an answer that is expedient."

Right now, his greatest concern is that Canada's peacekeeping resources are not stretched too thin. In recent memory, the demand for Canadian expertise has never been greater.

When pledges to Somalia and Bosnia are fulfilled, more than 4,000 Canadians will be keeping the peace worldwide.

"Eventually," he says, "we could say (to the United Nations) we're sorry but we cannot take part in this operation because we've got too many people involved already.

"We haven't reached that point yet."

But there's a further warning: "You can't keep replacing one engineer unit with another engineer unit with another engineer unit, ad infinitum.

"We only have so many engineers."

Canada can double its commitment to Yugoslavia, provide for Somalia and maintain its peacekeeping job in Cyprus, he says, "but how long we'd be able to sustain that is something else.

"The United Nations understands there is a limit.

"But we can do more than we're doing now."

De Chastelain this month begins what is likely his last year at the helm.

Prime Minister Brian Mulroney has extended his term for a year, but de Chastelain expects this to be his final year.

Most former generals either lobby for the defence industry or analyze for the media. Not de Chastelain.

"I don't know what I'll do, but I know what I'm not going to do," he says. "I'm not going to work for the defence industry.

"I'd be a lousy businessman anyway.

"I have no intention of becoming a politician. I think they take on an awful lot without much thanks.

"I won't fade away and garden, or anything like that.

"I might play my bagpipes if someone will pay me to— or not, if they'll pay me not to."

Canada's quiet nuclear export

'Depleted' uranium originally from Canada is used to make tanks, shells and other conventional weapons

Dorothy Goldin Rosenberg

Dorothy Goldin Rosenberg is a member of Masters in Environmental Studies (MES), Consultant in Global Education, Board of Directors, Canadian Coalition for Nuclear Responsibility.

On August 6th, exactly 47 years ago today, the U.S. dropped an atomic bomb on Hiroshima. Three days later, it dropped another on Nagasaki.

It is particularly fitting that Canadians pause and reflect on this day, because, although we may not wish to be reminded of it, Canadian scientists and Canadian uranium played a major part in this destruction.

Nor can we, in 1992, allow ourselves to be complacent on nuclear issues. Canada is the world's largest exporter of uranium, which is not only the fuel of nuclear bombs but, increasingly, in its present form, a key ingredient in another kind of radioactive warfare: military armament. Scores of missiles, tanks and various sorts of ammunition made with depleted uranium were used by our allies in the gulf war.

The United Kingdom Atomic Energy Authority (AEA) last year estimated that at least 40 tons of depleted uranium (DU) was left on the gulf war battlefield, from the tens of thousands of armor-piercing rounds of ammunition fired at Iraqi vehicles by American aircraft and British and U.S. tanks.

This chemically toxic and radioactive waste threatens the long-term health of thousands of Kuwaitis, Iraqis and western clean-up teams. It may also pass through the food chain and affect the water supply.

Underlying this picture is a uranium waste cycle in which a Canadian raw material and toxic warfare reinforce each other.

When it is mined, uranium is 99.3 per cent useless in its natural form; only the fissionable U-235 can be used in nuclear power plants or in bombs. The leftover U-238, depleted of over half its U-235 content, is low-level radioactive waste.

DU is extremely heavy. Compared to a gallon of water weighing 8 pounds, or a gallon of steel at 60 pounds, or of lead at 90 pounds, a gallon of uranium weighs 152 pounds.

Concentrating maximum force upon a single point is what ordinance designers do, and multiplying the weight of a projectile by 2.5, as happens when uranium is substituted for steel, increases the moment of force to the same extent.

DU is also pyrophoric (it catches fire spontaneously) when finely divided. Ammunition is specially made to take advantage of one or more of these attributes. In addition, DU combines with other materials to make tank armor harder and less vulnerable.

As an inevitable consequence, more and more DU ammunition, alloyed for hardness with 2 per cent molybdenum, has been introduced into military arsenals over the last two decades. More and more of it is being incorporated into tank armor.

(The 1991 U.S. federal budget called for the acquisition of 36 million pounds of DU metal for the "National Defence Stockpile" over the next 10 years.)

According to the U.S. Food and Drug Administration, tank crews could receive the equivalent of one chest X-ray every 20 or 30 hours. The British AEA report explained the danger from uranium dust produced when depleted uranium shells hit and burned out Iraqi armored vehicles. The depleted uranium is spread around the battlefield in varying sizes from dust particles to full size shells. If airborne particles are inhaled, they can lead to unacceptable levels of exposure.

Because they are fired at high velocity they also tend to skip and ricochet when they hit the ground. DU shells oxidize in air forming uranium oxide that can flake off and remain in the soil even after the shells are removed. These could be hazardous to both clean-up teams and the local population.

The use of DU in weapons systems illustrates the symbiotic relationship between the domestic nuclear industry and the military.

The military improves ammunition and tank armor while the nuclear industry gets rid of its low level radioactive waste. The DU is given to the military free of charge, saving a great deal of money. Finally, as no safe way to dispose of nuclear waste is known, the nuclear industry is left with less uranium to worry about.

10. DEFENCE AND FOREIGN POLICY

It is well known that Canadian uranium is regularly shipped to nuclear weapons countries to be enriched for customers requiring it to power reactors. (Canada has no enrichment plants.) When Canadian uranium, now mostly from Saskatchewan, goes to French, U.S. and British enrichment plants (operated by the state agencies which also produce bomb materials), for every pound of uranium that is enriched, five pounds of depleted uranium can be stockpiled for weapons use.

The commingling of the civilian and military atoms at enrichment plants is no accident. Each of the major enrichment plants in the world (except for a Dutch plant), are in nuclear weapons states.

In 1965, Canada announced a ban on all exports of uranium for military purposes—a policy still nominally in effect.

But the shipments of "peaceful" uranium continued to go through the same U.S. enrichment plants, with predictable results. U.S. records show that Canadian uranium accounts for most of the depleted uranium in the U.S. stockpile.

The civilian enrichment process has always been a marriage of convenience for weapons states—it brings in extra cash and helps soften the image of the bomb factories. The U.S.–Canada Free Trade Agreement, for instance, created unrestricted U.S. access to Canadian uranium.)

We Canadians like to think of ourselves as peacemakers and peacekeepers and indeed many of us are. At this time of remembering the horrors of Hiroshima and Nagasaki, what better way to honor the victims—and our own self-image—than to stop the export of our uranium.

Is Ottawa breaking word on arms sales?

Tim Harper

Toronto Star

OTTAWA

From the ashes of the Persian Gulf war, a bold new Canadian legacy was to be forged.

So we were told, in those late winter days of 1991. Prime Minister Brian Mulroney announced that Canada was poised to become the world leader in curbing the world's arms trade.

He even offered to host a world summit aimed at ending the proliferation of arms. His external affairs minister of the day, Joe Clark, said Canada's record on arms control gave it the right to place the item "high on the world's agenda."

Today, that would-be policy appears to be in shambles.

With U.S. President George Bush and his allies again lobbing rhetorical Scuds at Iraq's Saddam Hussein, Ottawa and the Canadian weapons industry are rushing to skim their share of the billions available in the Middle East arms bazaar.

At very least, government critics say, Ottawa is breaking a 1991 pledge that a moratorium on arms sales to the Middle East would remain until an all-party subcommittee could study ways to revamp our arms export policy.

At worst, they say, the government is guilty of hypocrisy and immorality: pledging one thing on the world stage while trying to arm players in a highly volatile part of the world.

A year and a half after Mulroney sketched his vision of a brave new world with fewer destructive weapons, the defence department is working hard with Montreal-based Oerlikon Aerospace. They are major players in the race to sell an air defence system known as the Air Defence Anti-Tank System (ADATS) to potential buyers from the Persian Gulf.

Potential clients are believed to include Kuwait, Bahrain, Saudi Arabia and the United Arab Emirates. The company says there are "several" potential buyers in the Gulf region.

Gulf states representatives watched—and were reportedly impressed—when ADATS was displayed at CFB Suffield, Alta., in June.

Last year, the defence department and Oerlikon worked together to exhibit the system in Dubai.

Only days before the Suffield show, the government released its annual report of military exports. It showed the value of exports to the Middle East almost doubled from 1990 to 1991, from $12.8 million to $25.3 million. Sales included helicopters, aircraft and large-calibre weapons.

The customers included Bahrain, Egypt, Israel, Kuwait, Oman, Turkey, Saudi Arabia and the United Arab Emirates.

Such numbers are microscopic compared with the estimated $22 billion in U.S. sales to the region since the end of the gulf war, but the trend has a number of observers upset.

"The world is being given a very expensive and very persuasive lesson on how dangerous these weapons are," Mulroney told an audience of diplomats in February, 1991. "This problem must be brought under control and the time to act is now."

The Prime Minister even chided Bush for his arms export policy.

The first sign that Mulroney's words would not translate into action came less than three months later, when Trade Minister Michael Wilson introduced amendments to the Criminal Code, allowing the sale of more than 1,000 Canadian-made light armored vehicles to Saudi Arabia.

In return for an opposition pledge to allow the amendments to pass the House of Commons before the summer recess that year, Wilson set up the subcommittee to study our arms export policy.

Committee members say he also promised a moratorium on Middle East sales until the all-party committee finished its work.

Although the committee has not reported, defence sources believe they are close to an ADATS sale to a Gulf nation.

"There's a great deal of interest in this system out there," says Col. Dennis Hopper, who heads the defence

From *The Toronto Star,* August 26, 1992, p. A17. Reprinted with permission from The Toronto Star Syndicate.

239

department's low-level air defence project. "Some people consider it a very urgent requirement."

Oerlikon's Christiane Beaulieu says the company is in "discussion but not negotiation" with clients.

The signing of just one ADATS contract would be worth hundreds of millions of dollars to Oerlikon.

But that doesn't placate committee members. "It will be a real slap in the face to Parliament if they go ahead with these sales," says Liberal MP Lloyd Axworthy.

"This government has not just returned to business as usual in the region, it is increasing efforts to get on the gravy train."

Axworthy says the government commitment was simple—no sales to the Gulf region until the government had a new arms export policy.

Victoria New Democrat John Brewin calls the intensive sales effort in the Middle East a clear breach of government policy.

"There was a clear undertaking that there would no more sales to areas of tension like the Middle East," he says.

"They have no details of the committee's work and they're out flogging this system. Meanwhile, we've travelled the country trying to craft a policy.

"This is sheer lunacy. The government learned nothing from the Persian Gulf war."

An official in Wilson's office denies that the minister agreed to a moratorium.

Richard Lecoq says Wilson merely agreed to limit sales to Saudi Arabia for a period that ended Dec. 31, 1991.

Tariq Rauf of the Arms Control Centre says the Canadian military is exploiting its role in the Gulf war to boost sales, which is completely contrary to the stated government intention.

"Their subtle message is 'We saved your ass (in the gulf war), now how about buying something?'" Rauf says.

At issue are two opposite views of what Oerlikon is trying to sell: Is it an offensive or defensive weapon?

The ADATS system is an armored vehicle outfitted with radar and eight laser-guided missiles.

Its role is to shoot down incoming aircraft. Its range is about 10 kilometres (6 miles) while the more publicized American-made Patriot has a range of about 100 kilometres (62 miles).

"This is strictly a defensive system—you can't fire it 50 kilometres (31 miles) into another country," a defence source says. "We're not trying to sell tanks which can be used in an invasion."

Oerlikon's Beaulieu goes even further.

"This is the type of product that Canada can sell and still leave us proud to be Canadians," she says.

The ADATS, she says, fits a government policy that acknowledges countries' rights to defend themselves.

Rauf says the system is quite capable of being used offensively simply by providing cover to advancing or invading troops.

"It's known as a force multiplier; it adds to your offensive punch," he says.

Axworthy says ADATS is offensive simply because if one Middle East state buys it, its neighbors will feel pressure to keep pace in the race. "Each side just keeps ratcheting up its arsenal," he says.

Also at stake are as many as 500 jobs at Oerlikon, which has been hurt by defence cutbacks caused by the end of the Cold War.

To keep the jobs, Oerlikon says it must test the export market, particularly the non-NATO countries of the Middle East and Asia.

"The government supports this and the minister (Defence Minister Marcel Masse) supports this," Beaulieu says. "Five hundred jobs are at stake to a certain point.

"Without new contracts, there is no need for those jobs."

Martin Shadwick, a defence analyst at York University's Centre for International and Strategic Studies, says Oerlikon's plight shows the need for more attention to conversion or diversification of this country's weapons manufacturers.

"Total conversion is not always the best option," he says. "You don't go from missiles to toasters overnight unless you can find a market for $5,000, military-style toasters.

"But jobs cannot be the final arbiter in all this.

"The truth is that everybody's out there flogging everything these days. The market is so tough that even if you totally opened the door and dropped all restrictions on arms sales you might not save a single Canadian job."

Meanwhile, the subcommittee is racked by infighting and has not been able to finalize a draft report it wants to table in the House of Commons.

Opposition MPs, sources say, want to submit a report that would leave an open door for sales to the United States but tighten exports to other countries.

That policy, which would tighten export controls, is being challenged by Conservative MPs on the subcommittee.

Credits/ Acknowledgments

Cover design by Charles Vitelli

1. Canada: A Nation in Limbo

2. The Supreme Court of Canada and the Constitution

Facing overview—Industry, Science & Technology (ISTC).

3. The Parliamentary System

Facing overview—Industry, Science & Technology (ISTC).

4. Participation and Elections

Facing overview—Reuters/Bettmann Newsphotos. 104—
Reprinted from *Toronto Star,* September 10, 1992, p. A26.
Reprinted with permission from The Toronto Star Syndicate.

5. The Politics of Culture

Facing overview—Industry, Science & Technology (ISTC).

6. The Regionalism of Federalism

Facing overview—Le Château Frontenac.

7. Quebec

Facing overview—© S. Silverman/Gamma-Liaison. 164—
Illustration by Jerzy Kolacz. 165-168—Computer graphics by
Kaspar de Line.

8. Aboriginal Issues

Facing overview—Photo courtesy of Museum of the American
Indian, Heye Foundation.

9. Free Trade

Facing overview—Reuters/Bettmann Newsphotos.

10. Defence and Foreign Policy

Facing overview—U.S. Air Force photo.

ANNUAL EDITIONS ARTICLE REVIEW FORM

■ NAME: _____ DATE: _____

■ TITLE AND NUMBER OF ARTICLE: _____

■ BRIEFLY STATE THE MAIN IDEA OF THIS ARTICLE: _____

_____

_____

_____

_____

■ LIST THREE IMPORTANT FACTS THAT THE AUTHOR USES TO SUPPORT THE MAIN IDEA:

_____

_____

_____

_____

_____

_____

■ WHAT INFORMATION OR IDEAS DISCUSSED IN THIS ARTICLE ARE ALSO DISCUSSED IN YOUR TEXTBOOK OR OTHER READING YOU HAVE DONE? LIST THE TEXTBOOK CHAPTERS AND PAGE NUMBERS:

_____

_____

_____

_____

_____

_____

_____

■ LIST ANY EXAMPLES OF BIAS OR FAULTY REASONING THAT YOU FOUND IN THE ARTICLE:

_____

_____

_____

_____

■ LIST ANY NEW TERMS/CONCEPTS THAT WERE DISCUSSED IN THE ARTICLE AND WRITE A SHORT DEFINITION:

_____

_____

_____

_____

_____

*Your instructor may require you to use this Annual Editions Article Review Form in any number of ways: for articles that are assigned, for extra credit, as a tool to assist in developing assigned papers, or simply for your own reference. Even if it is not required, we encourage you to photocopy and use this page; you'll find that reflecting on the articles will greatly enhance the information from your text.

ANNUAL EDITIONS:
CANADIAN POLITICS, Third Edition
Article Rating Form

We Want Your Advice

Here is an opportunity for you to have direct input into the next revision of this volume. We would like you to rate each of the 63 articles listed below, using the following scale:

1. **Excellent: should definitely be retained**
2. **Above average: should probably be retained**
3. **Below average: should probably be deleted**
4. **Poor: should definitely be deleted**

Your ratings will play a vital part in the next revision. So please mail this prepaid form to us just as soon as you complete it.
Thanks for your help!

Annual Editions revisions depend on two major opinion sources: one is our Advisory Board, listed in the front of this volume, which works with us in scanning the thousands of articles published in the public press each year; the other is you—the person actually using the book. Please help us and the users of the next edition by completing the prepaid article rating form on this page and returning it to us. Thank you.

Rating	Article	Rating	Article
	1. Canada: Continuing Constitutional Crisis		31. Ending Regional Favoritism
	2. Canada's Constitution: A New Austria-Hungary in the Making?		32. Sharing Canada's Power: At What Cost?
	3. The Constitutional Debate: A Straight Talking Guide for Canadians		33. O Atlantica, We Stand on Guard for Thee?
	4. Text of the Charlottetown Agreement		34. Bitter on the Rock
	5. And Justices for All		35. Slow Death of a Nation's Heartland
	6. How the Charter Changes Justice		36. Action and High Energy: British Columbians Confront Radical Change
	7. The Hidden Opposition/The 'Court Party' in Practice		37. The Death of Denendeh
	8. Better Ways to Choose a Judge		38. Too Little, Too Late to Save N.W.T.?
	9. Wrestling in Court Over Charter Goals		39. What If Quebec Separates?
	10. Supreme Court Charts New Direction for Canadian Values		40. Affirmative Action and the Sign Law
	11. The Perils of Executive Democracy		41. Duelling in the Dark
	12. Cleaning House		42. Hard Times and Quebec
	13. A New Top Gun		43. Our Culture's Native Roots
	14. Lobby Horse		44. The Honor of the Crown
	15. Interest Groups—the New Power in Ottawa		45. Drumbeats of Rage
	16. Premiers Design New Senate		46. What Is Self-Government?
	17. Anger at the System: Sources of Discontent		47. The Internal Exiles of Canada
	18. Financing Leadership Campaigns in Canada		48. Confronting the Global Trade Challenge—Canada Gets Ready to Take on the World and Win
	19. TV Advertising Limits Handicap Reform		49. Look Again at the Free Trade Deal
	20. Nomination Rules Rile Some Grass-Roots Liberals		50. Why We Must Join NAFTA
	21. A Better Way to Count the Votes		51. Gephardt Criticizes Trade Pact
	22. Direct Democracy: The Wave of the Future?		52. Canada: Love It or Lease It
	23. Plebiscites Common in Canada, Abroad		53. 'We're No Protectionist Bully'
	24. Canada Versus the United States		54. Fact, Fiction, and Mexico
	25. How Can Canada Maintain Its Cultural Independence?		55. This Time, Anti-Free Traders Aren't Alone
	26. Gotlieb Warns the Real Enemy Lies Within		56. The Bottom Line: A More Prosperous North America
	27. The Bell Tolls for Canadian Culture		57. A Jobs Policy for Peace
	28. Language in Canada		58. An Army for the 21st Century
	29. Writing Off Canadian Publishing		59. Closing Down Canadian Bases Marks End of Era
	30. How Come the *Digest* Qualifies as Canadian?		60. 'Peace Dividend' Costly
			61. Canada's Invisible General
			62. Canada's Quiet Nuclear Export
			63. Is Ottawa Breaking Word on Arms Sales?

(Continued on next page)

ABOUT YOU

Name_____ Date_____

Are you a teacher? ☐ Or student? ☐

Your School Name _____

Department _____

Address _____

City_____ State _____ Zip _____

School Telephone # _____

YOUR COMMENTS ARE IMPORTANT TO US!

Please fill in the following information:

For which course did you use this book? _____

Did you use a text with this Annual Edition? ☐ yes ☐ no

The title of the text? _____

What are your general reactions to the Annual Editions concept?

Have you read any particular articles recently that you think should be included in the next edition?

Are there any articles you feel should be replaced in the next edition? Why?

Are there other areas that you feel would utilize an Annual Edition?

May we contact you for editorial input?

May we quote you from above?

ANNUAL EDITIONS: CANADIAN POLITICS, Third Edition

BUSINESS REPLY MAIL

First Class   Permit No. 84   Guilford, CT

Postage will be paid by addressee

The Dushkin Publishing Group, Inc.
Sluice Dock
DPG **Guilford, Connecticut 06437**

No Postage
Necessary
if Mailed
in the
United States